MW00715675

Teach
Yourself
PowerBuilder™ 4

in 14 Days

Teach Yourself
PowerBuilder™ 4
in 14 Days

Judah J. Holstein
Michael Lessard
Adam Marturana
Basant Nanda
Robert Quinn
Chris Tierney

SAMS
PUBLISHING

201 West 103rd Street
Indianapolis, Indiana 46290

Dedicated to my loving wife, Jackie, and my unborn son, whose name will probably be Matthew.

Copyright © 1995 by Sams Publishing

FIRST EDITION

International Standard Book Number: 0-672-30676-X

Library of Congress Catalog Card Number: 94-69268

98   97   96   95   4   3   2   1

Interpretation of the printing code: the rightmost double-digit number is the year of the book's printing; the rightmost single-digit, the number of the book's printing. For example, a printing code of 94-1 shows that the first printing of the book occurred in 1994.

Composed in AGaramond and MCPdigital by Macmillan Computer Publishing

Printed in the United States of America

Trademarks

Overview

Contents

Acknowledgments

A lot of effort by a lot of people went into this book, and I would like to take the time to thank them. First, I would like to thank all of the people at Sams Publishing, without whom this book would not be possible. Most especially, I would like to thank my Acquisitions Editor, Rosemarie Graham. Her encouragement and guidance were invaluable. I would also like to thank the five authors who took the time and effort to contribute to this book. Thanks for dealing with my last-minute changes and my anal attitude. You guys all did a great job! Special thanks go to Michael Lessard, who not only did many of the Q&A and Quiz questions, but who also took the time to read my entire manuscript and helped keep it honest, even though it wasn't his responsibility.

In addition, there are countless others who have helped me indirectly in the writing of this book, some of whom whose names I will undoubtedly forget to mention. To my in-laws (yes, you read that right) for their support and encouragement throughout this whole process. Thank you for not being mad for all of the times that we came over, and I sat in the living room with my laptop writing away instead of coming in with everyone else for coffee and cake. Thanks to Steve and Keith for having the vision to see PowerBuilder as the tool of the future and for introducing it to me as early as you did. And thanks to everyone else who had anything to do with helping me write this book.

Most importantly, however, there is one person who was not directly involved in the writing of this book, but who was affected by it more than anyone else. When my wife Jackie told me that she was pregnant with our first child, I had more than three months of work left for the book, and two-and-a-half months left of school, not to mention a full-time job with a one-hour commute each way. Her patience and understanding while I continued to spend all my free time on everything but her was way beyond the norm, and I love her very much for it—and for everything else that she does to help make my life as wonderful as it is. Thank you, Jackie, for dealing with me all these months, and all these years.

—*Judah J. Holstein*

About the Authors

Judah Holstein

Judah Holstein is a certified PowerBuilder Developer-Professional who has been developing applications in PowerBuilder since version 1.0. He was a C and xBase developer since 1989, although he began programming computers on an Apple // in his basement with the help of a Beagle Brothers cheat sheet. He is the author of the "Builders Block" column in *Power Programmer* magazine. He was a contributing author in the book, *Secrets of the PowerBuilder Masters*. He holds a Bachelor of Science degree in Computer Applications and Information Systems from Iona College. He can be reached through AADM Consulting, Inc., of Watchung, NJ, at (908) 756-2443, via the Internet at mrdj@aol.com, on America Online with the screen name "Mr DJ," or on CompuServe at 73512,2676. He encourages you to drop him a line if you have any questions or comments, or if you just want to let him know how you liked the book.

Michael Lessard

Michael Lessard is a certified PowerBuilder Developer-Professional and a certified PowerBuilder Instructor. He is a Systems Design Engineer from the University of Waterloo (Watcom University) who teaches for PC Strategies & Solns. He, too, has been programming in PowerBuilder since version 1.0. Michael wrote many of the Quiz and "Putting PowerBuilder into Action" sections for the book.

Adam Marturana

Adam Marturana has contributed to the evolution of rapid application development techniques since the early 1980s. He has used PowerBuilder since its initial release and was one of the first to earn Powersofts CPD Professional rating. Adam is the founder and CEO of AADM Consulting, Inc. and can be reached there at (908) 756-2443 or at CompuServe ID: 74312,457. Adam wrote Chapter 26, "Using the Debugger," and Chapter 27, "Creating an Executable."

Basant Nanda

Basant Nanda works for a major investment bank in New York City. He is a certified PowerBuilder Developer and an experienced PowerBuilder architect. Basant has been developing with PowerBuilder since 1992 and has designed and deployed numerous applications. He can be reached at 72643.3251@compuserve.com. Basant wrote Chapter 13, "Standard User Objects," and Chapter 28, "Advanced Topics."

Robert Quinn

Robert Quinn has over ten years of experience in software development. Robert's experience ranges from business applications to systems software, mainframe to client/server, and assembler to PowerBuilder. He is currently involved in a project to efficiently manage extremely large databases. Robert is a certified PowerBuilder Developer and is employed by AADM consulting. Robert wrote Chapter 25, "Using Structured Query Language (SQL) in Your Scripts."

Chris Tierney

Chris Tierney coaches PowerBuilder programming teams and fabricates object classes for client companies. As a senior developer for AADM Consulting, he promotes object reuse and standards for large PowerBuilder application shops. Chris was previously a systems manager at a Fortune 500 corporation and has been an avid user of PC application development tools since the mid 1980s. Chris wrote Chapter 9, "The Library Painter."

Introduction

Who Should Read This Book

If you are not currently a PowerBuilder programmer but would like to become one, or if you are just beginning a new PowerBuilder project and want to quickly learn how to do it right the first time, this book is for you. This book teaches you how to develop applications by using PowerBuilder 4.0, whether you are an experienced programmer eager to learn a new language or have never "programmed" anything more complex than a spreadsheet before. This book teaches you everything you need to know about PowerBuilder programming, so you don't need to be a programmer to learn PowerBuilder with this book. In fact, if you are already developing with a structured programming language, you may find some of the first few chapters to be a review of familiar information. However, this book does require that you are at least marginally familiar with your computer, your mouse, and the Microsoft Windows Operating Environment.

What This Book Will Do for You

This book is not a reference book. This book is not the book that will sit next to your computer for many years to come so that you can refer back to it every time you forget which parameter comes first in a function. This book has one purpose, and that is to teach you how to develop applications by using PowerBuilder. After you have finished reading (or should I say, experiencing) this book, you will have acquired the fundamental tasks needed to develop PowerBuilder applications. This is not the kind of book you can read on the bus or train. You should read this book while sitting in front of your computer, and follow the step-by-step instructions that will teach you, in 14 days, how to create Windows applications with PowerBuilder. Programming computers is more than just telling a computer what to do. It is an art form, a form of creation, where you take bits and bytes and cryptic code words and create from them an intelligent, user-friendly interface between man and his information. Learning the skills you will need to create good computer programs requires a serious effort, but is well worth it. Read this book, and then read it again; and when you are done, you will have thrust yourself into the growing gallery of PowerBuilder programmers.

What This Book Will *Not* Do for You

The purpose of this book is to give you the foundation you need to be a PowerBuilder programmer. However, there are certain aspects of computer programming that you simply cannot learn from a book. Just as with any art form, computer programming is a very personal thing, and as your development experience grows, you will begin to pick up your own personal styles and preferences. People develop computer applications to solve problems, and there is always more than one correct solution to a problem. Sometimes, there is even more than one best solution to a problem. As you continue to be challenged by puzzles and attempt to solve them by using PowerBuilder, you will learn new algorithms, techniques, and ideas that help you build your own styles. In this way, you grow and evolve as a programmer. No book can teach you that which you can only learn from experience.

What You Need before You Get Started

Well, of course, you need a PC Compatible Computer, 386 or better (although a 486 is preferred), running either Microsoft Windows 3.1 or higher, or Microsoft Windows NT 3.5 or higher, with a mouse. You also need to have Powersoft's PowerBuilder. Whether you have PowerBuilder Enterprise Edition, PowerBuilder Team/ODBC Edition, or PowerBuilder Desktop Edition is not critical. For the purposes of this tutorial, the different editions are identical, with the exception of the additional software, support, and materials you get with the more advanced Editions. Oh, and of course, you need about 14 days.

What You Should Come away With

When you have finished reading this book and performing all of the step-by-step tasks outlined here, you will have created your first PowerBuilder application. You will learn all of the fundamentals you need to go out into the field and start creating PowerBuilder applications for yourself, your company, or your clients. You will not be a PowerBuilder guru or expert, but you will have enough of an exposure to PowerBuilder to be able to create many solutions to problems by using PowerBuilder. If you're working with a team of people, you will understand what the experts are talking about when they outline their design for you. Of course, what you come away with, in many ways, has much to do with your own aptitude and talent. Not everyone can be a great programmer, but there is no question that anyone can write computer programs, especially with PowerBuilder. When you finish this book, you will at least be able to understand what techniques are required to write computer programs with PowerBuilder.

Conventions Used in This Book

This book uses specific conventions to help you in your learning. KEYWORDS will appear in a monospaced font, and generally will be in UPPERCASE. Code listings will also appear in a monospaced font and will usually appear in separate listings, on a line by themselves, to prevent confusion. The first time a new word or phrase of interest is introduced, it will appear *italicized*. Things the user types will appear in **bold**. Throughout the book, there are also notes, tips, and cautions that will help you with your developing skills, even when it is not directly related to the topic at hand. Icons appear in the margin to denote a PowerBuilder button you are working with.

There is a Workshop section at the end of each chapter, which includes a Quiz and a hands-on example using PowerBuilder titled, "Putting PowerBuilder into Action." The answers to the Quiz questions appear in the back of the book in "Appendix A."

WEEK

1

AT A GLANCE

In your first week, you will be learning about the basics of PowerBuilder as well as its environment. By the end of this week, you should be able to recognize, understand, and use many of the features within PowerBuilder, such as windows, controls, the PowerScript language, User Objects, and much more. You will start right away on Day 2 with making your first functional application.

Chapter

1

Getting Started

Congratulations, and welcome to the world of PowerBuilder development! If you are reading this book, it means that you have decided to take it upon yourself to learn a new language—a new skill that you can take with you and use for the rest of your life. Over the next 14 days, I will teach you the art of PowerBuilder programming, and when you are done, you will be able to go forward and build your own computer applications by using this exciting and wonderful tool.

This morning, you will learn:

- ☐ What PowerBuilder is
- ☐ About some important tools that work with PowerBuilder
- ☐ How to install PowerBuilder
- ☐ How to launch PowerBuilder after it is installed
- ☐ How to select an application if one hasn't been selected for you already

What Is PowerBuilder?

PowerBuilder is a visual application workbench. It allows you to create applications in a graphical environment, such as Microsoft Windows. PowerBuilder is an application workbench that has quickly taken over as an industry leader in software development. This is because it enables you to develop applications quickly and easily. It has an exceptional interface to a large selection of Relational Database Engines. This interface enables you to easily code your applications to communicate with these databases to transfer and act upon your data. Powersoft released the first version of PowerBuilder in 1991. It was originally developed by a small team of C Programmers. In 1994, Powersoft acquired Watcom, the makers of Watcom SQL (which is included with PowerBuilder), Watcom C++ (the most optimal C++ compiler available on the market, the one used to compile DOOM), and other fine developers' products.

Since its initial release, PowerBuilder has quickly become a mainstream competitor for application development in the software development industry. Many large companies have been using PowerBuilder to build mission-critical applications—applications that are critical to the achievement of their company's mission. PowerBuilder is the language of choice in these companies because it affords them the opportunity to create data-active applications more quickly and easily than just about any other language.

PowerBuilder is not a compiler, though. When you create a PowerBuilder application, you are creating a set of files, called *libraries*, that are read by a PowerBuilder interpreter, called a *runtime module*. The runtime module then uses the information stored in these libraries, called *P-Code*, to perform certain actions—the actions you have specified in your libraries. With a compiled language, like C++, your code is converted into computer instructions that can be executed by the Windows Engine directly. With PowerBuilder, an interpretive language, the Windows Engine executes the PowerBuilder runtime module. The PowerBuilder runtime module reads

in the code that you have written and translates it into commands that can be understood by the Windows Engine. It then sends these commands to the Windows Engine, which creates the buttons and windows, gets the data, and does everything else your code has instructed it to do.

Unfortunately, there is a cost to using an interpretive language, and that is generally in speed and control. Because there is an extra layer of translation being used to run your applications, your application will take longer to execute instructions than if it were compiled. Also, your application becomes dependent on the runtime module. For example, you must rely on the runtime module for cross-platform support and the features of the operating environment your application can take advantage of. And most importantly, you must rely on the runtime module for the lowest levels of performance tuning because the code you write is translated at runtime.

Two fortunate circumstances, however, have allowed PowerBuilder to run at acceptable speeds even though it is an interpretive language. The first circumstance is obviously the dropping cost of hardware. With the endless innovations in faster chips, cheaper hard drives, and more memory capacity, you can buy a computer with a Pentium processor in it for as low as $2,000. In fact, by the time you read this book, there will probably be a new generation of computer chips available on the market, and the Pentium will be even less expensive. With a machine as fast as a Pentium, the number of executions per second your computer can perform is generally not the bottleneck in execution time of a Windows application. Performance of a compiled application should approach double that of an interpreted application. While at 4.77MHz that may translate into minutes, on a machine that executes at over 100MHz, your perception of the slowdown will be much less significant.

Another factor that plays an important role in the performance of PowerBuilder is Powersoft's recent acquisition of Watcom. Watcom has been a leader in the development of high-performance compilers for many years. And now that Watcom is a Powersoft company, the developers of PowerBuilder can share "secrets" with the developers of the other Watcom compilers on how to tune performance. Benchmarks have shown PowerBuilder 4.0, the first release after the Watcom/Powersoft relationship, to be substantially faster than PowerBuilder 3.0, which was developed before the relationship.

So, what is PowerBuilder? It is a visual workbench that may not be perfect, but offers things that the other application workbenches do not—speed, ease of use, and most importantly, power.

The Integrated Powersoft Solution

It's important to know that besides PowerBuilder, Powersoft offers several programs that make up a complete set of database-interactive, front-end tools for use with a Graphical User Interface (GUI) environment, such as Windows. Each tool has its own target audience. Although this book doesn't teach you how to use these other tools, it's important that you're familiar with them. The availability of these other tools may allow you to create more robust, integrated solutions without having to "rebuild the wheel."

One of these other tools, a stand-alone Database Engine called Watcom SQL, comes with PowerBuilder itself. Another tool is a tool that uses PowerBuilder-like interfaces to let your users access their data and build PowerBuilder-compatible queries that you can even integrate into your PowerBuilder applications. This tool is called *InfoMaker*. Powersoft also offers some developers' tools and an application framework to assist you in building and maintaining your applications. These tools are included with the PowerBuilder Enterprise Edition, but not with PowerBuilder Desktop Edition. However, you can purchase them separately if you own PowerBuilder Desktop.

Third-party vendors have also developed tools and application frameworks you can purchase and/or license for incorporation into an application you have developed. PowerBuilder even allows you to use Custom Control DLL files and VBX files written for C++ or Visual Basic in your applications. All in all, there is a plethora of external controls and frameworks available on the market today that you can use when building your applications. Because it's always cheaper to buy than to build, you should always keep abreast of the available tools and frameworks when initiating a new software development project.

Installing PowerBuilder: History Lesson Is Over! Let's Get Started!

So you've bought PowerBuilder, and you need to install it. Well, installing PowerBuilder is relatively simple. On my computer, my hard drive is drive C: and my CD-ROM drive is drive D:, so those are the drives I'll use for installation. However, your CD-ROM drive may be drive E:, and you may prefer to install PowerBuilder on a drive other than C:. Therefore, you should use the drive letters that are appropriate for your machine when following the installation guidelines that follow. If you are using floppy disks, you will probably install from drive A: or B: instead of D:. Also, be aware that if you are using a shell other than the standard Program Manager Windows shell, things may look slightly different. If you are running on a Network, you should talk to your network administrator about where to install PowerBuilder.

Before you can install PowerBuilder on your computer, you will need to verify that you have the proper equipment. PowerBuilder for Windows requires that you at least have Microsoft Windows 3.1 with an 80386 computer and 8MB of RAM. PowerBuilder for Windows NT requires at least Windows NT version 3.5, an 80486 computer, and 12MB of RAM. They both require VGA graphics and about 20MB of hard disk space to install the complete system with all of the options. These are the basic, minimum requirements. Obviously, if your system is better, you will have no problems with the installation process. If, however, you are using a system that does not meet the minimum requirements, you should consider upgrading your system before installing PowerBuilder.

If you are using a CD-ROM drive, simply place the PowerSoft Installation CD inside it. If you are using floppy disks, find the disk that is labeled "Disk 1 of 11" and insert it into your floppy drive. From the Windows Program Manager, select Run from the File menu. The Run dialog box will appear on the screen so that you can enter a command to be executed (see Fig. 1.1). At the Command Line Prompt, simply type

`a:\setup`

and press the **ENTER** key. The disk will whir and spin a bit, and then the system will ask you which products you want to install. Figure 1.2 lists the available products for PowerBuilder Enterprise Edition. The first one is `PowerBuilder Enterprise 4.0 for Windows`. However, if you are using PowerBuilder Desktop, you will not see all of these options, and the first one will read `PowerBuilder Desktop 4.0 for Windows`. Either way, select the first item in the list, and then click the **Install** button. The system will then ask you to register your copy of PowerBuilder by entering your Name and Company Name (see Fig. 1.3). Enter the information in the boxes provided. After Setup confirms this information with you, it asks you which components of PowerBuilder you want to install and where you want to install them (see Fig. 1.4 and Fig. 1.5).

Figure 1.1.
The Run dialog box.

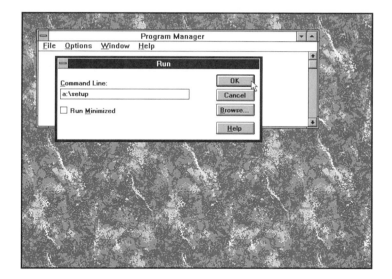

Figure 1.2.
The products available to install (for PowerBuilder Enterprise Edition only).

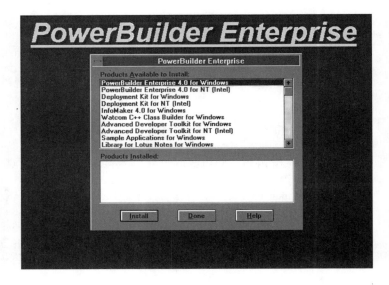

Figure 1.3.
Registering your copy of PowerBuilder.

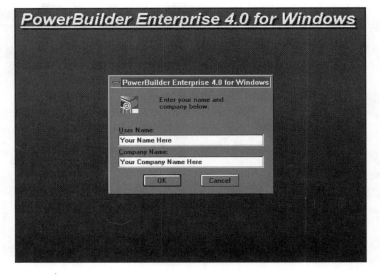

Figure 1.4.
Setup confirms your registration information.

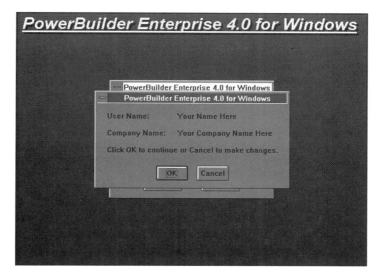

Figure 1.5.
Telling PowerBuilder which components you want to install and where you want to install them.

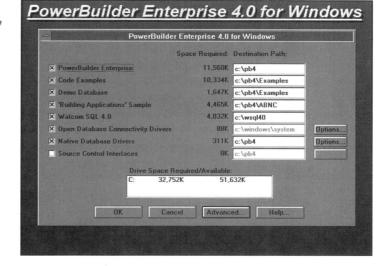

Each available component is listed in the Main Setup window with a check box next to it. You can toggle the check box to either checked or unchecked by clicking on it with your mouse. You tell the setup program to install a particular component by checking its check box. To the right of each component is a number indicating how many bytes of hard drive space are required to install that particular component, and an entry box where you may enter the path where you want that component installed. On the bottom of the screen is a box that shows you the total number of bytes you need to install all of the checked components, along with the number of bytes available on each of the hard drives where components are being installed.

For now, leave the default options checked and don't check or uncheck anything else. If you are installing to a drive other than your C: drive, enter the full path name of the path where you want to install these files in the box that says c:\pb4. The box on the bottom tells you if you have enough hard drive space to install the checked components.

DO   **DON'T**

DO Make sure that you have enough space on your hard drive to install PowerBuilder by using File Manager to organize your files and archive them if necessary. You will need anywhere from 10 to 20MB of free hard drive space to install PowerBuilder, depending on which edition of PowerBuilder you are installing and which options you decide to install.

DON'T Try to "cheat" on the installation process by just unchecking components until it tells you that you have enough room. If you don't install all of the checked components, you won't be able to complete the material in this book properly.

Click on the **OK** button, and setup will begin to install the PowerBuilder components to the locations you have specified. If the location you specify for any of your PowerBuilder component directories does not exist, setup confirms creation of a new directory in case you make a mistake (see Fig. 1.6). If you did make a mistake, you will be able to cancel the installation here by pressing the **No** button.

A screen will appear with a box in the bottom left corner that tells you how far along the installation has gone, which file is being copied, and to where it is being copied (see Fig. 1.7). The box at the top of the screen contains installation notes about PowerBuilder that are not in the manual.

Figure 1.6.
Confirmation before creating the c:\pb4 directory.

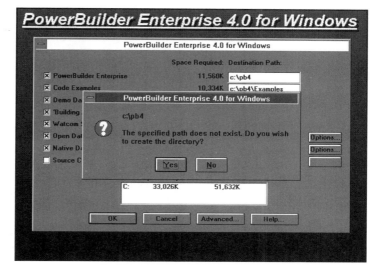

Figure 1.7.
The Installation Status screen.

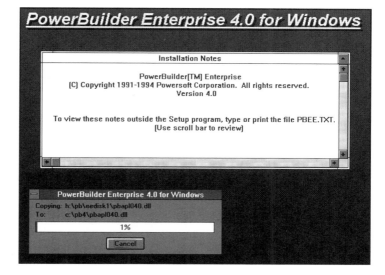

If you are using floppy disks, then every so often Setup prompts you to replace the disk in your floppy drive with the next disk in the set (see Fig. 1.8). At the end of this process, Setup asks you for one of the disks from the ODBC DDDK Set. If you specify that you want to install other ODBC drivers, it may ask for more than one of the ODBC disks.

Figure 1.8.
Prompt for Disk 2.

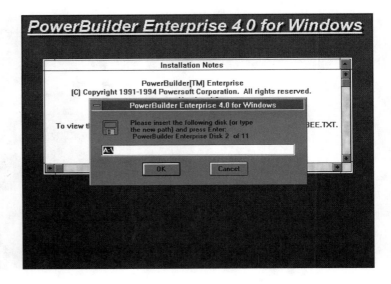

Setup then asks you to update your AUTOEXEC.BAT file to include the necessary directories in your path (see Fig. 1.9). Selecting to update your AUTOEXEC.BAT enables PowerBuilder to run properly even when you are doing development in a directory other than the PowerBuilder directory. If your path is not updated properly, you may run into problems later on that may be very difficult to troubleshoot. Therefore, it is recommended that you allow Setup to update your path. Setup will also ask if it can update your *system registry*, which is also often referred to as the *registration database* (see Fig. 1.10). Applications register themselves in the registration database to allow Windows to use them as servers for Object Linking and Embedding (OLE). In other words, by registering PowerBuilder with Windows, you will be able to embed PowerBuilder objects right into other Windows applications, and Windows will know how to run them. You'll learn a little bit more about OLE in Chapter 14, "Other Types of User Objects."

Finally, Setup asks you if you want to create a PowerBuilder Program Manager Group (see Fig. 1.11). Choose **Yes** to have setup create a Program Manager Group with the PowerBuilder and PowerBuilder Demo Database icons (see Fig. 1.12). After Setup creates your Program Manager Group, it informs you that setup is complete with a bright and exciting dialog box (see Fig. 1.13). Exit Windows and reboot your machine by pressing **Ctrl-Alt-Delete** so that your computer will recognize PowerBuilder and Watcom in your path.

Figure 1.9.
*Updating
AUTOEXEC.BAT.*

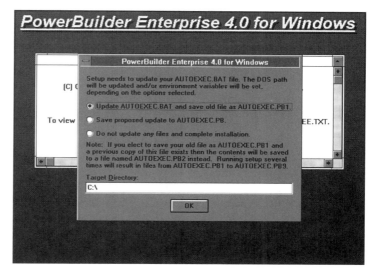

Figure 1.10.
Update the System Registry?

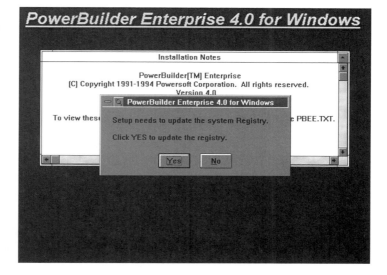

Figure 1.11.
Prompt to create a Program Manager Group.

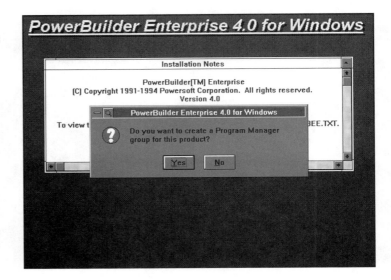

Figure 1.12.
The Powersoft Program Manager Group.

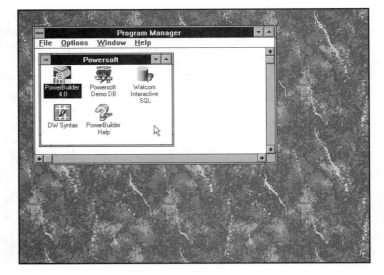

Figure 1.13.
Setup is complete!

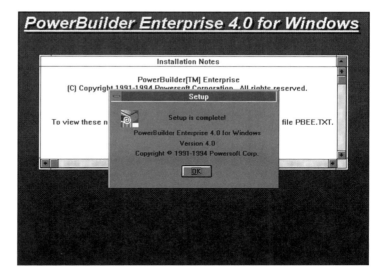

Using PowerBuilder with Other Databases

If you are developing in a Corporate Environment, you will probably be using a server-based Database Management System (DBMS), like Oracle, SQL Server, or Watcom-NLM. If this is the case, you received a set of SQL interface disks with your edition of PowerBuilder that includes the drivers PowerBuilder needs to use to connect to your server. While this book deals only with the single-user Watcom SQL Database engine that comes with PowerBuilder, you may also want to install the driver for your other DBMS. Simply insert the first disk into your drive and run its Setup program in the same way you ran the setup program for PowerBuilder itself. The Setup procedure gives you the option to install the SQL Interface Drivers as well as the Distribution Kit.

You will need the Distribution Kit to distribute your compiled applications to users who don't have PowerBuilder. If you choose to install the Distribution Kit, be sure to install it into its own directory, and not in the PowerBuilder (c:\pb4) directory. Be sure to install the SQL Interface files into the same directory that you installed PowerBuilder, though.

Congratulations! You have just completed your first step into the world of PowerBuilder development!

Launching PowerBuilder

Now that you have prepared your system to run PowerBuilder, you need to learn how to run it and set it up so you are comfortable in your PowerBuilder environment. When you start Windows, you should again see the PowerBuilder Program Manager Group on your screen (refer to Fig. 1.12). Double-click on the PowerBuilder Icon on the screen. After a number of hard drive revolutions, a box appears informing you that you are now running PowerBuilder, and the main PowerBuilder desktop appears (see Fig. 1.14). The title bar (the top line of the screen) should say PowerBuilder - Exampl40. The first part is the name of the application you are running—PowerBuilder. The second part is the name of the application with which you are working. In PowerBuilder, you create applications and, as such, you are always working within the context of the application you are creating. Therefore, the application that is displayed on the title bar, Exampl40, is the name of the application that PowerBuilder thinks you want to work with now, which also happens to be the sample application you installed in the last section.

Figure 1.14.
The Initial PowerBuilder screen.

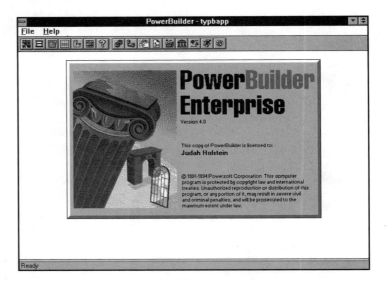

If during the installation process earlier in this chapter you chose not to install the sample application, PowerBuilder asks you to select an application. Because applications are stored in libraries, PowerBuilder first asks you which library the desired application is in (see Fig. 1.15).

Figure 1.15.
*Select a PowerBuilder
Application Library.*

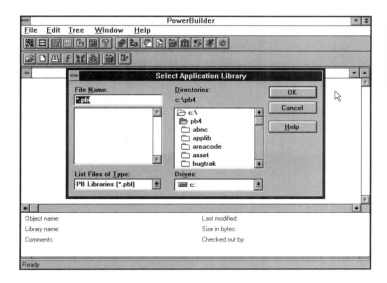

Choosing an Application

If you have been prompted to select an application, you need to either select one that already exists, or create a new one. The first dialog box in which you do this looks very much like other dialog boxes used to open files from inside Windows (refer to Fig. 1.15). At the bottom right, you can change which drive you are looking at. Above that in the Directories list box, you can select the directory to look in for the application. Next to the Directories list box, on the right side, is the File Names list, which lists all of the libraries in the specified directory. From that list, you can select the library file that houses the application with which you want to work. Also, above that is the File Name entry box where you can type in a library name directly if you already know it. We will talk more about libraries later on in Chapter 9, "The Library Painter," which is devoted specifically to them. For now, just know that applications are stored in library files, and in order to select an application, you first need to select the library within which it is stored.

After you select a library (or type in its name), the Select Application dialog box appears, listing all of the applications in the library you just selected (see Fig. 1.16). The first application is highlighted, meaning that it is selected. Its name also appears in the Applications entry box. Also, if there are comments about the application, they appear in the Comments box. You can select a different application by either clicking on its name in the Applications list box, scrolling up and down with the arrow keys inside the Applications list box, or by typing the name of the application you want in the Applications edit box. Finally, you can indicate that the currently selected application is the one you want by pressing the **OK** button. If you have made a mistake somehow, you can press the **Cancel** button, and PowerBuilder will forget you even asked to open a new application.

Figure 1.16.
Select a PowerBuilder application.

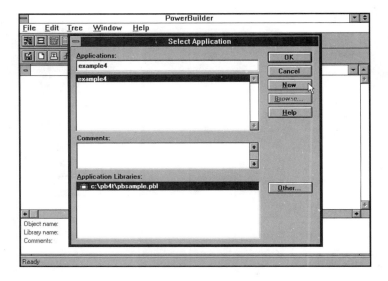

Note: PowerBuilder requires that some application be "active" in order for you to do any development. Therefore, if you have just installed and are without any application at all, PowerBuilder will prompt you with a message explaining that you are required to select an application (see Fig. 1.17). If you ignore that message, PowerBuilder will terminate your session, prompting you with a message stating so (see Fig. 1.18). (They think they're real tough when they do that, don't they? Little do they know that all we have to do to get back in is to double-click on the PowerBuilder icon again as we did in the preceding section, and just start again.)

Figure 1.17.
PowerBuilder requires an application.

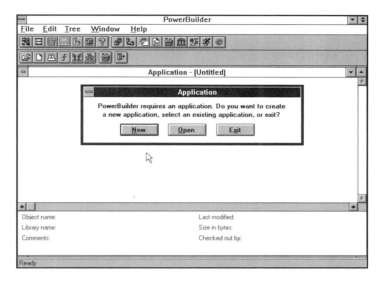

Figure 1.18.
Warning that this will end your PowerBuilder session.

Morning Summary

PowerBuilder is a visual development environment that is rapidly becoming an important contender in the battle of Windows development tools. It is an application workbench that allows you to quickly create applications that can run under the Microsoft Windows environment. This morning you learned a bit of the history and semantics of PowerBuilder, and also about some of the other tools that can help you make robust solutions by using PowerBuilder. Some of these other tools are Powersoft products, like InfoMaker, Watcom SQL, and the Application Framework. Before you can use PowerBuilder, however, you must install it onto your system.

Installing PowerBuilder properly copies all of the necessary files from the disks that come in your PowerBuilder package to your hard drive; it also sets up your Windows environment so that you can run PowerBuilder. You have learned about the different installation components and options and what the PowerBuilder Setup program does to your computer during the installation process. After PowerBuilder is installed on your computer, you can launch it by double-clicking on the PowerBuilder icon in the Powersoft Program Manager Group. After you have launched PowerBuilder, you see the initial PowerBuilder window, which uses the Exampl40 application, a sample application that comes with PowerBuilder to help demonstrate some of the things you can do with the tool.

Chapter

2

The PowerBuilder Environment

This afternoon, you will learn about the PowerBuilder Development Environment. You will learn:

☐ About some of the common menus you will find in PowerBuilder

☐ How to make the most of the toolbars that PowerBuilder provides for you

☐ How to select the sample application

☐ About the kinds of applications that PowerBuilder lets you build

An Introduction to the PowerBuilder Environment

After you have launched PowerBuilder and haves chosen an application, you are faced with a big, almost empty screen (see Fig. 2.1). The colors for the different components of a window are handled internally by Windows and can be set in the Colors applet of the Control panel, so things may look slightly different on your computer.

Figure 2.1.
The main PowerBuilder screen.

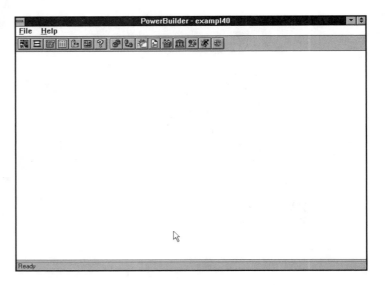

On the title bar on the top line of the screen is the name of the application you are running, *PowerBuilder*, and then a dash, and then the name of the PowerBuilder application you are working with, in this case *exampl40*. On the right side of the title bar are two buttons with which you may already be familiar. They are the *Minimize button* and the *Maximize/Restore button*. If you click on the Minimize button, which looks like a down arrow, your window minimizes and shrinks down into a PowerBuilder icon in the bottom-left corner of the screen. If you then double-click on the minimized PowerBuilder icon, your PowerBuilder window appears again on-screen and is the size it was before you minimized it.

If you click on the Maximize button, which looks like an up arrow, your window maximizes, meaning it grows in size to fill up the entire screen. Also, the Maximize button changes into a Restore button. Instead of looking like an up arrow, it looks like an up-and-down arrow. If you click on this button, your window restores itself again to the size it was before it was maximized. Finally, on the left corner of the window is a box that looks like it has a long dash running through its center. This is the *control menu*. When you click on the control menu, a menu appears in which you can minimize, maximize, or restore your window (depending upon its current state); move, size, or close your window; or switch to another application using the Microsoft Windows Task Manager. It's important to recognize the different components of your title bar because in Microsoft Windows, nearly *every* window has a title bar, and nearly every title bar looks and works the same way. Even most of the windows that you create in your own applications will have title bars, and so you must be aware of their existence and of how they work.

Note: If you have ever done any GUI development, you will probably recognize the control menu by a different name—the *system menu*. There are actually two different "flavors" of control menus. The first one has a long dash in it and appears on the main window of an application. The other one has a smaller dash in it and appears on some of the windows that are contained inside the main window of an application, but not on the main window itself. The **C**lose menu item of the smaller-dash control menu only closes the window on which it lies. The accelerator for the close function on this menu is **Ctrl-F4**. Also, the last menu item of this control menu appears as Nex**t** Window, which takes you to the next window inside the application. The accelerator for the Nex**t** Window menu item is **Ctrl-F6**. However, the control menu with the larger dash has **Alt-F4** as its **C**lose accelerator, and choosing **C**lose will close the entire application, even if there are many windows inside the main window. Additionally, there is no Nex**t** Window item, but instead there is a **S**witch To item that brings up the Windows Task Manager when you select it. The accelerator key for this menu item is **Ctrl-Esc**. Take note of the two different types of control menus. In Chapter 10, "The Multiple Document Interface (MDI)," these are discussed in more detail.

Immediately under the blue title bar is a white menu bar. Starting from left to right, the menu bar has some words on it, in this case, **F**ile and **H**elp. Each of these words represents a menu that you can use to select things to do and places to go. If you click with your mouse on either of these two menus, a list of menu items appears under the menu you click. Clicking on different menu items causes different things to happen. Go ahead and try it—click on the **F**ile menu, and then click on the E**x**it menu item that appears at the end of the list that shows up under the **F**ile menu. Whoa! You probably realize that by doing this you have exited the PowerBuilder environment, but that's okay. Restart PowerBuilder again, and you can continue.

Notice that some letters in many of the menus and menu items are underlined, for example the "F" in File and the "H" in Help. These letters are called *accelerators*. They are meant to allow the user to work more quickly by allowing him/her to use the keyboard to navigate through the system. How does it work? Well, if you hold the **Alt** key and then press the letter of the menu that is underlined, it will act as if you clicked it. So, if you hold down the **Alt** key and press **F** at the same time, the File menu will appear. Then, if you let go of both **Alt** and **F** and just press **X**, you exit the system again. Of course, you probably have had enough of me making you get in and out of PowerBuilder, so you don't have to exit again; this time you can try it with different menu items. The rule is that to get to a menu that is on the menu bar (like **F**ile and **H**elp) you need to hold down the **Alt** key for the accelerator key to work. Once the menu is open, you can get to its menu items and submenus by using the accelerator key without holding down the **Alt** key.

Note: Sometimes, accelerators are referred to as *hot keys*.

Note: The reason that the accelerator keys may seem to be inconsistent is actually because using **Alt-*Accelerator*** is in itself a shortcut. In the "olden" days of Windows, the way to use an accelerator key was to first press the **F10** or **Alt** key alone, which would bring you to the menu bar, and then press the accelerator key for the letter of the menu item you were interested in. In later versions of Windows, this process is shortened into a single keystroke. However, you can still press just the **Alt** key or just the **F10** key to get to the menu without selecting any particular item on the main menu.

There is also another kind of accelerator key. Some menu items have other words and letters to the right of the menu item text itself. For example, under the **F**ile menu, the third menu item reads **P**owerPanel.... To the right of this menu item appears Ctrl+P. This means that if you hold down the **Ctrl** key and press the letter **P** at the same time, PowerBuilder executes the same function that executes when you select the **P**owerPanel... menu item from the **F**ile menu.

Right now, there are only two menu items on the menu bar. That's because only two menus are available for the screen you're looking at. However, at other times, you may find other menus available based on the screen you are looking at. Some very common menus you will see in PowerBuilder are:

- A **F**ile menu, where you can load and save files and data (see Fig. 2.2)
- An **E**dit menu, where you can do things that edit the controls and text you are working with

- ☐ A **W**indow menu, where you can arrange windows on your screen or select a different window
- ☐ A **H**elp menu, where you can ask the system for help and helpful information
- ☐ A De**c**lare menu, where you can declare variables and functions
- ☐ A **D**esign menu, where you can manage and preview the design of your application components

Figure 2.2.
The File menu.

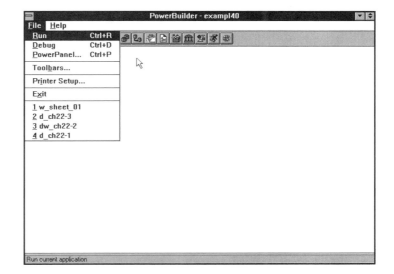

There are many menus in PowerBuilder to help you build your applications. As you learn about each application component, you are also introduced to each of the important menu items for that component.

The Toolbar

Under the menu bar is a toolbar with a bunch of picture buttons (see Fig. 2.3). Each of the buttons on the toolbar actually corresponds to a menu item in one of the menus. Developers like to create toolbars to allow mouse users to quickly access frequently used menu items, in the same way that they give accelerator keys to keyboard users. Each toolbar button has on it a picture that tries to make it easy for you to understand the purpose of that toolbar on-screen. For example, on the toolbar that is on-screen now, the second button looks like a window. That's because if you want to create a window, you can click on that button. (But don't do it yet! We'll get to that in the next couple of days.)

Figure 2.3.
The toolbar.

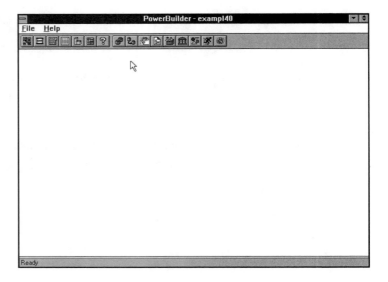

Toolbars, like menus, sometimes change, appear, and disappear, depending on what window you are looking at. Certain options and commands are only available when you are looking at certain windows, so PowerBuilder doesn't give you the opportunity to execute something you're not supposed to. In fact, in PowerBuilder, there are multiple toolbars that can appear on-screen at any time. The *PowerBar*, the toolbar that's on your screen now and appears in Figure 2.3, contains buttons that correspond to actions that you can perform from just about anywhere in PowerBuilder. A second toolbar, the *PainterBar*, appears on-screen with buttons that change depending on where you are in the system.

Because toolbars are offered as a facility for mouse users, Powersoft has tried to make it as convenient as possible for mouse users to take advantage of toolbars. Therefore, they have added additional toolbar features to make them easier to work with, like the capability to move them, customize them, and show short descriptions of what they do.

The first thing that Powersoft has given you to help facilitate your use of toolbars is a collection of "cues" to help you determine what each toolbar is intended to do. The first of these cues is manifested in small descriptive phrases that appear on the status bar when you click and hold your mouse down on a toolbar button. The toolbar button's action won't actually occur until you release your mouse button. If you click and hold down the mouse button on your toolbar, the status bar will show a brief description of the action that releasing your button will cause. If you decide that you don't want to perform that action, you can simply move your mouse cursor outside of the area of the toolbar button and release the mouse button there.

Alternatively, you can simply leave your mouse stationary on top of any icon in the toolbar. After a few seconds, the PowerBuilder *ToolTips* will appear, displaying the name of the toolbar button that your mouse cursor is pointing to inside a small yellow bubble, and describing the toolbar button's function on the status bar, as well (see Fig. 2.4). By moving the mouse cursor over different toolbar buttons, you can see ToolTips for each one. This information can be very useful for you when you remember or can figure out what some of the buttons do, but need a little one- or two-word push to remember what happens when you click on some of the less frequently used buttons.

Figure 2.4.
The PowerBuilder ToolTips.

Another feature of toolbars you will often find useful is the capability to easily move the toolbar around the screen to any position that you like. To move a toolbar, you can just grab it and move it. This can sometimes be a little bit tricky, though, because you have to grab it in an area that indicates to the toolbar that you want to move it, and not that you want to click on any of its buttons. You can try to grab it, then, either in one of the gaps between buttons, or in the margin between the edge of a button and the edge of the toolbar.

Warning: Be aware that to the right of the toolbar is a large amount of empty toolbar space, but only a small piece of that actually "belongs" to the toolbar itself. If you try to grab the toolbar too far to the right, it will not move.

Grab the toolbar with your mouse and drag it around the screen. Drag it to the middle of the screen, then to the bottom, then back to the top, then to the left, and then to the right. Notice how the shadow that is created changes shape. That's because when it's on the edges of the screen, it becomes a toolbar that aligns itself with its edge, but when it is not on the edge of the screen, it becomes a *Floating* toolbar (see Fig. 2.5). Try dragging your toolbar to the middle of the screen and then let go of your mouse. See what happens? The toolbar is no longer a bar on the edge of your screen, but is instead a set of buttons inside a box that can be placed anywhere inside your screen.

27

Figure 2.5.
The Floating toolbar.

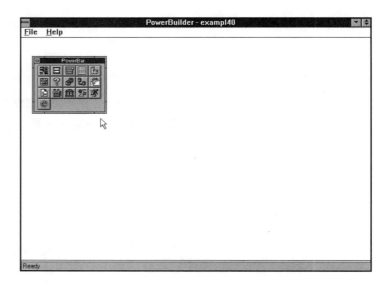

You can quickly move the toolbar from one edge of the screen to another by using the right button of your mouse. Click on the toolbar with your right mouse button instead of your left mouse button, and a popup menu appears (see Fig. 2.6). There are a number of menu items on this popup menu. The first one says "PowerBar" and has a little check mark next to it. In PowerBuilder, there are actually a few toolbars that you can work with at certain times. The main one that you are working with right now is called the *PowerBar*. The PowerBar is the main PowerBuilder navigational toolbar that contains buttons that perform functions that are always available. You learn more about the PowerBar in the next section. For now, just be aware that the toolbar that you are playing with is called a PowerBar. The check mark means that the PowerBar is visible. If you now click on PowerBar, the check mark turns off, and the PowerBar disappears. To get it back, select **File|Toolbars**.... This brings up the Toolbars window, where you can control the appearance of the toolbars in PowerBuilder, as well. Click on the **Show** button to show the PowerBar, and then click on the **Done** button to close the Toolbars window. The next five menu items on the right mouse menu do exactly what you just did when you were dragging the toolbar around the screen with your mouse. They move the PowerBar to the position on-screen that you specify: left, right, top, bottom, or floating.

Let's jump down to the last menu item for a moment. The last menu item reads Show Text. Click on that menu item and watch what happens. All of your toolbar buttons get really big and have a word or two under them to describe what they do (see Fig. 2.7). For the first few weeks when you use PowerBuilder, you will probably like the Show Text to be on to remind you of what each toolbar button does. After you have some experience with PowerBuilder, the pictures and ToolTips will be enough of a reminder by themselves, and you'll probably want to turn off the toolbar text so that the toolbar takes up less room on-screen. To turn off the toolbar text, just right-click on your toolbar again. The popup menu appears, and this time the Show Text menu item will have a check mark next to it. If you click on the Show Text menu item this time, it will turn off the toolbar text, and the next time you right-click on the toolbar menu, you will find the Show Text menu item unchecked.

Figure 2.6.
The toolbar popup menu.

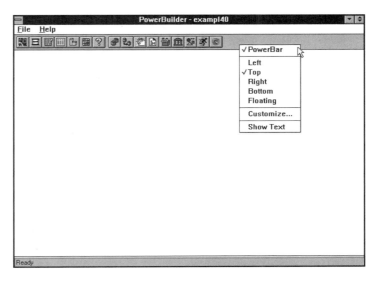

Figure 2.7.
The toolbar with text.

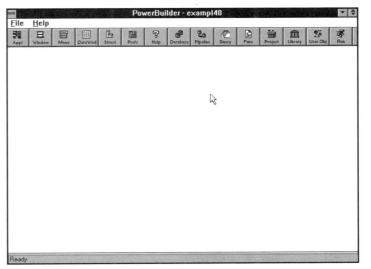

> **Warning:** Unfortunately, there is a little bit of a problem if you leave the Show Text on in PowerBuilder. If you are using standard 640-×-480 video mode and you leave Show Text on, some of the PainterBars don't fit into the width of the screen. Generally, I prefer to leave the text off, and stick to using ToolTips and status bar help if I can't remember what a button does.

The menu item that hasn't been discussed is labeled Customize.... By using Customize, you can do really neat things to your toolbar, like add buttons, remove buttons, and change the order of buttons on your toolbar. When you click on Customize, the Customize toolbar window appears (see Fig. 2.8). At the top of this window, you can select your palette. In PowerBuilder, there are three palettes that you can choose from: the **P**ainterBar, the Power**B**ar, and the **C**ustom palette. The PainterBar palette is only available when you are customizing a PainterBar, and the PowerBar palette is only available when you are customizing the PowerBar. Right now, you are working with the PowerBar, so the PainterBar button is disabled and grayed out. Conceptually, though, both the PainterBar and PowerBar palettes work the same way. Toolbar buttons that are on the PainterBar and PowerBar palettes are preset by PowerBuilder and map directly to functions that are available in PowerBuilder itself. For example, there is an Exit toolbar button in the PowerBar palette. The Exit toolbar button maps directly to the Exit command in PowerBuilder, which can also be accessed by choosing the **F**ile|**Ex**it menu item. If you want to be able to quickly exit by clicking on the Exit toolbar button, click on the Exit toolbar button in the palette (the first set of icons in the middle of the screen) and hold down the mouse button while you drag it onto your toolbar (on the bottom of the screen). When you let go, the Exit button appears on your toolbar not too far from where you left it, between other buttons. If you want to move it because you prefer it to be in a different spot, you can drag it in the same way to a new position. If you want to get rid of it, you can drag it anywhere off the toolbar, and it disappears. If you want to move a button onto the end of the toolbar, you need to scroll the toolbar to the end by using the scroll bar under it so you can drop your button there. Notice, also, that if you click on any of the buttons, either in the palette or in the toolbar, the status bar displays some information about the function that is mapped to that button.

The Custom palette has other icons that are built into PowerBuilder but that are not mapped to any functionality inside PowerBuilder. Instead, when you drag a button from the Custom palette to your toolbar, PowerBuilder prompts you for some information about the toolbar item (see Fig. 2.9). The first thing you need to enter is the command line to run when you click on the toolbar button. For example, if you want to run File Manager every time you click on the button, in the Command Line box enter `winfile.exe`, which is the command line that runs the Windows File Manager. If you don't remember the name of the command line that you want your toolbar button to run, you can search for it by pressing the **Browse** button. The second thing you need to tell PowerBuilder about your toolbar button is its toolbar text. That's the text that will appear in your toolbar button's ToolTips and when you choose Show Text to show the text of the toolbar. In the box labeled `Item Text`, you can specify a word or phrase to be used as the toolbar text of your custom button. If you prefer, you may specify two toolbar text items to use, a short one and a long one, separated by a comma (,). The first one appears beneath the toolbar item when Show Text is on, and the second one appears in the toolbar button's ToolTips bubble. The final thing you need to tell the toolbar item is its Microhelp text. The Microhelp text is the text that appears on the status bar at the bottom of the screen when you click on the toolbar button. At the bottom of the Customize screen also notice two buttons, labeled Query and Report. Although you haven't learned what they are yet, just be aware that by using those two buttons, you can have your toolbar run a query or generate a report instead of running an external command line when you press your custom button.

Figure 2.8.
The Customize toolbar window.

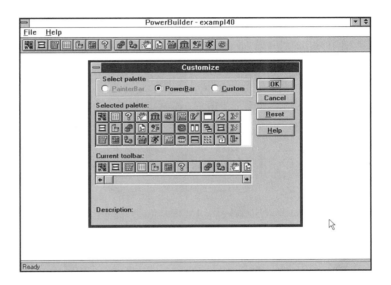

Figure 2.9.
Custom Toolbar Item Command window.

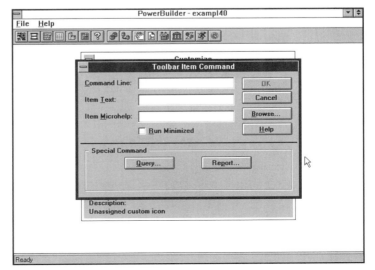

31

In addition, when editing certain toolbars, you may be offered the capability to click other buttons to put other items on the toolbar. For example, when editing the Window PainterBar, you will be able to create a custom toolbar item out of a User Object.

You can also create a custom toolbar item that corresponds to a menu item. To do this, enter the command in the following format:

`@<menu>.<menuitem>`

For example, if you want to create a custom toolbar that corresponds to the **File|Close** menu item, enter the following command:

`@File.Close`

In addition, you can use the menu item position number instead of the menu item name. For example, if the **C**lose menu is the fourth menu item under the **F**ile menu, which is the first menu item, you can enter,

`@1.4`

This is extremely useful for some menu items you will encounter later that allow you to perform important tasks, but whose names are not clear. For example, later you will learn about aligning text and objects in your windows. The menu item to do this, however, has no name, but instead uses pictures to explain its purpose. In order to create a toolbar from this menu item, then, you need to use the menu item position number.

Note also that the command must correspond to a menu item that performs an action, and not one that has a submenu. If a menu item is inside a submenu, you can simply separate the menu item from its submenu item with a period, as you do between the menu and its menu item; for example,

`@Edit.Align.3`

which corresponds to the third menu item under the Edit|Align menu.

Clicking on the **OK** button saves your changes, inserts your toolbar button onto your toolbar, and brings you back to the Customize Toolbar window. If you then want to save your new, custom toolbar, click the **OK** button on the Customize Toolbar window, and it will return you to the main PowerBuilder screen with a brand new, personalized PowerBar.

The PowerBar/PowerPanel

The last section talked extensively about how to use and customize the PowerBuilder toolbars, but it didn't actually talk very much about what the toolbars do.

The main PowerBuilder toolbar, the one that you have been working with in the previous section, is called the *PowerBar* (see Fig. 2.10). On it are buttons that help you get around within PowerBuilder. For less frequently used global actions, PowerBuilder has something called the

PowerPanel (see Fig. 2.11), which is a window with buttons for all of the *Painters* you can access to paint (or create) PowerBuilder objects, as well as several other important things you can do in PowerBuilder. To bring up the PowerPanel, select **File|PowerPanel**, or press **Ctrl-P**. This action displays all of the buttons in a small window on-screen. While this window is up, you cannot do anything else except click on a button to perform an action, or close the window. You can close the window either by choosing **C**lose from the control menu (the one with the dash in it in the top right hand corner) or by clicking on the **Cancel** button.

Figure 2.10.
The PowerBar.

Figure 2.11.
The PowerPanel.

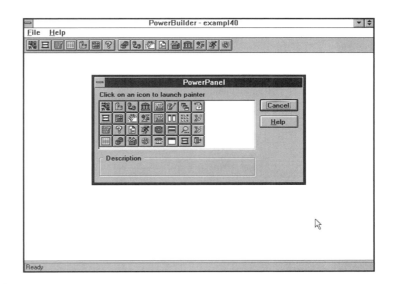

With PowerBuilder, you learn to paint your windows, controls, reports, and other things by using *Painters*. To get to the different Painters inside PowerBuilder, you use the PowerBar or PowerPanel. Each button on the PowerBar gets you to a different Painter:

 Application Painter—Edits attributes of your application, like the application's icon

 Window Painter—Creates windows and dialogs that will be displayed to the user

 Menu Painter—Creates menus and toolbars of your own that the user can use in your application

 DataWindow Painter—Creates layouts for data entry and data display

33

Structure Painter—Creates structures to group related variables

Preferences Painter—Changes the way your PowerBuilder environment looks and feels

Online Help—Gets help about PowerBuilder

Database Painter—Creates and modifies data in your database

Data Pipeline Painter—Converts and copies your data with Data Pipelines

Query Painter—Creates and saves queries for incorporation into your application

Function Painter—Creates global functions that can be called by your application's scripts

Project Painter—Manages the creation of executable applications with projects

Library Painter—Organizes and manipulates the components you have developed

User Object Painter—Creates user objects to group common functions and components or communicate with external objects

Run—Runs your application

Debug—Debugs your application

Additionally, there are other toolbar items that are PowerBar items you can place on the toolbar by using the Customize Toolbar function described in the previous section.

Space—Adds a space to make room between sets of toolbar buttons

Report Painter—Creates and runs reports (The Blue one is for run-only mode, where you cannot create reports, only run them)

Database Profile Painter—Selects and edits database profiles, which tell PowerBuilder how to communicate with your database

ODBC Driver Configuration—Configures your Open Database Connectivity Driver, the database drivers provided by Microsoft to permit communication to multiple database types using a single SQL standard

Tile Vertical—Arranges the open sheets as tiled vertically

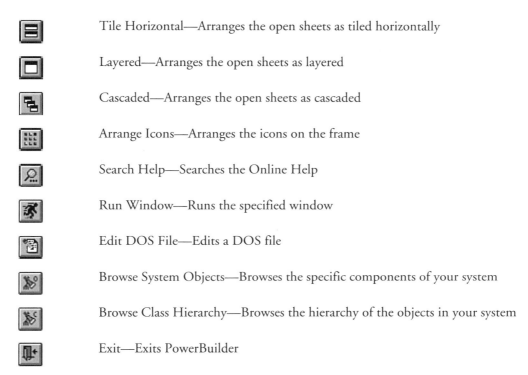

Tile Horizontal—Arranges the open sheets as tiled horizontally

Layered—Arranges the open sheets as layered

Cascaded—Arranges the open sheets as cascaded

Arrange Icons—Arranges the icons on the frame

Search Help—Searches the Online Help

Run Window—Runs the specified window

Edit DOS File—Edits a DOS file

Browse System Objects—Browses the specific components of your system

Browse Class Hierarchy—Browses the hierarchy of the objects in your system

Exit—Exits PowerBuilder

The toolbar buttons on the PowerBar are ones that are at the highest level of functionality and are applicable to PowerBuilder as a whole, and not to any one single component, painter, or editor. The PowerBar stays on your screen at all times (except if you turn it off), so you can access those toolbar buttons no matter what else you are doing. It is important to recognize this structure because when you develop your own applications, you may want to use that as a guideline.

PowerBuilder Preferences

PowerBuilder has many options that you can control besides the ones that you have already learned about. To discuss them now would be premature because many of them relate to things about which you have not yet learned. However, most of the options in PowerBuilder can be managed from a single, central location, called the *Preferences Painter*. You open the Preferences Painter by clicking on the Preferences button that appears on the PowerBar or PowerPanel. You are then presented with the Preferences window, which allows you to view and edit your preference settings (see Fig. 2.12).

Figure 2.12.
The Preferences window.

The preferences are split up into sections based on what they control. For example, preferences that relate to your application are contained in the Application section. Preferences that have to do with the database appear in the Database section. Preferences that have to do with the PowerBuilder environment appear in the PowerBuilder section. Each section appears as an icon in the area labeled Section. You change to the section you want to work with simply by clicking on its icon. When you click on the icon of a section, the list of preference variables, sometimes referred to as *keywords*, will appear in the list labeled **V**ariable:. You can then select a keyword from the list, and its value will appear in the box on the bottom of the screen labeled Va**l**ue:. You may change the value for the selected preference variable simply by changing the value that appears in this box.

Note: Throughout this book, I will mention preferences that you may be interested in that apply to the specific topic we are discussing. However, for the complete list of preferences and their possible values, you will need to refer to the PowerBuilder documentation.

PowerBuilder uses a special type of file, called a *Profile file*, to store the values for your preference variables. If you are using Microsoft Windows, this file is called *PB.INI*, and by default is located in your PowerBuilder directory. Microsoft Windows provides a standard for Profile files that is

used by PowerBuilder and not just for the PowerBuilder preferences. There are even PowerBuilder functions that you can use to create and use profile files in your own applications. As an alternate to using the Preferences Painter to control your PowerBuilder environment, you can use other utilities to edit your PowerBuilder Profile file. However, if you do this, your changes may not take effect until you restart PowerBuilder.

Selecting the Sample Application

PowerBuilder includes a sample application that was installed onto your hard drive during the installation process if you followed the directions in the previous chapter. If you did not install the sample application, you must either install it now or skip the rest of today's lesson. To install the sample application, follow the installation instructions from Chapter 1.

To run the sample application, you must first make sure that your PowerBuilder environment is using it. If you are currently set to use the sample application, your title bar will read PowerBuilder - exampl40, indicating that exampl40 (the "official" name of the sample application) is the current application. You can skip to the next section, "The Sample Application," if your system is currently set to exampl40. However, if it does not say that, you need to select the sample application as your current application. Open the Application Painter on the PowerBar by clicking on the Application Toolbar button. Select the **F**ile|**O**pen menu. The Select Application Library window appears (see Fig. 2.13). Find the directory where you installed PowerBuilder in the right side of the window, under where it says Directories. Select the "examples" directory that appears under the PowerBuilder directory by double-clicking on it. On the left side of the window, in the box labeled File Name, enter

`pbexamfe.pbl`

or select it from the list. Click on the **OK** button. The Select Application window appears (see Fig. 2.14). The top line of the window, labeled Application, reads `exampl40`. Click the **OK** button to return to the Application Painter. From the **E**dit Menu, select **L**ibrary List. At the bottom left of the screen, double-click on each entry in the Library list box. As you double-click on each entry, its name and path are added to the list at the top of the screen. After you have added all of the libraries, click on the **OK** button. Once again, you are returned to the Application Painter. Close the Application Painter by selecting **F**ile|**U**pdate. This accepts your selection of the exampl40 application, and your title bar reads PowerBuilder - exampl40.

Figure 2.13.
The Select Application Library window.

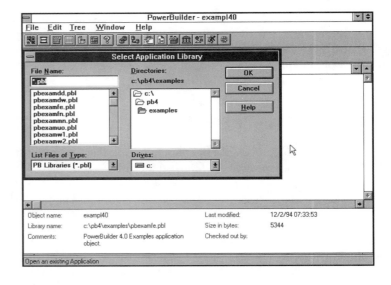

Figure 2.14.
The Select Application window.

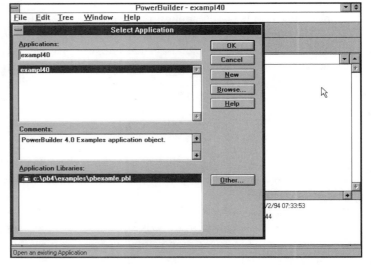

The PowerBuilder Sample Application

The PowerBuilder sample application that comes with PowerBuilder is an application that the people at Powersoft created and collected to demonstrate many of the exciting features of PowerBuilder. By spending a few minutes with the sample application, you can get a glimpse of just a few of the exciting things you can do with PowerBuilder in your own applications. I won't review all of the sample application; I'll leave some of the experimenting up to you.

To start the sample application, all you need to do is click on the **Run** button on the toolbar—the one that looks like a little man running. The PowerBuilder environment minimizes to show a pretty, purple title screen, and your disk may begin whirring for a few moments until the Sample Application main window appears on your screen (see Fig. 2.15).

Figure 2.15.
The Sample Application main window.

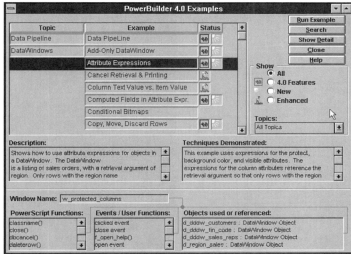
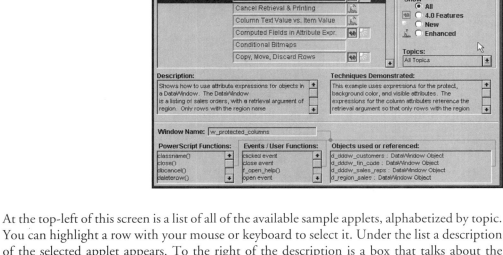

At the top-left of this screen is a list of all of the available sample applets, alphabetized by topic. You can highlight a row with your mouse or keyboard to select it. Under the list a description of the selected applet appears. To the right of the description is a box that talks about the PowerBuilder techniques that the applet illustrates. Under the description is yet another box that tells you the name of the window that it will open to run that applet, and also tells you some information about that window, including the functions and events that it uses and references. At the top right of the screen, there are a number of buttons. The first button, **Run Example**, is the button you press to run the selected example. Underneath that is a **Search** button you can use to search for a specific example. Beneath that one is the **Show Detail** button, which runs a report that explains the example that is selected in detail. Below that are the **Close** and **Help** buttons, which close the window and get help about the window, respectively.

Under the buttons is a set of radio buttons and a drop-down list box that lets you limit the list of examples to a more specific set of examples. By selecting a topic in the drop-down list box, you can show just the examples for that topic. By selecting one of the radio buttons, you can limit the list to show only those that demonstrate 4.0 features, new features in PowerBuilder version 4.0; New examples that weren't available in previous versions of the sample applications; or Enhanced examples that were available in previous sample applications, but have been updated. By using these radio buttons and the drop-down list box, you can limit the list on the left to only those examples that you are interested in, so that it is easier to work with. Now, let's take a look at a few of my favorite examples.

Let's start with something simple, and perhaps relatively unexciting. PowerBuilder has functions that allow you to ask the system for the current time and date. The "Digital Clock" example in the DataWindow Topic uses these functions to display a digital clock on-screen (see Fig. 2.16).

Figure 2.16.
The digital clock.

A more interesting example, the "Presentation Styles" example of the DataWindow Topic, demonstrates the built-in presentation styles of data that PowerBuilder offers (see Fig. 2.17). If you look at the one labeled GRID, you can see the data in its most flat format. PowerBuilder lets you easily build things like groups, cross-tabulations, and graphs with your data. You'll learn more about this feature when we discuss DataWindows at the end of the week.

Another interesting example is the "Change Employee Status" example of the Drag and Drop topic, which demonstrates a feature called *Drag and Drop* (see Fig. 2.18). Drag and Drop allows the user, in this case you, to pick up things on-screen with your mouse by pointing to them and holding down the left mouse button. Once you have picked up an item, you can drag it around the screen and drop it on drop targets by letting go of the mouse button. In this example, you can drag a person's name into the DataWindow drop target on the bottom-right of the screen to see his record appear there. Then, you can drag the picture that appears inside his record onto one of the status buttons on the left side of the screen to change his status. Although this particular example may not be the most appropriate implementation of Drag and Drop, I think Drag and Drop is a very exciting, user friendly feature that, when implemented properly, is a wonderful feature. You've already used it to quickly and easily drag your toolbars around your PowerBuilder screen.

Figure 2.17.
The DataWindow
Presentation Styles.

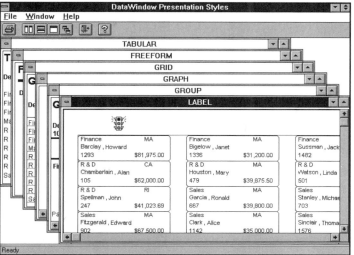

Figure 2.18.
The Change Employee
Status example.

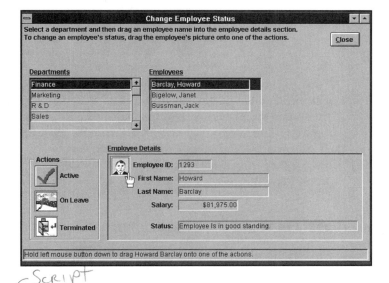

The last example that I'll talk about at any length is the "Draw( ) - Aquarium Fish" example of the "Functions - PowerBuilder" topic (see Fig. 2.19), which demonstrates how you can create animations in your applications. Although it is rare that you will want an animation such as the one demonstrated in the Aquarium example in your applications (unless you are building a game), it is possible that you will want to spice up your applications with a little animation, as is done in the Main Example window. Another reason that I like this example is that it was one

41

of the examples originally developed by David Litwak, CEO and founder of Powersoft. David Litwak actually wrote several of the examples that you see here. So have confidence in yourself; you'll be able to write applications by using PowerBuilder, even if you're a corporate executive!

Figure 2.19.
The Aquarium Fish example.

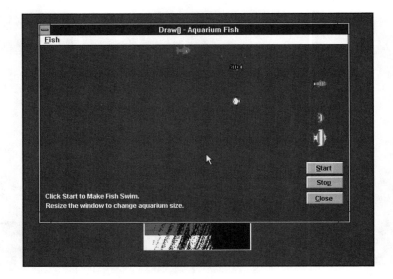

All of the examples that are available will eventually be interesting to you as you learn about the concepts they are trying to demonstrate in the coming chapters. After you have finished with the lessons in the 14 days ahead, you should be sure to come back to the examples, peruse them all, and even look at the source code that was used to create them. Some of the examples, though, may still be interesting to you at this stage, and you should be sure to take a look at them now. These are the examples in the topics of Graphs, MDI, Object Communication, and most of the User Objects. Also, be sure to take a look at the Towers of Hanoi example in the Recursion topic.

Afternoon Summary

Once you have launched PowerBuilder, you will see the main PowerBuilder desktop. On this screen there is a title bar that tells you the name of the application you are working with, and also several controls to move and size the screen inside the Microsoft Windows workspace. Under the title bar is a menu bar that contains several menu items you can access with the mouse or keyboard to perform actions in the PowerBuilder environment. The items that are on the menu bar may change based on what you are currently doing. Even so, many menus in PowerBuilder will stay the same no matter where you are in the system, because they allow you to perform functions that are available almost anywhere.

There are shortcuts you can use to access the functionality in the menu bar. One shortcut, called an *accelerator*, allows you to use the **Alt** key and the underlined letter of a menu item to jump to a specific menu item using the keyboard. The other shortcut is a shortcut for mouse users that places frequently used menu items as buttons on a *toolbar* so you can quickly click on them with your mouse. PowerBuilder uses two toolbars: the *PowerBar* and the *PainterBar*. The PowerBar contains buttons on it that allow you to perform actions that can be performed anywhere inside PowerBuilder. The PainterBar contains buttons that perform actions that are specific to your current state inside the PowerBuilder environment. Additionally, for navigation, there is a *PowerPanel*, which is a small window that contains all of the buttons that map to actions you can perform anywhere in the system.

There are many exciting things you can do with PowerBuilder. PowerBuilder provides a sample application containing a large number of examples to show you some of the exciting things you can do with PowerBuilder. Later, after you have learned more about PowerBuilder and how to use it, you will be able to go into the sample application and actually see the code that is used to perform the actions the examples perform. Be sure to spend some time playing with the sample application because it will surely give you an idea of the power of PowerBuilder.

Q&A

Q What is PowerBuilder used for? What can I do with it?

A PowerBuilder is a visual workbench that allows you to create applications you can run inside the Microsoft Windows operating system. PowerBuilder is especially suited for building applications that access data in databases.

Q When I install PowerBuilder, the installation directory defaults to C:\PB4. Is it required that I install all of the components to that directory?

A It doesn't really matter where you install PowerBuilder, as long as you allow PowerBuilder to set up your Program Manager icons and AUTOEXEC.BAT and CONFIG.SYS files so that they point to the proper directory. In fact, I generally recommend that you place the Watcom database components in a separate directory, rather than in the PowerBuilder directory itself.

Q You have two windows open on your screen. One of them, of course, is PowerBuilder, which is maximized and in front. The other one is the Calculator. You need to perform a calculation to figure out a value. How can you navigate to the Calculator window if it's behind the maximized PowerBuilder window?

A There are several ways that you can do this. The first is by minimizing the PowerBuilder window. If you minimize the PowerBuilder window, you will be able to see the Calculator and click on it to bring it up front and enter in a calculation. Also,

you can select the "Switch To..." menu from the Control menu, and choose Calculator from the Task Manager that will appear. Finally, if you're an experienced Windows user, you will know that there are several "shortcut keys" you can use to switch to other Windows tasks, like **Ctrl-Esc** and **Alt-Tab**, but this wasn't covered, so if you knew it, give yourself extra credit.

Q Help! I can't find the example application! There are no libraries in my PowerBuilder directory!

A By default, the example application is in a subdirectory of the PowerBuilder directory called Example. If this directory is missing, it means that you probably unchecked the Example Application box when you installed PowerBuilder, causing it not to be installed. You need to install both the example application and sample database if you want to be able to properly follow the actions put forth in this book. If you didn't install them in the last chapter, you can go back and re-install just those two components, and you should be able to take over from there with no problem.

Q What is the value of the example application? How come there are so many examples that look like they do the same thing?

A Many of the examples included in the sample application are specifically included to demonstrate multiple ways to achieve the same end result. In programming, there are many ways you can approach a problem, and PowerBuilder gives you several options that are worth noting. Until you are more familiar with PowerBuilder, though, you may not be able to distinguish many of the differences.

Workshop

You can find the answers to the Quiz questions in Appendix A.

Quiz

1. So you've bought PowerBuilder, and you have this pretty purple and white package in front of you. What do you have to do to be able to start?
2. What kind of different buttons can you put on your toolbar?
3. How do you move the toolbar?
4. How do you select menu items?

Putting PowerBuilder into Action

1. Install PowerBuilder.
2. Launch PowerBuilder from your Program Manager.
3. Make sure that the sample application, exampl40, is selected. If it is not, select it.
4. Move your PowerBar to the bottom of the screen.

Chapter

3

Your First PowerBuilder Application

This morning, you will learn:

- [ ] What an application is and why you need it
- [ ] How to create an application
- [ ] What the attributes of an application are
- [ ] Some other things that you can do from the Application Painter

What Is a PowerBuilder Application?

Your computer doesn't really speak English, even though it may sometimes seem like it does. There is a computer language that your computer does, in fact, speak and understand. This language is known as your computer's *instruction set* because it is the set of instructions that your computer knows how to interpret. When you write programs in languages like PowerBuilder, C/C++, Pascal, Basic, or even assembly language, your English-like computer programs need to be translated from one of these languages that people can understand into your computer's instruction set. This enables your computer to execute the commands that you have instructed it to in your computer program. The result of this translation is an *executable file*, generally an .EXE or a .COM file, that when run, performs the tasks you have outlined. This .EXE or .COM file is a computer application.

PowerBuilder is a little bit different, though, than C/C++ or Pascal. In these other languages, everything you develop is written as English-like code words in an editor of some sort. If you want to build a window in C, you need to write English codes to draw the lines and pictures by hand. You write your lines of code in your favorite editor, and then use command-line compilers to compile your code into computer language. Even if you just want to test a small piece of your code, you have to recompile the entire thing into an application to see it. If you want to see what your window looks like, you have to recompile. If you don't like the height of the window and need to make it a little bigger, you need to recompile. If it's too big now and you want to make it just a little smaller, you have to recompile. If the height was okay to begin with and it was really the width that was wrong, you need to recompile. Even if each time you compile, it only takes two or three minutes (which is a very low estimate for a large application), you are talking about a lot of wasted time.

In PowerBuilder, though, the English-like code component is only part of the way you build your applications. You will learn later that a large part of your PowerBuilder development effort is with visual components as well. You visually build windows, buttons, lists, and entry fields, instead of having to write code to create them. You visually set certain attributes of the windows and buttons and other visual objects, like height and width, instead of writing code to set these attributes. You interactively create the visual component of your application and immediately see what the user will see on-screen.

Because of this, PowerBuilder is more than just another computer programming language. It is a computer programming environment, a complete set of programming tools to make it as easy as possible for you to develop your computer applications. When you create a program using PowerBuilder, you are not just writing a bazillion lines of code, you really are building a computer application.

When you are running PowerBuilder, then, it is safe for the environment to assume that your intention is to build an application. However, in order for the PowerBuilder environment to be an application-building environment and not a compiler, it allows you to define something that is referred to as an *Application Object*. In the Application Object, you tell PowerBuilder a little bit about the application you are building.

Creating a New Application

Creating a new application is very easy. First, you have to open up the Application Painter like you did in the last chapter. Click on the **Application Painter** button on the PowerBar. When we last left off, we were running the Sample Application, so you will see the exampl40 application appear on the screen. Now choose the **F**ile|**N**ew menu item. Because every application is stored in a library, the Select New Application Library screen will appear (see Fig. 3.1).

Figure 3.1.
The Select New Application Library window.

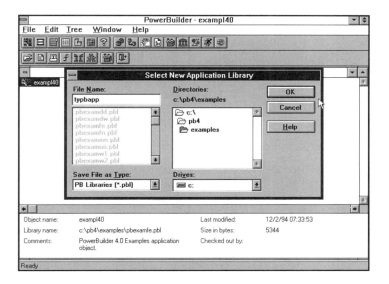

Let's call our application *typbapp* and place it in its own library, also called *typbapp*. Type

`typbapp`

in the box labeled File Name. Click on the button that says **OK**. This creates a library named *typbapp* in your current directory. Then, the Save Application screen will appear (see Fig. 3.2).

Figure 3.2.
The Save Application window.

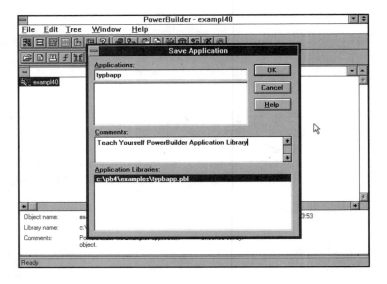

Now, you can type in the name of the application that you want to create. Type

`typbapp`

into the top line of the Save Application window, where it says **A**pplications. Then, press the **Tab** key twice so that your cursor is in the box that is labeled Comments and type

`The Teach Yourself PowerBuilder Application`

and then press **Enter**. You should be returned to the main Application Painter screen (see Fig. 3.3) and see typbapp as your application, indicated by the application icon next to the name of the application. PowerBuilder asks you if you want to create an Application template. If you respond **Yes**, PowerBuilder will create several components for you that you can modify to meet your needs. However, because that wouldn't be learning, you should respond No for now by clicking on the **No** button with your mouse. After you have finished with your lessons, you can go back and intelligently check out the components that make up the Application Template. In the meantime, you have just created the PowerBuilder Application Object that we will be using throughout this book. It's just that simple.

Figure 3.3.
TYPBAPP as your
PowerBuilder application.

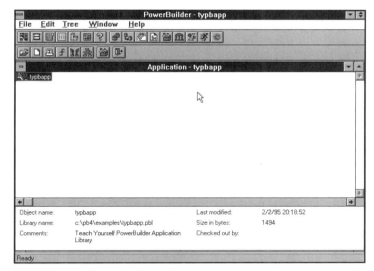

The Application Painter

I want to take some time to introduce you to the *Application Painter*. Compared to most of the other PowerBuilder Painters, the Application Painter is relatively simple because there really isn't much you can do with your application. First, notice that there is now a second toolbar under the PowerBar. This is the *PainterBar* that was mentioned in yesterday's lesson. The PainterBar changes depending on what Painter you are in. For example, now you are in the Application Painter, so the PainterBar has things on it that you can do for Applications. If you were in the Database Painter, the PainterBar would have different buttons on it to allow you to do things you might want to do in the Database Painter. Each Painter has its own functionality and, therefore, each Painter also has its own PainterBar.

The top of the Application Painter contains the name of your application. Then there is mostly just white space, until you get to the bottom of the screen, where you can see certain information about that application. The left column of the window shows you the name of the object that is selected in the screen above, in this case, the *TYPBAPP* application. Under that appears the name of the library in which this object is stored. Under that you can see the comments that have been entered for that object.

The right column tells you the last time this object was modified, the size of the object in bytes, and the name of the person who checked it out. For now, it's not important to know what that means, just to know that it is there. You'll learn more about checkout next week.

You may be wondering why you need all of this information for just a lousy Application Object. What I didn't tell you is that if you have other objects you have built to use in your application, and you will, you will be able to see a list of all of those objects and see information about each one at the bottom of this screen.

Application Attributes

In PowerBuilder, every object has attributes. *Attributes* are those characteristics that make an object work the way it does, and some attributes need to be set at development time. Now that you've created an application, there are certain attributes of that application that you need to set in order to make your application work the way you want. The attributes you can set are:

- ☐ The Icon
- ☐ The Default Global Variables
- ☐ The Default Fonts
- ☐ The Library List

Note: Actually, the Application Object has several other important attributes that you cannot get to from the Application Painter, but can only get to by placing code in scripts. These attributes include things like the English name of your application, the name of the toolbars in your application, the default title for your DataWindows, the default Microhelp message, and the timeout length for a DDE conversation—all things you will learn about in the next two weeks.

The Application Icon

The *application icon* is the icon that appears in a Program Manager group and that your user will double-click on to start running your application. It is also the default icon for all of the windows in your application, so that if you minimize one of these windows, the application icon is the one that is displayed on-screen. For example, the PowerBuilder icon is the icon that you double-clicked on to start running PowerBuilder. If you minimize your PowerBuilder screen by clicking on the down arrow in the top-right corner of the PowerBuilder screen, you will see this icon in the bottom-right corner of your screen. To create your icon, you will need an icon editor. There are a number of shareware icon editors that you can download from any local bulletin board or online service, like CompuServe. Or, if you are using PowerBuilder Enterprise Edition, you may install and use the Watcom Image Editor that comes with that edition.

To edit the application's icon, either click on the Icon button on the toolbar or choose the **E**dit|Application **I**con menu item. You are presented with the Select Icon screen (see Fig. 3.4), where you can choose the icon you want to use for your application icon. For now, though, since we don't have an icon for you to use, you can press **Cancel** and return to the Application Painter.

Figure 3.4.
The Select Icon screen.

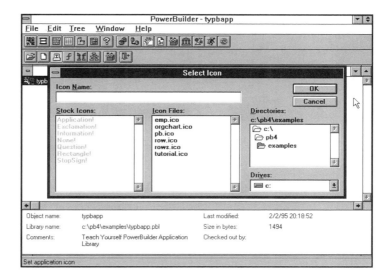

Note: Unfortunately, Windows doesn't come with an icon editor, only Paintbrush, which allows you to edit bitmaps, but not icons. However, there are a large number of software programs that you can get either commercially or even on the shareware market that you can use to edit your icons. If you are using PowerBuilder Enterprise Edition, it is packaged with the Watcom Image Editor, which allows you to edit icons, bitmaps, and cursors. Alternatively, you can download an Icon Editor from your favorite online service. I've used a program called IconMaster with much success. You can download a shareware version of IconMaster from CompuServe or America Online, or any number of other online services.

The Default Global Variables

There are some global variables that are used by PowerBuilder throughout the system internally that you can also control. Each of these global variables will eventually be discussed in turn, but for now, just take for granted the fact that PowerBuilder allows you to modify the datatype of these global variables. For example, there is an error global variable that handles system errors that occur inside PowerBuilder. If you extend the default error construct, you can have PowerBuilder use your error construct instead of its own internal one by changing the default datatype of the global error object to point to your construct. To do this, select the **Edit|Default Global Variables** menu item, or click on the Default Global Variables toolbar button on the application PainterBar. You are prompted with the Default Global Variables Types screen that appears in Figure 3.5. Next week you learn about how and why to extend the default constructs that PowerBuilder supplies. For now, though, just know that this window is here, and click on the **Cancel** button to close it.

Figure 3.5.
The Default Global Variables Types window.

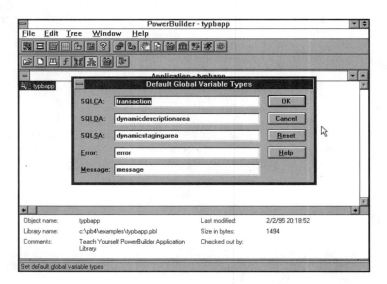

The Default Fonts

When you create text in your application, you can change the font to any font your heart desires. However, if most of your text is going to be of a particular font, instead of always having to change it, you should make it the default font for your application. This way you can be more productive and only spend time changing the font for text that is special. PowerBuilder allows you to specify the default font for your application for four different types of text you can create in PowerBuilder. You can specify a default font for Data that comes from your database, for Headings and Labels that describe data in your database, and for all other text in general. To do this, press the Default Fonts button on the PainterBar, or select the **Edit|Default Fonts** menu item. You are presented with the Default Fonts window, where you can select the default fonts for each of the aforementioned types of text (see Fig. 3.6). In the top-right corner of the window, you can select which type of text you are setting the default for. Click on the radio button for the type of text that you want to change, for example, Headings. In the middle of the screen, you can change the defaults for this type of text. For example, the font name, color, background,

and style. At the bottom of the screen are displayed a few letters in the style that you have created so you can get an idea of what your selection will look like. I prefer my text to use MS Sans Serif, Size 8 for the default text font. I like headings and labels to be Bold, though. You can set these settings by selecting each of the text styles and changing the font, size, and style appropriately for each. First select the **T**ext radio button. Then select MS Sans Serif in the Font drop-down list box. Then select 8 in the Size drop-down list box. Then select the **D**ata radio button, and change the font and size the same way. Then select the **H**eadings radio button and choose the font and size, but this time also click on the **B**old check box so that it becomes checked. Finally, select the **L**abels radio button and do the same as you did for the Headings. Press the **OK** button, and you're all done setting your fonts.

Figure 3.6.
The Select Default Fonts window.

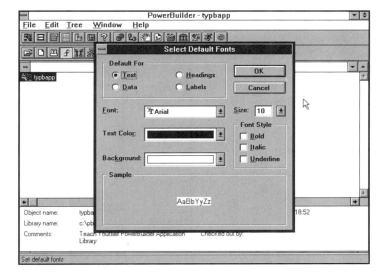

Note: In PowerBuilder, the default fonts are not dynamic. That is, once an object is created with a default font, the font is stored in the object. If you later change the default font in your application, it has no effect on already existing objects, only newly created ones.

The Library List

As you develop applications using PowerBuilder, you will start to find yourself creating separate libraries to hold the objects you create so that you can better organize yourself and your code. Although we won't talk about strategies for organizing your libraries until next week, it is important to recognize that you will often find yourself with more than one library for your applications. In order for your application to find all of the objects it needs, you have to tell it which libraries to look in. Just like you tell your computer which directories to look in when you run commands in your DOS path, you tell your application which libraries to look in for objects by listing them in your *library path*. To change your library path, click on the Library Path button on the toolbar or select the **Edit|Library** List menu item. The Select Libraries window will appear on your screen (see Fig. 3.7). At the top of the window is where you can enter in the path names and library names of the libraries that contain objects used by your application. If you prefer not to type in the names, you can select the directory from the list labeled **D**irectories, and then double-click on the library name in the **P**aste Libraries list, and the name will appear in the box on the top. When you are finished, click on the **OK** button, and you are returned to the Application Painter.

Figure 3.7.
The Select Libraries window.

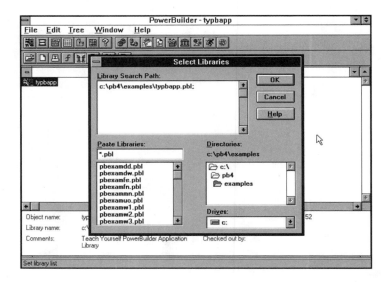

Note: When you are developing applications in PowerBuilder, the library path is not stored in the application itself, but is instead stored in the PB.INI file of the developer. This means that if you have multiple developers working on an application, each one will need to set his/her own library path independently. However, when you eventually compile your application into an executable file (which you will learn about in Chapter 27), the library path will be stored inside the application.

There is one last attribute of Applications that you can modify. These are the application scripts. *Scripts* are the components of objects where you actually get to type in your code. However, we are going to skip scripts for now and talk about them in detail tomorrow.

Viewing the Application Reference Tree

In PowerBuilder, you create an Application Object that will be used to call other objects to communicate with your users, communicate with your database, and perform other tasks as well. Initially, your PowerBuilder application probably opens a main window. Then, that window opens other windows and communicates with other objects. Each of those windows and other objects communicates with their friends. And their friends tell their friends, and their friends tell their friends, and so on, and so on, and so on.... Until there are so many people buying PowerBuilder shampoo that...no...wait...I mean until there are so many objects talking to other objects that its just impossible to figure out what's going on. In the Application Painter there is a new menu, the *Tree* menu, that allows you to examine the hierarchy of references in your applications. You can expand and collapse the tree of any of the displayed objects using this menu. Additionally, you can jump right into the painter for any of the objects you see in the tree.

Create Executable

At the end of the entire programming process, you are going to want to distribute your PowerBuilder application, or at least run it "standalone." In other words, you may want to run your application not from inside PowerBuilder, but directly from Windows like you might run any other program. In order to prevent you from having to run it from the PowerBuilder Development Environment, you need to make it into an *executable* file, a file that can be executed by the Windows Operating System, all by itself. You can do that from the Application Painter either by selecting the **F**ile|Create **E**xecutable menu item or by clicking on the Create Executable icon on the PowerBar. Of course, because we haven't actually created anything yet, it's clearly too early to talk about creating an executable now. Instead, we'll talk more about it at the end of next week, after we have built something worth making into an executable.

Morning Summary

The purpose of programming is to create applications that our users can run. Unlike many other programming languages, though, PowerBuilder is a complete programming environment. In PowerBuilder, you develop applications in a visual workbench type of environment. When you want to create functionality to be linked to your visual components, you create code to perform those functions. The first step in building an application using PowerBuilder, though, is telling PowerBuilder about the application you are building. PowerBuilder allows you to define an Application Object for exactly this purpose. You can then modify certain attributes of the Application Object to meet your needs. You can change the Application Icon, the Default Global Variable Types that will be used by the application, the Default Fonts that will be used in the application, and the list of libraries that will contain objects in your Application.

There is, of course, more to an application than the Application Object. By the end of these two weeks, you will have created a large set of windows, objects, and other controls that together make up the components that will be used in your application. As you build more and more of these components, you will want to be able to trace which components communicate with which other components. You can use the Reference Tree of the application to see this information.

Finally, once you are done building all of the components of your application, you will want to build an executable out of it so that your users can run it without having to use the PowerBuilder development environment.

Chapter

4

Doing Windows

This afternoon, you will learn about:

☐ The Window Painter, what it is, and how it is used

☐ Creating a new window

☐ The different types of windows you can create in PowerBuilder

☐ Changing the appearance of the new window to meet your needs

☐ Different attributes of the window and different ways to change them

The Window Painter

In general, programs that you write need to communicate with your user, either by displaying information or by allowing the user to enter input into the system. When you develop applications using Microsoft Windows, the component you will use to communicate with your user is the window. Inside a window, you can display to the user things like text and pictures, as well as allow the user to input information either by entering it with the keyboard or by clicking buttons and other visual controls. Generally, related information is displayed in a single window. For example, you may create a customer window that your user can open to display information about a customer. If there is more customer information than can fit on a single window, perhaps you'll have a main customer window that displays the most commonly used information about the customer, like Name, Account Number, and Phone Number. Then you can allow the user to open additional customer windows for less-frequently accessed information, like Street Address and Date of Birth. In some other environments, like on the mainframe and in most DOS applications, screens are just screens, and information is placed directly on the screen. In Microsoft Windows, however, your screen contains many *windows*, each of which is in itself a screen with information in it. The user can select the information he/she wants to see by opening or switching to the appropriate window. While we won't yet discuss the details of how to give the user the capability to open and switch to windows, you should be aware that the window is the fundamental component of your PowerBuilder applications to display output to and retrieve input from, or *interface* with the user. For this reason, let's start with the Window Painter, where you will spend time painting the windows that will be used to interface with your user.

To get to the Window Painter, click on the Window Painter button on the PowerBar. If you prefer to use the keyboard, you can press **Shift-F2**, instead. A screen appears asking you which window you want to work with (see Fig. 4.1). Click on the **New** button. The Window Painter appears with a new, empty window on it (see Fig. 4.2). A new toolbar, the Window PainterBar, should appear on your screen under the PowerBar. Well talk more about the Window PainterBar in the next section.

Figure 4.1.
The Select Window screen.

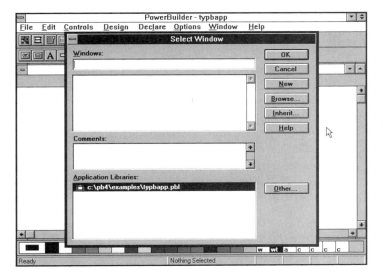

Figure 4.2.
The Window Painter.

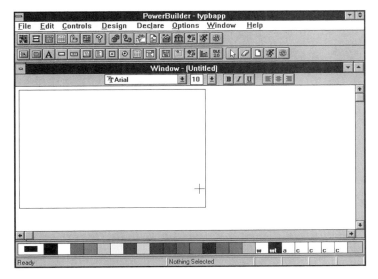

The Window Painter is itself a window inside your PowerBuilder main window (sometimes referred to as the *frame*). Like most other windows, the Window Painter screen has a title bar, which should now read, "Window - [Untitled]" in the center. When the only thing you are working with is the Window Painter, this probably seems redundant. But as you become more experienced with developing PowerBuilder applications, you will see that often times you may have multiple painters up on-screen at any given time, maybe even multiple Window Painters. When that happens, it is helpful to be able to see which painter you are working with and which window you are working with inside the Window Painter. This is very similar to the main title bar, which tells you the name of the Windows Application you are using as well as the name of the application you are editing; for example, "PowerBuilder - typbapp." Each of the PowerBuilder painters uses a similar convention to help you find your way around by telling you the name of the painter you are working with, as well as the name of the painted object that you are editing in that painter. Because we have not yet given our window a name, though, it simply tells us that the window is "[Untitled]." After we save our window and give it a name, that name will appear instead of "[Untitled]." This is a convention that you will find in most windows applications, especially those that support multiple documents open at the same time.

In the last chapter, you spent some time learning about the title bar. As you may remember, I said that almost all windows have a title bar and that they generally work the same way. As promised, the Window Painter does, in fact, have a title bar. You should be aware that there are some differences between the main window's title bar and the title bar that is in the Window Painter. For example, if you look at the control menu of the Window Painter's title bar, you will notice that it is slightly smaller than the control menu on the main title bar. This is because the Window Painter is a sheet inside the main PowerBuilder frame. If you click on the control menu of the Window Painter, you'll see that most of the items on the control menu look the same as the main control menu, except the last one. Instead of switching between applications in windows, when you are working with a sheet you can only switch between windows in your application, this one being PowerBuilder. So the last menu item says "**N**ext," and selecting it takes you to the next open Painter Window in your current PowerBuilder session.

Also on the title bar of the Window Painter window are the Minimize and Maximize boxes that look and work just like those that are on the main title bar. However, when you minimize and maximize your Window Painter window, it is not relative to the entire screen like it is with the PowerBuilder frame. Instead, it is relative to the PowerBuilder frame itself (see Fig. 4.3). When you minimize the PowerBuilder frame, a PowerBuilder icon appears in the bottom-left corner of the screen. When you minimize your Window Painter, though, the Window Painter icon appears at the bottom of the PowerBuilder frame. Likewise, when you maximize your PowerBuilder frame, it adjusts itself to take up the entire screen. When you maximize your Window Painter, however, it only adjusts itself to take up all of the screen that is inside the PowerBuilder frame, and not the entire screen. You may also notice some other interesting changes in the appearance of your screen when you maximize and minimize your Window Painter. I will talk more about these nuances, though, later in Chapter 10, "The Multiple Document Interface (MDI)."

Figure 4.3.
The maximized Window Painter.

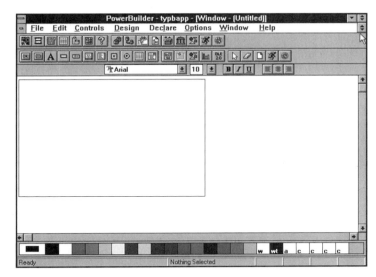

The Style of a Window

If you double-click with your mouse inside the window you are painting, the Window Style window appears on your screen (see Fig. 4.4). The Window Style window allows you to change the style of the window with respect to a number of different factors. First, at the bottom left, in the Window Type group, you should select the type of window that this is. There are several different types of windows from which you can choose. Actually, windows come in two categories. The first category of window includes windows like your PowerBuilder frame and the main window of any windows program that you run. They are the main windows that are called up by Windows Program Manager when you first double-click on the icon of an application. Every application you create is going to have to have one and only one window in this category. The window types that you can use to create a window in this category are *Main*, *MDI Frame*, and *MDI Frame with Microhelp*. For now, let's not discuss the differences between these three types of windows. I will go into more detail about these differences in Chapter 10, "The Multiple Document Interface." Your main application window will be one of these three types of windows.

For additional communication with your user, your main window may open other windows, which are called *children* of the main window. Child windows come in three flavors: *popup windows*, *response windows*, and just plain *child windows*. The only major differences between the three have to do with something called *clipping*, and something called *modality*. Let's start

61

with the plain vanilla child window. When a window opens a child window, that child window actually lives inside its parent. You can move the child window around anywhere inside its parent, but you cannot drag the window outside of the borders of the parent. If you try to drag a child window outside its parent, any portion of the child window that is outside of the borders of the parent window disappears and is hidden behind the borders of the parent window. If you minimize the parent window, the child window is minimized with it, as if it were literally contained inside of it. This is referred to as *clipping*. The portion of the child window that is outside the borders of the parent window are clipped off.

Figure 4.4.
The Window Style window.

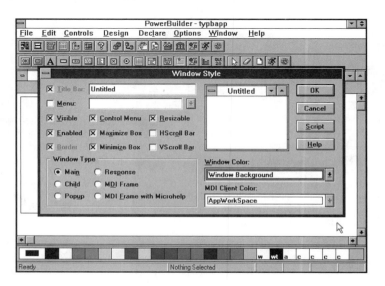

Sometimes, however, you will want to interact with the user in such a way that he/she cannot proceed until he/she responds to a particular message or answers a particular question. For example, if your application attempts to perform some function and an error occurs that prevents the function from completing successfully, you will want to put a message on the screen to inform the user of the error and not proceed any further until your user acknowledges that he/she is aware of the error. You may even want to give the user the opportunity to choose one of several reactions to the error; for example, to abort the function, ignore the error, or retry the function that caused the error. In this case, a vanilla child window will not suffice, and instead you will want to use a *response window*. The response window is a window that can exist outside of the borders of the main window, so it is not clipped. Also, the response window is *modal*, which means it suspends all execution of your applications functions until the window is closed. The user cannot ignore a response window because the application is halted until the user closes the response window. You might use a response window to inform your user that their printer ran out of paper or that their hard drive is full, among other things.

Note: Response windows are *Application Modal*, meaning that the user cannot perform other actions within the application until he/she closes the response window. However, the user may still switch to perform other tasks within the Microsoft Windows Operating System and run them normally. In Microsoft Windows, you can also create *System Modal* windows, which prevent the user from doing anything else on the system until the modal window is closed. However, PowerBuilder does not directly provide a way to create System Modal windows.

The final style of window is almost like a compromise between the vanilla child window and the response window. Sometimes you want to open a window on-screen that is not modal (so other components of the application can continue running) and is not clipped (so it can be placed outside of the borders of the main window). For example, you may want to open a window that displays status about an action that is being performed. Perhaps it shows what percent of the job is complete. It needs to be open on the screen outside of the borders of the main window so that the user can see what's going on in there. It also cannot halt the rest of the application because then the application would go into limbo. There would be no function running to check the status on since the status window prevents the function from running. Instead, you can use a *popup window* to perform this function. A popup window can be placed anywhere on-screen, even outside the borders of its parent. It is also not modal, and therefore your application can continue running even after the window is opened. A good example of a popup window is a spell-checker window, which pops up in a separate window and displays suggested spelling corrections but is not modal, so that you can switch away and correct the text of the document even while it is up on-screen.

Note: In truth, there is one additional style of window that can be opened: an *MDI sheet*. However, you don't set an MDI sheet's style during the creation of a window. Instead, you open a child window as an MDI sheet with a special Open command. Well save a detailed discussion about MDI frames and MDI sheets when we talk about the Multiple Document Interface in Chapter 10.

Above the window style group of radio buttons is a set of check boxes where you can control certain features of the window you are painting. Based on the window style you have selected, some of the attributes are forced to either be checked or unchecked and are grayed out (disabled) so that you cannot change the state. However, if the check box is not grayed out, you may toggle the check on or off by clicking on it. At the top-right of this window is a model of the window that you are painting. In that model, you can see some of the features of how your window will look, like the title bar, title, border, scroll bars, and menu. Go ahead and try it—toggle the state of the check boxes in the middle column; turn off the control menu and the Minimize and

Maximize boxes. Notice how the model's title bar is now devoid of any of these features. Now go ahead and turn them back on and watch them come back onto the title bar. Now try it with the next column: turn off the Resizable check box. Notice that the border of the model window has changed. Turn on the scroll bars and watch them appear inside the window. Go up to the top line and enter in a title for the window. Notice how the title bar of the model changes to show your newly entered title. If you change the windows style to a popup window, none of the check boxes will be grayed out, and you can play with each of them to see what they do. To give you an idea of what each one does, see the following list. These are the attributes of a window that you can control by checking boxes in the window style dialog box:

- ☐ **Title Bar:** Gives your window a title bar.
- ☐ **Menu:** Gives your window a menu bar.
- ☐ **Visible:** Makes your window visible or invisible.
- ☐ **Enabled:** Allows your window to accept input from the user, such as a mouse or key click.
- ☐ **Border:** Gives your window a border.
- ☐ **Control Menu:** Gives your window a control menu.
- ☐ **Maximize Box:** Gives your window a Maximize box.
- ☐ **Minimize Box:** Gives your window a Minimize box.
- ☐ **Resizable:** Makes the border of your window allow the user to resize it.
- ☐ **Hscroll Bar:** Gives your window a Horizontal scroll bar.
- ☐ **Vscroll Bar:** Gives your window a Vertical scroll bar.

Additionally, you can change the color of your window by selecting a color from the palette of colors contained in the drop-down list box labeled Window Color. If the window type is an MDI frame, you can also select an MDI client workspace color from the MDI Client Color drop-down list box. We'll talk more about the application workspace when we talk about the Multiple Document Interface in Chapter 10.

DO   DON'T

DO Make your window colors standard and user-friendly by setting them to the *Window Background* and *Application Workspace* colors whenever possible. This way, your user can make your application whatever color he/she wants by changing the Control Panel color settings.

DON'T Necessarily follow the preceding rule rigidly in all cases. If you want to allow for 3-D effects for your controls, you will probably want to set your window color to light gray (the one directly above the "Window Background" color).

The Window Painter Menus and PainterBar

Notice again that under the main title bar is a set of menus. However, whereas before there were only two menus to select from, File and Help, now there are quite a few more menus available. This menu, even though it's on the window in the position where we left the PowerBuilder main menu, now belongs to the Window Painter. This is because the Window Painter is the currently displayed, or *active*, sheet inside the PowerBuilder frame. In other words, the menu bar on the PowerBuilder frame doesn't actually belong to the main PowerBuilder frame alone. It will take on different characteristics based on which sheet you are looking at. Because you are now looking at the Window Painter, it shows you the list of actions you can perform inside the Window Painter. This is another feature of Windows that we will talk about more in Chapter 10, "The Multiple Document Interface (MDI)."

In the Window Painter, you can perform a number of different types of commands, all of which are accessible from the menu. First, notice that on the left side of the menu are the standard **F**ile and **E**dit menus where you can perform functions like saving, opening, and printing files (in this case windows), cutting and pasting data, and undoing your most recent edits. All of these functions are functions that you will become more familiar with because almost every menu in Windows offers you the capability to perform these functions. In fact, you should become so familiar with this type of organization of menus that when you build your own applications with PowerBuilder, you will organize your menus in much the same way. The two rightmost menus on the screen are the **W**indow and **H**elp menus, which are also standard menus you should become very familiar with. The Window menu allows you to rearrange and select your windows inside the PowerBuilder frame, and the Help menu allows you to get help with your programming efforts.

In between these two familiar sets of menus, however, is a set of menus that you probably are not already familiar with. Each menu has a selection of functions that you can perform to help paint your window. The menus are:

☐ **Controls:** The **C**ontrol menu allows you to turn your cursor into a control painter so that you can paint a *window control* on your window. Window controls are the objects that appear in your windows to interact with your user. For example, buttons, labels, lists, and edit fields are all types of controls. We will talk more about the different controls in the next chapter.

☐ **Design:** The **D**esign menu has functions under it that help you in the design of your window and its controls. Each of the things that you can do are important enough that we will discuss each one in turn.

☐ **Preview:** The Preview function allows you to see what your window will look like to the user when it is opened on-screen. However, when you are previewing a window, it does not actually function as if it were running. Instead, only default behavior for all of the controls and the window itself will be available. However, it is a very effective way of testing the layout of your window, even though it will not help you with functionality.

☐ **Window Style:** The Window Style function allows you to edit certain attributes of the window itself. Selecting this menu item brings up the Window Style window (refer to Fig. 4.4), which you learned about in the previous section.

☐ **Window Position:** Selecting the Window Position menu item brings up the Window Position window, which you will learn how to use in just a few minutes.

☐ **Control Style:** The Control Style menu item is probably grayed out right now. That's because this menu item allows you to manipulate the style of a control on your window in much the same way that you learned to manipulate the style of your window itself. In order to use it, though, you must be in the process of selecting a control.

☐ **Tab Order:** In Windows, the currently selected control is referred to as having *focus*. The control that is in focus is the one that gets the input when the user enters it. This is how Windows can allow you to have multiple edit fields on-screen at one time—only one of them can have focus at any given time. One way to get a control into focus is by clicking on it with your mouse. The user can also use the Tab key to toggle which control has the focus. If the user presses Tab once, it will tab to the first control; if the user presses tab again, it will tab to the next control, and so on. The order in which the controls get focus when the user presses tab is defined here by selecting the Tab Order menu item. When you select Tab Order, it becomes checked, and your window is in Set Tab Order mode. Little numbers appear next to each control, and you can change those numbers to change the tab order. Then, when you are finished, select the Tab Order menu item again, and your window will return to Edit mode with the new tab order.

☐ **Show Invisibles:** Sometimes when you are creating a window, you need to make a control invisible. Perhaps it is a control that is used to store data that the user cannot see, or perhaps it is a control that should only appear on-screen under certain conditions. Because PowerBuilder tries to make your development environment work as closely as possible to the real application, it makes invisible controls disappear off the screen, unless the Show Invisibles menu item is checked.

☐ **Grid...:** If you think of the Power Grid, you think of the intersecting power lines that are arranged to make your town light up with electricity. Well, inside your PowerBuilder window is a grid you can use to help you place and align your controls

on-screen. When you select the **G**rid menu item, you are prompted with a box that allows you to manipulate this grid (see Fig. 4.5). You can show the grid by clicking on the Show Grid check box. You can change the size of each cell inside the grid by changing the X and Y sizes of the cell. The X size is the horizontal size, and the Y size is the vertical size. You can also select to have your controls "snap" to the grid. This means that if you place a control in your window, it will automatically adjust its position so that it is aligned with the nearest corner of a cell on the grid. Although I personally find this behavior to be quite annoying, some people prefer using this method to align their controls. PowerBuilder offers some much better methods of alignment that we will discuss in the next chapter.

Figure 4.5.
*The Alignment Grid
window.*

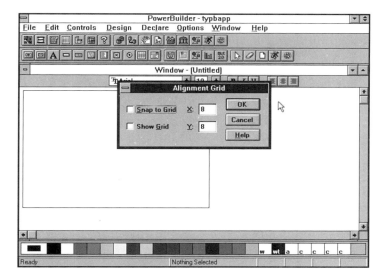

☐ **Declare:** The Declare menu contains menu items that allow you to declare special programming constructs, like certain types of variables and functions for use in your application. We will talk more about these types of constructs later in the week.

☐ **Options:** The Options menu allows you to control certain options having to do with the Window Painter environment. For example, you can decide where on-screen to place your color and style toolbars, as well as if you want your controls to have a 3-D look and feel to them when you place them on-screen. Notice that to the right of the menu items inside the Options menu there are little, black arrows pointing to the right. What this means is that this menu item has another menu under it where the actual commands can be found. When you click on this menu item, another menu will appear to the right of this one.

The **E**dit Menu contains several standard items beneath it that you may be familiar with if you have used other Windows applications. They are:

☐ **Undo**: The **U**ndo menu item allows you to undo your most recent change in case you make a mistake. The text of this menu item changes to tell you what will be undone when you select it, or if there is nothing to undo; it reads Can't Undo and is disabled.

☐ **Cut**: The **Cu**t menu item takes anything that you have selected and stores a copy in the Windows clipboard. It also removes that item from the screen.

☐ **Copy**: The **C**opy menu item also takes anything that you have selected and stores it in the Windows clipboard. However, it does not remove the item from the screen.

☐ **Paste**: Once an item is in the clipboard, you can take a copy and paste it back onto your screen by selecting the **P**aste menu item. This menu item will be disabled if there is nothing on the clipboard that you can paste.

☐ **Clear**: The **Cl**ear menu item deletes the selected controls off the window.

Additionally, the Edit menu has some new menu items. They are:

☐ **Control List:** You can select any of the controls that are on your window with the Control **L**ist menu item. When you select this menu item, the Control List window appears on your screen (see Fig. 4.6). Inside this dialog box is a list box that lists all of the controls in the window. You can select controls by highlighting their names in the list box and by clicking the **Select** button. Or, you can directly edit the style of the controls you select by clicking the **Control Style** button. Well talk more about controls and their styles in the next chapter.

Figure 4.6.
The Control List window.

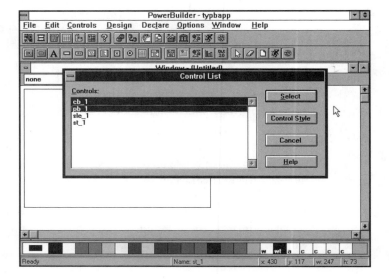

- [ ] **Select All:** You can select all of the controls in your window with the Select **A**ll menu item.

- [ ] **Select Control:** The Select Co**n**trol menu item returns your cursor to Select Control mode, instead of Create Control mode. We'll talk more about this in the next chapter.

- [ ] **Tag List:** Every control has a general purpose storage area where you can store any string you want as an attribute of the control. This is called the *Tag value*. You can assign tag values to your controls by selecting the Ta**g** List menu item.

- [ ] **Bring To Front**: It is possible for one control in a window to overlap another. By selecting the Bring To **F**ront menu item, you can bring a control that was behind another to the front.

- [ ] **Send To Back**: In the same manner, you can select the Send To **B**ack menu item to push a control behind other controls that it is overlapping.

- [ ] **Align Controls:** You can let PowerBuilder move a group of controls so that they are lined up nicely and neatly. The little pictures in the submenu that appear when you select the Al**i**gn Controls menu item show you how to align them, either horizontally or vertically, either left, right, or centered. You must have at least two controls selected for this menu item to be enabled.

- [ ] **Space Controls:** You can let PowerBuilder space controls evenly by selecting the Space C**o**ntrols menu item. You can either space your controls horizontally or vertically. You must have at least three controls selected for this menu item to be enabled.

- [ ] **Size Controls:** You can let PowerBuilder size a group of controls so that they are all the same size vertically or horizontally by selecting the Si**z**e Controls menu item.

- [ ] **Reset Attributes:** The **R**eset Attributes menu item resets a control attribute so that it matches the attributes of a control from which it is inherited. We will discuss this more later in the week when we talk about object-oriented concepts in Chapter 11, "An Introduction to Object-Oriented Software Constructions."

Some of the more common functions that you can perform from your Window Painter menus can be performed quickly by clicking on a particular menu item on the Window PainterBar (see Fig. 4.7). The first set of 16 buttons on the Window PainterBar are actually controls that you can place on your screen. These controls correspond to many of the more common controls that you find in the Controls menu. The next five toolbar buttons actually perform functions within the PowerBuilder Window Painter environment. The first one returns your cursor to selection mode in case you select a control button and then change your mind about wanting to place a control on the window. The next button is the Erase button, which deletes the currently selected item(s). The next button is the Script Painter button, which allows you to write scripts for your window and for your Window controls. And the next two buttons you have already seen on the PowerBar, and they are the Run and Debug buttons, which allow you to run your application.

Figure 4.7.
The Window PainterBar.

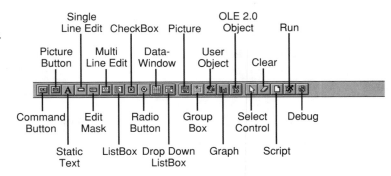

The Style and ColorBars

There are two other toolbars that you have not yet seen that first appear here in the Window Painter. At the bottom of your screen, you'll see there is a palette of colors. This palette is called the *ColorBar*. By clicking on a color in the ColorBar, you can quickly change the color of an object you are working with. Most objects in PowerBuilder have a foreground color and a background color. To change the foreground color, you click with the left mouse button; and to change the background color, you click with the right mouse button. We'll talk more about the ColorBar later in this chapter.

At the far left of the ColorBar, there are a few colors that have little letters in them. The first three are system colors that are read from your systems Window Color settings. The box with a "w" in it is the color that has been set up in your Windows Color Settings as the Window Background color. The box with a "wt" in it is the Window Text Color, and the box with an "a" in it is the Application Workspace color. By using these colors, you can keep your application consistent with respect to the rest of your user's desktop. This is because your window and object colors will be the same as all of the other window and object colors in the user's system. The user can change color settings in the Color applet of the Control Panel and change the color of applications to whatever the user wants. Your application will simply respond by changing its color to match the user's settings.

The boxes with little "cs" in them are custom colors that you can change to whatever color you want. Because the ColorBar has room for only 16 of the many colors that can be displayed, you can add your own colors to the toolbar inside these boxes if the color you want is not already there. To add your own color to the toolbar, double-click with your left mouse button on a box with a "c" in it. The Custom Color window will appear on your screen (see Fig. 4.8). You can choose one of the basic colors by clicking on it from the palette of basic colors, or you can create a custom color by clicking inside the left pane of the window in the color grid and adjusting the hue, saturation, and luminescence with the thin color pane at the far right of the screen. The box in the center labeled "Color|Solid" shows you the true color value in the left column and the solid color value in the right column. Some colors become "grainy" when you select them

because of limitations in the number of colors that can be displayed on your screen at any given time. The solid color is the closest solid color that PowerBuilder can find relative to the color that is selected.

Figure 4.8.
The Color window.

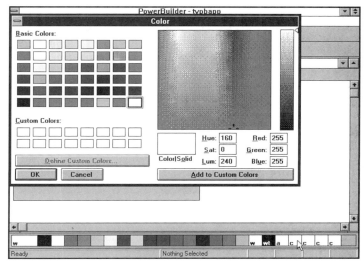

In the real world, all visible color can be "generated" from three basic colors: Red, Yellow, and Blue. That's why if you have ever seen a projection TV, you see three big light tubes that shoot out the picture—one each of red, yellow, and blue. In computers, colors are made up of three basic colors, too; however, instead of yellow, the second basic color is green. When you select a color in the Customize Color window, notice that the values that are displayed in the Red, Green, and Blue boxes for that color show different numbers. The numbers represent the amounts of each of the basic color that is used to generate the color on your screen. The values range from 0 to 255. If all three values are set to 255, the resulting color is white. If all three values are set to 0, the resulting color is black. If one of the values is set to 255, and the other two are set to 0, then the color is "pure"—either pure red, pure green, or pure blue. You can actually type in color values for each if you would like to use that method to change the color, as well.

You can also type in color values in the Hue, Saturation, and Luminescence boxes. Hue, Saturation, and Luminescence is another method you can use to determine color. These work like the Color, Tint, and Brightness knobs on your television set. It was a very popular method back in the "pre-Windows" days, and even in an earlier version of Windows, but has since become less popular among application developers. This method is still popular in Desktop Publishing and Imaging applications, though.

After you have selected the color you like, you can click on the button labeled **Add to Custom Colors**, and it will add the color you have selected to the toolbar in the current custom color value, over on the left side of the screen. Notice that there is room for 16 custom colors on this screen. Only the first four custom colors will appear on your ColorBar. So why is there room for 16 of them? Because you can also use this window to change the color of your objects, and so you get the ability to save up to 16 custom colors in your palette, even though you can only quickly select four of them on the color bar. When you have finished adding custom colors, you can save your changes by pressing the **OK** button.

Note: The Custom Color Selection window is a remnant from an old version of PowerBuilder that was never really changed for this version. Because of this, it is not one of the most intuitive windows in PowerBuilder. Because there is rarely a wide range of colors inside Windows applications anyway, this window is not that critical, and you probably won't access it often, if ever again at all.

Back to the ColorBar, then. At the far left of the ColorBar is a box that has two colors inside it. It doesn't change anything when you click on it, but changes when you click on other colors. That is the Color Selection box where you can see what the colors are for the currently selected object. The inside box shows the foreground color, and the outside box shows the background color. As you already know, you can change the color of the object you are working with by clicking on any of the colors along the bottom of the Color Bar. However, what you may not have realized is that if you want to select a color that is not on the color palette, you can double-click on the Color Selection box, and it will bring up the Custom Color window where you can change the color of the currently selected object to any color you like, even if it is not on the color bar. In general, most Windows applications stick to some basic colors, so the colors on the color bar should suffice. However, if you find yourself wanting to build objects with a wide range of colors, you'll find this capability invaluable.

Inside the Window Painter window, at the top of the Window Painter, you should see another new toolbar called the StyleBar (see Fig. 4.9). The StyleBar allows you to control the style of text inside your controls. For example, if you create your own OK button, you want to make the text a certain font, size, weight, and so on. Perhaps you have text fields on your screen, and you want to make them appear in a particular way. You can use the StyleBar to quickly manipulate certain things about text in your controls.

Figure 4.9.
The StyleBar.

StyleBar ——

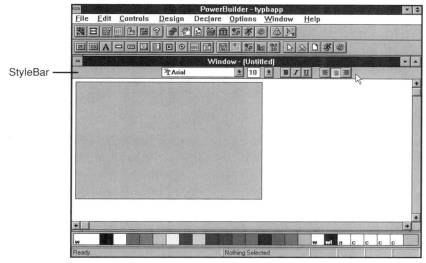

At the left side of the StyleBar, you should now see just empty space. However, if you were editing a control that could have text in it, there would be an entry box in this space to allow you to edit the text in that control. Entering text in that edit box causes the text you have entered to appear inside the control. The first visible control inside the StyleBar, however, is the Font drop-down list box. Here, you can select the font for the text of the currently selected control. Next is the Pitch drop-down list box. This is where you can enter the size of the text inside the currently selected control. Notice that the arrow of this drop-down list box looks like it is disconnected from the display box. This means that you can actually type a number into the box as well as choose one from the list.

Next to the pitch box are three buttons that control some other factors about the style of your text—Bold, Italic, and Underline. You may recognize them from other applications. These three buttons are toggle buttons. Each one can appear either in the up or down position. If the background color is light, and the button looks like it's pressed, the button is down, and is on. If the background appears slightly darker, and the button looks raised, it is up and is off. The first button allows you to toggle whether the text of the current control is boldface or not. If this button is down, the text of the current object is bold. If it is up, it is not. The next button toggles whether or not the text is italicized, and the last button toggles whether or not the text is underlined. Any combination of bold, italic, and underline is acceptable, even if it is not visually appealing!

The next three buttons determine the alignment of the text. Only one of these three buttons must be down. If the left one is down, the text is left justified; if the middle one is down, the text is centered; and if the right one is down, the text is right justified.

You'll find the StyleBar very useful as you begin to create forms for data entry and data display. Although there are other ways to manipulate the style of text in your controls, the StyleBar is very convenient and very standard, and soon you'll be using it quite a lot.

Resizing and Positioning Your Window On-Screen

Often, when you have created a window with controls for input and output on it, you may find that your controls don't fit snugly into the space provided by default for your window. Generally, you will need to make the window either bigger or smaller. And when you change the size of the window, you will also usually find it necessary to change the position on the screen where it opens up. There are a couple of ways to do this.

If you look back at the Window Painter screen in Figure 4.2, you'll notice that your window has a border. One way of resizing your window is to pick up a piece of either the right or lower border with your mouse and drag it to the size that you want it to be. Notice that as you pass your mouse over the right border of the window, your mouse cursor changes shape to look like a right-and-left pointing arrow. When you pass your mouse over the lower border, the cursor changes shape to look like an up-and-down pointing arrow. When you pass your mouse over the bottom-right corner of the window where the right and lower borders meet, the cursor changes shape to look like a set of diagonal arrows. This change in the shape of the cursor indicates to you that you can size the window in the direction of the arrows by clicking and dragging to the size that you like. So, to make the window wider, pass your mouse cursor over the right border until you see the cursor shape become a right-and-left pointing arrow. Then click and hold your mouse button, which essentially "picks up" the right border. Then you can drag the right border to the new desired position. The same applies to the lower border as well. And if you want to quickly adjust both the right and lower borders in one shot, you can pick up the lower-right corner of the window and place it in the new desired position, which effectively moves both the right and lower borders.

There is also another way of resizing the window. Select Window **P**osition from the **D**esign menu, and the Window Position screen appears (see Fig. 4.10). The screen is essentially split up into entry fields in the top half where you can enter information in manually, and a model of the screen in the bottom half where you can drag and reposition a window placeholder to adjust the size and position of your window. The window placeholder inside the model works a lot like the window itself in the Window Painter. To change the size of the window, you can drag any of the four sides or four corners to a new position (which is slightly better than in the Window Painter, where you can drag only the bottom and right edges and corner). The window placeholder's size will adjust and the window will move with respect to the model. The model itself is meant to emulate the user's Microsoft Windows screen, and the position of the window inside the model indicates the opening position of the window—the position on the entire

screen where the window will open when it is instructed to. For most windows, the user can move the position of the window after it is open; but even for those windows, you will generally want to have the window open in a particular position on-screen when the user clicks on the button that opens that window. Immediately above the model are two check boxes, one labeled "Center Vertically" and the other labeled "Center Horizontally." They work exactly as they sound. If you check them, they will force your window to be centered relative to the screen as you make your adjustments. However, if you uncheck them, you can move your window anywhere you like. You may have already moved your window out of center by resizing it. Or, if you want to move the window without adjusting the size, you can simply click anywhere inside the borders and drag your window to its new position. At the top left of the screen there is also a set of entry fields where you can type in the X and Y coordinates of the starting point (the top-left corner) of the window, as well as the width and height of the window. The X coordinate represents the horizontal position of the window on-screen. The larger the number, the farther to the right your window is placed. The Y coordinate is the vertical coordinate on the screen. The larger the number, the farther to the bottom the screen is placed. The numbers inside these fields are updated when you make changes to the size and position of your window.

Figure 4.10.
The Window Position screen.

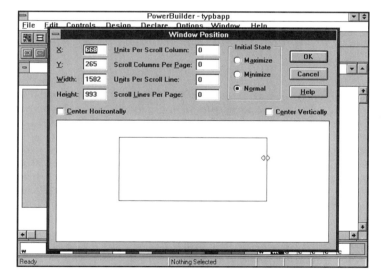

Note: It is probably rare that you will want to enter specific values for these fields, especially with how easy it is to adjust the position of the window using the other methods; but it's there if you need it.

To the right of these entry fields is a set of entry fields for adjusting the behavior of the scroll bars that appear inside your window. By default, all of these values are set to 0, which enables the default behavior for scroll bars in your window. For now, I am going to skip these fields and save their discussion for when we discuss scroll bars in the next chapter, "Controls." Besides, most applications use the default behavior of the window scroll bars because trying to manage the scroll bars yourself generally "costs more than it buys," as they say in the computer business.

To the right of the scroll bar section is a group of radio buttons where you can select the initial state of the window when it is opened. By default, the window opens in "Normal" or restored state. That means that it will pop up on the user's screen in much the same way that it looks when you create it. However, sometimes you may want a window to start on your user's screen either as maximized or minimized. If that is the case, simply click on the appropriate radio button, and it shall be. Even if it starts out in maximized or minimized mode, it will still become the "normal" size if the user chooses to restore their window. This is a very effective and user-friendly way of opening your own frames for your user so that they take up the entire screen, without making the actual size of the frame so big that it is annoying.

The Role of the Right Mouse Button

There is also another way to edit all of the window attributes that we have talked about in this chapter—by clicking with your right mouse button anywhere inside the window. When you click with your right mouse button on the window, a menu will pop up that allows you to perform most of the actions you have seen on the main menu. In fact, there are several functions that you can perform from the right mouse menu that you cannot perform from anywhere else inside the Window Painter!

Note: The first item on the right mouse menu is Script. You may have noticed that up until now, I have been skipping references to Script buttons and menus altogether. We'll talk about Scripts in the next couple of days, in Chapter 6, "Putting It All Together," but there is quite a bit of groundwork to cover before we get there.

Note: Incidentally, this is poor design on the part of Powersoft. For your own applications, you should always offer all functions from the main menu somehow, even if you also offer the function using the mouse with a button or a right mouse menu. That way, the user can always perform all functions even if he/she doesn't have a mouse, or if it's in the shop.

Under the Script menu item, there are menu items that allow you to change the color, icon, pointer, position, style, title, and window type. Here you find two new attributes that you can modify that you cannot modify from anywhere else. These two new menu items are **I**con and **P**ointer. When you select the **I**con menu item, notice that the same icon window that you saw in the application painter comes up. The difference is that this time, the list on the left is not disabled (grayed out). Inside that list box is a list of "Stock Icons." No, these icons are not statues traded over the open market. These stock icons are icons that are built into windows and your application. This is indicated by the fact that their names are all followed by an exclamation point (!). By default, all of your windows will have the same icon as your application, the Application! stock icon. However, you can change it to one of the built-in icons, like an exclamation point or a stop sign, or you can choose an icon file that you have created.

When you select the **P**ointer menu item from the window's right mouse menu, a window that looks almost identical to the icon selection window appears on your screen. The only difference is that this time, the type of file that is displayed in the list of files is a cursor file, and the stock icons are replaced by stock pointers. As you may have guessed, the stock pointers are the pointers that are built into Windows and your application, and include things like the Arrow pointer, Hourglass pointer, and I-Beam pointer—pointers you must have seen if you've ever used Windows at all. When you change the pointer for your window, the pointer you have selected appears on-screen when your user's mouse passes over this window.

DO	DON'T

DO Get used to using the right mouse button. It's quickly becoming a Windows standard for object attribute editing.

DON'T Worry if your mouse has three buttons. You won't need to use the middle button, just the left and right ones.

The window isn't the only thing that you can right-click on to get a convenient popup menu to quickly edit attributes. Actually *all* controls in PowerBuilder have a right mouse menu that you can use to quickly edit the control's attributes. In fact, you'll find that the right mouse menu is quickly becoming the de-facto standard as an attribute editor for many applications, and PowerBuilder is no exception. The right mouse button is available for use quite a bit in PowerBuilder, so you should really start to get used to using the right mouse button if you want to become very proficient in PowerBuilder.

Afternoon Summary

The method by which your application interfaces with your user is via a window. A window is simply another term for a screen. However, in Microsoft Windows, you can have multiple windows placed on your screen at any given time, and each window works independently. In PowerBuilder, you create windows by using the Window Painter. You can open the Window Painter by clicking with your mouse on the Window Painter button inside the PowerBar, or by pressing **Shift-F2**. Then, you can create a new window by clicking on the **New** button.

When you click on the **New** button, the Window Painter appears inside your PowerBuilder frame. Also, new menus and a new toolbar, called the Window PainterBar, appear at the top of your PowerBuilder frame. These new menus offer functionality that allows you to manipulate the window's attributes, and also create and edit controls on the window. You can change the type of window, the size and position of the window, the tab order of the controls inside the window, and much more by using the menus inside the Window Painter.

In addition, there are two new toolbars that appear when you are in the Window Painter: the StyleBar and the ColorBar. The StyleBar allows you to quickly edit the text and style of certain controls inside your window. The ColorBar allows you to quickly change the color of objects inside your window.

Finally, you should be aware that there is another important menu that you may need to use to modify certain attributes of your window, and that is the right mouse menu. You get to the right mouse menu by clicking on the window with your right mouse button. The right mouse menu contains items that allow you to edit all of the attributes of your window, including some of those you may be able to get in other ways. The right mouse menu is used consistently throughout the PowerBuilder environment, so you need to be familiar with it.

Q&A

Q What's the point? Why do I need an Application Object?

A PowerBuilder creates applications. In order to tell PowerBuilder which application to create, you need to define an Application Object. In other languages you have to tell the compiler what the application you want to create is, and what modules to include, and other things about the application you are creating. You do this by specifying parameters on the command line of a compiler and linker. PowerBuilder is a complete application building environment, however, and there is no separate compiler or linker with command lines. Instead, you tell it these parameters right in the Application Object.

Q **Can I use PowerBuilder to create real applications that I can send out to users to run on their own?**

A Of course! That's exactly what PowerBuilder is for! Over the next two weeks, you will learn everything you need to build real Windows applications using PowerBuilder. While you are developing, you will be using the PowerBuilder development environment to create, test, and run your application's objects. But when you're all finished, you will make your PowerBuilder application into an executable .EXE file that is completely independent and self-contained. Actually, you'll also need to distribute .DLL files with your application for it to run, but your users won't need to run PowerBuilder to run your executable application.

Q **I noticed another available button on the Select Window screen that you kind of skipped over called "Inherit." What does that mean, and why did you skip it?**

A Later this week, you will learn object-oriented techniques that include inheritance, and you will learn how to use that button and why it's important. You gotta crawl before you can walk, though, and you'll need to learn how to create a window before you can learn how and why to inherit one!

Q **In the Window Style screen, when I select a different window type, some of the check boxes and radio buttons turn gray. Why is that?**

A For most of the window attributes, the check boxes and radio buttons are user-defined controls. You, as the user, can define your window to either have or not have the particular attribute. However, certain window types have certain requirements that can't be overridden by you. For example, if you are making a main window, a title bar is *required* as part of the window; therefore, it becomes disabled and is set to on. By the same token, child windows cannot have menus. Each window type has its own rules, and PowerBuilder helps you enforce them by using this method.

Q **Isn't the ColorBar supposed to change the color of the window? When I click on colors on the ColorBar, it doesn't change!**

A Actually, the ColorBar is supposed to change the color of controls in the window, and it does. But you can't use it to change the color of the window itself. To change the color of the window itself, you must open the Window Style screen.

Q **Why do you love that right mouse button so much? I've never had to use it in any other application before!**

A The right mouse button is a relatively new Windows standard but is quickly becoming more popular among developers of Windows applications. It has become the standard method of editing attributes in many Windows applications and is a standard for exactly that purpose in PowerBuilder. After all, most Windows users have a mouse with two or more buttons, why not take advantage of this?

Workshop

Quiz

1. What's the first step in creating a PowerBuilder program?
2. What are the different attributes of the Application Object?
3. What is the name of the primary visual PowerBuilder component that you use to interface with your user?
4. What are the different methods that you can use to change the style of your windows?

Putting PowerBuilder into Action

1. Open up the Window Painter.
2. Create a new window.
3. Double-click on the window to bring up the Window Style screen.
4. Try out each of the different window types, and pay attention to which of the other check boxes and radio buttons turn on and off based on the window types.
5. Size your window as it appears on-screen. Now look at it in the Window Position window. Notice how much easier it is to judge the size and position of the window in the Window Position screen, even though you can perform your sizings in the Window Painter itself.

Chapter

5

Controls

In this chapter, you will learn:

☐ How to place controls on your window

☐ Three different ways to modify the attributes of your controls

☐ Some of the more important and common attributes of different controls

☐ How to preview your window

☐ How to save your window

☐ How best to name your controls

Placing Controls on Your Window

When you are in the Window Painter, your cursor can be in different "modes." By default, when you first enter the Window Painter, your cursor is in the "Selection" mode. This means that your cursor can be used to select items to manipulate and edit them. In the last chapter, you used your selection cursor to select the window itself and change things like its size and shape. However, your cursor can also be put into control Creation mode. When you want to place a control on your window, you tell the cursor which control you want to create, either by selecting it from the Control menu or by clicking on the control you want on the Window PainterBar. This action makes your cursor become a control creation cursor. To place an instance of that control inside the window, simply click on the window with the control cursor in the spot where you want it. The object will appear on the window, and then the cursor will return to the selection cursor so you can manipulate and edit that object.

There are a number of different controls that you can use to communicate with a user. Let's place a few of the more common ones on our window to help us communicate with our user.

You should be familiar with the Command button. Most of the windows that you have looked at so far, in fact most windows in general, have Command buttons on them to allow you to perform actions by clicking on them with your mouse. For example, almost all windows that you see in Microsoft Windows have an OK and a Cancel button. Coincidentally, the Command button is a very good first control to place on your window.

Make your cursor into a Command Button Creator either by choosing Command**B**utton from the **C**ontrols menu or by clicking on the Command Button button on the Window PainterBar. Your cursor will become a Command Button Creator, and PowerBuilder visually shows this to you by displaying the Command Button toolbar button in a depressed state. (But don't worry, we'll cheer it up in just a minute.) Move your cursor into the window on-screen. Notice that the cursor changes shape to look like a crosshair instead of the usual arrow shape. Click with your left mouse button, and a Command Button control appears on-screen directly under your crosshair cursor. Inside the Command Button control appears the word None. Your cursor does not change shape, but notice that your cursor has returned to Selection mode, which is indicated

by the fact that the Command Button toolbar button returns to its normal state. Also, the Command button that you just placed on the window is selected, indicated by the four little black dots that you see at the corners of the button. At the bottom of your screen, also notice that the status bar no longer reads Nothing Selected, but instead shows some information about the currently selected control. It shows you the name of the button you just made is cb_1, and further over to the right it shows the X and Y Coordinates of the button, as well as its height and width. We'll talk more about the status bar later.

Let's place some more controls on our window. Make your cursor into a Static Text Creator by either selecting **S**taticText from the **C**ontrols menu, or by clicking on the Static Text toolbar button with your mouse. This time the Static Text button goes down. If you move your cursor into the window and click on your mouse button, a Static Text object appears on the window under your cursor. The text of this static text will also say None. Place a single line edit control on the window. Select SingleLine**E**dit from the **C**ontrols menu, or click on the Single Line Edit icon and place it inside your window. Notice that the Single Line Edit control doesn't come up with any text in it by default. Now that you're starting to get the hang of it, try a few by yourself. Place a list box control inside the window. I'll give you a hint—the List Box toolbar button is pictured in the sidebar. Place a check box and a radio button inside your window. Place a drop-down list box and a picture in your window. When you're finished, your window should look something like Figure 5.1. Your controls may not appear in exactly the same location on-screen. If you like, you can move your controls around the screen to make them look more like what is in Figure 5.1. Or, because this is your window, you can move your controls around the screen anywhere you want them.

Figure 5.1.
A window with some controls.

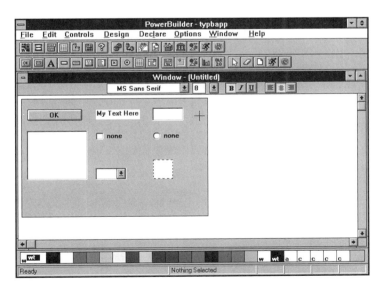

83

To move your controls inside your window, you first have to make sure that your cursor is in Selection mode. If you just placed a control on the window, your cursor should already be in Selection mode. If it's not, you can put it in Selection mode by clicking on the Selection tool on the toolbar. Either way, Selection mode is indicated by the fact that the Selection control on the toolbar is down. After you're in Selection mode, simply click on the control that you want to move and drag that control to a new position on-screen. As you drag the control, the outline of the control appears to help guide you as to where it will be placed if you let go of your mouse button and drop the control (see Fig. 5.2). If you want to select multiple controls to move, you can "lasso select" them by clicking on an area outside the controls but inside the window, and then by dragging your lasso through all of the controls that you want to select (see Fig. 5.3). Any control that is inside the area of your lasso will become selected. You can also toggle the Select status of any control by holding down the **Ctrl** key while clicking on the control. When you have selected multiple controls, all selected controls appear with black dots in the corners (see Fig. 5.4). By selecting multiple controls, you can move all the selected controls as a single group. As with single controls, when you move multiple controls, shadows of each control appear and help guide you as to where the controls will be placed if you let go of your mouse button and drop the group of controls (see Fig. 5.5). You can also move your controls with the arrow keys on your keyboard. Simply press the arrow key that faces the direction that you want to move the selected control. For example, if you want your control to move right, press the right-arrow key.

Figure 5.2.
Moving a control on a window.

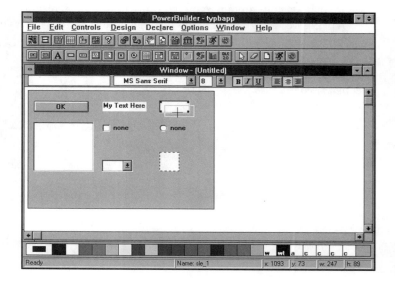

Figure 5.3.
*Selecting controls
with a lasso.*

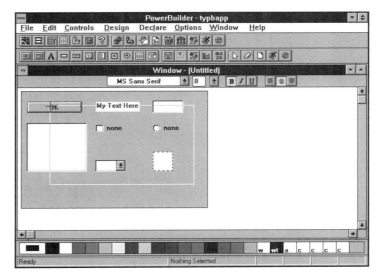

Figure 5.4.
Selecting multiple controls.

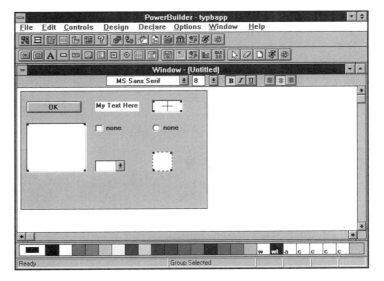

Figure 5.5.
Moving multiple controls on a window.

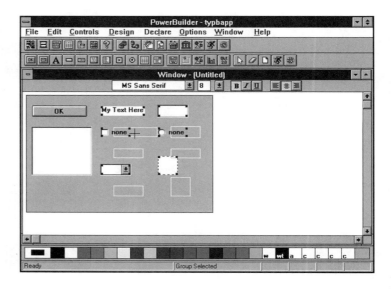

Of course, there is more to building exciting windows than moving controls around on-screen. You may also want to make a control bigger or smaller to fit the way you want it in your window. For example, our Command button is the wrong size. Every other Command button in Microsoft Windows is wider and shorter. Let's make our Command button look more like the standard Windows Command button. To do this, select the Command button with your Selection cursor. Then, move your cursor to the right side of the Command button until it changes shape to a right-and-left pointing arrow, as seen in Figure 5.6. Then click and hold your left mouse button, and drag the mouse to the right until the button is the right size (see Fig. 5.7). Then do the same for the vertical size of the button by moving your mouse cursor to the bottom border of the button (see Fig. 5.8). If you want to do it more quickly, you can move the corner of the control, which allows you to adjust both the height and the width of the control at the same time (see Fig. 5.9). Does this all seem familiar? It should—you did the same thing with the window itself yesterday afternoon in Chapter 4.

For some, fine-tune adjustments using a mouse require more of a steady hand than is available. In realization of the fact that not everyone is mouse-dexterous, PowerBuilder gives you the capability to easily make the controls on your screens look nicer by automatically aligning, sizing, and spacing selected controls for you. If you select multiple controls, you can quickly align them by selecting Align Controls from the Edit menu (see Fig. 5.10). You can align your controls horizontally or vertically so that an edge aligns or so that their centers align. The pictures that you see in the Align Controls menu describe the alignment that your selected controls will take on. Additionally, you can make all of your controls the same size by selecting the Size Controls menu of the Edit menu. You can size them either horizontally or vertically. Finally, if you have selected three or more controls, you can space them out evenly so that there is an equal amount of space between each of them by selecting the Space Controls menu from the Edit menu. Again,

you can space your controls either horizontally or vertically. When aligning and sizing your controls, the control that you selected first is used as the *anchor* for all other selected controls. This means that all of the controls will size themselves or align themselves with the first control. In a similar manner, when you space your controls, PowerBuilder sets the amount of space between each of the controls equal to that amount of space that is between the first two controls you have selected. Sometimes, if you are not paying attention to the order in which you selected your controls, these menu items may not do what you expect. Using these techniques, however, you can quickly position controls on your screen so that they look nice and professional.

Figure 5.6.
*The Horizontal
Sizing cursor.*

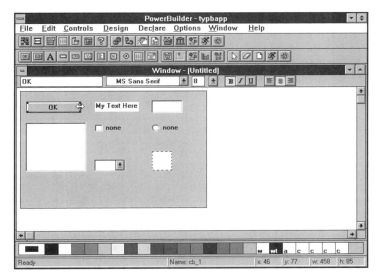

Figure 5.7.
*Horizontally sizing the
Command button.*

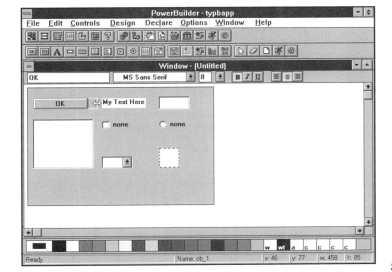

Figure 5.8.
The Vertical Sizing cursor.

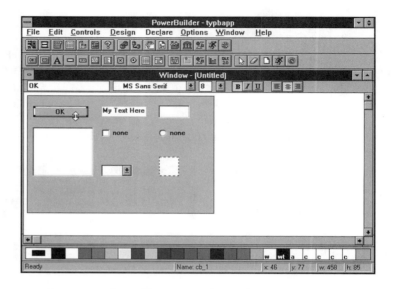

Figure 5.9.
The Corner Sizing cursor.

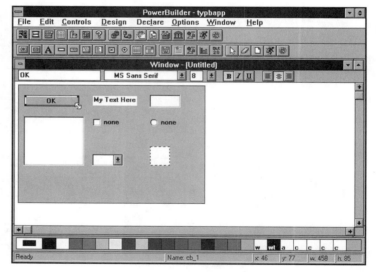

Figure 5.10.
The Edit/Align Controls menu.

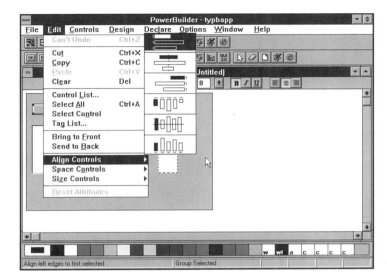

Double-Clicking to Change Control Attributes

There are other things about controls that you will need to change in order to make full use of their capabilities. Some of the more common features of each control can be accessed by double-clicking on the control itself. For example, if you double-click on the Command button, you will see the CommandButton attributes dialog box (see Fig. 5.11). In that window, you will notice that you can change some of the attributes of the Command button. The first attribute is the name of the button. In PowerBuilder, every control has a name. By default, when you create a control, PowerBuilder assigns that control a name based upon the type of control that it is, followed by an underscore, followed by a sequential number. So, your Command button's default name is *cb_1*: *cb* stands for Command Button, and 1 is the first Command button. Each control has its own prefix, so if you look at the name of the Static text, it will be st_1. The Single Line Edit's name is sle_1, and so on. The default prefixes are listed in the documentation and in the on-line help. These names are intuitive enough that you will remember them with ease after you have worked with PowerBuilder for a while. In general, it is a good habit to change the name of your controls to something that is a little bit more representative of what the control is for. Because this button will eventually become an OK button, let's change the name to cb_ok.

Figure 5.11.
*The CommandButton
dialog box.*

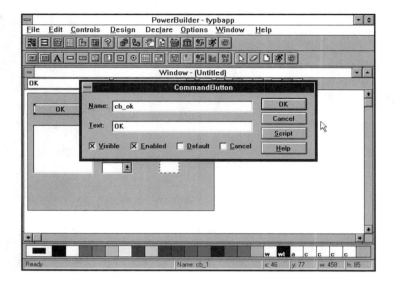

The next attribute you can change from the CommandButton attributes dialog box is the text of the button. Right now, it is set to read None. Of course, we don't want our OK button to say None; we want it to say OK. To change the name, move your cursor first to the Text Edit box, either by pressing the **Tab** key on your keyboard or by clicking in the Text Edit box with your mouse. You can also get to it by holding down the **Alt** key and pressing the letter **T**. This is indicated by the underlined "T" in the label for this box, **T**ext. After you are in the text box, you can delete the word None from the box with your **Backspace** or **Delete** key, and instead type in the word **OK**.

Under the text box of the Command Button attribute dialog box is a set of check boxes. As with the Window Style window that we talked about yesterday, these check boxes are either on or off, indicating whether the attribute of the command button is set to true or false. For example, if the visible check box is checked, the button is visible. If you uncheck the Enabled check box, the Command button becomes disabled and becomes grayed out so the user cannot click on it. You can also make the button into a Default button by checking the Default check box. If the button is a Default button, when the user presses the **Enter** key, the button acts as if the user has clicked it. This is a good behavior to associate with an **OK** button, so let's make our button the Default button by checking the Default check box. On many windows, there's also a Cancel button that gets clicked when you press the **Escape** key. You can make a button behave that way by checking the Cancel check box. When you're done making all of the changes to the

Command button, you can press the **OK** button, and the changes will be accepted. Or if you decide you don't want to accept the changes you have made, you can press the **Cancel** button. Some controls also allow you to create scripts for them, which you can do by clicking the **Script** button. We'll talk more about scripts tomorrow. Finally, at any time, you can get help about the current control attribute dialog box by clicking on the **Help** button.

Each of the controls has its own Control attribute dialog box window. Some of the attributes that you can change are common among most, if not all, of the controls in your window, such as Name, Visible, Enabled, and Text. Many controls also have a Border attribute so that you can give the object an underline, box, shadow, or even a three-dimensional border. To see an example, double-click on the Static Text control that you created earlier. The StaticText attribute dialog box appears on your screen (see Fig. 5.12). In this dialog box, you will see a place to enter the name and text of the static text, as well as check boxes for Visible and Enabled and even some new attributes that you have not seen before—Focus Rectangle and Alignment. The Focus Rectangle is a dotted box that appears just inside the borders of a control to indicate that the control is currently in focus, or selected. The Alignment attribute controls how the text inside the static text is displayed. You can align your text to the left or right, or you can center it. As you double-click on each control in your window, you can see that the most popular attributes of that control appear in a dialog box where you can edit them.

Figure 5.12.
The StaticText attributes dialog box.

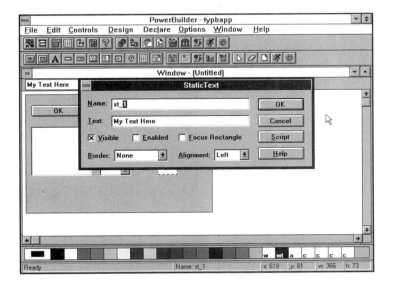

Right-Clicking to Change Control Attributes

It is important to realize, though, that there are attributes of these controls that you are not seeing when you double-click on them. For example, what if you want to change the color of the text of your Static Text control? The StaticText attributes dialog box doesn't have color as one of its attributes that you can edit. Does this mean that you cannot change the color of this control? Of course not! There is a way to get access to all of the possible attributes of a control that you can edit, and that is by clicking on the control with your right mouse button.

If you remember, yesterday you used the right mouse button to see a popup menu listing all of the attributes of a window that you can edit. Well, by the same token, you can use your right mouse button to click on any control and see all of the attributes of that control that you can edit. Go ahead and right-click on the Command button control that is now our **OK** button. You should see a popup menu appear that looks just like Figure 5.13.

Figure 5.13.
The Right Mouse menu for a Command button.

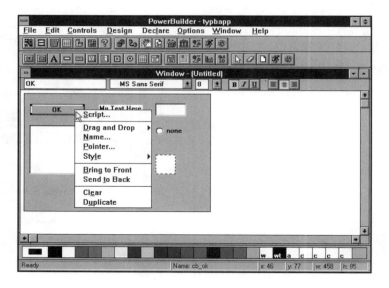

The Right Mouse menu for the Command button has the following menu items:

☐ **Script:** Clicking on the **S**cript menu item takes you to the Script Painter. You've already seen me evade detailed discussion of the Script Painter, and I'm not going to stop now. We'll talk in detail about the Script Painter in the next lesson.

☐ **Drag and Drop:** The **D**rag and Drop menu has a couple of submenus on it where you can edit attributes having to do with drag and drop of your controls. They are **D**rag Auto and Drag **I**con.

- **Drag Auto:** The Drag Auto menu item is a True/False selectable attribute, which appears checked when you click on it and make it True. If a control's Drag Auto attribute is set to True, your user can click on the control and drag it automatically, similar to the way in which you can drag the controls in the development environment to move them around the screen.

- **Drag Icon:** Clicking on the Drag Icon menu item allows you to change the icon that appears when the user drags this control. By default, when your user drags a control, a rectangle about the size of the control appears, which is what you see in the PowerBuilder development environment. However, you can make your application more intuitive by showing a different icon to your user when he/she drags certain controls. Furthermore, at runtime, you may want to change the icon that appears to the user, depending on certain factors. For example, if you've ever copied or moved files using File Manager, you probably noticed that the document icon that you drag to the destination point appears differently when you are going to copy a file than when you are about to move it. You can create similar, user friendly effects by changing the Drag icon.

- **Name:** Clicking on the Name menu item opens the CommandButton attributes dialog box, in the same manner that double-clicking on the button does.

- **Pointer:** Clicking on the Pointer menu item opens the Change Pointer dialog box, which you learned about yesterday.

- **Style:** Under this menu item, you will find the same Command button attributes that you find at the bottom of the CommandButton attributes dialog box. Clicking on one of these menu items toggles its check status On or Off, which also toggles the attribute's own status to True or False.

- **Bring to Front/Send to Back:** The next two menu items are not really attributes but are commands that you can use to control *Z-Order positioning* of your controls within the domain of your window. If two controls overlap, one of the two controls is on top, and the other is on the bottom. The one on top covers the ones under it. This is often referred to as the *Z-Order position* of an object. You can control which object is on top by bringing it to the front with the Bring To Front menu item, or by sending it to the back, by clicking on the Send To Back menu item.

- **Clear:** The Clear menu item deletes the control.

- **Duplicate:** The Duplicate menu item creates a new control that is an (almost) exact copy of the control. This new copy will be given its own unique name, using the same naming conventions that we talked about yesterday, but it will not contain any scripts—even if the original did.

There are two other very common attributes that you can control from a Right Mouse menu that don't apply to a Command button but that apply to a number of other controls, and so I will mention them here.

☐ **Border:** You can change the border of your control by selecting one of the border styles from the submenu of the Border menu item.

☐ **Color:** You can change the color of different parts of your control. When you select the Color menu item, you can select what you want to change the color of: the text color or the background color. Sometimes there are other choices, as well. After you select what you want to change the color of, you see a list of colors from which you can select one.

Of course, there are other attributes that are specific to each individual control, but I will discuss these "custom" attributes later in this chapter. In the meantime, feel free to spend a few minutes looking at the different Right Mouse menus for each of the different controls that you currently have on your screen.

Using the ColorBar and StyleBar to Change Control Attributes

Of course, you've already learned quite a bit about the semantics of the ColorBar in the last chapter, so I won't spend a lot of time reviewing that information. But this is where the ColorBar actually comes into play. When you want to change the colors of your controls, you can click with your left mouse button on the ColorBar to change the foreground or text color of the control you are working with. You can right-click on the ColorBar to change the background color of the control you are working with.

Note: Certain standard Microsoft Windows controls, like the Command button, have colors that cannot be changed with the color bar, but instead must be changed with settings in the Microsoft Windows Control Panel. Of course, because it's generally a bad idea to mess around with the user's Control Panel settings at runtime, it's best not to try to mess around with the colors of these controls.

Other controls, like the Static Text control and the Single Line Edit control, can have their color changed right from the ColorBar. So to change the text color of your Static Text, select your Static Text by clicking on it. Then click on the dark blue spot on the ColorBar, and this will make your Static Text appear dark blue. Then, right-click on the yellow box on the ColorBar to make the background yellow. This illustrates how to change the colors of your controls with the ColorBar.

One thing that you may have noticed so far is that there doesn't seem to be a way to change the font of the text that you are working with by using any of the aforementioned methods. This is true, and in my opinion is probably just a bit of an oversight on the part of the developers of

PowerBuilder. Of course, they didn't leave us totally without any way to change the font of text inside the objects that we are working with; they just gave us a really nice toolbar to help us do it. But you should take note of the problem here. If you were working without a mouse, you would have a very difficult time figuring out how to change your text's font and size with the keyboard. Eventually, you might find in the documentation that you can in fact get to the StyleBar with the keyboard with some accelerator keys, but the fact that you have to look in the documentation means that the method is not intuitive enough. When you create your applications, always offer a simple, intuitive keyboard equivalent for any action that they can perform. But soapbox aside, let's learn how to use the StyleBar.

You already learned that you can change the text of your controls from the Control attribute dialog box. But a quicker way is to change the text from the StyleBar. If you select the control whose text you want to edit, say the Static Text control, and then click on the StyleBar in the box on the left side, you can change the text of your control to match your own preferences. Select your Static Text control and click on the Text Edit box on the StyleBar. Clear out the text that is currently in there, and type

`My Text Here`

Then, click on the font drop-down list box and select the MS Sans Serif font. Finally, click on the Size box, and select a size of 8 points. The resulting window should look something like what you see in Figure 5.14. You can also change the text to be bold, italic, or underline by toggling the state of those three buttons. Finally, you can change the text to be right-, left-, or center-justified by clicking on the appropriate button on the style bar.

Figure 5.14.
Changing the style of your static text object.

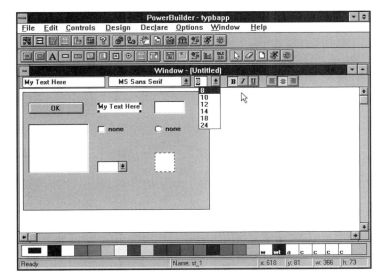

Previewing Your Window

Certain attributes, like the font and style of the controls on your window, are represented in the Window Painter the way they will look when you run your application. However, certain behaviors of your controls are not visible inside the Window Painter. While you are creating your windows, you may want to get a feel for things like the tab order, window placement, or just how the buttons click and the edit boxes allow data entry. PowerBuilder recognizes this need to test out the feel of your window and has given you the capability to preview your window by selecting Preview from the Design menu.

While previewing your window, you will be able to see how the window opens when you open it in your applications (see Fig. 5.15). Then, you can actually "work the controls" in the same way your user will when he/she runs your applications. Your button will click, your edit box will accept input, and your check box will check. But keep in mind that only the default behavior of your window's controls will be available. Later, you will learn how to extend the behavior of your window and its controls by using scripts. However, in Preview mode, even if your controls have scripts, they don't get run. The Preview window is for layout and default behavior only.

Figure 5.15.
Previewing your window.

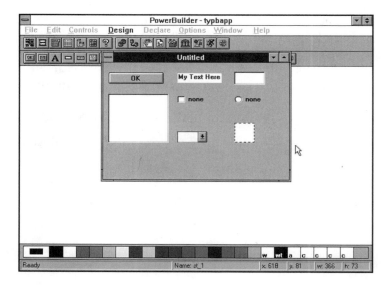

When you are finished previewing your window, you can turn off Preview mode in one of two ways. The first way is to close your previewed window by using the Control menu in the top-left corner. By double-clicking on this control menu, or by selecting Close from this Control menu, you can close open windows, including this one. Closing this window restores

Development mode. However, some of the windows that you create will not have Control menus. And if they don't, you can't use a Control menu to close your previewed window. So instead, you must click again on the **D**esign menu and turn off Preview mode by selecting Preview again.

> **Note:** You've seen a few of the window controls that are available for placement on your window. You've also been given the tools that you need to see how these controls can be changed, and how they work. You should spend some time experimenting with all of the window controls to learn a little bit about how they work and what the different attributes of the different controls are. The *Objects and Controls* PowerBuilder manual describes each of the controls, what their attributes are, and how they work, to help guide you through your explorations. Exploration and experimentation is the key to acquiring knowledge.

Saving Your Window

When you develop your PowerBuilder applications, you will spend some time placing controls on your window and then previewing your window to make sure that you are happy with it. After you are happy with the way your window looks, you will want to save your window so that you don't have to re-create it. Saving your window permanently stores a copy of your window on your hard disk so that you can call it up again and use it. You may want to call it up so that you can make changes to it. Or, more importantly, you may want to call it up to have it run as part of your application. Either way, you must first save your window so that you can use it again.

There are actually a number of ways you can save your window. The first and most definitive way of saving your window is by selecting **S**ave or Save **A**s from the **F**ile menu. Doing this instructs PowerBuilder to immediately save your window, regardless of its status. If this is the first time that you are saving your window, and in this case it is, PowerBuilder prompts you by asking you for the name and location of where you would like to save the window (see Fig. 5.16). Type in

`w_ch5`

as the name of your window in the box labeled `Windows`. Then, tab over to the box labeled `Comments` and enter in a comment about this window, perhaps something like

`The window that I created in Chapter 5`

Figure 5.16.
Saving your PowerBuilder window.

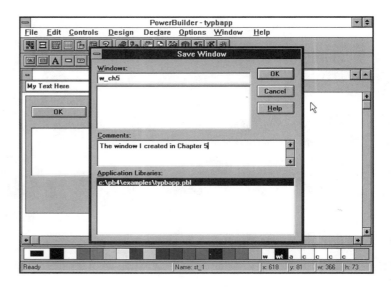

Notice at the bottom of your screen that you can select which library you want to save your window in. However, since we are only working with one library in this application, we don't really get much choice. If we had more libraries in our application, we would specify which library we want to save our window in by selecting that library in this box.

After you have finished filling in the information about the window you want to save, simply click on the **OK** button, and PowerBuilder will save your window in the library you have specified, with the name you have specified, and the comments you have specified. After you have saved your window the first time, if you make additional changes, you can save your window again by choosing **S**ave from the **F**ile menu, and it will simply update the window with your changes without prompting you. If you prefer to change the name of the window, you can choose Save **A**s from the **F**ile menu, and PowerBuilder will prompt you again so you can enter a new name, new library, and new comments.

Another good technique that you can learn from the makers of PowerBuilder is to help prevent your user from losing data. If you make changes to your window and try to close it without saving your changes, PowerBuilder prompts you to save your changes before closing (see Fig. 5.17). If you click on the **Yes** button, PowerBuilder will save your window and then close it, as if you had selected the **S**ave menu item from the **F**ile menu. If you click on the **No** button, PowerBuilder closes the window and abandons your changes. If you press the **Cancel** button, PowerBuilder aborts your attempt to close and allows you to keep working on your window, assuming that your attempt to close was a mistake.

Figure 5.17.
PowerBuilder prompts you to save your changes.

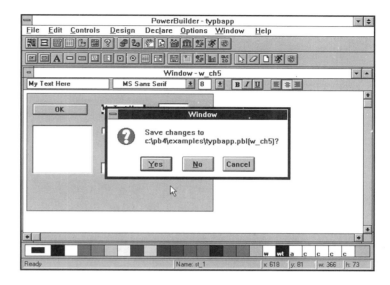

5

DO	DON'T

DO Save your changes frequently. It is very frustrating to lose hours worth of changes that you made because you didn't save and the power went out, or you got an error of some sort.

DON'T Forget to back up your files frequently. Backing up your files will also help prevent loss in case you make (and save) a change that you don't like.

What's in a Name?—Naming Your Controls

Every control on your window has a name. The name of the control defaults to the acronym of the control type followed by an underscore, followed by a number. However, when you begin to put code into your applications, you will find that most of your coding statements are commands that are directed at controls on your window, or commands that read and write attributes of your window controls. For this reason, you should be sure to give your controls names that make it easy for you to understand what the control is. Earlier today, I asked you to change the default name of your **OK** button, cb_1, to a name that is more indicative of what our

button is, cb_ok. Imagine if you had placed five buttons on your window, and they were named cb_1, cb_2, cb_3, cb_4, and cb_5. Which one is the **Cancel** button? You would be much better off if you named your controls cb_ok, cb_cancel, cb_options, cb_search, and cb_help. Now can you guess which one is the Cancel button? As you begin to build windows with many controls on them, you will find it very useful to use naming conventions that will make it as easy as possible for you to have a clear concept of the controls you are working with.

DO	DON'T

DO Name your controls as unambiguously as possible. I can't stress enough how important this is and how much your productivity will increase just by doing this.

DON'T Limit your good naming practices to window controls. Give everything you create a clear, concise, unambiguous name. Name your windows and other objects clearly when you save them, too. It will reap large rewards.

Note: You can control the default prefixes that will be used for your control names by adding lines in your PB.INI file. If you edit your PB.INI file by using Notepad, you may add these lines to the section entitled [Window]. Simply add a single line for each prefix that you want to change that contains the name of the control type, followed by an equal sign, followed by the prefix that you want to use. For example, to change the prefix for list boxes, simply add a line to the [Window] section that reads as follows:

```
Listbox=list_
```

Notice that there are no spaces here. If you insert spaces, it will not find the Listbox keyword, and will not use this prefix. Also, after you make changes to PB.INI, you should be sure to restart PowerBuilder so that it can read in your changes.

Morning Summary

After you have a window, you will want to place controls on it to interface with your user. In the Window Painter, your cursor has several different "modes." One of the modes is Create mode. If your cursor is in Create mode, it can create a control of the type that it is set to create. For example, you can turn your cursor into a Command Button Creator and place a Command button on-screen. After you place your Command button on the window, your cursor goes into

Selection mode, where you can click on controls on-screen to select them.

By using the selection cursor, you can move, size, and edit your controls, as well. By double-clicking on your controls, you open a window for the control where you can change some of the more common attributes of your control, like the control's name. Additionally, you can click with the right mouse button on the control to bring up a popup menu that allows you to edit the other attributes of the control. If the control has text on it, you can change the text, the font, the size, and the style of the text by clicking on the StyleBar. You can change the color of your controls with the ColorBar. By clicking on the ColorBar with the left mouse button, you change the foreground or text color of the object. By clicking on the ColorBar with the right mouse button, you can change the background color of the object.

After you have placed your controls on your window, moved them around, sized them, edited them, and given them pretty colors, you will want to see more of what your window will look like when it is run. You can do this by selecting Pre**v**iew from the **D**esign menu. When you are satisfied with the way your window appears, you should save it in a library by choosing **S**ave from the **F**ile menu. When you save your window, you will be asked to give it a name. The name of your window should help you figure out what it is for.

In PowerBuilder, you give names not just to your windows, but to all of your controls. It's always a good idea to use names that will allow you to recognize what the control you are referring to is, as well as what it is used for. For example, if you name your OK button `my_cntrl`, it will be very difficult for you to remember what it is. But if you name it `cb_ok`, you should have no trouble realizing that this is your OK Command button.

5

Chapter

6

Putting It All Together

In this chapter, you will learn:

- ☐ How to make your window open when you run your application
- ☐ How to use the Script Painter
- ☐ How to run your application
- ☐ About the Windows Engine and the Event-Driven Programming Paradigm
- ☐ About PowerScript Scripts and some of the more common events of the PowerBuilder controls

What Is a Script?

By now you have created a window and placed a number of controls on it. You've learned how to save your window, and you've learned how to preview what your window will look like when you run it. Now it's time to make your window run as part of your application.

In the last chapters, I spent a bit of time discussing the attributes of controls, applications, and windows. And during the discussion of each one, I referred to the fact that one of the attributes of the control is something called a *script*, and then kept telling you that we would talk about scripts later. I've devoted an entire chapter, this chapter, to scripts because they are the essence of your PowerBuilder programs. *Scripts* are used to give functionality to your controls, windows, and other objects. They are the attributes that you use to create instructions that can be communicated to your computer and peripherals to make them react. They are the pieces of the puzzle that allow you to make your controls react to input from your user, and allow you to define your own custom behavior for your controls. Scripts are what PowerBuilder programming is all about. And scripts are what you need to make your application open your window, the first step in seeing your work in action.

> **Note:** There are several different types of commands that you can place in scripts—*keywords*, *expressions*, *function calls*, and *declarations*. You will learn about each of these types of script commands in the next couple of chapters.

Making Your Application Open Your New Window

Open the Application Painter again by clicking the Application Painter button on the PowerBar. The current application, typbapp, should open in the Application Painter. If it does not, review Chapter 3 to see how to open or create it. After you look at typbapp, edit the script

by selecting **S**cript from the **E**dit menu, or by clicking on the Script Painter button on the Application PainterBar. The Script Painter will appear on your screen (see Fig. 6.1). Type in

```
Open( w_ch5)
```

Figure 6.1.
The Script Painter.

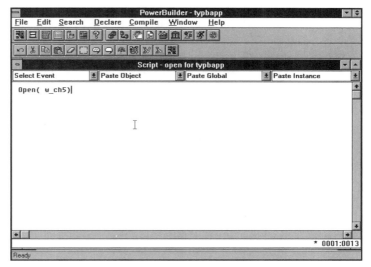

That's all of the code you need to open your window from Chapter 5. That instruction, when encountered by PowerBuilder, causes PowerBuilder to perform whatever actions necessary to open the window named w_ch5, which we created in the last chapter. Return to the Application Painter by selecting **R**eturn from the **F**ile menu, or by clicking on the Return to Application Painter button on the Script PainterBar. You can now save the changes you have made to your application by selecting **S**ave from the **F**ile menu. Notice that your Script Painter button has changed a bit to indicate that there are scripts for your Application Object. Before, the button was empty because there were no scripts. But now that we have entered a script in the Application Object, the icon for the Script Painter informs us that there is code in this Application Object. Later, when we start working with the scripts of multiple objects on a window, this will prove to be a very exciting and helpful feature.

Running Your Application

You have just created a script for your application that tells it to open your w_ch5 window when you start your application. Although don't yet understand why this is the case, suffice it to say that I have stepped you through all that you need to get your application to open the w_ch5 window when you start it. If you now select **R**un from the **F**ile menu, or click on the Run Button on the PowerBar, your w_ch5 window should open up.

Script Painter Basics

Before we go any further, I would like to spend time explaining the intricacies of the Script Painter. When you develop your PowerBuilder applications, you will find yourself spending most of your time in the Script Painter. Therefore, it is very important that you are intimately familiar with its features and usage so you can be as efficient as possible when developing your applications. Open the Script Painter for your application again. Recall again the Script Painter window that you saw in the last section (refer to Fig. 6.1). This time, instead of just typing some code, though, let's pay attention to what we're looking at.

A Bit of Coding Standards

First, let's talk about the big white space area on the screen. This is the script editing area where you place your code. When you want to define behaviors for your controls, you will type in the instructions you want your objects to perform in this area. In general, statements inside PowerBuilder take up a single line of code. When you have finished that line, you press the **Enter** key and proceed to type the next line. A good practice that will help readability is to indent code using the **Tab** key inside constructs that begin and end. For example, you may have an IF statement (which we talk about in tomorrow's lesson when we talk about "Other Conditionals") that performs several statements in between an IF and an END IF statement. To help make it easy to recognize that these statements are inside the IF statement, code the statements in the following manner:

```
IF Today is Monday THEN      (1)
     Get Up On Time          (2)
     Take a Shower           (3)
     Take kids to school     (4)
     Go to Work              (5)
END IF                       (6)
```

Of course, the preceding statements aren't really executable within PowerBuilder, but it illustrates the point—lines two through five are tabbed over so that it is easy to see that they only occur within the scope of the IF statement. If the IF statement is false, then these statements will not execute, and we can visualize jumping down immediately to line six without even paying attention to the code in lines two through five. Illustrate the structure of your code with these tabs. Anything that "belongs" to a complex statement like this (you'll learn these statement types in the next chapter) should be tabbed over to indicate that they appear inside a group of other statements. We'll talk more about this practice in the next chapter.

Comments

It is a good practice to narrate your code using comments so that if you come back to your code at a later time, you will be able to understand what your code is supposed to do. Additionally, if someone else has to maintain your code, they can read the comments to help understand what

your code is trying to do. Of course, that assumes that you create comments that are useful and make sense.

There are two ways you can indicate comments in your scripts. The first method is to create *block comments* using one symbol, a forward slash and asterisk (/*), to represent the beginning of the comment block and a different symbol and an asterisk and then a forward slash (*/), to represent the end of the comment block. Anything inside these two symbols is ignored by the PowerBuilder compiler and is there solely for your benefit. Your block comment can even be on multiple lines. A block comment might look something like this:

```
/*
This next piece of code parses the input of the user into multiple
command strings, then validates each clause of the input, and then
returns an empty string if there is an error, or the result of the
user's query if it is OK.
*/
```

Another type of comment is a *line comment*. In a line of code, everything after the line comment indicator, a double forward slash (//), is ignored by the compiler as a comment. You can comment out an entire single line by placing the double slash at the beginning of the line, or you can even comment out just part of the line by placing the double slash in the middle of the line. This is very useful for one line comments, as well as for temporarily commenting out changes to your code while you are testing or debugging. A few examples of line comments are:

```
// Everything after the double slash is ignored by the compiler.
IF x > 0 THEN //But everything before it is still "seen" by the compiler!
```

Note: When I first started learning how to program, I was programming in my own environment and writing programs for my own needs. I was the only programmer on the "project," and so I figured that I didnt need to comment my code. After all, who else would ever try to read it?

The programs were relatively good—they lasted about a year before I needed to make changes because of new input requirements. But when I went to make those changes, it had been a year since I had looked at that code, and I had since written many other programs. Although I was eventually able to figure out my own programs, it took a very long time. Had I commented my code from the beginning, the process would have been much simpler.

Good, understandable, relevant comments are critical to allowing maintenance of an application and are an essential part of the development process. Don't be lazy about commenting your code. You may pay for it yourself in the end!

One of the best justifications for good comments, and in fact, good documentation as a whole, is often referred to in the industry as the "Hit By A Truck" theory. The theory proposes that programmers can, and will, get hit by trucks or other large moving vehicles. When a programmer

6

gets hit by a truck, even if he/she survives, it's very unlikely that the programmer will be able to maintain his/her code for a while. And if **you** need to maintain that programmer's code, it will be most critical that the programmer has properly documented the code; otherwise, it will be nearly impossible to maintain it.

DO	DON'T

DO Create comments that describe the purpose and results of statements inside your code.

DON'T Create comments that simply repeat the syntax of your code in English. For example, the following comment is useless:

```
// Add 3 to X

X = X + 3
```

A better comment might look like this:

```
/* Increment X to the value that
        we need later for some purpose  */

X = X + 3
```

Script Painter Menus

The Script Painter has a number of menus to help you with your script editing. Let's spend a few minutes discussing each one:

File: The File menu is a standard menu, and you should already be familiar with most of its menu items. However, in the Script Painter, you are presented with some new File menu items that you may not have seen before.

☐ **Import:** By selecting Import, you can import the contents of a flat file into your Script Painter. This is very useful for quickly loading script headers.

☐ **Export:** By selecting Export, you can export your script into a flat file in case you want to use it again somewhere else.

Edit: The Edit menu is also a relatively standard menu, although some new menu items appear under the Edit menu when you are in the Script Painter. They are:

☐ **Comment Selection:** By selecting Comment Selection, you can quickly place double slashes in front of your code to comment it out. When you select this menu item, it will comment out the line with your cursor on it. If you have highlighted several lines, it will comment out all of the lines that you have highlighted.

□ **Uncomment Selection:** The Uncomment Selection menu item will remove double slashes from the front of any line that is highlighted. If no lines are highlighted, it will remove the double slashes from the line with your cursor on it. If there are no double slashes at the front of the selected line(s), nothing will happen.

□ **Paste Function:** You can quickly paste a function into your code. When you select the Paste Function menu item, the Paste Function window appears (see Fig. 6.2). At the right side of the window, you can specify the type of function that you want to paste by clicking on the appropriate radio button. You can specify either Built-In PowerBuilder functions, User-Defined functions (we'll talk about these in the next chapter), or External functions (we'll talk about these next week). By selecting a function in the list box on the left side of this window and by clicking **OK**, or by double-clicking on the name of the function itself, you can place the function directly into the script that you are working on at the current cursor position.

Figure 6.2.
The Paste Function window.

□ **Paste SQL:** If you want to put *embedded SQL* into your scripts, you can access the SQL Painter to help you build it by selecting the Paste SQL menu item. Next week, in Chapter 20, we will spend a great deal of time talking about PowerBuilder's incredible SQL Painter for building queries. Figure 6.3 illustrates the SQL Statement Type window.

□ **Paste Statement:** PowerBuilder also allows you to quickly paste standard PowerBuilder constructs that are commonly used and are sometimes more complex than we are able to remember. You do this by selecting the Paste Statement menu item. These constructs are discussed in the next chapter. Figure 6.4 illustrates the Paste Statement window, where you can select a PowerBuilder statement to paste.

Figure 6.3.
*The SQL Statement
Type window.*

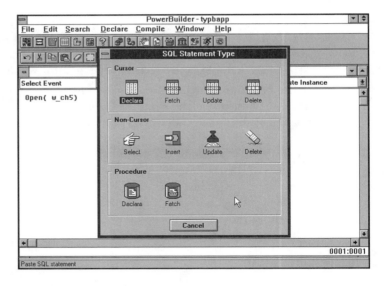

Figure 6.4.
The Paste Statement.

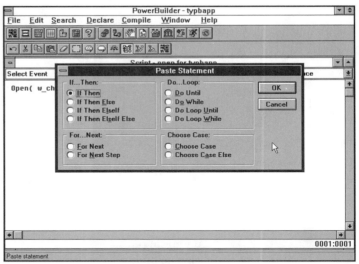

☐ **Browse Object:** You can browse certain information about the object whose script you are writing. You can see what attributes that object has, as well as what functions that object can call. When you select the Browse **O**bject menu item, the Browse Object window appears (see Fig. 6.5). If you select an attribute or a function and click on the **Paste** button, it will paste the selected attribute or function into your script.

Figure 6.5.
The Browse Object window.

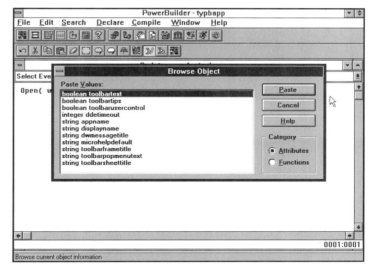

☐ **Browse Objects:** The **B**rowse Objects menu item opens the Browse Objects window, which contains the PowerBuilder Object Browser (see Fig. 6.6). This will surely become one of your favorite utilities within PowerBuilder to help you code your applications. Using the Object Browser is similar to using the Browse Object window, except that you can browse additional components of your objects, like instance variables and shared variables (which we'll talk about later); and you can browse components of any object in your library path, and even some internal system components. Using the Object Browser allows you to easily paste in function proto-types for functions that you are calling from other objects in your system.

Figure 6.6.
The Browse Objects window.

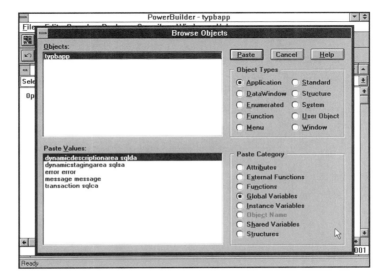

☐ **Select Object:** Although it is probably grayed out in the Applications Script Painter, you will find the Select Object menu item very useful when you start building scripts for objects in your windows. When you click on this menu item, a list of objects appears in the Select Object window (see Fig. 6.7). By selecting one of these listed objects, you can quickly and easily switch the script that you are editing to the script of the object that you selected.

Figure 6.7.
The Select Object window.

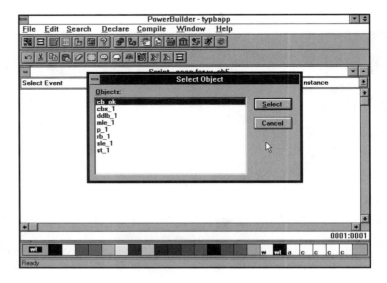

Search: The Search menu contains several menu items that allow you to navigate to specific locations within your script. You can either search for a specific set of characters in your text, optionally replacing them with a different set of characters, or jump to a specific line number in your script. Because these are features that are available in any word processor, discussing them in any further detail would be redundant.

Declare: From the Declare menu, you can declare certain types of functions and variables. You will learn more about these different types of language constructs in the next chapter. You can declare three types of these constructs: Scoped Variables, Object Functions and Structures, and External Functions. You can also declare special events that you want to control.

☐ **Scoped Variables:** These include Global Variables, Shared Variables, and Instance Variables. When you select any of these menu items, you are prompted with the appropriate declaration window, where you can declare variables of the type that you requested. Figure 6.8 shows the Declare Global Variables window where you can declare your global variables. Similar windows appear for the other types of variables that you can declare.

Figure 6.8.
The Declare Global Variables window.

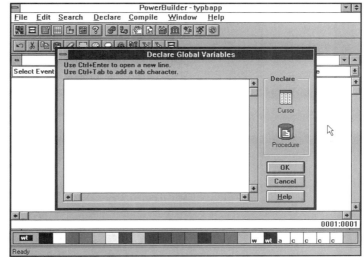

☐ **Object Functions and Structures:** Because we are working on the Application Object, the functions and structures we can create here are **A**pplication Functions and Application **S**tructures. However, if we were editing a Window, these would be **W**indow Functions and Window **S**tructures. This has to do with something that is referred to as the *Scope* of the function or structure. You will learn more about Scope in the next chapter.

☐ **External Functions:** External Functions are functions that you would want to call from a Windows .DLL file, external to PowerBuilder. We will discuss them in more detail in Chapter 14, "Other Types of User Objects." In the Application Painter, we can only declare a Global E**x**ternal Function; however, in other painters, we can also declare **L**ocal External Functions. This is another technicality that has to do with Scope, so I will save discussion of this matter for when we talk about that in the next chapter.

☐ **User Events:** By default, PowerBuilder gives you a specific set of supported events for which you can create code. If you want to create your own events (we'll talk about the reasons you might want to do this at the end of the chapter), you can do that by selecting the User **E**vents menu item.

Compile: You can compile your script from this menu. Also, you can set some compiler options here. When you learn about object-oriented development in Chapter 11, you will also learn about some additional options that appear under the **C**ompile menu.

☐ **Script:** Selecting the **S**cript menu item will attempt to compile the script that you have entered into the Script Painter. If there are any errors in your code, a Message window will appear, telling you what the error was and on which line it occurred (see Fig. 6.9).

Figure 6.9.
The Script Painter with a Message window on the bottom.

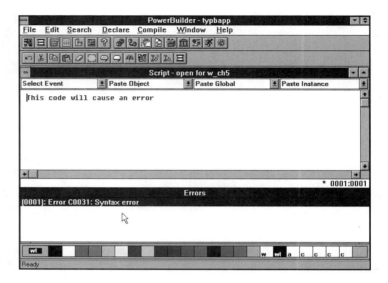

☐ **Display Compiler Warnings:** If the Display **C**ompiler Warnings menu item is checked, then both errors and warnings are displayed in the Message window. If it is not checked, then warnings are ignored and not displayed.

☐ **Display Database Warnings:** If the Display **D**atabase Warnings menu item is checked, then Database Warnings are displayed in the Message window when they are encountered; otherwise, they are ignored and not displayed.

The **W**indow and **H**elp menus remain unchanged inside the Script Painter.

The Script PainterBar

As with other painters, the Script Painter has a toolbar of its own, referred to as the *Script PainterBar* (see Fig. 6.10). As with other PainterBars, the Script PainterBar contains buttons that allow you to quickly perform some of the most common actions that are available to you from the menus. Following is a list of the buttons that appear on the Script PainterBar, along with a brief description of their functions.

 Undo: Undo the most recent change in your script.

 Cut: Cut selected text to the clipboard.

 Copy: Copy selected text to the clipboard.

 Paste: Paste text from the clipboard into the current script.

Erase: Erase the selected text.

Select All: Select the entire set of text in the Script Painter.

Comment Selection: Place line comment marks (//) in front of the selected lines of code.

Uncomment Selection: Remove line comment marks from in front of the selected lines of code.

Paste SQL: Paste a SQL Statement into the Script Painter.

Paste Statement: Paste a PowerBuilder statement into the Script Painter.

Browse Object: Browse the current object.

Object Browser: Open up the Object Browser (inside the Browse Objects window) to browse any object in the system.

Return to Application Painter: Save script changes and return to the Application Painter. This button position is reserved for returning to whatever painter you were in before the Script Painter, and would therefore be returning to when you clicked on it. For example, if you were working on a script for a window from inside the Window Painter, this would be a Return to Window Painter button.

Figure 6.10.
The Script PainterBar.

Script PainterBar

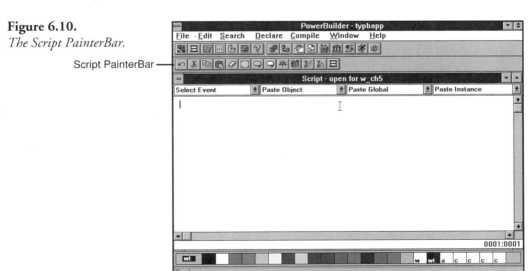

Script Shortcuts

At the top of the Script Painter window are four drop-down list boxes that you can use to help write your scripts. When you select one of the drop-down list boxes, it shows you its list of items. For all but the first drop-down list box, when you select one of the items in the list, it pastes that item into your PowerBuilder script at the current cursor position. For example, the second drop-down list box, labeled Paste Object, displays a list of all of the objects that might be of interest to you in your current script. In the Application Painter, your scripts are probably going to open windows, so when you select the Paste Object drop-down list box, you should see a list of the windows that are available to your application, in this case the window that we created in the last chapter, w_ch5. If you select w_ch5, it will paste w_ch5 into the Script Painter at the current cursor position. The same applies for the other two drop-down list boxes. The one labeled Paste Global displays all of your application's global variables that you may have declared from the **D**eclare menu. The one labeled Paste Instance lists all of the instance variables for the current object that you have declared from the **D**eclare menu. These tools allow you to quickly paste information that you might have to search for otherwise.

I have already mentioned, however, that the first drop-down list box, labeled Select Event, works slightly differently. This drop-down list box does not paste information into your scripts. Instead, it allows you to select which script you are working with. As you already know, each object can have its own script. Your application has a script, your window has a script, and each of the controls inside your window has a script. But it goes deeper than that. Each object actually has multiple scripts. You've already learned that scripts are what you use to control the behavior of your objects. The manner in which they do this is based on the manner in which they are engaged, or triggered, because of events that occur in your environment. Each control has a number of *events* that correspond to specific conditions within your environment. When a condition is met, its event gets triggered. Most of these events correspond to input from the user. For example, when your user clicks on a button, he/she causes a `clicked` event for that button to be triggered. Each event can have a script attached to it, so when your button's `clicked` event gets triggered, a script for the `clicked` event, if there is one, will run. We'll talk more about the events of your controls and the mechanics of how the events occur later. In the meantime, it is important to realize that your PowerBuilder objects have multiple events, and that each event's script is accessible by using the Select Event drop-down list box.

When you click on the Select Event drop-down list box, it displays a list of the available events for the object whose script you are editing. When you click on one of the listed events, the Script Painter will attempt to compile and save the current script, and then switches to the script for the event that you selected. If there was script for that event beforehand, then that script will appear in the Script Painter. An icon will appear next to the event name of any event that has script in it to let you know that there is a script for that event already (see Fig. 6.11). The Script Painter's title bar tells you the name of the script and the object that you are currently editing to prevent you from getting lost.

Figure 6.11.
The Select Event drop-down list box with script for some events.

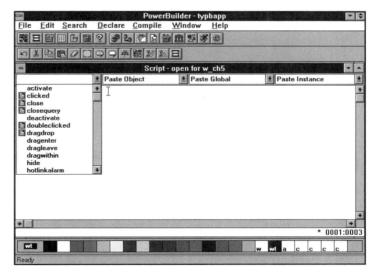

6

Giving Life to Controls in Your Window with Scripts Coding

PowerBuilder applications primarily involve defining reactions of specific objects to specific conditions by using PowerBuilder scripts. In other words, when your user clicks on your **OK** button, you want that action to elicit a specific reaction, perhaps close the window. As we briefly mentioned in the previous section, when your user clicks on the **OK** Button, it eventually causes the button's clicked event to be triggered. So you can make your application react to the clicked event of the **OK** button by writing a script for it. In the next lesson, you will learn the syntax of the PowerScript language that can be used to perform these reactions. But first, let's spend a few moments discussing the exact process of how events work.

Warning: The following discussion refers specifically to the method of handling events that is used by the Microsoft Windows Engine. The details of how other GUI environments handle events may be slightly different. However, the general idea is the same, and the resulting event mapping that occurs within PowerBuilder is identical. Nonetheless, it is important to recognize that there may be minute differences at the Operating System level of the management of events.

Event-Driven Windows

In Microsoft Windows, everything that appears on-screen (and even a thing or two that doesn't) is considered an object and is given an identification reference, called a *handle*, that Microsoft Windows uses to communicate with that object. Every window, button, drop-down list box, and so on, in every application has a unique handle that Windows uses when it wants to talk to that object. As you have already learned, each of these objects has events that are triggered when certain conditions are met. Internally, the Microsoft Windows Engine monitors the environment for any new conditions, and then uses a dispatcher to send the appropriate message to the proper object, referring to it by using its handle. The message tells the object to trigger the appropriate event. In truth, it's only slightly more complex than that—the Microsoft Windows Engine keeps a queue of messages that are being triggered within the system, and each application has to poll that queue to pick up its own messages and place them on its own application queue. The application then services its own queue by passing each message to the appropriate object within the application, triggering the appropriate event. Figure 6.12 illustrates this process.

Figure 6.12.
The Event Dispatching process.

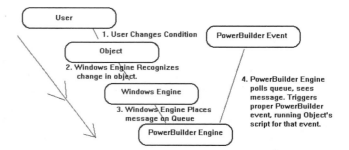

At an introductory level, it is not critical to understand the details and complexities of the different queues. It is important to understand that each event that gets triggered in a Windows application is caused by a message that is passed to it from a message queue, which contains, among other things, the handle of the object that is the recipient of the message, the message number (which tells the object which event to trigger), and sometimes certain parameters that may be needed by the recipient of the message to help it perform the proper action. Using our previous example, when your user clicks on your button with the mouse, the Windows Engine monitors this condition and interprets it as a mouse click by creating a new message on the queue. It places the handle of the button in the message because it is the button that is the recipient of the message (it is the button that is clicked). It figures out which event number is the proper message ID for "Clicked," and places that in the message number. It sees that in the clicked message, it is required to place the X and Y coordinates of the mouse cursor into the message parameters, and so it does. Finally, it places the message at the end of the system queue to be picked up by your application's queue. Your application, when it is ready, then polls the system queue and sees that there is a new message for it to retrieve. It retrieves the message off

the system queue and sticks it onto the end of its own message queue. Eventually, the message reaches the front of the application queue. At this point, the application sends the message to the button. The button then interprets the message as a clicked message and performs the script that is placed in the `Clicked` event of the button object. All of this happens in a few microseconds. By using this event-based method of program flow, the Microsoft Windows Engine can effectively multitask its applications. By simply dispatching messages and leaving the actual work to the object itself, the engine's job is simply building up its queue of messages. As each event occurs in the system, its message is simply added to the end of the queue. If there are other messages at the front of the queue, they will be dispatched first. Each dispatched message causes a specific task to be performed. As soon as that task is complete, the next message on the queue can be dispatched, and so the process continues.

It is this dispatching of events that controls the flow of execution in Microsoft Windows, and therefore Microsoft Windows is often referred to as an *Event-Driven Operating System*. There are both advantages and disadvantages to programming in an event-driven environment. In an event-driven environment, each object must react to events as they are received by the object, but the sequence of those events is controlled by an external source, specifically the Windows dispatcher. This is both an advantage and a disadvantage, depending on your perspective. Because the object doesn't control the sequence of events, each event must be almost completely isolated and independent of other events in the system, and must simply be a reaction to a message based on the current state of the recipient object. This requires additional thought and good planning and design. However, if you plan well, it also means that your code will probably be better organized and easier to maintain.

Note: If you don't plan and design well, you will probably end up with what is known in the industry as *spaghetti code*. Imagine looking at a plate of spaghetti. Now imagine trying to follow along a single strand of that spaghetti from start to end without actually touching that plate of spaghetti. Sounds like a neat trick that might be part of a summer camp intramural game or something. When a programmer must spend as much effort to follow a single thread of code in an application as to follow a single strand of spaghetti on a plateful of spaghetti, this code is referred to as spaghetti code. Even though the code may work, debugging, enhancing, and modifying this code requires countless hours of effort and is usually more difficult than scrapping it and starting over. Although poor programming practices can lead to spaghetti code even in the most elegantly designed system, a good, clear, well-documented design is the first step to preventing spaghetti code in your applications.

If you have previously done development in a structured environment, then this event-driven thought and planning process will take some getting accustomed to. Inside an event, the code

is still structured code. However, each event's code is like its own function that gets called when the event gets triggered. Using certain language constructs such as Instance and Shared Variables, you can still communicate between different events, for example, to verify that a specific event occurred first. After you get used to developing your applications in an event-driven architecture, you will find it actually becomes easier to organize your applications because your code simply falls into the right event naturally.

In Microsoft Windows, certain objects have a default mechanism for reacting to the triggering of an event. For example, by default when you click on a Command button, it changes its appearance to look like it has been pressed. Then when you release it, it changes its appearance again to look normal. This reaction is already built into all Command buttons and is the default behavior of two events, called *WM_LBUTTONDOWN*, which is the Windows message that occurs when you push down on the left mouse button, and *WM_LBUTTONUP*, which is the Windows message that occurs when you release (or let up) the left mouse button. Together, a `WM_LBUTTONDOWN` event followed by a `WM_LBUTTONUP` event causes a `BN_CLICKED` event to occur. As a programmer, you don't have to do any work to create this effect—it is built right into the control. When you create scripts to perform actions upon the `BN_CLICKED` event, you are simply extending the default behavior of the control to include the behavior that you have coded. There are also ways to override the default behavior of a control, but in most cases, overriding the default behavior of a control would mean violating "Windows standards." This would make your applications inconsistent with the rest of the Windows applications on the market today and is generally a bad idea.

When you are using PowerBuilder to develop your applications, there is one additional step in the event dispatching process. When the Windows Engine dispatches a message to your application, you don't control the polling of the messages off the system queue. "Invisible" code inside your PowerBuilder application is handling all of that for you. When the PowerBuilder Engine inside your application finds a Windows message, it translates it into a PowerBuilder event and passes the message on to that event. Your PowerScript code, then, responds to the events that are triggered by this PowerBuilder Engine in response to a message by the Windows Engine. For example, PowerBuilder passes the `BN_CLICKED` Windows message on to a PowerBuilder `clicked` event. However, in some cases, PowerBuilder handles messages differently than the Windows Engine, translating a Windows message or sequence of Windows messages into a PowerBuilder message that doesn't directly correspond to any particular Windows message. For this reason, you may occasionally find events in PowerBuilder that don't seem to correspond directly to any single Windows event. One of the main reasons that this is done is to permit you to take your PowerBuilder libraries and run them on any other platform (for example, Mac, Windows NT, or Motif) that PowerBuilder supports, without having to worry about the events being handled differently by the different platform. For example, if you are using a Macintosh, there is no right mouse button. But there is a right mouse button `clicked` event (called `rButtonDown`) that PowerBuilder supports. On the Macintosh, the `rButtonDown` event will get triggered if the user holds down the **Option** key and presses the mouse button. PowerBuilder

handles this translation for you. Otherwise, you would have to either trap this condition yourself or lose the right mouse button functionality because it would never get triggered by the operating system. You will especially see events that don't map directly to operating system events in the DataWindow control, which you will start to learn about in Chapter 23.

> **Note:** Did you ever try to tell someone a story, and it was really, really, really involved and complex, so you decided to skip some of the less-important, trivial details to make the story a little more understandable? Perhaps you even went as far as to change the story ever so slightly just to be able to have it still make sense without going into too much detail and sidetracking the conversation altogether? Well, it's a technique that I have unfortunately taken upon myself in the last section. Some of the nitty-gritty details of the event dispatching process in the previous section have been omitted, or slightly altered, to try to give you an idea of the big picture, without spending two weeks just explaining the way Windows and PowerBuilder handle messages and events. If you prefer a full, in-depth discussion that includes all the details and is 100 percent accurate, feel free to spend some time reading the Microsoft Windows Software Development Kit books, specifically the Overview volume, which spends a great deal of effort discussing Windows tasking and memory management. And in the meantime, please forgive me if some of the details in the previous discussion are missing or slightly exaggerated.

A Description of Some Common Events

So far, in my discussion of scripts and events, I have continually remarked that events are reactions to "specific conditions in the environment." I have been rather explicit in using this terminology because it is important to recognize that user input is not the only thing that can cause an event to be triggered. Nonetheless, most of the conditions that cause events to be triggered in a Windows application occur as a direct result of user input, either with the keyboard or the mouse. When a user clicks with the mouse, the Microsoft Windows Engine immediately recognizes this condition and evaluates which control it must send the clicked message to.

As I am sure you can guess, user input with the mouse and keyboard is probably the most common cause of an event being triggered. It would only make sense to ensure that most, if not all, of the Windows controls know how to react to input from the mouse and keyboard. In this way, the user is not confused by inconsistent input methods, but instead is immediately and intuitively aware of how to deal with new controls and applications. And so you will find that there are many objects inside PowerBuilder that all have events with the same names, which respond to the same conditions, such as input.

Let's look at an example. You should still be in the Script Painter for the Application Object. Click on the down arrow of the Select Event drop-down list box and notice the four events that you can select for an application: Close, Idle, Open, and SystemError (see Fig. 6.13). Each of these events is triggered by a specific condition. The Open event, for example, is the event that gets triggered when the user opens the application—when he starts it up from the Program Manager. The Close event occurs as the application is about to end. The SystemError event occurs when there is a runtime error within the application. And the Idle event gets fired when the user is idle for a certain amount of time.

Figure 6.13.
The list of events for an application.

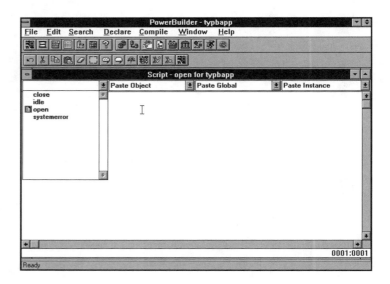

Note: When you look at the event name in the Select Event drop-down list box, it will look slightly different. Event names in PowerBuilder are forced to all lowercase. However, to make the event names easier to read, this book uses mixed case for event names. This way, it will be easier to figure out what the events refer to, especially when the event name is made up of multiple words concatenated together.

Now close this Script Painter. You can either click on the Return to Application Painter icon or double-click on the Control menu for the Script Painter. If you are prompted to save your changes, you can select No because we haven't made any changes that we want to keep. Open up the Window Painter and select the w_ch5 window from the list. Now, click on the Script Painter button on the Window PainterBar. You will be in the Script Painter for the w_ch5 window itself. Now, click on the down arrow of the Select Event drop-down list box. A list of events that are available for the window should appear (see Fig. 6.14). There are quite a few events that a window can respond to. A few of the event names, however, may look familiar—specifically Open and Close. Just like the application as a whole, each individual window can be opened and closed by the user in some manner—perhaps by clicking on a button or by selecting a menu item. And each window, therefore, can have its own specific reaction to being opened or closed, perhaps initializing the window to accept input or to display the proper values on-screen. Also notice the names of some of the other events, specifically events like Clicked, DoubleClicked, DragDrop, DragEnter, DragLeave, DragWithin, and rButtonDown. These events map directly to some common types of input by the user. For example, the Clicked event is triggered when the user clicks the left mouse button inside the boundaries (often referred to as the *client area*) of the window. The DoubleClicked event gets triggered when the user double-clicks with the left mouse button inside the client area of the window. The DragDrop event gets triggered when the user drops a dragged object onto the client area of the window. The DragEnter, DragLeave, and DragWithin events also respond to a dragged control being dragged into, out of, and within the client area of the window. And the rButtonDown event is triggered when the user clicks with the right mouse button inside the client area of the window.

Figure 6.14.

The events for a window.

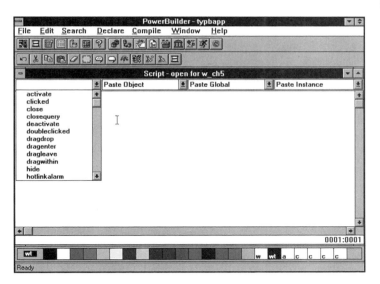

Now close the Script Painter again. This time, select your **OK** button that you created inside w_ch5 with your mouse and click on the Script Painter icon on the toolbar. Once again, the Script Painter will appear. Open up the list of available events for the button by clicking on the Select Event drop-down list box. Notice the names of the events that are triggered in a button—Clicked, DragDrop, DragEnter, DragLeave, DragWithin, Other, and rButtonDown. All of these are events that appear for the window as well. We haven't talked about the Other event just yet, but we will in a moment. But with regard to the other events, they work just like their counterparts in the window, except that they get triggered when the user performs their appropriate action

within the client area of the button, instead of the window. In other words, when the user clicks on the button, the button's `clicked` event will get triggered, not the window's.

Additionally, there are a few other events that you'll see that can be triggered for a button. These are the `Constructor`, `Destructor`, `GetFocus`, and `LoseFocus` events. The `Constructor` event gets triggered as the button is being constructed, before it displays on-screen. It's sort of like an `Open` event for the button. You can place any initialization code inside the `Constructor` event. In a similar manner, the `Destructor` event gets triggered as the button is about to be destroyed. It is like a `Close` event for the button.

A control is said to be *in focus* when it is the control that is going to receive input from the keyboard or mouse. Most controls indicate that they are in focus with a dotted rectangle around the control, often called a *caret*. You can change which control currently has focus in a few ways, most notably either by clicking on it with the mouse or by pressing the **Tab** key. When the focus is changed from one control to another, a `LoseFocus` event is triggered in the control that previously had focus, and a `GetFocus` event is triggered in the control that is about to receive the focus. The `Constructor`, `Destructor`, `GetFocus`, and `LoseFocus` events are four more events that nearly every control in PowerBuilder can react to.

If you choose the **S**elect Object menu item from the **E**dit menu, you can choose to see the script of each of the controls that you placed in your w_ch5 window. Notice for each control that most of the preceding events exist. In addition, two other events are relatively common. For controls that can accept text entry, such as single-line edits, edit masks, multi-line edits, and drop-down list boxes, there is an event called `Modified`. When the user edits the contents of the text entry field and accepts the changes either by changing the focus or by pressing the **Enter** key, the `Modified` event is triggered for each of these controls. In lists, such as list boxes and drop-down list boxes, there is an event called `SelectionChanged` that gets triggered when the user changes the item in the list that has been selected. You've probably also noticed that nearly every control has the `Other` event. Let's take a moment to talk about the `Other` event.

As you now know, Windows sends many messages to your controls whenever conditions change. And PowerBuilder allows you to react to these messages by placing code in events that get triggered in response to a message from the Windows dispatcher. Even though PowerBuilder has built-in events for many of the messages that Windows sends, there are other messages that may be sent that PowerBuilder doesn't translate into an event. For example, every time your mouse moves, even if you aren't clicking or dragging, Windows sends a message to the control that is under your mouse pointer to tell it that the mouse has moved. However, the actual movement of the mouse is already handled, and there is almost never a need to react to the movement of the mouse over your control. So, PowerBuilder does not translate that message into an event and simply ignores it. What if you are writing an application for users who need to see the exact X and Y coordinates of the mouse displayed on-screen whenever it is moved? This is a very realistic requirement for a painting or CAD (computer-aided design) type of application, right? So there really is no reason that we shouldn't be able to do this, especially since Windows sends messages to tell us when the mouse moves. But PowerBuilder ignores these

messages! Should we switch to a new development tool? No way! PowerBuilder doesn't ignore the messages that it doesn't translate into events; it passes them to you by triggering the Other event so that you can catch them in there! Inside the Other event you can use a special global variable called *message* to find out about the message that triggered the Other event. Then, all you need to know is the message number of the message you want to trap, and you can place code in the Other event that reacts to that message based on its message number. So, if we want to react to the message that Windows sends to our objects when we move the mouse, we simply need to find the message that gets posted by Windows when we move the mouse. If we look in the Windows Software Developer's Kit documentation, we should find an event called WM_MOUSEMOVE. We look up the message number of the WM_MOUSEMOVE event, place code in the Other event to test to see if the message that triggered it was WM_MOUSEMOVE, and then display the X and Y coordinates of the mouse in our window if it was this message.

In Windows, there are many, many events. And many of the events that Windows posts as messages are not translated into their own events by PowerBuilder, but are instead posted to the Other event of your controls. Because of this, it is a good idea to keep the amount of code that you place in the Other event to a bare minimum. Otherwise, each time you move the mouse, or the time changes, or just about anything else happens, your code in the Other event will run, and your application will be really, really slow. Instead, there is a better way to deal with the need to react to events that PowerBuilder doesn't give us by default, and that is by using *User Events*.

DO   **DON'T**

DO Use User Events whenever you need to trap a message that PowerBuilder does not handle automatically.

DON'T Place code in the Other event unless you really need to; for example, if you need to trap a Windows message that does not get dispatched to *any* PowerBuilder event, even a User Event.

User Events

A *User Event* is just what it sounds like it should be. It's an event that is defined by you, the user. (In this case, the user is the PowerBuilder developer, not the user of the resultant application.) As we briefly mentioned earlier in this chapter, you can declare User Events by selecting the object for which you want to create the event and choosing the User **E**vents menu item from the **D**eclare menu. When you do this, the Declare User Events window will appear on-screen (see Fig. 6.15). To create the user event, type in the name of your user event in the box on the left side of the screen labeled Event Name. The name you type here will be the name of the event in your object. Now, you have to assign that event name to a real PowerBuilder event that will be triggered in response to a condition within the system. Type in the name of the PowerBuilder

125

event in the box labeled Event ID. On the far right, in the list box labeled Paste Event ID, is a list of all of the available PowerBuilder Events that you can use as your event IDs. You can even paste the event ID right in by double-clicking on the event ID that you are interested in. Most of these events directly correspond to Windows events and notification messages. PowerBuilder uses the "pbm_" prefix for all of its events, but Windows uses "wm_" as its prefix for standard events, and different prefixes for special events that it refers to as *notification messages*. If you are searching through the list of PowerBuilder User events for a notification message, the first two letters of the notification message (before the underscore) will not appear as the first two letters of the User Event, but instead appear as the fourth and fifth letters of the User Event (after the underscore). For example, the BN_CLICKED Windows message appears as pbm_bnclicked in PowerBuilder. Other than that, and a few special events that we'll talk about in a minute, all of the User Events should map to their corresponding wm_ Windows message.

Figure 6.15.

The Declare User Events window.

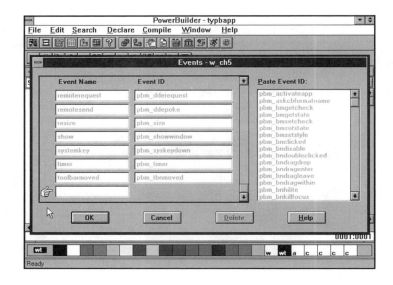

Additionally, there are some special PowerBuilder event IDs listed that don't correspond directly to their wm_ counterparts. For example, there are about 75 messages that start with the phrase pbm_custom??. These events actually map to special Windows messages called *wm_user messages*. Windows and PowerBuilder allow you to create your own messages that you intend to trigger when you monitor a specific condition within your own application. For example, you might monitor an error condition that occurs as a result of some sequence of events that is specific to the context of your application. Maybe the user tried to press some set of keys or click on some set of buttons in an order that is not acceptable. However, because this condition can be monitored from a number of places (for example, there are several buttons that will check for this error condition), you don't want to duplicate the code in each button. So instead, you can create a pbm_custom event that each button triggers if it monitors this error condition. Then, you place the code to handle that error condition in the User Event.

Note: In addition to being triggered as a result of input, you can create code that triggers any event manually. The `TriggerEvent()` function will cause a specific event to fire immediately, and the `PostEvent()` function will cause an event to be posted at the end of the message queue, to be processed when its turn comes. You can specify both standard, built-in events, as well as User Events. In this way, you can use events like generic subroutines that are called from other scripts.

There are some other events that PowerBuilder builds for us that are specific to PowerBuilder and don't map directly to Windows messages. Additionally, there are some messages that are used to allow you to interact with special external controls called *Custom Controls* and *VBXs*. We'll talk more about these in Chapter 14.

DO	**DON'T**

DO Be aware that if you use User Events to trap Windows messages that PowerBuilder doesn't internally support, you run the risk of compatibility problems with future releases and multi-platform operating capability. Officially, Powersoft does not support this type of User Event anyway.

DON'T Worry if you are using `PBM_CUSTOMnn` events to create events that only you will trigger, though. This type of user event is supported by PowerBuilder and should not cause you any problems on other platforms or in future releases.

Afternoon Summary

By default, the controls and windows that you create have certain behaviors. They already know how to perform certain actions. However, in order to make them perform the actions that you want them to, you need to create *scripts*. Scripts are where you place your code—your instructions to the compiler to perform actions. By creating scripts for your controls, you can make certain things happen. For example, you can make your Application Object open your main window with a script. Then, you can run your main window by selecting **R**un from the **F**ile menu, or clicking on the Run button on the PowerBar.

You create scripts in the Script Painter. In a structured language, like PowerBuilder, you will benefit dramatically simply by following several simple standards. For example, you should always properly indent your code. Also, be sure to place comments in your code wherever possible. Comments will help you remember why you wrote a piece of code and what that piece of code is intended to do. If a month later you need to make a change or find a bug, you will have a much easier time if your code is well commented.

The Script Painter has several menus that you can use to perform certain actions. For example, you can quickly comment and uncomment lines of code, paste certain types of PowerBuilder statements into your code, search and navigate throughout your code, and compile your script. Additionally, there is a toolbar to enable you to quickly perform some of the more common actions. At the top of the Script Painter, there are three drop-down list boxes that allow you to quickly paste certain information into your scripts, as well as a fourth drop-down list box that allows you to assign your current script to a specific event.

The Windows Engine monitors the state of the current Windows environment and responds to changes in the environment by sending a message to the object that has changed. For example, when you click with your mouse on a button, Windows monitors that click, recognizes that it occurred over the button, and then sends a message to the button to tell it to react to the click. When PowerBuilder receives a message from the Windows Engine for one of your controls, it reacts by triggering the proper event for that control. Your control then executes the script in that event.

Some events are common among many controls in PowerBuilder. For example, there are several controls that all have events to react to the clicking of mouse buttons, dragging and dropping, changing of focus, and editing of text inside the control. Additionally, all controls in PowerBuilder have an Other event that allows you to react to events that PowerBuilder doesn't translate otherwise from the Windows API into a PowerBuilder event.

However, because there are many Windows messages that cause the Other event to be triggered, putting code in the Other event is a last resort among PowerBuilder developers. Instead, you should create a User Event that will be triggered by PowerBuilder when it receives only a specific message from the Windows API, or a customized message from another PowerBuilder object.

Q&A

Q Why can I both double-click on a control and right-click on it to get to the attributes of the control?

A Right-clicking is a relatively new standard and new feature. In earlier versions of PowerBuilder, there was no right mouse button support at all, only double-click support. When they introduced the right-click support, there was no point in eliminating the double-click support. After all, it never hurts to give the user the capability to do something in multiple ways.

Q Is there any way to select more than one control at a time?

A Yes, there are several ways you can do this. First, you can "lasso select" a set of controls by clicking on the window outside of any controls and by holding down the mouse button. Then, as you drag the mouse cursor around the screen, a rectangle appears starting at the point where you started lassoing and meets your current mouse pointer. When you let go of the mouse, everything inside this rectangle is selected.

A second way to select multiple controls is to hold down the **Ctrl** key while you click on a control. This action toggles the select status of the control you clicked on without affecting the select status of any of the other controls.

Finally, you can select any number of controls from the Control **L**ist menu item under the **E**dit menu.

Q **If I have multiple controls selected, what can I do with them as a group?**

A You can move them as a group, size them as a group, align them as a group, space them as a group, even delete them as a group. You can also change any attributes that the selected controls have in common with the right mouse button.

Q **Can more than one event be triggered as a result of a single action?**

A Sure! In fact, it happens regularly. Often, a single action triggers multiple events! For example, when you close your window, it triggers, of course, the Close event of the window. When the window closes, it attempts to destroy all of the controls inside it. If there are controls inside the window, their Destructor events will each get triggered in turn as the window attempts to destroy them. This is just one example, but there are many other examples of events that "string along" each other. Nonetheless, you should not write code that assumes that a particular event will be strung along, nor that a particular event will occur first. If you need to write code that depends on other events, be sure to first check in your code to verify that the other event has occurred.

Q **It looks like all the Windows events that I may want to write code for are available as User Events. If that's the case, why would I ever use the Other event?**

A Actually, there are User Events for just about every event that you can find in the Windows API documentation. However, there are times that you will find an event or notification that does not have a corresponding user event. Additionally, there are times that PowerBuilder does not pass the event through to your control even though it receives it from the Windows API. In these extremely rare cases, you may use the Other event to trap these events that you can't otherwise trap.

Workshop

Quiz

1. Name two ways that you can edit the attributes of a control.
2. Which control would you use to allow the user to enter in a number?
3. Which event will get triggered when your user actually enters a number into the control?
4. Which control would you use to allow your user to close your window?

5. In which event would you place the code to perform the closing of the window?

6. When the user clicks on that button and closes the window, what other events do you think will be triggered?

Putting PowerBuilder into Action

1. Open up the w_ch5 window if it is not already open.

2. Place one of each of all the controls on your window.

3. Double-click on each control and change the attributes that you see there.

4. Preview your window after you add and edit your controls. Tab to each one and see how it works.

5. Right-click on each control and edit all of the different attributes of the control.

6. Preview your window again and play with each control as you make changes. Notice how the different attributes affect each type of control.

7. Open the Script Painter for each control. Notice the different events that each control has.

7

The PowerScript Language

In this chapter, you will acquire a detailed understanding of the PowerBuilder programming language constructs you can use in your scripts. If you are already a developer in any structured language, this chapter will probably be somewhat of a review for you. However, I encourage you to at least peruse it anyway because you will need to become familiar with the specific keywords that PowerBuilder uses in its syntax. These keywords may be slightly different than the keywords you have used in the language with which you currently develop. You will learn:

☐ About the architecture of the computer

☐ How the computer translates your code into instructions

☐ How these instructions can be executed to cause things to happen in your system

☐ Techniques for writing good, well-organized, structured code in PowerBuilder

Computer Architecture 101

If you have ever taken an introductory computer course, you have probably learned a little bit about the internals of how a computer works. Although I won't spend too much time reviewing this information, it is important to recognize a few fundamentals about how the computer works in order to write good programs.

A computer is really not much more than a spruced-up calculator. Unlike a calculator, a computer has memory, disk storage, and a pixel-based monitor instead of a character-based LCD panel. But at the heart of the computer is something called a *Central Processing Unit (CPU)*. The heart of the CPU is something called an *Arithmetic Logic Unit (ALU)*. The CPU accepts instructions from your programs and then processes these instructions. There is a limited set of instructions that any CPU can understand, which is defined by the manufacturer of the CPU. Eventually, all of the programs that you write will be translated into instructions that your CPU can execute. We touched on this concept earlier in the week.

There are really only two basic types of instructions that are fundamental to the CPU of any computer. These are instructions to store and retrieve data from different areas of memory and instructions to perform calculations on numbers. In other words, all of the cool things that you can do on your computer are derived from commands that either calculate or store numbers.

Of course, sometimes different things happen when you store the right number in the right place. For example, if you store certain numbers in certain places in your computer's memory, certain pixels on your computer's monitor light up in a certain color. If you store certain numbers in a different place in your computer's memory, a command is sent to your hard drive to store a magnetic blip on your hard drive media. All of the peripherals you may already take for granted actually have their own components that receive information from your CPU and act upon it. Together, your CPU and your peripherals make up this wonderful thing called a computer.

The art of computer programming at the lowest level involves telling the CPU to store the right numbers in the right locations to produce the right effect. If you want to make a pretty picture

on the screen, you have to send a message to the monitor to light up the correct pixels in the correct colors. If you want to write a file to the hard drive, you have to send a message to the hard drive to put the drive head in the right place and send the proper sequence of magnetic blips to the media inside. Because the CPU holds only enough information to perform the instructions that it is capable of, we will often need to build up sets of data in memory and then dump that data, one piece at a time, to the hard drive or to the monitor through the CPU.

Fortunately, PowerBuilder shelters us from that level of interaction. We have the capability to do all of these things in a very easy way with a language that is at a much higher level than the CPU's language. We have been given a finite set of functions and keywords that we can use to produce the effects we want without having to know the details of how they get translated into action. Ultimately, PowerBuilder translates our commands into commands that the CPU can understand. It also translates our data into the proper format that can be understood by our peripherals. At the lowest level, programming a computer is simply a matter of storing the right data in the right place so that it can cause certain components to react.

Variables

At a higher level, though, you are sheltered from this level of component interaction. Still, when you are creating applications, you will often find it necessary to hold information in storage so you can use it again later. For example, you may need to calculate a series of numbers. Quick: what's $5 \times 4 \times 3 \times 2 + 6 \times 2$? Well, if you take a minute to figure it out, you should get 132. But how did you come up with that answer? You probably thought to yourself, $5 \times 4 = 20$, and then $20 \times 3 = 60$, and then $60 \times 2 = 120$, and then $6 \times 2 = 12$, and then $120 + 12 = 132$. Am I right? Well, even if you didn't actually think it through that way (maybe you used a calculator), many people would think it through that way. They break up the calculation into smaller pieces and store the result in a temporary location in their mind until they need it again later for the next step of the calculation. That's an example of why you use a variable. Each time you store a value somewhere in your mind, you are essentially making it into a variable that can be recalled again for the next calculation. In programming, you often need to store information to be used again at a later time. You store information in variables. You may use a variable to temporarily store the results of complex calculations or to temporarily store data you want to use more than once. As an example, take the calculation that I asked you to figure out earlier: $5 \times 4 \times 3 \times 2 + 6 \times 2$. I asked you to tell me what the answer was. In programming, in order to tell the user what the answer is, you must first store the result of the equation in a variable, which you can then output to the user. In order to store a value in a variable, you code something that looks like the following:

```
MyVar = 132
```

This statement tells the computer to store the value 132 into the memory location that it refers to as MyVar. This is called an *assignment statement*. You *assign* the variable MyVar a value of 132.

Sometimes, you may want to store the result of an equation in a variable, instead of just a simple number. You might, for example, want to store the results of the preceding calculation in a variable called `result`. In order to code such a statement, you say

```
result = 5 * 4 * 3 * 2 + 6 * 2
```

> **Note:** Computers use the asterisk (*) to represent multiplication because the letter x can mean other things, and the compiler might get confused. Computers also use the slash (/) for division and the caret (^) for exponents.

This statement says to assign the variable `result` the value that is returned by calculating `5 * 4 * 3 * 2 + 6 * 2`. The equal sign (=) tells PowerBuilder to assign the result of the equation on the right side of the statement to the variable on the left side of the statement. Computers use the asterisk (*) to represent multiplication instead of an x in order to prevent confusion between multiplication and the letter x. Similarly, because there is no symbol on your keyboard that looks like the division symbol you learned in Algebra (÷), computers use the slash (/) to indicate division. So, when PowerBuilder encounters the preceding line of code, it calculates the value of the equation on the right side of the statement, which is 132, and assigns it to the variable `result`. Later, in our program, we might code the following statement to make use of our newly created variable:

```
newresult = result / 6
```

The preceding statement tells PowerBuilder to evaluate the equation on the right side and assign it to the variable on the left side. However, one of the values on the right side is our old variable, `result`! That's okay, PowerBuilder will substitute the actual value of our variables for us—that is their purpose. So, when PowerBuilder goes to evaluate the right side of the formula, it evaluates it as

```
newresult = 132 / 6
```

because the `result` variable contains the value 132. Therefore, when PowerBuilder evaluates this expression, it places the quotient of 132/6, which is 22, into the variable `newresult`. Only the data on the right side of the equation is changed in an assignment statement. The contents of the variable `result` have not changed, and `result` is still equal to 132. As a rule, in an assignment statement, the left side of the statement must be a single variable, and the right side of the statement can be any expression or equation that PowerBuilder can interpret and resolve to a single value. This expression can include other variables, as well as *literals*. Literals are expression components whose values you want to be taken literally, as opposed to *variables*, whose values you want to be translated into a different value (that is, the contents of the variable) based upon the name of the variable.

Variable DataTypes

So how does the compiler recognize the difference between a variable and a literal? In order to store information in a variable, you must first *declare* your variable's name and the type of variable you want it to be. Declaring your variable is only slightly different than declaring your independence. When you declare your variable, you are telling the compiler, "Hey! The variable named here is a variable that holds a value of a particular type." In our preceding example, we would have had to declare the variables MyVar, result, and newresult as variables that can hold numbers in them. I know that you never really expected to have to use something that you learned in high school, but in your high school math class you probably learned that there are different kinds of numbers. There are integers, which are whole numbers that can't have fractions or decimals, and there are real numbers, which are numbers that can have fractional parts or decimals. Well, in computers, real numbers are stored differently in memory than integers, so we must declare to the compiler which type of number we want our variable to be. In other words, in order for the compiler to recognize that MyVar is a variable, we need to tell the compiler, "Hey! The variable MyVar is a variable that will hold a value that is an integer." To make such a declaration, we code the following line:

```
integer MyVar
```

When declaring a variable, you first declare the variable type (in this case, integer) and then the variable name. You can also declare multiple variables of the same type on the same line, separated by commas. For example, you could have said

```
integer MyVar, result, newresult
```

which tells the compiler that you want it to recognize all three names as variables of type Integer.

You can store almost anything in a variable: numbers, letters, words, and more, as long as your variable is the right type. PowerBuilder checks that the value you attempt to insert into a variable matches that variable's type. For example, PowerBuilder does not allow you to store letters in a variable that is an Integer. If you attempt to assign a letter to a variable of type Integer, PowerBuilder tells you that the types of data in your assignment are incompatible. However, there is a datatype that is meant to hold letters. That type is the Char datatype. If you declare a variable as a Char, you can store a single character in that variable. If you want to hold words in a variable, you may declare it as a String type, which may hold up to 65,535 characters in a single String. There are also some other interesting datatypes that you may find useful in your development journeys. These datatypes are listed in Table 7.1.

Table 7.1. The different datatypes.

Datatype	Description	Example
Integer (Int)	A variable of type Integer holds a whole number between 32,767 and –32,767. It uses up two bytes of storage.	5,000

Table 7.1. continued

Datatype	Description	Example
Long	A variable of type Long holds a whole number between 2,147,483,648 and –2,147,483,648. It uses up four bytes of storage.	1,000,000
Double	A variable of type Double holds a whole number between about 1.7×10^{308} and -2.2×10^{308}. It uses up eight bytes of storage.	10,000,000,000
Real	A variable of type Real holds a real, positive number between 3.4×10^{38} and 1.7×10^{-38} and can have a precision of up to six decimal places.	99,999.9999
Decimal (Dec)	A variable of type Decimal holds a number with up to 18 digits (not including the decimal point).	9.9999999999
Character (Char)	A variable of type Character holds any single ASCII character. It takes up one byte of storage.	B
String	A variable of type String holds a sequence of up to 65,535 ASCII characters. It requires one byte of storage for each character in the string, plus one additional byte.	Hello World!
Date	A variable of type Date holds any specific calendar date in the format yyyy-mm-dd.	1999-12-31
Time	A variable of type Time stores a time of day in the format hh:mm:ss.ffffff. It has a precision of up to one microsecond.	23:59:59.999999
DateTime	A variable of type DateTime stores a value that holds both the date and the time of day in a single variable.	2000-01-01 0:0:0.000001
Boolean	A variable of type Boolean holds a value of either TRUE or FALSE.	FALSE
Blob	A variable of type Blob holds a value that can contain up to 4MB of any data in any format. You can use it to store long strings or images.	"¡kÂ|ōŌe"

Some datatypes are somewhat compatible and can be converted if you try to assign them. For example, because it is perfectly legal for a variable of type Long to contain values between 32,767 and –32,767, there is no reason why you shouldn't be able to store an Integer value inside a variable of type Long. Therefore, PowerBuilder permits you to assign an Integervalue to a Long variable; PowerBuilder even allows you to assign a variable of type Integer to a variable of type Long and converts it for you. However, PowerBuilder will not allow you to store the contents of a Long variable into a Date variable. Because a Long variable can contain values that are not permissible in a Date, PowerBuilder will not allow you to make this assignment. Although this type of datatype-checking may seem excessive and prohibitive, in reality it is a discipline that, as a programmer, you may one day appreciate. In lower-level languages where there is no datatype-checking, errors of incompatible assignments can be extremely difficult to debug.

In general, you will probably find yourself using Strings, Integers, Longs, and Booleans most frequently; but you should be familiar with all the datatypes because you may find yourself needing one of the others as well.

DO	**DON'T**

DO Use the right datatype to hold your values. If you are storing a value that exceeds the maximum capacity of an integer, use a Long, not an Integer.

DON'T Use a larger datatype, however, if you don't need it. If you only need an Integer, using a Long wastes memory.

Enumerated Types

In addition to the standard datatypes you can use within PowerBuilder, there are some special types of variables that can take on a specific set of values, similar, in a way, to the Boolean variable that takes on either TRUE or FALSE. Suppose that you have a variable that represents the alignment of text within an object. Because you can align text only to the left, right, or center, your Alignment variable will probably only have three acceptable values: left, right, or center. This type of variable is referred to as an *enumerated type* because its set of values is enumerated to a specific list of possible values. The possible values for a variable of type Alignment are enumerated to Left!, Right!, and Center!. PowerBuilder makes it easy to recognize enumerated values by placing an exclamation point after their names.

The benefit of enumerated types is primarily for readability and for type-checking. As with standard variables, PowerBuilder does not allow you to insert values of a different type into enumerated variables. You cannot, for example, assign a value of 14 to a variable of type Alignment. It just doesn't fly. You get the same kind of message that you get if you try to assign a letter to an Integer variable.

Additionally, enumerated types shelter the programmer from the "real" values that are being used internally by the compiler or receiving functions. Using our alignment example again, the values for Left!, Right!, and Center! may be 0, 1, and 2, respectively; or they may be -1, 0, and 1; or they may be L, R, and C—whatever is easiest for PowerBuilder to deal with internally. However, for us to use these values, we don't need to know what PowerBuilder uses internally for these values. In fact, we usually don't know. This way, if in a later version the value changes for some reason, that change is invisible to us because we have used an enumerated type. Its much easier to understand a line that reads

```
Alignment = Right!
```

than it is to understand

```
Alignment = 1
```

In some other programming languages, the developer is allowed to create his/her own enumerated types. In PowerBuilder, though, we cannot create our own enumerated types, but we can make use of a large number of enumerated types PowerBuilder supplies for us. Most of the enumerated types that PowerBuilder gives us are for setting attributes of our objects and for calling functions. There are quite a few of them; unfortunately, too many to be listed here. However, you can look up the enumerated types and their possible values in the PowerBuilder documentation.

The secret to good programming is writing effective code that is readable, understandable, and optimal. PowerBuilder gives us many tools to help make our code as readable and understandable as possible. Enumerated types are one effective tool for making our code readable. Another one of these tools is something called a *structure*.

Structures

Sometimes, you may need to store multiple variables that are in some way related to each other or that are used together for some purpose. For example, let's say you want to store a fraction in its original fractional form. In order to do this, you need two variables of type Integer—one to hold the numerator and one to hold the denominator. Together, they make up a single fraction, and by dividing the numerator by the denominator, you get the decimal representation of the fraction. If you want to store a value of $^{12}/_{100}$, you store a 12 in the numerator variable and a 100 in the denominator variable. You can later show the user the fraction in its native form. To do this, code the following three lines:

```
Integer numerator, denominator
numerator   = 12
denominator = 100
```

So far, this is nothing new. It's just two variables that are intimately related, and that's all. But these variables are so intimately related that it doesn't make sense to have one without the other. What good is a numerator without a denominator or a denominator without a numerator? In reality, it would be much nicer if we could have a single variable of type Fraction that contained

a numerator and a denominator. Well, that's where a *structure* comes in. By using a structure, we can actually create a Fraction datatype that contains a numerator and a denominator. Open up the Structure Painter from the PowerBar or PowerPanel by clicking on the Structure Painter button. A window appears prompting you to open an existing structure (see Fig. 7.1). However, because we have no structures to open, you can click on the button labeled **New** to create a new structure. The New Structure definition window appears where you define the contents of your structure (see Fig. 7.2). In the left column, you can enter the name of your structure components: in this case Numerator and Denominator. Then in the right column, you specify the datatype of the subcomponents: in this case integer.

Figure 7.1.
Opening an existing structure.

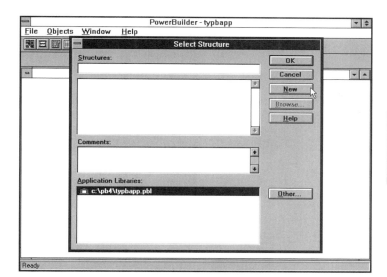

Figure 7.2.
The New Structure definition window.

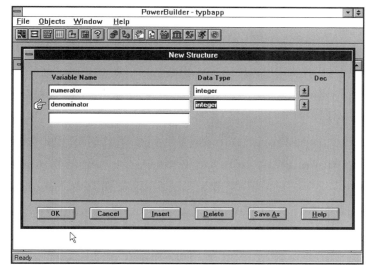

After you have specified the definition of your structure, you can save it by pressing the **OK** button. You are prompted to save your structure and give it a name (see Fig. 7.3). In this example, call your structure `fraction_struct`. Type in the name

`fraction_struct`

in the entry box labeled Structures. In the Comments field, you can type in a comment describing the structure. Finally, press **OK**, and the structure is saved.

Figure 7.3.

Saving the structure as
`fraction_struct`*.*

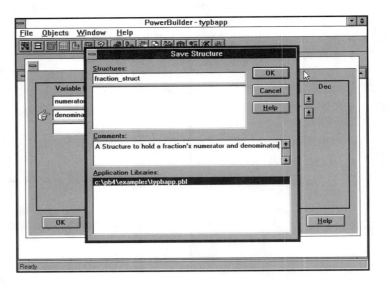

Now in your code, you can create variables whose datatypes are `fraction_struct` to store fractions, instead of declaring variables separately for your numerators and denominators, as follows:

```
fraction_struct StockValue
```

Then, when you want to reference the values inside each of the structure's components, for example, numerator and denominator, you simply use *dot notation*. Dot notation means you refer to the name of the structure variable, followed by a period (.), followed by the name of the component you are interested in, as follows:

```
StockValue.numerator   = 12
StockValue.denominator = 100
```

Again, it's important to recognize that the most significant benefit with structures is readability. If you didn't have structures and you wanted to create three stocks that held fractions, you would need to declare three variables, each with a unique name, to represent each of your numerators and denominators, for a total of six variables. You might do something like this:

```
integer numerator_IBM
integer numerator_GM
integer numerator_AAPL
integer denominator_IBM
integer denominator_GM
integer denominator_AAPL
```

Now, instead of doing this, you can declare three variables of type `fraction_struct`. Each one's numerator is referenced simply as `numerator`, and each one's denominator is referenced simply as `denominator`, as follows:

```
fraction_struct IBM
fraction_struct GM
fraction_struct AAPL
IBM.numerator = 16
AAPL.denominator = 8
```

In practice, this may not be a perfect example. After all, if you were writing a stock portfolio tracking system, you probably wouldn't create a variable to store each possible ticker on the stock market. Instead, you might extend your structure even further by creating a stock structure that contained the name as a `string`, the price as an `integer`, and the fraction as a `fraction_struct` (see Fig. 7.4). Notice that I used the structure `fraction_struct` as a datatype for one of the components of my stock structure. This is perfectly legitimate and acceptable. In order to reference the numerator of the fraction of the stock, simply use dot notation, as you have already learned. To refer to the stock fraction of a stock variable named `MyStock`, you would use `MyStock.fraction`; and so to refer to the numerator of the fraction, you would use `MyStock.fraction.numerator`.

Figure 7.4.
The Stock structure.

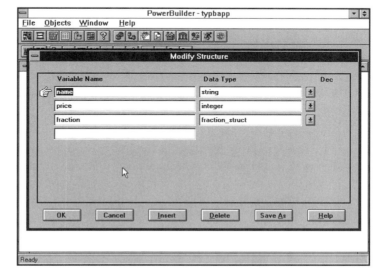

<table>
<tr><td>

DO

</td><td>

DON'T

</td></tr>
</table>

DO	DON'T
DO Use structures to create "complex" datatypes that contain multiple variables that are tightly related and don't make sense individually.	

DON'T Overuse structures by trying to take unrelated variables and grouping them into a structure. If you declare a structure and don't actually store data in all of the elements in the structure variable, your structure variable still takes up as much memory as if you did store data in all of its elements. In other words, if you have a structure with three elements and only store data in one of those elements, your structure variable still reserves space in memory for the other two elements in case you decide to use them later. If you don't use them, you are wasting memory.

Now, suppose that we are creating a stock portfolio tracking utility to track 15 stocks. We need to have 15 stock variables to track one of the 15 stocks in each one of the variables. We can easily declare 15 separate variables of type stock to do this, as follows:

```
stock mystock_1
stock mystock_2
...
stock mystock_15
```

In fact, there is nothing really wrong with declaring these 15 variables. However, as with before, these variables are somehow related, and by declaring each one separately, we really lose the relationship between each of the variables. They're not so closely related that they belong inside another structure because you really don't save anything by declaring a structure with 15 stock variables anyway. However, you can relate them to each other by making the 15 stocks into an *array* of 15 stocks.

Arrays

An *array* is defined as an indexed collection of a single data type. In other words, an array is a group of variables that are all of the same type that have an index you can use to point to any one element in the group. So, in our example of 15 stocks, we can create an array of 15 stocks that we then later can refer to with an index number. If we want to insert data into the first stock, we can specify the first stock by using an index of 1. If we want to insert data into the 15th stock, we can specify that stock by using an index of 15.

To declare our array of 15 stocks, all we have to do is specify the datatype, variable name, and in brackets the number of elements that we want in the array, as follows:

```
stock stock_array[15]
```

Note: By default, when you define an array in the format array[n], where n represents any value you like, it defaults to an array with elements indexed 1 through n. You can also specify indexes other than 1 to n. You may want an array with indexes from 0 through 10. You can specify an array like that by declaring it in the format

```
string str_array[0 TO 10]
```

You can even declare arrays whose indexes are negative!

Sometimes you will not know exactly how many elements of the array you will need at runtime. For this purpose, you can create an *unbounded array* by placing nothing inside the brackets in your declaration. When you declare an unbounded array, you can add an unlimited number of elements to the array. However, internally unbounded arrays are quite memory inefficient, and so you should carefully consider your options before using them.

While sometimes these features can be handy, you probably will only declare arrays from 1 to n using the standard format.

The preceding line of code declares an array of 15 stock values, numbered stock_array[1] through stock_array[15]. If we want to assign a value to one of our stocks, we simply refer to it with its proper index number. For example, examine the following four lines of code:

```
string      stock_names[15]
stock_name[1]  = "IBM"
stock_name[5]  = "GM"
stock_name[10] = "AAPL"
```

Here we are declaring an array of 15 stock names. Then, we are assigning the first stock name to the value of "IBM". We assign the fifth stock name the value of "GM", and finally we assign the tenth stock name the value of "AAPL". Let's go back to our original example of 15 stocks, though. If you remember, in order to assign a value to a structure, you need to use dot notation. Well, because we have an array of 15 stocks, we still must use the dot notation to assign a value to a structure element of one of our array elements. We simply indicate which stock we are referring to with its index number, as follows:

```
stock_array[5].name="GM"
```

This assigns the value "GM" to the name of our fifth stock in the stock array.

Because the index is just a numeric value, we can actually use a variable to indicate which element in the array we are interested in. Take a look at the following code snippet:

```
stock    stock_array[15]
integer index
index = 1
stock_array[ index].name = "IBM"
```

```
index = 5
stock_array[ index].name = "GM"
index = 10
stock_array[ index].name = "AAPL"
```

After executing this snippet of code, we end up with what we might expect—the name in `stock_array[1]` is `"IBM"`, the name in `stock_array[5]` is `"GM"`, and the name in `stock_array[10]` is `"AAPL"`. Although you may not yet be able to appreciate it, you will soon come to understand why the capability to index an array with a variable is one of the most powerful features of an array.

There are some other interesting aspects to arrays that you need to be aware of. Suppose that you want to declare a storage structure to hold a deck of cards. At first glance, you may want to declare an array of 52 cards, as follows:

```
string card[52]
```

However, if you've spent as much time at the Poker table as I have, you'll at least know that there is more to a deck of cards than just 52 pieces of plastic-coated paper. Actually, there are four suits of 13 cards each. Ideally, you would store the deck of cards as a 13×4 matrix that would look something like the data in Table 7.2.

Table 7.2. A deck of cards as a 13×4 matrix.

♠:	A	2	3	4	5	6	7	8	9	10	J	Q	K
♥:	A	2	3	4	5	6	7	8	9	10	J	Q	K
♦:	A	2	3	4	5	6	7	8	9	10	J	Q	K
♣:	A	2	3	4	5	6	7	8	9	10	J	Q	K

In fact, you can create an array that stores your cards just the way you want them very simply, as follows:

```
string card[13,4]
```

This declares an array with two dimensions. You may want to think of it as an array of 13 elements, each of which is itself an array of 4 elements. You get a total of 52 elements, but now you can refer to them in their own dimension. To refer to the 7 of diamonds, you need to refer to `card[7,3]`. There is no limit to the number of dimensions you can define for an array in PowerBuilder.

Loops

As I mentioned before, the capability to use variables as your index numbers in arrays is extremely powerful. The reason this capability is so powerful is because there are ways to increment your index variables in rapid succession so you can quickly and easily populate your arrays with values in small amounts of code. After all, whats so special about an array of 52 cards if you have to use 52 statements to populate the array with data?

FOR..NEXT Loops

But what would you say if I told you I could populate the array of 52 cards with just five lines of code? Well, it's no lie. I can. I can populate the array in five lines using something called a *loop*. By using a loop, I can repeat a section of code many times. Sometimes I know the exact number of times that I want to repeat a certain section of code. In this case, I use something called a *FOR..NEXT loop*. For example, if I have 52 cards, I can use a FOR..NEXT loop to repeat my one assignment statement 52 times, as follows:

```
integer card[52]                (1)
integer counter                 (2)
FOR counter = 1 TO 52           (3)
     card[ counter] = counter   (4)
NEXT                            (5)
```

When PowerBuilder encounters the FOR statement in line 3, it sets the variable counter to a value of 1. Then, it continues on to the next statement and assigns the value of 1 to the first element of the card array. Then, it encounters the NEXT statement in line 5, which tells it to jump back to the line 3 with the FOR statement on it. Then, it executes the FOR statement again, but this time it increments the value of counter to 2. Then, it again repeats the assignment statement on line 4. But this time, counter contains a value of 2. So this time it assigns a value of 2 to the second element of the card array. It continues looping through these three lines, incrementing the value of counter each time, until the value of counter reaches 52. Once the value of counter is 52, it recognizes that it has finished all of the iterations of the loop; and when it hits line 5 this time, instead of looping back to the FOR statement in line 3, it will continue on with your code.

By default, your counter variable in a FOR..NEXT loop is incremented by one for each iteration of the loop. However, you don't have to increment your counter by one; you can increment your counter by any number, even a negative number! So, if we want to count down from 52 to 1 to arrange our card array backwards, we can do so by using the FOR..NEXT..STEP command, indicating a STEP value of -1, as in the following:

```
integer card[52]                (1)
integer counter                 (2)
FOR counter = 52 TO 1 STEP -1   (3)
     card[ counter] = counter   (4)
NEXT                            (5)
```

This time, the loop works its way down the array. It first sets the value of the counter variable to 52, and during each iteration of the loop, it subtracts 1 from the counter variable until it reaches 1.

Sometimes, we don't know exactly how many times we want to loop through a certain section of code. Instead, we want to loop through that code continuously until a certain condition is

met. In that case, we can use a different type of loop called a *DO..LOOP loop*. There are four flavors of a DO..LOOP loop, but we'll start with the most common: a DO WHILE.

DO..WHILE Loops

In a *DO..WHILE* loop, you tell the compiler to continue repeating your code while a particular condition is true. Generally, the condition is changed inside your loop based on some sort of calculation or some other factor.

```
Integer counter                    (1)
Integer card[52]                   (2)
counter = 52                       (3)
DO WHILE counter > 0               (4)
    card[ counter] = counter       (5)
    counter = counter - 1          (6)
LOOP                               (7)
```

In this example, we are populating our deck of cards backwards, starting with 52, and working our way down to 1. First, we declare our variables. Then we initialize our counter variable to 52. Then in line 4, we tell the compiler to continue executing lines 5 and 6 as long as the value inside counter is greater than 0. Because the value of counter is 52, which is greater than 0, the compiler then executes line 5, which sets the value of card[52] to 52. Line 6 then decrements the counter variable to 51, and finally, line 7 tells the compiler to jump back up to line 4. Line 4 executes again, and determines that the value of the counter variable, 51, is still greater than 0, and so the process repeats. Eventually, the value of counter reaches 0, at which point the statement in line 4 executes and determines that the value of counter, 0, is not greater than 0 but is equal to 0. And so it skips lines 5 and 6 and continues directly to line 7, and then continues past.

You need to recognize an important facet of this last step. When the value of counter reached 0 and line 4 executed, PowerBuilder evaluated the condition to be false and skipped immediately to line 7. If the condition were false to begin with, for example, the value of counter was 0 before line 4 was reached the first time, then lines 5 and 6 would never get executed. Instead, it would skip immediately to line 7. So PowerBuilder gives us another alternative to the DO WHILE..LOOP that ensures that the code inside the loop gets executed at least once, even if the condition is false. To do this, you use the DO..LOOP WHILE loop construct. In a DO..LOOP WHILE statement, your condition isn't actually tested until the end of the loop, which means that if the condition is false the first time, it still executes the statement inside the loop. A DO..LOOP WHILE statement to perform our array population might look something like this:

```
Integer counter                    (1)
Integer card[52]                   (2)
counter = 52                       (3)
DO                                 (4)
    card[ counter] = counter       (5)
    counter = counter - 1          (6)
LOOP WHILE counter > 0             (7)
```

As you can see, the only difference in this entire construct is the position of the `WHILE counter > 0` statement. However, the implications of this small difference are very large.

DO..UNTIL Loops

PowerBuilder has also given us one other major variation on the `DO..LOOP` construct, and that is a `DO..UNTIL..LOOP`. Instead of performing the contents of the loop as long as a condition is true, it loops through the statements in the loop for as long as a condition is *not* true. When the condition is true, the loop stops repeating; and as with the `DO..WHILE` version, you can also `DO..LOOP UNTIL` to ensure that the function executes at least once.

> **Note:** You can do some other important things inside of a loop. If for some reason you want to exit a loop prematurely, for example, before the main condition of the loop is satisfied, you can use the `EXIT` keyword to do this. When PowerBuilder encounters an `EXIT` statement in your loop, it immediately jumps to the end of the loop and continues on, as if the end of the loop had been reached.
>
> If for some reason you want to skip all or even just part of an iteration of the loop, you can do so by using the `CONTINUE` statement. When you issue a `CONTINUE` statement inside of a loop, PowerBuilder jumps immediately back to the beginning of the loop and then continues on.
>
> These two statements are available to both `DO..LOOP` loops and `FOR..NEXT` loops.

Other Conditionals

Sometimes, instead of looping based on a condition, you simply want to evaluate a condition as either true or false, and then execute a specific set of statements based on that condition. PowerBuilder gives us two other kinds of statements that we can use to do exactly that, the `IF..THEN` statement (which has several variations) and the `CHOOSE CASE` statement.

The *IF..THEN* Statement

The first statement is an `IF..THEN` statement. It sounds just like what it is. You simply say, "If" a condition is true, "then" do this; otherwise, skip it. The format for an `IF..THEN` statement is

```
IF counter > 0 THEN
    counter = 0
END IF
```

If the condition `counter > 0` is true, then PowerBuilder sets `counter` to `0`. Otherwise, if `counter` is less than or equal to `0`, then it skips directly to the `END IF` statement.

The *IF..THEN..ELSE* Statement

Alternatively, you may want to execute one set of statements if a condition is true and a different set of statements if that same condition is false. In that case, you use an *IF..THEN..ELSE* statement, which looks like this:

```
IF counter > 0 THEN        (1)
    counter = 0            (2)
ELSE                       (3)
    counter = 10           (4)
END IF                     (5)
```

When PowerBuilder encounters this statement, it evaluates the condition counter > 0. If it is true, then it executes line 2, setting counter to 0. Then, when it reaches the ELSE statement on line 3, it jumps past line 4 to the END IF statement on line 5, and continues on. If, however, the condition in line 1 is false, then this time instead of jumping down to the END IF statement, PowerBuilder jumps down to the ELSE statement in line 3. Then, it executes the statement in line 4, setting counter to 10.

The *IF..ELSEIF..ELSE* Statement

But what if you want to execute one set of code if the counter is greater than 0, and a different set of code if the counter is equal to 0, and yet a third set of code if the counter is less than 0? You can use the *ELSEIF* statement to do this, as follows:

```
IF counter > 0 THEN        (1)
    counter = 0            (2)
ELSEIF counter = 0 THEN    (3)
    counter = 10           (4)
ELSE                       (5)
    counter =-5            (6)
END IF                     (7)
```

PowerBuilder evaluates the condition in line 1. If its true, it executes the statement in line 2 and then jumps down to line 6, as before. If it is not true, then PowerBuilder jumps to line 3 and evaluates the condition there. If counter is equal to 0 and the condition is true, it executes line 4 and then jumps down to line 7; otherwise, it jumps down to line 5 and executes line 6. By using this method, you can add a little bit more power to your conditions. In fact, there is no limit to the number of conditions you can test by using an IF..ELSEIF..ELSE set of statements. You can have two ELSEIF clauses, or three, or four, or as many as your heart desires. Of course, after one or two ELSEIF clauses, your IF statement becomes quite a bit less readable—and if you remember, the mark of excellent code is readability.

The *CHOOSE CASE* Statement

For this reason, PowerBuilder gave us another conditional statement we can use to test a result for many values. This statement is the *CHOOSE CASE* statement. By using the CHOOSE CASE statement, we can choose a set of code to execute based upon a value that can come from the

contents of a variable, or even the result of a calculation. We could have coded the previous code snippet as a CHOOSE CASE statement, as follows:

```
CHOOSE CASE counter          (1)
      CASE 0                 (2)
            counter = 10     (3)
      CASE > 0               (4)
            counter = 0      (5)
      CASE < 0               (6)
            counter = -5     (7)
END CHOOSE                   (8)
```

When PowerBuilder encounters a CHOOSE CASE, it evaluates the expression in line 1, counter. Then, it looks for the first CASE statement. If counter is 0, it performs the code in line 3, and then skips directly to the END CHOOSE in line 8; otherwise, it skips to line 4. If counter is greater than 0, it performs the code in line 5 and then skips down to line 8. If counter is less than 0, it performs the code in line 7; otherwise, it skips to line 8. Using a CHOOSE CASE statement, you can test for a large number of values very easily.

Note: Although the example presented earlier only has one line of code for each CASE, your CASE statements may contain more than one line of code per CASE. PowerBuilder determines that you are finished with a particular CASE statement when it sees the next CASE statement, or when it sees the END CHOOSE keyword if there are no more CASEs.

7

As with an IF statement, you can use a CASE ELSE statement to handle results of your CHOOSE CASE expression that aren't found in any of the other CASE statements, as follows:

```
CHOOSE CASE counter          (1)
      CASE 0                 (2)
            counter = 10     (3)
      CASE > 0               (4)
            counter = 0      (5)
      CASE ELSE              (6)
            counter = -5     (7)
END CHOOSE                   (8)
```

This snippet performs identically to the previous snippet; however, the reason is slightly different. This time, when it reaches line 6, CASE ELSE, it determines that it has not satisfied any of the other conditions, and so it performs this code. It does not evaluate counter to be less than 0, but instead simply understands that counter does not match any of the other criteria. A better example of why you may want to use a CASE ELSE is if you are reacting to user input, as follows:

```
CHOOSE CASE keyhit           (1)
      CASE 'A'               (2)
            counter = 10     (3)
      CASE 'B'               (4)
            counter = 0      (5)
```

```
        CASE ELSE               (6)
              counter = -5      (7)
END CHOOSE                      (8)
```

In this case, CASE ELSE replaces a statement that would have to otherwise be coded in some way to indicate if keyhit were not 'A' or 'B' but something else. Of course, you could have coded a CASE statement for every other key on the user's keyboard, but that would be too much.

DO	DON'T

DO Use IF..ELSEIF instead of CHOOSE CASE for two or three cases, or for very complex conditions. The code will execute slightly faster.

DON'T Use IF..ELSEIF for more than three or four choices. Even though the code in a CHOOSE CASE may execute a few microseconds slower, it can become very difficult to read code with more than three or four ELSEIFs in it.

Relational Expressions Used in Conditional Statements

Now, let's discuss the kinds of expressions you can use in the conditional statements we learned about in the previous section. Basically, you must use any expression that PowerBuilder can evaluate to a single result of TRUE or FALSE. This expression can be as simple as a Boolean variable containing a value of TRUE or FALSE, or it can be a complex set of logical and relational comparisons. As you have already seen, there is a type of conditional statement that compares one value to another. This comparison is referred to as a *relational expression* because you are attempting to evaluate one value's relationship to the other. A relational expression evaluates the relationship of operands on the left side of the expression (preceding a relational operator) to operands on the right side of the expression. In our example, we compared the value of the counter variable to 0. First, we checked to see if it was equal to 0. To do this, we used the equal sign (=). Then, we checked to see if it was greater than 0 by using the greater than symbol (>). Finally, we checked to see if its value was less than 0 by using the less than symbol (<). All of these symbols can be used to compare two values to each other. Additionally, we can test two values to see if they are not equal to each other. To do this, we combine the less than symbol with the greater than symbol (<>). Its almost as if we are testing to see if the value on the left is either greater than or less than the value on the right. (If the value is greater than or less than the value on the right, then it cannot be equal to the value on the right!) For example, to see if our counter variable was not equal to 0, we would have said

```
IF counter <> 0 THEN
```

The Components of an Expression

The term *expression* is used to refer to any set of operators, variables, literals, and keywords that can be evaluated by the compiler to a single result. Although there are syntactical rules as to what kinds of things can make up an expression, there is no limit to the number of operators and operands that can make up an expression—as long as they follow the rules. An example of an expression is

```
a ^2 + b ^2 + c ^2
```

Assuming a, b, and c are variables, this expression tells the compiler to take the value of a and square it (the caret (^) is exponential operator), and then add to that the square of b, and add to that the square of c. The compiler can resolve that entire expression into a single value. If a, b, and c are each equal to 2, the result would be $2^2 + 2^2 + 2^2$ which, of course, equals 12.

In this example, we have several *operators* and *operands*. An operator is an expression term that operates on the values in the expression. In our example, the plus sign (+) is an operator because when the compiler reads in the plus sign, it adds the next value to its result, operating on the result. The caret (^) is also an operator, which tells the compiler to perform an exponential calculation. These operators are called *arithmetic operators* because they cause arithmetic operations to be performed. Additionally, there are also *relational operators*, like the greater than (>) and less than (<) operators you have already learned about. Relational operators cause the compiler to perform a relational comparison. Assignment operators are another kind of operator that causes the compiler to perform an assignment, which you learned about earlier in this chapter. So far, the only assignment operator you learned about was the equal sign, but there are several other assignment operators, called *unary assignment operators*, that are used to assign a value to a variable. Finally, there are *logical operators*, which are operators that tell the compiler to perform Boolean logic. You'll learn about Boolean logic later in this chapter.

Between the operators are values that are not operators but that the compiler uses in relation with the operator to evaluate the result of the expression. These values are referred to as *operands*. Very simply, operands are basically anything in an expression that is not an operator. They can be literal values, variables, or even expressions. But all of the operands in an expression must evaluate to the same resulting datatype. For example, "A" + 1 is not a legal expression because "A" and 1 are not the same datatype.

The order in which an expression is evaluated is based upon certain rules of *precedence*. As with mathematics, certain operations need to be evaluated first to come up with the right answers, and so the order of precedence determines which part of the expression will be evaluated first. As with mathematics, you can override

7

the default order of evaluation by using parentheses. The default order of precedence is listed as follows:

1. ( ) (Expressions inside parentheses override the natural order of precedence.)
2. ++, -- (Unary Plus and Minus)
3. ^ (Exponentials)
4. *,/
5. +,-
6. =,<,>,<=,>=,<>
7. NOT
8. AND
9. OR

You can also test whether a value is greater than or equal to another value in a single relational statement with the symbol >=, or if it is less than or equal to another value with the symbol <=.

You can also compare non-numeric values. For example, you can compare a string variable to a literal string, as follows:

```
IF mystring = "HELLO" THEN
```

If the variable mystring contains the value "HELLO", then the result is true; otherwise, it is not. Be aware, however, that the value "Hello" is not equal to "HELLO" because the case is different. String comparisons must match exactly. Also, strings are compared using a *lexical comparison*. A lexical comparison compares a value one character at a time. Even though numerically 100 is greater than 25, lexically "100" is less than "25" because "1" is less than "2".

Another type of comparison involves two or more relationships. Let's say you want to test for a condition where the value of one variable is equal to 0, and the value of a different variable is less than 0. Separately, these comparisons are pretty simply to do; and together, it's just as simple. All you need to do is use a logical operator to link the two relational expressions into one. The logical operators you can use are AND, OR, and NOT. Logical operators essentially compare two Boolean values. Ultimately, each relational clause in your expression will be evaluated to a single Boolean value, either TRUE or FALSE. Logical operators take two Boolean operands and return the result as a Boolean based on the two operands.

Table 7.3 lists the results of logical comparisons. In order for an AND to return TRUE, both sides of the AND must evaluate to TRUE. If either side is FALSE, then the AND is FALSE. For an OR to be TRUE, either side of the OR can be TRUE. If neither side is TRUE, however, the OR is FALSE. NOT takes a Boolean expression and returns the opposite. NOT TRUE is FALSE, and NOT FALSE is TRUE.

Table 7.3. Logical comparisons.

Comparisons with AND		
AND	**TRUE**	**FALSE**
TRUE	TRUE	FALSE
FALSE	FALSE	FALSE
Comparisons with OR		
OR	**TRUE**	**FALSE**
TRUE	TRUE	TRUE
FALSE	TRUE	FALSE
Comparisons with NOT		
NOT	**TRUE**	**FALSE**
	FALSE	TRUE

To put all this into practice, you can have an expression that looks like this:

```
IF a * b + c > d / e AND NOT q ^ r < 0 OR z = "HELLO" THEN
```

This is a perfectly legal, although quite complex, logical expression that the compiler can evaluate to a single result of TRUE or FALSE. Based on the values of the variables inside the expression, it will break this expression into something that looks like this:

```
IF TRUE AND NOT FALSE OR FALSE THEN
```

Eventually, the compiler will have converted the expression into either

```
IF TRUE THEN
```

or

```
IF FALSE THEN
```

which it can then use to determine whether it will perform the code inside the IF statement.

Functions

I think you may have heard me say it before once or twice. In case you weren't listening, I'll say it again. The most important features of a structured language are readability and understand-ability. You have already learned about many of the constructs that you use to create your programs: variables, loops, conditionals, and expressions. You've also seen that these statements can become very complex all by themselves. Now, imagine that you have a long set of code to perform some action that contains multiple lines of very complex code. All of a sudden, your readability factor has gone down the tubes.

PowerBuilder gives you the capability to take several lines of code and put them into a separate construct, called a *function*, that you can call from your main body of code. When PowerBuilder encounters a function call in your code, it immediately begins executing the code that is contained inside the function. The format for a function is simply

```
function()
```

Take a quick look at Listing 7.1 and see if you can figure out what it does. Not really very readable, is it? But now, take a look at the code in Listing 7.2. Isn't that much more readable? Even though you may not understand every little detail of what either code listing is attempting to do, isn't it much easier to venture a guess as to what the code in Listing 7.2 does than the code in Listing 7.1? Isn't it also easier to see that there is some duplicate functionality being performed for rows whose type is A and B as well as for rows whose type is D and E? The reason that it is so much more readable is because we've separated out some of the related code into functions and given the functions names that make it easy to understand what the functions are supposed to do, which in turn makes it easier to read the code.

Listing 7.1. A complex code listing.

```
long    ll_row, ll_count, ll_pos
string  ls_row_type, ls_row_data
ll_count = RowCount()  // Find out how many rows we have to deal with
FOR li_row = 1 TO ll_count  //Loop through each row
  ls_row_type = GetItemString( ll_row, "rowtype") // Find out the type of row this
  ➥is
  CHOOSE CASE ls_row_type
    CASE "A"
      ll_pos = Pos( GetItemString( ll_row, "aColumn"), "A")
      DO UNTIL ll_pos = 0
        ll_pos = Pos( GetItemString( ll_row, aColumn), A, ll_pos + 1)
        SetItem( ll_row, "info" + String( ll_pos), Mid( ls_row_data, ll_pos, 3)
      LOOP
    CASE "B"
      ll_pos = Pos( GetItemString( ll_row, "bColumn"), "B")
      DO UNTIL ll_pos = 0
        ll_pos = Pos( GetItemString( ll_row, "bColumn"), "B", ll_pos + 1)
        SetItem( ll_row, info + String( ll_pos), Mid( ls_row_data, ll_pos, 3)
      LOOP
    CASE "D"
      ll_row = dwFind( "aColumn=  "+ GetItemString( ll_row, "dColumn"), 0,
      ➥ll_count)
      IF ll_row = 0 THEN
        SetMicroHelp( Parent, "Bad Row")
        EXIT
      END IF
    CASE E
      ll_row = dwFind( "aColumn=  "+ GetItemString( ll_row, "dColumn"), 0,
      ➥ll_count)
      IF ll_row = 0 THEN
        SetMicroHelp( Parent, "Bad Row")
        EXIT
```

```
         CASE ELSE
             SetMicroHelp( Parent, "Bogus Row")
             Beep(1)
      END CHOOSE
NEXT
```

Listing 7.2. Functions make code readable.

```
long    ll_row, ll_count, ll_pos
string  ls_row_type, ls_row_data
ll_count = RowCount()  // Find out how many rows we have to deal with
FOR li_row = 1 TO ll_count  //Loop through each row
   ls_row_type = GetItemString( ll_row, "rowtype") // Find out the type of row this
   ➡is
   CHOOSE CASE ls_row_type
     CASE "A"
       f_parse( "A")
     CASE "B"
       f_parse( "B")
     CASE "D"
       f_skip_row( "D")
     CASE "E"
       f_skip_row( "E")
     CASE ELSE
         SetMicroHelp( Parent, "Bogus Row")
         Beep(1)
   END CHOOSE
NEXT
```

7

Warning: It is also possible to create functions that cause your code to actually be **less** readable. If you name your functions poorly, people who try to read your code will be unable to do so because the function references are not helpful. Name your functions so that they describe what the function does, or what it returns. A function named `f_perform_func()` is useless—of course, you are performing a function! A function named `f_get_password()`, however, clearly describes what this function does—it gets the password. Using descriptive names is not just important for functions, but for all of your PowerBuilder objects, including variables, structures, controls, and objects.

Another important reason that you would create a function is to take code that you want to use in more than one place and be able to call it as a single function call, instead of having to copy the same code multiple times. For example, if you have a utility routine that reacts to errors that occur in your application, instead of rewriting the error-handling code after each time an error can occur, you can simply write a single error-handling function and call it each time instead. This way, if later you need to make a change to the error routine, you can change it once inside the function instead of having to change it in each place where the function is called.

> **Note:** Generally, it is a good idea to create functions for code used more than once. However, it is not always a good idea to create functions for code used only once. There is a very small performance price to calling a function, and if you are calling functions where you don't need to, you might be unnecessarily slowing down your applications. In addition, it can be very difficult to debug and trace through code that has functions that call functions that call functions that call functions, and so on. And so functions should be used to eliminate duplication, not to cause havoc.

To create a function, you open up the Function Painter by clicking on the Function Painter icon on the PowerBar. The Select Function window appears (see Fig. 7.5) asking you if you want to open an existing function. Click on the button labeled **New** to indicate that you want to create a new function. Then, the New Function definition window prompts you for information about your function, including the name of the function, the return value, and any arguments that you may want to pass to the function (see Fig. 7.6).

Figure 7.5.
The Select Function window.

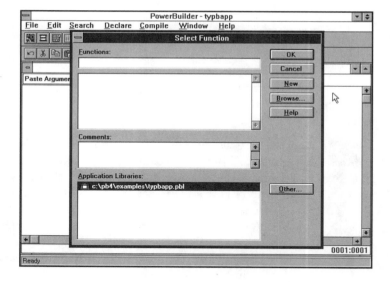

Figure 7.6.
*The New Function
definition window.*

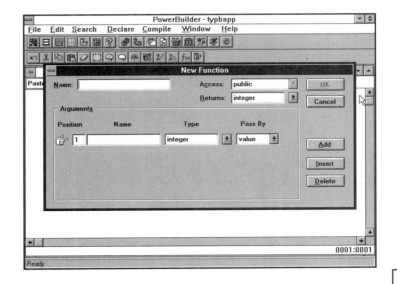

If you create a function to handle errors, you will probably need the function to know what error condition has occurred so that the function can log it, display a message, halt the program, or act upon it in some other way. To do that, you need to pass some information about the error to the error-handler function so that it can react to the error in an appropriate manner. The information that you pass is referred to as the *arguments* to the function. You pass arguments (sometimes also called *parameters*) inside the parentheses of the function, separating each argument with a comma. Inside the function definition window, you must declare those arguments so that your function can make sense out of them when it is called. You give each argument a name and tell the compiler its datatype. Inside your function, you can refer to that argument as you would any other variable. In fact, you can basically treat an argument as a variable whose value is set inside the call to the function.

Function arguments can be passed in two ways: either by *value* or by *reference*. When you pass an argument to a function by *value*, you are simply passing the value of the argument to the function so that the function can use it or change it as it pleases with no effect on the calling code. However, when you pass an argument by *reference*, it's more like you are passing the function the actual variable that you placed in its parameter call. If the function then changes the content of that variable, the calling code will also be affected by that change. For example, let's say you have a segment of code that contains a variable called counter, and you set the value of counter to 15. Then, you call a function to increment the counter, f_increment, which receives a single argument of type Integer. Inside your main code, you call

```
f_incrememnt( counter)
```

and the function increments the value of the argument that it received, as in the following code:

```
int_arg = int_arg + 1
```

If the argument is defined as an argument by value, then when your function is called, your function allocates space in memory to hold the int_arg argument and then sets it to the same value as the variable counter which was passed to it, in this case 15. However, the location in memory of the counter variable is different than the memory location of the int_arg argument, even though they both contain the same value. The function increments the value of int_arg to 16 and returns. But when it returns, it eliminates the memory reference of the int_arg argument because that reference only lives as long as the function. Hence, the change is lost. However, if you declare the int_arg argument as an argument by reference, the function does not allocate new memory for the argument int_arg. Instead, it makes the argument int_arg refer to the same location in memory where the counter variable itself is stored. When the function increments the int_arg variable, it is changing the value at the same location in memory that is pointed to by the counter variable. Then, the function ends, which terminates the name int_arg as a reference to the location in memory where the 16 is stored. However, the counter variable still points to that location in memory! And so, if you read the contents of the counter variable, you will see that it now contains a value of 16.

Creating arguments by reference is one way to allow your functions to manipulate data that is used by the calling program. Your function can actually change the value of its callers parameters. However, there is often a much simpler manner in which you can have your functions communicate with their calling programs, and that is by returning values.

When you declare your function, one of the things you declare is the *return type* of the function. Your function can opt to return a single value of any datatype that there is, and then some! You tell your function to return a value with the *RETURN* keyword, (not to be confused with the **Return** key!). In your code, you can simply state

```
RETURN <returnvalue>
```

<returnvalue> can be any literal, variable, or even an expression that can be evaluated to a single value of the type that is declared as the return type. The following are all legal return statements:

```
RETURN TRUE
RETURN 1
RETURN "HELLO"
RETURN my_var
RETURN 10*50
RETURN f_error_code()
```

Notice that you can even return the result of another function. This is all legal if the return type matches the declared return value of the function. However, if you declare your function to return a value, it must *always* return a value of that type. If a function you define as having a return value attempts to end without returning a value or attempts to return a value of a different type that it cannot convert, PowerBuilder will generate an error. This feature of functions, however, makes them very powerful indeed. Because functions can be evaluated to a single return value,

they can be used in expressions, as parameters to other functions, or even as return values for other functions! You will find functions to be one of your most frequently used tools in development of your PowerBuilder applications.

Note: A question that is often asked is if there are two ways to return a value to a caller of a function, how do you determine when to use a return value and when to use a reference argument? There is no real right or wrong answer to this question, but it's generally a good practice to have your functions return values that indicate the result of the function; for example, if it succeeded or failed. However, if your function is returning incidental data, you should pass reference arguments to get the data to return that information. Many of the PowerBuilder functions use this as their standard. For example, the dwDescribe() function that is used to get information about a DataWindow accepts two parameters and returns a string. The first parameter is a string containing the request for information, for example, it tells the function which information to return. The function itself returns a string containing the information you requested. There is also a second parameter, which is a reference parameter. If there is an error, PowerBuilder will place an error message in the second parameter so that you can read the error message out later.

Morning Summary

Your computer isn't all that much more than a fancy calculator. It contains a *Central Processing Unit (CPU)* and memory. The CPU recognizes only a limited set of instructions that you can use to place information into memory and to retrieve information from memory. While most memory is available for execution and storage of your programs, some memory is shared by external components, like your hard drive and video monitor. You can make your external components perform certain functions by placing specific values at specific memory locations that the external components are monitoring. In the old days, programmers did this at a very low level, by writing code in languages, like Assembly Language, that are very close to the native instruction set of the computer. However, PowerBuilder is a high-level language, meaning that it provides a more English-like interface to the computer that shelters the programmer from the instruction set of the computer. It is the job of the translator, in this case, PowerBuilder, to translate the code into the computers native instruction set.

The first language construct you should be familiar with is called a *variable*. You declare variables to store values in memory. You can then recall the data that you stored in your variable later. When you declare your variables, you have to tell the compiler what type of data you are going to store in the variable. There are several different types of data that you can store in your variables. You can store integers, strings, real numbers, Boolean values, and other things as well.

You can also make use of predefined English-like variable values, called *enumerated types*, that allow you to specify parameters and attribute values in a more English-like manner. For example, instead of setting the alignment of a static text control to 1, which might be difficult to interpret, you can set it to Right!, whose meaning is pretty clear. You can also create *structures*, which allow you to take multiple variables and group them together into a single structure. You declare structures in the Structure Painter.

When you want to store large sets of repetitive data of the same type, you can do so by using an *array* of that datatype. You declare an array by placing the number of elements you want in brackets, as in

```
string    my_array[10]
```

The value of an array is that you can access its elements very easily by using something called a *loop*. A loop, like it sounds, allows you to loop through the same statements multiple times. There are two types of loops: those where you know the number of iterations, a FOR..NEXT loop, and those that continue until a certain condition is met, the DO..LOOP loop. Additionally, you can test a single condition using an IF..THEN statement. You can test multiple condition sets using the IF..THEN..ELSE and IF..THEN..ELSEIF variations, as well. If you have many conditions to test, however, it is more readable to use the CHOOSE..CASE statement to test a single condition and react to a large number of different results. When you are creating your conditional statements, you need to create expressions to be tested. There are several types of expressions that you can use in PowerBuilder: logical, relational, and arithmetic. Each expression has its own purpose, resulting either in a Boolean value or a numeric result.

When you put all of these constructs together to build your applications, you will find that it can be very confusing—especially if you are working on a large application. However, PowerBuilder provides something called a *function* to allow you to place certain pieces of code in their own logical unit and call it from your applications. By placing specific functional code in a separate unit, you can make your code more readable. In addition, you can gain savings by using functions when you need to run a specific set of code in more than one place. To make functions useful, they return values and can take arguments. The arguments that they take can be passed by value or by reference. If you pass them by reference and if the function modifies the value, the caller will be able to see this modification.

Chapter

8

Getting around
with Menus

In this chapter, you will learn:

☐ How to build your own menus using the Menu Painter

☐ How to create a toolbar from your menu

☐ How to create scripts for your menus

☐ How to communicate between your menus and your windows

The Menu Painter

Probably the most popular method of interfacing with your user is through a *menu*. Even in the olden days of computer applications, before Microsoft Windows, menus were a common method of presenting options to the user. In Microsoft Windows, though, menus are standard. Any and every available function in your application should be accessible from a menu item. In Microsoft Windows, menus take two forms: menus that appear on the menu bar in a window and menus that pop up on-screen somewhere besides the menu bar. Both types of menus are created in the Menu Painter.

Open the Menu Painter by clicking on the Menu Painter button on the PowerBar, or by pressing **Shift-F3**. You are prompted with the Select Menu window (see Fig. 8.1). Click on the **New** button to create a new menu. The Menu Painter appears (see Fig. 8.2). The top line of the Menu Painter, under where it says `Menu Bar Items:`, is a virtual menu bar that, in effect, represents the menu bar of the menu you are creating. You enter the menu items that you want to appear on your menus menu bar in entry boxes above the black line. To create a new menu bar item, you can simply type your menu item name in the edit box. In Windows, the first menu item on a menu is usually the **F**ile menu, so type

&File

in the first menu bar box. As with the other controls in your system, you can create an accelerator for your menu items by placing an ampersand (&) in front of the letter that you want to become the accelerator, and it will appear with an underscore.

Notice that as you type in the name of your menu item, the word `m_file` automatically is entered in the box labeled Menu Item Name on the right side of the screen. Just as each of the controls inside a window has a name, so does each of the menu items in a menu. This single line edit box is where you edit the name of your menu, and just as the controls that you place on your windows each get a default name, so do each of the menu items in your menu. However, it's a little bit easier for PowerBuilder to evaluate a default name in the case of the menu because the name can be inferred from the text of the menu item itself, which is required as part of the creation of the menu item.

Figure 8.1.
The Select Menu window.

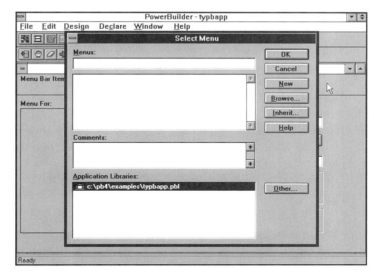

Figure 8.2.
The Menu Painter.

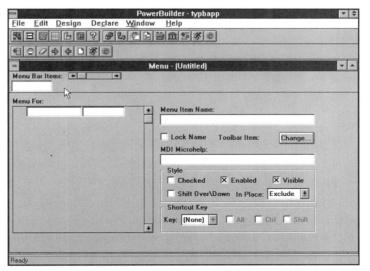

Notice that on the right side of the screen, under the Menu Item Name box, there are several other attributes of the menu item that you can control. Unlike the Window Painter, the Menu Painter lets you edit the menu items attributes right from the same window in which you create the menu items. You don't have to double-click or right-click with your mouse. Although this may seem a little bit inconsistent, this is primarily because there really isn't much to creating a menu item except giving it attributes. So, let's spend a moment talking about the menu item attributes that you can modify.

The Attributes of a Menu

The first thing that you can do is *lock* or *unlock* the name of the menu item. If the menu item name is unlocked, changing the text of the menu item will change the name of the menu item as well. However, generally after you set the name of the menu item the first time, you may not want to change it again for minor wording changes to the text. In that case, keep the menu item locked, and changes to the text will not be translated into changes to the menu item name. You need to keep the menu item locked because after the first time you enter the menu item text and you tab off to edit or create another menu item, it will automatically lock itself for you—assuming that you don't want to change the name. To have it change the name of the menu based on the text of the menu item, you need to uncheck the box. Locking the menu item doesn't prevent you from changing the name of the menu item in the Menu Item Name box, only from having it change automatically when you edit the menu item text.

Beside the Lock Name check box is a text item labeled Toolbar Item:, and then a bit of space, and then a button labeled Change. You can make toolbars in your application just as there are toolbars in PowerBuilder itself. In fact, you can make your toolbars work the same way that the toolbars in the PowerBuilder environment work. We'll talk more about this later in the lesson.

Under the Lock Name check box is an edit box labeled MDI Microhelp. If you have created your application by using MDI windows, and specifically an MDI Frame with Microhelp, whatever you type in this box will appear on the Microhelp Bar of your MDI Frame with MicroHelp. The Microhelp Bar is the status bar on the bottom of the screen. When the Multiple Document Interface (MDI) is discussed tomorrow, you will learn more about the Microhelp Bar and how to use it.

Under your Microhelp text are several other attributes that you can change. You can toggle the status of your menu items checked, visible, and enabled states with the check boxes that are labeled by the same names. If your menu item is not enabled (disabled), it will appear gray. If it is not visible (invisible), it will not appear on the menu at all. If it is checked, it will have a small check mark next to it.

Beneath these three check boxes is a check box labeled Shift Over\Down and a drop-down list box labeled In Place. By using these attributes, you can force your menu items to appear in a particular position in the menu, even if they are inherited from another menu with new menu items at the descendant level. This is an advanced technique that is used when you inherit menus, and you will need to learn about the object-oriented programming techniques that we will discuss in Chapter 11 before you can use this feature.

Finally, you can create a shortcut key for your menu items in addition to the accelerator key that you may have defined with the ampersand (&). First, select the key itself that will be the shortcut key. Then, check whether the user will need to hold down the **Alt**, **Ctrl**, and/or **Shift** keys while they press the shortcut key. For example, if you want to have a shortcut key of **Ctrl-F7** for your menu item, you first select the **F7** key from the Key drop-down list box, and then check the Ctrl check box by clicking on it.

That's really all there is to creating a single menu item. But of course, most menus have more than one menu item. Now let's spend a moment talking about how to create a full menu for your application.

Creating a Menu

In general, when you create a menu, you start off by creating the first menu item that will appear on the menu bar. You already did this when you entered the word &File earlier. After you enter in the first menu item, you will probably set up the attributes to meet your needs, like you did earlier. Then you can take either of two paths. One path, the path I personally prefer, is to enter in the rest of the items that will appear on the menu bar. There is a Windows standard that says the menu bar should contain a File menu, an Edit menu, a Window menu, and a Help menu. Because you have no reason to violate the standard right now, let's start off by creating these menu items on your menu bar.

First, let's create the Edit menu. In order to do this, you have to create a new menu item on the menu bar. The easiest way to do this is to click on the virtual menu bar in the gray area next to the edit box where you typed in the word &File. Don't click the mouse button too far over from the edge of the edit box—click right next to it, maybe within a quarter of an inch from the edge. This opens a new, empty edit box where you can type in the name of the next menu item—in your case, the Edit menu item. Type in the word

&Edit

This will create your Edit menu on the menu bar, and call it m_edit. Now, you can edit whatever attributes you feel you need to change for the Edit menu. For example, you may want to type some information about the Edit menu in the Microhelp edit box, or you may want to make the menu item invisible. However, for your purposes, let's leave everything as it is by default for now.

Now, let's create the next menu item. Click again to the right of the Edit menu on the menu bar, and in the new menu box type

&Help

Notice that this time, it will create a menu item on the menu bar called m_help. There's nothing new about the Help menu. For now, again, leave its attributes alone.

Now, let's create your fourth menu item: the Window menu. Wait a minute! The Window menu is supposed to be *before* the Help menu! Oh, no! What have you done?! Don't get nervous. All you need to do is create the Window menu in between the Edit menu and Help menu, instead of after the Help menu. To do this, open an empty menu edit box in front of your Help menu instead of after it. You can do this either by selecting **I**nsert from the **E**dit menu, or by clicking

on the Insert icon on the Menu PainterBar. This will open an edit box in between your Edit menu and Help menu, where you can place another menu bar item. This way, you can now type

`&Window`

and the Window menu will appear in the right place.

Beside the Menu Bar Items label, above the virtual menu bar, is a horizontal scroll bar that you can use if you create more menu items on the menu bar than can fit inside your screen. It works pretty much like any other scroll bar—if you scroll the menu bar to the right, menu items on the left side of the menu bar will drop off into cyberspace and be hidden to make room for menu items on the right.

Now that you have a menu bar, you can create some items to appear under each of the menus on the menu bar. Start by clicking on your File menu (not the File menu of the Menu Painter, but the File menu that you created on your virtual menu bar). Notice that under the virtual menu bar is a line that now reads `Menu For: File` and has an arrow pointing to the right next to it. We'll talk about the significance of that right arrow in a few moments. In the meantime, notice that under that line in the list box is a pair of edit boxes. Click on the edit box to the left, and a hand will appear pointing at the line that you clicked on. In the edit box, you can enter the text of your first menu item under the File menu. So for this example, type in the word

`&New`

As you may have guessed, the name of the menu item will default to `m_new`. You can now edit the attributes of this menu item. For now, don't worry about that, though. Let's create a few more menu items. Press either the **Enter** or **Tab** key on your keyboard. A new menu edit box will appear under your recently created **N**ew menu item. Enter

`&Open`

and press **Enter** or **Tab**. Now you can enter another menu item under the **O**pen menu. Enter

`&Close`

and press **Enter** or **Tab**. By now, you should be getting the feel for how this works. Go ahead and create menu items for the rest of the File menu on your own. Create menus with the following text:

```
&Save
Save &As
&Restore
Pr&int Setup
Print Pre&view
&Print
E&xit
```

DO	**DON'T**

DO Pay attention to the placement of the ampersand (&) in your menu items.

DON'T Assign the same accelerator key to more than one menu item in a drop-down menu if you can avoid it.

There is nothing in PowerBuilder or Windows that prevents you from assigning the same accelerator key to two or more menu items in a single drop-down menu. If you do create more than one menu item with the same accelerator key, pressing that accelerator key will highlight the menu item without actually clicking on it. The user will need to press **Enter** or click with the mouse to get the menu item to execute.

Now, just like in the Window Painter, the Menu Painter allows you to preview your menu to see how it will look when it is placed on a window. To see this, select Previe**w** from the **D**esign menu, or press **Ctrl-W**. PowerBuilder displays an empty window whose menu is the menu you are creating. You can then select the File menu from the window and see all of the items under the File menu drop down (see Fig. 8.3). But something about this menu doesn't look right. Everything in the menu is piled right on top of each other. It doesn't look as neat and organized as the menus you may have seen in other Windows Applications.

8

Figure 8.3.
Your File menu.

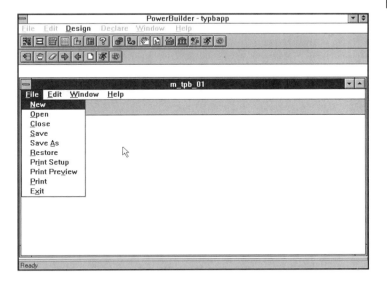

That's because there are no *separator bars* in your menu. Separator bars are lines between groups of menu items. If you go to the PowerBuilder File menu, you should see a menu structure that looks somewhat similar to the menu structure that you just built in your menu. However, different logical groups of menu items are separated with lines. It makes the menu easier to read and understand. You should put menu separator bars in your menu, as well.

To create a menu separator bar, you need to create a menu whose text is just a dash (-). That's it. Just a dash. PowerBuilder will recognize this to mean that you want a separator bar to appear on that line of the menu. Now, let's put some separator bars in your menu.

Wait! There's no room to put separator bars in! All of the menu items in your menu are contiguous! What are you to do? Actually, the answer to that is quite simple. You'll need to *insert* empty menu items into your menu in the places where you want your separator bars to appear.

Inserting Menu Items and Separator Bars

To insert a menu item in a menu, you must first indicate where on the menu you want the new item to appear. You do this by clicking on the menu that will appear after the new menu item that you insert. In other words, the menu item you insert will appear between the menu item you select and the one immediately before it. Click on the menu item you have labeled Save. Now, you can insert a new menu item that will appear between the Save and Close menu. You can do this either by selecting **I**nsert from the **E**dit menu or by clicking on the Insert icon on the Menu PainterBar. You did this once before when you created your Menu Bar items, specifically the Window menu. However, in that case, inserting your new menu item moved your Help menu to the right. Now, it moves your Save menu down. The bottom line, however, is that when you insert your new menu item here, an empty menu entry box will appear exactly where you expect it to be—between Close and Save—and your cursor will be waiting in the newly created menu entry box.

Now, you can create your Menu Separator bar by typing a dash (-) in the box. That's it—just a dash—nothing else. Go ahead and preview your menu again if you don't believe me. Select Previe**w** from the **D**esign menu, and then select your File menu on the Preview window. Notice this time that there is a line between the Close and Save menu items. That line is your separator bar.

Let's go back and create some more separator bars so that your menu looks really nice and really standard. Get out of Preview mode either by closing the Preview window or by selecting Previe**w** from the **D**esign menu. Now insert another menu item between Restore and Print Setup. Click on your Print Setup menu item and then insert the new menu item either by selecting **I**nsert from the **E**dit menu or by clicking on the Insert button on the toolbar. Type a dash (-) in the new menu item. Now, let's put one last separator bar before your Exit menu. Click on the Exit menu.

WHOA! What's that?!? You should see a small window appear on your screen telling you that the name of your menu is invalid (see Fig. 8.4). As with other objects, each menu item in a single menu must have a unique name so that you can reference it. With menu items, PowerBuilder generates the name of the menu item based on its text. You just entered a menu item with a dash as its text, so the name that PowerBuilder assigned to it should be m_-. However, only moments ago, you created a menu item with a dash as its text between the Close and Save menu items, and PowerBuilder gave it the name m_-. Therefore, when you indicated to PowerBuilder that you were finished changing the name of this new menu item by clicking on the Exit menu item, it tried to assign it a name that is already being used in the menu. PowerBuilder cannot allow you to give two menu items the same name within the same menu object. Otherwise, there is no way for PowerBuilder to be able to tell which of the two menu items you are talking about when you try to reference it in your scripts. In reality, it is unlikely that *you* will ever reference a menu separator bar in your scripts. However, internally PowerBuilder has to reference all of your menu items, even the menu separators, to do things like create and destroy them.

Figure 8.4.
The Invalid Menu Item Name window.

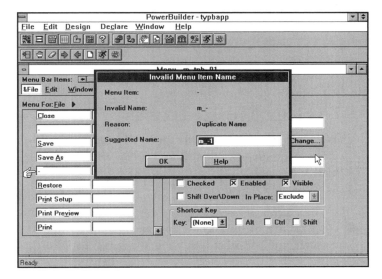

Warning: PowerBuilder by default allows you to create variables and object names (such as menu item names) with a dash (-) contained inside of them. However, some developers prefer to disallow this because it is nonstandard and can cause confusion with the Subtraction operator—a minus sign. You can prohibit dashes in identifiers by changing the DashesInIdentifiers setting in the PowerBuilder Preferences section (in the Preferences Painter) to 0. By default, it is set to 1, which allows dashes in identifiers.

PowerBuilder displays the Invalid Menu Item Name dialog box that you see now to tell you about your problem and to allow you to change the duplicate name of your menu item. It even goes as far as to recommend a new name, which is the menu item name that it tried to assign, followed by a sequential number, in this case the number one. The first line tells you the text of the menu item, which in this case is just a dash. The next line tells the original proposed name of the menu item, which is m_-. Next it tells you the reason that it cannot use this menu item name, which in this case is because it is a duplicate menu item name. Finally, it shows you the recommended, automatically generated menu name, and allows you to edit it if you like. For now, let's just keep the recommended name (m_-1) and keep going. Click on the **OK** button to accept the newly recommended name and return to the Menu Painter.

Now, let's finish off with the separator bars in this File menu. Click on the Exit Menu item and insert another separator bar. By now, you should already know how to do this. Click on the Insert button on the toolbar or select **I**nsert from the **E**dit menu. Enter a dash (-) into the Menu Item entry box. Press **Enter** and accept the new menu item name, which should now be m_-2. Notice that PowerBuilder incremented the sequence number to 2, instead of 1, because it already used 1 in your last separator bar. PowerBuilder will keep track of that for you. You can insert as many separator bars as there are numbers, and it still keeps track for you, prevents you from entering any duplicates, and recommends the next highest sequence number when you try to enter a duplicate name.

Moving Menu Items

You know what? I made a mistake. I told you to create that Restore menu item in the wrong place. It was supposed to be directly under the Close menu item. Now, how can you go about getting it there?

The answer is actually relatively easy. Put your cursor into Move mode by selecting **M**ove from the **E**dit menu, or by clicking on the **Move** button on the toolbar. Then, pick up the menu item you want to move by clicking on it and holding down with your left mouse button. Then, you can drag it to any other position in the menu. Let go of it when you are satisfied with its new location. Try it. Move the Restore menu item to be directly under the Close menu item. Put your cursor into Move mode by selecting **M**ove from the **E**dit menu, or by clicking on the Move button on the toolbar. Now pick up the Restore menu item and drag it to the space between the Close menu item and its separator. That's all there is to it!

Deleting Menu Items

You know what, though? You won't even need that Restore menu anyway. Let's get rid of it altogether. To do this, simply click on the menu item to delete—in this case the Restore menu item—so that the little hand is pointing to it. Then, select **D**elete from the **E**dit menu, or click on the **Delete** button on the toolbar. Voila! The menu item disappears! Unfortunately, there is no Undo in the Menu Painter, so if you have deleted the wrong one, you'll need to insert it again and start over.

Preview your menu one more time. Click on Preview from the **D**esign menu. Now, click on your File menu. You will see a pretty menu with separator bars that looks very much like the one in Figure 8.5.

Figure 8.5.
A File menu with separator bars.

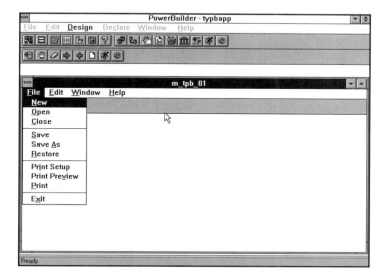

Multi-Level Menus

Now, suppose that in your system, the user can open multiple types of documents, such as reports or graphs. So, let's show that on the menu bar.

Click on the New menu item in your menu. Now, create a menu level under the New menu item either by selecting **N**ext from the **E**dit menu or by clicking on the Next Level button on the toolbar. Now, the list of menu items disappears, and the title above the list reads `Menu for: File > New >`. This means that you are now editing the submenu that appears beneath the New menu item in your File menu. Enter in the following two menu items:

```
&Report
&Graph
```

But now how do you get back to the File menu? All you have to do is select **P**revious from the **E**dit menu or click on the Prior Level button on the toolbar. Now, you are returned to the File menu. Notice this time that a small right arrow has appeared next to the New menu item in your menu. This tells you that there is another level beneath your New menu item.

Lets preview the menu again and see what it looks like with your submenus. Select Preview from the **D**esign menu. Click on your File menu. Notice that the New menu has a little, black right arrow next to it. Click on the New menu, and up comes the submenu with Report and Graph as options (see Fig. 8.6). In Windows, menus with multiple levels are often referred to as a *cascading menus*.

171

Figure 8.6.
The cascading New menu.

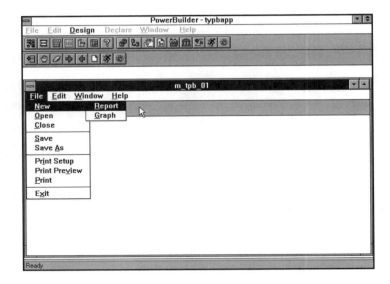

Note: There is no limit to the number of menu levels that you can have in a cascading menu; however, from a practical standpoint, most users will get annoyed if you have more than three levels.

Toolbar Attributes—Giving Your Menu a Toolbar

Earlier in the lesson, I mentioned that PowerBuilder allows you to create toolbars for your application that work in the same way that the toolbars in PowerBuilder work. This means that you can create toolbars that can be dragged around the screen, shown with or without text, have Microhelp explaining them on the status bar, and even have ToolTips. In PowerBuilder, every toolbar button must correspond directly to a menu item. The first step in making your menu item appear on the toolbar is to select that menu item and click on the **Change** button. Go ahead and select your Open menu item and click on the **Change** button.

When you click on the **Change** button, you are presented with the Toolbar Item dialog box (see Fig. 8.7). Here you define information about your menu items toolbar button. This includes the picture(s) that will be used for your menu items toolbar button, the text of the toolbar button that will appear in the ToolTips and ShowText, the toolbar buttons position, including spacing and sequence, and whether or not the toolbar button is visible.

Figure 8.7.
The Toolbar Item dialog box.

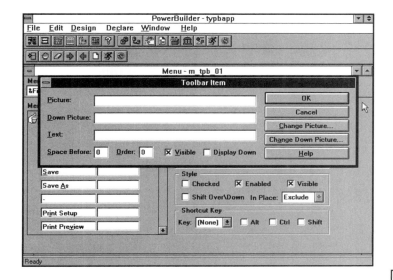

By default, your toolbar buttons will work in the same way that the PowerBars toolbar buttons work. When the user clicks on the button, it will immediately release and perform its action. However, you can also make toolbars whose buttons stay down and don't come up until you tell them to. For example, you may want your button to stay down until the user completes the requested action; or you may want the button to represent a state and have the button stay down when the user clicks it the first time and go up when the user clicks it again—kind of like the buttons on the style bar that change your text to bold, italic, and underlined. This is also possible.

The toolbar item, though, always has a picture that is displayed when the button is up. You can select the picture you want to appear on the button when it is up, either by typing its name in the edit box labeled Picture or by clicking on the **Change Picture** button. When you click on the **Change Picture** button, you are presented with the Select Toolbar Item Picture dialog box (see Fig. 8.8), where you can either select a built-in toolbar icon from the leftmost list or select your own bitmap file to use for the toolbars picture in the middle list. The picture that you select is displayed to the right of the Picture Name box. You can also type in the name of the picture you want in that box. You can also change which bitmap files appear in the Picture Files list box by changing the drive and directory that you are in. Change the current drive and directory with the Drive and Directory list boxes. When you are satisfied with your choice, press the **OK** button, and you are returned to the Toolbar Item dialog box. The name of the picture you have selected will appear in the Picture edit box. Go ahead and select the picture called Custom007! as the picture for the Open button on the toolbar.

Figure 8.8.

The Select Toolbar Item Picture dialog box.

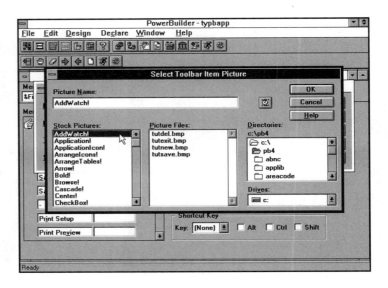

By default, when you select the picture for a toolbar button, it's the picture that is used when the button is either up or down. However, if you prefer, you can also change the picture that appears when the button is pressed down. Changing the down picture is the same as changing the regular picture. You can type in the name you want in the Down Picture edit box, or click on the **Change Down Picture** button. When you create a down picture, it will display while the button is pressed down, even if the button is not going to stay down. In other words, the down picture may display only for an instant as you click on the button itself. However, you may also want to make the toolbar button stay in the down position for an extended period of time, like the Boldface, Italic, and Underline buttons on the style bar.

To do this, you must write scripts that change the status of one of the attributes of the menu item; this attribute is called ToolbarItemDown. When you set this attribute to TRUE, it makes the button appear in the down position, showing the down picture if there is one. If you set it to FALSE, the button is in the up position, and clicking on it pushes it down (although by default this means that letting go will let it back up again). By changing the value of this attribute in the Clicked event of the menu item, you can make your button into a toggle button instead of an action button. You can set the initial state of the ToolbarItemDown attribute by clicking on the check box labeled Display Down. If it is checked, the toolbar is initially displayed in the down position.

Note: You can even use the ToolbarItemDown attribute of a menu item to make your buttons work like the Left, Right, and Center Justification buttons that appear on the StyleBar. Only one of these buttons can be down at a time. Putting one down brings the other two up. To do this, you could write code in the Clicked

event of the menu item that would set its `ToolbarItemDown` attribute to `TRUE` as you did before. However, you would also set the `ToolbarItemDown` attribute of the other two buttons to `FALSE` at the same time to ensure that the other two are both up. If you placed this code in all three buttons (or better yet, created a single function to do it, and called it from the `Clicked` event of each menu), you will achieve the desired result. Use your imagination—it is the only thing that will limit you when developing your applications.

In addition, there are a couple of other attributes of your toolbar that you can control. Normally, each button on your toolbar is directly adjacent to the next. However, you may want some spacing in your toolbars. If you want to place some space before a button on the toolbar, simply enter the number of spaces that you want into the edit box labeled Space Before. The width of the space between toolbar buttons is about one third of the width of the toolbar button itself.

PowerBuilder puts the buttons on your toolbar in the same order that they appear in the menu, starting with the first menu on the menu bar, working its way down that menu's drop-down menu, and then going to the next menu on the menu bar, and so on. However, you may not want your buttons to appear in this order. If this is not the order you want, you can change the order of your toolbar buttons by changing the value in the entry box labeled Order. As with the tab order of your controls, the order of the buttons on the toolbar appear sequentially based on their number.

When you are finished setting up your toolbar item, you can click on the **OK** button of the Toolbar Item dialog box to accept your changes. Then, if you haven't already guessed, you can preview your menu with its toolbar by selecting Previe**w** from the **D**esign menu. When you preview your menu this time, you will see a toolbar beneath the menu bar containing all of your toolbar buttons, with their spacing and order as you have specified. Because you are only in Preview mode, they will not actually work; but at least Preview will give you an idea of how it looks. Later, you'll assign the menu to a window and see how your toolbar really works.

Menu Scripts

Of course, in order to actually make your menu do anything, you will need to write scripts to react to the users selecting a menu item. PowerBuilder gives you two events for each menu item to which you can react. These are the `Selected` and `Clicked` events. When you first click on a menu item, and the menu item becomes highlighted, that triggers the `Selected` event. In the `Selected` event, you might want to do things like turn on and off submenu items based on the users security, or check and uncheck submenu items based on other conditions. But you don't want to spend too much time inside the `Selected` event because the code for that event will be executed before any of the submenus are opened.

Most of the time, however, the user will click on a menu item to get something to happen: for example, to make the menu item perform a function or to check and uncheck it. You've been using the PowerBuilder menus all along in the previous several lessons, so you should already be familiar with clicking on a menu item. When your user clicks on a menu item, the click triggers the Clicked event of that menu item. Inside the script for the Clicked event is where you will place most of your menu's code; and if you are using menus properly, you probably will not have too much code there, either. Generally, a menu's job is to make something happen inside one of the windows in the application and generally, the window that performs the function is the window that houses that menu. In PowerBuilder, this window is referred to as the *Parent* window of the menu. In your scripts, you can use the keyword ParentWindow to refer to your menu's Parent window. This is helpful if you want to trigger an event in the Parent window as a result of an action in the menu. For example, suppose that you want to allow the user to save a file. Instead of placing the code to save a file in your Save menu, you can declare a user-event in the Parent window called ue_save, and then trigger that event when the user clicks on the Save menu. The code inside the Save menus Clicked event will look something like this:

```
TriggerEvent( ParentWindow, ue_save)
```

When the user clicks on the Save menu, the code inside automatically triggers an event called ue_save in the Parent window, whichever window that may be, which could then save whatever information it had to save back to the database or to the disk. By using this technique, each window is responsible to manage its own save functionality. The code to perform the save is not in the menu but in the Parent window. It doesn't matter which window is the Parent window. If it has an event called ue_save, it works together with this menu to save its data when the user clicks Save. If it doesn't have an event by that name, that's okay. The message is simply ignored, and the TriggerEvent function fails. You can even trap the return value of the TriggerEvent function into a variable and check it to see if the triggering of the event has failed. If it fails, you can display a message indicating that Save is not available. TriggerEvent returns a 1 if it succeeds and a -1 if it fails.

DO	DON'T

DO Try to limit the code in your menus to things that are contained in the menu itself or in the Parent window. Stick to changing the attributes of the menu items, like Checked, Enabled, Visible, ToolbarItemDown, and so on, and to triggering events in the Parent window.

DON'T Hard code the name of the Parent window (or any other window) into your menu if you in any way can avoid it. Doing so tightly couples the window and its menu, making the menu useless without its Parent window. If you instead use the ParentWindow keyword, you can reuse your menu with other windows, possibly even other applications.

Saving Your Menu

After you have finished creating all of the menu items that you want, and you have placed scripts inside them, you can save your menu object into a library so that you can use the menu in your application. To save your menu object, simply select **S**ave from the **F**ile menu. When you do this, the Save Menu dialog box appears on-screen (see Fig. 8.9). In this window, you are prompted to enter the name you want to give the menu, comments for the menu, and the library in which you want to save the menu. Go ahead and enter the name of your menu as

`m_typb 01`

Figure 8.9.
The Save Menu dialog box.

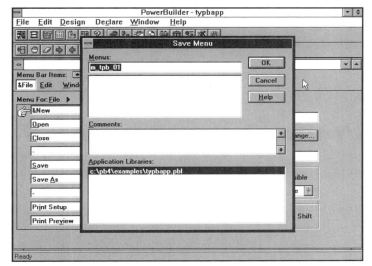

Enter the following comment:

`The Teach Yourself PowerBuilder Menu from chapter 9`

Click on the **OK** button. PowerBuilder saves your menu in the typbapp library. Now, you can close your menu. If you haven't saved your menu, you are prompted to save before closing by the dialog box that appears in Figure 8.10.

Figure 8.10.
The Save Menu Changes prompt.

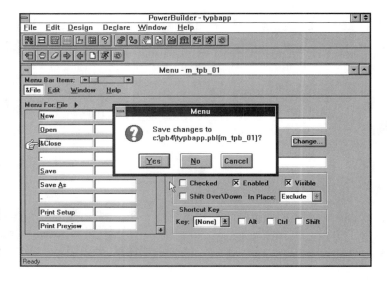

Putting Your Menu in a Window

Now that you have created and saved a menu, you need to place it inside a window for it to have any effect. For now, let's place this menu inside your w_ch5 window that you created way back in Chapter 5. Open up the w_ch5 window inside the Window Painter. Click on the Window Painter icon on the PowerBar, or press **Shift-F2** to open the Window Painter. Select w_ch5 from the list of windows to open. PowerBuilder brings up your w_ch5 window for you to edit. Double-click on the window to bring up the Window Style dialog box (see Fig. 8.11). Click on the Menu check box to turn it on, and all by itself the name of your menu appears in the drop-down list box next to the check box. That's really all there is to it.

Save the window and see how it looks—menu, toolbar, and all. Run the application by selecting **R**un from the **F**ile menu or by clicking on the Run button on the PowerBar. You can now see your window with its menu up on-screen (see Fig. 8.12). Spend a few moments to play around with your window and menu a bit, and close the window when you are done by double-clicking on the Control menu.

Note: Even though you can define toolbars for any menu, they only appear on your windows when you use the Multiple Document Interface (MDI). We'll talk about the Multiple Document Interface in Chapter 10.

Figure 8.11.
The Window Style dialog box.

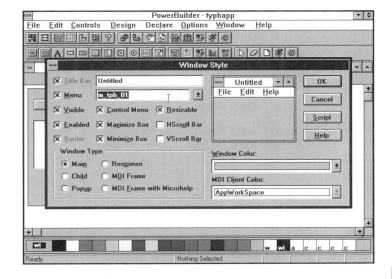

Figure 8.12.
The w_ch5 window with a menu.

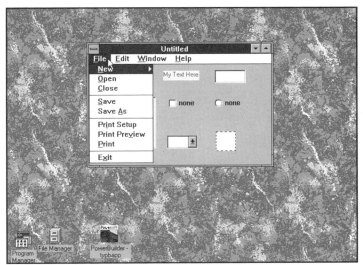

In addition to placing your menu inside a window, you can also make it pop up anywhere on-screen by using the PopMenu() function. You can call the PopMenu() function anywhere inside your script. Simply enter

```
PopMenu( menu name, x-coordinate, y-coordinate)
```

The *x-coordinate* and *y-coordinate* are numbers that tell the menu where to pop up. They need to be specified in PowerBuilder units. The *menu name* is the name of the menu that you want to pop up. You can pop up any of the menu items on the menu bar by using the name that it is assigned in the Menu Painter. You must qualify that name by specifying the name of the menu in which it resides. For example, if you want to pop up your File menu, you use

```
PopMenu( m_typb01.m_file, 10, 15)
```

This pops up your File menu 10 PowerBuilder units from the left side of the screen and 15 PowerBuilder units from the top. This is exactly the type of menu that pops up when you right-click on objects inside the Window Painter.

> **Note:** You can create your own Right Mouse Menus by using the `PopMenu()` function! All you need to do is figure out the X and Y coordinates where you want to place the menu. This can be based on the position of the object that the user clicks on, or you can use the `PointerX()` and `PointerY()` functions to get the X and Y coordinates of the mouse pointer relative to an object or window in the system, and pass those coordinates. For more information on these functions, see the PowerBuilder Function Reference or on-line help.

You are now equipped with the knowledge you need to make menus for your application. You can make menus that appear on the menu bar, and menus that appear anywhere else on-screen. As a general rule, make sure that the user can do everything from the menu so that even if the user doesn't have a mouse to click or drag, he/she can still perform all of the operations necessary to complete tasks from the menu by using the keyboard. A true user-friendly application ensures that *anyone* can utilize it, even if they do not have a mouse. A well-organized menu system is an excellent way to make your Windows applications more user-friendly.

Afternoon Summary

The most common method of allowing your user to control your application is through the use of a *menu*. Menus were common navigation tools even before Windows was around. They allow the user to choose what he/she wants to do and where he/she wants to go. In Windows, the menu goes on its own menu bar, or it can pop up as a popup menu, as well.

PowerBuilder menus are created in the Menu Painter. When you open the Menu Painter, you can create items on a virtual menu bar. Then, under each menu bar item, you can create the menu items that will appear under that menu bar menu. You enter the text for the menu item inside edit boxes for each menu item, and as you do so, PowerBuilder assigns the menu item a name. You can create an accelerator for each of your menu items by placing an ampersand (&) in front of the letter that will be the accelerator.

You can edit the currently selected menu items attributes by manipulating the controls on the right side of the window. You can lock the menu name to prevent the menu name from automatically changing when you change the text of the menu. You can create a toolbar button that corresponds to this menu item. You can enter Microhelp text that appears on the status bar when the user selects the menu item. You can make the menu item checked, invisible, or disabled. And you can give your menu a shortcut key.

As you create menu items on the menu bar, simply click in the area to the right of the menu item to get a New Menu Text edit box. You can then create a new item on the menu bar. After you create the menu items that appear on your menu bar, you can fill them in with their own menu items that will appear under them. You can insert menu items in front of other menu items by selecting **I**nsert from the **E**dit menu or by clicking on the Insert button on the toolbar. You can also move menu items around by selecting **M**ove from the **E**dit menu or by clicking on the Move button on the toolbar. You can delete menu items by selecting **D**elete from the **E**dit menu or by clicking on the Delete button on the toolbar. After creating all of your menu items, you can see how your menu will look to the user by previewing it. To preview your menu, select Previe**w** from the **D**esign menu.

There is a special menu item called a *separator bar* that separates menus into groups by placing a line on the menu. You can place separator bars on your menu by using a dash in the menu text. PowerBuilder translates this to a separator bar for you. If you create multiple separator bars, you may get a warning message from PowerBuilder that the menu name is not valid because it is a duplicate menu name. Menu names in PowerBuilder menus must be unique, and so when PowerBuilder tries to assign the same menu to your separator bars (because they have the same text), it gets an error. However, the error dialog recommends a new menu name and allows you to just press the **Enter** key and continue with the new name.

You can create menus that open submenus: these are called *cascading menus*. To create a cascading menu, select the menu item that you want to be the parent item and then select **N**ext from the **E**dit menu—or click on the Next Level button on the toolbar. This opens the next level of menu items, displaying where you are in the title above the list. You can then enter your cascading menu items. Then, you can return to the previous level by selecting **P**revious from the **E**dit menu or by clicking on the Prior Level button on the toolbar.

You can create toolbars in your applications that work just like the PowerBar and PainterBar. Each button on the toolbar maps directly to a menu item in your menu. To make a toolbar button that maps to a menu button on the menu, simply click on the **Change** button. You are presented with a dialog box that allows you to pick the toolbar buttons picture, down picture, text, order, and spacing.

Each menu item has two events that it can respond to: the `Selected` event gets triggered when the user highlights the menu item, and the `Clicked` event gets triggered when the user actually selects the menu item by clicking on it. In order to help make your window generic, PowerBuilder supplies you with the `ParentWindow` keyword, which refers to the window that owns the menu.

In order to place your menu in a window, you must first save it as a menu object in a library. To do this, select **S**ave from the **F**ile menu and give your menu a name. Then, you can place your menu in the window in one of two ways. The simplest way is to place the menu on the menu bar of the window by editing the style of the window in the Window Painter and by choosing the menu in the Menu drop-down list box. Alternatively, you can use the `PopMenu()` function to open the menu as a popup menu anywhere on-screen.

Q&A

Q Are the standard data types listed in Table 7.1 the only variables I can declare in PowerScript?

A No, in addition to the standard data types, PowerBuilder supports enumerated types, arrays, structures, objects, and controls. Any of these types can be declared and used in scripts or passed as arguments in functions.

Q I want to know more about structures. Are there other uses for them?

A Many people use structures to pass multiple data values between windows by using the `Message.PowerObjectParm` attribute. Functions that allow you to pass variables to windows or user objects like `OpenWithParm`, `OpenSheetWithParm`, `OpenUserObjectWithParm`, or `CloseWithReturn` pass only one variable parameter. This is carried in the global `Message` object. The `StringParm` attribute is used to pass one string value, the `DoubleParm` attribute will pass one numeric value, or the `PowerObjectParm` can pass one structure containing many variable types and values.

Create a structure named s_customer with variables

```
customer_id integer
customer_name string
```

From a menu item, you can open window `w_sheet` as a sheet within MDI frame `w_frame`:

```
//declare a local variable of type s_customer
s_customer lstr_customer
//assign values to customer structure
lstr_customer.customer_id = 15
lstr_customer.customer_name = "Jupiter Motors"
//the structure lstr_customer is passed to w_sheet as it opens
OpenSheetWithParm(w_sheet,lstr_customer,w_frame)
```

The opening script of `w_sheet` could look like this:

```
//declare a local variable of type s_customer to match the structure passed
s_customer lstr_customer
//get the structure passed from the PowerObjectParm
lstr_customer = Message.PowerObjectParm
```

The customer ID is available in `lstr_customer.customer_id` (15) while the customer name is in `lstr_customer.customer_name` ("Jupiter Motors").

Q **I have an array with 100 elements that I want initialized. Is there a way to initialize or reset this array without looping through 100 iterations to assign values to all the elements?**

A You can declare an array of the same type and set the array to initialize equal to the new array. This will either reset all the elements to default values or initialize the entire array with no elements.

The following example describes array resetting and initializing:

```
//li_test and li_initialize are unbounded integer arrays and initially have
no elements
//li_reset has 100 elements all set to default value 0
int li_test[], li_reset[100], li_initialize[], li_count
//li_test will have 100 elements with non-zero values after 100 loop
iterations
FOR li_count = 1 TO 100
    li_test[li_count] = li_count
NEXT
//all 100 li_test elements are set to default value 0
li_test[] = li_reset[]
//li_test is essentially initialized, it has no elements with values
li_test[] = li_initialize[]
```

Q **How can I stop execution of a script and exit from an event?**

A At any point within your script, you can code a RETURN, which stops further processing of that script and allows the event to end. However, you must be careful when doing this, because code following a RETURN will not get executed, even if you are paying attention.

Q **Is there a way to group or compare multiple conditions within a CHOOSE CASE statement?**

A Yes, this example illustrates the different ways:

```
CHOOSE CASE li_number
    CASE IS > 2
        //relational <, <=, >=, >, <> using keyword IS
    CASE 7 TO 11
        //range of values using TO
    CASE 4,6
        //multiple values separated by comma
    CASE IS <4,5
        //combination of above options
END CHOOSE
```

Q After editing my menu, the item labeled `Print` is named `m_-2`. Why did this happen?

A When you first created the menu, the menu item was - (a separator bar), and the name was set to `m_-2` and became locked. You later edited that item and changed the label to `Print` but did not unlock the name, so `m_-2` stayed. Simply change the Menu Item Name to something you want, like `m_print`.

Q Is there a quick way to tell if a control contains script?

A When you select a control, if it contains script, the script icon will show lines as opposed to a control with no script.

Q You mentioned that `ParentWindow` could be used in menu scripts to refer to the menus associated window. Why do I get a compile error when I use `ParentWindow` to reference window functions and controls?

A `ParentWindow` can be thought of as a variable of type `window`. Because the base window class has no window functions or controls placed on it, the compiler will not recognize references to window functions or controls. Instead of `ParentWindow`, you must use the specific window object name or variable of that type to reference window functions or controls. You can assign the `ParentWindow` to this variable and then call these functions in that manner.

Q What do I need to code to allow my toolbars to have the same placement and `ShowText` capability as the PowerBar and PainterBars in PowerBuilder?·

A No extra script is necessary. The toolbars in your application will have this functionality by default.

Workshop

Quiz

1. Throughout this book, object and variable attributes are set and accessed by using the dot notation. What is the general syntax of this notation?

2. Why are naming conventions so important?

3. Name two ways arguments can be passed to a function.

4. What's the difference between a shortcut key and an accelerator for a menu item?

5. How do you associate a menu to a window?

Putting PowerBuilder into Action

1. Finish off the menu that you started in this chapter. Place the following items into the menu:

    Under the Edit menu:

```
&Undo
-
Cu&t
&Copy
&Paste
```

Under the Window menu:

```
Tile &Vertical
Tile &Horizontal
&Layer
&Cascade
-
&Arrange Icons
-
&Toolbars
```

Under the Help menu:

```
&Contents <F1>
&Search For Help On...
-
&About
```

2. Create toolbars for the following items in the menu. As the text for each item, use the name of the menu item itself. For example, the text for the File/Save menu should read Save. Place space before the ones that are marked by entering a **1** in the Space Before entry box.

MenuItem	*Picture Name*
File/Open	Custom007!
File/Save	Custom008!
File/Print	Print!
File/Print Preview	ScriptYes!
File/Exit	Exit! (Space Before)
Edit/Undo	Undo!
Edit/Cut	Cut!
Edit/Copy	Copy!
Edit/Paste	Paste!
Window/Tile Horizontal	Horizontal! (Space Before)
Window/Tile Vertical	Tile!
Window/Layer	Layer!
Window/Cascade	Cascade!
Window/Arrange Icons	ArrangeIcons!
Help/Contents	Help! (Space Before)

3. Enter in Microhelp text for each of the menu items, as follows.

MenuItem	*Microhelp*
File/Open	Open a new sheet
File/Close	Close the active sheet
File/Save	Save the data in the active sheet
File/Print Preview	Preview the contents of the active sheet
File/Print	Print the contents of the active sheet
File/Exit	Exit "Teach Yourself PowerBuilder"
Edit/Undo	Undo the most recent change
Edit/Cut	Cut the selected text to the clipboard
Edit/Copy	Copy the selected text to the clipboard
Edit/Paste	Paste text from the clipboard
Window/Tile Horizontal	Tile the Windows Horizontally
Window/Tile Vertical	Tile the Windows Vertically
Window/Layer	Layer the Windows
Window/Cascade	Cascade the Windows
Window/Arrange Icons	Arrange the Icons
Help/Contents	Display the Help Index

4. Place the following line of code inside the File/Exit menu item:

```
Close( w_ch5)
```

5. Place the following line of code in the File/Close menu item:

```
Close( ParentWindow)
```

6. Place the following line of code in the File/Print Setup menu item:

```
PrintSetup()
```

7. Place a line of code in each of the following menus that reads as follows:

```
TriggerEvent( ParentWindow, ue_<menu item name>)
```

where the second parameter is the letters ue and an underscore, and the name of the menu item. For example, for the File/Save menu, the line of code should read:

```
TriggerEvent( ParentWindow,"ue_save")
```

Do this for the following menu items:

MenuItem	*Second Parameter*
File/Save	ue_save
File/Save As	ue_saveas
File/Print	ue_print
File/Print Preview	ue_preview
Edit/Undo	ue_undo
Edit/Cut	ue_cut
Edit/Copy	ue_copy
Edit/Paste	ue_paste

8. Save your menu.

Chapter

9

The Library
Painter

This morning, you will learn:

- [ ] What the PowerBuilder Library Painter is used for
- [ ] What a PowerBuilder library is
- [ ] How to effectively organize your objects within libraries
- [ ] How to view and manipulate objects and libraries

Using the Library Painter

The *Library Painter* provides tools for the developer to view and organize the contents of objects and libraries. A *PowerBuilder library* (often referred to as a "pibble" because the library file uses the DOS file extension ".pbl") is a container that PowerBuilder uses to store objects.

The Library Painter's tools work on either of two views of library objects: physical and logical. The physical view is concerned with the contents and arrangement of objects in the library disk file, while the logical view deals with the relationship of objects in an application.

This chapter will review mostly the tools that work with the physical view. We will also look at some of the logical view tools, but their purpose may not be immediately clear until the book progresses.

Clicking on the Library button in the PowerBar opens a Library Painter. A dialog box similar to the one in Figure 9.1 opens and displays the physical view of the objects you have created in library typbapp.pbl.

A drive and directory "tree" like the Windows File Manager is shown, but note that only PowerBuilder library files and objects within those libraries are displayed. Each entry includes a bitmap of the entry's object type that corresponds to the associated PowerBuilder painter.

Note: An object is referred to as an *entry* in the Library Painter, but both terms are used interchangeably throughout this chapter.

When you open the Library Painter for the first time in a PowerBuilder session, it always displays the library where the current application object resides (see Fig. 9.1).

By clicking and double-clicking on libraries and entries (or using the up/down arrow keys and the Enter key), the similarity to File Manager becomes apparent as objects and libraries get selected, and directory tree and library branches expand and collapse.

Double-clicking or pressing **Enter** on a selected entry launches the associated PowerBuilder painter loaded with the selected object. If you have launched a painter, just close it to return to the Library Painter.

Figure 9.1.
A Library Painter dialog box.

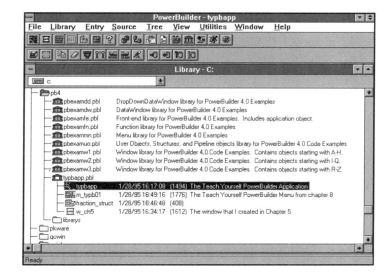

Each click on the PowerBar's Library button opens another Library Painter. After a while, you'll probably find it convenient to open one or more Library Painters at the beginning of every PowerBuilder session to quickly locate the objects that you want to work on.

PowerBuilder Libraries

A PowerBuilder library is physically a single DOS file (in PowerBuilder for Windows 3.1), and contains three components: the *header*, the *source code*, and the *p-code*.

The *header* is a "directory" that tells PowerBuilder where to find library objects in the file, and it keeps track of information such as object revision dates, comments, and so on.

The *source code* is what the developer writes to instruct PowerBuilder to perform tasks. Source code is saved separately for each object in the library file. The *p-code*, if you recall from Chapter 1, is the instruction set that PowerBuilder generates from source code so that the runtime module can run the code you've written. P-code is generated every time an object is saved.

Note: You've seen how PowerBuilder maximizes productivity by generating source code automatically through the use of painters. Both the automatically- and manually-generated source code (that developers type in) are represented in the library using a standard syntactical format for each object type. This format can be viewed by using the Library Painter Export feature, which we will explore later in the chapter.

In Chapter 3, you created a library automatically with the Application Painter. The Create Library feature manually generates and initializes new PowerBuilder library files. Figure 9.2 displays the Create Library dialog box prompting the developer to specify the drive and path in which the library will reside.

Figure 9.2.
The Create Library dialog box.

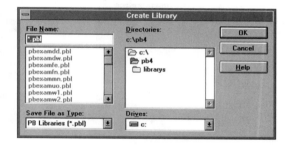

Organizing Objects within Libraries

The arrangement of objects within PowerBuilder libraries is largely dependent on whether or not you plan to use (or have used) PowerBuilder's Object Inheritance feature.

When Object Inheritance is not used, the arrangement of libraries is fairly straightforward. If the number of objects used in the whole application totals 60 or less, and the library file size is less than 800K, all the application's objects can be stored in a single library. Otherwise, libraries can be arranged by object type, like the sample application libraries shown in Figure 9.3. Here, a library pbexamdd.pbl has been created for application Exampl40 to only store drop-down DataWindow objects. An arrangement like this makes it easy to find objects of certain types.

If objects do follow an inheritance strategy, however, libraries of objects should be created for each major application function to facilitate the creation of PowerBuilder Dynamic (runtime) Libraries. As an example, look at Figure 9.4, which shows the libraries for the application a_pubs, a publisher's tracking system. Here, a developer has created one library each to store the objects for dealing with authors, publishers, stores, and titles. Notice the comments for each library entry.

Manipulating objects in PowerBuilder is very simple. Developers can use the Library Painter options Copy, Move, or Delete (by selecting library objects and pressing the appropriate buttons or the menu item **E**ntry | **C**opy/**M**ove/**D**elete. Alternatively, using the right mouse button to click on an entry will display a floating menu also containing the **C**opy/**M**ove/**D**elete options, as shown in Figures 9.5 through 9.7.

Figure 9.3.
Library object arrangement when inheritance is not used.

Figure 9.4.
Library object arrangement when inheritance of objects is used.

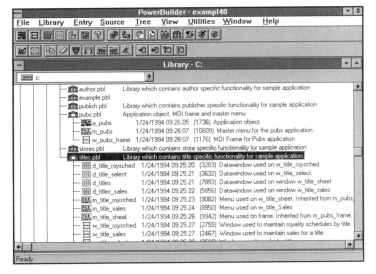

Figure 9.5.
*The **C**opy entry floating menu option.*

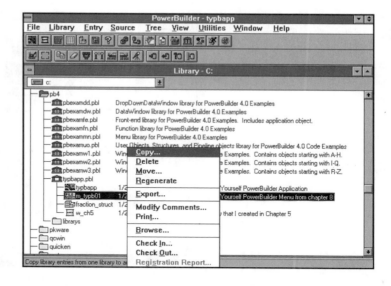

Figure 9.6.
*The **M**ove entry floating menu option.*

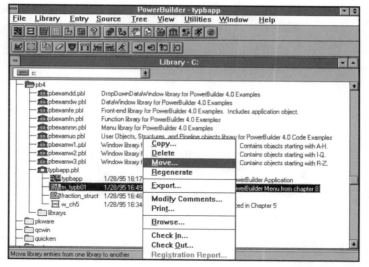

Figure 9.7.
*The **Delete** entry floating menu option.*

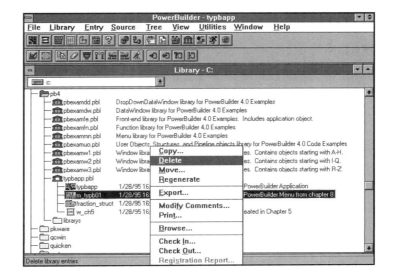

When copying objects, the Copy Library Entries dialog box will prompt for the destination library file name (see Fig. 9.8). The procedure and dialog box for moving objects is similar to the procedure for copying entries.

Figure 9.8.
The Copy Library Entries dialog box.

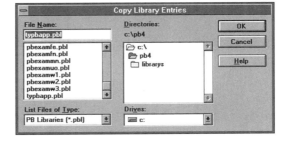

When deleting objects, a confirmation message will prompt for deletion of the object as a precaution box (see Fig. 9.9).

Figure 9.9.
Delete Object Confirmation message box.

Modifying Comments for Libraries and Objects

Comments can be associated with both libraries and objects using the Modify Comments function.

To create or modify the comments for a library, select the library file using the mouse or keyboard and invoke the menu option **L**ibrary | **M**odify Comments (see Fig. 9.10). (Alternatively, using the right mouse button to click on a library file will display a floating menu also containing the **M**odify Comments option.)

Figure 9.10.
The Modify Comments option as selected from the floating library menu.

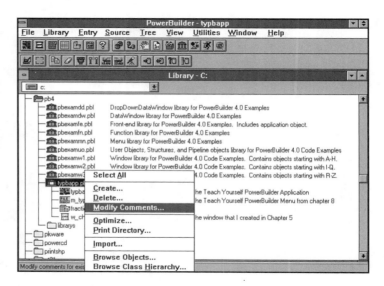

A dialog box like the one in Figure 9.11 will prompt you to enter comments. Use this dialog box to enter some comments that describe the library's scope.

Figure 9.11.
The Modify Library Comments dialog box.

To create or modify the comments for an entry, select the entry using the mouse or keyboard and invoke the menu option **E**ntry | Modi**f**y Comments (see Fig. 9.12). (Alternatively, using the right mouse button to click on an entry will display a floating menu also containing the Modi**f**y Comments option.)

Figure 9.12.
The Modify Comments option as selected from the floating entry menu.

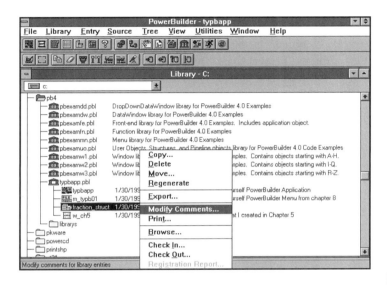

A dialog box like the one in Figure 9.13 will prompt you to enter comments. Use this dialog box to enter some comments that describe the entry's function.

Figure 9.13.
The Modify Library Entry Comments dialog box.

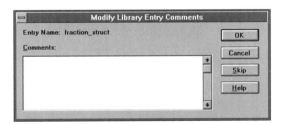

Browsing Objects

As stated at the beginning of this chapter, the logical view deals with the relationships of objects within an application. An example of a logical view is the Application Reference Tree (Expand Branch) feature of the Application Painter that was mentioned in Chapter 3. There, we can view only the objects that make up an application, regardless of the library in which they are stored.

There are three types of object browsers that are accessible from the Library Painter: *Browse Objects* (discussed in Chapter 6, "Putting It All Together"), Browse Class Hierarchy, and Browse Library Entries.

When you start to inherit objects later in the book, you'll notice that a hierarchy of objects (or classes) will emerge, starting with the first ancestor (the superclass) through to the last descendant (subclass). It is often helpful to see the logical view of this class hierarchy during development. Using the Class Browser, which is invoked by using the Library menu option **U**tilities | Browse Class **H**ierarchy, a view of inherited and non-inherited classes in the current application's library list can be displayed by four object types (**M**enu, **S**ystem, **U**ser Object, and **W**indow).

System classes represent those that are hard-coded into the PowerBuilder system; these are the classes you use to create objects of type Window, Menu, Structure, and so on. Note that the Regenerate button is disabled when System object types are being viewed.

Because the Class Browser is intended to be used to view class hierarchies, only the inheritable object types (**M**enu, **U**ser Object, and **W**indow) are appropriate to the view. Other object types like Functions and DataWindows cannot be viewed in the Class Browser because the capability to inherit from them is not supported in PowerBuilder.

Figure 9.14 shows the Class Browser displaying a list "tree" (again like File Manager) of all of the windows in the application library list. Descendant windows are shown as "branches" nested under ancestor windows.

Figure 9.14.
The Class Browser showing the hierarchy of window objects used in the PowerBuilder sample application Exampl40.

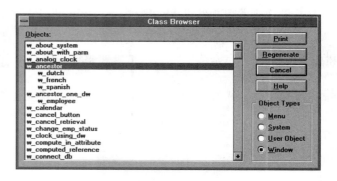

 The Browse Library Entries dialog box looks through an object's (or a group of objects when selected) source code for a specific string, and is invoked by using the Browse PainterBar button or through the **E**ntry | **B**rowse menu option (see Fig. 9.15). (Alternatively, using the right mouse button to click on an entry will display a floating menu also containing the **B**rowse option.) The developer can also limit the scope of the search to just certain areas of the source code (only scripts, attributes, and so on) as well as the information displayed by the search (line numbers, event names, and so on).

Figure 9.15.
The Browse Library Entries looking for the string "title" in the source code of an object.

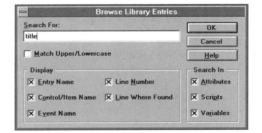

The result of the search for the specific string is shown in Figure 9.16. Here we can see that the string "title" was found in two attributes in the source code for window class w_ch5.

Figure 9.16.
The Matching Library Entries dialog box displays a match in two attributes in window class w_ch5.

Printing Libraries and Objects

Reports of library and object contents can be printed by using the Print Directory and Print functions, respectively.

The Print Directory option is invoked by using the menu option **Library | P**rint Directory (see Fig. 9.17). (Alternatively, using the right mouse button to click on a library file will display a floating menu also containing the **P**rint Directory option.)

A dialog box like the one in Figure 9.18 will prompt you to verify the printing of the correct library. Pressing OK will print the Library Directory report on the default printer.

The Print function is invoked by using the menu option **E**ntry | **P**rint. Alternatively, using the right mouse button to click on an entry will display a menu also containing the Prin**t** option, shown in Figure 9.19.

Figure 9.17.
*The **P**rint Directory option as selected from the floating library menu.*

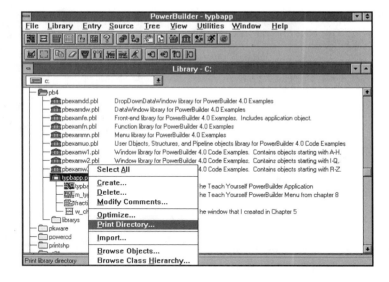

Figure 9.18.
The Print Library Directory dialog box.

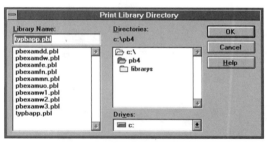

Figure 9.19.
*The Prin**t** option as selected from the entry menu.*

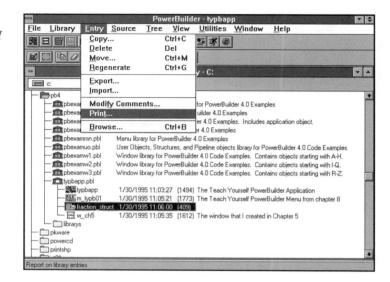

A dialog box like the one in Figure 9.20 will allow you to verify the correct printer, specify the number of report copies, and select components of the entry to include in the report. Be aware that more components selected translates to a more voluminous report!

Figure 9.20.
The Print Options dialog box.

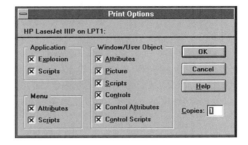

Regenerating and Optimizing Libraries

The Regenerate feature gives developers two methods of operation for manually regenerating p-code for selected library entries.

There are three reasons why Regenerate is used:

☐ An ancestor object has changed

☐ A new release (or build) of PowerBuilder itself has been installed

☐ A library file is suspected to be corrupt

The first method of regeneration is accomplished simply by selecting an object or set of objects and using the Regen PainterBar button or menu option **E**ntry | **R**egenerate. (Alternatively, using the right mouse button to click on an entry will display a floating menu also containing the **R**egenerate option, (as shown in Figure 9.21). Regeneration will then occur, which will revise the object(s) modification date to the current system date and time.

The second regeneration method is to be used when objects in the application are inherited. In an inheritance hierarchy, it is more effective to regenerate p-code using a sequence ordered from ancestor through descendant object. PowerBuilder conveniently provides this method of regeneration from the Class Browser dialog box. The Regenerate button here forces regeneration through the sequence by just selecting the ancestor object.

For example, Figure 9.22 shows ancestor window w_ancestor selected in the Class Browser list. Upon pressing the Regenerate button, PowerBuilder will begin regenerating w_ancestor, then it will continue regenerating w_dutch, w_french, and w_spanish.

Figure 9.21.
*The **Regenerate** option as selected from the floating menu.*

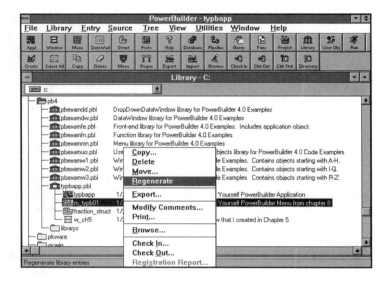

Figure 9.22.
*The Class Browser dialog box with the **Regenerate** button enabled.*

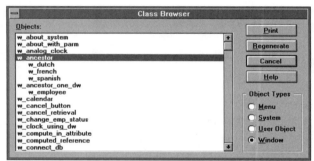

Application development tools like PowerBuilder tend to place heavy demands on disk drives, which are usually the hard drive(s) of the developer's Windows 3.1 workstation and/or server. This dependency results in a lot of disk writing of source code and object code to library files. After many library edits have occurred, particularly when running PowerBuilder in a multi-developer environment, the Optimize function must frequently be used against the library files (see Fig. 9.23).

Optimization replaces the contents of a library file after reorganizing it, like a disk defragmentation program. This ensures integrity and performance during reads and writes to these files.

The Optimize Library option dialog box includes a check box indicating Save Original Library As .BAK File (see Fig. 9.24). When checked, PowerBuilder creates a backup file of the same filename as the library but with the .BAK extension before the optimization takes place. This guarantees recovery of the file if an error occurs during optimization. Developers are advised to use this option at all times.

Figure 9.23.
The Library | Optimize menu option.

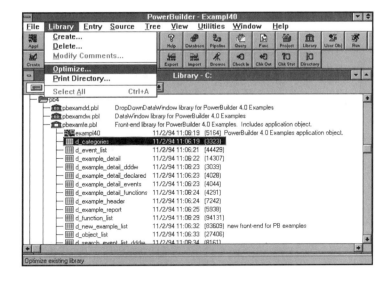

Figure 9.24.
The Optimize Library option dialog box.

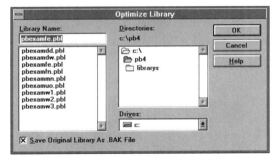

It is good practice to optimize library files just prior to regenerating whole libraries or before generating .EXE files.

Building a PowerBuilder Dynamic Runtime Library (.PBD)

A *PowerBuilder Dynamic Runtime library*, or *.PBD*, is a version of your library containing only the p-code. PBDs are used when you are creating an executable version (.EXE) of a PowerBuilder application that uses objects stored in multiple libraries. PBDs are similar to Windows dynamic-link libraries (.DLLs), but are not compatible with anything except PowerBuilder.

In PowerBuilder version 4.0, the Project Painter automatically generates PowerBuilder Dynamic Runtime libraries, or .PBDs. However, developers can also generate PBDs manually by using the Library Painter's Build Dynamic Library function.

To manually generate a PBD out of a library file (.PBL), select the library file by using the mouse or keyboard and invoke the menu option **U**tilities | Build **D**ynamic Library (see Fig. 9.25).

Figure 9.25.
*The Build **D**ynamic Library menu option.*

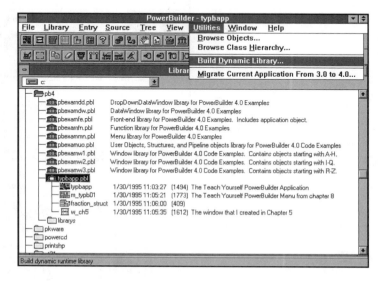

A dialog box like the one in Figure 9.26 will prompt you to verify generation from the correct library. The Resource File Name box with the associated Files button allows the references contained in a PowerBuilder resource file to be compiled into the PBD. Pressing OK will generate the PBD into the same directory path as the original .PBL.

Figure 9.26.
The Build Dynamic Runtime Library dialog box showing "typbapp.pbl" awaiting conversion to a .PBD.

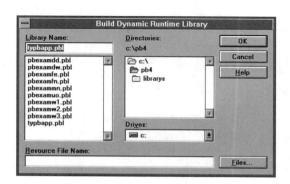

Exporting and Importing

Earlier in the chapter, it was stated that source code was saved in the library in a standard syntactical format. The Export option creates an ASCII file containing the source code for selected library entries and is intended to be used for archiving and version control.

The dialog box shown in Figure 9.27 shows the floating menu bar's **E**xport option highlighting entry w_ch5.

Figure 9.27.
Export floating menu option selected for window w_ch5.

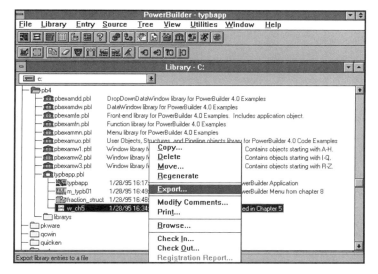

Selecting this option displays the Export Library Entry dialog box, as seen in Figure 9.28.

Figure 9.28.
The Export Library Entry dialog box.

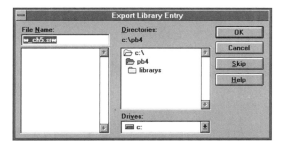

Notice that in the File Name edit box in the Export Library dialog box, PowerBuilder has suggested a name for the export file by using the first eight characters of the object's name, followed by the extension .srw. (This file extension is different for each object type; for example, windows use extension .srw while menus use the extension .srm, and so on.) This file name can be overridden, if desired.

The Import option takes the source code file created by the Export function and automatically regenerates a library object from it. After displaying a file dialog box similar to the one from the Export function, the Import File Into Library Entry dialog box prompts for a destination library to import from (see Fig. 9.29). Note that only those libraries in the current application's library list are displayed.

Figure 9.29.
*The Import File Into
Library Entry dialog box.*

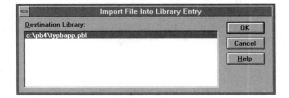

Developing with Others—Check In/Check Out

Neither the Check In nor the Check Out function is critical to teaching yourself PowerBuilder. However, if you are (or are planning to become) a professional developer, you need to acquaint yourself with their capabilities.

The options Check In and Check Out are used when developing PowerBuilder applications in a team environment. The two functions exist to prevent overwrites of objects by disallowing edits to checked-out objects.

Check Out involves copying an object to a private library and placing a "lock" on it so other developers can't make changes to it. Editing takes place on the copy of the object in the private library, which typically resides on a disk only accessible to the developer who checks out the object. The Library Painter includes a facility for the other developers to view the currently checked out objects, and they can also open and copy (but not change) the checked out object.

When an object is checked back into its original library, the original object is replaced with the newly edited copy, and the lock is removed. If for some reason the developer who checked the object out wishes to revert back to an object's original (unchanged) state, s/he can clear the object's check-out status. This option also lets the developer erase or retain the copy of the checked-out object in the private library.

Morning Summary

The Library Painter is similar to the Windows File Manager in that it provides tools for the developer to view and organize the contents of objects and libraries. A PowerBuilder library is a container of PowerBuilder objects and is physically a single DOS file containing three components: the header, the p-code, and the source code.

The arrangement of objects within PowerBuilder libraries is largely dependent on whether or not you plan to use (or have used) PowerBuilder's object Inheritance feature.

There are three types of object browsers that are accessible from the Library Painter: Browse Objects, Browse Class Hierarchy, and Browse Library Entries. The Browse Class Hierarchy dialog box displays inherited and non-inherited classes in the current application's library list by any of four object types. The Browse Library Entries dialog box looks for a specific string in an object's source code.

The Regenerate option offers two methods of manual generation of p-code for selected library entries. Optimization replaces the contents of a library file after reorganizing it, ensuring file integrity and performance.

The Export option creates an ASCII file containing the source code for selected library entries. The Import option takes the same source code and automatically regenerates a library object from it.

The Check In and Check Out functions are used when developing PowerBuilder applications in a team environment. Check Out prevents overwrites of objects by disallowing edits, or "locking," checked-out objects. Check In removes the lock and updates the object to reflect the latest edits.

10

The Multiple
Document
Interface (MDI)

In this chapter, you will learn about the Multiple Document Interface (MDI). You will learn:

☐ What the Multiple Document Interface (MDI) is

☐ How an MDI application works

☐ How to make your application an MDI application

☐ How to make MDI sheets

☐ How to give your MDI application toolbars and menus

An Overview of the Multiple Document Interface

So far, the application that you have built has a main window where all of the action takes place. The menu is directly on the window, as is the toolbar and all of the controls. The window itself is the center of all the action. You may also have other popup windows and response windows to get information from the user, but the application's focus is in the main window of the application.

Some applications, though, have many windows of interest where each window performs a similar function on a different object, or a different function on the same object. For example, in PowerBuilder itself, you open different painters to create different components of your application, like windows and menus. In Microsoft Word, you create and edit different documents. In Microsoft Excel, you create and edit spreadsheets. Each of these applications allows you to open multiple windows at the same time and use each one independently, editing a different object, spreadsheet, or document in each window. Microsoft has built a Windows standard for applications that allow your user to open multiple documents at the same time. They call this standard the *Multiple Document Interface (MDI)*.

According to Microsoft, an application that uses the Multiple Document Interface will always contain a special main window, called an *MDI frame*. Instead of just floating around your Windows desktop, all of the other windows of your application will be limited to the area inside the frame, which is referred to as the *MDI client area*. In other words, they will be children of the MDI frame. Each of these windows is referred to as an *MDI document* or an *MDI sheet*. Although each sheet is completely independent, the user can only edit one sheet at a time. The sheet that is currently being worked on is called the *active sheet*. Even though each sheet can have a menu and toolbar of its own, the menu of the active sheet appears on the menu bar of the frame, and the sheet itself has no menu bar. By the same token, only the active sheet's toolbar appears at any given time. The frame also can have a menu and toolbar of its own, which appears when no sheet is active; however, you can separate the frame's toolbar from the active sheet's toolbar so that it is displayed even if there is a sheet open. For example, the PowerBar in PowerBuilder is a frame toolbar, which is available even when there is a sheet toolbar, a PainterBar, on the screen.

In order to make this transition from a single-document environment to a multiple document environment as smooth as possible, the developers of Windows included several other important standards that help users navigate among MDI sheets. For example, in an MDI application, there is always a menu item on the menu bar called **W**indow. This menu will contain a set of menu items that allow you to quickly arrange the sheets inside your MDI Frame. In general, you can arrange your windows in the following ways:

☐ **Tile:** Tiling will make your MDI sheets fill the area inside the MDI frame completely, but without any one of the sheets overlapping the other (see Fig. 10.1). You can tile your sheets with an inclination toward vertical alignment or horizontal alignment.

Figure 10.1.
Tiled sheets.

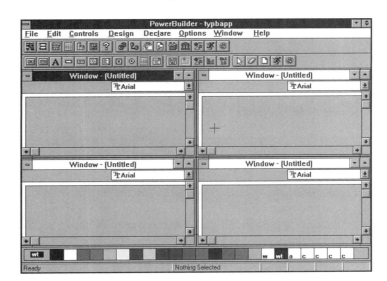

☐ **Layer:** Layering your sheets will make them all size themselves to exactly fit the space inside the MDI client area (see Fig. 10.2). Each window will overlay the next, since they are all the same size, and all in the same position.

☐ **Cascade:** Cascading your sheets will arrange them so that they are all the same size but take up about one eighth of the client area instead of the entire client area. In addition, each sheet is slightly offset from the next so that it is slightly lower and to the right of the one behind it. This way, you can see the title bar of each of the sheets in the arrangement (see Fig. 10.3).

Most single document applications allow you to minimize your main window into an icon that appears at the bottom of the Windows desktop. In an MDI application, you can minimize the MDI frame and have it become a single icon appearing at the bottom of the Windows desktop as well. However, you can also minimize any of the sheets inside the MDI frame, but instead

of appearing at the bottom of the Windows desktop, they appear at the bottom of the MDI client area inside the MDI frame. For this reason, there is generally also a menu item called Arrange **I**cons in the **W**indow menu that allows you to quickly arrange the icons inside the MDI client.

Figure 10.2.
Layered sheets.

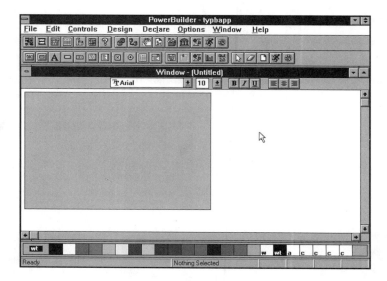

Figure 10.3.
Cascaded sheets.

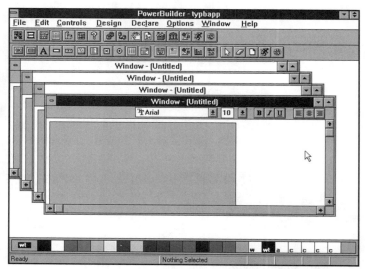

Sometimes other menu items that are not part of the MDI Window standard but are functions that the user performs on windows also appear in the Window menu. Things like **N**ew Window, to open another copy of the same document inside a new window, **S**plit, to split the current window, and so on. This is perfectly acceptable, as long as they fit within your overall menu metaphor.

Finally, beneath the last item in the **W**indow menu appears a list of all of the open documents of the application. Selecting a window from the list of windows on the **W**indow menu makes that sheet become active. Each window listed in the **W**indow menu will be sequentially numbered, and each number will actually be the accelerator key of the menu item. So, if you have seven windows open, the **W**indow menu displays each sheet's name in the list, and each sheets accelerator will be its sequential number: **1** for the first one, **7** for the seventh (see Fig. 10.4). The list allows up to nine windows. If there are more than nine, a tenth item will appear, reading **M**ore Windows.... If you click on this menu item, it will bring up a small dialog box containing a list of the windows that are open, even if there are more than nine. You can select the window you want from this list.

Figure 10.4.
The Window select list.

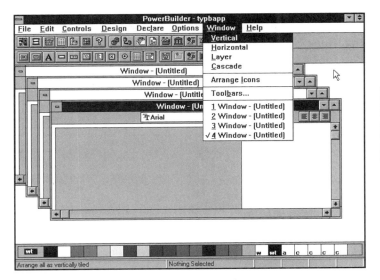

The Control Menu of the MDI Sheet

There are a couple of other important shortcuts that Windows provides to make it more simple to use an MDI application. First, notice that each sheet has a control menu of its very own. In each sheet's control menu, you can Ma**x**imize, Mi**n**imize, **R**estore, **M**ove, and **S**ize the sheet. These functions work just like their counterparts in the MDI frames control menu, except that they adjust the window with respect to the MDI frame and not the Windows desktop. So, as was stated before, minimizing the window turns it into an icon not at the bottom of the

Windows desktop, but at the bottom of the MDI frame. By the same token, maximizing the sheet makes it take up the entire space within the MDI frames client area, as opposed to the entire space on the Windows desktop.

Finally, in each sheet's control menu, the last item is Next Window and has an accelerator key of **Ctrl-F6**. This means that you can quickly switch to the different sheets inside your MDI frame by selecting this menu or by pressing **Ctrl-F6**. Doing so makes the next window in the window list active, bringing it up front, changing the color of its title bar to the active color, and giving one of its controls the focus.

As a prime example of an MDI application, how it works, and its advantages, you can take into consideration PowerBuilder itself. When you first open up PowerBuilder, you are simply staring at an empty screen. In order to actually do anything, you probably will open one of the MDI sheets that you can open in PowerBuilder; for example, a painter. Then, you will begin to do your work inside your painter. Perhaps you will open another painter or two simultaneously and do work in there, too. And with a few exceptions, this is generally a legal operation. You can build your window in one painter, your menu in another, and have your library painter open in the background as well. You can even have two or three different windows open at the same time. This is what MDI is all about—you can open multiple documents and work on them at the same time. As long as the open documents don't depend on each other, you don't even have to save one to switch to the other. You can arrange your documents so that you can see more than one at the same time. The Multiple Document Interface allows the user to be more productive because the menus that the user sees are consistent across all sheets, even though they may not be identical.

The Parts of an MDI Frame

Now that you have been introduced to the MDI standards, let's talk a bit more in depth about the components of the *MDI frame*. In general, an MDI frame will be an empty window with a menu, and perhaps a toolbar and status bar as well. However, for some applications, you may need an MDI frame that also contains other controls on it. When the frame contains no additional controls on it but is simply an empty window, we refer to it in PowerBuilder as a *standard* MDI frame. However, PowerBuilder labels an MDI frame that has controls on it as a *custom* MDI frame. Custom MDI frames are perfectly acceptable, although I recommend avoiding them if at all possible until you have more experience with PowerBuilder. The reason has to do with the *MDI client area*.

The MDI Client Area

The area inside an MDI frame that can contain other windows is called the *MDI client area*. In Windows, the MDI client area is actually itself a control. In PowerBuilder, this control is given the name `mdi_1`. Every MDI frame has an MDI client area, and in PowerBuilder it is always called `mdi_1`. In fact, although it has some special attributes and behaviors that are specific to MDI

client area objects, including the fact that you don't really have control over whether it exists in your window or not, it works in much the same way as any other control in a window. It has attributes and functions that you can modify and execute. For example, you can modify the size and position of the MDI client area if, for some reason, you want your MDI sheets to appear in a space that does not take up the entire MDI frame's window space.

When you create a standard MDI frame, for example, an MDI frame that contains no controls inside it, PowerBuilder automatically manages the size and position of the MDI client area, mdi_1, so that it fits exactly within the space inside the MDI frame. If your user changes the size of the MDI frame, PowerBuilder automatically changes the size of the MDI client area, mdi_1. However, as soon as you place a control inside your MDI frame, it becomes a custom MDI frame, and PowerBuilder can no longer automatically handle the size and position of the MDI client area because the mdi_1 control may overlay the other controls on your MDI frame, hiding them from view. So, when placing controls on your MDI frame, you need to adjust the size and position of mdi_1 yourself. You generally do this in the Resize event of the MDI frame window.

To size the MDI client area inside the MDI frame, you need to first get the size of the area inside the MDI frame. The area inside a window is referred to as the *workspace*, and you can get its height and width by using the functions WorkSpaceHeight() and WorkSpaceWidth(), respectively. After you have the height and width, you can figure out how to calculate the size and width of the MDI client area. Let's take an example. Suppose that you have a static text at the bottom of your MDI frame called st_status, inside which you want to put status messages. You need to size mdi_1 so that it exactly fits within the space from the top of the MDI frame to the top of st_status. Well, in that case, you can set the height of mdi_1 so that it is equal to the Y coordinate of st_status. And then you can set the width of mdi_1 to the WorkSpaceWidth() of the frame. That one is pretty easy. Listing 10.1 shows how you deal with the same situation, except that st_status is at the top of the MDI frame instead of at the bottom. This time, you have to do some calculations based on the height of st_status to get the proper height of mdi_1, and you have to place the top of mdi_1 at the bottom of st_status. In addition, you can let mdi_1 fill the workspace of the MDI frame, and simply move the controls on the MDI frame to the front using the BringToFront attribute. However, this will allow the sheets that you open to cover your controls, which cosmetically may not be desired.

Listing 10.1. Sizing the MDI client area.

```
int li_Width, li_Height
// Get the size of the workspace
li_Width = WorkSpaceWidth()
li_Height = WorkSpaceHeight()
// Calculate workspace left after the bottom
// of the static text.
li_Height = li_Height - ( st_status.y + st_status.height)
// Move the the client area to the bottom of the static text.
Move (mdi_1, 0, st_status.y + st_status.height)
// Resize the client area.
Resize (mdi_1, li_Width, li_Height)
```

It is very important that you recognize that the space in which your MDI sheets can reside is the MDI client area, `mdi_1`, and not the workspace of the MDI frame. In a standard MDI frame, of course, these are the same. However, in a custom MDI frame, they are different, and the MDI client area may not take up the entire workspace of the frame. And so, in a custom MDI frame, you have to position and adjust the MDI client area yourself.

Microhelp

In our last example, I cited one reason you may need to use a custom MDI frame. That was to create a status bar at the bottom of the MDI frame; a feature which is commonplace in Windows MDI applications, and is almost in itself an MDI standard. If your users want a status bar, they are probably not out of their minds, but are in fact very reasonable. As a matter of fact, even PowerBuilder itself has a status bar! Does this mean that any time you create an MDI frame you need to use a custom MDI frame so that you can place a status bar in your frame?

Of course not! The people at Powersoft had some insight into the fact that many, if not most, MDI frames have status bars on them, and the status bars can be easily integrated into the MDI frame itself because they themselves follow certain standards. And so, they created a different style of standard MDI frame, called the *MDI frame with Microhelp*, which allows you to create a standard MDI frame with a status bar, without the headache of having to manage the MDI client area yourself. They refer to the status bar as the *Microhelp Bar*, and so from now on I will use the same terminology.

When you create an MDI frame with Microhelp, PowerBuilder creates a pretty, three-dimensional, one-line status bar at the bottom of your MDI frame. It then automatically sizes the client area so that it fits inside the workspace of the MDI frame, minus the height of the Microhelp bar. In other words, the Microhelp bar itself is not covered in the MDI client area, `mdi_1`. In this way, you can have your MDI Microhelp inside your application without having to expend too much effort on maintaining it.

If you remember yesterday, we mentioned Microhelp when we talked about the Menu Painter. Each menu item has an attribute called Microhelp. You can type in text that you want to appear on your frame's Microhelp bar when your user selects that menu item (or clicks on that toolbar item), and PowerBuilder automatically handles that for you. So, just as in PowerBuilder, you can have your menu items be truly very friendly by explaining themselves on the Microhelp bar, and you can do it with little or no effort. This is one way to get text onto the Microhelp bar.

When you first start up an application that contains an MDI frame with Microhelp, the Microhelp bar will simply display the word Ready. In addition, any time your user clicks on a menu item that does not have any text in its Microhelp attribute, or if the user clicks in between two menu items, the Microhelp bar displays the word Ready. This is the default text on the Microhelp bar and appears at different times. You can change the default text of the Microhelp bar by changing the value of the `MicroHelpDefault` attribute of the application. In addition, you can read in the value of this attribute and manually display it to your user when you complete a task. But you haven't yet learned how to do that, now have you?

The last, and most important method of placing text on your Microhelp bar is manually, by using the `SetMicroHelp()` function. The `SetMicroHelp()` function takes one parameter, and that is a string representing the text to be displayed on the Microhelp bar. This function can only be used on an MDI frame with Microhelp window; otherwise, it returns an error. However, because most MDI frames have little or no functionality, this function is probably called instead from an MDI sheet. In that case, you need to find out the name of the MDI frame in your application and call the function for the MDI frame window and not the current window. You can do this either by specifying the name of the MDI frame window as a quasi-parameter in front of the first parameter of the function call, as in

```
SetMicroHelp( w_mdi_frame, This is the microhelp message)
```

Or you can specify the window name in front of the function name, followed by a period, as follows:

```
w_mdi_frame.SetMicroHelp( This is the microhelp message)
```

Either notation is acceptable, and we'll talk more in detail about why you might use one notation over the other in the next lesson, when we talk about Object Oriented Software Construction.

Making an MDI Frame for Your Application

Now its time to actually build an MDI frame for your application. Open up the Window Painter by pressing **Shift-F2** or by clicking on the Window Painter button on the PowerBar. Create a new window by clicking on the **New** button on the Open Window dialog box. The Window Painter opens with an empty Window inside. Double-click on the window to edit the Window Style attributes, and enter the following title:

`Teach Yourself PowerBuilder`

Then, click on the Menu check box, and the menu we created yesterday, `m_typb_01`, should automatically appear in the drop-down list box portion. If it doesn't, select it from the drop-down list box. Finally, turn on all of the check boxes and change the window type to an MDI frame with Microhelp. When you are done, press the **OK** button to accept the changes. Now, open the Window Position dialog box either by selecting Window **P**osition from the **D**esign menu, or by right-clicking on the window and selecting **P**osition... from there. Have your application open the MDI frame right into the Maximized state by choosing the Maximize radio button from the Initial State group of radio buttons. Then, click on the **OK** button to accept that change. Finally, save your frame as `w_mdi_frame` by choosing **S**ave from the **F**ile menu. As the comment, enter

`The Teach Yourself PowerBuilder MDI Frame (Ch. 10)`

When Saving a MDI frame need to assign a menu

215

Congratulations! You have just built your MDI frame! If you want to see how it looks, you can preview it by selecting Preview from the Design menu. Your MDI frame should appear and look very much like the window that you see in Figure 10.5.

Figure 10.5.
Previewing your MDI frame.

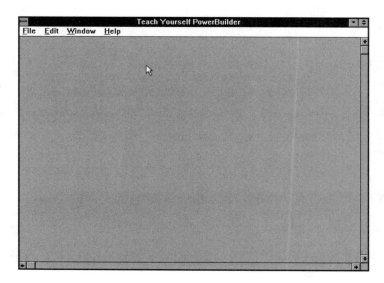

Feel free to change the size and position of the window if you like. You can even change any other attributes that you find interesting. However, for now, don't place any controls on the window. Let's leave this as a standard MDI frame for this example. When you are satisfied with your MDI frame, you may save it and close the Window Painter.

Opening Your Frame when You Run

Now, let's link the MDI frame into your application so that it opens when you run. Open up the Application Painter by pressing **Shift-F1** or by clicking on the Application Painter button on the PowerBar. Edit the application's script either by selecting Script from the Edit menu or by clicking on the Script Painter icon on the Application PainterBar. If you remember, in Chapter 5, we placed code in the Application Painter to open the w_ch5 window. Let's modify that code so that your MDI frame opens instead. Delete the word w_ch5 from the line of code that currently exists in your Application Open Script. Replace that word with the name of your MDI frame, w_mdi_frame. When you are finished, your Application Open Script should look something like this:

```
Open( w_mdi_frame)
```

That's all there is to it! Its really that simple. Instead of opening the window from Chapter 5 when you run your application, it will now open your MDI frame window. If you don't believe me, try it! Close your script painter by selecting **R**eturn from the **F**ile menu or by clicking on the Return to Application button on the Script PainterBar. Then, run your application by either selecting **R**un from the **F**ile menu or by clicking on the Run button on the PowerBar. Your MDI frame will now open, maximized to fill the entire screen, with nothing in it but a menu bar, toolbar, and Microhelp bar (see Fig. 10.6). The word Ready should appear on the Microhelp bar. If you placed Microhelp messages in the items on your menu bar, you can select a menu item or toolbar item and see its description appear on the Microhelp bar, instead.

Figure 10.6.
Your new MDI frame.

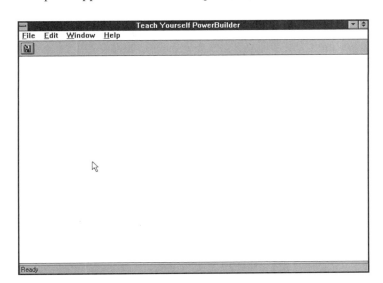

Give yourself a few minutes to calm down from the excitement of setting up this MDI frame window, and then go ahead and close it by selecting E**x**it from your **F**ile menu. Wait a minute! Nothing happened! Of course nothing happened! There's no code in the Clicked event of the E**x**it menu to get triggered when you click on it! Are you stuck? Of course not! Remember, you can close any window, including this MDI frame, by choosing **C**lose from the Control menu, or by just double-clicking on the Control menu. Go ahead and do that, and you should be returned to the Application Painter. Close up the Application Painter, and let's move on.

Creating MDI Sheets

So your application now opens the MDI frame. But there's more to an application than the MDI frame. In fact, if you haven't already figured it out, the MDI frame is probably one of the least complex components of your application from a coding standpoint, especially if you are using

a standard MDI frame. However, the MDI frame itself is the center of your MDI application. It is the almighty Window of Windows, lord of all of the other windows in your MDI application. In almost all MDI applications, all of the windows in your application will be opened either by the MDI frame itself, or by a window that was opened by the MDI frame. From a development standpoint, the MDI frame is the parent of all of the other windows. Perhaps not directly—perhaps there is a chain of windows, each successively opened by the window before it in the chain. But eventually, if you follow that parental chain back to the top, you will find the MDI frame. The MDI frame is center stage for your application, not only visually but programmatically.

In fact, this is one of the beauties of the MDI frame. To end your application, all you have to do is close it. Then, it will close all of its children, who will close all of their children, and so on, and so on. Windows deals with this for you so that you don't have to be bothered.

Note: Where do window children come from? Well, it all starts with a bird, a bee, and a flower. Oh, wait...sorry, wrong story.

Actually, whenever you open a window, it is a child of either another window or the Microsoft Windows desktop itself. If you open the window as a main window, or as an MDI frame, it becomes a child of the Desktop. If you open the window from another window, it becomes a child of that window. In addition, however, you can open the window as a child of a different window by specifying that windows name in the Open command. A single window can have many children, but only one parent.

One feature of a child window is that it must close before its parent can. Before any window closes, either as a result of user input or otherwise, it attempts to close all of its children first. So, if you want to make your windows close automatically when another window closes, open it as a child window.

Making the Frame Open Sheets

Earlier, we talked about how to make your windows open from your script by using the Open() function. However, MDI sheets are opened by using a special Open command. Because of the way Windows handles MDI applications, instead of just setting your MDI sheet to an MDI sheet Window type, you actually can make your MDI sheets any style except MDI frame and open them with the special OpenSheet() function, and they will become MDI sheets. The OpenSheet() function requires several arguments. The first argument, of course, is the name of the sheet to open. Lets have your MDI frame open the w_ch5 window as an MDI sheet.

Open up the Menu Painter by pressing **Shift-F3** or by clicking on the Menu Painter button on the PowerBar. Select your menu, m_typb_01, from the Open Menu dialog box. This opens the menu you created yesterday into your Menu Painter. Click on your **O**pen menu item under the **F**ile menu. Edit the script either by selecting **S**cript from the **E**dit menu, or by clicking on the Script Painter button on the toolbar. Enter the following line of code into the script for the clicked event of the **O**pen menu item.

```
OpenSheet( w_ch5, w_mdi_frame)
```

Return to the Menu Painter, by selecting **R**eturn from the **F**ile menu or by clicking on the Return to Menu Painter icon on the Script PainterBar. This is the basic method of opening an MDI sheet. However, there are other parameters that the OpenSheet() function can take. We'll talk more about these other parameters in a moment. For now, though, let's take a look and see how this works.

Run your application by selecting **R**un from the **F**ile menu or by clicking on the Run icon on the PowerBar. Your MDI frame should open up as the application's main window. Select **O**pen from the **F**ile menu and amazingly your w_ch5 window from Chapter 5 should open up inside your MDI frame. Its size and shape, though, may be different than the way you left it. That's because by default, when you open an MDI sheet, it immediately cascades the window to the default MDI sheet size, unless you specify otherwise. We'll talk about how to do that in just a moment.

First, though, click on the **W**indow menu. The last menu item that you created was Arrange **I**cons. However, under the Arrange **I**cons menu item, there is a separator bar and the title of the w_ch5 window. Whenever you open an MDI sheet, PowerBuilder automatically places your sheet's title right on the menu. By default, the OpenSheet() function assumes that the menu on which you want to place the window list is the second-to-last menu. If you follow Windows standard, it is likely that this is the case. However, if for some reason you want your window list to appear somewhere else, you can override the placement of your sheet list by specifying a third parameter to the OpenSheet() function. Specify the third parameter to the OpenSheet() function as the sequential number of the menu item that should contain the sheet list. For example, in your case, the **F**ile menu is number 1, the **E**dit menu is number 2, and so on. If for some reason you want your sheet list to appear under the **E**dit menu instead of the **W**indow menu, you simply code the **O**pen of that sheet as follows:

```
OpenSheet( w_ch5, w_mdi_frame, 2)
```

This opens w_ch5 as a sheet inside w_mdi_frame and places the sheet list in the second menu bar menu item, which in your case is the **E**dit menu.

If you recall, I also mentioned that by default when you open a sheet inside PowerBuilder, the size of the window is determined internally by Windows as the default size for an MDI sheet for cascading purposes. What if you have created an MDI sheet, and you **don't want** Windows to change the size of the sheet when it opens? Well, fortunately, the OpenSheet() function offers a fourth parameter that you can use to override this behavior. You can specify as the fourth parameter any one of the following Enumerated datatypes:

☐ **Cascaded!:** This is the default, and specifying this parameter enables the default behavior described earlier.

☐ **Layered!:** This causes the sheet to be automatically layered when you open it.

☐ **Original!:** This causes the sheet to open at its original size: the size it was when you saved it.

Remember, that in order to specify the fourth parameter, you must specify the third as well. So, if you change your `OpenSheet()` call in your **File|O**pen menu to read as follows,

```
OpenSheet( w_ch5, w_mdi_frame, 0, Original!)
```

your `w_ch5` sheet will open as normal, without resizing it at all. Specifying `0` as the third parameter—the menu number to use for the sheet list—makes PowerBuilder place the sheet list in the second-to-last menu item on the menu bar. I use this function call quite frequently because most of my users like their windows to come up in the same size that they were developed. You will probably find yourself using this function call quite frequently, too.

There is one more optional parameter, the *window class* parameter, for the `OpenSheet()` function, which you can use to dynamically open multiple instances of the same window or a window whose class type is determined at runtime. The way in which you do this is to declare a variable of type `window`, and open that variable instead of the window itself. Then, as the second parameter, specify a string containing the class of the window that you want to open. Listing 10.2 demonstrates this technique.

Listing 10.2. Dynamically opening the `w_ch5` window.

```
Window  lw_sheet
String  LCS_WIN_TYPE = "w_ch5"
OpenSheet( lw_sheet, LCS_WIN_TYPE, w_mdi_frame, 0, Original!)
```

By placing the code in Listing 10.2 inside your **O**pen menu in `m_typb_01`, you will be able to open multiple copies of the `w_ch5` window inside your MDI frame. You could even change the value of the `LCS_WIN_TYPE` variable to another window class name, and it will open an instance of that window instead. We will talk more about why this works tomorrow. In the meantime, be aware that you can do this. You will find it a very useful technique.

Note: You can allow your user to arrange all open sheets in any of these formats, even after they are open. In general, this functionality is offered to the user when the user selects items from the Window menu of the frame. Generally, the Window menu has several items under it, specifically Tile, Layer, Cascade, Arrange Icons, and sometimes Tile Horizontal. PowerBuilder has a function that allows you to rearrange the sheets in any of these formats with a single function call. This function is the `ArrangeSheets()` function. To arrange the sheets on the window as Layered, simply code the following line:

```
ArrangeSheets( w_mdi_frame, Layer!)
```

Notice, by the way, that the message to arrange the sheets is sent to the MDI frame and not to any particular sheet. The MDI frame internally finds all of its sheets and arranges them properly in the format specified by the second parameter. Valid formats are `Layer!`, `Cascade!`, `Tile!`, `Icons!`, and `TileHorizontal!`. We'll actually put this function into our MDI menu in the Putting PowerBuilder into Action section at the end of this lesson.

Finding Open Sheets

Once you have multiple MDI sheets open, you may find it necessary to find out which sheet is currently active. To do this, you can use the `GetActiveSheet()` function. The format for this function is simply

```
<MDI Frame Window>.GetActiveSheet()
```

It returns a handle to the sheet that is currently active inside the MDI frame. You can store the result inside a Window variable or use it directly.

In addition to getting the currently active window, you can also use the `GetFirstSheet()` and `GetNextSheet()` functions to navigate through the list of MDI sheets in the MDI frame. This list is the same list that you see in the **W**indow menu of the frame. The `GetFirstSheet()` function returns a handle to the first sheet in the list. The format for the function is identical to the `GetActiveSheet()` function; that is, it has no parameters. The `GetNextSheet()` function returns a handle to the next sheet in the list. You pass to it the window whose next sheet you want to find. This does not have to be the first sheet or even the active sheet; but if you do not pass a valid sheet or if there is no next sheet, the window returned will be invalid. You can use these functions, for example, to navigate through each of the copies of `w_ch5` window that you opened.

Using MDI Menus

When you open the `w_ch5` window, the only menu that appears is on the MDI frame's menu bar. In addition, because you set `w_ch5`s menu to be the same menu as the frame's menu, `m_typb_01`, the menu bar is the same whether or not the sheet is opened. However, in real life, you probably will not use the same menu for both your frame and your sheet. In fact, you will probably have slightly different menus for all of your windows.

10

Planning Your Menus

When you plan out which menus your windows will have, you must consider several issues. First of all, there are some menus that will be available from all of your windows. For example, you will probably be able to open a new sheet, regardless of which sheet you are looking at. You will probably be able to exit the application, no matter where in the system you are. You will probably be able to arrange your sheets, regardless of which sheets are open. And surely, you will be able to get to the help index, regardless of what you are doing in the system.

For this reason, it is likely that many of your menu items will be available at all times within your application (see Fig. 10.7). The menu shell that you created in the recent lesson about menus actually contains mostly functions that are globally available. However, some of the functions will not make sense if you are looking at an empty frame.

Let's make a new frame menu that looks like the menu that already exists. However, this frame menu will be a menu that you will use when the frame is empty and has no open sheets inside. So, some of the menu items won't make sense. For now, just copy the menu and turn off the menu items that you are not interested in by making them invisible. In the next lesson, you'll learn of a technique that you can use instead of copying, called *inheriting*, that is actually a better way of implementing this feature.

Open the menu painter by pressing **Shift-F3** or by clicking on the Menu Painter button on the PowerBar. Open your menu, m_typb_01. Select Save **A**s from the **F**ile menu. This prompts you to enter the name of the menu to save. Enter

`m_tpb_frame`

and enter the following comment:

`The copied frame menu`

and save the menu. Then, go ahead and click on your **C**lose menu item. The little hand should point to it. Click on the Visible check box so that it is unchecked. Do the same for each of the next three menu items: for the separator bar, **S**ave menu item, and Save **A**s menu item. Skip the next two items and then make the Print Preview and **P**rint menu items invisible. If you like, preview your menu and notice that the **F**ile menu looks somewhat smaller and the items that you asked to be invisible are invisible.

Now, let's turn off the rest of the wasteful menu items. Since this menu is for use in an empty MDI frame, there is no need for any of the **E**dit menu functions, so let's turn off the entire **E**dit menu. Select the **E**dit menu on the menu bar, and then uncheck the Visible check box. In fact, since there are no sheets, you don't need a **W**indow menu either. Turn off the **W**indow menu by clicking on it and unchecking the Visible check box. Now, preview your menu, even if you have just before.

Figure 10.7.
The MDI frames menu.

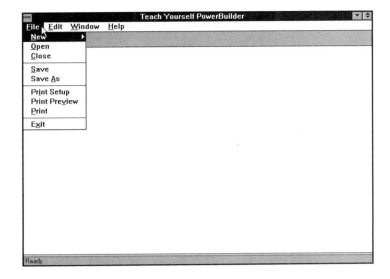

Now, let's learn about how you can implement this menu scheme so that there is a different menu displayed when a sheet is open versus when the frame is empty.

Frame Menus and Sheet Menus

First, you need to spend a moment to understand how MDI menus work. When you open your MDI frame, it will probably have a menu. You may not want it to have a menu, but implementing an MDI frame without a menu is not a very good idea. The reason this is the case is because of how Windows handles the menus of MDI sheets.

When you open the MDI frame, its menu appears on the menu bar. This is relatively normal as far as windows and menus go, so I won't dwell on it too much. However, when you open an MDI sheet, its menu is placed on the menu bar of the MDI **frame**, not the sheet itself. When you open another MDI sheet, its menu also appears on the MDI frame. When you have multiple MDI sheets open, the menu of the active sheet will appear on the frame. If you switch to a different sheet, its menu will appear. If you close all of the sheets, the empty frame's menu returns. This is what happens when each sheet has its own menu.

However, if you have sheets without menus, when you open them, the current menu on the MDI frame remains, even if the menu is left over from a previous MDI sheet! And in fact, internally, things can sometimes get out of whack if you have some sheets with menus and other sheets without menus. Therefore, the rule of thumb is that if you need menus for any of your MDI sheets in an application, you should place menus in **all** of your MDI sheets for that application. In addition, you should always place a menu in your MDI frame.

Remember, of course, that each sheet can have its own distinct menu, and you give your sheets menus in the same way you have already learned—simply by assigning the menu to the window in the Window Styles dialog box. Let's give your MDI frame window its new menu to illustrate the affects. Open the Window Painter by pressing **Shift-F2** or by clicking on the Window Painter button on the PowerBar. Open the w_mdi_frame window by selecting it from the Open Window dialog box. Double-click on w_mdi_frame in the Window Painter to bring up the Window Styles dialog box. The Menu check box should still be checked, but the m_typb_01 menu should be selected. Instead, select the new m_tpb_frame menu from the menu drop-down list box. When you're finished, click the **OK** button and save the frame. Run the application by selecting **R**un from the **F**ile menu or by clicking on the Run button on the toolbar. Flip through the MDI frame's menu now and notice that it looks quite different—the items that you made invisible no longer appear. Now, open the sheet by selecting **O**pen from your **F**ile menu. Notice how now the menu changes to look more like the one you created originally. Close the sheet and notice that the frame's menu returns.

DO	DON'T

DO Create a menu for your MDI frame window if you are using menus in any of your sheets.

DON'T Create some sheets without menus and others with menus in the same MDI application.

MDI Toolbars

Perhaps you have also noticed that there are two toolbars on the MDI frame when you open the sheet. The first one is for the frame, and the second one is for the sheet. Right now, they look the same. However, they are taken from the menu of the frame and active sheet, respectively. This allows you to create a separate toolbar for menu items that are globally available versus functions that are only available for a specific sheet. Wait a minute, that sounds somewhat familiar, doesn't it? Yes, that's right! It works just like the PowerBar and the PainterBars. In fact, if you open multiple sheets, only the active sheet's toolbar will appear. When you switch to a different sheet by making it active, its toolbar will replace the previous sheet's toolbar.

Good candidates for items that can appear on the frame's toolbar are items like the Sheet Arrangement items that appear inside the **W**indow menu, like **L**ayer and **C**ascade, the **H**elp functions, **F**ile|**N**ew, and **F**ile|**O**pen. Because these types of functions are available all the time, or at least most of the time, there is no reason to place them on every toolbar. Then, you can save space on the sheet toolbars and place only sheet-related buttons on those toolbars.

It is possible, of course, that you might not want two toolbars. After all, some users just get confused by so many toolbars. If this is the case, you can eliminate this problem by making the name of the two toolbars the same. If you recall, when you make a toolbar float, it has a title bar just like most windows do, and in that title bar is a name. You can change this name in your code using the Application Objects `ToolbarFrameTitle` and `ToolbarSheetTitle` attributes. For example, in your application script, you can say

```
ToolbarFrameTitle = Frame Toolbar
ToolbarSheetTitle = Sheet Toolbar
```

In fact, you can even modify these attributes from your windows; however, to do this, you must specify the name of the application object itself because it is an attribute of the application.

If both the Frame Title and the Sheet Title are the same, however, the frame toolbar will be replaced by the active sheet's toolbar when any sheet is open, effectively producing a single toolbar. Of course, when there are no sheets open, the frame's toolbar will appear. This technique can be used to develop applications that only have one toolbar instead of two.

> **Note:** Alternatively, you can make a toolbar invisible by changing the `ToolbarVisible` attribute of the toolbar's parent Window to `FALSE`. So, if you want to turn off the MDI frame's toolbar, you can do so by setting the frame's `ToolbarVisible` attribute to `FALSE`. You can even let the frame check to see if there are any sheets open by using the `GetActiveSheet()` and `IsValid()` functions. If the `GetActiveSheet()` function returns an invalid value, there are no sheets open within the frame, and you can display the frame's toolbar. Otherwise, you can turn off the frame's toolbar because there is a sheet open whose toolbar will be visible. The following line of code demonstrates this technique.
>
> ```
> w_mdi_frame.ToolbarVisible = NOT IsValid( w_mdi_frame.GetActiveSheet())
> ```
>
> The `IsValid()` function returns a boolean value, and the `NOT` keyword flips it to the opposite. So, if the active sheet is valid, the `ToolbarVisible` is `NOT TRUE`, which is `FALSE`.

10

Afternoon Summary

The Multiple Document Interface (MDI) is a standard Microsoft Windows interface that allows you to develop applications with multiple, independent documents open at the same time. Applications like Microsoft Word, Microsoft Excel, and even PowerBuilder itself are MDI applications. The Multiple Document Interface implements certain standards to make applications that use this interface look and feel the same. There are several components of an MDI

application that are introduced as a result of this standard. First, you need a main window wherein all of your documents may reside. This window is referred to as the *MDI frame*. Inside of this frame, you may open multiple documents called *sheets*, each of which are independent but probably related. Human beings can only interact with one window at a time, and so the sheet that is currently being worked with in an MDI application is referred to as the *active sheet*. The menu of the active sheet appears not on the menu bar of the sheet but on the menu bar of the MDI frame. The toolbar of the active sheet also appears inside the MDI frame and not on the sheet itself.

Because MDI applications allow you to work with multiple sheets, there are generally functions on the menu to arrange the sheets in different ways. These menu items appear in the Window menu and allow you to tile, cascade, and layer your MDI sheets, as well as arrange your icons. Some applications even let you split your window or open new copies of the same window. There is also a list of open MDI documents inside the Window menu. You can switch to any sheet by selecting it from the Window list. In addition, each window has its own control menu where you can minimize, maximize, restore, and close the window. You can also switch to the next window in the list. PowerBuilder itself is an MDI application and having played around with it quite a bit now, you probably have already used a number of the features that come with an MDI application.

An MDI frame is actually composed of several parts. Inside the MDI frame is the MDI client area, which is the area inside which sheets can appear. In a *standard* MDI frame, the client area fills the inside of the MDI frame completely and automatically. In a *custom* MDI frame, because you have your own controls in the MDI frame's window workspace, you also need to size the MDI client area yourself. You do this by referring to it like any other object in PowerBuilder, with the name `mdi_1`. You can find out the size of the MDI frames workspace by using the `WorkSpaceHeight()` and `WorkSpaceWidth()` functions. In addition, the MDI frame may have a status bar. In PowerBuilder, the status bar is referred to as the Microhelp bar. Of course, in order for a Microhelp bar to appear, your MDI frame must be an MDI frame with Microhelp style.

When you use an MDI frame with Microhelp, PowerBuilder displays the text that is in the Microhelp attribute of your menu items on the frames Microhelp bar automatically when the user selects a menu item. In addition, PowerBuilder will place the word `Ready` on the Microhelp bar when there is no other text to place there. You can change this text by changing the value of the `MicroHelpDefault` attribute of the application. You can also place text on the Microhelp bar by using the `SetMicroHelp()` function in the MDI frame window, passing to it the text that you want to have appear on the Microhelp bar.

All that you have to do to create an MDI frame is create a window whose style is MDI frame or MDI frame with Microhelp. Then, you can have your application open the frame. However, you have to take some special measures to have your frame open MDI sheets. There is no MDI sheet window style. Instead, you create with one of the other window styles, usually Main or Child, and open them from the MDI frame (or its menu) by using the `OpenSheet()` function.

The OpenSheet() function takes four arguments: the name of the sheet to open, the name of the frame that will be its parent, the position of the sheet list on the menu, and the manner in which to open the sheet. The last two parameters are optional.

In an MDI application, the MDI frame's menu appears as you expect, on the MDI frame's menu bar. However, the MDI sheet's menu also appears on the MDI frame's menu bar. The MDI frames menu bar always displays the active sheet's menu. Also, only the active sheet's toolbar appears. By default, the MDI frame's toolbar and MDI sheet's toolbar are separate, like they are in PowerBuilder itself. However, you can make your application have only one toolbar by giving the frame's toolbar and the sheet's toolbar the same title. The titles are controlled as attributes of the Application Object—ToolbarFrameTitle and ToolbarSheetTitle. You can make a toolbar invisible by using the ToolbarVisible attribute of the window.

Q&A

Q What is the difference between a physical view and a logical view of objects?

A The physical view looks at the contents and arrangement of objects in a library disk file. The logical view looks at the contents and arrangement of objects in an application.

Q Help! I've pressed the Enter key while an entry was selected or double-clicked on; now I'm no longer in the Library Painter. What happened, and how do I get back?

A For convenience, the Library Painter launches other PowerBuilder painters that are associated with selected entries. If you have launched a painter, just close it to return to the Library Painter. Alternatively, you may use the menu option **W**indow to get back to the Library Painter without closing the launched painter.

Q Why are libraries limited to 50 or fewer objects and a file size of less than 600KB? Why are Powersoft's recommended limits larger?

A These limitations are based on experience developing PowerBuilder applications in a wide range of environments. The recommendations given by Powersoft are indeed more liberal than those in this book; but because objects can grow very large in an enterprise application, it is better to err on the conservative size to avoid problems.

Q Why does the Class Browser only let me see my windows, menus, and user objects and not my functions or DataWindows?

A The Class Browser is intended to be a tool to facilitate object-oriented programming (OOP). Because PowerBuilder does not support inheritance (an OOP concept) of function, DataWindow, structure, and other types of objects, their inclusion in the Class Browser would have been inappropriate. Instead, the Application Reference Tree (Expand Branch) option in the Application Painter should be used for a full logical view of application objects.

Q **I created an MDI frame, and it is opened as the main window for my application. But, when I open my MDI sheets, they don't show up? What is going on?**

A Remember, MDI sheets are not opened inside of an MDI frame but inside of the MDI client area that is contained inside the MDI frame. If you place **any** control **anywhere** on the MDI frame, it becomes a custom MDI frame, and the MDI client area, mdi_1, must be sized manually in the Resize event of the MDI frame. If you do not resize mdi_1, there is no visible MDI client area in the MDI frame window. When you open the sheet, it does in fact open in the MDI client area, but because you can't see the MDI client area, you can't see the sheets inside of it. To resolve this, either remove all controls from the MDI frame or place script in the frame's Resize event that will resize mdi_1.

Q **Some very weird things are happening in my application. I select menu items from my MDI menu or toolbar, and the results that appear on-screen are from a sheet that is open, but not active (for example, behind another window). How do I get my menus to work properly?**

A This problem is a symptom of an MDI application with menus assigned to some sheets, but not all. Here's what happens. You open your first MDI sheet, and its menu takes over on the MDI frame's menu bar. Now, you open a second MDI sheet, except this one does not have a menu assigned to it. Because this is an MDI application, the menu on the menu bar will be the one that belongs to the last active sheet that has a menu. So, the current menu belongs to the sheet that you opened first. If inside that menu there are references to the ParentWindow of the menu, they will resolve not to the active sheet, but to the sheet that is in fact the parent of this menu—the one that you opened first. This is one of the reasons you must always create a menu for all MDI sheets in an MDI application, including the frame.

Workshop

Quiz

1. How do I delete a library?
2. How do you create an MDI sheet? What is the Window Type of an MDI sheet?
3. Which common sheet arrangement types **cannot** be used as the initial arrangement sheet type of an MDI sheet?

Putting PowerBuilder into Action

1. Click on the Library Painter button in the PowerBar now to open a Library Painter window. Create a new library called typbapp2.pbl in the c:\pb4 directory.

2. Give library `typbapp2.pbl` the comment `Temporary library for Chapter 9 exercises`.

3. Select the window entry `w_ch5` from the library `typbapp.pbl`. Copy this object to `typbapp2.pbl`. Now close and reopen the `typbapp2.pbl` library to refresh the view of `typbapp2.pbl` to ensure that the window was correctly copied.

4. Repeat Step 2, copying the entries `fraction_struct` and `m_typb01` from the library `typbapp.pbl` into `typbapp2.pbl`.

5. Give the entry `fraction_struct` in library `typbapp2.pbl` the comment `This is a temporary structure`.

6. Regenerate all the entries in library `typbapp2.pbl`. (Hint: Use the Select All menu option from the floating library file menu.)

7. Optimize the library `typbapp2.pbl`.

8. Build a PowerBuilder Dynamic Runtime library (PBD) from library `typbapp2.pbl`. (Don't fill in the Resource File Name box.) Using the Windows File Manager, verify that the PBD was created in the same directory path as the original library.

9. Export entry `w_ch5` from the library `typbapp2.pbl` by using the Export dialog box defaults for file name and directory path. Using the Windows Notepad or another text editor, look at the contents of the export file to see the syntactical layout of `w_ch5`'s source code. Jot down or remember this file name and path because you'll be using it again.

10. Delete `w_ch5` from the library `typbapp2.pbl`.

11. Import entry `w_ch5` from the file you specified in Exercise 8. (Ensure that you are importing this source code back into `typbapp2.pbl`.) View library `typbapp2.pbl` to verify that the object imported successfully.

10

12. Open the ~~`m_typb_frame`~~ m_typb_01 menu in the Menu Painter. Edit the script for the Tile **H**orizontal menu item under the **W**indow menu. Place the following code inside that menu.

```
ArrangeSheets( w_mdi_frame, TileHorizontal!)
```

13. Place the following code inside the Tile **V**ertical menu item under the **W**indow menu.

```
ArrangeSheets( w_mdi_frame, Tile!)
```

14. Place the following code inside the **L**ayer menu item under the **W**indow menu.

```
ArrangeSheets( w_mdi_frame, Layer!)
```

15. Place the following code inside the **C**ascade menu item under the **W**indow menu.

```
ArrangeSheets( w_mdi_frame, Cascade!)
```

16. Place the following code inside the Arrange **I**cons menu item under the **W**indow menu.

```
ArrangeSheets( w_mdi_frame, Icons!)
```

17. Try it out! Run the application, open a few sheets, and see how it works. Minimize some sheets and try the Arrange **I**cons menu item.

Chapter

11

An Introduction to Object-Oriented Software Construction

In this chapter, you will learn:

- [ ] The meaning of the key terms that are used to describe and explain object-oriented software construction
- [ ] The purpose and advantage of using object-oriented programming techniques
- [ ] The different object-oriented techniques themselves, including inheritance, encapsulation, and polymorphism
- [ ] Special keywords that allow you to namelessly refer to certain objects in your scripts

What Is Object-Oriented?

The answer to that question is actually simpler than it may seem. Of course, it depends upon how you read the question. One possible answer to the question is, People are object-oriented; and in fact, they are. Even before a baby is one year old, it learns to recognize objects like its mother, its father, its bottle, and its favorite teddy bear. People are taught to look at the world as a set of objects, without giving any thought to the complexities of the makeup of the objects they look at. You take the objects that you look at for granted; additionally, each person has his or her own individual perceptions of the same object. For example, if you look at a car, you probably see a vehicle you use to get back and forth from work every day. I have an uncle who is a used-car dealer (we don't hold it against him). When he looks at a car, he's looking to see if the body looks nice so he can get a good price for it. I have a friend who is a mechanic. When he looks at a car, he goes straight for the hood and looks at the engine, the carburetor, the radiator, the transmission, the spark plugs, and all of the other components inside. He doesn't care how it looks; he's more interested in how it sounds. But in reality, a car is made up of a body, an engine, spark plugs, and everything else we see and hear—and it also brings most of us back and forth to work. As an object, the car serves many functions and has many attributes. The color of its body is an attribute. The sounds it makes are attributes. The make and model of the engine inside is an attribute. Driving us back and forth to work is a function. Making us a profit is a function. Even though any particular viewer may find interest in only a specific set of attributes and functions, the car still has all of its attributes and functions.

Let's take it a step further. One of the attributes of the car is its engine. However, the engine itself has functions and attributes. The year, model, and size of the engine are all attributes of the engine. The number of cylinders is an attribute of the engine. The alignment of the cylinders is an attribute of the engine. The engine has a function to turn the crankshaft at a specific rate. It has a function to burn certain amounts of gasoline at a certain rate. Why, it sounds like the engine itself is an object! After all, it can be the subject of someone's interest just like the car itself is. In fact, each of the pistons inside the engine is also an object! They can be a subject of interest to someone who is investigating the engine, and each of the pistons has attributes and functions that it performs.

The car as a whole is a system that is made up of all of the objects inside it. It is a successful system because it has a simple, user-friendly interface, but internally it is an extremely complex arrangement of objects. When you step on the gas pedal, gas is injected into the engine. Air is taken into the engine from the carburetor. The spark plug ignites the spark. The piston has to be in just the right spot for it to be airtight. The gasoline must ignite, causing the piston to be pushed down. This allows the fumes to be released into the emission system. It also causes the crankshaft to turn. When the crankshaft turns, the wheel turns. When this process happens many times a second, the car goes. All in all, the process is a very complex one, but when the user wants to interface with the car to make it go, all he has to do is simply press on the gas pedal with his foot. The user doesn't have to be concerned with what happens inside the system—he presses the gas pedal, the car goes, and that's all the user needs to know.

But the car manufacturer is responsible for sheltering the user from the complexities of the car. When the car manufacturer builds your car, he has to build all of the objects that make up the car first. Then, he has to put the objects together in the proper way so that they can communicate with each other properly. He must hook up all of the proper connections in order to elicit the proper reactions to the user's actions. He has to hook up the fuel injector to the gas pedal, the carburetor to the engine, the gas lines and the water lines. He has to measure the crankshaft and pistons and set up the timing belts to make sure everything fits properly in the process.

That is the essence of what object-oriented development is. Object-oriented development means building a system (in the preceding case, a car and in our case, software) as a set of objects. Each object has its own properties—attributes and behaviors—and can itself contain other objects. Each individual object is responsible for its own input and output and communicates with other objects to react to a particular command. Each object has a defined interface that users or other objects can use to communicate with it. The system itself is an object that accepts and responds to input from the user. Internally, though, most reactions are implemented as messages to other objects inside it, that in turn implement their functions as messages to the objects inside and next to them, and so on, until the entire process is complete.

11

Note: Most objects have some attributes to store the *state* of the object. The state of an object can then be used to determine how the object will respond to certain stimuli, such as input from other objects in the system. For example, a car might be in the *parked* state, *igniting* state, or *driving* state. If the car is in the parked state, and the user presses the gas pedal, the car floods. If the car is in the igniting state, and the user presses the gas pedal, the car starts (pre-fuel-injection). If the car is in the driving state, and the user presses the gas pedal, the car drives faster.

Note: In reality, the term object-oriented software construction is a waste of words. After all, we all look at the world as a set of objects, and everything else that we construct in the world is constructed in an object-oriented manner, from tangible objects—why shouldn't software work the same way? But because software construction itself is a relatively new discipline and because so many people have been developing software in a non-object-oriented manner, we need to explicitly announce our use of object-oriented software construction techniques. Many developers are still developing in a process-oriented manner, which only takes into account the processes that occur and the flow of the data in your system without looking at software components as objects. Object-oriented software construction is not a separate programming language, though. If you've programmed before in a process-oriented way, you will find that object-oriented software construction is mostly a different way of looking at the problems we have to solve as developers. It's thinking of the things that you create as objects, not just as functions.

What Is an Object?

The *American Heritage Dictionary* defines the word o*bject* as, "Something intelligible or perceptible by the mind."[1] Grady Booch, a leader in object-oriented technology, says, "An object has state, behavior, and identity; the structure and behavior of similar objects are defined in their common class; the terms *instance* and *object* are interchangeable."[2] I'll try to make it more simple: *Everything* is an object—you just have to look at it that way. The application is an object; the windows in the application are objects; the controls in the windows are objects; even functions and events are objects. In order to build your software with objects, you must figure out what different objects you need. Then you can put together blueprints for your system to describe each of your objects, show which objects are connected, how they are connected, and what they do. By using these blueprints, you can create the molds you need to create your objects; then, from the molds, you can create all of your objects for your system and put them together according to the blueprints.

In object-oriented theory, the blueprint of the system is referred to as the *design* of the system; the molds that you create are called the *classes*; and of course, the *objects* are generated from the molds—the classes. You spend time designing your system so that you know which objects you will need, what they will need to do, and how they will interface with each other. This way, you can start to build the classes you have identified and instantiate them into objects in your system.

Abstraction

The first step in this design process, then, is figuring out what classes you need. Amazingly, this is thought of as the most difficult part of object-oriented design. However, once you get into an object-oriented mindset, this process becomes easier and more natural and before long, you will have no trouble getting started.

In order to determine what classes you need, you have to think about what objects your system will have, what their properties are, and how they will behave, forgetting about how the objects work internally. You then can group your objects together based on similarities. For example, even though your engine may have eight spark plugs, each of them works the same way and does the same thing. You don't need eight molds to create the eight spark plugs; you only need one. Therefore, you don't need to create eight spark plug classes; you can create just one spark plug class and have it appear eight times in your system. In object-oriented terms, you can say that there are eight *instances* of the spark plug class in your system. (You can say an *object* is an *instance* of a *class*.)

The first step of designing and building an object-oriented software system simply involves figuring out what all of the objects in the system are and which ones can be grouped together into classes. You can do this by listing out the different objects in your system, their properties (or attributes and variables), and their behaviors (or functions and events), and by figuring out which objects have the same or similar responsibilities. Then, you build your classes from what you have learned from this study, by grouping similar objects into classes. This process is called *abstraction*—looking at your objects in an abstract manner to figure out how they are related and which objects belong to the same classes. Then, you can build your classes and create instances of your objects from the classes to make up your system.

Abstraction may also be thought of as *classification*. In the same way that scientists classify animals and organisms, computer scientists classify software objects. By using our example again, regardless of whether the engine itself is a four-cylinder, a six-cylinder, a V6, or an eight-cylinder, or even if it's an airplane engine or a steamboat engine, it pretty much does the same thing and has similar attributes. They are all different types of engines with slightly different attributes: the number of cylinders, the alignment of the cylinders, and the intended recipient of the engine. But they are all instances of the engine class of objects. This is the process of classification.

The science of classifying animals and other organisms is very empirical. Great care and effort is taken to ensure the proper classification of living organisms. First, you must determine the Kingdom of the organism. Then, there are things like the Phylum, Class, Order, and Family, until you finally can express the Genus and Species, the most significant and unique components of the classification of the organism. I'm sure you know that the human being is classified as Homo Sapien. Homo is the Genus, and Sapien is the species. Perhaps you aren't aware, though, that the human being is in the same class as the cat, dog, horse, ape, and even whale! That's

right—we're all mammals. From a biological standpoint, we share certain similar attributes and behaviors: We all give birth to our children live and not in eggs, and we all have the ability to nurse our children. However, we are more closely related to the ape than to any of the other mammals mentioned. We don't have flippers like the whale; we have an even number of fingers and toes, unlike the horse; and we are not carnivorous, like the cat and dog. However, we do have opposable thumbs like the ape, but we are not apes: We don't have tails, we stand erect, and we have larger brains. Therefore, we are classified as our own unique species, Homo Sapien.

Scientists classify organisms based on their attributes and behaviors, and have done so for many, many years. There is some level of hierarchy that helps determine the class of an organism based on its attributes and behaviors. If an organism is determined to exhibit attributes and behaviors of a particular Kingdom, it can be defined as a member of that Kingdom. If it exhibits attributes and behaviors of a particular Phylum, it is classified as a member of that Phylum. As you work your way down the Class, Order, and Family, it becomes increasingly more specific as to the organism's attributes and behaviors. Eventually, if it is determined to be a unique species, it will be assigned a new species name; otherwise, it will be classified as a member of an already existing species.

Software developers can use this proven model to develop their software classes. First, you have to design or determine the attributes and behaviors of your objects. Then, you must evaluate these attributes and behaviors to determine how they are similar to other objects you know about and that are available to you. You can begin to define the attributes and behaviors that make up your classes, and then you can define a hierarchy of classes based on their attributes and behaviors. Common attributes and behaviors can be used to define new classes that are promoted up the hierarchy, such that all classes based on that class share those common attributes and behaviors. Classes that have been promoted up the hierarchy can also be compared, and promotions can occur within those classes until eventually, there is a complete, hierarchical definition of all of the classes in the system. This completes the first step in an object-oriented design.

> **Note:** The preceding method of analysis and design is most commonly referred to as the *bottom-up* design approach. It starts at the bottom, looking at each potential class in the system, and then builds a hierarchy of classes in an upward direction when it finds common attributes and functions in multiple classes. There is also a *top-down* design approach, which starts at the top, attempting to define the most general objects first, and then building hierarchies in a downward direction to support more specific functionality. Either approach is appropriate, and both are studied extensively.

Inheritance

Of course, there are actually more practical reasons behind the classification of software programs than for the sake of the science, and those are reusability, extensibility, and, indirectly, cost savings. You can use an object-oriented technique, called *inheritance* to create classes that inherit their attributes and behaviors from other classes. So, if you have defined a particular class that represents common behaviors and attributes, you can then define other classes that will inherit the behaviors and attributes of that class. Using inheritance, you can implement a hierarchical system of classes such that classes in the hierarchy inherit attributes and behaviors of the classes that have been promoted above them.

To demonstrate how this might translate into a cost savings, let's go back to our car manufacturer. When he creates the cars on his assembly line, he doesn't have to actually create all of the objects that go into the car himself. Generally, he buys many of the other objects already built. For example, his assembly-line workers don't have to build the spark plugs they put into the car; the spark plugs come already built. Even the engine is completely built before it is put in the car. It would be inefficient to have to build each engine as you are about to place it in the car. Henry Ford would turn over in his grave, and car makers everywhere would still be filling orders from the 70s! Instead, most of the objects inside the car are bought from factories that specialize in creating those objects and are placed in the car already assembled. Perhaps after they are placed in the car, they are adjusted slightly to meet the car's needs. But the fact that the car manufacturer can buy these objects to place in his car means that he doesn't have to build them himself, even if he needs to adjust the object he bought to fit into his car. This is cheaper and more efficient than if he were to build the entire car from the ground up. But you can't do that in software, right? How can you buy an object off the shelf and fit it to meet the needs of your system? Wouldn't you have to change the source code of the object you bought to be able to do that?

Actually, by using object-oriented technology, you can create classes that are completely self-contained, with a defined interface of input and output. Well-designed, self-contained classes can then be sold to other developers and used in their systems. And even if the objects you buy from other developers don't exactly meet your needs, you can use inheritance to create new classes from them that you can adjust so they properly fit into your system.

Inheritance in software is much like inheritance in human life. A child inherits many of the characteristics of his or her parents. In the same way, a *descendant* class inherits the properties and behaviors of its *ancestor* class. Unlike people, though, classes in PowerBuilder generally have only one parent (although some other object-oriented languages allow for multiple inheritance). So, when you create your descendant class, it's as if you are creating a new class that contains all of the code of its ancestor class, almost as if it were a copy of the ancestor class.

Of course, there would be no added value to the inheritance of objects if it just meant making copies of classes that you bought. Inheritance, instead, allows you to extend or override ancestor code in your descendant so you can modify the attributes and behaviors of the descendant.

237

However, if the descendant class were actually just a copy of the ancestor class, that would corrupt the relationship. The two classes would be completely separate, distinct classes whose relationship would be effectively terminated when you change either of them. Any changes in one would be unmatched in the other, and the two would very quickly become out of synch with each other. With inheritance, however, the descendant class is not a copy of the ancestor class, but instead points to code in the ancestor class. If the code in the ancestor class is changed, the code in the descendent class also reflects this change.

At the descendant level, though, you can *extend* functionality simply by adding the code you want in the descendant class, and it is invisible to the ancestor class. Then, if the ancestor class changes, the behavior in the descendant class is also changed, even if it has extended the functionality of the ancestor class.

On the other hand, there may be certain behaviors in the ancestor that you *don't* want the descendant to have. In this case, you can *override* this functionality in the descendant, and even add functionality to replace it. When you override the ancestor's behavior, you are simply telling the descendant class not to point at the ancestor class, but instead to point at your code. Then, in your code, if you like, you can call the ancestor function yourself.

Let's take one more car example. Let's say that you are an automobile manufacturer, Loyola Auto. You've been manufacturing cars for years and years, but you've gotten an offer from another manufacturer, Major Motors, to proceed with a joint venture to build a brand new line of cars, called the Geode Prison. Now, you've been manufacturing cars for years and years, and this Geode Prison really sounds like a great idea, but it also sounds a lot like a car you are currently manufacturing, the Loyola Corona. So, to save money, you decide to use whatever you can from the Loyola Corona design to build the Geode Prison. So, you take the Corona molds for the chassis and the body and use them to build the chassis and body of the Prison. But, because Major Motors is an American car manufacturer, they decide they want some changes in the car design. So, they recommend a number of changes to the Prison, including moving the antenna slightly up toward the roof, using different tires made, of course, by Goodmonth, an American tire company, and changing the rear direction signal to red instead of yellow. They even recommend a different engine be used inside the car.

So, you begin production of this new car. In essence, the Geode Prison is actually very much inherited from the Loyola Corona. The next year, the companies decide to make both cars' bodies more rounded to fit in with the more modern, aerodynamic look of cars being produced by other companies, like that new competitor, Jupiter. Because both cars use the same mold, all you need to do is change the mold once so that its corners are more rounded, and all of the cars will be affected. But, the two cars can still maintain their differences with little or no affect. The Geode Prison can still have a higher antenna, different engine, Goodmonth tires, and red rear direction signals. Because the molds are the same, though, you only have to change them in the ancestor, for example, in the Loyola Corona. This is the beauty of inheritance. If you make a change in the ancestor, the descendant will automatically integrate that change, but will still be able to keep the attributes that it has developed on its own.

DO	DON'T

DO Be aware that it may take a bit longer to instantiate an object that is of a class that is inherited more than four or five levels deep.

DON'T Worry too much, though. Even though it may take a few seconds longer to open, after the object is opened, it will still perform as normal, and the developers at Powersoft are always looking for ways to improve the instantiation performance!

Polymorphism

But how would this work in software? How can a descendant class override or extend attributes or behaviors in the ancestor? After all, isn't the functionality performed by the same functions in both the ancestor and descendant? Can you make the same functions in a descendant point to different functionality than the functionality in the ancestor? The answer is that you can, because of an object-oriented concept known as *polymorphism*. Polymorphism allows you to use the same name to mean different things, depending on who you are talking to. For example, birds fly. airplanes fly. Both classes, birds and airplanes, have similar but different manners of flying. However, both functions are called *fly*. When a bird performs the function to *fly*, it flaps its webbed, feathered wings so it can catch enough air beneath them to exert pressure against the wind to give it lift. On the other hand, when an airplane performs its *fly* function, it uses engines to generate a forward momentum that is fast enough to force enough wind underneath its wings to exert enough pressure against the wind to give it lift. The results of flying in both cases are the same: the object gains enough lift to get off the ground and travel through the air. However, the two functions are implemented very differently; still, they produce the same result, and therefore are named *fly*. When you tell the bird to fly, it performs its fly function. When you tell the airplane to fly, it performs *its* fly function. If the bird were to attempt to perform the plane's fly function, it would never get enough forward momentum to get off the ground. And the airplane doesn't have joints in its wings to be able to even attempt to use the bird's fly function!

11

The point is that in the real world, there are functions that are given the same name that are implemented differently by different classes. And in the same manner, object-oriented software permits you to create functions with the same name for different objects and implement them differently, depending on the object performing the function. When a class is inherited from another, the descendant is automatically given all of the functions from its ancestor. However, the descendant class can then create its own function with the same name. Then, when an object calls that function in the descendant class, it performs the function at the descendant level, not the ancestor level. The descendant's function can even have different arguments and return values different than the ancestor's function. This may all seem very confusing, so let's create a bona fide example.

Let's create a window, called `w_sheet_base`. It will be the base class for a set of windows in your application. Open up the Window Painter by pressing **Shift-F1** or by clicking on the Window Painter button on the PowerBar. Create a new window by clicking on the **New** button on the Open Window dialog box. Create a window function by selecting the **W**indow Functions from the Dec**l**are menu. The function that you create will be a function that is owned by the window object, as opposed to the global functions that we talked about the other day, in Chapter 7. Click on the **New** button to create a new window function. You will again be presented with the New Function definition dialog box that we saw in Chapter 7. In the box labeled Name, enter

`f_message`

Then tab over to the box labeled Returns and select (None). Then click on the **OK** button. You will be in the function painter (which looks and works very much like the script painter). Enter the following line of code:

`MessageBox( title, I am the Ancestor)`

Now return to the Window Painter either by selecting **R**eturn from the **F**ile menu or by clicking on the Window Painter button on the toolbar. Now, open the Script Painter to edit the Open event of the window. Select **S**cript from the **E**dit menu, or click on the Script Painter button on the Window PainterBar. The Open event should be the event that appears. If it is not, select it from the Select Event drop-down list box. Enter the following line of code:

`f_message()`

Then return to the Window Painter. Double-click on the window and change the title to read

`Base Window`

Then click on the **OK** button. For good measure, let's also place something inside the window. Place a command button in the window by selecting Command**B**utton from the **C**ontrols menu or by clicking on the CommandButton button on the toolbar. Then click on the window to place the command button there. Finally, save the window with the name you used before, `w_sheet_base`. Enter the following comment:

`The Sheet Window Base Class`

Now, open the menu that you created yesterday, `m_tpb_01`, and click on the **O**pen menu item of your **F**ile menu (not of the main PowerBuilder menu). Place the following line of code in its `Clicked` script:

`OpenSheet( m_sheet_base, w_mdi_frame)`

Return to the Script Painter and save your changes in the menu. Finally, run your application. You should see your MDI Frame come up. Select **O**pen from the **F**ile menu. You should see a message box appear (see Fig. 11.1). The title reads `Base Sheet`, and it says `I am the Ancestor`. Click the **OK** button, and the Base Sheet should appear.

Figure 11.1.
The Base Sheet message box.

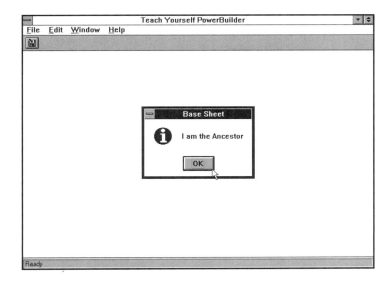

Now, exit the application and return to the PowerBuilder environment. Close the Menu Painter and instead, open up the Window Painter again. This time, when it comes up with the Select Window dialog, click on the button that says `Inherit`. You will be prompted with the Inherit From Window, which invites you to select the ancestor for the window you are about to create (see Fig. 11.2). Select `w_sheet_base` and click **OK**. On your screen, you should see a window that contains a single command button. The title bar should read `Window - (Untitled)` `inherited from w_sheet_base`. If you double-click on the window, you will see that the title bar attribute is set to read `Base Sheet`, like you set in the Ancestor. Now, change that to read

`Descendant Sheet`

Click **OK**. Then, save the window as `w_sheet_01` and enter the following comment:

The First descendant

Then, open your menu `m_tpb_01` again in the menu painter and select the **O**pen menu item again. Edit its script so that it opens `w_sheet_01` instead of `w_sheet_base`. The resulting script should read as follows:

`OpenSheet( w_sheet_01, w_mdi_frame)`

Now, close the Script Painter, save and close the menu, and run the application again. Select **O**pen from the **F**ile menu. Again, you should see a message box appear, but this time the title reads `Descendant Sheet`. This time, it is actually using the title bar information from the descendant to display the message box, but it is still calling the message box function from the ancestor! If you click **OK**, you will see the descendant sheet `w_sheet_01` come up in the frame, indicated by its title bar. Close the application and let's take this one step further.

Open up w_sheet_base in the Window Painter again. Change the text of the button so that it reads OK and make sure that its font is MS Sans Serif, size 8, boldface. Move the button across the screen to the other side. Now, save the window and run the application again. Open the descendant sheet by clicking on the **O**pen menu item in the **F**ile menu. Click **OK** when the message box comes up and notice the descendant window. The **OK** button on your descendant window appears not where you last left it, but where you moved it in the ancestor! That's the beauty of inheritance. I changed the position in the ancestor, and the button was also moved in the descendant. If you had created four or five windows that were inherited from w_sheet_base, they would all have picked up (inherited) this change, unless they had overridden it themselves.

Figure 11.2.

The Inherit From Window dialog box.

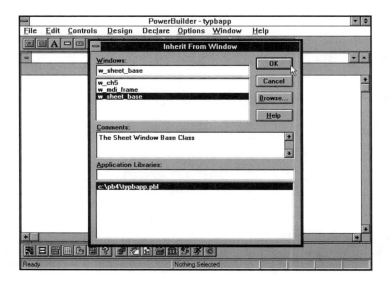

Now, let's demonstrate polymorphism. Close the application and open the w_sheet_01 window in the Window Painter. Declare a window function in this window by clicking on the **W**indow Functions menu item from the De**c**lare menu. Notice that the f_message function does not appear in the list of functions. Click on the **New** button to create a new f_message function. Enter **f_message** in the Name entry box and select (None) from the Returns box, and then click **OK**. Enter the following two lines of code as the code for your function:

```
SetMicroHelp( w_mdi_frame, I am the descendant)
Beep( 1)
```

Return to the Window Painter, save the window, and run the application. Select **O**pen from the **F**ile menu. Notice that you are not prompted with a message box; instead, the message I am the descendant appears on the Microhelp bar, and the computer beeps. *That* is polymorphism. The function name is the same in the ancestor as in the descendant, and so it is called the descendant function instead of the ancestor function. This is how you can override functionality in a descendant by using functions.

In addition, you can extend functionality of the ancestor in the child by calling the ancestor's function at some point in the descendant function. To call an ancestor function, simply preface the function name with the name of the ancestor and two colons (::). So, in this example, you can add a line at the end of the `f_message` function in the `w_sheet_01` window that reads

```
w_sheet_base::f_message()
```

This line of code forces the window to call its ancestor's function after performing its function. Run the application with this change, and you first see the Microhelp change, then hear the beep, and then see the message box.

You can also override and extend functionality in an event script. However, because the list of events always appears the same, this process works a little differently. When an event in an ancestor has code inside of it, that event has a pink script icon next to it in the Select Event drop-down list box (see Fig. 11.3). You can then place your code in the script to extend that script by default. If there is code in both the ancestor and descendant, the icon will appear half pink and half white. When you extend a script, the ancestor code will run first, followed by the descendant code. If you aren't sure what the ancestor code looks like, you can select the Display Ancestor Script menu item from the Compile menu. This brings up the Display Ancestor Script dialog box, which displays the script of the immediate ancestor of the current object (see Fig. 11.4). However, because there is no limit to the depth of the hierarchy, you can actually see the scripts for objects higher in the hierarchy of objects for this descendant by clicking on the **Ancestor** button. Then, you can work your way back down the hierarchy with the **Descendant** button. The object and script that you are looking at are displayed in the top-left corner of the dialog. If there is only one level of hierarchy, however, there is no ancestor or descendant to navigate to, and so these buttons are disabled. In addition, you can quickly select the entire text of the ancestor script and copy it to the clipboard by using the **Select All** and **Copy** buttons, respectively. Actually, you can even select only a small part of the text if you want to by using the cursor because the script is displayed in a multi-line edit box. Finally, you can close the window by clicking on the **Cancel** button.

Once you are reminded of the script that occurs in the ancestor, you may decide that you want to override that script in this descendant. If that's the case, you may select **O**verride Ancestor Script from the **C**ompile menu. Doing so prevents the ancestor code from executing when this event is triggered in the descendant. If you change your mind, you can go back to extending your script by selecting **E**xtend Ancestor Script from the **C**ompile menu. Notice that selecting one of these two items toggles the position of the check mark.

You may decide, however, that you don't want to override the script, but you don't really want to extend it, either. What you want is for your code to execute first, and then to have the ancestor code execute afterward. What you should do is leave the **O**verride Ancestor Script checked so that the ancestor code does not get called first. Then write your code and where you want to call the ancestor code; use the CALL and Super keywords to do this.

Figure 11.3.
A script with ancestor code.

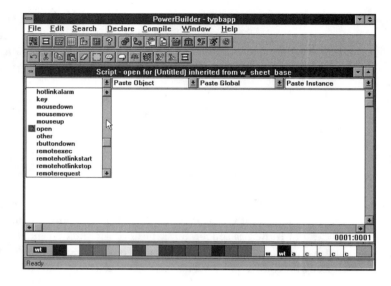

Figure 11.4.
The Display Ancestor Script dialog box.

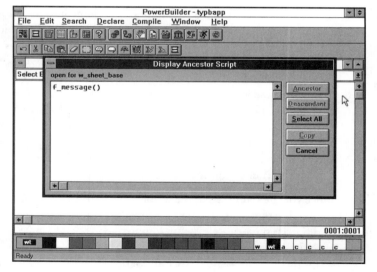

CALL and *Super*

The CALL keyword enables you to call a script in an ancestor object from its descendant. The Super keyword refers to the direct ancestor of the object that you are currently in. If you are calling the ancestor script for the Open event of the window, you can simply use

```
CALL Super::Open
```

The code for the ancestor's Open event will be executed at that point. When it is finished, it returns to the statement after the Call. You are permitted to call the ancestor script for any ancestor in your hierarchy, even if it is not the direct ancestor of your object. In other words, if the ancestor that you are interested in is three levels up the hierarchy, you may still call it, but you cannot use the Super keyword to refer to it. Instead, you must refer to it specifically by name. Place the name of the ancestor you want to refer to where you had the name Super in the preceding example. For example, in this case, you might use

```
CALL w_sheet_base::Open
```

Note: Even though you could have used the Super keyword in the last example, we just wanted to demonstrate the technique.

If you are trying to call the ancestor script not for the window itself but for an object inside the window, you may use the Super keyword as well. However, if you are calling script from an ancestor that is not the direct ancestor, and you want to specify the script by name, you must take one additional step. You must additionally preface the name of the event with the name of the object in the ancestor for which you want that event to occur. For example, if you are editing the Clicked event in the command button on the window, cb_1, and you want to call the ancestor command button's Clicked event, use the following line of code:

```
CALL w_sheet_base'cb_1::Clicked
```

You must do this because although the command button is indirectly inherited as a result of the inheritance of the window, it is the window that is actually inherited, and it is the window that knows how to resolve the reference to cb_1's Clicked event, not cb_1 itself. And so, you kindly give the descendant a little more information to make it easier for the PowerBuilder compiler to resolve the reference. Another advantage of using the Super keyword becomes apparent here. If you use the Super keyword inside an object like a command button, PowerBuilder actually resolves the reference to the ancestor object, and you don't have to specify the name of the object by name. It replaces the w_sheet_base'cb_1 part of the CALL statement as follows:

```
CALL Super::Clicked
```

11

Note: You can use the Super keyword anywhere you may refer to the immediate ancestor for object-oriented purposes—in other words, wherever you may call an ancestor function or event. So, earlier, where you were calling the ancestor function f_message(), you could have used the Super keyword as well.

DO	DON'T

DO Try to use the Super keyword whenever you are calling scripts from an ancestor object.

DON'T Reference your object by name if you can use the Super keyword. Doing so causes problems if you make a change in the ancestry or change the script to be in a different ancestor.

Referencing Your Objects

Because you can give the same name to functions and variables within different objects, there needs to be some way for you to figure out which function is executed when you call it by name. For example, if I have two windows open and both have a function called f_message() in them, how does the compiler determine which one I am talking to when I call the f_message() function? The answer is that you have to tell the compiler which object you are talking to. You specifically name the object that you are talking to either as the first parameter of the function, as in

```
f_message( w_sheet_01)
```

or you can prefix the function call with the name of the recipient object, followed by a period, as in

```
w_sheet_01.f_message()
```

This is referred to as *dot notation* and is conceptually similar to the dot notation covered in the discussion about structures in Chapter 7. Either of the two methods of telling the compiler who you are talking to is acceptable. Academically, dot notation is probably preferred, but I personally prefer the first parameter method because it works better with the PowerBuilder editor. You are invited to make your own decision as to which notation you prefer.

Dot notation is also used to refer to attributes and instance variables that belong to an object. Of course, because there are no parameters to attributes or instance variables, only dot notation can be used.

Referential Shortcuts

In the English language, there are certain words that serve as pronouns that you use instead of proper names when you are communicating. These pronouns make it easier to communicate because they are easier to deal with than proper names. In the same manner, PowerBuilder offers a number of keywords that you can use in your scripts as pronouns to replace properly named references.

The first pronoun that you can use is *This*. This refers to the current object. It's similar to the pronoun *I* in the English language. It replaces any reference to the object that is the caller. So, if you want to call your own f_message() function, instead of saying

```
w_sheet_01.f_message()
```

you can simply say

```
this.f_message()
```

In the English language, the pronoun You is often understood and skipped, especially in command form. You can say things like, "Come Here!," or "Go Home!," but really you mean, "**You**, Come Here!," and "**You**, Go Home!." In a similar manner, the pronoun This in PowerBuilder is implied whenever there is no other reference specified. That's why you can say

```
f_message()
```

without any reference at all.

Another important pronoun that you need to be aware of is the *Parent* keyword. You can use the Parent keyword to refer to the object that is the direct parent of the object that uses it. For example, the parent of a Command button on a window is the window itself. Using the Parent keyword, you can create generic code to refer to parents of your objects. You can even create special objects, called *user objects*, out of controls like Command buttons, and use the Parent keyword in their code to refer to the parent object, no matter which window it happens to be. We'll talk more about user objects in the next several chapters.

You have already learned about the final pronoun that you can use. That is the Super keyword, used to refer to the immediate ancestor of an inherited object.

Scope

Before you learn about the next object-oriented concept, *encapsulation*, it is important to mention the traditional concept of *scope*. Perhaps scope should have been mentioned when variables and functions were discussed in general. However, without the concept of scope, the concept of encapsulation will not make sense. In many ways, scope is one component of encapsulation, but there are many more.

Scope refers to who has access to a particular variable, function, or object. Quite a bit of time has been spent talking about variables that are declared inside your script. These variables are referred to as *local* variables. They are only available to the script in which they are declared. Once the script terminates, the variables are gone.

At the other end of the spectrum, there are variables that you can declare, called *global* variables, that are available to every single object, function, and script in your system. They are declared from the Global Variables menu item of the Declare menu of any object or Script Painter. They are stored, however, as part of the application object.

In between, there are two different types of variables: *instance* variables and *shared* variables. *Instance* variables are variables that live as long as the instance of the object and can be accessed by any script inside the object that has the instance variable. For example, if you have a window, you can modify the value of the instance variable from any script inside the window, as well as any script inside any object inside the window, like a Command button. Once the window is closed, the variable disappears. Each instance of the window has its own copy of the variable so if there are many instances of the window, there are many instances of the instance variable. By declaring instance variables for an object, it is almost like creating new attributes for that object. As with globals, you declare instance variables from the Declare menu.

Finally, *shared* variables are similar to instance variables in that they exist for the window or object in which they are defined. However, unlike the instance variable, there is only one copy of the variable that is created, even if there is more than one instance of the object that defines it. So, if you have two instances of the shared variable, each instance can modify the shared variable, and one instance's modifications are reflected in the other instance. This is a very good method for communicating between like objects. As with instance and global variables, you declare shared variables from the Declare menu.

It should also be mentioned that function and structure definitions have some limited scope as well. While you can declare a local structure variable, you cannot create local function and structure definitions inside a script. You can, however, define your functions and structures globally by using the Function and Structure Painters, or as instance functions and structures that are defined for a specific object, like a Window Function or a Window Structure. When you define a Window Function, you are defining a function as an instance function for a specific window.

Encapsulation

The traditional concept of scope has been around since the early days of structured programming. However, object-oriented programming extends the concept of scope a step further by declaring three new types of access methods you can use with your instance variables and object level functions. These methods allow you to *encapsulate* the variables and functions of one object so that they are protected from access by certain other objects.

By default, all of the instance variables and object functions will be *public*. This means that other objects in the system can access them by using the referencing methods like dot notation, discussed in the last section. Even though the variable is an attribute of the object for which it is defined, other objects can modify or retrieve the value of that variable.

The other end of the spectrum is the *private* instance variable or object function. When you declare an object function or instance variable as private, only objects inside the window itself will be able to access the variable or function. The attribute will be invisible to all outside callers, even objects that are descendants of the object itself.

Between the two extremes is the *protected* variable or function. If you define a variable or function as protected, other unrelated objects will still not be able to access the function or variable, but descendants of the object *will* be able to.

As I've already mentioned, by default the access of an instance variable or function is public. However, you can change this very easily. If it is for a function, you can simply change the access by choosing it from the Access drop-down list box in the New Function definition dialog, which you saw earlier in this lesson and you also worked with in Chapter 7. To control the access for an instance variable, you must place the appropriate keyword in front of the declaration. You can place it once in front of each declaration as follows:

```
Private String is_name
Private String is_address
Private String is_zip
Protected String is_count
Protected String is_num
```

There is a shorthand for this notation that involves simply stating the access, followed by a colon (:). Each variable that is declared after that will be assumed to be of that access, until a different access is declared, as in the following example:

```
Private:
  String is_name
  String is_address
  String is_zip
Protected:
  String is_count
  String is_num
```

By protecting your variables from outside influence, you help guarantee the integrity of your variables. As a general rule, programmers like to use the tightest scope and access possible. This way, you minimize the risk of corrupting the contents of the variable and maximize the predictability of the value of the variable within your scripts. Keep in mind that in an event-driven environment like Windows, it is unacceptable to attempt to write code that depends on the order of task-independent events. That means that if you have an event that modifies a global variable, and another event interrupts the first one and modifies the same global variable, the system becomes corrupted. Therefore, try to protect your variables as much as possible by limiting their scope and access to the objects that need them.

Further Study

Although I have given you an introduction, if you are serious about building your systems architecture skills, you will need to learn more about designing your systems by using object-oriented analysis and design techniques. Although object-oriented technology isn't all that new of an idea, it has only recently become part of the mainstream of programming. Therefore, this science is rapidly growing, and new techniques, styles, and methodologies are being developed and updated.

The topic of object-oriented software construction could take up volumes all by itself, and in fact, it has. If you are interested in following the leaders of object-oriented technology, there is a large number of books and periodicals on the subject that you can read to learn about the different concepts, methodologies, and even languages, that are based on the object-oriented paradigm.

Morning Summary

People look at everything in the world as an object. They see the object with their own perspective. However, the object may have attributes and behaviors that some viewers don't take into account in their perspective. The objects that you look at may be made up of other objects. Object-oriented development means implementing a system using objects that have their own attributes and behaviors and may be made up of other objects. Everything is an object; you just have to look at it that way.

When building software systems by using an object-oriented methodology, you need to spend time *designing* your objects. You need to create *classes*, which are the molds that are used to generate the objects. The first step in the design process is *classifying* your objects. This process is referred to as *abstraction*. It is similar to the classification of animals that biologists perform. If two or more objects can be derived from the same class, then you only need one class to create them both.

If two classes share some behavior or attributes, but not all, you can use *inheritance* to share between the two classes. You can create an *ancestor* class that contains the common behavior and attributes, and then create other classes from this ancestor, called *descendants*, that inherit the behavior of the ancestor. In addition, the descendant can *extend* or *override* the functionality that it inherits.

Polymorphism allows you to use the same name for functions and attributes in different objects. Descendant classes can redefine functions in the ancestor by creating a function of the same name and placing different code in there. For example, you may create a function in the ancestor class called f_message(), that displays a message box; you then create a function in the descendant class, also called f_message(), that displays its message on the Microhelp Bar. When you open the descendant class, the message box of the ancestor does not appear, but instead the message from the descendant appears on the Microhelp bar. If you want to extend the ancestor function in the descendant, you call it from the descendant by prefacing it with the name of the ancestor and two colons (::). Because events are defined for a descendant object automatically, you can change them to override or extend their ancestors from the Compile menu. You can also see the script from the Ancestor from that menu as well. In the same manner that you call the ancestor function from a descendant function, you can also call the ancestor script from the descendant script. However, to do this, you must use the CALL keyword. You can also use

the keyword Super to refer to the direct ancestor of the object. Simply use the format CALL Super::<*Event*>, where <*Event*> is the name of the ancestor event that you want to trigger. If the ancestor event that you want to trigger is not the immediate ancestor but several levels up, you can refer to it specifically by name and use the same format.

Because you can have functions with the same name in different objects, you need to refer to your objects when calling their functions specifically to indicate which function you want. You can do this by specifying the object as the first parameter of the function, or by using *dot notation*—specifying the name of the object, followed by a period, followed by the name of the function. You use dot notation to refer to attributes and instance variables of an object, too.

There are certain pronouns that you can use to reference objects that help make your code more generic. You can use the *This* keyword to reference the current object. *This* is an implied pronoun that can be omitted if you prefer. In addition, you can use the *Parent* keyword to refer to the direct parent object of the current control. For example, a command button's parent is usually the window on which the button resides. Finally, you can use the *Super* keyword to refer to the immediate ancestor of an object.

Scope refers to who has access to a particular variable, function, or object. Variables that are declared inside your scripts are called *local* variables and are only available to code within the same script that is executing. *Global* variables are available to any code anywhere in the application or any of its objects. *Instance* variables are variables that are available to any script or function within a single instance of the object for which they are defined. *Shared* variables are available to *all* instances of the object for which they are defined. They are all declared from the Declare menu of the script or function painter. You can also create instance functions and instance structure definitions.

Object-oriented programming takes the concept of scope a step further. You can encapsulate your instance variables and functions to prevent other objects from accessing it improperly. By default, instance functions and variables are *Public*, meaning that anyone can access them. However, you can also declare them as *Private*, which will prevent any object except the owner from accessing that variable or function. Or, you can declare them as *Protected*, which allows only the owner and its descendants to access them. You control the access of a function from the Access drop-down list box in the function definition. You declare the access of instance variables by placing the access type in front of the declaration.

Works Cited

1. *The American Heritage Dictionary*, Second College Edition, (Boston: Houghton Mifflin Company, 1985), 857.

2. *Object-Oriented Analysis and Design with Applications*, Second Edition, (Redwood City: The Benjamin/Cummings Publishing Company, Inc., 1994), 83.

12

User Objects

In this chapter, you are introduced to the PowerBuilder User Object. You will learn:

☐ What a User Object is
☐ What User Objects are used for
☐ How to figure out when you should use a User Object

What Are User Objects?

In the last lesson, you learned about how windows can be inherited and how you can create instance variables, window functions, and structures to make windows object-oriented. However, I didn't tell you that there is a way to make the controls inside your window object-oriented as well. To create object-oriented controls that can have their own instance variables, object functions, and inheritable attributes and behaviors, you use the PowerBuilder *User Object*.

By using User Objects, you can create customized controls, or even groups of controls, that have their own attributes and behaviors. These custom behaviors and attributes can even be inherited! Then, you can place your User Object on your windows, and it integrates into your application like any other control. In fact, you can even distribute your User Objects and use them among different applications. The User Object is a completely encapsulated object, just as a Command button or Static Text object is. Therefore, in your PowerBuilder programming, if you have a well-designed object-oriented application, you will spend a significant amount of time inheriting or creating User Objects to incorporate into your applications.

You create User Objects in the User Object Painter. The User Object Painter is accessible by pressing **Shift-F11** or by clicking on the User Object button from the PowerBar. When you enter into the User Object Painter, you are prompted with the Select User Object dialog box, where you can select a User Object to open if you have some already in your libraries, or you can create a new one by clicking on the **New** or **Inherit** button (see Fig. 12.1). Go ahead and click on the **New** button now to create a new User Object.

You are then prompted with the New User Object dialog box, which asks you which type of User Object want to create (see Fig. 12.2). There are several different types of User Objects; therefore, when you attempt to create a new User Object, PowerBuilder asks you which kind of User Object you want.

Figure 12.1.
The Select User Object dialog box.

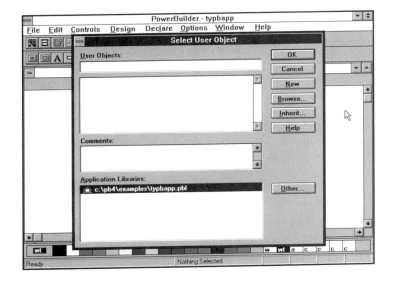

Figure 12.2.
The New User Object dialog box.

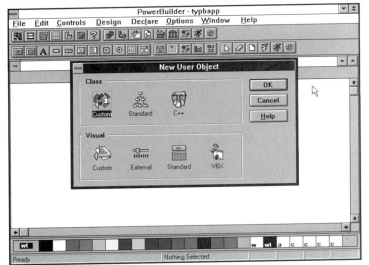

An Introduction to the Different Types of User Objects

With PowerBuilder, you can create six different types of User Objects, based on their source, purpose, and function. There are two major categories of User Objects, as indicated in the New User Object dialog box. There are *Visual* User Objects, which become visual controls or groups of controls that appear on-screen, and there are non-visual, *Class* User Objects, which can also be created inside your applications but do not correspond to visual controls or components of PowerBuilder. We'll talk a bit about each type of User Object in turn.

Standard Visual User Object

This is probably the most common type of User Object that you create. By using the Standard Visual User Object, you can create extensions to the PowerBuilder controls. You can create special-purpose controls you can place inside your windows. Why in the world would you want to do this? Well, suppose that you are building an application that has a standard OK button on every window. You want to have your OK button work exactly the same way on each window. You want it to validate the data in the window by calling the window's f_validate() function. If this succeeds, you want to save the changes in the window by calling the window's f_save() function (these functions are created by the programmer). Finally, if this succeeds, you close the window. So now, your application has 15 windows, and therefore 15 OK buttons, each with the exact same code inside. But wait! You made a mistake! The f_validate() function needs to take a parameter in order to determine the type of validation this is! Now, you have to go into 15 windows and change the code for each of the buttons.

By using the Standard Visual User Object, you can instead create a single OK button User Object that has the required functionality placed inside of it. Then, you can place this User Object inside all 15 of your windows by selecting User**O**bject from the **C**ontrols menu, or by clicking on the User Object button on the Window PainterBar. Now, if you need to change the functionality of the OK button in your windows, you only change it in one place—in the User Object definition in the User Object Painter. Your single change will automatically translate itself down to all the windows containing that User Object.

This technique is also very popular for creating special custom controls that can be distributed to other users or other applications. Did you ever see a hierarchical list box or a set of tab folders used in a PowerBuilder application? Well, their specific functionality is probably defined as a standard User Object created from a DataWindow.

Custom Visual User Object

In some cases, you want to create a custom control, not out of just one control, but out of a set of multiple controls. Perhaps you want to create a ribbon bar for your data so that the user can navigate through data with buttons that look like VCR controls. You probably have seen some of this effect in the Sample Application. In order to do this, you can create a Custom User Object. The Custom User Object may have several buttons and text items on it that each elicit some specific action. One button may move you forward a page in your data, and another may move you back a page. Once you have combined all of these controls into a Custom Visual User Object, you can place that User Object inside your window and hook it in with whatever protocol it requires. It will handle all of the functionality invisibly. Be aware, though, that Custom Visual User Objects must be well designed and well thought out in order to be efficient and be integrated easily.

Standard Class User Object

If you remember from the early lessons when the Application Object was discussed in Chapter 3, an attribute of the Application Object called Default Global Variables was mentioned. You learned about several internal global variables that PowerBuilder uses, and you learned how to reassign their datatypes to your own classes. I said that doing so is something that is a bit more advanced, and we'd learn about it later. Let's talk about it now.

PowerBuilder supplies certain global variables for you that are used internally by PowerBuilder itself. One clear and classic example is the Message variable, which contains the information about the Windows messages that are being passed from object to object and event to event. Whenever any event is triggered, the message is stored in the default Message Object.

However, as it currently stands, the object that receives the message has no way to know who the caller of the message is. In addition, there is a limited number of message parameters that can be passed to the receiving object. If you want to pass additional parameters to a receiving object, including perhaps the calling object, you can create a Standard Class User Object of type Message and add variables and functions that would permit you to save additional information in your Message Object. Then, you can make your object the default global Message Object, and any object in the system can use these new message attributes to pass information back and forth. The message is perfectly simple, and the meaning is clear.

Another example of why you may use a Standard Class User Object is to extend the database objects to permit use of Sybase Remote Procedure Calls. If you don't know what I am talking about, don't worry. Sybase is a popular Database Server, and you can do some special function calls using something called Remote Procedure Calls. In PowerBuilder, you need to use the Standard Class User Object to use Remote Procedure Calls. You can read more about using Remote Procedure Calls in the PowerBuilder and Sybase Documentation.

Custom Class User Object

In addition to standard classes, you can also create your own classes. Instead of having attributes and functions built in, a custom class is a completely empty, nonvisual shell that you can use to create your own classes with attributes and functions. You can create instances of these objects and use them in your application. An example of why you may use a custom class is to encapsulate common utility functions into a single class for use in multiple applications. Another prime candidate for custom classes are utility managers in general. Many designs call for a transaction manager to manage database transactions, an error handler to handle errors, and other such items. Since they are generally composed of functionality and attributes without any visual components, they are prime candidates for custom classes. After you build your utility manager once, you should be able to take it from project to project and application to application to reuse again and again.

C++ Class User Object

The next type of User Object that PowerBuilder offers is the *C++ Class User Object*. If you are using PowerBuilder Enterprise Series and have installed the Watcom C++ Compiler that came with the system, you can use the C++ Class User Object to help you build .DLL files. If you build a .DLL file with the C++ Class User Object, it will be easier to integrate your .DLL into your PowerBuilder application because PowerBuilder takes care of a lot of the overhead for you. This is an extremely advanced topic that requires knowledge of building .DLLs as well as of C++, and so we'll save this topic for a more advanced book.

VBX User Object

PowerBuilder, of course, is not the only front-end development tool available on the market today. Another popular front-end tool is produced by Microsoft Corporation and is called Visual Basic. You probably have heard of it, but even if you haven't, you may have heard of a special type of control called the *.VBX*. The .VBX is a special kind of control that is created specifically for use in Visual Basic. It allows developers to create programs in other languages, like C and Assembler, and link them into their front-end applications. This is one very powerful method that programmers can use to extend their front-end environment; for example, when they come across functionality that is not available internally by the front-end tool but is available through a lower-level language like C or Assembler.

PowerBuilder allows you to incorporate .VBX controls into your applications by creating an interface with the .VBX control. That interface is the VBX User Object. You create the VBX User Object to specify to PowerBuilder how to interact with the .VBX, and then you can insert the User Object into your PowerBuilder applications like any other control. You can often find useful .VBX controls on bulletin boards or on CompuServe. Some common .VBX controls that you might find interesting are the Animated Cursors and Meters.

External User Object

Finally, the last type of User Object that PowerBuilder offers is the External User Object. PowerBuilder and Visual Basic are not the only front-end development tools on the market today. Before either of them was available, Microsoft created a standard for developing controls that could easily be shared between programmers using the Microsoft Software Development Kit to develop their Windows applications, regardless of the tool they were using. The standard object that was created was called the *Custom Control*. Although newer standards like .VBX and OLE are becoming more popular and making the Custom Control less popular, there are still quite a few Custom Controls available on the market today. PowerBuilder allows you to incorporate any Custom Control into an object that can be placed in your PowerBuilder application by using the External User Object.

Note: "Buying is cheaper than building," is a common axiom in the software industry. By giving you the ability to use external objects like the .VBX and Custom Control .DLL, you have more options for building your applications. This might not hold true, though, if you want to distribute your application across multiple platforms. Since .VBX and .DLL controls are not supported on all platforms, you may need to re-create them or find other alternatives for other platforms anyway. For example, you may not be able to use your .VBX meter on Windows NT, and so you would need to substitute something else for your Windows NT version of your application.

Sharing Code: A Brief History

12

In the earliest days of application development, sharing code meant typing it in again. One day, some developer with tired hands created *function libraries* to save commonly used functions in his libraries and to link those functions into applications that needed them. This was a big help because now he could share his function libraries with other developers, and then they could use his code, too. The function library idea caught on—so much so that other companies took this even a step further, and built protocols for linking functions in dynamically at runtime instead of at compile time. They called this the *.DLL* file for *Dynamic Link Library*.

Eventually, people learned about the object-oriented and object-based concepts and started building not just functions, but classes and objects that they could share with all their friends and co-workers. They extended the .DLL protocol to allow for the creation of Custom Controls to easily share these objects that they created, without sharing the code behind them. Custom controls became increasingly popular for exactly that reason. Before long, there were custom

controls to do everything from acting like other, standard controls with 3-D special effects, to emulating a complex spreadsheet; and they were all being distributed everywhere because they were so easy to distribute.

Later, when Microsoft released Visual Basic, they extended the custom control standard so that it would be easier for Visual Basic developers to incorporate custom controls into their applications. And again, because they were easy to create and distribute, VBXs became quickly popular and available.

But as applications became more complex, somebody said, "Why not just give the owner of a data file the ability to work on its file even if the file is embedded within a different application?" And so, *Object Linking and Embedding* (OLE) was born.

Object Linking and Embedding (OLE)

Object Linking and Embedding (OLE) is a protocol that allows you to link a file to its serving application, embed it into another application, and let the server take over functionally if the user attempts to edit the object. In other words, suppose that you have a word processing document that you are writing, and you want to place a spreadsheet inside your word processing document. If the word processing program you are using knows how to manage the links for the embedded spreadsheet, you can embed the spreadsheet into your word processing document. When the user edits the spreadsheet, the user is actually running the spreadsheet application, not the word processing application. The spreadsheet's menus will replace the word processor's menus. This automated integration of a document inside another application is referred to as *OLE Automation*, and is growing even more popular even more quickly. This is because now you don't even need to create special controls anymore—just special links! Microsoft is even expecting to release a new version of the Windows operating system that will incorporate this feature directly into the operating system itself. This technology is new and exciting, and you can use it right inside your PowerBuilder applications!

Note: Even though an OLE object is not really a User Object, it works in much the same way that a User Object does and serves a similar purpose. Therefore, the OLE object will be included in the discussion of User Objects. Unlike the User Object, however, the OLE object has some additional features and additional requirements. We'll discuss the OLE object in extensive detail tomorrow.

Note: Originally you could use OLE to embed objects from one application into another. Then, you could double-click on the OLE object, and it would open the application that "owned" the embedded object so that you embedded it. Later, Microsoft updated the OLE specification to allow you to edit your embedded objects directly inside your applications. This updated specification is often referred to as *OLE 2*. PowerBuilder supports the OLE 2 specification, even though some other Windows applications do not.

Why Use User Objects?

It is important to realize that when you create a User Object, you are creating a true class definition. If you are developing object-oriented applications, you will want to use a large number of User Objects in your application. You can encapsulate functionality inside a User Object so that it can be used in multiple places inside your application but maintained in only one. Essentially, User Objects allow you to create your own custom controls, but instead of being .VBXs or .DLLs, they are simply PowerBuilder objects that can be used in your applications.

The PowerBuilder User Object, however, has another major advantage. Each User Object is its own library entry, and therefore each User Object is very modular. This means that if you are developing applications with a team of people, you can design each component individually and allow each member of the team to be exclusively responsible for a single component of the application, developed as a User Object or collection of User Objects. Each member can even stub out the functionality of his User Object until it is complete, allowing other developers to develop their components referencing the other stubbed, but incomplete, User Objects. As developers replace the stubbed functions with real working code, the application as a whole will start working.

User Objects are very useful tools. They allow you to truly build and design object-oriented PowerBuilder applications. Learn to use, build, and design them, and your PowerBuilder development efforts will be extremely successful.

12

Afternoon Summary

You can use User Objects to create controls and classes that can be used in your windows and that are object-oriented. You create User Objects in the User Object Painter, which is opened by pressing **Shift-F11** or by clicking on the User Object button from the PowerBar.

There are six different types of User Objects that you can create in PowerBuilder. The type of User Object that you create will depend on the purpose and source of the User Object. *Visual* User Objects will become visual components of your window, like controls or groups of controls. *Class* User Objects are nonvisual objects that will be instantiated in your application for functionality and structure only.

The most common type of User Object you will probably define is the *Standard Visual User Object*. You use this type of User Object to create special-purpose controls that you can place inside your windows, or even distribute to other users for use in other applications. *Custom Visual User Objects* are User Objects that are created out of multiple controls and that work together as a group to serve some common purpose, like a ribbon bar. You can create a *Standard Class User Object* to extend or override the behavior of the Default Global Variables that are used by the application, like the Message and Error objects. You can also create your own *Custom Class User Object* that allows you to encapsulate attributes and functions into a class that doesn't have any visual component, like a transaction manager or error handler. In addition, you can interface PowerBuilder with .VBX controls that are used in Visual Basic by creating a *VBX User Object*. And finally, you can interface with any custom control that follows the Windows Custom Control specifications by using an *External User Object*. In addition, to use data from other external applications, you can use *Object Linking and Embedding (OLE)* to embed an external object into your window, link it to its source application, and allow the user to edit it with the source application from right inside your application.

User Objects allow you to truly design and build object-oriented applications using PowerBuilder. Since each User Object is an independent entity that can be placed in its own module with its own attributes and behaviors, it is the true essence of what object-oriented experts refer to as an object.

Q&A

Q How do I make my descendant script execute before my ancestor script, instead of after it?

A From within the Script Painter, select **O**verride Ancestor Script from the **C**ompile menu. At this point only the descendant script will execute. At the end of the descendant script, enter `CALL w_ancestor'object::event` or `CALL Super::event` (one ancestor level up), to cause the ancestor script to execute when the event is triggered.

Q Why do I get a compile error when I try to call an ancestor window's function from a descendant window's command button?

A Ancestor window functions can be called directly, with the general syntax `w_ancestor::wf_function()`, from a descendant window event or function, but not from any control events. If a control requires access to an ancestor window's function, then create a window function in the descendant to call the ancestor function. Within the control event, you will call the descendent window function. Controls on a window can only call ancestor functions of the control itself if, for example, they are inherited from a User Object.

Q Do I always have to use `w_ancestor::wf_function()` to use ancestor window functions in my descendent window and controls?

A No, just the function name. Even though you don't see it, you inherit it. Use `w_ancestor::wf_function` only if you want a specific ancestor window's function because, by default, another function would be called, like a window function with the same name and parameters in the descendant window.

Q I created a function in an ancestor window. Why can't I access it from any descendant scripts?

A You gave the window function `Private` access rights so that only scripts within the ancestor window can call it. `Protected` access rights would allow descendant windows to access the function and still restrict the rest of the application from calling it.

Q I tried to create a custom User Object, but PowerBuilder just beeps when I try to select a command button from the toolbar to place on the object. Why?

A By default, you enter `Class:Custom`, a non-visual Custom Class User Object. Because it's non-visual, you cannot place graphic controls on the User Object. The menu items for selecting graphic controls are disabled, but there are no visual cues on the toolbar for this. You should create a `Visual:Custom` Custom Visual User Object.

Workshop

Quiz

1. What is the general syntax for calling ancestor scripts and functions?
2. List three frequently used script pronouns other than `Super`.
3. Name the four variable scopes.
4. Give the three access levels you can declare for variables and functions.
5. List the different types of User Objects.

Putting PowerBuilder into Action

1. Open the Base Sheet window (`w_sheet_base`) in the Window Painter.
2. Create a window function that will validate any changes in the sheet, called `f_validate()`. The function is a private function that returns an integer value and has no parameters. If the return value is positive, the data was successfully validated. If it is negative, a validation error occurred. If it returns a 0, there was no data to validate. Because in the base class there is no data to validate, the code inside should simply return a 0 value. Insert the following comment and line of code into the function:

```
/*******************************************************
* Integer f_validate
* Parms: None
* Returns: 1 - Successful Validation
*          0 - No Validation Occured
*         -1 - Validation Failed
* Descr: This function will validate data in the window.
*        It will check to see if there is any data to be
*        validated as well. It will be overriden in the
*        descendant window.
*******************************************************/
RETURN 0
```

3. Create a window function that will save any pending changes in the sheet, called
   f_update(). The function is a private function that returns an integer value and has no
   parameters. If the return value is positive, then the data was successfully updated. If it
   is negative, an error occurred. If it returns a 0, there was no data to update. Because in
   the base class there is no data, the code inside should simply return a 0 value. Insert
   the following comment and line of code into the function:

```
/*******************************************************
* Integer f_update
* Parms: None
* Returns: 1 - Successful Update
*          0 - No Update Occured
*         -1 - Update Failed
* Descr: This function will update data in the window.
*        It will be overriden in the descendant window.
*******************************************************/
RETURN 0
```

4. Create an OK button for the Base Sheet. Change the button text of the cb_1 button to
   read OK. Change the name of the button to cb_ok and set its Default attribute to
   TRUE. Change the script for the Clicked event to read as follows:

```
/*******************************************************
* CommandButton cb_ok
* Event: Clicked
* Descr: When the user clicks the OK Button, attempt to
*        validate the data and save it. Then close the
*        window.
*******************************************************/
Integer li_result
li_result = f_validate()
IF li_result > 0 THEN
// Validate succeeded with rows, update changes.
  li_result = f_update()
END IF
IF li_result >= 0 THEN
// Validation and Update Succeeded or was unnecessary
  Close( Parent)
END IF
```

5. Create a Cancel button by creating a new button on the window, making its text read Cancel and naming it cb_cancel. Set its Cancel attribute to TRUE. Place the following script in its Clicked event:

```
/*****************************************************
* CommandButton cb_cancel
* Event: Clicked
* Descr: Close the Parent window without saving.
*****************************************************/
Close( Parent)
```

6. Create a script for the CloseQuery event of the window that will prompt the user to save changes if the user tries to close without saving. Set the Message.ReturnValue attribute to 1 in the CloseQuery event to prevent the close from occurring. The code in the CloseQuery event will read as follows:

```
/*****************************************************
* Window w_sheet_base
* Event: CloseQuery
* Descr: When the user tries to close the window, check
*        for pending updates, and allow the user to update
*        or cancel if there are.
*****************************************************/
Integer li_result
li_result = f_validate()
IF li_result > 0 THEN
// There are rows to be saved. Prompt the User.
  li_result = MessageBox( Window.Title, &
                "Changes have been made, Save Changes?", &
                Exclamation!, YesNoCancel!)
  CHOOSE CASE li_result
    CASE 1 // Yes
      li_result = f_update()
      IF li_result < 0 THEN // Update Failed, Prevent Close
        Message.ReturnValue = 1
      END IF
//    CASE 2 // No Close as normal, don't do anything
      CASE 3 // Cancel - Prevent Close
        Message.ReturnValue = 1
  END CHOOSE
END IF
```

7. Save your new Base Sheet. It should look something like the base class window that appears in Figure 12.3.

12

Figure 12.3.
*The New Base Class
window.*

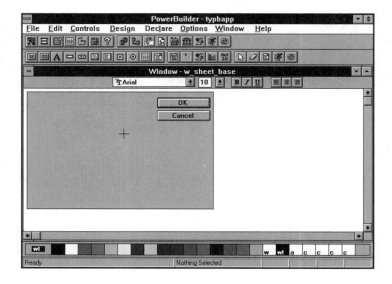

Chapter

13

Standard User Objects

In this chapter, you will learn:

☐ How to build your own Standard User Objects by using the User Object Painter

☐ How to create scripts and functions for your Standard User Objects

☐ How to integrate your Standard User Object as a control in a window or Custom Visual User Object

Standard User Objects

PowerBuilder has provided an object-rich development environment by providing a suite of basic objects and controls, such as DataWindows, command buttons, static text fields, and so on. These are well encapsulated objects providing a basic set of behaviors and, as you have discovered, have reduced the task of developing an application to that involving assembly of objects interacting with one another to provide the desired functionality and behavior.

Let's assume that many DataWindows in your application are required to highlight the selected row. Instead of reinventing the object wherever required, you can create what is called a *Standard User Object* having this behavior.

PowerBuilder enables developers to extend the functionality of PowerBuilder controls and create customized objects, as described earlier, called *User Objects*. Standard User Objects are those User Objects that are derived from one standard PowerBuilder control. They have events and behaviors of the standard PowerBuilder control. These standard User Objects can then be used in windows and your Custom User Object repeatedly. They can be of two types: visual User Objects or non-visual Class User Objects.

In general, User Objects need to be well encapsulated and have a friendly interface to access their state information and behavior. Variables and functions need to be scoped as private, protected, or public. User-defined events need to be used whenever the parent window needs to respond to customized behavior.

In the next chapter, which describes Custom User Objects, you will create a StyleBar that lets you select the font, style, alignment, and size of the text. In this chapter, you will create a *picturebutton* Standard Visual User Object that you will use as a toggle button in the StyleBar Custom Visual User Object. A picturebutton and a command button display the same behavior, but the picturebutton has a picture attribute for each of its two states (up and down).

The User Object Painter

Open the User Object Painter by clicking on the User Object Painter button on the PowerBar or by pressing **Shift-F11**. You are prompted with the Select User Object window (see Fig. 13.1). The open User Object window has a number of buttons for various options. Click on the New button to create a new User Object. The open User Object window closes, and you are prompted with a New User Object window. You can select the style of your new User Object from this

window (see Fig. 13.2). The selections are grouped in two categories: Class, with the choices being Custom, Standard, and C++, and Visual, with the choices being Custom, External, Standard, and VBX. Select Visual Standard. You are now prompted with the Select Visual Standard Type window (see Fig. 13.3). The scrollable list box presents all the types of Standard User Objects that can be created. In this list, double-click on picturebutton or select picturebutton and click **OK**.

Figure 13.1.
Select User Object window.

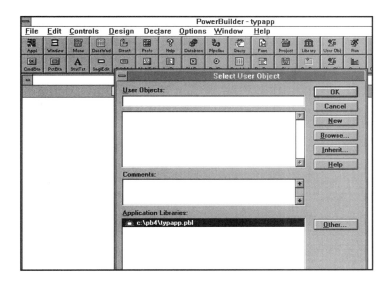

Figure 13.2.
Select Category of User Object.

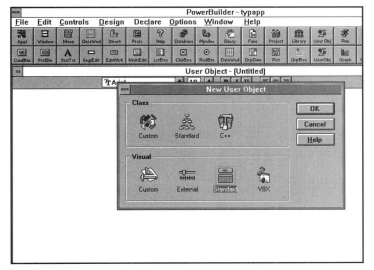

Figure 13.3.
Select Visual Standard User Object window.

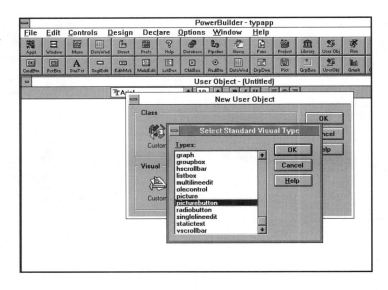

In the User Object Painter, a picturebutton is placed at the top-left corner (see Fig. 13.4). The StyleBar above this picturebutton lets you set the style of the text on the picturebutton. Starting from left, the first edit field lets you set the text itself; the next drop-down list box gives you a list of available fonts; the next editable drop-down list box lets you set the points for the font size; the next set of three buttons lets you set the style of the text as boldfaced, italicized, and/or underlined, and lets you align the text as left, centered, or right aligned. The Microhelp area at the bottom of the screen should display additional attributes of this picturebutton, such as name of the object, the x and y coordinates, and its height and width.

Figure 13.4.
The User Object Painter.

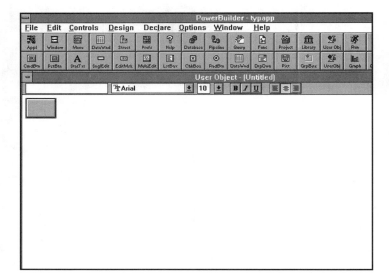

In the User Object Painter, you can declare shared variables, instance variables, User Object structures, User Object functions, global external functions, local external functions, and user events for the User Object by selecting the appropriate menu item from the Declare menu. You can set the scope of the instance variables and User Object functions to `private`, `protected`, or `public`. It is recommended to scope your functions and variables correctly in order to create well encapsulated objects.

Now let's go over each of these menu items in detail. You are prompted with the familiar Declare Global Variables window when you select the **G**lobal Variables menu item. This window lets you edit and add to the list of global variables in your application. By selecting the **S**hared Variables menu item, you are prompted with the Declare Shared Variables window. Declare all the variables that will be shared by objects inherited from the User Object that you are going to create. You will be prompted with the Declare Instance Variables window when you select the `Instance Variables` menu item. Use this window to edit or add to the list of instance variables for this object. Keeping with good object-oriented techniques, your instance variables need to be correctly scoped as private or protected to insulate the inner operations of your object from other objects. User Object functions need to be provided to enable other objects to access the value of instance variables in your User Object. By selecting the **U**ser Object Functions menu item, you are prompted with the Select Function in User Object window. You can either select an existing function or click **New** and create a new User Object function. By clicking on the User Object S**t**ructures, you are prompted with the Select Structure in User Object window. You can select and edit an existing structure or create a new structure. The Global E**x**ternal Functions and **L**ocal External Functions menu items enable you to declare the prototypes for external functions used globally or locally in this object. The User **E**vents menu item enables you to declare user events in your User Object for responding to windows events that are not declared as the default events for that type of object in PowerBuilder—and for enabling the window or custom User Object, where you will use this User Object as a control, to respond to customized messages.

Let's briefly go over the attributes of a picturebutton so you are comfortable with developing this type of a Standard User Object.

You can specify attributes of the picturebutton in the User Object Painter. Clicking the right mouse button on the picturebutton displays a pop-up menu. This pop-up menu enables you to set the following attributes: the name of the bitmap file that this picturebutton displays when it's enabled or disabled; the drag and drop attributes; the cursor file to display when this button is in focus (by default it's set to arrow); and the style of the picturebutton. The name of the bitmap to display can also be set by double-clicking on the picturebutton and selecting the appropriate bitmap when prompted with the Select Picture window.

Now let's go over each of these attributes in detail. The picture or the bitmap file that the picturebutton displays is called the `pictureName` attribute. This attribute can be set by either selecting the **N**ame option from the pop-up menu or by double-clicking on the picturebutton; in either case, you are prompted with a Select Picture window. If the bitmap is referenced

13

dynamically, it is advisable not to set the bitmap with the path unless the bitmap is qualified with the path name in the resource file while building the executable. You can also set the picture that will be displayed when this button is disabled by setting the `disabledName` attribute. This attribute is set by selecting the **Ch**ange Disabled option from the pop-up menu and by selecting a bitmap using the Select Picture window you will be prompted with. Drag and Drop options for this picturebutton can be set by selecting the **D**rag and Drop cascading menu option from the pop-up menu, and appropriately setting the `dragAuto` and the `dragIcon` attributes. When the `dragAuto` is set to true, PowerBuilder automatically puts the control into Drag mode, hence a click will trigger the `dragdrop` event and not the `Clicked` event. When `dragAuto` is set to false, you have to programatically initiate the Drag behavior. Selecting the Drag **I**con menu item from the pop-up menu prompts the user with a Select Drag Icon window. You should select the .ICO file you want to be displayed when the user drags the control. You can set the `pointer` attribute by selecting the **P**ointer menu item from the pop-up menu, and selecting the appropriate pointer file to display when prompted with the Select Pointer window. The `Style` menu item in the pop-up menu lets you set the `Cancel`, `Default`, `VerticalAlignment`, `HorizontalAlignment`, `OriginalSize`, and `Enabled` attributes.

Building the User Object

The picturebutton User Object will be used as a toggle button in the StyleBar, so let's determine the functionality that this toggle button will have to provide. When clicked, this picturebutton should display a picture to visually indicate that the style it represents is selected; and when clicked again, it should display a picture to visually indicate that it is no longer selected. The picturebutton should have no text, and other controls or objects should be able to determine its state.

The toggle User Object will be used to create different buttons to set the text style as boldfaced, underlined, and so on; therefore, you need to create a function to set the pictures this button will display in its two states: button up and button down.

The toggle button does not display any text, so set its text attribute to a blank string. This button requires instance variables to store the name of the bitmap that it displays when it is not selected—or up and the name of the bitmap that displays when it is selected, or down and a variable to store its selected state. Select the **I**nstance Variables menu item from the De**c**lare menu. You are prompted with the Declare Instance Variables window. Enter the following private variable declarations:

```
Private string is_dnBmpName
Private string is_upBmpName
Private boolean ib_isSelected
```

The variable `is_dnBmpName` stores the name of the down bitmap; `is_dnBmpName` stores the name of the up bitmap; and `ib_isSelected` stores the selected or not selected state.

Now you have to create a function to set values of the two variables is_dnBmpName and is_upBmpName, another function to access the variable ib_isSelected, and another function to set its initial state to up or down.

First let's create a User Object function called f_reg_buttons. This function does not return a value, but it requires two parameters: ps_dnBmpName and ps_upBmpName, which set the values of the private instance variables is_dnBmpName and is_upBmpName, respectively. Select the **User Object Functions** menu item from the Declare menu. You are prompted with the Select function in the User Object window. Because this is a new function, click **New,** and you are prompted with a New Function window. Name the function as f_reg_buttons. Set the access of the function to Protected. This function returns no value, so set Returns as (None). This function expects two variables, so set the first argument name as ps_dnBmpName. Set its Type as String and set Pass By as Value. Set the second argument name as ps_upBmpName. Set its Type as String and set Pass by as Value. Click on **OK,** and you are now ready to write the script for this function. The script of this function reads as follows:

```
/**********************************************************
* f_reg_buttons
* Parms:        ps_dnBmpName     string by value
*               ps_upBmpName     string by value
* Returns:      None
* Descr:        This function sets the private instance variables
*               is_dnBmpName and is_upBmpName
**********************************************************/

is_dnBmpName = ps_dnBmpName
is_upBmpName = ps_upBmpName
```

Do not forget to compile the script after you have finished typing it. Now let's create a function to set the initial state of the button as up or down and let's call this function f_set_initial_state. This function expects one parameter of the type integer. If the value of this parameter is 1, its state is set as selected, the down bitmap is displayed, and the private boolean instance variable ib_isSelected is set as TRUE. On the other hand, if the value of the parameter to this function is 0, the button's state is set as not selected, the up bitmap is displayed, and the private boolean instance variable ib_isSelected is set as FALSE. Let's repeat the steps taken while creating the previous function to create f_set_initial_state. From the Declare menu, select the **User Object Functions** menu. Click on **New** and declare the name of this function as f_set_inital_state. Set the Access of this function as Protected and set Returns to (None) because this function does not return a value. This function requires one parameter, so set the first argument name as pi_initialState and set its Type as Integer and Pass By Value. Click **OK** and type in this script for this function:

```
/**********************************************************
* f_set_initial_state
* Parms:        pi_initialState           integer by value
* Returns:      None
* Descr:        This function set the initial state as down if
* pi_initial_state = 1 or sets the initial state to up if
* pi_initialState = 0
**********************************************************/
```

13

```
if pi_initialState = 1 then
    this.pictureName = is_dnBmpName
    ib_isSelected = TRUE
elseif pi_initialState = 0 then
    this.pictureName = is_upBmpName
    ib_isSelected = FALSE
end if
```

Don't forget to compile the script after you have finished typing it. This button toggles between its selected or down state and not selected or up state when a user clicks on it. Let's add a script for its `Clicked` event, which will flip the state of the button. Right-click on the picturebutton and from the pop-up menu, select the **S**cripts menu item, which happens to be the first menu item. Now select the `Clicked` event from the list of events in the leftmost drop-down list box, which displays the label Select Event. The script in this event should read as follows:

```
/*********************************************************
* event: clicked
* Parms: None
* Returns: None
* Descr:    Toggle the state and the bitmap of this picture
* button by checking the value of the instance variable
* ib_isSelected
*********************************************************/

if ib_isSelected then
    //toggle the state to not selected
    ib_isSelected = false
    this.pictureName = is_upBmpName
else
    //toggle the condition to selected
    ib_isSelected = True
    this.pictureName = is_dnBmpName
end if
```

Do not forget to compile the script after you have finished typing it. Now let's create a function called `f_is_selected` to enable other controls to determine its state. This function returns the value of the instance variable `ib_isSelected`. Let's repeat the exercise of creating a function. From the Declare menu, select the **U**ser Object Functions item. Click on **New** and declare the Name of this function as `f_is_selected`. Set the Access of this function as `Public`; this function returns a boolean value so set Returns to `boolean`. This function expects no parameters so click **OK** and type in the following script for this function:

```
/*********************************************************
* f_is_selected
* Parms:    None
* Returns: boolean
* Descr:    This function returns the value of the instance
* variable ib_isSelected.  This function return TRUE if the
* button is in a selected state OR returns FALSE.
*********************************************************/

return ib_isSelected
```

Don't forget to compile the script after you have finished typing it.

Note: The function `f_is_selected` has its Access set as Public because this function is used by other controls to determine the state of the toggle button.

Now that you have created all the functions and scripts to provide the desired functionality and behavior, save the picturebutton User Object that you have created. From the **F**ile menu, select the **S**ave menu item. You are prompted with the Save User Object window (see Fig. 13.5). Name this object as `uo_toggle_button`, select the Application Library you want to save it in, and click **OK**. You have now created your first Standard User Object and are on the way to becoming an adept object-oriented programmer!

Figure 13.5.
Save User Object window.

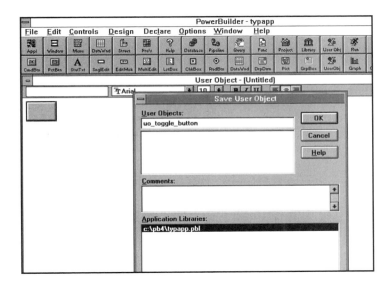

Putting User Objects in Your Windows

After you have created your Standard User Objects in the User Object Painter, they have to be incorporated in your windows and Custom User Objects to provide the desired functionality. Let's create a window that has a toggle button that displays the bitmap files cut1.bmp and cut2.bmp in its up and down states, respectively (both of these bitmaps come with PowerBuilder), and the initial state of this button is up.

At this stage, you should be familiar with creating windows. From the PowerBar, click on the Window Painter button or press **Shift-F11**. You are prompted with the Select Window window. Click on the **New** button to create a new window. Now from the Window PainterBar, click on the User Object button. You are prompted with the Select User Object window (see

Fig. 13.6). From the application libraries section in the Select User Object window, select the .pbl file in which you stored the User Object uo_toggle_button. Now from the list of User Objects stored in this .PBL file, select uo_toggle_button and click **OK**. Now place this User Object on the window by clicking on the spot where you want to locate it (see Fig. 13.7).

Figure 13.6.
Select User Object Window in Window Painter.

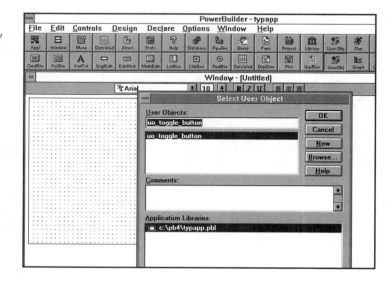

Figure 13.7.
Window with toggle button User Object.

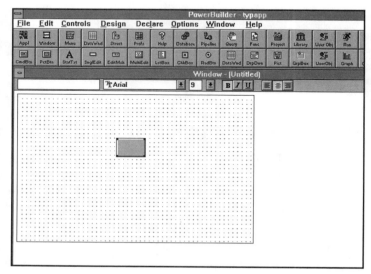

You can change its location on the window by dragging it to the new location. Now let's write the code to provide the desired functionality.

Recall the behavior that you earlier encapsulated in this User Object. This button in its up or not selected position should display cut1.bmp and in its down or selected position displays cut2.bmp, and its initial state is up. Initialize these attributes and this behavior by the following code in the constructor event of the User Object control. (Right-click on the toggle button and select **S**cript from the pop-up menu; then select the constructor event from the list of events in the drop-down list box in the top-left corner.)

```
/********************************************************
* constructor
* Parms:    None
* Returns:  None
* Descr:    Set the initial up picture as cut1.bmp
* and down pciture as cut2.bmp, and set the inital
* state of the button as up
********************************************************/

//set the pictures
f_reg_buttons(cut2.bmp, cut1.bmp)
//set the initial state as up
f_set_initial_state(0)
```

Do not forget to compile the script after you have finished typing it. Now save the window and call it w_toggle_button_test. Run the window by pressing **Ctrl-W** and by selecting the window w_toggle_button_test (see Fig. 13.8). Now as the window comes up, the toggle button initially displays cut1.bmp, and when you click this button, it toggles between its up and down states by displaying the appropriate bitmaps.

Figure 13.8.
Run Window selection window.

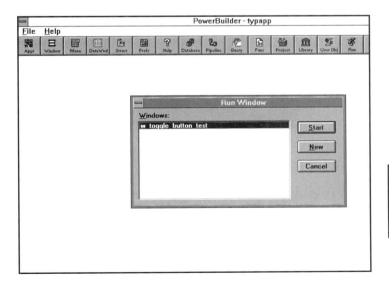

Other Standard User Objects

Standard User Objects make application development and code maintenance much easier. There are many examples of other useful Standard User Objects. Almost all windows have a Close button; click on this button, and the window closes. You can create a Standard User Object of the type commandbutton, which closes the parent window in the Clicked event and has its text attribute set to Close. Instead of duplication of code in every screen to provide this functionality, all you have to do is create a control in every window inherited from this User Object. Another common requirement that you will notice while developing applications using PowerBuilder is for DataWindows that highlight the selected row. You can create a Standard User Object of the type DataWindow which, in the Clicked event, checks if the clicked row is valid and highlights it.

Morning Summary

PowerBuilder has provided an object-rich development environment by providing a suite of basic objects and controls, such as DataWindows, command buttons, static text fields, and so on. These are well encapsulated objects providing a basic set of behaviors. You can extend the behavior of any of these objects and create what are known as Standard User objects. These objects have the events and behaviors of the standard PowerBuilder control from which they are derived. They can then be used repeatedly in windows and your custom User Objects.

Standard User Objects can be classified into two categories: Visual and non-visual Standard User Objects. In this chapter, we discussed and created a picturebutton Visual Standard User Object.

Remember that the user objects have to be well encapsulated and require a friendly interface to access their state information and behavior. Variables need to be scoped as private, protected, or public. It is recommended to use user-defined events wherever the parent window needs to respond to customized behavior.

Other Types of
User Objects

In this lesson, you will learn how to create and use the other types of PowerBuilder User Objects. These User Objects include:

- [ ] The Custom Visual User Object
- [ ] The Standard Class User Object
- [ ] The Custom Class User Object
- [ ] The External User Object
- [ ] The VBX User Object
- [ ] The C++ Class User Object
- [ ] The OLE 2.0 Control

Custom Visual User Object

You have learned how to extend a single PowerBuilder control by using the Standard Visual User Object. However, what if you want to create a special control that is really made up of a group of controls? Let's say you want to make a Text StyleBar similar to the one that you use in the Window Painter to control the font, size, and style of text in your windows? There's no reason that you cannot emulate that behavior with your own controls; but there is more than one control on a StyleBar, and so it cannot be a Standard Visual User Object. Does this mean that if you want to place a StyleBar in three of your windows, you have to recode all of the functionality in each of the three windows where you want to place the StyleBar? Well, you might, if it weren't for the *Custom Visual User Object.*

The Custom Visual User Object is similar to the Standard Visual User Object in that you can extend PowerBuilder controls to add your own behavior to them. The Standard Visual User Object allows you to extend a single control. However, the Custom Visual User Object is used to take multiple PowerBuilder controls and create a brand new control out of them. The Custom Visual User Object is like a shell on which you place individual PowerBuilder controls. Then you code behavior for those controls and save them as a single unit. You can then place that unit onto a window or even onto another Custom Visual User Object.

The Custom Visual User Object shell, however, works slightly differently than the Standard Visual User Object. Unlike the Standard Visual User Object, the Custom Visual User Object has no events to speak of, except for the standard events: `Constructor`, `Destructor`, the `Drag...` events, the *Other* event, and the `RButtonDown` event. Each control on the Custom Visual User Object has its own events as well; however, they are not visible to the window upon which you place the Custom Visual User Object. Instead, you must make interfaces between the parent of the Custom Visual User Object and controls of interest to it. For example, if you are developing a StyleBar, you will need to create some way for the parent window to respond to your user changing the font or the size of the text by using your StyleBar object. Because the parent window

cannot place code inside the SelectionChanged event of the Font drop-down list box, the StyleBar object will instead have to find a different way to allow the parent to respond.

Generally, the way this is done is by declaring User Events in the Custom User Object that correspond to each of the actions of interest that take place, and User Object functions that the parent can call to get the information that causes the event. Continuing with our example, you may decide to create a User Event for the StyleBar called ue_fontchanged, which is triggered manually (for example, with a TriggerEvent() function call) from the SelectionChanged event of the Font drop-down listbox. Then, there would be a Public User Object function called f_get_font() that would return the currently selected font from the Font drop-down list box. The user calls the f_get_font() function from the ue_fontchanged event and changes the font accordingly. Similarly, the size of the font, style of the font, and so on, can all be transmitted in the same manner.

DO	DON'T

DO Encapsulate all of the code that is used to make the Custom Visual User Object work. Place this functional code in places where the window or object that houses the Custom Visual User Object cannot access it. This includes private or protected functions and instance variables, and events of the objects that are within the Custom Visual User Object. Limit public functions and user events of the Custom Visual User Object itself to functions that are used to tell the parent that something happened, and to let the parent get the information it needs to respond to such events.

DON'T Allow the parent object to access information about the insides of a Custom Visual User Object that it doesn't need.

By using these object-oriented techniques, the parent window of your User Object doesn't have to deal with this code and doesn't even have the opportunity to mess it up.

2..4..6..8...ENCAPSULATE..ENCAPSULATE!!

Let's go ahead and build an object-oriented StyleBar Custom Visual User Object that you can use in your applications.

Open the User Object Painter by pressing **Shift-F11** or by clicking on the User Object Painter button on the PowerBar. You will then be presented with the Select User Object dialog box that you saw in the last lesson. Click on the **New** button from the Select User Object dialog box to create a new User Object. When prompted for the type of user object that you want to create, select Custom from the Visual section. Pay attention, though; you can also choose to create a Custom Class User Object, and you don't want to do that yet. (You'll do that later.) You'll be presented with an empty Custom Visual User Object screen that looks a lot like the Window Painter (see Fig. 14.1). In fact, in many ways, the Custom Visual User Object is a lot like a window.

Figure 14.1.
The Custom Visual User Object window.

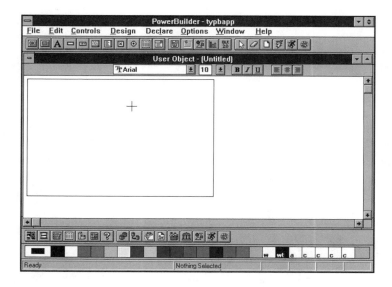

The Font Selection Control of the StyleBar

Let's place a font selection control on the Custom Visual User Object. Remember in the Window Painter how the cursor changed modes? Sometimes it was in Selection mode and could move things around and edit their styles, and other times it was in Control Creation mode where you could use it to create a control on your window. Well, the cursor in the Custom Visual User Object Painter works exactly the same way. So, in order to place a control on your Custom Visual User Object, you have to put your cursor into Control Creation mode with the control that you want to put on your User Object.

Select DropDownListbox from the **C**ontrol menu or click on the drop-down list box button on the User Object PainterBar. Place the drop-down list box on your User Object in the top-left corner. Double-click on it to edit its style. In the area where it says Item, enter the following list:

```
Arial
Courier
MS Sans Serif
MS Serif
System
Terminal
Times New Roman
```

Warning: When editing text in the Item list, pressing the **Enter** key by itself will trigger the default **OK** button of the drop-down list box Style dialog box. So instead, separate each line by holding down the **Ctrl** key when you press **Enter**.

Change the name of the drop-down list box to `ddlb_font` and click on the check box labeled Allow Editing. Click **OK** to accept your changes. Now, size the drop-down list box so that all of the fonts in the list fit properly.

Let's also create a drop-down list box to let the user choose the size of the font. Again, make your cursor into a drop-down list box creator. Place another drop-down list box immediately to the right of the first one. Double-click on the new drop-down list box and enter the following list for its items:

```
8
9
10
12
14
16
24
32
```

Change the name of this drop-down list box to `ddlb_size` and click on the check box labeled Allow Editing. Then click the **OK** button to save your changes. To make your drop-down list boxes look really sharp and standard, change their fonts to MS Sans Serif 8 by selecting each (or both) of them and by choosing MS Sans Serif from the StyleBars Font drop-down list box, and then choose 8 from the StyleBars Size drop-down list box. Pay attention when you do this—this is exactly the behavior you will be emulating.

The Style Buttons of the StyleBar

In the last lesson, you built a toggle button User Object. Now, let's place some toggle buttons on your StyleBar. In order to create a toggle button, you need to turn your cursor into a toggle button user object creator. Select User**O**bject... from the **C**ontrol menu or click on the User Object button on the User Object PainterBar. You are then presented with the Select User Object dialog box, where you can select the exact user object that you want your cursor to create (see Fig. 14.2). Select the Toggle Button you created this morning and click **OK**. Now, place a toggle button on your User Object next to the Size drop-down list box. Since you'll need six of them, quickly place six of them into your StyleBar User Object by duplicating your first one five times. To duplicate an object, right-click on the object and select **D**uplicate from the Right Mouse menu, or press **Ctrl-T**. Repeat this five more times until there are six toggle buttons on-screen.

Line up your toggle buttons so that they are all right next to each other and horizontally aligned. Make some space between the middle two buttons so that you have two sets of three toggle buttons. Now, let's set up the first toggle button. Double-click on the leftmost button to see its Style window. Notice that the Style window you are presented with is the Style window you see for *any* picture control (see Fig. 14.3). This is because PowerBuilder gives you the same interface for Standard User Objects as the base class control from which they are derived. Change the name of the first toggle button to p_bold. Go into the Script Painter by clicking on the Script button on the User Object PainterBar, then choose the Constructor event from the Select Event drop-down list box, and enter the following line of code:

```
f_reg_buttons( "pb_b_up.bmp", "pb_b_dn.bmp" )
```

Figure 14.2.
The Select User Object dialog box.

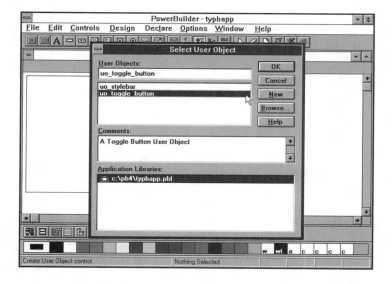

Figure 14.3.
The Toggle Button User Object Style dialog box.

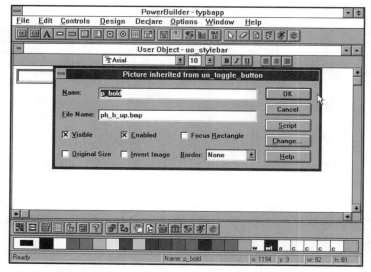

Then close the Script Painter. That should be all you need to do to make this toggle button work.

> **Note:** Certain things that I've been talking about in the last several lessons should be starting to become clearer now. You've created a standard user object called the toggle button to extend the Picture control to more closely meet your needs because none of the other controls have met them. Then, you have used this new control inside of your StyleBar object. With only a small amount of code, you have been able to integrate the toggle button into your StyleBar. Even though you have six toggle buttons in your StyleBar, you have coded all of the functionality for your toggle button only once. If you later decide to change the way your toggle button works, or worse yet, find a bug, you will only have to change code in one place. The advantages of object-oriented design and development should be starting to wake up inside your mind now. Even if they are not, though, don't worry—you'll get it soon enough.

Communicating User Events

Now, let's do a few last things to the StyleBar to make it functionally usable. Declare a User Event for the StyleBar that will be used to communicate a style change to the parent window. Select User **E**vents from the Declare menu. Enter the following event name:

```
ue_style_changed
```

Select or enter `pbm_custom01` as the PowerBuilder User Event that it will map to. Now, click **OK**. Next, you'll create a User Object function that will allow the user to get the current style settings. Select **U**ser Object Function from the Declare menu. Click on the **New** button to create a new User Object function. As the name of the function, enter

```
f_get_font
```

Make the function a Protected function with a return type of `string`. There are no parameters to the function, so click the **OK** button. Enter the following line of code:

```
RETURN ddlb_font.text
```

Then, return to the User Object Painter by selecting **R**eturn from the **F**ile menu or by clicking on the Return To User Object Painter button on the Function PainterBar. Finally, let's make the Font drop-down list box trigger the `ue_stylechanged` event so that the parent of the StyleBar can react to a font change. Open up the Script Painter for the Font drop-down list box and enter the following line of code:

```
TriggerEvent( Parent, ue_stylechanged, 1, 0)
```

Recognize that this is a slightly different version of the TriggerEvent function than what you've used before. Here's why. The third and fourth parameters represent numbers that will be passed to the triggered event, ue_stylechanged, in the Message.WordParm and Message.LongParm components. This is how you can pass parameters to events. You can in this way indicate to the ue_stylechanged event which style component has been changed. Pass a 1 to the ue_stylechanged event in the Word Parameter to indicate that the font has changed. Better yet, let's create some Instance Variables to represent the different types of changes to the style that can happen. This way, when you place this object inside a window, you don't have to remember abstract numbers but instead can use your English-like variable names to check the type of style change that has occurred.

Open the Declare Instance Variables dialog box by selecting **I**nstance Variables from the **D**eclare menu. Enter the following variable declarations—don't forget to use **Ctrl-Enter** to create a new line:

```
Protected:
  Int  ICI_CHG_FONT = 1
  Int  ICI_CHG_SIZE = 2
  Int  ICI_CHG_BOLD = 3
  Int  ICI_CHG_ITALIC = 4
  Int  ICI_CHG_UNDERLINE = 5
  Int  ICI_CHG_JUSTIFY = 6
```

Now, replace the 1 in your script with the constant for a Font change, ICI_CHG_FONT. The line of code should now read:

```
TriggerEvent( Parent, ue_stylechanged, ICI_CHG_FONT, 0)
```

This way, anyone who reads this code will be able to more easily understand what you are trying to do.

Note: In some languages, there is a concept of a *constant*—a special type of variable that cannot be changed once you set a value to it. In general, the constant is used almost like an enumerated datatype, to make your code more readable by allowing you to give your own name to a value that is used for a particular purpose—much like what you have done earlier by giving your ue_stylechanged parameters names instead of numbers.

PowerBuilder doesn't have a special *constant* datatype, though. Even though you have set the values of your constant-like variables to meet your needs, PowerBuilder will not prevent you from changing their values. However, you can use naming conventions to indicate that the value is a constant and enforce the constant values yourself by following your conventions, thereby producing the same effect.

Close the Script Painter and return to the User Object Painter. Then, save the StyleBar. Select **S**ave from the **F**ile menu. You are presented with the Save User Object dialog box (Fig. 14.4). Enter

```
uo_stylebar
```

as the name, and then enter in the following comment:

```
The StyleBar user object from chapter 14
```

Figure 14.4.
The Save User Object dialog box.

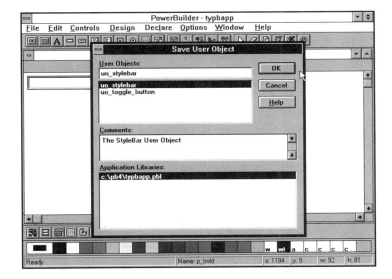

Later, you'll actually use the StyleBar in a window and see how it can be used to modify the style of other objects.

Standard Class User Object

Another type of User Object that you can create is a *Standard Class User Object*. The Standard Class User Object, like the Standard Visual User Object, allows you to extend a Standard PowerBuilder construct to meet your needs. However, in the case of the Standard Class User Object, the construct that you are extending is a PowerBuilder class, not a visual control. The PowerBuilder classes that you can extend are the DynamicDescriptionArea, DynamicStagingArea, Pipeline, and Transaction, which have to do with the Database (you'll learn about that later, in Chapters 19 through 25); the OLEObject, OLEStorage, and OLEStream objects, which are for Object Linking and Embedding; the MailSession object, which handles mail sessions with a server that follows the Microsoft Mail Application Programmer Interface (MAPI) standard; and the Error and Message classes, which are used internally by PowerBuilder to handle system errors and windows events, respectively.

These PowerBuilder classes are functional, but not visual. In other words, they perform functions and contain logic without ever appearing on-screen. The Message class stores information about the PowerBuilder messages that are being passed between objects, but you can never see it on-screen. The Error class holds information about any errors that occur in the system, but again, it cannot be seen on-screen. The OLE and MailSession classes communicate with assorted server applications, and the rest communicate with the database. All in all, though, each of these classes has attributes, events, and functions, but they lack visual characteristics because they cannot be made visible on-screen.

To create a Standard Class User Object, open the User Object Painter, as you have been, by pressing **Shift-F11** or by clicking on the User Object Painter button on the PowerBar. Then, click on the **New** button on the Select User Object dialog box to create a new User Object. When prompted for the type of User Object you want to create, select Standard from the Class section. You are prompted with the Select Standard Class Type dialog box, where you can select the type of standard class that you want to create (see Fig. 14.5). Highlight the type of standard visual object that you want to extend and press the **OK** button, and you are presented with the User Object Painter window. However, because you cannot place visual controls on your Standard Class User Object, all of the menu items inside of the **E**dit, **C**ontrols, and **D**esign menus do not apply and are disabled. In addition, you will not be able to select any of the controls buttons on the toolbar. However, you may still perform all of the actions that are available inside the Dec**l**are menu. This includes declaring Instance and Shared variables for the class, declaring User Object functions and structures for the class, and even declaring User Events. In addition, you can open the Script Painter for the Standard Class Object and write code for each of these events, along with any events that come stock with the object. In this manner, you can extend the default behavior of the Standard Class that you have selected from the list.

Figure 14.5.
The Select Standard Class Type dialog box.

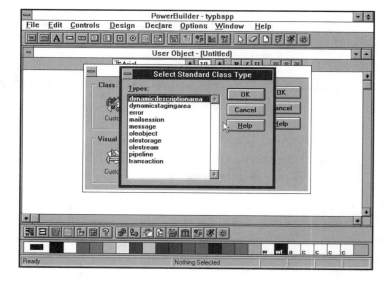

At first glance, it may be difficult to understand why you even need such a feature. After all, if these standard classes are only used internally by PowerBuilder, why would you want to extend them? Well, the answer is that these classes are managed internally by PowerBuilder but are accessed both by your code and, in some cases, by external sources such as the Database server, OLE server, or Mail server. Because of this, you may find it necessary to extend the features of these classes to support features of the server, or to facilitate your code. Table 14.1 lists several examples of the kinds of extensions you may want to add to Standard Classes. However, as you begin to develop applications of your own by using PowerBuilder, you may find other opportunities and reasons to extend the PowerBuilder classes.

Table 14.1. Example Standard Class extensions.

Class	Extension
Message	Include additional data in an `OpenxxxWithParm` call to permit receipt of multiple parameters without a structure. Build a message logging function that will log information about the current message to a file.
Error	Encapsulate error handling functions right into the Error Object.
Pipeline	Transfer database data and structure between multiple servers in an application script.
Transaction	Encapsulate transaction management functions directly into the Transaction Object. Also to use *Remote Procedure Calls*, special database calls that require special function prototypes in the transaction object. See your database interface documentation for details.

Once your new Standard Classes are built and saved, you will need to incorporate them into the application itself. To do this for the ones that are used by PowerBuilder, you simply open up the Application Object (either via the Library Painter or the Application Painter) and change the name of the default global variable object to the name of your new Standard Class. For example, if you create a new error object called my_err, you will replace the data type of the Error global variable with my_err. Then, when your application starts, it will declare its Error global variable as a variable of type my_err instead of type error. For the other datatypes, or in a case where you don't want the variable to be a PowerBuilder Default Global variable but are declaring a local, shared, or instance copy that will be used by your application in a different manner, you need to *instantiate* the variable yourself. Instantiating the variable refers to creating a live instance of the object that has memory allocated for its variables, functions, and events, and can then be used by the rest of the application. We'll talk more about how to instantiate a variable in a few minutes.

Custom Class User Object

The capability to extend the PowerBuilder classes with a Standard Class User Object is a very powerful one. In addition, however, you may want to create a non-visual class of your own. For example, you may want to create some sort of utility class, like an error handler, a communications handler, or even a multimedia class. Or, you may want to create some kind of class to handle your users' business logic. There are any number of reasons that an application designed using the object oriented methodology would require a non-visual class definition, and by using the Custom Class User Object, you can implement that class definition.

To create a Custom Class User Object, you open the User Object Painter as you have done previously by pressing **Shift-F11** or by clicking on the User Object Painter button on the PowerBar. Then, click on the **New** button on the Select User Object dialog box to create a new User Object. When prompted for the type of user object you want to create, double-click on the Custom icon in the Class section. The User Object Painter window will open again. The environment works very much like the environment when you create a Standard Class, except that the only events that are defined for a Custom Object are the Constructor and Destructor events and the object does not have any attributes or behaviors. You will put in all of the attributes and behaviors yourself by declaring Instance and Shared Variables, User Events, and User Object Structures and Functions. Then, as with most of the Standard Class User Objects, you will need to instantiate them inside your applications so that you can use them.

Using Classes in Your Application

When you use a visual object like a window or a button, and you open it, PowerBuilder instantiates the object for you as part of the Open of the window, and so you don't have to do anything else to it. When you declare a standard variable like a string or an integer, internally PowerBuilder knows how to allocate the memory for it, so you don't need to do anything else to use that either. Even when you tell PowerBuilder to use your Standard Class as the datatype for one of its default global variables, PowerBuilder instantiates it for you, and you don't need to do anything else to be able to use it. However, when you want to use a class variable in your code, you need to instantiate it yourself.

To instantiate a non-visual class variable you must use the CREATE command. The syntax for the CREATE command is

```
<class variable> = CREATE <class type>
```

You must, of course, declare the variable before you attempt to CREATE it, and you must CREATE it before you attempt to use it. When you are done with it, you can release the memory that was allocated for the object by using the DESTROY command. The syntax for the DESTROY command is

```
DESTROY <class variable>
```

Once the variable is destroyed, it can no longer be referenced by your code without re-CREATE-ing it.

Let's say you have created a new error object called my_err, and you want to use it to generate some error message in your code. The following code listing demonstrates how you would go about declaring this object:

```
my_err luo_error_obj
luo_error_obj = CREATE my_err
luo_error_obj.f_generate_error( 21)
DESTROY luo_error_obj
```

If the object has been declared locally, you must create and destroy that object inside the same event because it will not live past the end of that event's script. However, if the object has been declared as an Instance, Shared, or Global Variable, you do not have to create and destroy your classes inside the same event. You may decide to CREATE a class in the Constructor event of an object and then DESTROY it in the Destructor event of that same object. This is especially useful if the object is declared as an Instance variable and is used in more than one event in the system. Remember, if you create and destroy your classes in different events, you need to ensure that no event will attempt to access it if it hasn't already been created or if it has already been destroyed. You can use the *IsValid()* function to determine if the object has been created. The format for the IsValid() function is

```
IsValid( <object> )
```

It returns TRUE if the object is valid and FALSE if the object is not valid. The IsValid() function does not just test the validity of class objects. You can also check if a window is valid or if a control is valid, or if just about anything else is valid by using the IsValid() function, as we demonstrated in Chapter 10.

Other Types of User Objects

So far, we have discussed all of the User Object types that extend standard PowerBuilder constructs and controls. These User Objects all have something in common—they are defined completely as PowerBuilder objects. In addition, however, there are several other User Object types that you can create that allow you to interact with objects that are external to the PowerBuilder environment. Let's talk about these User Object types now.

External User Object

Developers develop most applications for a specific purpose or for a specific user. There are a large number of vendors who are now developing controls for other developers to use in their applications. By saving their controls in special library files, other developers can use their *Application Programmers Interface (API)* to interact with their controls and make them work.

There are two flavors of this type of control. The first is the *Windows custom control*, which is a control that follows the guidelines specified by the Microsoft Windows Software Developers Kit for creating custom controls. These controls are stored in *Dynamic Link Library* files (.DLLs). PowerBuilder allows you to incorporate a custom control that is stored in a .DLL file into your PowerBuilder application by creating an *External User Object*.

As you may have guessed, you create an External User Object by opening the User Object Painter. You do this by pressing **Shift-F11** or by clicking on the User Object Painter button on the PowerBar. Then, click on the **New** button on the Select User Object dialog box to create a new User Object. When prompted for the type of user object you want to create, double-click on the External icon in the Visual section. You will then be prompted to select the .DLL file that contains the control that will become your External User Object (see Fig. 14.6). For now, select the cpalette.dll file from the \PB4\EXAMPLES directory where you stored your PowerBuilder example files. This .DLL file contains a number of custom controls by a company called Blaise that are included with the PowerBuilder sample application (although if you want to redistribute this .DLL, you will need to purchase it directly from the company). Included among these is a progress meter control, which you can use to display the progress of something that is happening. The progress meter usually looks like a rectangle that fills to the right until it reaches 100% complete. For example, as PowerBuilder installed files to your hard drive, it used a progress meter to display how far along the installation process was. Selecting the cpallete.dll file is the first step toward integrating a progress meter into your application—by creating an External Custom User Object out of it.

Figure 14.6.
Pick a .DLL, any .DLL.

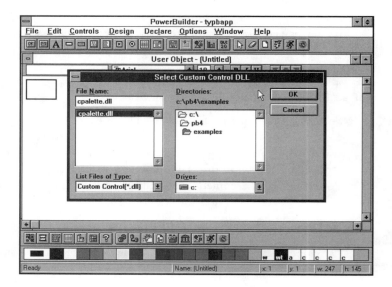

After selecting the .DLL file that you are interested in, you are then presented with the External User Object Style dialog box, where you can specify the settings for your External User Object (see Fig. 14.7). The first line of this dialog box allows you to specify the name of the .DLL file within which the control is housed. The next edit box labeled Class Name: is where you specify the class name of the control that you want to incorporate into your application. By default, PowerBuilder will specify the .DLL name as the class name. However, in the case of the progress meter, the name of the class is cpmeter. Type **cpmeter** into the Class Name: edit box. The last edit box is labeled Text:, and you can enter any text that might be inside the control. However, with a progress meter, there is no text, so leave it blank for now.

Figure 14.7.
*The External User Object
Style dialog box.*

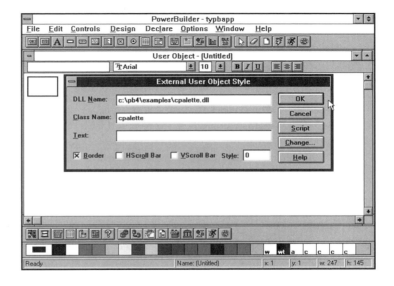

Beneath the edit boxes are three check boxes that allow you to specify if the control will have a border and scroll bars. Your progress meter comes with its own border, so let's turn the PowerBuilder border off. Finally, there is a small edit box labeled Style:, where you can enter in the *style number* of the control. Many custom controls have special characteristics that you can set using the style number. For example, there are several different styles of progress meter: horizontal or vertical, dial or bar, and so on. Generally, the controls documentation will indicate which numbers correspond to which styles. By placing a style number in the box, you can specify certain features of the control. For your progress meter, for example, you can use the default style of 0, or you can select from other features by specifying other styles. For example, you can turn off the display of the number in the meter by specifying a style number of 16.

Warning: Actually, since most custom controls are designed to be integrated into applications that were written in C, they usually use special names called *constants* for their styles instead of numbers. A C program can simply include a special *header file* in its code, and the constants will automatically be converted into numbers by the C compiler. However, PowerBuilder does not use these header files. If your custom controls documentation only lists the style name and not the style number, look for a header file that ends with the extension .h or .hpp. You can use a standard text editor (such as Notepad or Write) to edit this file and find the line containing the definition of your style. It should read something like

```
#define <style name> <number>
```

You can then use the number that you see here as the style number in your External User Object.

If you decide you have picked the wrong .DLL, you can change it by clicking on the **Change** button, and you will once again be presented with the Select .DLL File dialog box (refer to Fig. 14.6). In addition, you can get right to the Script Painter for this control by clicking on the **Script** button. You can indicate that you are finished here by clicking on the **OK** or **Cancel** buttons.

After you click on the **OK** button, the User Object Painter window will open again, this time with your custom control displayed. If you entered in all of the settings that I specified earlier, your window will look like Figure 14.8. As with the other windows in the system, you can drag the edges and corners to resize the custom control. Go ahead and drag the edge of the meter so that it looks like more a rectangle instead of a square. Let's say you want to change the style of the control. You can bring back the External User Object Style dialog box by either double-clicking on the control or by selecting **U**ser Object Style from the **D**esign menu.

Interacting with Your External User Object

In addition to setting up the style of the control, you may want to create functions that will help the user interact with your control. For example, in the case of your progress meter, you need to provide a method for the user of this control to set the amount of progress on the meter. According to the Blaise documentation, you set the amount of progress on the meter by sending a special user-defined message to the control. The message that you need to send is WM_USER + 3018. In Windows, each message has a specific number. WM_USER is equivalent to number 1024, so WM_USER + 3018 is 4042. You send the new position of the meter as the Word parameter of the message. In PowerBuilder, you send a message to a control by using the Send() function. The first parameter of the Send() function is the handle of the control to which you want to send your

message. In order to get the handle of a control, you use the *Handle()* function, passing to it the name of the control whose handle you want. Then, as the second parameter to the Send() function, you pass the message number to send—in your case, 4042. The last two parameters to the Send() function are the Word parameter and Long parameter, respectively. Rather than require the user to remember all of these details of the Blaise Progress Meter, you can create a User Object function that handles the job. Lets create a User Object function called f_set_position(). Select **U**ser Object Function from the **D**eclare menu, and you are presented with the User Object Function dialog box. Then, click on the **New** button to create a new function. Finally, enter the name of the function in the Name: box and create a single argument of type Int called pi_position. The function is public and does not return any value (indicated by the word (None) in the box labeled Return:). Then, click the **OK** button. Now, enter the following line of code:

```
Send( handle( THIS), 4042, pi_position, 0)
```

This line of code will send the message WM_USER + 3018 to itself (indicated by the THIS keyword) using the pi_position parameter passed in by the caller of the function. Now, the developer who uses this control in their system simply has to say

```
uo_meter.f_set_position( 100)
```

to set the meter's position to 100 percent and doesn't have to look up in the Blaise documentation how to use this meter.

Figure 14.8.

The progress meter custom control (in User Object Painter).

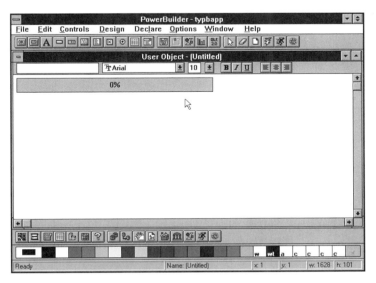

User Object Notification Messages

While some controls communicate with their callers by using user events, others also communicate with their callers by using special user notification command messages. Without discussing the reason why each one is used, the only difference has to do with the way you can trap these messages. As a developer, you will probably never need to send a notification message to elicit a reaction from a control. This kind of behavior is usually handled as you did earlier with the user message that you sent to the control to change the meter position. However, you may have to trap user events and notifications that are being received by an external control in response to input within the control. For example, you may have an external button control and need to trap the Clicked event. However, instead of corresponding to a PowerBuilder Clicked event, you may need to have the Clicked event correspond to a user event or notification message. In order to do this, simply declare a user event that corresponds to the correct event or notification, and then you can place code inside that event to respond to a message from the control. The user event name for messages that are WM_USER messages are pbm_custom*nn*. The first message, pbm_custom01, is equivalent to WM_USER; the second, pbm_custom02, is equivalent to WM_USER + 1; and so on, all the way to pbm_custom75, which corresponds to WM_USER + 74. If you need to react to a notification message, you can trap the pbm_uonexteral*nn* messages. These messages correspond to special notification messages that are sent from the control to its parent window. The pbm_uonexternal01 message corresponds to notification number 0, all the way through pbm_uonexternal25, which corresponds to notification message 24. If you check the documentation that comes with your custom control, you should be able to determine which events you need to trap and then trap them by using these messages.

External Functions

The last method of communicating with an external .DLL file is through the use of functions. Although not limited to use in custom controls, you can allow PowerBuilder to interact with a function in a .DLL file by declaring it as an external function. As with variables, your external functions can be global to the application, or local to the object (or window) for which they are declared. With External User Objects, you will probably declare them as local, so let's declare a local external function. The format for the declaration of an external function is

```
{ SUBROUTINE ¦ FUNCTION <return type> } <function_name>( [REF] type1 arg1, [REF]
➡type2 arg2, .. [REF] type3 arg3) LIBRARY <lib_name>
```

If the function does not return a value, you start by specifying so with the keyword SUBROUTINE. Otherwise, you specify the function with the keyword FUNCTION, followed by the <return type>, the datatype of the value that will be returned when the function is called. Then, you specify the

name of the function, followed in parentheses by the datatype and argument name of each argument in the function. By default, the argument is passed by value. However, if it is passed by reference, simply specify the REF keyword in front of the datatype. Finally, you specify the name of the .DLL file that contains the function in quotes. For example, the following declaration prepares PowerBuilder to use the FlashWindow() function of the Microsoft Windows SDK, which flashes a window:

```
FUNCTION Boolean FlashWindow( UINT hWnd, Boolean fInvert) LIBRARY USER.EXE
```

Now, you can use the FlashWindow() function in your code, and PowerBuilder will know how to find it and how to translate the parameters into the proper parameters to pass to the USER.EXE file that accepts the function call.

By using the preceding methods, you can interact with external controls stored in .DLL files. You can send them messages and functions and receive input from them from by trapping their user and notification messages in user events.

VBX User Object

In addition to controls that are stored in .DLL files, Microsoft has created an API for a special kind of custom control specifically designed to interact with Visual Basic, and stored in a special kind of .DLL file, called a .VBX. PowerBuilder allows you to easily integrate these special controls into your application. To do this, you create a VBX User Object.

By now, you should already know that you create a VBX User Object by opening the User Object Painter. You should also know that you do this by pressing **Shift-F11** or by clicking on the User Object Painter button on the PowerBar. Then, click on the **New** button on the Select User Object dialog box to create a new User Object. When prompted for the type of User Object that you want to create, double-click on the VBX icon in the Visual section. You will then be prompted to select the .VBX file that contains the .VBX control that you want to create as a User Object (see Fig. 14.9). For now, select the vbdia.vbx file from the \PB4\EXAMPLES directory where you stored your PowerBuilder example files. This .VBX file contains a diamond button that allows the user to click in four directions: up, down, left, or right. When you select the vbdia.vbx file from the list, the name diamond will appear on the right in the box labeled Class Name:. As with .DLL files, there can be any number of controls in a single .VBX file. Unlike .DLL files, though, .VBX files have more information inside of them, so PowerBuilder can figure out what classes, attributes, and events are available to the user of this control. So, it lists the available controls in the Class Name: box. After you select one (in this case, the diamond,) you can click on the **OK** button, and you will be presented with the User Object Painter, containing your .VBX control.

14

Figure 14.9.

Select a .VBX File and Class.

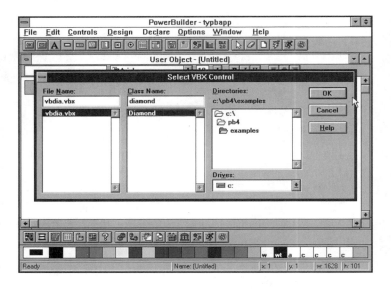

Once inside the User Object Painter, you can edit the attributes of the .VBX control by either double-clicking on it or by selecting **U**ser Object Style from the **D**esign menu. You will be presented with the VBX properties dialog box, where you can set the specific attributes of the .VBX control (see Fig. 14.10). In addition, you can edit the scripts of the .VBX control and even add user-defined events to trap other .VBX events. This works in a similar manner to the pbm_uonexternal*nn* message; however, with a .VBX control, the events are called pbm_vbxevent*nn*. Using this method, you can integrate a .VBX control right into your application.

Figure 14.10.

The VBX properties dialog box.

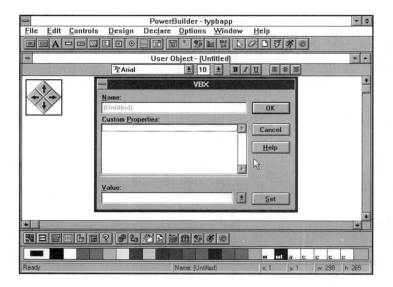

C++ Class User Objects

In addition to the above types of controls, those of you using PowerBuilder Enterprise Edition will also be able to create .DLL files of your own out of C++ classes that are compiled with Watcom C++ (assuming you installed this option). PowerBuilder allows you to easily integrate these .DLL files into your applications, and takes care of some of the overhead of declaring a C++ object for you. However, this is an advanced topic, and requires knowledge of C or C++ programming, so we will keep our discussion of this type of User Object very brief.

To create a C++ Class User Object, you open the User Object Painter as you have done previously, by pressing **Shift-F11** or by clicking on the User Object Painter button on the PowerBar. Then, click on the **New** button on the Select User Object dialog box to create a new User Object. When prompted for the type of user object that you want to create, double-click on the C++ icon in the Class section. You will now be prompted to enter the name of the .DLL file that you want to create. Then, you will be presented with the User Object screen. This time, you cannot create scripts or place controls on the User Object window. You can only declare variables (Global, Shared, and Instance) and User Object Functions from the Declare menu. In addition, when you select any of these items, they look slightly different than when you perform these operations in other places. Finally, notice that even though you can declare a function name and parameter list, you cannot actually code the function—you are simply returned to the User Object Painter.

When you are finished declaring your variables and functions, you can select Invoke C++ **E**ditor from the **D**esign menu, which will convert your declarations into C++ syntax and invoke the Watcom C++ editor with that syntax prepared for you. You can then code your functions and compile them into a .DLL file, which can then be used by your PowerBuilder application.

OLE 2.0 Objects

One other important method of incorporating external objects into your application is by taking advantage of a Windows feature called *Object Linking and Embedding*, or *OLE*. Using OLE version 2.0, you can embed objects, including data, from one application into another. Then, when activated inside the receiving application, referred to as the *client application*, the source application, referred to as the *server application*, can automatically be activated and activate the object. For example, you could embed an Excel Spreadsheet into your PowerBuilder application by using OLE 2.0. Your PowerBuilder application would be the client application, and the server application would be Excel. When you click on the Excel Spreadsheet object inside your PowerBuilder application, Excel comes alive automatically. If you edit that spreadsheet, you are actually editing it from Excel, not from your PowerBuilder application. Using this method, however, you can easily integrate objects from other applications into your PowerBuilder applications, providing a complete solution and saving you the time and money that you need to duplicate that functionality yourself. You can even create PowerBuilder reports and embed

14

them in other applications. The details of creating OLE Clients and Servers is too advanced to discuss in any length here. However, you should be aware of this extremely powerful feature and the capability to use it in your PowerBuilder applications. This way, if you find yourself wanting to incorporate functionality from an OLE Server compatible application into your PowerBuilder application, you know where to start.

Afternoon Summary

The Custom Visual User Object is used to take multiple PowerBuilder controls and create a brand new control out of them and extend their behavior. Each of these individual controls has its own events, but they are not visible to the parent window of the Custom Visual User Object. You must declare User Events in the Custom User Object that the parent can intercept, and then create functions that the parent can call to get information out of the Custom User Object. You create Custom Visual User Objects by opening the User Object Painter and specifying that you want to create a Custom Visual User Object.

Another type of User Object that you can create is a Standard Class User Object. The Standard Class User Object allows you to extend a Standard PowerBuilder class to meet your needs. The PowerBuilder classes that you can extend are the DynamicDescriptionArea, DynamicStagingArea, Pipeline, and Transaction, which have to do with the Database (we'll learn about that later in Chapters 19 through 25); the OLEObject, OLEStorage, and OLEStream objects, which are for Object Linking and Embedding; the MailSession object, which handles mail sessions with a server that follows the Microsoft Mail Application Programmer Interface (MAPI) standard; and the Error and Message classes, which are used internally by PowerBuilder to handle system errors and windows events, respectively.

In addition, you can create a Custom Class User Object, which is a class that you create from scratch, usually to encapsulate specific object-oriented functionality. When you create a custom class, you will need to instantiate that class in your script using the CREATE command. Then, when you are finished with that class, you can eliminate it from memory using the DESTROY command. You can also check if a class has been instantiated using the IsValid() function.

You can use the External User Object to link to Windows Custom Controls that are stored in Dynamic Link Libraries. When interfacing with an external custom control, you will need to specify things like the name of the .DLL file, the name of the control class, and the number of the style of the control. You can use the Send() function to pass messages to your external user object and the Handle() function to get the windows handle of the object that you are talking to for use in the Send() function. You can declare user events that will allow you to trap messages sent by the control to your application. You can declare function prototypes of external functions so that you can call functions in your .DLL. In addition to controls that are stored in .DLL files, PowerBuilder allows you to easily integrate .VBX controls into your application using a VBX User Object. If you are using PowerBuilder Enterprise Edition, you may also be able to build your own .DLL files using Watcom C++ and the PowerBuilder C++ Class User

Object. You can also use OLE Objects in your applications to incorporate external functionality into your application.

Q&A

Q **I created a Visual Standard User Object with several User Object functions and placed it on a window. Why can I only call the object's functions from within the User Object events and not other control events on the window?**

A You created user object functions with `Protected` access rights. If you had used `Public` access rights, script from anywhere in the application could call the function, as long as the object was in an open window. Placing the User Object on a window creates an instance of that object like a descendent, so if the access right was `Protected`, you could call the object's functions from the user object's events on the window, but not from any other window script.

Q **Why do you initialize a User Object in its `Constructor` event instead of the window open event?**

A Coding the initialization procedure for the User Object in its `Constructor` event encapsulates the code to some extent, from other controls and events of the window.

Q **I created a Custom Visual User Object with just one command button. The `Clicked` event of the button has `Parent.BackColor = RGB(0,0,255)`. After placing this object on a window, I ran my application and clicked the button, but nothing happened.**

A When `Parent` is used in control events that are part of the User Object, the User Object itself is the parent object. In User Object functions or events, `Parent` refers to the window that it is placed on. The script should be placed in a User Object function or event and the script within the command button should call the User Object function or trigger the event. You may not have seen the color change if the command button was hiding the User Object background.

Q **If I want my window scripts to send messages to a Class User Object, do I have to use User Object functions?**

A No, PowerBuilder 4.0 also lets you use functions `TriggerEvent()` and `PostEvent()` in Class object types. You can declare user events for Class User Objects and access the script in these events by calling either `TriggerEvent()` or `PostEvent()`.

Q **Do I have to substitute Standard Class User Objects, like transaction objects associated to remote procedures, with application default global variables to use them?**

A No, Standard Class User Objects, like transaction objects, can be used in script by declaring then creating them first, then destroying them when their use is finished.

Workshop

Quiz

1. How do you declare access rights for variables?
2. How do `Public`, `Private`, or `Protected` access rights limit a variables use?
3. What is the main reason to create a Standard Visual User Object?
4. How do you use a Class User Object in script?
5. List some benefits of encapsulation.
6. What is the syntax for using `TriggerEvent()` on an objects `Clicked` event and a declared user event, `ue_custom_event`?

Putting PowerBuilder into Action

1. Let's finish off your StyleBar. Go back and open your StyleBar in the User Object Painter.
2. Change the names of the other toggle buttons. The second one will be `p_italic`, the third one is `p_underline`, the fourth one is `p_justleft`, the fifth is `p_justcenter`, and the last one is `p_justright`.
3. In the constructor event of each of the buttons, initialize the button with the `f_reg_buttons()` function, passing to it the appropriate up and down picture names. The up bitmap names are pb_?_up. The down bitmap names are pb_?_dn. Replace the question mark (?) with the appropriate letter. For `p_italic`, it is *i*; for `p_underline`, *u*; for `p_justleft`, *l*; for `p_justright`, *r*; for `p_justcenter`, *c*.
4. In the `Clicked` event of each of the toggle buttons, trigger the `ue_stylechanged` event of the parent user object with the appropriate message. The message for `p_bold` is `ICI_CHG_BOLD`. For `p_italic` it is `ICI_CHG_ITALIC`, and for `p_underline` it is `ICI_CHG_UNDERLINE`. The message that will be triggered for all of the last three buttons is `ICI_CHG_JUSTIFY`. Then, it will be the responsibility of the function to determine the proper justification state.
5. Set it up so that the three justification buttons are mutually exclusive. In the `Clicked` event of each of `p_justleft`, use the following code segment to ensure that the other two buttons will not be in the Set state at the same time as this one.

```
IF p_justcenter.f_IsSelected() THEN
    // If its selected, then trigger a click to unselect it.
    p_justcenter.TriggerEvent( Clicked!)
END IF
IF p_justright.f_IsSelected() THEN
    // If its selected, then trigger a click to unselect it.
    p_justright.TriggerEvent( Clicked!)
END IF
```

6. Place the same code in each of the other two justification buttons. In p_justcenter, replace the references to p_justcenter in this code with p_justleft. And in p_justright, replace the references to p_justright with p_justleft.

7. Create a new window and place a StyleBar in it, and try it out!

14

AT A GLANCE

Now that you have familiarized yourself with PowerBuilder, you will be learning about one of its most important features: the Database Interface. Throughout this week, you will learn about the Database Painter, DataWindows, SQL, and more. Don't let these topics intimidate you if you've never worked in a database environment. Days 8 and 9 will help you understand key concepts on how a database works. If you already understand these concepts, a little brush up never hurt anybody.

Chapter

15

Database Concepts

In this lesson, you will be introduced to *databases*. You will learn:

☐ What a database is and how it is used

☐ About the different constructs that make up a *relational database*, including Tables, Keys, Indexes, and Views

☐ About some common *Relational Database Management Systems (RDBMSs)* that you can use with PowerBuilder, including the Open Database Connectivity kit

What Is a Database?

The computer's capability to perform complex mathematical computations is clearly one of the main reasons that computers are valuable tools in today's world. In fact, historically it was nothing more than a big adding machine that was christened with the name *computer*. Since then, however, computers have become much more than devices for adding and subtracting numbers. Computers have taken us into the Information Age, not for their capability to calculate but for their capability to deal with information.

People have been dealing with information since the beginning of history. You know that because you can retrieve information about it from bibles, scrolls, books, files, and other similar types of archives, mostly recorded on paper (or papyrus). These archives are simply collections of information stored by assorted people (or deities) for retrieval by others like us later. The manner in which others are able to retrieve this information is by reading it from the archive.

As information became more abundant, people began to realize that they needed a way to organize their information so they could find and retrieve it faster and more easily. So people began to develop complex filing and organization systems. The Dewey decimal system that is still used by libraries today is one popular example of such a system. Other systems are used by hospitals to store patient records, by governments to store census records, and by companies to store customer, sales, and tax records.

Then came the Information Age of computers! Information was abundant for a very long time—long before the Information Age began. Most people just didn't know how to deal with their information until they started playing with computers. With the introduction of computers came software manufacturers who began to develop applications that could take information, store it on your computer in an organized fashion, and then allow you to find and retrieve your information quickly and easily. The information that they stored was referred to as *data*, and the programs that allowed you to store your data were called *Database Management Systems (DBMSs)*. The collections of data inside a DBMS became known as a *database*.

As people began to see how well computers dealt with data, they began to convert all of their information to computer data that could be stored in the databases of their DBMSs. Software vendors spent time enhancing their DBMSs to be able to handle more data and to search more quickly. They researched different data storage paradigms, or *data models*. They began to use these models when developing their products. Some of the more popular data models used were the Relational data model, the Hierarchical data model, the Network data model, and the Object-Oriented data model.

Then they began to develop standards. There were standard file formats and standard command syntaxes that could be used to query data in a database. Products using the standard file formats and command syntaxes were even more friendly to the user because the user didn't have to learn a new syntax to access data from another database. Some DBMSs could even share their database files!

The Relational Data Model for Databases

Eventually, however, one standard stood out from the rest and grew to be popular enough that all of the major database vendors now use that standard in their products. That standard uses the *Relational data model* as its organization paradigm, and the *Structured Query Language (SQL)* as its command syntax. It is the standard that is supported by PowerBuilder for data access.

What Is a Table?

The *Relational data model* was first developed by IBM Research by a man named E. F. Codd in San Jose, CA, in 1969. The Relational data model dictates that data is stored in matrices, referred to as *tables*. The tables are made up of *columns* and *rows*. Each row represents a single record of information, for example, a single tax return or customer order. Each column in the table represents a single field, for example Gross Income or Customer Name. Sometimes, a specific field in a specific record is referred to as a *cell* in the table. There is (theoretically) no limit to the number of rows or columns that can be created for any table, and there can be any number of tables stored in a single database. Table 15.1 demonstrates an example of a table of customer information. Figure 15.1 illustrates the different parts of a table.

Figure 15.1.
The different parts of a table.

1	Mary Peters	2 Everything Tpke	(800) 555-1212
2	Sam Iyam	10 Queue Drive	(212) UR-WELCM
3	I.M. Not	1 Animal Way	(508) ELE-FANT
4	Dr. Rexx	2I Light Zone Street	(800) ROD-SRLNG

Table 15.1. A sample customer table.

#	Name	Address	Phone
1	Mary Peters	2 Everything Tpke	(800) 555-1212
2	Sam Iyam	10 Queue Drive	(212) UR-WELCM
3	I.M. Not	1 Animal Way	(508) ELE-FANT
4	Dr. Rexx	2I Light Zone Street	(800) ROD-SRLNG

Note: In its original form, the Relational data model did not use many of the terms that are used here. Instead, because Dr. Codd was of a mathematical background, very precise mathematical terms were used to describe the components of the Relational data model. Most significant was the term *Relation* itself, which was used to name the model. In mathematics, a relation basically refers to a table (with some interesting elaboration that I will leave to you to explore on your own if you want to). According to the Relational data model, a database is composed of a set of relations. What are now called rows or records were originally referred to as *tuples* and were given a specific definition of their own. Finally, what is referred to as columns or fields were originally named *attributes*. The names that are used in this discussion, however, are the now popular among most database professionals. This discussion will stick with these more popular terms instead of the original ones, even if it does mean sacrificing some linguistic precision. If you want to study the original Relational data model, you can do so by reading an article entitled, "A Relational Model of Data for Large Shared Data Banks," published in the magazine *Communications of the ACM*, Vol.13, No. 6, June 1970. There are also a lot of other books and publications that describe this model in further detail.

In order to view the data in your tables, you can perform *queries*. The result of a query is, itself, a table, often referred to as a *result set*. The command syntax that is used to perform these queries and generate result sets is called the *Structured Query Language*, often referred to as *SQL* and pronounced *SEE-quel*. When building a query, you specify which columns and rows you want to see. You can even join columns from multiple tables based on some common information between the two tables. For example, suppose that you have two tables: One table holds customer information, such as customer number, name, address, and phone number; the other one holds order information, including part number, price, and order date, as well as the customer number of the customer who ordered that particular item. By using SQL, you can ask to see the order information for a specific customer number or for a specific part number, or even for a specific price range. You can even create a result set that contains the name of the customer on the same line as that customer's order. The process of specifying specific criteria to determine

which rows are included in the result set is often referred to as *filtering*, and the process of including columns from different tables is referred to as *joining*. When joining two tables, there is always at least one column in common between each of the two tables. Using the preceding example, you need to have a customer number in the customer table that can be joined to the customer number column in the order table.

The Primary Key

According to the Relational data model, the manner in which the rows are stored in a table is arbitrary. It is left up to the engine how to order the data to allow for maximum performance efficiency. Therefore, you cannot use the record number to refer to a record. Instead, you can only find specific rows based on data values in the table. You may decide to use some column (or columns) of data as a unique identifier to help you pinpoint specific rows. This value that represents the unique identifier is referred to as the *primary key*. Can you guess which customer table column that we have discussed is the primary key? If you guessed the customer name, that would be a pretty good guess, but it would also be incorrect. After all, how many people do you know with the same name? Maybe not that many, but it only takes one duplicate record to compromise the integrity of the primary key. In fact, you get an error message if you attempt to insert into a table a row having a duplicate value for the primary key, and the row will not be inserted. So even though, theoretically, you can use the customer name as the primary key column for your customer table, if you happen to have two customers named Joe Smith, you won't be able to have records for both of them in your customer records.

Instead of using the customer name as the primary key, you can use the customer number. The customer number is arbitrarily assigned and is intended to be unique for each customer. Therefore, you can easily use this customer number as the primary key of your table. In fact, you can take any table that you have and create an artificial primary key in the same manner. For example, in the order table, it is unlikely that any combination of columns is unique. After all, the same customer may order the same quantity of parts at the same price twice on the same day. So, if you want to create a primary key for the order table, you *must* create an artificial primary key that is an order number or order code.

Foreign Keys

By creating a method whereby you can identify a single, unique row in your table, you can point to that row in another table simply by referencing its primary key. For example, customers place orders. If you want to have information about your customers with their orders, you can include the customer name, address, and phone number right in each order record. However, because your customers are repeat customers and call in orders every month, you are wasting a lot of space by including the same customer information for all of these order records. Instead, you have a customer table where you store one record for each customer. The primary key of this table is the customer number; therefore, by placing the proper customer number in the order record,

you know which customer has placed the order. If you want to know the name, address, and phone number of the customer who has placed a particular order, you can simply look up that customer number in the customer table. In fact, you can use a SQL join to view the customer information together with the order information, even though they are stored in separate tables. Figure 15.2 illustrates this method. By using this method, you can minimize the amount of space that your database takes up because there is only one copy of the customer information.

Figure 15.2.

Joining two tables by their keys.

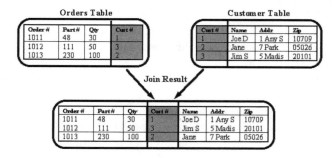

In the Relational data model, the reference to the customer number inside the order table is called a *foreign key*. A foreign key is a column in one table that identifies a unique row from another table using its primary key column. A foreign key points to the primary key of its *parent table*, as the customer number in the order table points to the customer number of the customer table. When using a Relational DBMS, you can define your primary keys and your foreign keys, and the database will enforce the integrity of your data. In other words, after you have defined your primary and foreign keys, your DBMS will prevent you from inserting invalid data into your tables. For example, it does not make sense to have an order from a non-existing customer; so if you have defined the customer number of the order table as a foreign key into the customer table, the DBMS will not permit you to insert a row into the order table if it contains a customer number that does not exist in the customer table. This process of automatically coordinating and protecting the data in foreign and primary keys is referred to as *referential integrity*. Referential integrity also works backward. In other words, if you delete a customer from your customer table, all of the orders that point to that customer will no longer be valid. In order to maintain your referential integrity, you will either need to delete the referenced rows from the order table and reassign their customer numbers to a valid customer number (or null), or prevent the parent row from being deleted. The rules the DBMS uses to enforce the referential integrity of the database are referred to as *constraints*.

> **Note:** Although most DBMSs require that you point your foreign key columns at primary keys, the ANSI standard does not require the parent key to be the primary key of the parent table. It is required to be unique, though, and is usually the primary key.

Warning: Some DBMSs require a little effort to make them automatically enforce referential integrity constraints. For example, a SQL Server requires you use *triggers*, special stored database commands that are run automatically by the DBMS when data in a table is modified. Other DBMSs, like Watcom and Oracle, automatically enforce your referential integrity constraints once they are defined in the foreign key. Check your DBMS's documentation for details.

Note: Although in this example you have created a single field that holds an arbitrary number to play the role of the primary and foreign keys, you have done this only because of the logical role of the data. Remember that the purpose of a primary key is to uniquely identify a single row in a table. This means that if there were a data column that logically served this purpose, you could have used that column as the primary key instead of creating a new one. For example, if you have a supermarket that has a table of products, one of the fields is probably the SKU Number, the number that is used to create the barcode. Because this number is by definition already unique, there is no reason to create an artificial product key as the unique ID—you can just use the SKU Number. You can even create a key that contains multiple columns that together make up a unique value. For example, perhaps you need to determine the county of a particular city and state. You may have a table with three columns: city, state, and county. Clearly, by itself, state is not unique because there is more than one county in any state. Also, by itself, city is not unique because there are multiple cities with the same name that are in different counties (generally because there are cities in different states that have the same name: there is a Kansas City in Kansas as well as one in Missouri). However, together city and state are unique because there is no duplication of city names within a single state. So, the primary key of this table will be City and State. This is perfectly legal and is often referred to as a *composite key*.

Also, it should be pointed out that the ANSI Standard does not require that a foreign key point to a primary key. In fact, according to the ANSI Standard, you can create a foreign key that points to any column or set of columns from any other table. However, from a practical standpoint, your foreign keys should always point to primary keys in the parent table.

One of the primary values of the relational data model is in the fact that you can use primary and foreign keys to minimize, or possibly even eliminate, duplication of data. The process of analyzing your table structure and creating tables with less data and more referential integrity is often referred to as *normalization*. The process of normalizing data involves analyzing the fields

15 • Database Concepts

of your tables and determining which fields are duplicates. You can then separate out certain columns into a separate table and give them a unique key so that you can replace these columns in the original table with their key, and use joins to get the data back. Figure 15.3 illustrates two environments—a denormalized database and a normalized database that contain the same data. Data that is completely *normalized* is theoretically ideal in a relational database, even if practically it is not always desired or even achievable.

Figure 15.3.

A database before and after normalization.

Denormalized Database

Date	Part	Qty	Price	Customer	Addr	City	State	Zip
2/1/95	Nuts	30	$150	John Doe	5 Madis	New	NY	10003
2/1/95	Bolts	50	$500	John Doe	5 Madis	New	NY	10003
2/5/95	Nuts	100	$500	Jim Willi	7 Park	New	NY	10004

Normalized Database

Orders Table

Date	Part #	Qty	Cust #
2/1/95	1	30	1
2/1/95	2	50	1
2/5/95	1	100	2

Customer Table

Cust #	Name	Addr	Zip
1	Jim W	7 Park	10004
2	John	5 Madis	10003

Parts Table

Part #	Name	Price
1	Nuts	$5
2	Bolts	$10

ZipCode Table

Zip	City	State
10003	New York	NY
10004	New York	NY

Warning: A completely normal database is not always practical because of the manner in which a DBMS handles joins. When using joins, the DBMS has to search through multiple tables to find the data, so there may be a performance cost to normalizing your data. For most simple joins, this performance cost is negligible, and the savings of normalization much outweigh the cost. However, in most DBMSs, there is a limit to the number of joins that can be performed in a single query before performance is adversely affected, and sometimes you have to denormalize your data so that you can achieve acceptable performance.

Indexes

Although the use of keys to identify data is one very effective method of finding a specific row in a table, it is unlikely that this is the only method you will want to use for retrieving your data. Our earlier discussion spoke about being able to build queries that retrieve result sets from a table based on certain criteria. In general, the criteria that you include will be based on the values of the data in your tables. For example, you may want to find all orders that have been placed in the last three days that are still unfulfilled. Building this query is not a problem at all. However, when you build this query, the DBMS is going to have to search through your data to find the rows that meet this criteria.

Even in the earliest days of computers, quick search algorithms were a hot research topic. The search for the algorithm that will locate a piece of data in the shortest amount of time is still a hot research topic today. One of the most effective ways of searching data is implemented through the use of *indexes*. An *index* is a special type of file that stores information that can be used to quickly find a particular row of data in a table based on a column or set of columns. The columns that are used by the index are referred to as the *key* of the index. Although today's indexes are somewhat more complex, at the simplest level an index is simply a list of values and pointers. The values are the different values of the key of the index, and the pointers are pointers to the records in the table that hold the value specified. However, unlike the table itself, the values of the index are sorted specifically to make it possible to quickly pick out the records from the table based on the values in the column. Figure 15.4 demonstrates how an index is used to find rows in a table.

Figure 15.4.
How indexes make finding data faster.

City Table

City	County	State
Eastchester	Westchester	NY
Stamford	Fairfield	CT
Montclair	Bergen	NJ
New York	New York	NY
White Plains	Westchester	NY
Greenwich	Fairfield	CT
Brooklyn	Kings	NY
Poughkipsee	Dutchess	NY
New Rochelle	Westchester	NY

County Index on City Table

County	Record Numbers		
Bergen	3		
Dutchess	8		
Fairfield	2	6	
Kings	7		
New York	4		
Westchester	1	5	9

For example, suppose that you create an index on the Name column of the customer table. The index will contain a list of names, probably in alphabetical order, along with pointers to the records containing the names. In many ways, the index itself is a table, too; although the database does not treat it that way. If you ask the DBMS to find the customer whose name is Sam Iyam, it can quickly search through the name index to find out which records contain the name Sam Iyam. Then, it can just jump to those records in the table that it found in the index. Of course, the savings on a small table of four or five records are probably not as recognizable as the savings on a much larger table with hundreds or thousands of customers. But the savings are there, nonetheless.

Indexes aren't supported by the ANSI Standard; however, every major DBMS supports indexes because in the real world, database users are more concerned with maximum performance than maximum standard compliance. Indexes are also crucial for effective performance on large tables; so indexes are pretty much a fact of life in the relational database world, even if ANSI isn't prepared to define a standard for them.

There are two types of indexes: standard and unique. The standard index simply handles sequencing of the data columns, as described earlier. However, you can also create a *unique index* that permits only distinct, unique key values. If you attempt to insert a duplicate row into a table with a unique index, you get an error message similar to the way you get an error message if you try to insert two rows into a table with the same value for their primary key. In other words, if you have a unique index on the name column of your customer table, and you try to insert a new

customer that has the same name as an existing customer, you get an error and cannot insert the row. Many DBMSs also offer other index options, but because the other options are generally DBMS dependent, I will leave it up to you to read your database documentation to learn about them.

Views

The collection of normalized tables stored in the database is generally referred to as the *physical model* of the database. The physical model represents the actual storage of the data in tables, and is organized in such a manner as to maximize storage space and integrity and to minimize waste. However, to someone who is not a database expert, normalized data is difficult to read. It requires the user to search through tables looking for values in one, to find keys in another, and to find values in yet a third. Of course, an expert user, one who is familiar with the physical model of the database, can probably figure out the proper commands to do this rather easily. However, the novice database user probably is not capable of dealing with a completely normal database.

In general, database users are business people who are experts in the intricacies of their business and data, not in the intricacies of relational databases and the SQL language. They will have trouble thinking of their data in normal form and will probably not be able to quickly formulate the commands required to view the data in the form that they are logically more comfortable with. To make life easier for these users, you *can* create new tables that are more consistent with their *logical model* of your database. However, by creating these new tables, you defeat the whole purpose of normalizing your data because these new tables are denormalized, and probably waste space. Instead, you can show your users how to build the queries they need to see the data in the form they like. You can write those queries down on paper so that your users can remember them. Of course, this is rather impractical, especially if you have a large, widespread user base with a heavy turnover rate. Instead, because the result of a query is in itself a table, you can store your queries in special constructs called *views*, which allow your users to view the results of these queries like they are tables themselves, without having to remember the query syntax that builds them. You can create views that are based on queries that result in denormalized tables so that your users can simply query the views to see what they want. The only extra space that is taken up by a view is the space that the DBMS needs to store the query syntax.

For example, you can create an Orders view from a query that shows the order information together with the customer and product information. Then instead of having to look up each set of information separately, the user can simply look at the Orders view and perform his queries on that view, as if it were in itself a table. However, when using a view, the data itself is not stored separately, and so you still maintain maximum normalization of data and therefore maximum storage efficiency and integrity. Views are a very efficient and useful tool for creating user-friendly logical views of your system-friendly physical data. They can also be used to help control security by permitting a user to see data through a view that he/she might otherwise not be permitted to see.

Note: Under certain conditions, your users can even update data using views. We will learn more about these conditions when we talk about the SQL Language in Chapter 19.

Some Common Relational DBMSs (RDBMSs)

There are a large number of relational database management systems (RDBMSs) that support the standards that have been described in this lesson. Many of them are supported by PowerBuilder with the use of drivers so that you can use these database engines for your software development. If you have purchased PowerBuilder Desktop or PowerBuilder Team/ODBC, most of these drivers must be purchased separately. However, if you have purchased PowerBuilder Enterprise Edition, all available drivers are included right in your package.

All three editions of PowerBuilder come with a PowerBuilder driver to connect to the Microsoft Open Database Connectivity Interface (ODBC). They also include the Watcom SQL DBMS and an ODBC driver that allows you to connect to your Watcom SQL DBMS by using the ODBC Interface. You can also get ODBC drivers that allow you to connect to other databases besides Watcom by using the ODBC Interface. In fact, a number of them are included with your PowerBuilder kit. You'll learn more about the ODBC Interface in the next lesson.

If you own PowerBuilder Enterprise Edition, you will also find drivers for Microsoft's SQL Server, Sybase's SQL Server, Gupta's SQLBase, Informix, Oracle, XDB, IBM's Distributed Relational Database Architecture (DRDA), Allbase/SQL, and a couple of Gateway products that allow you to access DB2 databases. These drivers are direct interfaces into the appropriate database and are generally more efficient and flexible than their equivalent ODBC driver. By installing the appropriate driver, you give PowerBuilder the capability to talk to that database. Between the drivers that are included with PowerBuilder and the drivers that are available for use with the ODBC interface, you should be able to connect to almost any DBMS available on the market. Because PowerBuilder shelters you from the specific commands of the database, you should have no trouble creating tables, populating data, and performing all of your other database actions because your interface is the same. Even when you write your programs, you will be able to switch to different databases simply by changing the database driver you are using; and if you have stuck with standard database commands, you will not have to change any of your code. This is one of the most exciting features of PowerBuilder—the open interface to the database.

In the next several lessons, you'll learn how to take advantage of these features. You'll learn how to use several painters to prepare and manipulate your databases, and then you'll learn how to incorporate your database data right inside your applications.

Morning Summary

Computers have taken us into the Information Age, not for their capability to calculate, but for their capability to deal with information. Prior to the information age, people retrieved their information by reading it from a book. As information became more abundant, people developed complex filing and organization systems so that they could more easily retrieve their information. With the introduction of computers came software manufacturers who began to develop *Database Management Systems* (DBMSs) that could take information, or *data*, and store it on a computer in an organized fashion. Eventually, the Relational data model and the Structured Query Language became the standard systems that took over the industry. It is this standard that is supported by PowerBuilder for data access.

The Relational data model, first developed by IBM Research by a man named E. F. Codd in San Jose, CA, in 1969, dictates that data is stored in *tables,* made up of *columns* and *rows*. Each row represents a single record of information, and each column represents a single field. Sometimes, a specific field in a specific record is referred to as a *cell* in the table. In order to view the data in your tables, you can perform *queries* that return *result sets*. The command syntax that is used to perform these queries is called the Structured Query Language, often referred to as SQL and pronounced *SEE-quel*.

In the Relational data model, you cannot use the record number to refer to a record. Instead, you can only find specific rows based on data values in the table. You may decide to use some column (or columns) of data as a unique identifier. This value that represents the unique identifier is referred to as the *Primary Key*. You can use the Primary Key of a table to reference that row in a different table using a *Foreign Key*. A foreign key points to the primary key of its *Parent Table*. When using a relational DBMS, you can define your primary keys and your foreign keys, and the database will enforce the integrity of your data automatically using rules called *constraints* that prevent you from having invalid data in your table. This process of automatically coordinating and protecting the data in foreign and primary keys is referred to as *Referential Integrity*. You can *normalize* your data by using primary and foreign keys to minimize, or possibly even eliminate, duplication of data in your database.

The criteria that you include in a query is based on the values of the data in your tables. When the DBMS executes a query, it has to search through your data to find the rows that meet your query criteria. To do this, it uses *indexes*, special files that store information to quickly find a particular row of data. An index is based on a column or set of columns, referred to as the *key* of the index. At the simplest level an index is a list of values and pointers. The values are the different values for the key columns of the index, and the pointers are pointers to the records

in the table that hold the value specified. The values of the index are sorted to quickly pick out records from a table based on the values in a column. Many DBMSs offer a large number of index options. Read your database documentation to learn about them.

The normalized tables that are stored in the database are generally referred to as the *physical model* of the database. The physical model is generally organized to maximize storage space and integrity, and minimize waste. However, since normalized data is difficult to read, you can also create *views* of the *logical model* of your database. Views are simply queries that look like tables. They allow your users to view their data without having to remember query syntax. You can create views that are based on queries that result in denormalized tables so that your users can simply query the views to see what they want.

There are a large number of relational database management systems that support the standards that are described in this lesson. Many of them are supported by PowerBuilder with the use of drivers, so that you can use these database engines for your software development.

Chapter

16

PowerBuilder
Database Interface

In this lesson, you will be introduced to the Database Painter. You will learn about:

☐ Connecting to your database
☐ Setting up Database Profiles
☐ Creating and deleting local Watcom Databases
☐ Defining ODBC and how to set it up
☐ Maintaining display formats, edit masks, and validation rules

The Database Painter

The PowerBuilder *Database Painter*, as with the other subsystems within PowerBuilder, is referred to by PowerBuilder as a *Painter*. However, it is unlike the other Painters in that it does not let you build objects that are stored in Libraries. Instead, it lets you create and manipulate objects that are stored in your databases—the tables, indexes, keys, and data. It also allows you to navigate to a couple of other important data related painters, the *Data Manipulation Painter*, and the *Database Administration Painter*, each of which will be discussed later. However, these data-related Painters work slightly differently than the other Painters within PowerBuilder because they create database objects and not PowerBuilder Objects that can be saved in your libraries.

You can open up the Database Painter by pressing **Shift-F7** or by clicking on the Database Painter icon on the PowerBar. When you do this, the Database Painter will open and probably chug along for a couple of seconds before it finally displays a list of tables to select from (see Fig. 16.1). In the next lesson, you'll learn about some wonderful and exciting things you can do with the tables in the database. For now, though, just press the **Cancel** button, and the overview of the Database Painter will continue.

Figure 16.1.
The Select Tables list.

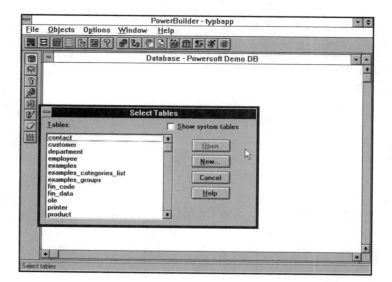

Note: In actuality, when you first open the Database Painter, it attempts to connect to the current database. If you've been in the Database Painter before, the current database is whatever database you last connected to. Otherwise, it will default to use the PowerBuilder Demo Database that is installed with Power-Builder. If you did not install the PowerBuilder Demo Database, an error message will appear, and you will not be able to proceed any further. Go ahead and install the PowerBuilder Demo Database (as well as the Watcom Database Engine, if you didn't install that either) if you want to proceed with the upcoming chapters. Most of the rest of this book will be dealing with the database, and if for some reason you do not want to install the database now, you will need to skip many of the next few lessons.

Warning: If you are using a Database other than Watcom, you may need to run certain scripts in order to prepare your database for use with PowerBuilder. Check your Database Interface documentation for details.

Most of the functionality that can be found in the Database Painter has to do with editing the structure of your tables, indexes, and keys. In addition, you can use the Database Painter to edit and query your data. Also, there are functions to help you set up and manage your database environment. However, before you can learn how to work with your databases, you must learn how to talk to them. Therefore, this lesson will start by talking about the first thing that you must do in order to use your database—connect to it.

Connecting to the Database

In order for PowerBuilder (or any other application, for that matter) to access data in a Relational Database, it must first *connect* to that database server. Connecting to a database server involves telling your computer which database server you want to use and who you are. You also must specify your password so that the database knows that you are who you say you are. Connecting to your database server is like picking up your telephone and dialing the telephone number. Just like there are many people whose number you can dial, there may be many servers that are available to connect to. In order to distinguish which one you are talking to, you must dial the right number.

The difference with database servers, however, is that there is usually more to it than dialing numbers. To connect to your database server, you need a bit more information about its name and address. Because PowerBuilder supports a variety of database server types, you need to know the type of server you are trying to connect to. You also need to know the name of the server and

your login ID and password. Although it's not necessary for the purposes of connecting, it is also useful to know which database you want to connect to. In addition, depending on the DBMS you are using, there may be other information you need to know, including parameters, user IDs, and so on. Be sure to check your PowerBuilder Interface documentation for any additional settings you may need in order to connect. The examples in this discussion are specific to the Watcom Database that comes with PowerBuilder.

When you installed PowerBuilder, assuming you followed the installation instructions presented in the first lesson, PowerBuilder installed the Watcom SQL DBMS and Microsoft's Open Database Connectivity (ODBC) Engine for you. We'll talk extensively about these things later in this lesson. For now, though, realize that because these components are supplied with PowerBuilder, the installation procedure was able to set up your system for you so that you could connect to the PowerBuilder Sample Database the first time you logged in. Had it not done this for you, you would have gotten an error when you first tried to open the Database Painter telling you that the system was not able to connect to the database. It would then have proceeded to ask you to supply the proper information it needs so that you can connect. However, because these settings were already set up for you, everything progressed smoothly. In fact, because of the way the ODBC driver and Watcom SQL work, PowerBuilder actually started the Watcom SQL Engine for you when you first opened the Database Painter, and will turn it off when you are finished! (That's why it took so long to open up.) Let's talk about what you would have had to do if you were unable to connect for some reason; that is, what you must do to connect.

Within the **F**ile menu, there is a menu item called **C**onnect that itself has a popup menu beneath it (see Fig. 16.2). The first menu item within the **C**onnect menu is Powersoft Demo DB. Choosing this menu item connects you to the Powersoft Demo Database you installed back in the first lesson. This menu item refers to what is called a *Database Profile*. In order to help make it easier to connect to your databases, you can set up PowerBuilder Database Profiles, which will appear on this menu above the separator bar. Then, instead of having to fill out all of the information to reconnect each time you want to switch to that database, you can just select its Database Profile menu item from the **C**onnect menu. This is more useful, of course, if you connect to more than one database, because PowerBuilder automatically reconnects you to the last database you were in each time you re-enter the Database Painter.

Beneath the separator bar, there are two more menu items. If you select the **P**rompt... menu item, you are presented with a prompt that allows you to enter the telephone number of your database, so to speak (see Fig. 16.3). Again, because you are using the ODBC driver, much of this information is already set up for you, and all you need to know in order to connect is the name of the *Data Source* you want to connect to. Later, though, you'll see what makes up a data source, and then it will be more clear how this process works. For now, simply select Powersoft Demo DB from the list and click **OK**.

Figure 16.2.
The Connect menu.

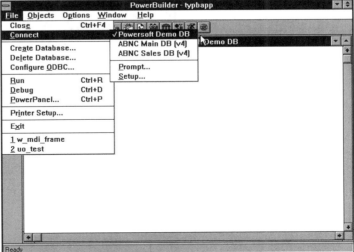

Figure 16.3.
The SQL Data Sources connection prompt.

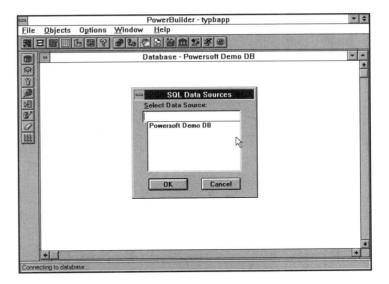

Beneath the **P**rompt... menu item is another menu item, **S**etup.... When you click the **S**etup... menu item, you are prompted with the Database Profiles dialog box (see Fig. 16.4). This dialog box lists the currently available profiles you have set up and allows you to choose a Database Profile to use. Right now, there is only one profile that is set up for you, that is the Powersoft Demo DB profile, and it is listed in the list box of this dialog box. Clicking **OK** selects this Database Profile in the same way as selecting it from the **C**onnect menu.

Figure 16.4.
The Database Profiles dialog box.

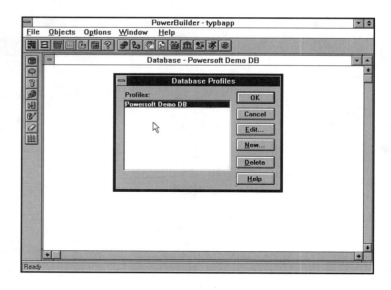

Note: If you are using PowerBuilder Enterprise edition, you may see two other Database Profiles called ABNC Sales DB (v4) and ABNC Main DB (v4) that were set up for you if you installed the Sample Applications for Windows product.

In addition to selecting a Database Profile, you can also edit existing profiles, delete ones that you don't need anymore, and even create new ones. You may want multiple profiles to be able to switch quickly between databases or even between DBMSs. When you create and save new profiles, they are stored in your PB.INI file and are listed in the **C**onnect menu, too. To edit an existing profile, click on the **E**dit button. When you click on the **E**dit button, you are presented with the Database Profile Setup dialog box, which contains the setup for the Database Profile you are now editing (see Fig. 16.5). In this case, you will be editing the Powersoft Demo DB profile because you should have no other profiles in your system. You can confirm this because the first edit box in the Database Profile Setup dialog box contains the name of the profile, Powersoft Demo DB, in the edit box labeled Profile Name:.

Warning: Even though your PowerBuilder Database Profiles are stored in the PB.INI file, your DBMS may store additional information about a database in its own files. For example, the ODBC engine that we'll talk about later uses an ODBC.INI file to store its database information, and the Watcom SQL engine uses a WSQL.INI file to store the information it needs about the database. In addition, there is general PowerBuilder information about ODBC drivers in the PBODB040.INI file. The point is, when you want to remove a Database Profile from PowerBuilder, deleting it from the Database Profiles Setup dialog box will only remove it from the PB.INI file. If you want to eliminate it from the database itself, you will need to check the documentation that came with your DBMS to see if other measures are necessary.

Figure 16.5.
The Database Profile Setup dialog box.

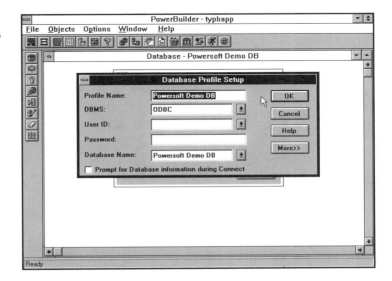

Beneath the name is a combo box labeled DBMS:. Inside that box is listed ODBC because that is the DBMS engine you are using to connect to your database, which is accessed through the Watcom engine as well. If you click on the drop-down arrow, you will see a list of DBMSs that you may select from (see Fig. 16.6). If you have not installed any other PowerBuilder Database Interfaces, then the list will only contain the ODBC driver, which you installed in the first lesson. Otherwise, whichever Database Interfaces you have installed will also appear in this list.

Beneath the DBMS:, you may need to enter a User ID: and Password:. This is not the database login ID but a user ID that is used to connect to the server itself, if such a connection is required. Beneath this, in the edit box labeled Database Name:, you specify the name of the database you are connecting to. When using the ODBC driver, the name of the database is ignored. However, for readability, it is a good idea to enter the name of the ODBC Data Source to which you want to connect. We'll talk more about configuring your ODBC Driver in just a bit. Beneath the Database Name: edit box is a check box that you can check if you want the system to prompt the user for database login information and a database name when this profile is selected. This

is an effective manner of dealing with database access if you are developing in a team environment with multiple developers. If you do not check this box, though, the system does not prompt the user but instead uses information that is stored in this Database Profile to connect. This information is not currently displayed on-screen. If you click on the **More>>** button, though, the screen gets bigger, and the connect options that you can store in a Database Profile appear (see Fig. 16.7).

Figure 16.6.
The list of DBMSs.

Figure 16.7.
The Connect Options of a Database Profile.

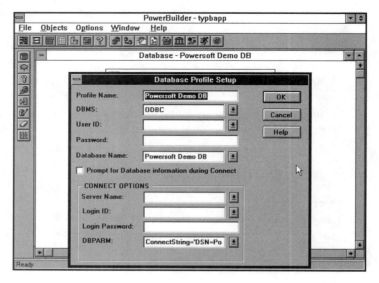

The connect options are the actual database options used to connect to your database. They are the options that would have been prompted for if you had checked the `Prompt for Database information during Connect` check box. These options include the name of the server, which can be entered or selected from the combo box labeled Server Name:; the ID that you are using to log in to the database, which can be entered or selected from the combo box labeled Login ID:; the password to use to connect, which can be entered in the edit box labeled Login Password:; and finally, any other database parameters that may need to be passed to the database and entered or selected in the combo box labeled DBPARM:. The database parameters are specific to the database vendor that you are using. Some database vendors permit you to enter supplemental information like a machine name. When using the ODBC driver, connect information is passed inside the DBPARM string in a parameter called the *ConnectString*. The format for this parameter is

```
ConnectString='DSN=<Data Source>;UID=<login id>;PWD=<login password>'
```

Note: The login ID and login password are optional—they can be set either inside the `ConnectString` or from the Login ID and Login Password edit boxes in the profile settings. Be aware, however, that if they are entered in both, the profile settings will override the `ConnectString`.

If you have checked the `Prompt for Database information during Connect` check box and have also entered Connect Option information, the prompt will use this information as a default.

When you have finished updating your Database Profile, you can save your changes by clicking the **OK** button. This action returns you to the Database Profiles dialog box, where you may find that there are other exciting things you want to do. For example, you may want to create a new Database Profile. To do this, click the **N**ew button, and you will be presented with the same Database Profile Setup dialog box. However, this time, it is empty, and you have to enter your information from scratch. From the Database Profiles dialog box, you may want to delete a Database Profile, which you do by clicking on the **D**elete button. Don't do this now, though, because this Delete button does not confirm your delete—it just deletes your profile without any warning.

In addition to creating Database Profiles, if you are using Watcom SQL, you can also create new local databases. To create a database, select Cre**a**te Database... from the **F**ile menu. This menu item creates a local Watcom SQL database file and also configures it to work with the ODBC driver. Upon selecting this menu item, you are prompted with the Create Local Database dialog box, which asks for information about the database that you want to create (see Fig. 16.8). The first edit box on this screen asks you to specify the name of the new database and is labeled Database Name:. Beneath that, you may enter a User ID: and Password: of a valid database user who has permission to create a database. By default, the system will use the DBA user ID and a password of sql.

Figure 16.8.

The Create Local Database dialog box.

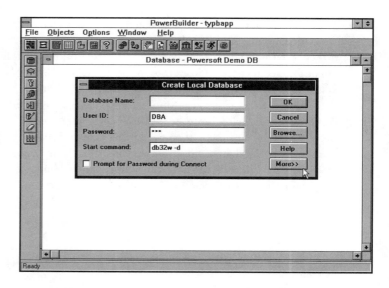

In the edit box labeled Start Command:, enter the name of the command that the system will use to start the database engine (specifically, Watcom SQL). You can also check the `Prompt for Password during Connect` check box and have the system confirm the password before logging you into the database. The **Browse** button allows you to specify the directory and name of the database you are creating. The **More>>** button opens up additional database options that can be set for the database (see Fig. 16.9). Most of these are check boxes that can be set to allow for a specific feature of the Watcom SQL database engine to be used. These settings are really only for advanced users who are familiar with the Watcom SQL engine and how it works. If you are not a Watcom SQL expert, you should probably just leave these settings alone. Still, I'll briefly describe what each setting controls so that you can take the initiative to learn about it on your own if you like.

The first of these database options is the `Use case sensitive names` check box. If you check this check box, your database, table, and column names will be case sensitive. This means that a column name of `ID` will not match a column name of `id` because one is uppercase and the other is lowercase. When names are case sensitive, the names of databases, tables, and columns must match **exactly**, even with respect to capitalization. The `Use transaction log` check box turns on or off transaction logging. If transaction logging is on, transactions will be saved in a log file that will be written back to the database file when the DBMS has free time, and the database will perform slightly better. If transaction logging is off, each transaction is written back to the database file as soon as it is committed. We will talk more about transactions in Chapter 23, "DataWindow Controls." The `Use ANSI blank behavior` check box has to do with how trailing blanks in the database are treated. If they follow the ANSI standard, they are ignored for the purpose of comparison. If they do not, comparisons with trailing blanks must match exactly.

For example, in ANSI, SPACE = SPACE, whereas in non-ANSI mode, they do not match because the extra blanks only appear in the first instance and not the second. You can also encrypt your database file by checking the Encrypt database check box.

Figure 16.9.
The Create Database dialog box expanded.

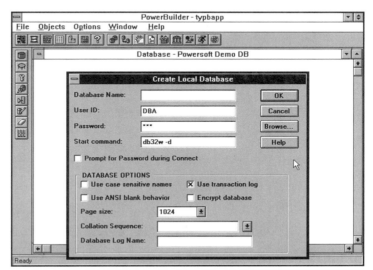

In addition to the above check boxes, there are three other options you can set. The first is the Page Size: of a *page* in the database. In Watcom SQL, a *page* is the term used to represent the unit of memory that the DBMS allocates for data. If the page size is 512, it means that the DBMS will read in 512 bytes of data at a time into memory. You can control how big a page of data is by selecting its size from the drop-down list box. Next, you can select the Collation Sequence: that will be used to determine the order of data in indexes and queries. This is based on the language you are using, and so you specify which sequence to use by specifying a language. Lastly, you can specify the name of the transaction log file that will be used to log your database activities by specifying a name in the Database Log Name: edit box. By default, the transaction log file has the same name as the database itself, with the extension .log; however, you can override the default by placing a name inside this box.

When you have set up all of the database information, you can create the new database by clicking on the **OK** button. PowerBuilder will attempt to create a new Watcom database file and will also set everything else up for you for so you can connect to it from PowerBuilder. This includes configuring the ODBC driver to be able to connect to your new database, as well as creating a PowerBuilder Database Profile for this database. Once the database is set up, PowerBuilder will connect you to it, and you'll be able to start working with your new database right away.

In addition to creating a database, PowerBuilder allows you to delete databases that you no longer use. To delete a database, select Delete Database... from the **F**ile menu. PowerBuilder

displays a list of database file names in the Delete Local Database dialog box, and you can select which one you want to delete (see Fig. 16.10). After you select it, PowerBuilder confirms that you are sure you want to delete this file (see Fig. 16.11). If you answer **Yes**, PowerBuilder will go right ahead and delete the file. However, it does not clean up the ODBC driver or PowerBuilder Database Profiles, so you will have to delete those manually. You already know how to delete a Database Profile but not how to configure your ODBC driver, so let's discuss that now.

Figure 16.10.
The Delete Local Database dialog box.

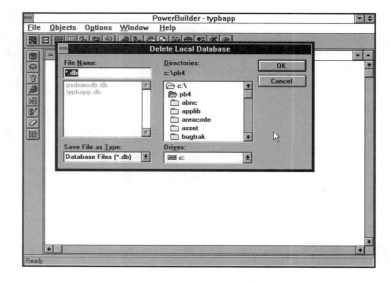

Figure 16.11.
Confirming delete request of a database.

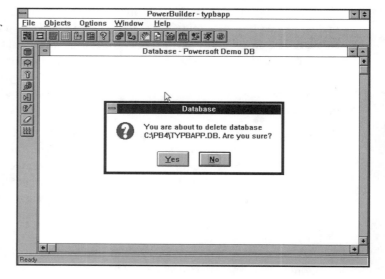

The ODBC Engine and Drivers

16

Not long ago, the people at Microsoft recognized the value of the Structured Query Language (SQL), a standard query language syntax. According to the Microsoft vision, any system that understands this standard language should be able to query any database, even databases that don't speak SQL. So, they created a system called the *Open Database Connectivity (ODBC)* engine that would allow for this dream to come true. Any application can perform queries against the ODBC engine using a standard query language, and let the ODBC engine worry about how to translate the query into the proper results. All you need is an ODBC *driver* to figure out how to convert your query to a query that is compatible with the database file that it's trying to read from. In addition, you need to configure a *data source*. Configuring your ODBC data source simply involves telling the ODBC engine what it needs to know in order to make the data source look to you like a database, including which driver it should use to perform queries. Then, when you tell the ODBC engine that you want to perform a query against a specific data source, it has all of the information it needs to execute the query, except perhaps the query itself, which it will get from you.

PowerBuilder provides access to the ODBC configuration system right from the Database Painter. To configure your ODBC Data Sources, you can select Configure **O**DBC from the **F**ile menu. You are presented with the Configure ODBC dialog box, which is split into two sections (see Fig. 16.12). The top half of the dialog lists the ODBC Drivers that you have installed in your system. You installed these drivers as part of the PowerBuilder setup back in the first lesson of this book. The bottom half of the dialog lists all of the data sources that have been created that use the driver that is selected in the top half. If you are using other applications that support ODBC, they may have installed their own drivers and data sources for you, or you may have selected additional drivers from the PowerBuilder setup in the first lesson. Otherwise, the only data source that is currently set up for you is the Powersoft Demo DB that was set up by PowerBuilder when you installed it. The driver that it uses is the *Watcom SQL 4.0* driver.

If you find Watcom SQL 4.0 in the list of drivers at the top and select it, you will see the Powersoft Demo DB appear in the list at the bottom half of the screen. (In addition, if you installed other sample applications from the installation procedure, you will see all of the other data sources listed there as well, so you may have to do some searching for the Powersoft Demo DB.) If you select the Powersoft Demo DB Data Source, you can attempt to modify it by clicking on the **E**dit button. However, you will get an error message indicating that you cannot modify the data source to which you are connected (see Fig. 16.13). Instead, though, you can just as easily create a new data source by clicking on the **C**reate button. When you click on this button, you are presented with the Watcom SQL ODBC Configuration dialog box (see Fig. 16.14). It is important to realize that this dialog box is specific to Watcom SQL, and other drivers use their own dialog box.

Figure 16.12.
The Configure ODBC dialog box.

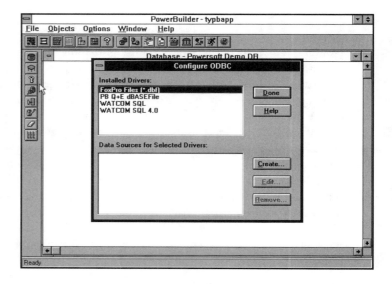

Figure 16.13.
Modifying your current data source.

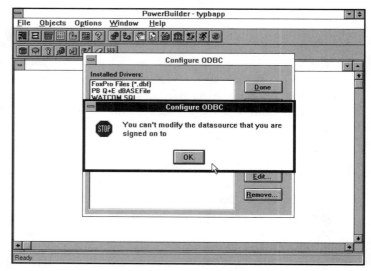

Figure 16.14.
The Watcom SQL ODBC Configuration dialog box.

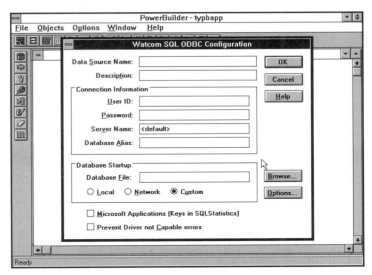

The first thing that every Configuration dialog box asks you is the name of the data source; in this case, it is prompted for in the edit box labeled Data **S**ource Name:. For example, the name of the data source that you are currently using is Powersoft Demo DB. In addition, you can place a small description of the data source in the next box, labeled Description:. Next, the system asks for connection information about the data source. This includes the **U**ser ID: and **P**assword:, which are optional and are overridden by the settings in your PowerBuilder Database Profile, so you can leave them out. With Watcom, you can start multiple database *Servers*, and if you like, you can specify in the edit box labeled Server Name: the name of a specific server to use for this data source; or you can leave it blank, and the ODBC Driver will use the default server. You can also specify the name that this database responds to (for connection purposes) in the Database **A**lias: edit box.

In addition to connection information, you must specify startup information for the data source to tell the database driver how to start a database connection the first time. This includes specifying the name of the Database File:, which you can either enter directly or search for by using the **B**rowse button. Also, you must specify the information as to which engine will be started by clicking on the appropriate radio button. You can search for a Local engine, meaning the engine is running on your local machine; or you can search for a Network engine, where the engine is running on a network server, and you are just connecting to it; or you can specify your own Custom settings and enter your own command line and startup information by clicking on the **O**ptions button.

In addition, there are two check boxes that you can set at the bottom. You check the first one, labeled Microsoft Applications (Keys in SQLStatistics), if you are going to be using this data

source with a Microsoft Application, which uses a nonstandard method of retrieving information about keys and indexes. In addition, if your system has trouble dealing with the `Driver Not Capable` error message, you can check the `Prevent Driver not Capable errors` check box, and the system will resolve the problem by eliminating this error. Because PowerBuilder does not have either of these problems, you may leave both check boxes unchecked for a data source that you are using with PowerBuilder. When you are finished, you can save the changes to your data source by clicking on the **OK** button; or you can click on the **Cancel** button, and your changes will be ignored. Either way, you will be returned to the Configure ODBC dialog box.

From the Configure ODBC dialog box, you can also delete a data source by clicking the **R**emove... button. When you do this, you are prompted to confirm deletion of your ODBC data source. If you say OK, the data source will be removed. When you are done making any changes to your data sources, click on the **D**one button, and you are returned to the Database Painter.

Once you are all set up and connected, the title bar of the Database Painter tells you that you are in the Database Painter and gives you information about your current database connection. The title bar that appears now at the top of the Database sheet should say something like

```
Database - ODBC.Powersoft Demo DB.dba
```

This tells you the driver name (`ODBC`), followed by the Database name (`Powersoft Demo DB`), followed by the user name (`dba`). This way, you can easily determine what database you are looking at, and who that database thinks you are.

The Database Menu and PainterBar

Once you are connected to your database, there are a number of things you can do with it. For one thing, you can create and edit tables, indexes, and keys in your database. You can also manipulate the data in your tables and administer database rights and privileges. We've already discussed the Connection options that are accessible from the **F**ile menu. In addition, there is a menu item called **O**bjects, where you can manipulate your database objects. We'll talk about most of these menu items in the next several lessons. For now, though, let's just take a moment to talk about a few of the menu items in this menu that you'll use in the next lesson.

Maintaining Your Format Styles

The first of these menu items is the Display **F**ormat Maintenance... menu item. In PowerBuilder, you use something called a *Display Format* or *Format Mask* to make your data display differently than it is stored. For example, lets say that you have a dollar value that you want to store in your database. Your user wants to see the dollar values appear on-screen with leading dollar signs ($) and proper resolution of cents with two decimal places. For example, even if the value is an integer, like four dollars and no cents, the two decimal places should appear anyway, with zeroes inside ($4.00). Simple, right? Just make the dollar value column into a column that can store string values, and store the value in the proper format, dollar sign and all! However, because

dollar values are also used to calculate other numeric fields, such as order totals, taxes, and other things, you need to store them as numbers! Because it's stored as a numeric value, you cannot store a dollar sign with it, and you cannot force two decimals to appear if there is no decimal value. So, how can you go about displaying the data in the proper format? You simply use a format mask that tells the column to display itself with a leading dollar sign and two decimal places. If you look at the list of formats, youll see one that looks like this:

```
$#,###.00;($#,###.00)
```

This display format actually contains two different format masks separated by a semicolon (;). The first format mask is for positive numbers, and the second format mask is for negative numbers. This display format means that when the number is positive, it will mask it so that it starts with a dollar sign, has a comma after every three digits, and has two zero-filled decimal places. If the number is negative, it will also be surrounded by parentheses to indicate that it is negative. Using this mask, you can store the number as a numeric value and still display it in the format that you want, without having to compromise the integrity of the data.

There are also other formats available for you to use if you like, and you can also create your own. Each datatype has its own format rules. With a numeric format, you use a number sign (#) to represent a numeric digit. Other characters can be displayed as well by enclosing them in quotes. In addition, dollar signs ($), percent signs (%), commas (,), a decimal point (.), and the letter *E* (for exponential notation, like 1.02e09) can be used in your numeric formats without quotes, and the system will recognize their meaning properly. When using a numeric display format, you can specify a different format for when the number is positive, negative, zero, and null. You separate each of these with semicolons. For example:

```
$#,###.00;($#,###.00);Zero;Null
```

will display a dollar value if positive, a dollar value inside parentheses if its negative, the word Zero if the value is zero, and the word Null if the value is null. Only the first section of the format mask is required. If you skip the rest, PowerBuilder will use that mask for all cases.

There are also special keywords that you can use to quickly represent a format in PowerBuilder. The keyword [General] can be used to let PowerBuilder figure out a format to use (generally to display the data as it is stored), and the keyword [Currency] will use the Microsoft Windows standard currency format as specified in your Control Panel.

In addition, you can use colors by specifying a color name or color value inside brackets in your formats. For example, the following format is identical to the one you last saw, but changes the color of the value to red if the number is negative:

```
$#,###.00;[red]($#,###.00);Zero;Null
```

You may use the following color keywords, enclosed in brackets, inside your display formats: black, blue, cyan, green, magenta, red, white, and yellow. In addition, you can specify the numeric value of the color you want inside brackets. The numeric value is calculated as the amount of red (1-255) + the amount of green (1-255) * 256 + the amount of blue (1-255) * 65536.

337

In addition to numeric format masks, you can also define masks for strings, dates, and times. String format masks use the at-sign (@) to represent a character of the string. Any other character, space, and so on is displayed in the string itself. You can also use color values in your string format displays. As with numeric formats, there is a format for the string, as well as a separate format for a null string. So, you can have a string format as follows:

```
[blue](@@@) @@@-@@@@;No Phone Number
```

This will display a blue string in the format of a telephone number if there is a string, or the words `No Phone Number` if the value is null. As with numbers, the null format is optional.

As with string formats, date format masks also only have two sections: the first for a date, the second for a null date. With date format masks, you can specify three special keywords. The [General] date format will use the format specified as the short date format in your Windows Control Panel. The [ShortDate] format also specifies the same thing. The [LongDate] format uses the long date format as specified in your Windows Control Panel. In addition, you can specify date formats using the letter *d* to represent the day, *m* to represent the month, and *y* to represent the year. The number of letters that you use determines the format of that component. For example, a single *d* will place the day number. Two *d*s (dd) represent a zero-filled day number. Three *d*s (ddd) are used to represent the abbreviated weekday name (for example, Sun). And four *d*s (dddd) represent the complete weekday name (for example, Sunday).

For the month, you can specify the month number using a single *m*. Two *m*s (mm) represent the month number, zero-filled. Three *m*s (mmm) represent the abbreviation of the month name (for example, Jan). And four *m*s (mmmm) spell the month name out completely (for example, January). Years are represented by the letter *y*. Two *y*s (yy) represent the two digit year (for example, 95), and four *y*s (yyyy) represent the complete year, century and all (for example, 1995). Characters besides these are used literally inside the date format, so a valid date format may look like this

```
dddd, mmmm d, yyyy
```

which displays the complete day name, month name, the day number, and the century-year. A date in this format appears as follows:

```
Sunday, January 1, 1995
```

Finally, you can create a format mask for the time. Again, there are two sections: the time format and the null format—the null format is optional. Again, there is a keyword you can use to read the Microsoft Windows time format from Control Panel, and that is [Time]. Or, you can display hours (h), minutes (m), seconds (s), and fractions of a second (f). Use one *h*, *m*, or *s* to denote a non-zero-filled component (hour, minute, or second, respectively). Or, you can use two *h*s, *m*s, or *s*s to denote zero-filled components. You can also place anywhere from one to six decimal places after your seconds by placing a single *f* for each decimal place you want. If you want 12-hour time format, specify that you want *AM* or *PM* to appear at the end of the time format. You can use *AM* and *PM* or just abbreviate it *A* and *P*, simply by entering the combination you want

separated by a slash (for example, A/P). This combination is case sensitive, too, so you can force the *AM* and *PM* (or *A* and *P*) to either uppercase or lowercase, whichever you prefer. Remember, if you omit an AM/PM representation in your format mask, the time will use 24-hour time. A valid time display format mask may, therefore, look like this:

```
hh:mm:ss.ffff a/p
```

which will display the time in a format something like this:

```
01:24:33.4324 p
```

When you select the Display **F**ormat Maintenance... menu item from the **O**bjects menu, you are presented with the Display Formats dialog box (see Fig. 16.15). Here you can maintain your display formats for use in the database. In the list box labeled Display Format, each of the format masks is displayed. You can select one by clicking on it. You can create a new format mask by clicking on the **N**ew... button. You are then presented with the Display Format Definition dialog box (see Fig. 16.16). This is the dialog box where you actually define the display format. You first assign it a name in the edit box labeled Name:, and then you select the datatype that this format will be used for in the Type: drop-down list box. Finally, you can enter the format itself into the combo box labeled Format:. If you want to select a display format from the list, you can use that as a starting point, or you can enter your format mask completely from scratch. Then, you can test the format mask and see how different values look using that format mask by entering a value (of the type specified in the drop-down list box above) into the box labeled Test Value: and click on the **T**est button. The resulting display value will appear below in the area labeled Result:. When you are done creating your format mask, you can press the **OK** button to save it or the **Cancel** button to cancel it. Either way, you are returned to the Display Formats dialog box.

Figure 16.15.
The Display Formats dialog box.

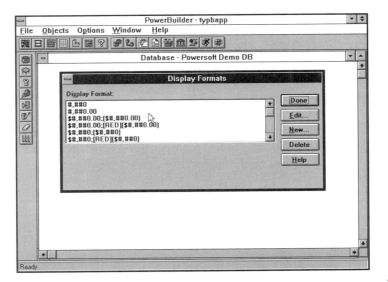

Figure 16.16.
*The Display Format
Definition dialog box.*

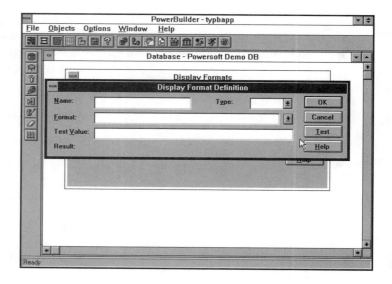

In addition to creating new format masks, you can delete format masks that you don't want
anymore by selecting them and clicking on the **Delete** button. You can also edit existing format
masks by selecting them and clicking on the **E**dit... button. However, when editing a format
mask, note that the name and datatype of the format mask cannot be changed. If you want to
change the name or datatype of an edit mask, you need to delete it and create a new one.

Maintaining Your Edit Styles

In addition to format masks that are used for display of data, you can also create format masks
that are used for entry of data. These edit masks are referred to as *edit styles*. The format for edit
styles is similar to display formats; however, because they are used for entry, there are several
different types of edit styles that you can create to facilitate entry of data into your database.

To maintain your edit styles, select Maintain **E**dit Styles... from the **O**bjects menu, and you are
presented with the Edit Styles dialog box (see Fig. 16.17). First, the existing edit styles are listed
in the list box labeled Style Names. Next to each style name is an icon to represent what kind
of edit style there is. The icon matches the picture on each of the buttons on the bottom right
of the dialog box. Each of these buttons creates a new edit style of the type specified. Let's take
a moment to discuss what each of these styles is.

Figure 16.17.
The Edit Styles dialog box.

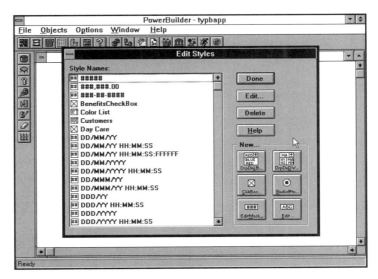

The first type of edit style is the *Drop Down Listbox Edit Style*. You can create an edit style that will allow your user to select a value from a list of choices in a drop-down list box. To define a new Drop Down Listbox Edit Style, click on the button labeled **DrpDnLB...**, and you are presented with the DropDownListBox Style maintenance dialog box (see Fig. 16.18). The first item that you can enter is the Name: of this edit style. Next, you can enter the Limit:, the maximum number of characters that can be entered into this field. Beneath that, you can enter an Accelerator: key, which will bring the focus to a field with this edit style when pressed by the user in combination with the **Alt** key. Next is a series of check boxes that you can set to make the drop-down list box react differently. For example, you can Sort the values in the drop-down list box, you can control whether the user will be able to type values into the check box or only select values from the drop-down list box by checking or unchecking the Allow Editing check box. You can make this field a Required Field, meaning that a value must be entered. You can check Empty String is NULL, or leave it blank to have PowerBuilder treat empty strings just as blank spaces. Additionally, you can set the field to automatically scroll horizontally when the user types into it by checking the Auto H Scroll check box. You can have the list display a Vertical Scroll Bar (V Scroll Bar). You can have the list of choices automatically pop up as soon as the user enters the field by checking the Always Show List check box. Finally, you can make the field always show the down arrow of the field, even when the field is not in focus, by selecting the Always Show Arrow check box. Lastly, if the field is editable, you can specify to force a certain case on the data inside the field by selecting a case style from the drop-down list box labeled Case:.

Figure 16.18.

The DropDownListBox Style maintenance dialog box.

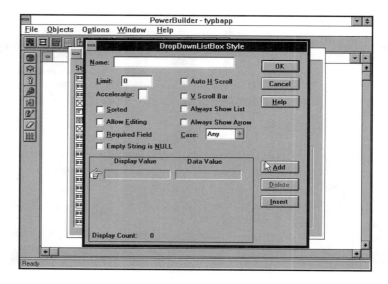

Beneath the check boxes, you can enter the list of display values and their corresponding data values. For example, you might want to create a drop-down list box that has the letter *A* display the word Active and the letter *I* display the word Inactive. To add an item to the end of the list, click the **A**dd button, and a new blank line will be added at the end of the list. You can delete an item from the list by selecting the line that you want to delete and clicking the **D**elete button. You can insert a blank line in front of the current line by clicking on the **I**nsert button. When you are done, you can click the **OK** button to save your new edit style or the **Cancel** button to ignore it.

The next type of edit style is called the *Drop Down DataWindow Edit Style*, which you can define by clicking on the DrpDnDW... button (refer to Fig. 16.17). This is similar to the Drop Down Listbox edit style, except that the list of values comes from something called a *datawindow*, which we'll talk about more in Chapters 21 through 24. Most of the fields in this window are similar to the fields that we talked about in the DropDownListBox Style dialog box. However, because you haven't yet learned about datawindows, we'll hold off on discussing this edit style for now.

Another type of edit style that you can create is the *Checkbox Edit Style* that allows the user to specify a value of a field by setting a check box on or off. You can create a Checkbox Edit Style by clicking on the button labeled ChkBox... (refer to Fig. 16.17). When you click on this button, you are presented with the CheckBox Style maintenance dialog box (see Fig. 16.19). Again, the first item you can enter is the Name: of the Edit style. Next, you enter the Text: that will be displayed for the check box. Beneath that, you can turn on or off several check boxes that control how your Checkbox edit style will appear. First, you can control whether the checkbox will appear to the left or right side of the text by clicking the Left Text check box. In addition, you can make this field look standard or have a three-dimensional look by checking the 3D check box. You can have the box portion of the check box remain the standard size, or you can have the box scale itself based on the size of the edit field by clicking the Scale Box check box. And finally, you can have either two states for your check box (checked and unchecked), or three states for your check box (checked, unchecked, and gray) by clicking on the 3 State check box. At the bottom of the screen, you can enter the data values that will be stored in the field when the check box is on or off. If the check box is a 3-State check box, you can also enter a third data value for the gray state (other). When you are done, you can click the **OK** button to save your edit style.

Figure 16.19.

The CheckBox Style maintenance dialog box.

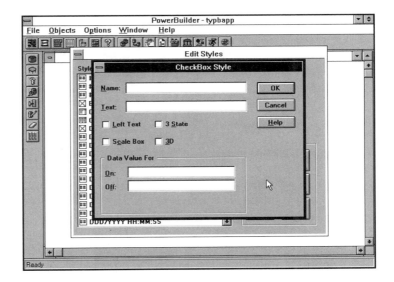

In a similar manner, you can specify a set of radio buttons that should be used to enter values. To do this, click on the RadioBtn... button (refer to Fig. 16.17), and you are presented with the RadioButton Style maintenance dialog box (see Fig. 16.20). The items that you can enter in the radio button dialog box incorporate items that you have already seen in the DropDownListBox Style maintenance dialog box as well as the CheckBox Style maintenance dialog box. The major difference is that instead of being selectable from a list, each of the items in the list of values is displayed in a group of radio buttons. There is no limit to the number of values you can enter. Each item in the list will appear vertically below the item before it, although you can have the items appear in more than one column by placing the number of columns you want in the edit box labeled Columns Across:.

If you prefer, you can create a simpler edit mask that works exactly like the edit mask control that you can place in a window, allowing the user to enter only specific characters with a specific format. To do this, click on the EditMask... button (refer to Fig. 16.17), which brings up the Edit Mask maintenance dialog box, which is the same dialog box that you saw in Chapter 4, Doing Windows (so we won't spend more time talking about it).

Figure 16.20.
The RadioButton Style maintenance dialog box.

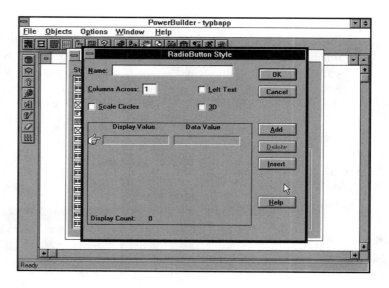

The last type of edit style is the plain, standard Edit Style. To create a standard edit style, click on the button labeled Edit... (refer to Fig. 16.17), and you are presented with the Edit Style maintenance dialog box (see Fig. 16.21). Many of the items that you see here have already been discussed in other edit styles. However, there are several new items that you can control. You can have your edit field display asterisks (*) instead of the values typed in to support Password Protection by checking the Password check box. By clicking on the Auto Selection check box, you can control whether PowerBuilder will automatically highlight the entire contents of the field when the user first tabs into it or not. Instead of automatically scrolling horizontally, you can set up your field to automatically scroll vertically by clicking on the Auto V Scroll check box. (It is recommended that you have the field scroll only horizontally or vertically, not both.) You can control whether the field will have horizontal and/or vertical scroll bars by clicking on the H Scroll Bar and V Scroll Bar check boxes. In addition, you can make the edit field Display Only, meaning that the user cannot edit the data in this field. You can also control whether the dotted rectangle that shows the currently active field will display or not by checking the Show Focus Rectangle check box.

When using a standard edit style, you can also control how the data in the field will be displayed. You can specify a display format mask, or you can create a code table of display values. You can also have the system validate input by using the Code Table, requiring that any data entered match an item in the table by checking the `Validate using code table` check box. When you change the display of a field, the data value displays when the user is inside the field, but the format mask or display value take effect when the user tabs out.

When you are done, you can click the **OK** or **Cancel** buttons to close the Edit Style maintenance dialog box. You will then be returned to the main Edit Styles dialog box (refer to Fig. 16.17),

where you can modify any of your edit styles by selecting one from the list and clicking on the **E**dit... button. When you do this, the appropriate style maintenance dialog box will appear. You can delete an unwanted edit style by selecting it and by clicking on the **D**elete button. When you are done, you can click on the **Done** button, and you will be returned to the Database Painter.

Figure 16.21.
The Edit Style maintenance dialog box.

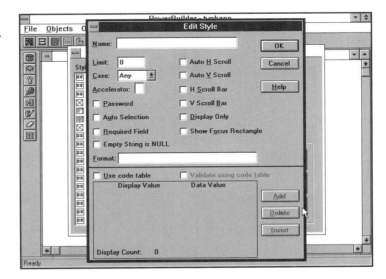

Maintaining Your Validation Rules

You can set up validation rules that will be used to validate data you attempt to enter into your database. To do this, select the **V**alidation Maintenance... menu item from the **O**bjects menu. You are presented with the Validation Rules dialog box (see Fig. 16.22). To create a new validation rule, click the **N**ew... button, and you are presented with the Input Validation rule definition dialog box (see Fig. 16.23). Here, you can again enter the Name: of the validation rule that you are defining. Beneath that, you specify the data Type: of the column for which this validation rule is defined. Then, you can specify the Rule Definition:, which is any expression that can be evaluated to TRUE or FALSE for any single value for a field (or column). You can use the keyword @col to represent the value of the column or field that this validation rule is used for. You can paste in this name by clicking on the button labeled @col. In addition, you can paste any function you like into your expression by clicking on it in the Functions: list box. One special, commonly used function for validations is the Match() function, which allows you to define text patterns that must match a string—generally the value of the column. If the value of the column matches the pattern, the Match() function will return TRUE; otherwise, the function will return FALSE.

Figure 16.22.
*The Validation Rules
dialog box.*

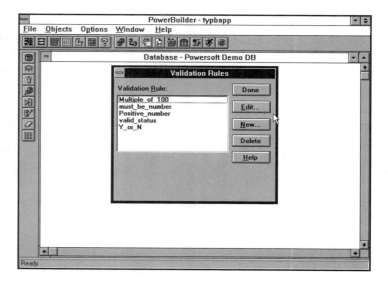

Figure 16.23.
*The Input Validation rule
definition dialog box.*

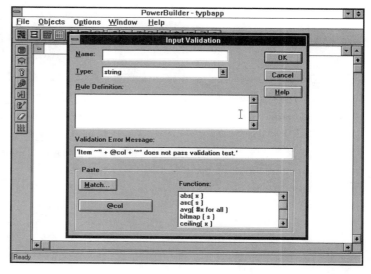

Because the Match() function is used so commonly with validation rules, there is a button right on the Input Validation rule definition dialog box labeled Match... that you can click to define a match pattern. When you click on this button, you are presented with the Match Pattern definition dialog box (see Fig. 16.24), where you can create a pattern of your own in the edit box labeled Pattern: or select one of the more common patterns from the list of patterns at the bottom of the page. Then, you can enter in a Test Value: and see if it matches or doesn't match by clicking the button labeled Test.

Figure 16.24.
The Match Pattern definition dialog box.

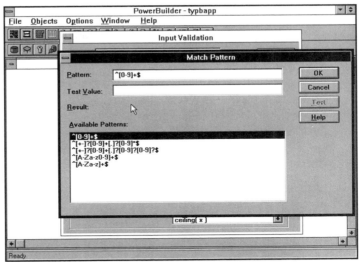

You can create your matching patterns by using standard characters in combination with special characters called *metacharacters*. The metacharacters are listed in Table 16.1. Any other character is a standard character. By specifying standard characters in combination with metacharacters, you can create even the most complex patterns to specify a certain number of certain characters in a certain order within your string. Then, when you are finished, you can click the **OK** button, and your match pattern will be pasted into the Rule Definition edit box. After you have created your rule expression, whether or not you use a match pattern, you can specify the error message that will be displayed if the validation fails. Again, here you may use the @col keyword to display the value of the column. Finally, when all is complete, you can click on the **OK** button; the validation rule will be saved, and you will be returned to the Validation Rules dialog box.

Table 16.1. The Valid Metacharacters.

Metacharacter	Description
Caret (^)	Matches the beginning of a string
Dollar sign ($)	Matches the end of a string
Period (.)	Matches any single character
Backslash (\)	Converts a metacharacter into a standard character
Brackets ([ ])	Matches any of the enclosed characters, or if the first character inside the bracket is a Caret (^), matches none of the enclosed characters

continues

Table 16.1. continued

Metacharacter	Description
Asterisk (*)	Indicates zero or more occurrences of a character
Plus (+)	Indicates one or more occurrences of a character
Question Mark (?)	Indicates zero or one occurrence of a character

Once you are returned to the Validation Rules dialog box, you can edit or delete validation rules by selecting the validation rule and clicking on the appropriate button. When you are finished, you can click the **Done** button, and your changes will be saved.

Afternoon Summary

The PowerBuilder Database Painter, which you can open by pressing **Shift-F7** or by clicking on the Database Painter icon on the PowerBar, lets you create and manipulate the tables, indexes, keys, and data that are stored in your databases. It also allows you to navigate to a couple of other important data related painters, the Data Manipulation Painter, and the Database Administration Painter.

In order for PowerBuilder to access data in a Relational Database, it must first *connect* to that database server. Connecting to your database server is like picking up your telephone and dialing the telephone number. In order to connect, you need to know the type of server you are trying to connect to, the name of the server, your login ID, and password. Depending on the DBMS you are using, there may also be other information that you need to know, including parameters, user IDs, and so on. You should be sure to check your PowerBuilder Interfaces documentation for any additional settings you may need in order to connect.

In order to help make it easier to connect to your databases, you can set up PowerBuilder Database Profiles, which will appear above the separator bar of the **C**onnect submenu of the **File** menu of the Database Painter. You can quickly connect to a different database by selecting a Database Profile from the **C**onnect menu, instead of having to fill out all of the information to reconnect each time you want to switch to that database. If you prefer, you can select the **P**rompt... menu item, which prompts you to enter this information. The **S**etup... menu item, allows you to set up the Database Profiles that will appear on your menu.

In addition to creating Database Profiles, if you are using Watcom SQL, you can also create new local databases. To create a database, select Cre**a**te Database... from the **F**ile menu. This menu item creates a local Watcom SQL database file and also configures it to work with the ODBC driver. In addition to creating a database, PowerBuilder allows you to delete databases that you no longer use. To delete a database, select De**l**ete Database... from the **F**ile menu.

Not long ago, Microsoft released the Open Database Connectivity Interface (ODBC), which allows any application to perform queries against the ODBC engine using a standard query language and an ODBC *driver*. The ODBC engine will figure out how to convert your standard query into a query that is compatible with the database file it is trying to read from. When using the ODBC engine, you need to configure a *data source*, which tells the ODBC engine what it needs to know to make the data source look like a database, including which driver it should use to perform queries. Then, when you tell the ODBC engine that you want to perform a query against a specific data source, it has all of the information it needs to execute the query, except perhaps the query itself, which it will get from you. PowerBuilder provides access to the ODBC configuration system right from the Database Painter. To configure your ODBC Data Sources, you can select Configure **O**DBC from the **F**ile menu.

Once you are all set up and connected, the title bar of the Database Painter tells you that you are in the Database Painter and also gives you information about your current database connection. Among other things, you can now maintain certain information that PowerBuilder stores in its dictionary to help you use the database; for example, your *display formats*, *edit styles*, and *validation rules*. *Display formats* make your data display differently than it is stored. Each datatype has its own format rules and uses different characters to represent different format components and values. There are also special keywords that you can use to quickly represent a format in PowerBuilder. You can also use colors by specifying a color name or color value inside brackets in your formats.

In addition to format masks that are used for display of data, you can also create *edit styles*, which are format masks that are used for entry of data. There are several different types of edit styles that you can create to facilitate entry of data into your database. To maintain your edit styles, select Maintain **E**dit Styles... from the **O**bjects menu, and you will be presented with the Edit Styles dialog box. There are several different types of edit styles, including the standard edit style, edit mask, drop-down list box, drop-down data window, check box, and radio button.

You can set up validation rules that will be used to validate data that you attempt to enter into your database. To do this, select the **V**alidation Maintenance... menu item from the **O**bjects menu. The rule definition is any expression that can be evaluated to TRUE or FALSE for any single value for a field (or column). You can use the keyword @col to represent the value of the column or field that this validation rule is used for.

Q&A

Q **Where are display formats, edit styles, and validation rules stored?**

A They are stored in the PowerBuilder repository—extended system tables unique to the PowerBuilder environment. In later chapters, you will learn about other column extended attributes.

Q In this unit you have created formats and edit styles, but how will they be used?

A These extended attributes are assigned to table columns. When any developer creates a DataWindow that has these columns in its result set, the extended attributes are copied to the DataWindow for these columns. Within the DataWindow Painter, these attributes can be overridden.

Q I created a table and assigned formats and edit styles to the columns. Why don't I see some of the column display formats when I view the table in the Data Manipulation Painter?

A Edit style settings will override display format settings. You will see edit styles first and see display formats only when edit styles are not associated with the column.

Q I'm confused about the difference between `@col` and `GetText()` in validation rules. How and where do I use these?

A `@col` is seen in the Database Painter and is required when creating a validation rule. The `@col` or `@column name` is simply a placeholder that is replaced with the `GetText()` function when the rule is copied to a datawindow. Because the Database Painter verifies a reference to a column with `@col` placeholder, `GetText()` should not be used in the Database Painter. When the validation rule is used in a data window, `@col` becomes `Real(GetText())` for number fields, `Date(GetText())` for date fields, and simply `GetText()` for string fields. You will use `GetText()` when creating or editing validation rules in the DataWindow Painter.

Workshop

Quiz

1. What is a primary key and why is it used?
2. What is a foreign key and why is it used?
3. What is table normalization?
4. What is the main purpose of table indexes?
5. What are views?
6. What is the display format definition for a date with style Jan/11/94?

Putting PowerBuilder into Action

1. Create a Watcom Local Database called TYPBAPP.
2. Browse through the display formats that come with a new database.

3. Create a new display format called *PhoneNum* that will display a string telephone number so that it looks like this:

   (800) 555-1212

4. Browse through the edit styles that come with a new database.

5. Notice that there are no validation rules that come with a new database.

6. Reconnect to the Powersoft Demo DB. You will be using that database in the next several lessons.

7. Create a new Edit Mask edit style called *Grade*. The edit mask type is Numeric, and the mask is ###. To make the mask really exciting, make it a spin control. Click on the Spin Control check box and make the spin increment *10*, the minimum value is 0, and the maximum value is 100.

8. Create a new validation rule called *lesson* that requires a value to be between 1 and 28. The message that should be displayed if the validation fails starts with the value that the user entered, followed by, "is not a valid lesson."

Chapter

17

Data Structure Using the Database Painter

In this lesson, you will learn how to use the Database Painter to view and edit the structure of your tables. You will learn:

☐ What the different icons and symbols in the Database Painter denote

☐ How to create, edit, and delete the different database structures, including Tables, Views, and Keys

☐ About the special PowerBuilder Data Repository, which allows you to store additional information about the tables and columns in your database that PowerBuilder will use to view and manipulate them

☐ About the Database Activity Log, where you can log each and every database command you execute to a log file

Viewing a Table

Go back and open the table list so you can select some tables to work on. Open the list of tables by selecting **T**ables... from the **O**bjects menu, or by clicking on the Select Tables icon on the Database PainterBar. The list of tables you should see is a list of the tables that are used by the PowerBuilder Sample Application and its example applets. You can also see the system tables by clicking on the check box labeled Show System Tables. The system tables are the database catalogs and the PowerBuilder tables that are used to store the structure of the tables, columns, and views. At this beginner level, though, you will probably neither need nor want to touch them.

> **Note:** Every DBMS uses *catalog tables* to store the structure of the data in the database. However, the catalog structure itself is nonstandard, and so each DBMS implements the catalog in its own way. Check your DBMS documentation for information about how the catalogs in your DBMS work.
>
> The PowerBuilder catalogs, however, are special PowerBuilder tables that store the repository information that we mentioned in the last lesson, along with other information about the structure of the tables in your database. The PowerBuilder catalogs are always the same, regardless of the DBMS you are using.

You can select a table by clicking on its name in the list box and then by clicking on the **Open** button. You can even select multiple tables—the first click selects a table name, and the second click unselects it. Clicking on **Open** will open all of the tables that are selected.

Note: If you double-click on a table in the list, it will also open up all of the selected tables without actually closing the dialog box.

Hey! Look at that! There is a table in the list called *employee*, and another table in the list called *department*. Let's take a look at those two tables and see what they look like! Highlight both of the tables (one at a time, of course) and then click **Open**. Your disk should spin for a moment while it opens the two tables onto your Database Painter desktop. Eventually, you should be presented with two big boxes with a bunch of lines and little boxes between them (see Fig. 17.1). The two big boxes are the table definitions of the two tables that you selected. The top line of each box (which is black if it is selected, and gray otherwise) contains the name of the table as well as a comment about that table. Underneath, each of the column names inside the table are listed, along with a short comment if it is available. Because the employee and dependent tables are related to each other, these relationships are depicted in the picture as well, using the lines and little boxes.

Figure 17.1.
The Employee and Department tables.

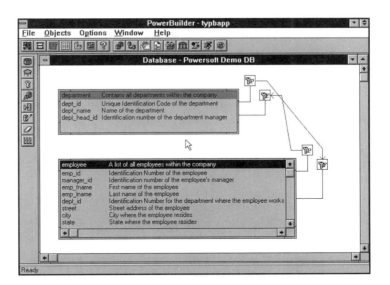

Note: Only one copy of a table can be opened on the Database Painter at a time. So as you open tables, their names will disappear from the list of tables that you can open.

17

Referential Integrity

 The little box with the capital P inside of it is a box that represents the Primary Key of the table. PowerBuilder displays the Primary Keys of open tables by using this icon, with lines drawn between the icon and the columns of the Primary Key. In the Department table, the Primary Key is the dept_id column. In the Employee table, the Primary Key is the emp_id column.

 In addition, there are also some boxes that have a capital F inside of them. These are the Foreign Key boxes, which represent the Foreign Keys of a table. In addition to the line between the icon and the Foreign Key column, there is also a line between the Foreign Key icon and its Primary Key icon if that icon is on the screen. For example, the department_head_id field of the Department table is a Foreign Key into the Employee table's Primary Key of emp_id. In addition, the dept_id field of the employee table is a Foreign Key into the department table's Primary Key of dept_id.

If you double-click on the Primary Key icon of the Employee table, or if you select the Employee table and select the **P**rimary Key menu item from the **O**bjects menu, you are presented with the Primary Key Definition dialog box, where you can redefine the Primary Key of the Employee table (see Fig. 17.2). Don't save it, but try this out now by clicking on the column names that are listed in the list of Table Columns. As you click on any column in the list, it appears on the list of Key Columns on the top line. You can change the order of the key columns simply by grabbing a column and dragging it to a new position in front of or behind another key column. Then, when you are finished setting up your Primary Key, you can click on the **OK** button, and it will save your changes in the database; or you can click on the **Log Only** button, and it will save your changes to a activity log that you can convert to a file later. (We'll talk more about the database activity log in a little while.) For now, though, because we don't want to go messing with the example tables, let's just press the **Cancel** button to cancel your changes and close the Primary Key Definition dialog box. You'll play with building your own Primary Keys with new tables in a little while.

If you right-click with your mouse on the Primary Key icon of the Employee table, you are presented with a menu of options (see Fig. 17.3). If you select the first menu item, **D**efinition..., you will go back to the same Primary Key dialog box as when you double-clicked on the Primary Key icon. Let's skip the second menu item for the moment and jump immediately to the third menu item. If you select the third menu item, D**r**op Primary Key..., you are prompted to drop the Primary Key definition (see Fig. 17.4). If you respond **Yes** (don't do this now), PowerBuilder will delete the Primary Key as well as any Foreign Keys that point to that Primary Key. If you respond **No**, PowerBuilder will cancel your request to drop the Primary Key. For now, respond **No** because this table has Foreign Keys that you don't want to lose yet.

Figure 17.2.
The Primary Key Definition dialog box.

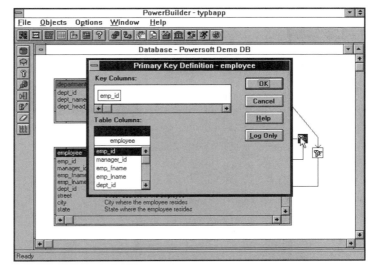

17

Figure 17.3.
The Primary Key right mouse menu.

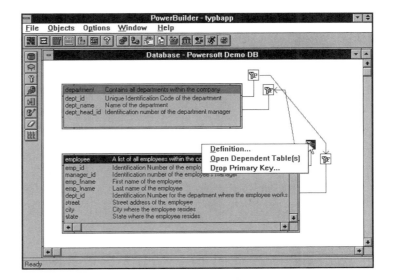

357

Figure 17.4.

*The Drop Primary Key
Confirmation dialog box.*

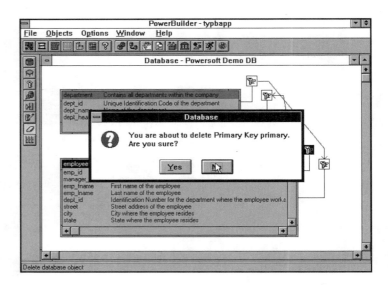

We skipped one menu item on the right mouse menu of the Primary Key, the **O**pen Dependent Table(s) menu item. If you click on this menu item, PowerBuilder will search through the database catalogs to find tables whose Foreign Key points to this Primary Key. Then, it will open them onto the Database Painter desktop, showing the Foreign Key to Primary Key relationship.

The Foreign Key icons also have a right mouse menu that you can use to manipulate the Foreign Keys (see Fig. 17.5). The last menu item, **D**rop Foreign Key, works exactly like its counterpart from the Primary Key's right mouse menu, **D**rop Primary Key. The difference between dropping a Foreign Key and a Primary Key is that when you drop a Foreign Key, it has no effect on other keys in the system. Above the **D**rop Foreign Key menu is the **O**pen Referenced Table menu item, which opens the table whose Primary Key this Foreign Key points to. Finally, the first menu item, **D**efinition..., allows you to define or redefine this Foreign Key.

When you select the **D**efinition... menu item from the Foreign Key right mouse menu, you are presented with the Foreign Key Definition dialog box (see Fig. 17.6). The Foreign Key Definition dialog box is not as simple as its Primary Key counterpart; however, it is not all that different, either. Unlike Primary Keys, Foreign Keys need their own unique names because there can be more than one Foreign Key on a table. The name of the Foreign Key that you are editing is displayed in the top right of the dialog box, in the box labeled Foreign Key Name:. Because all Foreign Keys point to Primary Keys, you must select the table whose Primary Key you want this Foreign Key to point to in the drop-down list box labeled Primary Key Table:. Then, it will display the names of the columns in the Primary Key of the table you selected in the box labeled Primary Key Columns: so that you can select the proper Foreign Key columns from the list of columns in the box labeled Select Columns. As you select them, the columns will appear in the box labeled Foreign Key Columns:, where you can reorder them like you did in the Primary Key

Definition dialog box, by dragging them to new positions. Finally, if your database supports it, you can select the Referential Integrity rule that you want to use for when dependent rows from the Primary table are deleted.

Figure 17.5.
The Foreign Key right mouse menu.

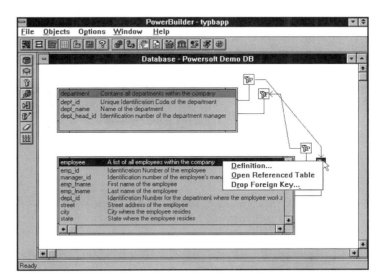

Note: Some DBMSs don't automatically support Referential Integrity rules, but instead give you alternate tools, for example *triggers* that you can use to implement Referential Integrity rules manually. Check your DBMS documentation for details.

Remember that the purpose of Foreign Keys is to enforce database integrity. It wouldn't make sense to have a row in the Employee table that had a department ID that didn't exist in the Department table. Employees must belong to some department, so the department ID in the Employee table is a Foreign Key to the Primary Key of the Department table. The Referential Integrity rule determines what action the database will take if you try to delete a department that has employees in it. You can either choose to RESTRICT dependent deletes, CASCADE dependent deletes, or SET NULL dependent deletes.

If you choose to RESTRICT dependent deletes, you will not be able to delete rows from the primary table if there are rows in the current table that depend on it. For example, you will get an error if you try to delete a department that still has employees assigned to it. This rule is enforced because there is a Foreign Key from the dept_id column in the Employee table that points to the Primary Key in the Department table, with the RESTRICT delete integrity option set.

Figure 17.6.
*The Foreign Key
Definition dialog box.*

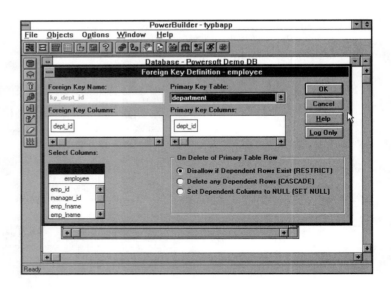

If you choose to CASCADE dependent deletes, you will force all rows in this dependent table to be deleted when their source row is deleted from the primary table. For example, you might want to have it so that if you delete a row in the Department table, it will delete all of the employees who work for that department. I know a few executives who have done this in the past, and so they prefer the CASCADE dependent deletes option over the RESTRICT.

The last option is the SET NULL option. You can set up your Foreign Key so that when a department is deleted, all employees with that department will have their department IDs cleared out to NULL. Perhaps this is less appropriate for a department-employee relationship than for other types of relationships, but it is a rule that you may use for your referential integrity in your database.

The Database Index

In addition to the Primary and Foreign Key icons, there is also an icon that is used to represent index keys. Indexes can be unique, or duplicate; therefore, there is an icon to represent unique index keys containing a picture of a single key, and duplicate index keys containing a picture of two keys. As with the other keys, there is a line from the key itself to the columns that make up that key. By double-clicking on the key, you can see the name of the index, what columns make up the index, if the index is clustered, and if the index is unique, in the Browse Index key definition dialog box (see Fig. 17.7). However, because indexes cannot be modified but have to be regenerated, you cannot modify the index from this window. If you want to modify the index, you need to drop it and then re-create it.

Figure 17.7.
The Browse Index key definition dialog box.

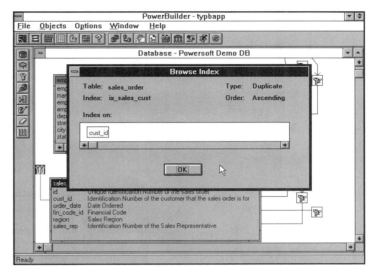

Like the other keys, you can right-click on the Key icon to see a menu (see Fig. 17.8). From that menu, you can select **B**rowse... to browse the index key definition, or select **D**rop Index... to drop the index altogether.

Figure 17.8.
The Index Key right mouse menu.

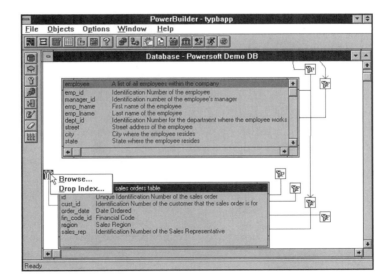

What You See Is What You Get

In addition to right-clicking on your keys and indexes, you can right-click on any empty space on the Database Painter desktop and get a menu of things that will help you control the Database Painter environment (see Fig. 17.9). The first menu item, Select Tables..., opens up the first dialog box you saw when you entered the Database Painter so that you can select additional tables that you want to work with in the Database Painter. Beneath that is the menu item Arrange Tables, where you can let PowerBuilder move your tables around on-screen so that they are more neatly arranged. Finally, the next three menu items are toggles that allow you to control what you want to see in the Database Painter.

Figure 17.9.
The Database Painter right mouse menu.

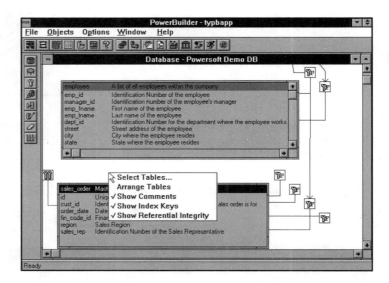

First, you can select to show or hide the comments that appear next to the table names and column names in the tables on-screen by selecting Show Comments from the menu. If the menu has a check next to it, then it is selected and comments will be displayed. Then, if you click on it, the comments will hide themselves and the check mark will disappear, indicating that comments are hidden. We'll talk more about these comments a bit later on, but just be aware that you can turn them on or off here.

You can select to show or hide the Index Key information by selecting the Show Index Keys menu item from the menu. As with the other menus, if the check mark is showing, then selecting this menu item will turn off the display of the index keys, as well as the check mark.

Finally, you can select to show or hide the Primary and Foreign Key information by selecting the Show Referential Integrity menu item from the menu. Again, as with the other menus, if the check mark is showing, selecting this menu item will turn off the display of the Primary and

Foreign Keys, as well as the check mark. If you like, go ahead and play with these settings to see how they affect your screen. Try arranging your tables after you turn each of the items on and off. However, when you are done playing, leave them all checked so that you can continue your lesson without any confusion.

Now, let's talk a bit about these table boxes that you've opened up.

The Database Painter Table Box

When you select a table from the Select Table window, it opens up in the Database Painter, allowing you to see its definition as well as its data. Let's start by looking at just the Department table, which you opened in the beginning of this lesson. On the screen is a box that describes the Department table. It displays the name of the table on the top line, followed by a comment. The top line itself is like a title bar, and you can move the table box by clicking on the top line and dragging the table with your mouse. Beneath the table's title bar is a list of the columns that make up that table, also followed by their comments. Each line represents a column in the table.

You can adjust the size of the table box as you would any sizable window—by dragging a corner or edge of the border around the box to the position that you prefer. Additionally, you can see the definition of the table by double-clicking on the table, or by selecting **E**xtended Definition from the **O**bjects menu. Double-click on the Department table box, and you will see the Alter Table definition dialog box, which describes the structure of the department table (see Fig. 17.10).

Figure 17.10.
The Alter Table definition dialog box.

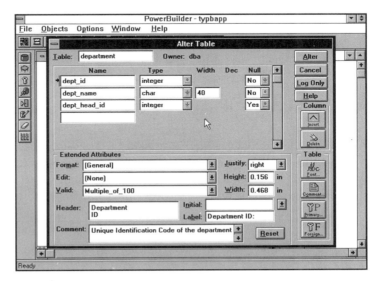

Table Definitions

At the top-left of the screen, the name of the table, *department*, appears. Immediately to the right, the name of the owner of the table appears. Beneath the table information is the column information. Each column is listed on its own line, first showing the name on the left, then the datatype, the width and number of decimal places (if appropriate for the datatype), and whether or not NULL values are permitted in this column. For example, in the Department table, the first column is named dept_id, is of type integer (which doesn't need width and decimal information), and does not allow NULL values.

Along the right edge of this dialog box are a series of buttons. The first button, labeled Alter, will accept any changes you made (assuming, of course, that they are legal), and then alter the table as you specify. Beneath that, the Cancel button allows you to cancel any changes that you may have made. Below that, the Log Only button will write your changes to an activity log that you can save as a file later on. This activity log is the same log that we talked about earlier in this lesson, and we will talk more about how to use the log later. Beneath that is the Help button, which will bring up online help about this window. Beneath the Help button are two buttons that are grouped as Column buttons. These buttons allow you to insert and delete columns, respectively. When you click on the **Insert** button, an empty column line is inserted into your table's list of columns immediately in front of (above) the line with the small arrow next to it, in this case the dept_id column line. If you click on the **Delete** button, the column with the arrow pointing to it will be deleted. Be aware, however, that the SQL Standard does not allow you to delete columns in an Alter Table statement, so you may get an error if you attempt to delete the dept_id column. However, if you were to create a new column and then decided that you didn't need it before you pressed **Alter**, you could delete that column without any problems.

Extended Attributes

Beneath the column list is a group of attributes labeled Extended Attributes. The attributes in this group box are related to the column that is currently selected, the one that has the little arrow next to it. PowerBuilder extends the system catalogs with its own system catalogs, called a *repository*, that it uses to help you when you are building PowerBuilder applications. It stores these extended attributes in that repository and then uses the repository when you build your DataWindow forms (which we'll talk about in Chapters 21 through 24), as well as when you view your data in the Database Painter using the Data Manipulation function (which we'll talk about in the next lesson). If you set a column's extended attribute here, it will then use that style as the default style when you create a form with that column (of course, you can override it if you prefer to).

The attributes that you can change are Format, Edit Style, Validation Rule, Justification, Height and Width, Initial Value, Header, Label, and Comment. I'll briefly describe each one in turn.

In the last lesson, you learned about maintaining your format masks, edit styles, and validation rules. The reason that you need to maintain them is so that you can use them in your database. One of the ways that you can apply them is through the extended attributes of a column. First, let's talk about the display format mask that you maintained in the last lesson. Here, you can apply a format mask to your column by selecting it from the Format drop-down list box. The list of available format masks is dependent on the datatype of the column; certain masks are only available for certain datatypes.

The edit mask works in almost the same way; however, the edit mask is used for editing data instead of just viewing it. If you want to allow your users to have formatted data entry, you can select an edit mask from the Edit drop-down list box. You can apply one of the edit masks that you created in the last lesson if you like, or you can apply one of the standard edit masks that come with PowerBuilder.

Beneath the Edit drop-down list box is the Valid drop-down list box, where you can select a validation rule to use for this column. As you learned in the last lesson, a *validation rule* is a PowerBuilder expression that must evaluate to either true or false, and will be used to determine if a value that is entered for this column is valid. If it is not, a validation error will occur, and a message box containing the validation error message will be displayed.

To the right of the Format drop-down list box, you can set the justification of this column. You can justify your columns to the right, left, or center. Beneath the Justify drop-down list box are the Height and Width entry boxes, where you can enter the height and width of the data in this column in inches. If you leave these blank, PowerBuilder will determine their values based on the width of the field and the font used. However, if you have a very long field and don't want to show the whole thing, you can set the width to a smaller value if you like.

Beneath that is the Initial drop-down list box. By default, when you insert a new row into a form or data manipulation window, the values for all of the columns in that row are empty. However, you may want to have a column default to a value when a new row is created. Here, you can enter this default value for the column. You can also select one of several from the list box. The values in the list box will change based on the datatype of the column. You can fill columns that hold strings with spaces, with an empty string, or set them to NULL. You can set integers, longs, and other numerics to zero (0) or to NULL. You can also set dates and times to the current time or to NULL.

Beneath the Initial combo box is the Label edit box, where you can enter a label that will be used in front of this column when the column is displayed in a Free Form mode. The Header edit box to the left of that is where you can enter a title that will be used when the column is displayed in Tabular or Grid mode. We'll talk more about the Free Form mode and other modes of viewing data in the next lesson, as well as later in Chapter 23 when we talk about DataWindows. For now, just be aware that if the label is on top of the column, the header will be used; but if the label is on the left of the column, the label field will be used.

> **Note:** A drop-down list box that also allows you to type into its display portion is usually referred to as a *combo box* by Windows programmers. This is because it is a combination of a drop-down list box and an edit box.

Finally, beneath the Header entry box is a Comment entry box, where you can enter the comment that will be used in the Database Painter (and in other places, too!) to describe this column. To the right of the Comment box is a button labeled Reset. If you click on that button, the values for all of the above settings will reset to their default settings. This does not reset your changes to the settings that were last saved but to the settings that PowerBuilder determined by default when the column was first built.

To the right of the Extended Attributes group box are some buttons that affect the entire table, labeled inside a group called Table. The first one, labeled Font, allows you to adjust the default font that will be used for the data in this particular table. If you remember, back when you learned about the Application Painter, we talked about the default fonts for tables. Well, if you click on the **Font** button here, you will be presented with the same Font dialog box where you can override the Application Default settings for this table only (see Fig. 17.11). As with its Application Painter counterpart, you can set the font, size, and style for Data, Headings, and Labels. A sample of the font selected is displayed at the bottom of the dialog box.

Beneath the Font button is the Comments button. When you click on this button, you will be prompted to enter a comment for the entire table, the one that will appear on the top line of the table box itself, next to the table name (see Fig. 17.12). If comments for this table already exist, they will be displayed in the dialog box as well, and you can overwrite the existing comment or add to it.

Beneath the **Comments** button is the **Primary Key** button. Here, you can define a Primary Key for the table if one does not already exist; or if it does, you can view and edit its definition. The window that appears when you click on this button is the same Primary Key Definition dialog box that you saw when you right-clicked on the Primary Key and selected Definition... (refer to Fig. 17.2).

Beneath the Primary Key button is the Foreign Key button. When you click on the **Foreign Key** button, PowerBuilder displays the Select Foreign Key dialog box, inviting you to select the Foreign Key that you want to edit, or to create a new one (see Fig. 17.13). You can select one to edit by selecting the Foreign Key you want to edit in the list box labeled Foreign Keys:, and then clicking on the **Edit** button, or by double-clicking on the Foreign Key name in the list.

When you do this, the Foreign Key Definition dialog box will appear on your screen, displaying the Foreign Key that you selected (refer to Fig. 17.6). This is the same dialog box that you saw when you right-clicked on the Foreign Key icon.

Figure 17.11.
The table's Font dialog box.

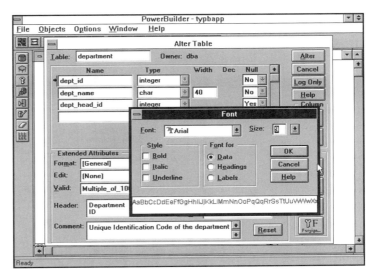

Figure 17.12.
The Comments for department dialog box.

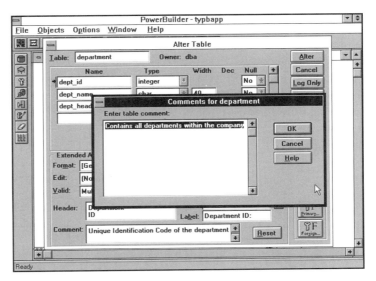

If you want to create a new Foreign Key, you can click on the **New** button, and you will be presented with an empty Foreign Key definition dialog box, where you may enter the information to build a new Foreign Key. When you have finished working on the Foreign Keys for this table, you can click on the **Done** button.

Figure 17.13.
The Select Foreign Key dialog box.

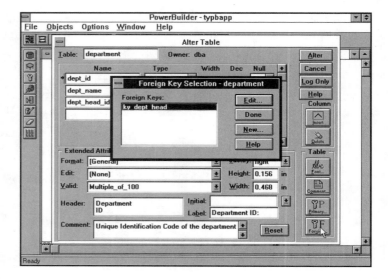

At this time, none of the changes you have asked for in the Table Definition dialog box have actually been made to the table, its keys, columns, or extended attributes. They are all being held in queue by PowerBuilder until you click on the **Alter** button. Once you are satisfied with all of your changes, you can click on the **Alter** button to accept your changes, the **Cancel** button to ignore the changes, or the **Log Only** button to save the database commands that execute these changes to an activity log file. The activity log file can then be used to make the changes later.

The Right Mouse Menu of a Table

For now, press the **Cancel** button to ignore any incidental changes that you may have made while reviewing the functionality of the Table Definition dialog box. You will be returned to the Database Painter window. Now, right-click on the department table near the top line of the table, which reads department. The title bar should turn black, and a popup menu will appear (see Fig. 17.14). The first item on the menu, Close, will close this table, removing it from the Database Painter desktop (but not the database itself). Most of the rest of the menu items in this right mouse menu map to functions that you have already seen because they are also available from the Table Definition dialog box. This is because the right mouse menu is supposed to be just a shortcut. The first of these menu items is the Definition... menu item, which will bring you back to the Table Definition dialog box, which you also get to by double-clicking on the table itself.

Figure 17.14.
The Department Table right mouse menu.

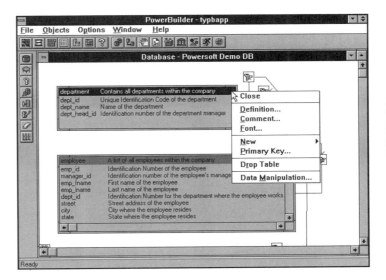

Beneath the Definition... menu item is the Comment... menu item, which opens up the Table Comments dialog box (refer to Fig. 17.12) that you saw inside the Table Definition dialog box when you clicked on the **Comments** button. Next on the menu is the Font... menu item, which opens the Table Font Selection dialog box. The next menu item is the New menu item, which itself has a submenu. From the New menu, you can select to create a new Index or a new Foreign Key. If you select New Foreign Key, you will see an empty Foreign Key Definition dialog box, where you can create a new Foreign Key on this table.

Note: You can also create a new Foreign Key by selecting Foreign Key from the New submenu in the Objects menu.

If you select New Index, you will be presented with the Create Index dialog box (see Fig. 17.15). In a similar fashion to the Create Foreign Key Table, you create an index by giving it a name in the edit box labeled Create Index:, and then select the columns of the index from the table picture in the bottom-left corner. Then, you can either select to have the index be unique or duplicate by clicking on the appropriate radio button in the top-right corner. In addition, depending on your DBMS, you may be able to choose the index to be Ascending or Descending, and Clustered or Non-Clustered. Finally, you can accept the index settings and generate it by clicking **OK**, or you can generate an activity log by clicking **Log Only**. You can also click **Cancel** to forget the whole thing.

> **Note:** You can also create a new index on a table by selecting the Index... menu item of the New submenu of the Objects menu, or by clicking on the New Index button on the Database PainterBar.

Figure 17.15.
The Create Index dialog box.

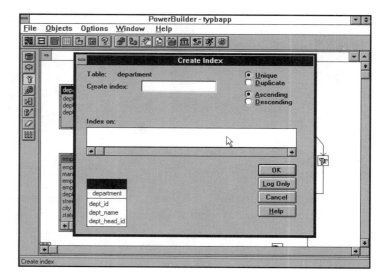

Beneath the New menu item is the Primary Key menu item, which will open the same Primary Key dialog box that you saw from the Table Definition dialog box. The next menu item is the Drop Table menu item. When you click on this menu item, you will be prompted to confirm that you want to drop the table (see Fig 17.16). If you say **Yes**, the table will be deleted from the screen as well as from the database.

>
> **Note:** You can also open the Primary Key dialog box by selecting the Primary Key menu item of the Objects menu.

Finally, the last menu item is the Data Manipulation... menu item. Let's skip this menu item and talk about it in the next lesson. Now let's take a look at the right mouse menu of a column. Right-click on the first column in the table box: dept_id (see Fig. 17.17). The first menu item that you can select is once again Definition..., and as you may have guessed, this will bring you back to the Table Definition dialog box. Each of the other menu items in the right mouse menu for a column gives you the capability to edit a few attributes of the column at a time; however, they all refer to attributes that you can also edit from the Table Definition dialog box.

Figure 17.16.
Deleting a table. "Are you sure?"

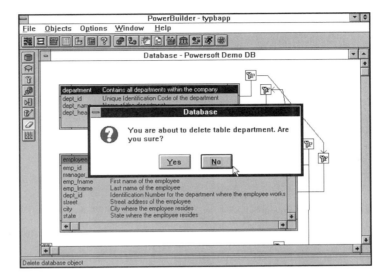

Figure 17.17.
The Column's right mouse menu.

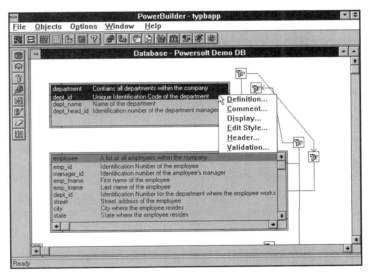

The Right Mouse Menu of a Column

The first of these menu items is the **C**omment... menu item, which opens the same Comment dialog box that you saw when you selected **C**omment... from the Table's right mouse menu—except that this time, you are editing the comment of the selected column and not of the whole table (indicated by the title bar of the dialog box).

Beneath the **Comment...** menu item is the **D**isplay... menu item. When selecting the **D**isplay...
menu item, you will be presented with the Column Display Format dialog box (see Fig. 17.18).
From this dialog box you can select a display format mask to be used when the column is
displayed by selecting it from the list of formats. Also, you can set the justification for the column
and set the height and width of the column. In addition, you can also edit the selected format
mask by clicking on the **Edit** button, or you can create a new Format Mask by clicking on the
New button. These display format masks are the same format masks that we talked about in the
last lesson. When you are finished editing the display format, you can save your changes by
clicking on the **OK** button, or you can ignore your changes by clicking **Cancel**.

Figure 17.18.

*The Column Display
Format dialog box.*

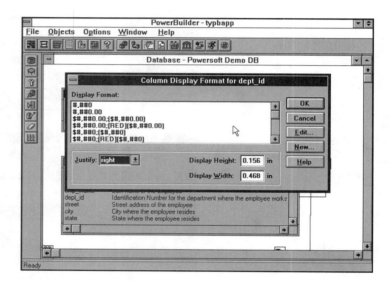

The next menu item is the **E**dit Style... menu item. When you select this menu item, you will
be presented with the Edit Style dialog box (see Fig. 17.19), where you can select an Edit Style
for this column, edit an Edit Style mask, or create a new Edit Style mask.

The next menu item is the **H**eader... menu item. When you select this menu item, the Column
Header dialog box appears on your screen (see Fig. 17.20). Inside this dialog box, you can change
the label and header texts. Also, you can set the justification for the label and header.

Finally, there is the **V**alidation... menu item. When you select this menu item, you are presented
with the Column Validation dialog box where you can select a validation rule for the column
and an initial value for the column as well (see Fig. 17.21). In addition, you can edit existing
validation rules and create new ones, too.

Figure 17.19.
The Edit Style dialog box.

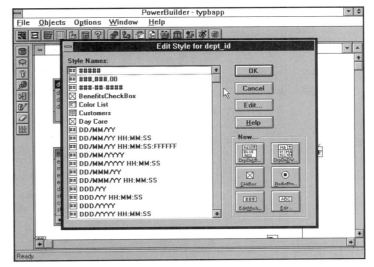

Figure 17.20.
The Column Header dialog box.

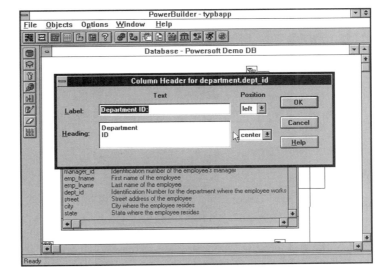

Figure 17.21.
The Column Validation dialog box.

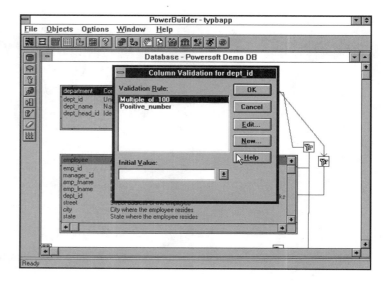

Creating a New Table

In addition to editing existing tables with their keys and indexes, you can also create new ones. To create a new table, you can click on the **T**able... menu item of the **N**ew submenu of the **O**bjects menu, or you can click the New Table button on the Database PainterBar. When you do this, you will be presented with an empty Table Definition dialog box where you can name and define a new table, much in the same way you edited the definition of an existing table earlier in this lesson.

Views

In addition to creating and editing tables, you can also create and edit *views*. If you remember, *views* aren't really tables, but they are queries that return result sets that look like tables. To create a view, select **V**iew from the **N**ew submenu of the **O**bjects menu, or click on the Create View button on the Database PainterBar. When you do this, you will be presented with the query builder, where you can create the query that the view will be based on. We will be spending quite a bit of time discussing the PowerBuilder query builder later, in Chapter 20, "Database Administration," and so I will leave this discussion for that chapter. When you are done building your query, though, you will be prompted to name your view, and the view will open up on the Database Painter window. Remember that once the view is created, it more or less works and looks like a table. So, to open an already existing view, you simply select it from the list of tables.

Once a view is open on-screen, it works pretty much like a table does; however, there are a few minor differences. First of all, a couple of the menu items that you see in the right mouse menu of a table have disappeared. For example, you cannot create Primary and Foreign keys on a view. More importantly, though, when you ask to see the definition of a view, you are not presented with the Table Definition dialog box but with the View Definition dialog box. Here you can inspect the *view syntax*, which is the query that was used to generate the view (see Fig. 17.22). Because views cannot be edited, that's pretty much all there is to seeing the view definition.

Figure 17.22.
The View Definition dialog box.

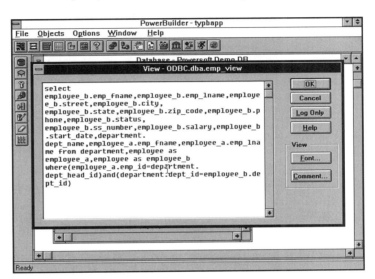

The Database Activity Log

Throughout this lesson, we briefly touched on something called the *activity log*. Whenever you perform any function in the Database Painter, PowerBuilder translates your actions into database commands that are sent to the database server. The activity log can store a log of these database commands and appears as an icon at the bottom left of the Database Painter screen (see Fig. 17.23). There are several methods to get commands into the log. We've already mentioned that you can click on a **Log Only** button in many of the dialogs you have seen in this lesson. However, you can also save the commands that would be used to create your tables and their extended attributes by selecting the E**x**port Table/View Syntax To Log menu item from the **O**bjects menu. Furthermore, you can have the activity log maintain a running log of all of the database commands that you have performed by selecting the **S**tart/Stop Log menu item of the **O**ptions menu. The first time that you select this menu item, the log file will begin collecting all of the commands that are sent to the database. The next time, the log file will stop.

Figure 17.23.
The Activity Log icon.

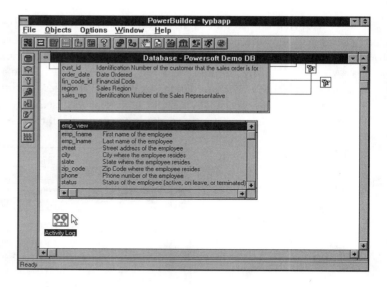

By double-clicking on the Activity Log icon, you can open a window that shows you all of the commands that have been saved to the activity log. If you like, you can save these commands to a file, which you can run later in the Database Administration Painter. To do this, select the **S**ave Log As menu item from the **O**ptions menu, and you will be presented with the standard Save File dialog box, where you can specify the name and directory of the file you want to save the log to. Finally, if you like, you can clear the log by selecting the **C**lear Log menu item from the **O**ptions menu, and all of the commands in the log will disappear, and you can start over again.

Morning Summary

You can open the list of tables by selecting **T**ables... from the **O**bjects menu or by clicking on the Select Tables icon on the Database PainterBar. You can also see the system tables by clicking on the check box labeled Show system tables. The system tables are the database catalogs and the PowerBuilder tables that are used to store the structure of the tables, columns, and views. You can select a table by clicking on its name in the list box and then by clicking on the **Open** button. You can even select multiple tables: the first click will select a table name, and the second click will unselect it. Clicking on **Open** will open all of the tables that are selected.

When you open a table in the Database Painter, it appears as a box that describes the table definitions of the tables that were selected. The top line of each box (which is black if it is selected, and gray otherwise) contains the name of the table as well as a comment about that table. Underneath, each of the column names inside the table is listed, along with a short comment if it is available. If any relations exist between two open tables, those relations are depicted by using pictures, lines, and little boxes.

The Primary Key of a table is represented by a little box with a capital P inside. PowerBuilder displays the Primary Keys of open tables using this icon, with lines drawn between the icon and the columns of the Primary Key. In addition, there are also some boxes that have a capital F inside them. These are the Foreign Key boxes, which represent Foreign Keys of a table. In addition to the line between the icon and the Foreign Key column, there is also a line between the Foreign Key icon and its Primary Key icon if that icon is on the screen.

If you double-click on the Primary Key icon of a table, or if you select a table and select the **P**rimary Key menu item from the **O**bjects menu, you will be presented with the Primary Key Definition dialog box, where you can redefine that Primary Key. You can change the order of the key columns simply by grabbing a column and dragging it to a new position in front of or behind another key column. If you right-click with your mouse on the Primary Key icon of the Employee table, you will be presented with a menu of options, including **D**efinition..., **D**rop Primary Key, and **O**pen Dependent Table(s). The Foreign Key icons also have a right mouse menu that you can use to manipulate them.

When you select the **D**efinition... menu item from the Foreign Key right mouse menu, or if you double-click on it, you are presented with the Foreign Key Definition dialog box. The Foreign Key Definition dialog box is not as simple as its Primary Key counterpart; however, it is not all that different, either. Because all Foreign Keys point to Primary Keys, you must select the table whose Primary Key you want this Foreign Key to point to in the drop-down list box labeled Primary Key Table:. If your database supports it, you can also select the Referential Integrity rule that you want to use for when dependent rows from the Primary table are deleted.

In addition to the Primary and Foreign Key icons, there is also an icon that is used to represent index keys. Indexes can be unique or duplicate, and so there is an icon to represent unique index keys, containing a picture of a single key, and an icon for duplicate index keys, containing a picture of two keys. As with the other keys, there is a line from the key itself to the columns that make up that key. By double-clicking on the key, you can see the name of the index, what columns make up the index, if the index is clustered, and if the index is unique, in the Browse Index Key Definition dialog box. Like the other keys, you can right-click on the key icon to see a menu. From that menu, you can select **B**rowse... to browse the index key definition or select **D**rop Index to drop the index altogether.

In addition to right-clicking on your keys and indexes, you can right-click on any empty space on the Database Painter desktop and get a menu of things that will help you control the Database Painter environment. The first menu item, Select Tables..., opens up the first dialog you saw when you entered the Database Painter so that you can select additional tables that you want to work with in the Database Painter. Beneath that is a menu item, Arrange Tables, where you can let PowerBuilder move your tables around on-screen so that they are more neatly arranged. Finally, the next three menu items are toggles that allow you to control whether you want to see keys, indexes, and comments in the Database Painter.

When you open a table box on-screen, it displays the name of the table on the top line, followed by a comment. The top line itself is like a title bar, and you can move the table box by clicking on the top line and dragging the table with your mouse. Beneath the table's title bar is a list of the columns that make up that table, also followed by their comments. Each line represents a column in the table. You can see the definition of the table by double-clicking on the table, or by selecting **E**xtended Definition from the **O**bjects menu.

In addition to the standard definition of a table, including information about the columns in the table, PowerBuilder extends the system catalogs with its own system catalog, called a *repository*, that it uses to help you when you are building PowerBuilder applications. It stores extended attributes in that repository and then uses the repository when you build your DataWindow forms, as well as when you view your data in the using the Data Manipulation Painter. The attributes that you can change are Format, Edit Style, Validation Rule, Justification, Height, Width, Initial Value, Header, Label, and Comment.

As with the other objects in the system, the table box also has a right mouse menu that you can use to extend the definition of a table. From this menu, you can create indexes, Primary Keys, Foreign Keys, and other functions associated with a table. To get to this menu, you must right-click on the top line of the table. If you right-click on one of the column lines in the table, you will be presented with the right mouse menu of the column, not the table. From this menu, you can perform functions associated with only that specific column, like changing the comment, changing the masks, header, and validation rules, and so on.

In addition to editing existing tables with their keys and indexes, you can also create new ones. To create a new table, you can click on the **T**able... menu item of the **N**ew submenu of the **O**bjects menu, or you can click the New Table button on the Database PainterBar. When you do this, you will be presented with an empty Table Definition dialog box, where you can name and define a new table.

In addition to creating and editing tables, you can create and edit views, by selecting **V**iew from the **N**ew submenu of the **O**bjects menu, or by clicking on the Create View button on the Database PainterBar. When you do this, you will be presented with the query builder, where you can create the query that the view will be based on. Once a view is open on-screen, it works pretty much like a table. There are a few minor differences, though, including some missing menu items and the Definition dialog box. Since a view is based on a query, the view definition dialog box displays that query and not a Table Definition dialog box.

Whenever you perform any function in the Database Painter, PowerBuilder translates your actions into database commands that are sent to the database server. The activity log can store a log of these database commands and appears as an icon at the bottom left of the Database Painter screen. There are several methods to get commands into the log. You can click on a **Log Only** button in many of the dialog boxes that you have seen in this lesson. Additionally, however, you can save the commands that would be used to create your tables and their extended attributes by selecting the E**x**port Table/View Syntax To Log menu item from the **O**bjects

menu. Furthermore, you can have the activity log maintain a running log of all of the database commands that you have performed by selecting the **S**tart/Stop Log menu item of the O**p**tions menu. The first time that you select this menu item, the log file will begin collecting all of the commands that are sent to the database. The next time, the log file will stop.

17

18

Data Manipulation Using the Database Painter

In this lesson, you will learn how to use the Data Manipulation Painter to view and edit the data inside your tables. You'll also learn about:

- [ ] Printing and zooming your data
- [ ] Saving your changes to the database or to local files of different type
- [ ] Importing data from a local file into the database
- [ ] Sorting and filtering your data to make it easier to work with
- [ ] Using DataWindow expressions

Viewing and Manipulating Data in a Table

If you recall, back when we first talked about the Database Painter, we skipped by one of the menu items in the menu structure of the Database Painter—the Data Manipulation... menu item. PowerBuilder has built an extensive, user friendly interface that allows you to view and manipulate your data without having to learn any special languages. This interface is called the *Data Manipulation Painter*.

To open the Data Manipulation Painter, right-click on the top line of the Department table and select Data Manipulation..., the last menu item. When you select this menu item, a new Data Manipulation window opens, containing all of the data from the Department table in *grid layout* (see Fig. 18.1). The layout of the data refers to the manner in which the data is displayed on-screen. In the grid layout, the column titles appear at the top of the screen, and each row of the table appears on its own line with the proper column value in its proper column. In addition, the grid layout looks and works very much like a spreadsheet; you can change the order of the columns simply by clicking on a column title and dragging it to a new position. You can change the width of the columns simply by clicking on the border between two columns and dragging the border to the new position, changing the width of the column immediately to the left of the border.

You can also get to the Data Manipulation Painter by selecting Data **M**anipulation from the **O**bjects menu. From this menu, you can also view your data in grid layout, but there are several other layouts you can use to view your data as well. Besides the grid layout, you can view your data in *tabular layout*, which is very much like grid layout in format but does not allow you to move or size your columns. Also, you can view your data in *freeform layout*, which makes your data look more like a form—each column is on its own line, and each row is a single page of information.

Figure 18.1.
The Data Manipulation window.

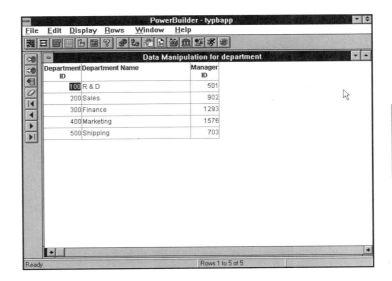

> **Note:** Internally, tabular layout and freeform layout are exactly the same. The only difference between the two is how the fields come up on the screen—horizontally or vertically. The grid layout, however, is a unique layout that is intended to look more like a spreadsheet than a form.

You can page through the data in the Data Manipulation window by using the scroll bars, or by using the **PgUp** and **PgDn** keys. You can also select the **N**ext Page menu item from the **D**isplay menu, which takes you to the next page of data, if there is more than one page of data in the current table. The **P**rior Page menu item takes you to the previous page of data if there is one. There are also buttons on the Data Manipulation PainterBar that correspond to these menu items.

In addition, there are two buttons on the PainterBar that are not reflected in the menu structure but help you navigate through your data. They are the First Page and Last Page buttons. Clicking on the First Page button quickly brings you to the first page of data in the window, and clicking on the Last Page button immediately brings you to the last page of data in the window.

> **Note:** The buttons that you use to navigate through the data in the Data Manipulation Painter look very much like the buttons that you may see on your VCR to fast forward and rewind through your video tape. For this reason, they are often referred to as *VCR buttons.*

Finally, the **Z**oom... menu item from the **D**isplay menu allows you to zoom the data inside the current window to help it fit better in your window. When you select this menu item, you are presented with the Zoom dialog box, where you can quickly select a zoom ratio by percentage, or you can type in your own zoom percentage in the box labeled Custom (see Fig. 18.2). The data in the window will zoom to that ratio. If you select 50%, for example, it will zoom the data to be half the size so that it can fit in the window. If you zoom the data to 110%, it makes it a little bigger and perhaps a little bit more readable.

Figure 18.2.
The Zoom dialog box.

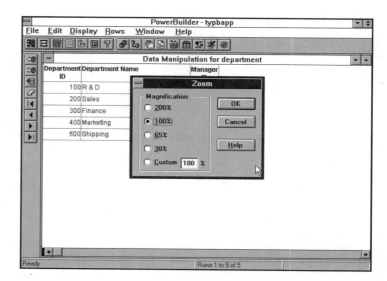

Printing Your Data

From the **F**ile menu, you can also print your data by selecting the **P**rint menu item. When you select this menu item, PowerBuilder will prompt you with the Print options dialog box (see Fig. 18.3). At the top of this dialog box, it tells you which printer is currently selected. However, you can change the current printer by clicking on the **Printer** button. Beneath that in the box labeled Copies:, you can specify the number of copies you want to print. Next, you can specify the range of pages to print. At the bottom of the dialog box, you can specify whether you want to print all pages, just the even pages, or just the odd pages. To the right, you can check to have the system collate your copies (printing each set of copies in page order), and to have your data print to a file instead of to the printer. Finally, you can click **OK** when you are done, and it will begin printing the data.

Figure 18.3.
The Print options dialog box.

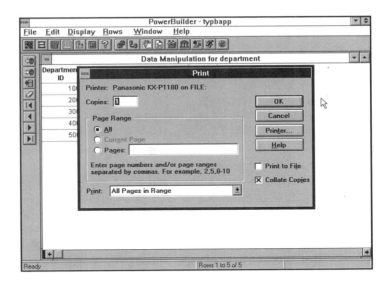

18

If you want to see what your hard copy will look like before you print it, you can select Print Preview. Once in Print Preview mode, you can use a set of Virtual Rulers to help you see how things will appear on the page, and you can adjust the margins by selecting the Print Preview Rulers menu item from the File menu. In addition, you can adjust the view of your page on-screen by zooming out to see more or by zooming in to see less. You choose the amount of zoom from the Print Preview Zoom... menu item from the File menu. When you select this menu item, you are presented with the Zoom dialog box that you encountered when you were looking at your data. This time, however, the zoom ratio that you enter just zooms in or out of the Preview screen, whereas selecting Zoom... from the Design menu zooms the actual picture of the data in the Data Manipulation Painter and actually zooms in our out what will be printed. As with other toggle menus, you can turn off Print Preview mode by clicking again on the checked Print Preview menu item.

DO	DON'T

DO Use the Display|Zoom menu item to control the zoom ratio of the data that appears in the Data Manipulation Painter. For example, if you need to zoom this data so that it will fit better in your window, this zoom function will control the size of the data in the window, as well as on the printed page.

DON'T Discount the value of the File|Print Preview Zoom... menu item, though. It allows you to see what a complete page of data will look like when it is printed out, even if the data is also zoomed using the Display|Zoom function.

Editing Your Data

If the table containing the data you are looking at has a Primary Key, you will be able to edit your data. You edit data in a grid DataWindow, one cell at a time, just like in a spreadsheet. Simply click on the cell you want to edit and change the value. Click on the cell in the Department ID column in the first row of data. The value of this cell contains the number 100. Now, change the number to 123. At this point, the data that you have entered has not yet been entered into the buffer of the window you are looking at. To attempt to accept the change that you typed in, press the **Tab** key. You are prompted with a message that the department number must be a multiple of 100 (see Fig. 18.4). This message is the result of a validation rule that has been placed on the column. Go ahead and change the number back to 100. Now, when you tab off, you don't get an error, and the data that you enter is accepted. Your focus will change to the second column, Department Name. At this point, your changes have not been saved back to the database. The Data Manipulation window buffers all of your input in the front end while you make your changes to the database. Only when you specifically ask to save your changes back to the database does it actually figure out what changes you have made. Then it creates and executes the SQL Statements that are required to save those changes to the database. This functionality is one of the more remarkable aspects of PowerBuilder. The fact that you can take advantage of this functionality right inside your own applications is what makes PowerBuilder the strongest relational database development tool available on the market today, especially for relational databases using client-server architecture. You can write programs that access relational databases without knowing a single word of SQL.

Figure 18.4.
The Department ID must be a multiple of 100.

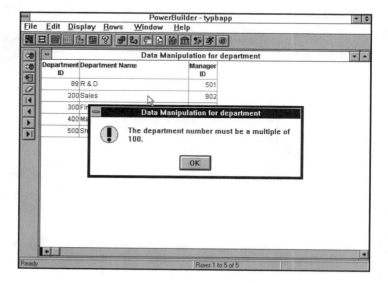

Deleting and Inserting Rows

The next menu in the Data Manipulation Painter is the **R**ows menu. From the **R**ows menu, you can **D**elete the current row of data from the table displayed on-screen; you can **In**sert a new row into the table in front of the current row; you can also **R**etrieve the data from the database again, which eliminates any unsaved changes that you may have made. You can use the buttons on the Data Manipulation PainterBar to perform these functions if you prefer, as well.

In addition, there are several other important functions that you can perform in the Data Manipulation Painter that are available from the **R**ows menu. You can import data from an outside source into your table by selecting the **I**mport... menu item. When you select this menu item, you are prompted to select the file that you want to import, as well as the file type of the file you are importing (see Fig. 18.5). PowerBuilder allows you to import Tab Delimited Text files and dBASE format database files. After you select the file that you want to import, PowerBuilder attempts to load the file into the Data Manipulation Painter. If there is an error, a message box is displayed describing the error and telling you which column the error occurred in. It will then ask if you want to continue importing the file or if you want to cancel the rest of the import. Either way, whatever data has succeeded upon import will be inside the table in the Data Manipulation Painter.

Figure 18.5.
The Select Import File dialog box.

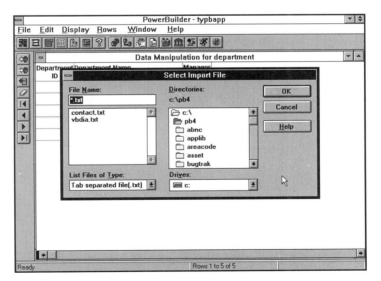

Saving Your Data

All of the changes you make—deleting rows, inserting rows, changing data, importing data, and so on—are only inside the data manipulation window that you are looking at, and are not saved into the database itself until you specifically ask PowerBuilder to save them for you. To tell PowerBuilder that you want to have it update your changes to the database, you simply select the **S**ave Changes To Database menu item from the **F**ile menu, or click on the Save Changes button on the Data Manipulation PainterBar. When you do this, PowerBuilder figures out what changes you have made and begins creating the appropriate statements that it needs to save your changes to the database. If, for some reason, the update does not succeed, PowerBuilder prompts you with an error message.

In addition, you can save the data that appears on your screen to your hard disk instead of (or in addition to) the database in a variety of formats; such as a spreadsheet, either Excel or Lotus formats, a tab delimited text file, a comma delimited .CSV file, a set of SQL commands, a dBASE database file, and a PowerBuilder Report file. To do this, simply select Save **R**ows As from the **F**ile menu, and you are presented with the Save Rows As dialog box (see Fig. 18.6). From this dialog box, you can select the file format that you want to save your file with, and you can specify the name of the file to save it with. In addition, you can have it save rows to the resulting file that represent the headers by clicking on the Include Headers check box. When you click the **OK** button, the file is saved to the directory that appears beneath the filename edit box in the format that you specified, and you are then returned to the Data Manipulation Painter.

Figure 18.6.
The Save Rows As dialog box.

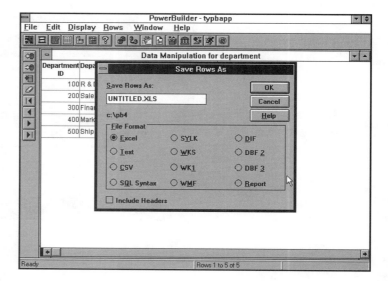

Data Buffers

It's important to understand how PowerBuilder handles all of this data. Somewhere deep inside the Data Manipulation Painter, PowerBuilder has made room for several copies of your data. First, there is the *Primary Buffer*, which is the buffer in which you are actually entering and modifying your data. This buffer is the only buffer that is "visible." All of the other buffers are "behind the scenes." The next buffer is the *Filtered Buffer*, which is where PowerBuilder puts rows that are filtered out. Next is the *Deleted Buffer*. When you delete a row from your DataWindow, PowerBuilder places a copy of this row in the Deleted Buffer. Finally, there is the *Original Buffer*, which holds a copy of the data as it appeared when it was first retrieved from the database.

This copy is also updated whenever you save your changes back to the database. As you make changes to data in the Primary Buffer, PowerBuilder sets flags to indicate that the data has been changed. When you ask to update the database, Power-Builder uses these flags to determine which rows need to be inserted, updated, and deleted from the database. It uses the data in the Original Buffer to tell the data-base the key values of the rows that are going to be updated so that even if you changed a key value, the database will change the proper row. It uses the Deleted Buffer to determine which rows to delete from the database. When it is done, it resets the flags and updates the Original Buffer to look like the Primary Buffer so that the next time you ask the system to update, the process works properly again. Using this process, PowerBuilder can quickly and easily create the proper state-ments to update your data for you.

Sorting

In addition to adding and removing data, you can also sequence your data by selecting the **S**ort... menu item from the **R**ows menu. When you do this, you will be presented with the Specify Sort Columns dialog box (see Fig. 18.7). In the left column labeled Source Data is a list of all of the columns available in the Data Manipulation Painter. You can drag the column that you want to sort on and drop it onto the list of columns on the right, labeled Columns. When you do this, the name of the column appears, and next to it is a check box where you can select whether to sort it in ascending or descending order. If the check box is checked, the data is sorted in ascending order. If there are duplicate values for one of your sort keys, you may want to sort on more than one column. In that case, you can drag another column over from the left column to the right column. You can place the new column either above or below the column that is already in there. The sort order of the data is based on the order of the columns in the list on the right, from top to bottom. You can change that order by dragging an item up or down in the list, as well.

Figure 18.7.
The Specify Sort Columns dialog box.

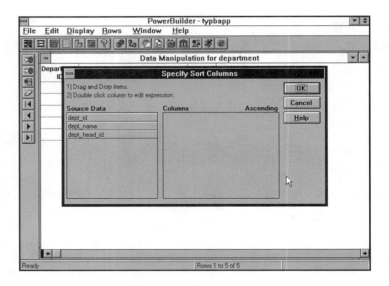

An Introduction to DataWindow Expressions

Another exciting feature of PowerBuilder is the fact that you can use an expression based on a column value (or even on several column values) to sort your data. The result of the expression is evaluated for each row in the table, and the result is used as a sort key. You do this by double-clicking on a column listed on the right side of the window. When you do this, you are presented with the Modify Expression dialog box (see Fig. 18.8). By default, the expression is simply the name of the column you placed in the list. This column name appears in the edit box labeled Expression:. However, you can place in this box any legal expression that you like, as long as it returns a single value for each row in the table that can be used for sorting. The value itself can be numeric or alphanumeric and is sorted based on its proper sequence; for example, numerically for numbers and lexically for strings. In order to help you build your expressions, you are supplied with a list of available functions in the Functions: list box and a list of columns in the Columns list box. Incidentally, the name of a column is not required to appear in the expression. You might want to have a sort key that is based on the status of the row, which you can get by using the IsRowNew() and IsRowModified() functions. For example, take the following expression:

```
if( IsRowNew(), 2, 1 ) * if( IsRowModified(), 3, 1 )
```

Figure 18.8.
*The Modify Expression
dialog box.*

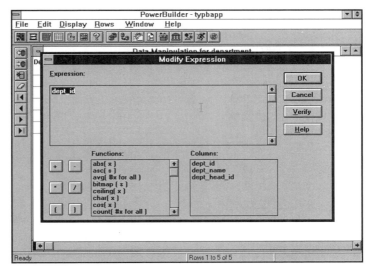

This expression demonstrates two things. First, it demonstrates the use of a special function that is only available for use inside a data expression; it is called the if() function. The if() function works much like the IF..THEN..ELSE language construct that you learned about way back in Chapter 7. The format for the if() function is

```
if( <boolean expression>, <Result if TRUE>, <Result if FALSE>)
```

The first parameter is a boolean expression that can be evaluated to either TRUE or FALSE. The second parameter is the value that the if() function will return if the expression evaluates to TRUE, and the last parameter is the value that the function returns if it is FALSE. Now, you can see how the preceding expression actually makes sense. It basically says that if the row is new, return a 2; otherwise, return a 1. Then, take that number and multiply it by 3 if the row is modified, or 1 if the row is not. The result of this expression will return four distinct values based on the status of the row, as demonstrated in Table 18.1. Rows that are neither new nor modified will appear first because they have the lowest result of 1. Rows that are new but not modified will appear second. Rows that are modified but not new will appear next. And finally, new rows that have been modified will appear last.

Table 18.1. The four values returned by the preceding expression, based on status.

IsRowNew	IsRowModified	Value 1	Value 2	Result
FALSE	FALSE	1	1	1
TRUE	FALSE	2	1	2
FALSE	TRUE	1	3	3
TRUE	TRUE	2	3	6

When you are done creating your expression, you can verify that it is a legal expression by clicking on the **Verify** button. When you click on this button, a message box will appear either telling you that the expression is OK or explaining what is wrong with it. If the expression is OK, you can save it by clicking on the **OK** button; or if you change your mind, you can press the **Cancel** button. When you're done, you are returned to the Specify Sort Columns dialog box, and your expression appears in the Column list. You can save your sort order by clicking the **OK** button and when you return to the Data Manipulation Painter, the data is sorted in the order you specify.

Note: Expressions can be used for other things besides sorting. We will talk more about the things that can use expressions in Chapters 21 and 22. In the meantime, pay attention to the Modify Expression dialog box since it will soon become one of your most commonly used PowerBuilder dialog boxes.

Filtering

To help you work with your data, you can filter out rows that you are not interested in by selecting **F**ilter... from the **R**ows menu. When you do this, you are presented with the Specify Filter dialog box, which allows you to enter an expression that will be used to filter out rows from your data display (see Fig. 18.9). Although this dialog box looks and works much like the Sort Expression dialog box, the expression that you use for your filter should evaluate to TRUE or FALSE for each row in the table. If the value is TRUE, the row stays; and if the value is FALSE, the row disappears to the Filter Buffer. And so, you can use expressions that contain Relational Operators as well. When a row is filtered out, though, it is not being deleted from the database. It's just being hidden from view.

Note: Actually, rows that are filtered out are internally moved to the Filter Buffer that we talked about earlier in this lesson.

Figure 18.9.
The Specify Filter dialog box.

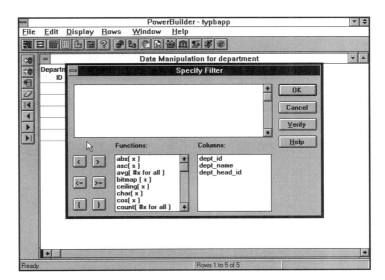

18

Describing the Data You Are Looking At

Finally, you can see a description of the rows on (and off) the screen by selecting Described... from the **R**ows menu. When you do this, you are presented with the Describe Rows dialog box, which indicates the number of rows deleted, the number of rows displayed, the number of rows filtered out, and the number of rows modified (see Fig. 18.10). This dialog box helps you understand what you are looking at, especially when it comes to figuring out why it looks like there is invalid or missing data. Often, you will look at this dialog box and realize that you forgot to reset your last filter, or that you deleted rows that you didn't intend to delete.

When you are finished manipulating your data, you can return to the Database Painter by choosing **C**lose from the **F**ile menu, or by selecting **D**esign from the **D**isplay menu. If there are changes pending, you are prompted to save your changes back to the database. Then, you are returned to the Database Painter, where you can continue working on building your tables, indexes, and keys.

Figure 18.10.
The Describe Rows
dialog box.

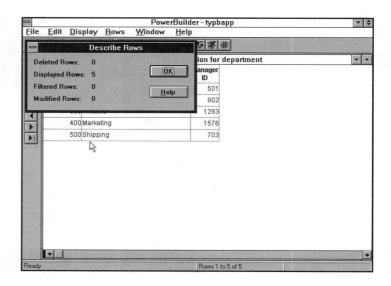

Afternoon Summary

PowerBuilder offers an extensive, user friendly interface that allows you to view and manipulate your data without having to learn any special languages or commands. This interface is called the *Data Manipulation Painter*, which can be opened in a number of ways. The first is by right-clicking on the top line of a table box and selecting Data Manipulation..., the last menu item. You can also get to the Data Manipulation Painter by selecting Data **M**anipulation from the **O**bjects menu. You can also click on the Data Manipulation icon on the Database PainterBar. There are several layouts that you can use to view your data. You can view your data in *Grid Layout*, *Tabular Layout*, or *FreeForm Layout*.

Once you have the data on your screen, you can page through it by using the **PgUp** and **PgDn** keys, or the **N**ext Page and **P**rior Page menu items from the **D**isplay menu. You can also use the VCR buttons that appear on the toolbar to page through your data. You can Zoom your screen in our out by selecting **Z**oom from the **D**isplay menu. You can print the data on your screen by clicking on the Print button on the toolbar, or by selecting **P**rint from the **F**ile menu. When you do this, you will be presented with a dialog box where you can control how your data will be printed. If you like, you can see what your printouts will look like before you print them by selecting Print Pre**v**iew from the **F**ile menu. Once in Print Preview mode, you can use a set of virtual rulers to help you see how things will appear on the page, and adjust the margins by selecting the Print Preview R**u**lers menu item from the **F**ile menu. In addition, you can adjust the view of your page on-screen by zooming out to see more or in to see less. You choose the amount of zoom from the Print Preview **Z**oom... menu item from the File menu.

If the table containing the data you are looking at has a Primary Key, you will be able to edit your data. You edit data in a grid DataWindow, one cell at a time, just like in a spreadsheet. Simply click on the cell you want to edit and change the value. From the **R**ows menu, you can **D**elete the current row of data from the table displayed on-screen. You can In**s**ert a new row into the table in front of the current row. You can also **R**etrieve the data from the database again, which will eliminate any unsaved changes that you may have made. You can use the buttons on the Data Manipulation PainterBar to perform these functions if you prefer, as well. You can import data from an outside source into your table by selecting the **I**mport... menu item from the **R**ows menu.

All of the changes you make—deleting rows, inserting rows, changing data, importing data, and so on—are only inside the DataWindow that you are looking at, and are not saved into the database itself, until you specifically ask PowerBuilder to save them for you. To tell PowerBuilder that you want to have it update your changes to the database, you simply select the **S**ave Changes To Database menu item from the **F**ile menu, or click on the Save Changes button on the Data Manipulation PainterBar. When you do this, PowerBuilder figures out what changes you have made and begins creating the appropriate statements that it needs to save your changes to the database. If, for some reason, the update does not succeed, PowerBuilder prompts you with an error message. You can also save your data to a local file in a number of formats by selecting Save **R**ows As from the **F**ile menu.

In addition to adding and removing data, you can also sequence your data by selecting the **S**ort... menu item from the **R**ows menu. You can use an expression to sort your data. You can also use expressions to filter out rows of your result set that you are not interested in by selecting **F**ilter... from the **R**ows menu. Rows for which the expression evaluates to TRUE will stay, and rows for which the expression evaluates to FALSE will disappear.

You can see a description of the rows on (and off) the screen by selecting D**e**scribed... from the **R**ows menu. When you do this, you are presented with the Describe Rows dialog box, which indicates the number of rows deleted, the number of rows displayed, the number of rows filtered out, and the number of rows modified.

Q&A

Q How can I print table definitions as they appear in the Database Painter?

A "How do you hold a moon beam in your hand?" may be an easier question to answer because there is no direct way in PowerBuilder to print table definitions. Using the Print Screen key, you can copy a bitmap image of the screen into Window's clipboard. The clipboard can be pasted into a program that can display and print the image. Unfortunately, this can be a laborious process. Instead, you might want to consider exporting the syntax of the table to a file and printing out the file. Even though it is not as intuitive to read as the pretty table box picture that you see in the Database Painter, it has all of the necessary information.

Q I created a table in the database painter and saved it to the log. After saving the log to a file, how can I use this log file?

A You can implement changes saved from your log file by entering the Database Administrator Painter and selecting **O**pen from the **F**ile menu, then select your log file. The log file will be in SQL format, which you can execute by selecting E**x**ecute SQL from the **O**bjects menu. We will discuss the Database Administration Painter in Chapter 20.

Q Why would you need to change the default height of a column when defining extended attributes in the Database Painter?

A Some edit styles, such as radio buttons, require more height than the default to enable you to see all the style's values. You would need to stretch the column higher in the Data Manipulation Painter if the default height was not modified in the Database Painter.

Q Why can't I insert or update rows in the Data Manipulation Painter for a table I just created?

A In order for PowerBuilder to be able to ensure that it is updating the proper row, it needs some unique constraint on the table, either a Primary Key or a Unique Index. By using the unique key, it can then properly ensure that the proper row is being updated because the unique key values will identify only a single row in the database. Within the Data Manipulation Painter, data can always be previewed even without keys or indexes on the table.

Q In the Data Manipulation Painter, I deleted rows of data, tried to return to the Database Painter, and got the message `Save changes back to database?`. Why does PowerBuilder prompt me to save changes when I thought I already saved them when I deleted the rows?

A All deletes, modifications, and insertions made within the DataWindow of the Data Manipulation Painter are stored in buffers. Changes to the data are not written to the database until an update command is issued. Selecting **S**ave Changes to Database from the File menu will issue an update to the database.

Q When I create sort criteria for my table in the Data Manipulation Painter, where is the sorting done?

A At the DataWindow level—more specifically, in the DataWindow Primary Buffer— locally each time data is retrieved from the database or the sort criteria is changed. We will discuss how to set sort criteria for DataWindows with the DataWindow Painter and in scripts in Chapters 21 through 24.

Workshop

Quiz

1. What are three referential integrity rules that can be associated with a foreign key?
2. List some extended attributes of table columns stored in the PowerBuilder repository.
3. Besides viewing, modifying, inserting, and deleting table data, what is another use for the Data Manipulation Painter?
4. From the Data Manipulation Painter, how do you save table data to a text file or a file of another format?
5. How do you bring text files into the Data Manipulation Painter and update the information to the database?
6. What rows go into the Filtered buffer when a filter is created and applied?

Putting PowerBuilder into Action

1. We will create a table that will hold a list of the lessons in this book, as well as a grade. Create a new table called *TYPB_LESSONS*. There are three columns in this table: *lesson*, whose datatype is number, *title*, whose datatype is varchar with a width of 25, and *grade,* whose datatype is smallint. We haven't yet learned what these specific datatypes mean yet; we will learn about them in the next lesson. For now, though, select these values from the list of datatypes.
2. Set the edit style for the grade column to the *Grade* edit style. Set the validation rule for the lesson column to the *Lesson* validation rule.
3. Create a primary key for the table. The primary key column is the *lesson* column.
4. Create an index on the table called *ix0_typb_lessons*. The columns for this index are first *grade* and then *lesson*.
5. Open up the Data Manipulation Painter for your new table. Insert 28 new rows in the table. Enter in the lesson numbers and chapter titles from the table of contents of this book.
6. Grade each lesson that you have already taken. Use your own criteria for grading, but follow any standard school grading system: 100 is a perfect score.
7. Save your changes back to the database. Then, save them to a text file. If you have a printer, print it out. If you like, you can e-mail them to me at the address listed in the "About the Authors" section in the front of the book.

Chapter

19

The Structured
Query Language
(SQL)

In this lesson, you will be taught the *Structured Query Language (SQL)*. This lesson will start off with a little bit of history about the SQL, and then you will learn how to build SQL statements that do the following:

- [ ] Query data from a table or set of tables
- [ ] Place new data into your tables
- [ ] Change data that is already in your tables
- [ ] Remove data from your tables
- [ ] Build and remove tables, views, and indexes
- [ ] Permit users to access your tables

An Overview of SQL

In the early days of databases, accessing your data meant picking a database vendor, purchasing that vendor's equipment, converting your data to that vendor's format, and learning that vendor's interface and command syntax. With most databases, if you changed database vendors, you needed to change to a new platform, and you needed to convert your data and learn a new command syntax. Companies who hired new employees to work on their databases needed to find people who were specialists with their specific vendor, or they had to retrain their new hires. But that was before the introduction of the *Structured Query Language (SQL)*.

The Structured Query Language (SQL) has been adopted as the standard database command language by nearly all of the popular database vendors. It is a descendent of relational database systems that were originally developed by IBM Research in San Jose, California, in 1979. As time passed and vendors began developing their own database engines, they needed to develop their own query command languages. Because the Relational Database model and the SQL Command syntax were being published by people with quite respectable credentials (IBM and Berkeley research departments), many vendors decided to use these models for their database products. Products like DB2, Ingres, Oracle, and even Sybase are descendants of the original DBMS prototypes that were developed by IBM and Berkeley research departments.

In 1986, the American National Standards Institute (ANSI) determined the value of a standard query command syntax and adopted a subset of the SQL Command Syntax as a standard that was intended to be platform independent. The SQL Standard was also adopted by the International Standards Organization (ISO) in 1987.

Later on, as software vendors developed DBMSs for standard platforms, they used the SQL standard as foundation for their command syntax, although most of them added extensions to it. Now, there are even DBMSs that can be run on your personal computer. Recently, Microsoft released the *Open Database Connectivity (ODBC)* engine. The ODBC engine is a Windows product that allows clients using Microsoft Windows to access different software systems as

relational database servers using SQL. Using special information files called *drivers*, you can access any type of file through the ODBC engine using standard SQL Syntax, even if the software vendor that creates that file doesn't use SQL as their engine's language. For example, dBASE does not use SQL Syntax as its language; instead, it has its own command syntax. Still, if you have the ODBC driver for dBASE, you can access dBASE files through the ODBC engine using standard SQL Syntax. The SQL Standard has become very popular and is now the mainstream database language. It is also the language that PowerBuilder uses for its database access.

In general, SQL Commands can be performed at an *interactive* level from a command prompt (usually supplied by the vendor), or they can be *embedded* inside your PowerBuilder scripts. Although there are some slight differences that will be discussed later when we talk specifically about embedded SQL in Chapter 25, the SQL Command language as a whole is pretty much the same regardless of whether you are in interactive or embedded mode.

When you are working with databases using SQL, you will come across two different types of commands. There are commands to view and edit your data, referred to as *Data Manipulation Language*, or *DML* for short, and then there are commands that you can use to define the structure for how your data will be stored, referred to as *Data Definition Language*, or DDL for short.

Note: Some people also refer to a third category of SQL Commands called the *Data Control Language (DCL)*. However, most authorities accept DCL to be a subset of DDL and not an independent category of commands.

Note: Don't be confused by the use of the term "language" for the different subsets of SQL Commands. In reality, they are not different languages, just different command sets inside the same language.

Data Manipulation Language Commands (DML)

You use the *Data Manipulation Language (DML)* commands to access your data in your database. There are four main commands that can be used to access your database. They are the SELECT, INSERT, UPDATE, and DELETE commands. Let's talk about each one in turn.

The *SELECT* Command

The SELECT command is used to retrieve data from the database. You tell the DBMS that you want to retrieve rows of data in a particular column or set of columns from a particular table or set of tables. You can retrieve the entire set of data from the table, or you can specify selection criteria to select only those rows that are of interest to you.

The format for a complete select statement looks something like this:

```
SELECT <column 1>, <column 2>, ... <column n>
   FROM <table 1>, <table 2>, ... <table n>
   WHERE <criteria>
```

Each of the components of a DML Command is often referred to as a *clause*. The clauses are based upon the keyword that is used to signify their beginning. Therefore, the list of columns you want to select is often referred to as the SELECT clause. The list of tables where those columns can be found is referred to as the FROM clause. The criteria that will be used to determine which of the rows is returned is referred to as the WHERE clause.

An example of a valid simple select statement is:

```
SELECT last_name, department, salary
      FROM employees
      WHERE state = "NY"
```

The set of data that is returned when you execute this statement, often referred to as the *result set*, is a list of all of the last names, departments, and salaries of employees listed in the Employee table that live in the state of New York. The result set is in table format and may look something like Table 19.1.

Table 19.1. The Results of a SELECT statement.

Last Name	Department	Salary
Jones	100	35000
Hanson	100	37500
Smith	200	47500
Simpson	300	27500
Ramsey	500	52500
Williams	400	32000

The *WHERE* Clause

The criteria that you use to specify the rows that you want to include in your result set is referred to as the WHERE clause. In the preceding example, it was relatively simple. However, you can make your WHERE clauses quite complex, and sometimes you may need to.

The WHERE clause in a SELECT statement at the simplest level is any expression that for each row in the result set can be evaluated to either TRUE or FALSE. The DBMS first creates a temporary result set including all of the rows available based upon the SELECT and FROM clauses. Then, one by one, it evaluates the WHERE clause for each row and determines whether to include that row in the final result set. If the WHERE clause is TRUE, then the row is included. If it is FALSE, the row is discarded. Although in reality most DBMSs optimize this procedure and achieve the same results without actually going through each possible row, this is the basic process that is being performed in creating a result set using SQL.

You can create your WHERE criteria expressions using the same relational and logical operators that you learned about in Chapter 7; and so, you can create complex expressions that may look like this:

```
WHERE ( state = 'NY'
        AND ( county = 'Westchester'
            OR county = 'Putnam'
            OR county = 'Rockland'
            OR county = 'Dutchess' ) )
    OR ( state = 'NJ'
        AND NOT ( county = city ) )
    OR ( state = 'CT'
        AND county <> 'Fairfield' )
```

The preceding WHERE clause will include rows if they are in New York state, in Westchester, Putnam, Rockland, or Dutchess counties. It will also include rows that are in the state of New Jersey in cities where the name of the city is not the same as the name of the county. It will also include rows that are in the state of Connecticut, as long as they aren't in Fairfield county. Any other rows will be discarded.

In addition to the standard relational operators, there are several additional keywords that SQL offers for use in your WHERE clauses as relational operators. The first one is the *IN* operator.

The *IN* Operator

Using an IN operator, you can specify an equality relationship between more than two values. In other words, you can compare one value to a set of other values and return TRUE if any of the values match. The syntax for a clause using an IN operator is as follows:

```
<value 1> IN ( <value 2>, <value 3>, ... <value n>)
```

For an example, take a look at the first five lines of the preceding WHERE clause, where you are looking for rows in the State of New York, in the county of Westchester, Putnam, Rockland, or Dutchess. By using an IN operator, you could have written this clause in two lines instead of five. The syntax for this statement would have been as follows:

```
WHERE ( state = 'NY'
        AND ( county IN ( 'Westchester', 'Putnam', 'Rockland', 'Dutchess' ) ) )
```

The *BETWEEN* Operator

Another SQL operator that you can use is BETWEEN. Use the BETWEEN operator to search for a value that is between two other values. BETWEEN is usually only useful for numeric values, although it is legal (and occasionally useful) for alphanumeric values. For example, instead of

```
SELECT name
  FROM employee
  WHERE salary > 25000
    AND salary < 50000
```

you can use the following statement:

```
SELECT name
  FROM employee
  WHERE salary BETWEEN 25000 AND 50000
```

As an example of a valid, even sensible, alphanumeric BETWEEN statement, you might use the following statement:

```
SELECT name
  FROM employee
  WHERE name BETWEEN 'G' AND 'H'
```

which would select all employees whose last name started with the letter *G*.

Note: Remember that when lexically comparing numbers (that are stored as strings), the values aren't necessarily sequential. For example, if you try to sort the numbers 1, 2, 3, 10, 100, and 1000 as numbers, they are already sorted as you might expect, numerically sequenced. However, the same numbers as strings would sort as '1', '10', '100', '1000', '2', '3'.

The *LIKE* Operator

Additionally, you can search for specific patterns using the LIKE operator. The LIKE operator allows you to compare a value to another value with *wildcards* in it. Wildcards are special placeholders in a pattern that match any character. You may have experienced wildcard characters in your work with DOS files. In SQL, the underscore (_) is a single character wildcard, similar to DOS's question mark (?) wildcard. It matches any single character. For example, 'n_t' matches 'net', 'not', and 'nut', but not 'nt' or 'neat'. The percent symbol (%) is a multi-character wildcard, like DOS's asterisk (*). It matches any sequence of characters, including no characters. For example, 'n%t' matches all of the above and others.

So, you can create a SQL statement that looks like this:

```
SELECT name
  FROM employee
  WHERE state LIKE 'N_'
    AND city LIKE '% %'
```

This statement will match rows that have a two-letter state abbreviation that starts with the letter *N*, and a city that contains a single space anywhere inside the name (including at the beginning or end of the name, as well).

The *IS NULL* Operator

In addition, there is one more special relational operator that is used only for NULL values. A NULL value means that there is no value for a column in that row. For example, let's say your Employee table has a column called 'm_name', which is the column where you place the employee's middle name. However, many people simply do not have middle names. So, if you don't have a middle name, your row in the database will instead contain a NULL value in the middle name column.

NULL values do not match any other value in a relational comparison, even another NULL value. For this reason, in order to select a NULL value, you need a special relational operator, which in SQL is called IS NULL. So, to select rows from the database that don't have a middle name, you can use the following statement:

```
SELECT name
  FROM employee
  WHERE m_name IS NULL
```

The *NOT* Operator

In all of these operators, you can also specify a NOT format. You can replace IN, LIKE, and BETWEEN with NOT IN, NOT LIKE, and NOT BETWEEN, respectively. Instead of IS NULL, you can say IS NOT NULL.

Subqueries

In certain cases, you may want to compare data in one table to data in another table, instead of to literal values. For example, you may want to select only those employees whose department names start with the letter *P*. However, the names of the departments are in the Department table, and the employee information (including the department number) is stored in the Employee table. One way to get this information out is by using a *subquery* inside the WHERE clause.

A subquery is exactly what it sounds like. It is a query within a query. The main query will specify what you want to select. Then, inside the WHERE clause, you compare a column in the base query to the result of another query. So, to use the preceding example, you use the following statement:

```
SELECT name
  FROM employee
  WHERE department IN
      ( SELECT id
          FROM department
          WHERE name like "P%" )
```

In order to really understand this query, you need to first look at the second SELECT statement. The second SELECT statement selects out all of the department IDs from the Department table where the department name starts with the letter *P*. The result of this statement may be a table containing a single column (the ID column) with two rows, containing the values 100 and 300. If so, the main SELECT statement will actually evaluate to

```
SELECT name
  FROM employee
  WHERE department IN (100, 300)
```

Using this method, you can select information from one table that relates to information in another table. When using subqueries, the table in the subquery is often referred to as the *inner table*, and the table in the main query is often referred to as the *outer table*. In the preceding case, the inner table is the Department table, and the outer table is the Employee table.

You can mix criteria in your WHERE clause so that it includes standard criteria as well as a subquery. For example, if you want employees in New York state that are in departments that start with the letter *P*, you can use the following statement:

```
SELECT name
  FROM employee
  WHERE state = 'NY'
    AND department IN
      ( SELECT id
          FROM department
          WHERE name like "P%" )
```

You can also use additional criteria in the WHERE clause of your subquery if you like.

Actually, there is an easier, more concise way of selecting information from one table that relates to information in another, and that is by using what is referred to as a *join*.

Joining Multiple Tables

So far, all of the columns in your main SELECT statements have come out of the same table. Although we have talked about using subqueries to compare data between two tables, I should mention that you can also select data from multiple tables in a single SELECT statement, without a subquery. In order to select data from multiple tables, though, you have to pay attention to a few details. First, of course, you will need to specify the names of all of the tables that you are

working with in the FROM clause. In addition, you will need to help the compiler deal with *ambiguous* column names. An ambiguous column name is a column name that appears in more than one table. Imagine walking into a room full of people and shouting, "Hey, Joe!" It is very likely that more than one person in the room is named Joe, and so more than one person will try to answer at once. However, if you say, "Hey, Joe Williamson," you are much more likely to elicit an answer from the person you really want to talk to. Well, in order for the compiler to understand which column you are really talking to in a SQL query, you need to tell it not only the column name, but also the table name that the column comes from; otherwise, the DBMS has no way of knowing which column you are really talking about. For example, let's say that you are selecting the employee name from the Employee table and the department name from the Department table. You may have a statement that looks something like this:

```
SELECT name, name
    FROM employee, department
```

Even as humans reading this, it is unclear which names you want to select. Imagine how the computer must feel when it sees this! It will simply return a message explaining that the column name is ambiguous. However, you can remove the ambiguity by specifying the table names of the columns in the preceding statement. You specify table names by using dot notation, in the following format:

```
<table name>.<column name>
```

Read the following SQL statement, which is the same statement as above, but with the column names made clear with dot notation:

```
SELECT employee.name, department.name
    FROM employee, department
```

Now it is pretty obvious which column names we are talking about, even though the name of the *name* column is the same in both the Employee and Department tables. You can prefix your column names with their table names even if the name of the column is not ambiguous. In fact, it is generally a good practice to do this because even though the computer doesn't need the additional information, it makes your SELECT statements more readable to the human eye.

DO	DON'T

DO Use prefixes in all of your SELECT and WHERE clauses that contain multiple tables so that you don't get confused and forget which column belongs to which table.

DON'T Worry too much about your SQL statements getting too lengthy. In the next section, I will teach you a trick to make your prefixed SQL statements a little shorter and more manageable.

Now, if you perform the preceding query, you basically get a Cartesian product containing every combination of employee names and department names between the two tables, even though the department name may not be the name of the employee's department number. That's not what you want, though. What you want is to display a list of employees with their department names. The way you do this is by *joining* the two tables.

You *join* two tables by specifying their relationship in the WHERE clause. In the preceding example, the two tables, Employee and Department, are related. Within the Employee table, there is a column called department. It contains a value that is the ID of the employee's department record in the Department table. Therefore, you should join these two tables from the employee's department column to the Department's ID column. The code to do this looks something like this:

```
SELECT employee.name, department.name
   FROM employee, department
   WHERE employee.department = department.id
```

This statement will first select the Cartesian product of the set of employees and departments, and then discard those rows where the employee's department ID is not equal to the department ID of the Department table. The result is a list of employees and their department names.

You can perform joins in this fashion against any number of tables, with any number of join columns between those tables. Joins are what relational databases are all about—being able to store information in a normalized form, with small keys to access larger descriptions. Although joins are most commonly used to lookup descriptions of keys, they can also be effectively used simply to compare data within two tables.

Self-Joins and Aliasing Your Tables

Sometimes, the data that you have to look up is not in a separate table but is in the same table as the table from which you are performing the lookup. For example, let's say you want to see an employee and his manager. If there were a separate Manager table, all you would need to do is join the Employee table to the Manager table. However, managers are also employees, and so you have to join the Employee table to the Employee table! How do you do this? After all, how can the compiler interpret the following select statement:

```
SELECT employee.name, employee.name
   FROM employee, employee
   WHERE employee.manager = employee.id
```

It is just too confusing to deal with. After all, which of the two Employee tables is which? Instead, then, you can use your own names, called *aliases*, for your table names so that you can figure out which table is which. Instead of using the name employee for your tables, you can call the first one employee, and you can call the second copy of employee manager. Then, in the FROM clause, you simply specify the alias by following the table name with the alias name. The following SQL

statement is nearly identical to the previous statement, except that it is now obvious what you are trying to do:

```
SELECT employee.name, manager.name
   FROM employee, employee manager
   WHERE employee.manager = manager.id
```

You can alias any table in your SELECT statement in the same manner, even your first table name. So, if you want, you can use the following statement:

```
SELECT emp.name, mgr.name
   FROM employee emp, employee mgr
   WHERE emp.manager = mgr.id
```

I recommend you use aliases whenever you build queries that contain more than one table. It not only helps make your queries more readable, but it also makes them more manageable. Aliases add a level of protection from changes in your data structure, most especially when you are saving your queries in files or in code. For example, if you decide to add a separate table to store managers, all you need to do is change the second table name in the FROM clause from employee to manager, and the rest of the preceding statement remains intact because the aliases are the same. Aliases are among the best features of the SQL Standard, and you should use them whenever you have more than one table name in your FROM clause to make your SQL Statements clear and concise.

DO	DON'T

DO Use aliases whenever you can to make your SQL Statements clear and concise. Use short aliases, between one and three letters, for the best effect.

DON'T Worry if the aliases don't actually mean anything. If the aliases are short, it will be easy enough to look at the FROM clause to decipher them because your SQL will be concise. Try to use aliases that in some way correspond to table names, though, so that you don't get confused. For example, you could use aliases of emp and mgr for the Employee table, and dpt for the Department table.

The *DISTINCT* Keyword

There are a few other things that you can do with your SELECT statements that I won't go into detail about but are worth mentioning. First, you can prevent duplicate rows from appearing in your result set by using the keyword DISTINCT. The format for a DISTINCT selection is as follows:

```
SELECT DISTINCT <column list>
  FROM <table list>
  WHERE <criteria>
```

The *UNION* Keyword

You can merge the result sets of two separate SELECT statements by using the UNION keyword. Be aware, however, that the formats of the result sets must match in order to be merged. In other words, you cannot merge result sets that do not have the same number of columns or that have different datatypes in different positions for each column. The format for a UNION statement is as follows:

```
SELECT <column list>
  FROM <table list>
  WHERE <criteria>
UNION
SELECT <column list>
  FROM <table list>
  WHERE <criteria>
```

The *ORDER BY* Keyword

You can sort the rows of your result set based upon the values of a particular column by using the ORDER BY keyword. You can specify to sort in ascending or descending order using the ASC and DESC keywords, respectively. By default, ascending is assumed so that if you do not specify ascending or descending, it will be ascending. The format for an ORDER BY is as follows:

```
SELECT <column list>
  FROM <table list>
  WHERE <criteria>
  ORDER BY <column 1> ASC, <column 2> DESC, ...
```

Selecting Literal and Calculated Values

You can select literal values in your SELECT statements. In fact, you can even combine column values with literal values and perform calculations upon column values (or literal values) in your SELECT statements. It is perfectly legal, for example, to use the following statement:

```
SELECT id, l_name + ', ' + f_name + ' ' + m_name + '.', salary / 12, 1994
  FROM employee
```

This statement will produce output that may look something like this:

```
14 ¦ Smith, John J.    ¦ 2500 ¦ 1994
15 ¦ Benson, Harvey M. ¦ 2250 ¦ 1994
```

Aggregate Functions

There are special functions in SQL called *aggregate functions* that allow you to perform calculations based on an aggregation (or group) of data. For example, you may want to see the

total number of records in a table. To do this, you use the Count() function. Simply use the following statement:

```
SELECT Count(*) FROM employee
```

and the system will return the number of records in the Employee table. The other aggregate functions are Avg(<column>), which tells you the average of all of the values of <column> in the table, Min(<column>), which tells you the smallest value of <column> in the table, and Max(<column>), which tells you the largest value of <column> in the table. For example, you can perform the following query to find out how many employees you have, what the highest and lowest salaries are, and what the average salary is:

```
SELECT Count(*), Max( Salary), Min( Salary), Avg( Salary) FROM employee
```

You may not use aggregate functions in your WHERE clause.

The *GROUP BY* Clause

You can group your data based on the value of a specific column or columns using a GROUP BY clause. This allows you to select distinct values of a column with information about those specific columns. For example, let's say you want to see the number of employees in a particular state, for example, New York. You can create a SELECT statement that looks like this:

```
SELECT state, count(*)
   FROM employee
   WHERE state = "NY"
```

However, suppose that you want to see the number of employees in each state. You can go through one by one, creating queries that look much like the one above. However, that is quite an effort, and if you don't know the values that you are interested in, it will be impossible. By using a GROUP BY clause, though, you can perform this query very simply by grouping the Employee table on the state column:

```
SELECT state, count(*)
   FROM employee
   GROUP BY state
```

The result will be a list of states with their counts (aggregate functions are smart enough to work for their group when you perform a GROUP BY). Just like you can include and exclude rows from your SELECT statements with a WHERE clause, you can include and exclude groups using the HAVING clause. The following statement will limit the results of the above query to include only those states that start with the letter *N*.

```
SELECT state, count(*)
   FROM employee
   GROUP BY state
   HAVING state like "N%"
```

The Correlated Subquery

Finally, you can create *correlated subqueries*, which are subqueries where the inner query refers to columns from the outer query for comparison. For example, if you want to select all employees that are managers in department 100, you can use the following statement:

```
SELECT name
   FROM employee outer
   WHERE 100 =
      (SELECT department
         FROM employee inner
         WHERE inner.manager = outer.id)
```

Remember that the terms inner and outer in this query are aliases, as was discussed earlier, and that you reference the ID of the outer table from the WHERE clause of the inner table. In reality, you could have performed the same query using a self-join, as in the following:

```
SELECT name
   FROM employee outer, employee inner
   WHERE inner.manager = outer.id
     AND inner.department = 100
```

However, in some cases, a correlated subquery is slightly more flexible than a join because you can nest your subqueries, build groups based on them, and even include joins in your subqueries. In general, though, joins are easier to read than subqueries, and most DBMSs will execute joins more quickly (although some DBMS Optimizers are smart enough to convert subqueries into joins anyway), so the decision as to which you prefer is up to you and your DBA.

The *INSERT* Command

In order to have data to select, the data has to get into the table in the first place. In order to get the data into the table, you must use the INSERT command. There are two variations on the INSERT command. The first one is an INSERT command that you use to place specific values into a table. The format for this command is as follows:

```
INSERT INTO <table>
    ( <column list> )
  VALUES ( <value list> )
```

Using this method, you specify the table that you are inserting data into, the list of columns inside that table that you want to insert your data into, and the values that you want to insert into those columns. If the values that you are inserting are in the same order as the column list and all of the columns in the table are being inserted into, you can skip the column list altogether, and the DBMS will resolve it to mean all of the columns in order. An example of a valid INSERT..VALUES statement is as follows:

```
INSERT INTO employee
    ( id, name, ssn, address, city, state, zip, phone, department, manager )
  VALUES ( 142, 'John Smith', '0112234567', '21 Hanover Lane', 'Anytown',
          'NY', 12345, '9145551212', 100, 85 )
```

In addition, you can insert data into one table by selecting it out of another table or set of tables. You can use the result set of *any* valid SELECT statement as input for insertion into a table. The format for this statement simply replaces the VALUES clause with a SELECT statement. As with the INSERT..VALUES statement, the INSERT..SELECT statement will also be able to resolve the column list automatically if the results of the SELECT statement match column by column to the list of columns in the table to be inserted. An example of an INSERT..SELECT statement may be

```
INSERT INTO employee
   ( id, name, ssn, address, city, state, zip, phone, department, manager )
  SELECT r.id, r.name, r.ssn, r.address, z.city, z.state,
         r.zip, r.phone, r.department, e.manager
    FROM raw_employee r, zipcode z, employee e
    WHERE r.zip = z.zip
      AND r.manager_name = e.name
```

This statement will insert into the employee table all of the employees in the raw_employee table with the proper city, state, and manager based on lookups in the zipcode and employee tables, respectively. This also demonstrates joins and aliases, and you can see where these techniques are surely valuable.

The *UPDATE* Command

After your data is inside of your table, you often will need to change it, giving certain rows new values in certain columns. The way that you do this is by using the UPDATE command. The format for the UPDATE command is as follows:

```
UPDATE <table>
  SET <column 1> = <value 1>,
      <column 2> = <value 2>,
      ...
      <column n> = <value n>
  WHERE <criteria>
```

The UPDATE statement is very similar in format to the SELECT statement, except that there is no FROM clause. The table that is being updated is the only table in the FROM clause, and so you can only use columns from it inside your WHERE criteria, unless you build a subquery (which is, of course, perfectly legal). A simple UPDATE statement may be

```
UPDATE employee
  SET department = 100,
      manager = 14
WHERE state = 'NY'
```

This statement replaces all department values with 100 and manager values with 14 for all employees in the state of New York.

Note: A number of database vendors have extended the UPDATE statement to support placing a FROM clause after the SET clause so that you can do joins in your UPDATE statements, and even replace values in one table with values from another. Although it is not standard, the format can be very useful and is often more clear and concise as well. Check your database documentation for information on using this format.

The *DELETE* Command

Finally, you may want to remove rows from a table. Perhaps an employee is terminated. Perhaps a record is outdated or a department is merged into another. In order to remove rows from a table, you need to delete them using the DELETE command. The format for the DELETE command is similar to the UPDATE command, as follows:

```
DELETE FROM <table>
  WHERE <criteria>
```

If you don't specify any WHERE criteria, the DELETE command will delete the entire contents of the table specified. The WHERE criteria, as with UPDATE, can contain any valid WHERE clause, including a subquery. However, as with UPDATE, there is only one table in the FROM clause, and so you cannot have joins in your DELETE WHERE clause.

Note: However, as with UPDATE, there are some vendors who permit you to specify a FROM clause with multiple tables so that you can do joins, even though it is not standard. Again, check your database documentation for details.

Data Definition Language Commands (DDL)

In order to be able to manipulate data in a table, you must first define the table structure using *Data Definition Language (DDL)* Commands. This includes specifying the names and order of the columns and the datatypes that can be placed inside each column. The command that is used to create a table is the CREATE TABLE command. The format for the CREATE TABLE command is as follows:

```
CREATE TABLE <table>
   ( <column 1> <datatype 1> [NOT] [NULL],
     <column 2> <datatype 2> [NOT] [NULL],
     ..
     <column n> <datatype n> [NOT] [NULL] )
```

You create a table by specifying the name of the table to create, followed by a list of column names, the datatypes for those columns, and whether or not the column permits NULL values. By default, the column will not permit NULLs, meaning that you will not be able to insert a row that does not have any data in that column, and you will not be permitted to update the value of that column to NULL. Each column must have a unique, alphanumeric name within the table and must begin with a letter. Spaces are not permitted in the column name, and in general, you use the underscore (_) to represent separation of words. Although the standard dictates that the names of the columns will always be UPPERCASE, most DBMSs permit mixed and lowercase names and allow you to set an option flag to determine whether mixed case will be used, or uppercase only will be used. These column names are the same column names that you will be using in your DML statements to manipulate the data inside these tables, putting it into the table, taking it out of the table, and looking at it.

The Database Datatypes

ANSI dictates that there are several standard datatypes that can be used in a relational database. These datatypes are listed in Table 19.1. Let's discuss each one in turn.

Note: The datatypes that are available to the database are slightly different than the datatypes that you use in PowerBuilder scripts. However, for each database datatype, there is a standard PowerBuilder datatype that is compatible.

Table 19.1. The Standard Relational Datatypes.

```
INTEGER

SMALL INTEGER

DECIMAL(n,n)

FLOAT

DOUBLE

CHAR(n)

VARCHAR(n)

DATE

TIME
```

The INTEGER is the most clear datatype of the set. You are probably already familiar with integers because you learned about them in Chapter 7. However, in database language, the INTEGER is actually equivalent to a PowerBuilder LONG integer, and not a standard INTEGER. Relational Databases were first introduced on mainframes, and INTEGERs on mainframes are eight bytes long. On PCs, INTEGERs are only four bytes long, and LONG integers are eight bytes long. Don't let this confuse you. Just be aware that on the database, you can store a number up to around four million in an INTEGER, whereas on a PC, you can only fit a number up to 65535 in an INTEGER, and you must use a LONG integer to fit numbers greater than that.

In Mainframe-speak, though, there is a datatype that corresponds to the PowerBuilder INTEGER in terms of storage and size, and that is the Small integer (referred to as SMALLINT). A Small integer will store a number up to 65535, and is directly related to a standard INTEGER in PowerBuilder. So, if you want to save space in your tables and are going to be using numbers less than 65535, use the Small Integer datatype.

For decimal values, you may choose between using the DECIMAL datatype and the FLOAT datatype. The DECIMAL datatype allows you to specify the size and precision of the values that will be stored. For example, you may want to declare a decimal that allows for 16 digits, and the last three digits are the decimal values. You indicate that by declaring it as a DECIMAL(16,3). FLOATs, however, work like integers in that the maximum value it can hold is based on the implementation, and it uses a binary encoded decimal scheme to store the number to the right of the decimal. In a similar fashion to integers, you can store larger decimal numbers in a datatype that is called a DOUBLE, which refers to the *double-precision* datatype. The FLOAT is equivalent to a SMALLINT, and the DOUBLE is equivalent to the INTEGER or LONG Integer. The terms FLOAT and REAL are interchangeable, and in fact in PowerBuilder, it is the REAL datatype that corresponds to a FLOAT.

CHAR and VARCHAR datatypes are both compatible with PowerBuilder strings and chars. In order to store string types in a database, though, you have to declare how many bytes wide the field is. In each case, you specify the width of the datatype by placing it in parentheses after the datatype itself. The maximum allowable width in the database is 255 bytes, even though the maximum length of a PowerBuilder string is 64K long. So, if your string is longer than 255 bytes, the data will be cut off when you try to place it inside the database. It's not necessarily a major issue, but it is something that you must be aware of.

> **Note:** Some DBMSs provide other datatypes that you can use to store strings that are larger than 255 bytes. For example, Sybase uses the TEXT and IMAGE datatypes to allow you to store data that is larger than 255 bytes. However, these datatypes are nonstandard and specific to your DBMS, so you should check your DBMS documentation for details.

CHAR and VARCHAR both work the same way regarding selection and manipulation. The only difference between the two is how they are stored. In a CHAR field, the field will always take up the same number of bytes, even if the data is smaller than the maximum size of the field. For example, if you create a database field that is of type CHAR(30) and store a string, "PowerBuilder," inside that field, physically the database will make that field fill up the entire 30 bytes when it stores the field on the hard drive. However, if you declare a VARCHAR(30) and store the word "PowerBuilder" inside of it, the DBMS will shrink the field so it fits neatly around the word, in this case to 12 bytes. In general, it is your Database Administrator (DBA) who will be most interested in the difference between a CHAR and a VARCHAR. From the developer's standpoint, the trade-off is size for speed. In order for the DBMS to deal with the variable-length character type (VARCHAR), it must do a little bit of extra processing and so takes a little bit more time to retrieve and update. So, if every row in the database will take up most of the field anyway, then you are probably better off using a CHAR datatype because the wasted space will be minimal, but the speed will be better. If, however, it is a rarely accessed field, where most of the data is small, but the field needs to be large for compatibility of the occasional long string, you are surely better off with a VARCHAR because the speed loss will be less critical, and the storage savings will be dramatic. Of course, in real life, most situations are a bit more gray than those two, but this will at least give you a bit of an understanding. In general, it is a good idea to talk to your DBA, or any other expert, when building your databases.

The DATE datatype holds a date in the format YYYYMMDD. It is not an ANSI Standard datatype; however, it is accepted by all of the popular databases. It is compatible with the PowerBuilder DATE datatype. Be aware that some databases will be very picky about accepting a DATE datatype update format, while others will convert common date format (like MM/DD/YY) to the proper format (YYYYMMDD) for you without even knowing it. The standard, however, dictates that dates are represented in YYYYMMDD format only. A valid date, for example, is 19941030, which is October 30, 1994.

The TIME datatype holds a valid time in the format HH:MM:SS. It, too, is a nonstandard datatype that, while not accepted by ANSI, is accepted by just about all of the DBMSs that are used today. It corresponds to the PowerBuilder TIME datatype.

By using these datatypes, you can build a table to store just the information you want. A legitimate table definition may be as follows:

```
CREATE TABLE EMPLOYEE
    ( ID INTEGER NOT NULL,
      NAME VARCHAR(65) NOT NULL,
      M_NAME CHAR(1) NULL,
      ADDRESS VARCHAR(100) NOT NULL,
      ZIP CHAR(5) NOT NULL,
      PHONE CHAR(10) NOT NULL,
      START_DATE DATE NOT NULL,
      DEPARTMENT SMALLINT NOT NULL,
      MANAGER INTEGER NOT NULL )
```

This will create an employee table with nine columns: ID, Name, M_Name, Address, ZIP, Phone, Start_Date, Department, and Manager. M_Name, for the middle name, is the only field in the table that will allow NULL values. All others are required. You can see where some fields are INTEGERs, others are CHARs and VARCHARs, and there is even a DATE. By using this method, you can build tables in your databases that will store your information so you can manipulate your information using the DML commands: SELECT, INSERT, UPDATE, and DELETE.

The *ALTER TABLE* Command

Once a table is created, you may modify its definition by using the ALTER TABLE command. You can use the ALTER TABLE command to add and remove columns from a table, or you can use it to change a columns datatype or NULL setting. The format for this command is as follows:

```
ALTER TABLE <table name>
    {ADD ¦ DELETE ¦ MODIFY} <column name 1> <datatype 1>,
        <column 2> <datatype 2>
        ...
        <column n> <datatype n>
```

When you add a column to a table, null values will be inserted into the new columns for rows that already exist in the table; therefore, when adding a column to a table, they will always be NULLABLE. Also, you should be aware that the ALTER TABLE command, while very popular, is not adopted as part of the ANSI Standard.

Warning: Because ALTER TABLE as a whole is not defined as part of the ANSI Standard, the implementation of the ALTER TABLE command is **extremely** DBMS dependent. Check your DBMS documentation for its specific implementation rules regarding the ALTER TABLE command.

Indexes

There is no reason that you cannot go right from creating a table to inserting and selecting data with that table. However, SQL offers something called an *Index* that you can build for your tables that will help make searching through your tables much quicker. If you remember, we briefly discussed what an index is in Chapter 15. An *index* is a sequential list of data from a table, with a pointer to its proper row in the table. The data that is listed is based on the columns of the index, often referred to as the *Key*. For example, you can create an index on your Employee table using the name column as the key. This will create an alphabetical list of all of the names of all of our employees, with a pointer to the rows containing that name. Then, if you want to search for a specific name, the DBMS can look at the index alphabetically to find the name you are searching for, to quickly find out which rows contain that name, and to then jump directly

to those rows in the table. This is much faster because the DBMS can search through the index for the specific value and stop after it finds a value that is greater than the value you are looking for. In addition, most DBMSs use highly optimal binary search algorithms that allow the DBMS to jump around inside the index almost directly to the rows you are looking for. This is much more efficient than a sequential search through volumes of extra data.

You create indexes on columns in a table. The command format for an index is

```
CREATE [UNIQUE] INDEX <index name>
   ON <table name> ( <column 1>, <column 2>, ... <column n> )
```

> **Note:** By default, indexes permit duplicate values. However, if you specify that the index is unique, then it will not. If there are duplicate values in the table when you create the index, the index creation will fail. If the index is created successfully, and you later attempt to insert a row with a duplicate key value into the table, that insert will fail.

The following statement creates an index called *ix0_employee* on the ZIP column of the EMPLOYEE table:

```
CREATE INDEX ix0_employee
   ON employee ( zip )
```

When creating a *composite key*, a key based on more than one column, the order of the columns in the list is generally significant. When you execute a query, the DBMS evaluates which index it can use based on its WHERE clause. If the WHERE clause specifies search criteria that are in an index, the DBMS will use that index to retrieve the results of that query. However, if the columns specified in the WHERE clause exist in an index, and the index is composite, the index may not be used. If the WHERE clause refers to the second key column of the index but not the first, that index cannot be used because the DBMS cannot look for key values in the index in a different order than the order in which the key columns of the index were built. Your Database Administrator can help you determine the indexes you need on your tables.

Views

If you recall, we talked about views as a method to shelter the user from the physical model of the database and learned that they are just queries that act like tables. Well, the way you create a view is rather simple. All you need to do is tell the DBMS the query that will be used to generate the result set when a user selects data from the view. The DBMS does the rest. The manner in which you do this is by using the following statement:

```
CREATE VIEW <view name> AS <SELECT statement>
```

19

The <SELECT statement> can be any legal SELECT statement that you can create. It can include a WHERE clause, Joins, Groups, Unions, and anything else you can dream up, as long as it is legal as a query. However, if the query contains more than one table in the FROM clause, or if it contains a DISTINCT, GROUP BY, or HAVING clause, or even if it contains constants or expressions, then you will not be able to perform UPDATEs or INSERTs against this view. In addition, you will be prevented from INSERTing a row into a view that does not contain each of the NOT NULL columns from the source table because, of course, you will not be able to insert a non-null value into those columns without having them in the view. To create a view that displays a user-friendly view of the orders in the system, you can create a view like this:

```
CREATE VIEW user_orders AS
    SELECT o.number, c.name, p.name, o.quantity, o.price
        FROM   order o, customer c, product p
        WHERE  o.customer = c.number
          AND  o.product = p.number
```

This will produce a view that shows the order number, customer name, product name, quantity, and price. It replaces the customer and product numbers with their names so the user doesn't have to look them up. This view is not updateable because there is more than one table in the FROM clause, but it surely is useful to a user who does not know about customer and product numbers.

Warning: Some DBMSs place restrictions on the type of SELECT statement that can be used as the source of a view. For example, Sybase SQL Server versions prior to System 10 do not permit UNIONs and do not execute GROUP Bys in a view. Again, check your DBMS documentation for details.

Get Rid of the Old

If you determine that a database object is no longer needed, regardless of whether it is a table, index, or view, you can delete it from the database using the DROP command. The syntax of the DROP command is as follows:

```
DROP <object type> <object name>
```

For example, to drop the Employee table, you can use the following statement:

```
DROP TABLE employee
```

Likewise, to drop the ix0_employee index, you can use the following statement:

```
DROP INDEX ix0_employee
```

Finally, to drop the user_orders view, you can use the following statement:

```
DROP VIEW user_orders
```

Be aware that when you drop a table, all of its indexes and keys are dropped along with it.

Accessing Your Data

As part of the ANSI standard, users must log in to the database server using a *login ID*. The process for logging in is DBMS dependent, and so we won't talk about that. However, once logged in, the user may have rights to manipulate data—or maybe not. The manner in which these rights are determined is handled by the DBA using two SQL Commands: GRANT and REVOKE.

> **Note:** The GRANT and REVOKE commands are sometimes referred to as *Data Control Language (DCL)* commands.

The *GRANT* Command

The GRANT command grants a specific user the right to perform specific actions on specific tables. The format for the command is

```
GRANT <right 1>, <right 2>, .. <right n> ¦ [ALL]
   ON <table 1>, <table 2>, .. <table n>
   TO <user 1>, <user 2>, .. <user n> ¦ [PUBLIC]
   {WITH GRANT OPTION}
```

There are four standard types of rights that you can grant to a user. They are the right to SELECT, INSERT, DELETE, and UPDATE. The WITH GRANT OPTION clause gives that user the right to grant rights to other users as well. The ALL keyword is equivalent to specifying all four rights, and the PUBLIC keyword is equivalent to specifying every user in the database. To grant user JUDAH the right to SELECT data from the Employee table, you can use the following statement:

```
GRANT select ON employee TO judah
```

When granting UPDATE access, you can limit the UPDATE access to specific columns by enclosing them in parentheses after the UPDATE right. For example, to grant update access to the name and address columns of the employee table, you can use the following statement:

```
GRANT update ( name, address) ON employee TO judah
```

Of course, if you do not specify any columns, it is equivalent to specifying all columns, and the user has unrestricted update access to the table.

Most DBMSs also offer other rights, like the right to create tables, indexes, and so on. However, these rights are not adopted by the ANSI standard and are DBMS specific, so you need to check with your DBA or with the documentation that comes with your DBMS on how to grant and revoke those rights. However, the format of the command should be more or less the same, with just a different right keyword.

The *REVOKE* Command

Someone famous once said, "The DBA giveth, and the DBA taketh away." That which can be granted can also be revoked. The format of the REVOKE command is essentially identical to the GRANT keyword. The REVOKE command is not officially supported by the ANSI standard, but of course it doesn't make sense not to give it an honorary mention here. The format of the REVOKE command is

```
REVOKE <right 1>, <right 2>, .. <right n> ¦ [ALL]
   ON <table 1>, <table 2>, .. <table n>
   FROM <user 1>, <user 2>, .. <user n>
```

Extensions and Variations

Most DBMSs offer other commands that you can use to build your queries; however, they are slightly more advanced features that I will leave up to you to discover. There are many excellent database books that you can read that will discuss all of the features of SQL in detail, and even discuss the specific variations or extensions of a specific DBMS vendor. Of course the first place to start would be your DBMS vendor's documentation. Also, C.J. Date is author and co-author of a number of excellent books that discuss specific database vendors, such as DB2, Oracle, and Sybase.

Morning Summary

The *Structured Query Language (SQL)* was adopted as the standard database command language by the *American National Standards Institute (ANSI)* and nearly all of the popular database vendors. It is also the database command language that is used by PowerBuilder. There are two different methods of creating queries using SQL: at an *interactive* level and at an *embedded* level. The SQL Language syntax is the same regardless of which way you are performing your queries.

The SQL language is broken up into two different subsets of commands. The commands that allow you to view and edit your data are referred to as the *Data Manipulation Language (DML)*. The commands that you use to define the structure for how your data will be stored are referred to as *Data Definition Language (DDL)*.

There are four Data Manipulation commands: SELECT, INSERT, UPDATE, and DELETE. The SELECT statement is used to retrieve data from your tables. It is broken up into several components called *clauses*.

The result of a select statement is a set of data that looks like a table, called a *result set*. The SELECT clause contains the columns of the result set table. The FROM clause contains the names of the tables that those columns belong to. The WHERE clause contains the criteria that will be evaluated for each row to determine if it will be included or excluded from the result set. The WHERE clause of a SELECT statement is made up of relational and logical expressions that are evaluated for each row. If the expression evaluates to TRUE, the row will be included in the result set. If the expression evaluates to FALSE, the row will be excluded from the result set.

There are several special relational operators in SQL that help make it easier to deal with multiple sets of values. The IN clause allows you to search for a set of values. The BETWEEEN keyword can be used to search for values that are in between two other values. The LIKE keyword can be used to perform pattern searches by using special characters called *wildcard* characters that allow you to build flexible patterns to find matching values. In SQL, the underscore character (_) is a single character wildcard that matches any single character. The percent symbol (%) is a multi-character wildcard that matches any combination of characters. To search for NULL values in your database, you can use the IS NULL keyword. All of the preceding keywords may be combined with the NOT keyword to search for rows that don't match the criteria.

In addition to searching for discrete values and patterns, you may want to search for a set of data based on a different set of data. To do this, you use a *subquery*. A subquery is a query that is contained within the WHERE clause of another query. The DBMS will essentially evaluate the inner query for each row selected by the outer query and treat the clause just like the expression that results. However, a more efficient method of retrieving data from multiple tables would be to use a *join*.

You can use joins to select data from two tables within a single SELECT statement. When using multiple table names in the FROM clause, you should be careful not to allow *ambiguous* column names. An ambiguous column name is a column name that exists in more than one table in the query. Because it exists in more than one place, the DBMS needs to know which column you are referring to. To specify the full name of a particular column, you preface it with the table name, followed by a period (.). Using this *fully qualified* notation to identify your column names prevents any ambiguity in your queries because column names within a single table are unique.

When querying data from multiple tables, you join tables by specifying their relationship within the WHERE clause. For example, if you select information from the Employee table and the Department table, you will need to show that there is a column in the Employee table that indicates which department that employee belongs to. To do this, you simply relate the proper column in the Employee table to its corresponding column in the Department table. You can join any number of tables in a single SELECT statement. In fact, you can even join a table to itself.

If you attempt to join a table to itself, you once again run into the problem of ambiguous column names. After all, how will the DBMS identify which of the two versions of a table you want a particular column to come from. In order to again eliminate the ambiguity, you must *alias* your table names, giving one or both of the duplicate table names a new name that can be used in the SELECT and WHERE clauses to help clear things up. To alias a table, you simply follow the table name in the FROM clause with its alias. You can alias any table in your SELECT statements, even if their names do not pose ambiguity problems.

There are several other keywords that you can use in a SELECT statement to build queries. You can eliminate duplicate rows with the DISTINCT keyword. You can merge the result sets of two SELECT statements using the UNION keyword. You can sort your result set using the ORDER BY keyword. You can select literal values and scalar expressions. You can use special *aggregate functions*, like Count(), Avg(), Min(), and Max() to perform functions on sets of data. You can group your data into sets of common rows by using a GROUP BY clause. You can filter out specific groups using the HAVING keyword. You can create special subqueries called *correlated subqueries*, where the inner query refers to columns from the outer query.

In addition to querying your data, you also need to put data into your tables. To put data into your tables you use the INSERT command. You can insert discrete values into your tables, or use the results of a SELECT statement as the input for an INSERT statement. Once the data is inside your tables, you can change it by using the UPDATE command. You use the UPDATE command to set the value of a column or columns based on specific criteria. To remove data from your tables, use the DELETE command.

In order to store data in a table, you must first define the structure of that table. You do this by using the CREATE TABLE command. ANSI offers several standard datatypes that can be used in your database. They are the INTEGER, SMALLINT, DECIMAL, FLOAT, DOUBLE, CHAR, and VARCHAR. In addition, there are two other datatypes, the DATE and TIME, that although not adopted by ANSI as a standard, are accepted in practice by most, if not all, DBMSs. Once a table is created, you can modify it by using the ALTER TABLE command, which is also nonstandard but very popular.

In addition to creating tables, you can create indexes by using the CREATE INDEX command. Indexes are based on the columns of a table, and can have one or more *key columns*. To create views, you can use the CREATE VIEW command. Any legal SELECT statement can be used as the source for a view. When you are done with your Tables, Indexes, and Views, you can delete them from the database by using the DROP command.

In addition to creating the structure of your database, ANSI also defines DDL commands to give users rights to access your structures. The command to give a user the right to access a specific database object is the GRANT command. In addition to granting rights, you can also REVOKE them. The REVOKE command is not supported by the ANSI standard but is supported by most DBMSs to some degree. Most DBMSs also offer extensions and variations to the ANSI standard. You should check your DBMS documentation for details.

424

Chapter

20

Database Administration

In this lesson, you will learn:

- [ ] How to use the Database Administration Painter to build and execute your SQL commands
- [ ] About the PowerBuilder query builder, which allows you to easily build your own queries and is used in a number of places within PowerBuilder

The Database Administration Painter

The PowerBuilder *Database Painter* and *Data Manipulation Painter* are extremely powerful tools that you can use to create and manipulate objects in your database. However, sometimes you just need a little bit more control than what these painters give you. You may want to execute a query using only certain columns of a table, or your own filter criteria, which these painters don't offer. You may want to control users' access to different databases and tables, which cannot be done from the other painters. You may want to define or execute *stored procedures*, which are special queries that are stored on the Database Server, or select information from multiple databases, which are supported by a number of vendors but cannot be done from these painters.

PowerBuilder provides you with a special painter, called the *Database Administration (DBA) Painter*, where you can execute any valid SQL Statement in an interactive mode. Even SQL statements that are not standard but that are supported by your DBMS can be executed within the PowerBuilder DBA Painter. The DBA Painter also offers additional features like a query builder and syntax viewer. Most DBMSs come with an interactive SQL utility of their own, often called *ISQL*. PowerBuilder provides the DBA Painter as a substitute to ISQL, especially designed for PowerBuilder programmers, but usable by anyone. PowerBuilder's DBA Painter is much more user friendly than most ISQL utilities and provides you with many tools that you can use to help you create your SQL statements. Most ISQL utilities do not offer these features and just leave you with a blank line where you can enter your SQL commands and see their results.

Note: In my own personal experience, I have seen a number of companies purchase PowerBuilder licenses for the people in their DBA group just so that they could use the PowerBuilder Database, Data Manipulation, and DBA Painters. Together, these three components of PowerBuilder provide you with a very powerful, intuitive manner in which to interact with your database.

There are several ways in which you can navigate into the DBA Painter. There is no shortcut key for the DBA Painter; however, you can select its icon from the Power Panel, or if you like, you can even place the DBA Painter icon right on the PowerBar using the Customize Toolbar function that we talked about way back on the first day of this tutorial. In addition, you may

find yourself in the Database Painter, and decide you need to build a query that cannot be built from within the Database Painter; therefore, you decide to open up the DBA Painter. In anticipation of this situation, PowerBuilder has also placed the DBA Painter button on the Database Painter toolbar as well. By clicking on this button, regardless of where you start, you are placed into the Database Administration Painter (see Fig. 20.1).

Figure 20.1.
The Database
Administration Painter.

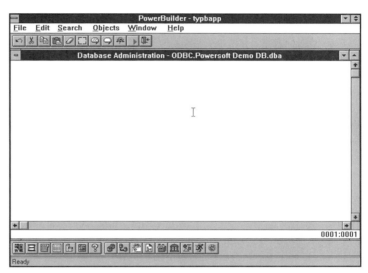

The title bar of the DBA Painter gives you a bit of information and probably reads something like this:

```
Database Administration - ODBC.Powersoft Demo DB.dba
```

This tells you that you are in the Database Administration Painter, using the ODBC Database Driver, connected to the Powersoft Demo DB Database, and logged in with the user ID dba. You've seen this title bar before when you've connected to the Database Painter.

The DBA PainterBar

When you first enter the DBA Painter, you are presented with an empty sheet, and you may feel like you are looking at an empty text editor document. In fact, the DBA Painter works like a notepad and supports many of the features that you may find in a text editor, but it also offers much more. Inside the DBA Painter notepad, you type in SQL commands. Your commands are displayed on-screen as you type them, as they may be in any other text editor, even the Script Painter. So far, nothing about the DBA Painter is all that different from the Script Painter or any other text editor. In fact, you may recognize some of the buttons on the DBA PainterBar.

Table 20.1 lists the buttons that appear both inside the Script Painter and the DBA Painter, and perform the same functions. We've discussed all of these except for the SQL Painter, which we will talk about later in this lesson.

Table 20.1. The Buttons in the DBA Painter that are also in the Script Painter.

Button	Description
	Undo the last edit
	Cut the selected text to the clipboard
	Copy the selected text to the clipboard
	Paste the contents of the clipboard at the current cursor position of the DBA Painter
	Clear the current selection
	Select the entire contents of the DBA Painter
	Comment selection
	Uncomment selection
	Open SQL Painter and Paste SQL
	Close DBA Painter

The Execute Button

In addition to these buttons, there is one new button on the DBA PainterBar that you have not seen before. This is the Execute Button, which executes any SQL Commands that you may have typed into your DBA Painter screen. You can also perform this function by selecting **Ex**ecute from the **O**bjects menu, or by pressing **Ctrl-U**.

In addition to the toolbar buttons, there are several important menu items that we will discuss that are not automatically represented by toolbar buttons (however, you can always put them there by using the techniques you learned about in Chapter 2, when you learned how to customize your toolbar). We'll address these menus as we discuss the features throughout this lesson.

Entering SQL Commands

We've begun discussing the procedures for executing your SQL. Let's finish that discussion by talking about the SQL that gets executed. When you ask the DBA Painter to execute your SQL, it starts at the very first line of the DBA Painter notepad and proceeds to read through your code until it finds a *Terminator character*. No, a terminator character is not a cyborg from the twenty-first century with an Austrian accent looking for a twelve-year-old kid. The terminator character is the character that tells PowerBuilder that it is time to send all of the information it has read from the DBA Painter notepad to the DBMS for execution. Then, assuming there are no errors, PowerBuilder continues reading your DBA Painter code until it hits the next terminator character, at which point it sends the command again to the DBMS.

Note: The default terminator character is a semicolon (;), but you can change your terminator character to any character you want by storing that character in the Terminator Character preference in the Database Preferences section in the Preferences Painter.

As PowerBuilder passes each SQL command to the DBMS, the DBMS attempts to execute it. However, it is possible that the SQL statement that you have entered is not valid. If this is the case, the DBMS will return an error message to PowerBuilder indicating the problem with your statement. PowerBuilder displays this message to you and asks if you want to continue processing the rest of the statements in the DBA Painter (see Fig. 20.2). If you answer No, you will be returned immediately to your DBA Painter, where you may correct any errors that were found. Or if you prefer, you can allow PowerBuilder to continue, attempting to execute the rest of your SQL.

There are certain SQL commands that return result sets. If your SQL statement has a result set, then that result set will be displayed to you in the Data Manipulation Painter and will be labeled accordingly. For example, a SELECT statement will be labeled Select *n*, where *n* is simply a sequential number (see Fig. 20.3). The first result will be 1, the second 2, and so on. If it is a stored procedure that returns your result set, the result set will be labeled Procedure Results *n*.

Figure 20.2.

*An error processing
DBA Painter.*

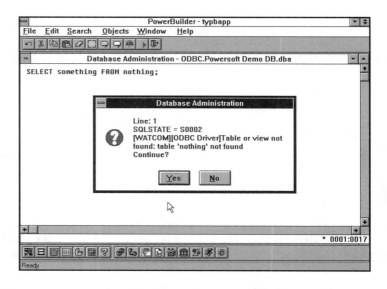

Figure 20.3.

*A DBA Painter
SELECT result set.*

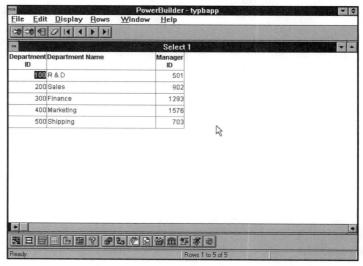

When you used the Data Manipulation Painter to manipulate the data in a single table, PowerBuilder displayed your data using the extended attributes that you set up in your table definitions in the Database Painter. It displayed the data with your format styles, edit masks, headers, and other attributes that you stored in the PowerBuilder Data Repository. In the same manner, when you enter the Data Manipulation Painter via the DBA Painter, the extended attributes of your tables will be used to display your data if they are available. If you are selecting a constant or a computed value, there will not be any information about that column in the Data Repository, and so PowerBuilder will use the name of the column or the value of the constant as the title.

Note: In some cases, you may even be able to edit the data that appears in the Data Manipulation Painter after you have executed a SQL statement. This will occur if you select data from only one table and include each of the columns that make up the Primary Key of that table. Since the Primary Key values of a table must be unique for each row in the table, PowerBuilder can use these values to build a WHERE clause for an UPDATE statement and still guarantee that it will update only the rows you change.

The capability to interactively enter and execute your SQL to see how the results will look is a very exciting, powerful feature of PowerBuilder. But that's not all! If you act now, you'll also learn about an *even more* exciting feature of PowerBuilder, the *PowerBuilder SQL Painter*.

Building SQL

The PowerBuilder SQL Painter is a graphical tool that helps you build SQL statements quickly and easily, even if you've never spoken a word of SQL in your life. You can open the SQL Painter from a couple of places besides the DBA Painter, like the Script Painter, but it always works more or less the same way. You enter the SQL Painter by selecting Paste S**Q**L from the **E**dit menu, by pressing **Ctrl-Q**, or by clicking on the Paste SQL button on the PainterBar. When you do this, PowerBuilder prompts you to select the type of SQL statement you want to build (see Fig. 20.4). You may build a SELECT, INSERT, UPDATE, or DELETE statement. Each of the different statement types works slightly differently, so we'll talk about each one in turn.

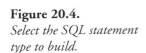
Figure 20.4.
Select the SQL statement type to build.

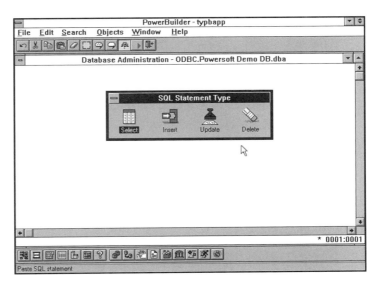

The SELECT Painter

First, let's click on SELECT and build a SELECT statement. When you click on the SELECT icon, you are presented with the SELECT Painter, which starts off by asking you which tables you want to select from (see Fig. 20.5). You should recognize this list because it is the same one that you saw in the Database Painter. Click on the Department and Employee tables and then click the **Open** button to open these tables into the SQL Painter. The tables will appear on the screen in table boxes that look exactly like the table boxes you saw in the Database Painter (see Fig. 20.6). However, this time, the tables boxes are not there for editing but instead are there for selecting.

Figure 20.5.
Select tables for building.

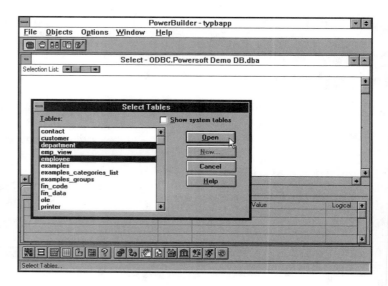

You specify the columns that you want to select by clicking on it in a table box. The name of the column that you selected will appear in a small box at the top of the screen, on the line that reads Selection List:. As you select columns from your tables, they are placed at the end of the selection list. However, if you want to change the order of your selected columns, you can simply pick up a column in the selection list and drag it left or right to a new position in the list. In addition, you can use the little scroll bar to scroll the list left or right if there are more columns than fit on-screen. You can quickly select or deselect all of the columns in a table by right-clicking on the table name of that table. When you do this, a popup menu will appear, allowing you to either select or deselect all of the columns in the table. In addition, from this right mouse menu you can close the table box.

Figure 20.6.
The SQL Painter (with Department and Employee tables open).

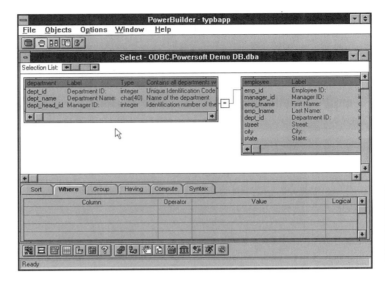

Joins

Besides selecting columns in a SELECT statement, there are some other very important components of your SELECT statement that you can build. Notice that there is a red line starting next to the dept_head_id column of the department table, proceeding through a funny looking box with an equal sign (=) in it, and finally to the emp_id column of the employee table. This line represents a join between these two columns of these two tables. PowerBuilder uses the Primary and Foreign Key information to attempt to determine what joins you may want to use when you are looking at two tables, and automatically puts those joins right on the screen for you. The symbol inside the join box tells us the type of join that it is; an equal sign, for example, represents a standard equijoin. However, you can change the type of join by clicking on the Join box. You will be presented with the Join style dialog box, where you can specify the type of join that this is (see Fig. 20.7). By default, your joins will be created as standard equijoins. However, you can change your join to a join where one column value is greater than or less than the other, by selecting the appropriate operator from the list. When you do this and press the **OK** button, you are returned to the SQL Painter, and the operator you have selected will replace the equal sign in the join box.

Figure 20.7.
The Join style dialog box.

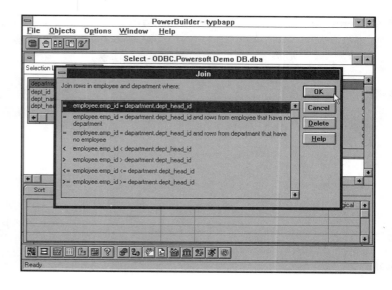

Outer Joins

In addition, the second and third join types in the list are special types of joins, called *outer joins*, which are nonstandard but are supported by just about all DBMS vendors on the market today. An outer join works like an equijoin, except it includes rows from one table even if there are no matching rows in the other table. For example, if you want to see all departments with their manager name, you leave the join as is. However, if there were a department that did not have a manager, that department would not appear in the result of this SELECT statement (because there is no row in the employee table where the emp_id column is equal to null). However, by making this an outer join, you can include that department in your result set and still see the department that was not led by a manager. Of course in real life, this particular situation is unlikely. After all, most companies assign at least one manager to each department. However, perhaps you are building a real estate sales system. In the homes table, there is a selling agent ID that stores the employee ID of the agent who sold the home. However, if the home has not yet been sold, that column will be null. In this case, you will surely find use for an outer join. There are innumerable valid uses for an outer join, and there will be some cases where you will be thankful that it is available. To create one, select the appropriate join option from the Join style dialog box.

Of the two outer join options, you can either choose to include rows from the left side, even if there is no matching row on the right, or rows from the right side, even if there is no matching row on the left. When you change your join to an outer join and return to the SQL Painter, a small circle will appear on the *outer* table of the outer join. The outer table is the one whose rows will appear even if there is no matching row in the other table. That is, when you choose

the second choice, to include rows in the Department table even though there is no manager for that department, a circle will appear on the department side of the join box.

Wait a minute! I don't want to see departments and their manager names! I want to see employees and their department names! That requires a different join than the one that we have now. So, let's first delete the join between `department.dept_head_id` and `employee.emp_id`. To do this, click on the **Delete** button in the Join style dialog box. This will delete the join and return you to the SQL Painter. Now, let's create the join that we really want, between `employee.dept_id` and `department.dept_id`.

Building New Joins

When we talked about the Window Painter, we talked about putting your cursor in different modes. The same concept applies to the SQL Painter. In order to create a join in the SQL Painter, you must put your cursor into *Join* mode. To do this, you can select **J**oins from the **O**bjects menu or click on the Join button on the SQL PainterBar. When you do this, clicking on a column in a table will no longer make it appear on the Selection List: line of the Database Painter but instead will select it as one side of a join. Then, when you click on a column from a different table, a new join will be created between the two columns you have selected. To create your join, set your cursor to Join mode and click on the `dept_id` column of the department table. Then click on the `dept_id` column of the employee table. When you do this, a red line with an equijoin will appear between the two columns. If you like, you can click on the Join box and change the type of join, as you did before. However, for your purposes, an equijoin is exactly what you want, so don't change anything.

When you are finished creating your joins, you can return your cursor to Selection mode so that you can pick columns that will be included in your Selection List by either selecting Display **C**olumns from the **O**bjects menu or by clicking on the Column Selection button on the SQL PainterBar.

The SQL Toolbox

Besides joins, there are still other SQL constructs that you may be interested in building. Many of these other constructs are built by using the *SQL Toolbox* at the bottom of the page. The SQL Toolbox is a funny looking control called a *Tab Folder*. You may have seen tab folders used in other applications that you have worked with. Tab folders contain multiple pages of information that are stored behind each other. At the top of the folder is a set of labeled *tabs*. By clicking on a tab, you can change the page that is displayed in the tab folder. For example, you may want to add filter criteria to your SELECT statement. To do so, open the Where page of the SQL Toolbox by clicking on the tab labeled Where. When you do this, the Where clause page of the SQL Toolbox is displayed (see Fig. 20.8). Here you can enter the criteria that you want in your WHERE clause.

Figure 20.8.
*The WHERE clause page
of the SQL Toolbox.*

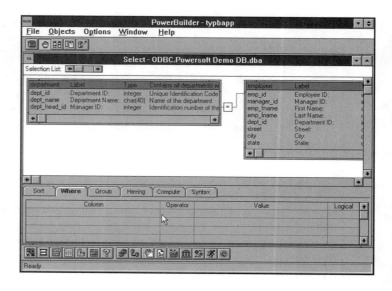

The *WHERE* Clause

The WHERE clause page is split up into four columns. The column at the far left is labeled Column and allows you to select a column from a drop-down list box. You can also type in a value into this column because there is no reason a WHERE clause must have a column name on the left side. The second column, labeled Operator, is where you select the operator for this line of the WHERE clause. By default, the operator is equals. However, you can use any valid SQL Operator, including IN, BETWEEN, and LIKE. Next is the Value column, where you can enter a value to which you can compare the item in the Column column. This can be the name of another column, a specific value, or a list of values if you are using an IN or BETWEEN operator, or a computed expression. In the last column, you can select a logical operator, And or Or, to link two lines of your WHERE clause, and then you may begin a new relational condition on the next line.

To help you build your WHERE clause, you can also use the right mouse button to quickly paste in things like column names and function templates into your Column and Value lists. If you are pasting into the Value column, you can also select the Values... menu item of the Right Mouse menu to see a list of all of the distinct values for the column listed in the Column column. You can then select one from the list, and it will be pasted right into the Value column. Also, if you want to create a subselect in your WHERE clause, you can select the Select... menu item from the Right Mouse menu, at which point you are presented with a new, empty Select Painter window, where you can build the SELECT statement that will be the subselect of this WHERE clause.

Sorting Your Data

Along with the Where tab, there are also several other tabs in the SQL Toolbox tab folder. If you click on the first tab, the Sort tab, you are presented with the Sort page of the SQL Toolbox, where you can define a sort order for your SELECT statement (see Fig. 20.9). Simply drag the columns that you want to use as your sort key from the left column to the right one. By default, the order is Ascending, and the check box is checked. However, if you prefer Descending order, you can simply uncheck the box. This page of the SQL Toolbox should look very familiar because it is nearly identical to the Sort dialog box that you saw in the Data Manipulation Painter. However, because standard SQL does not offer sorting based on an expression, you cannot edit the sort expression in the right column like you did with the Sort dialog box. Still, you can specify your sort keys and even arrange them within the list box on the right by dragging them up or down in the list.

20

Figure 20.9.
The Sort Page of the SQL Toolbox.

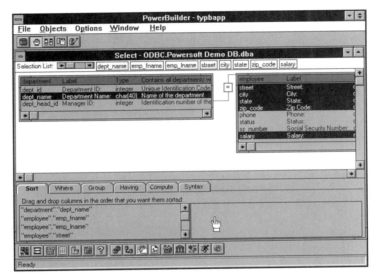

The Other SQL Toolbox Tabs

The tab that appears after the Where tab is labeled Group; it allows you to specify which columns will be used to group your data in a GROUP BY clause. This page works in pretty much the same way as the Sort page. You simply drag the column name over to the list box on the right side of the page. The Having page works exactly like the Where page, except that it specifies your HAVING clause.

The Compute page allows you to create your own computed columns that you can select (see Fig. 20.10). Here you can enter any expression that returns a single value per row, even a column name. In fact, you can paste in column names and functions using the right mouse button as you did in the Where page. Each line is a new expression, and each expression is displayed on the Selection List: as you enter it as another column.

Figure 20.10.

The Compute *page of the SQL Toolbox.*

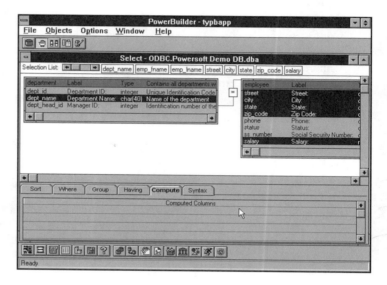

Finally, you can see what your painted SQL will look like by clicking on the Syntax tab (see Fig. 20.11). When you do this, the SQL that you have painted will be displayed on the page, and you can review it to make sure it meets your needs.

Figure 20.11.

The Syntax *page of the SQL Toolbox.*

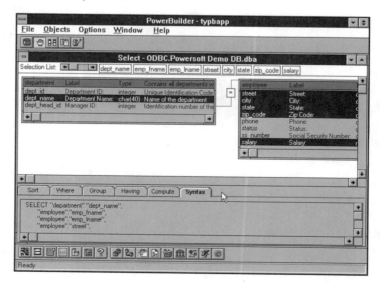

The SELECT Painter Menu

Besides the SQL Toolbox, there are several menu items that you can use to build your SQL statement. You can open the Table Selection dialog by selecting **T**ables... from the **O**bjects menu, by clicking on the Table button on the SQL PainterBar, or by selecting Select Tables... from the right mouse menu of the SQL Painter screen (which you can open by right-clicking on an empty area of the SQL Painter). You can create a union, which will open up a new SQL SELECT Painter window, by selecting Create **U**nion... from the **O**bjects menu. You can specify that you only want to see distinct result rows by checking or unchecking the **D**istinct menu item from the O**p**tions menu. You can arrange the tables by selecting **A**rrange Tables menu of either the O**p**tions menu or the right mouse menu. You can preview the results of your SELECT statement by selecting **P**review from the O**p**tions menu. If your SELECT statement is valid, you will be placed into the Data Manipulation Painter with its results; otherwise, an error message will display, and you will be left in the SQL Painter.

You can control your environment somewhat by using the **S**how menu that appears both in the O**p**tions menu and in the right mouse menu. You can choose to show the Datatypes, Labels, and Comments in the table boxes. You can show or hide the SQL Toolbox at the bottom of the screen from this menu. You can also show or hide the SQL Toolbox by clicking on the Show/ Hide SQL Toolbox button on the SQL PainterBar.

From the **F**ile menu, you can save your SELECT statement as a PowerBuilder Query Object by selecting the **S**ave Query or Save Query **A**s menu items from the menu. You can open an existing PowerBuilder Query Object into the SELECT Painter by selecting **O**pen Query, and you can clear your query and start from scratch by selecting **N**ew.... Finally, you can return to the DBA Painter by selecting either **C**lose or **R**eturn To Database Administration, or by clicking on the Return button on the SQL PainterBar. When you return, your select statement will be pasted in the DBA Painter notepad.

The INSERT Painter

Once back in the DBA Painter, you can create other SQL Statements. Open up the SQL Painter again by selecting Paste S**Q**L from the **E**dit menu, or by clicking on the Paste SQL button on the DBA PainterBar. This time, click on the Insert icon in the Select Statement Type dialog box. You will once again be presented with the list of tables to select from. However, because you can only insert rows into one table at a time, only select one table from the list to open.

 Warning: Even though you *should* only select one table from the list, for some reason you are *able* to select more. However, even if you do select more than one table from the list, when you click the **Open** button, PowerBuilder only opens the first table that you selected.

When you click on the **Open** button, you are presented with the Insert Column Values dialog box, which lists out each of the columns from the table you opened, followed by an edit box where you can enter in a value to insert (see Fig. 20.12). You can simply type in the value that you want to insert, or you can click on the **Null** button at the bottom of the dialog box, which places the word null in the edit box for the currently selected column (indicated by the little hand on the left) and inserts a null into that column. You can remove a column altogether from the insertion list by clicking on the **Delete** button. Then, if you like, you can reinsert the deleted column back into the list by clicking on it in the table box at the bottom of the dialog box. When you do this, the column is inserted at the end of the column value list, unless you have made space for it by clicking on the **Insert** button first. If you want to use a SELECT statement as the source of values for your INSERT statement, you can do that, too, by clicking on the **Select** button. This will open up the Select Painter described earlier.

Figure 20.12.
The Insert Column Values dialog box.

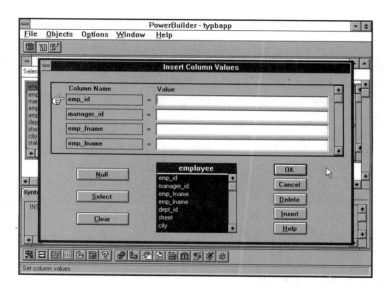

When you are done, you can click the **OK** button, and you are returned to the SQL Painter. Your INSERT statement will appear inside the Syntax tab of the SQL Toolbox, and your table will appear on the top half of the screen. If you want to change your INSERT statement, you can select Column **V**alues from the **O**bjects menu, or click on the Set Column Values button on the SQL PainterBar. When you are done building your INSERT statement, you can close the SQL Painter and return with (or without) your SQL INSERT statement to the DBA Painter.

The UPDATE Painter

The UPDATE Statement works like an INSERT statement with a WHERE clause. If you reopen the SQL Painter and choose Update as the SQL Statement Type, you will once again be presented with a list of tables. You should only select one table from this list. You are then presented with the

Update Column Values dialog box, which looks similar to the Insert Column Values dialog box, but is not exactly the same (see Fig. 20.13). This Update Column Values dialog box allows you to select the columns you want to update and enter update values for those columns. However, you cannot set a value equal to a SELECT statement, so that is not an option here. Furthermore, there is an additional set of buttons for your arithmetic operators. Finally, because most of the time you update only a few columns of your table in a single statement and not all of the columns, this dialog box starts off with none of the columns selected, unlike its INSERT counterpart, which starts off with all columns selected. However, selecting your columns and inserting your values works pretty much the same way in both dialog boxes.

Figure 20.13.
The Update Column Values dialog box.

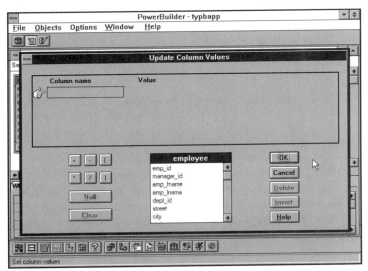

The other major difference between the INSERT Painter and the UPDATE Painter is the inclusion of the WHERE clause tab folder in the UPDATE Painter. Just like you did with your SELECT statement, you can enter in any valid WHERE clause as the criteria for your UPDATE command, even a subselect. And so by using the Update SQL Painter, you can build any standard SQL UPDATE statement that you like.

The DELETE Painter

Lastly, you can build a DELETE statement. If you return to the DBA Painter and open the SQL Painter again, you are once again presented with the Select Statement Type dialog box. This time, click on the Delete icon. When you do this, you are again presented with the list of tables, and you should again only select a single table from the list because you can only delete rows from one table at a time. The DELETE Painter works very much like the UPDATE Painter, but without the Column Values dialog box because you cannot delete columns, only rows. You can use the WHERE clause tab of the SQL Toolbox to enter any valid filter criteria, even a subselect,

to determine which rows will be deleted. When you are done, you can return to the DBA Painter, and your SQL statement will be painted.

Explaining Your SQL

Once you have entered a SQL statement into your DBA Painter notepad, regardless of whether you built it yourself or you used the SQL Painter to build it, you will often want to get information about the way the DBMS is planning to execute that statement. Most DBMSs come with an optimizer that attempts to determine the quickest way to execute a SQL statement. They do this by building something called an *execution plan*. An execution plan is exactly what it sounds like—a plan of how to execute the SQL statement that has been requested. The DBMS plans the statement by analyzing it and by attempting to determine which tables and indexes it should use in what order. By taking a moment to plan the execution of a SQL statement, a DBMS can test out different scenarios and come up with the scenario that will probably hit the database disk file the least number of times and return the result set in the quickest way possible. Since users are interested in good performance, it is usually helpful for developers to see the execution plan of our SQL statements so that we can attempt to either change our SQL or create new indexes to make our applications perform better.

You can see the execution plans of your SQL statements by selecting Explai**n** SQL from the **O**bjects menu. When you do this, the Explain SQL dialog box will appear, containing a description of the execution plan for the SQL statements that appear in the DBA Painter notepad. However, the language of the execution plan is very database dependent, so you should check with the database vendor's documentation to learn how to best read and understand it, as well as what you can do to make sure your SQL is performing at its best.

Importing and Exporting SQL Files

When you have built a set of SQL commands that you are happy with, it is generally useful to save those commands so that you can issue them again at will. For example, perhaps you have built scripts to create your table and index structures, or perhaps you have built a complex query that returns denormalized versions of your normalized data. Regardless of why this particular SQL script is important to you, if it is important, you will probably want a way to save it to your hard drive and then call it up later to be executed again.

You can save the contents of your DBA Painter notepad to a file by either selecting **S**ave, Save **A**s, or **E**xport from the **F**ile menu. Although there are minor differences between the three, all three basically save your DBA notepad contents to your hard drive, after prompting you to specify the filename that you want to save them with. In general, your SQL scripts will be saved with a .SQL file extension to make it easy to distinguish them as SQL scripts. However, you may specify any name and extension that appeals to you.

If later you decide you want to load your SQL script back into the DBA Painter notepad, you can simply select **O**pen or I**m**port from the **F**ile menu, and you are presented with the common

dialog that is used to select a file to open. Once you select it, it will be loaded into your DBA notepad. Here, the difference between the two menu items is a little more noticeable—if you use the **O**pen menu item, the .SQL file that you load will replace anything that is currently in the DBA Painter notepad; whereas if you simply I**m**port it in, it will be inserted into the DBA notepad at the current cursor position, without erasing the contents of the notepad.

Retrieving the Stored Syntax of Views and Procedures

In addition to retrieving your SQL from files on your local machine, PowerBuilder actually allows you to load SQL scripts into the DBA Painter notepad right from the database! You can import the SQL of *stored procedures* and *views*. Stored procedures are special SQL scripts that are saved on the DBMS and are supported by a number of the more popular DBMSs, including Watcom, SQL Server, and later versions of Oracle. And views, as you know, are simply cached SELECT statements that are stored on the server but look like tables. In both cases, you can load the SQL script from the server back into your DBA notepad by selecting the appropriate menu item from the **O**bjects menu.

To retrieve the syntax for a stored procedure, select the **P**rocedure Syntax... menu item. To retrieve the syntax for a view, select the **V**iew Syntax... menu item. Either way, you are prompted with the Syntax Selection dialog box, with either the list of procedures or views in the top half of the dialog box and the syntax of the selected procedure or view in the bottom half (see Fig. 20.14). If you select a line in the list box on top and click **OK**, that selected item's syntax will appear at the current cursor position in the DBA notepad.

Figure 20.14.
The Syntax dialog box (with Procedure Syntax inside).

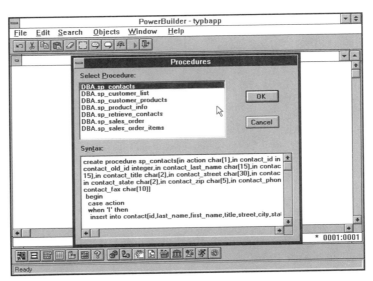

Maintaining Database Security

In addition to painting and writing SQL, the DBA Painter also offers a tool that is very useful to DBAs. It allows them to quickly and easily maintain database security, without having to know too much about the specifics of how that particular DBMS handles security, or even know the syntax that is used to create IDs, groups, and rights.

The security management process takes on three steps. First, you must create a login user ID. You can do this by selecting the Maintain **U**sers... menu item in the **O**bjects menu. When you do this, you are presented with the Maintain Users dialog box, where you can add a new user and modify or even delete an existing one (see Fig. 20.15). When you select the **New** button, you are presented with a dialog box that may look slightly differently for different DBMSs. However, the concept of the Create User ID dialog box will always be pretty much the same (see Fig. 20.16). You need to enter a unique ID and a password that the user of that ID will use to connect with. When you are done maintaining your users, you can click the **Done** button, and you are returned to the DBA Painter.

Figure 20.15.

The Maintain Users dialog box.

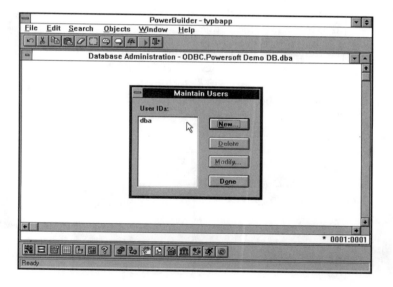

Most DBMSs allow you to create user groups and assign rights to the entire group so that any user in that group automatically inherits that right. To manage your groups, you can select Maintain **G**roups... from the **O**bjects menu. When you do this, you are presented with the Maintain Groups dialog box, where you can define new groups, delete existing groups, and assign users to specific groups (see Fig. 20.17). When you are done, you can click the **Done** button, and you are returned once again to the DBA Painter.

Figure 20.16.
The Create User ID dialog box for Watcom.

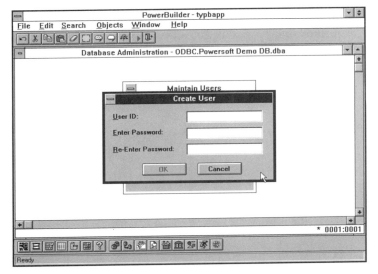

Figure 20.17.
The Maintain Groups dialog box.

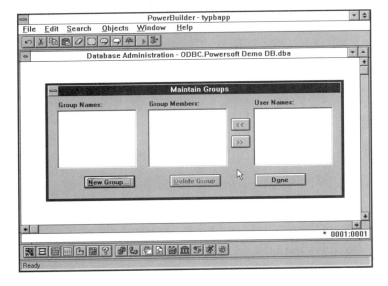

Once you've defined your users and groups, you can manage which users and which groups have what types of access to which tables by selecting Table Security... from the **O**bjects menu. When you do this, you are presented with the Table Security dialog box (see Fig. 20.18). In this dialog box, you first select a user ID or group name on the left side of the dialog box. Then you select a table in the middle and click on the check boxes at the right to establish which security

privileges that user or group will have to that table. In addition, you can select which columns that user may update by clicking the **Update** button at the bottom right of the screen. After you change the security, you must apply the changes by clicking the **Apply** button. And of course, when you are finished, you can click the **Done** button, and you are once again returned to the DBA Painter.

Figure 20.18.
The Table Security dialog box.

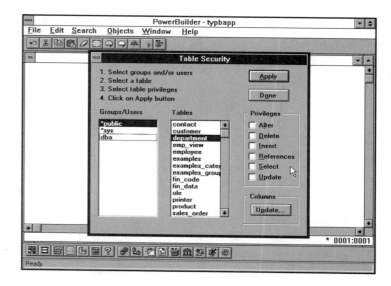

Warning: Database security is not part of the ANSI Standard, and so different DBMSs support it differently. For example, some DBMSs require separate server logins be set up before a User ID is created. Fortunately, if you are using native PowerBuilder drivers to connect to your database, any other security requirements will be available as menu items from the **O**bjects menu, and will work in a similar manner. Check the PowerBuilder documentation and your DBMS documentation for details if you are not sure.

Afternoon Summary

PowerBuilder provides you with a special painter, called the Database Administration (DBA) Painter, where you can execute any valid SQL statement in an interactive mode. It also offers additional features like a query builder and syntax viewer. When you open the DBA Painter, the

title bar gives you information about your database connection, including the driver, database, and login ID. The DBA Painter works like a notepad and supports many of the features that you may find in a text editor, but it also allows you to execute SQL commands that you type in. Many of the buttons on the DBA PainterBar are identical to buttons that you see on the Script PainterBar, except for the Execute button, which allows you to execute the statements inside your DBA notepad, line by line.

Each SQL command in the DBA notepad is separated by a terminator character, which tells the PowerBuilder SQL parser when it has reached the end of a single command. PowerBuilder then passes the command to the DBMS, at which point it is executed. If your SQL statement has a result set, then that result set is displayed to you in the Data Manipulation Painter and is labeled with a title indicating whether it is a result set or a stored procedure result and a sequential number. If you select data from only one table and include each of the columns that makes up the Primary Key of that table, you will even be able to edit your data in the Data Manipulation Painter.

In addition, you can build SQL statements quickly and easily by using the PowerBuilder SQL Painter. You may build a SELECT, INSERT, UPDATE, or DELETE statement. Most of the SQL Painters start off by listing the tables in the database, asking which tables you want to work with. When building a SELECT statement, you can select your tables, at which point you will be presented with table boxes, where you can select the columns from these tables that will be selected. In addition, you can also join columns graphically by using the Join tool on the toolbar. You can then use the SQL Toolbox at the bottom of the page to build other SQL clauses for your SELECT statement, including a WHERE clause, sort ORDER BY, GROUP BY, HAVING, and COMPUTE clause. You can also see the syntax of the SQL that you have painted from the SQL Toolbox. You can also build a union to another SELECT statement, and specify that you only want to see DISTINCT values.

Building INSERTs, UPDATEs, and DELETEs work in much the same way. However, there is one additional dialog box where you specify values for insertion or update. In addition, you can specify a subselect for your INSERT values. There are also a couple of other places from which you can get SQL into your DBA notepad. You can import and export your SQL from flat files on your hard drive, and you can retrieve the syntax of your views and stored procedures.

Once you have SQL in your DBA notepad, you can explain that SQL by selecting the Explain SQL Menu item. Explaining SQL will bring up a dialog box that shows the execution plan of the SQL on the server. The syntax that is used for this comes directly from the Server and is DBMS dependent. But it may help you optimize your SQL Statements.

You can also maintain your database security from the DBA Painter. You can maintain users, groups, and database logins, as well as grant and revoke rights on your tables and commands to your users and groups.

20

447

Q&A

Q **Is the Database Administrator the only place I can use SQL in PowerBuilder?**

A No, in addition to the Database Administrator you can use SQL in the Script Painter, DataWindow Painter, Query Painter, and Pipeline Painter.

Q **Do I always need a WHERE clause in my SELECT statement?**

A No, but the result set will include all rows from the table selected if no WHERE clause is specified. If you have multiple tables in your select statement, the result set will be generated as a product of the tables and could be very large and time consuming. It is best to use a WHERE clause to limit the result set to contain only data needed.

Q **There is so much SQL syntax to remember—how can I cope?**

A PowerBuilder hides much of the SQL when you create tables, create indexes, drop tables, assign database permissions, paint a DataWindow source, or use the SQL Painter in script because it enables you to create SQL graphically, without memorizing specific syntax. You don't need to remember all the syntax, but you need to understand it to help you take full advantage of SQL and PowerBuilder.

Q **I created a table by executing SQL script in the Database Administrator. Why doesn't the table show up when I go back into the Database Painter?**

A You created the table, but by default it will not show in the Database Painter. You must open the table from the table list to show it in the Database Painter workspace.

Q **From the SQL Toolbox, when I right mouse click on the WHERE tab under the Value heading, I notice Arguments... option is disabled. Is there any way to use arguments in the Data Administration Painter?**

A Arguments are not allowed in the Database Administrator because variables cannot be used. In other painters, where variables are allowed, you can enter arguments.

Q **While in the SQL Painter, I right mouse clicked under Value in the Where Page of the SQL Toolbox to select the Value... option for a column. Why does it take so long to paste data from this option?**

A The Value... option retrieves all distinct values for the column selected and shows them sorted in a Retrieve as Needed format. If the data values to paste are near the end of a large table, you will have to wait a while.

Q **Is there a way to have the SQL Painter sort based on an expression?**

A Yes, create a computed column with the Compute tab and then select that column in the Sort tab dialog box.

Workshop

Quiz

1. What are four main commands in Data Manipulation Language (DML) used to access the database?

2. List the three main components or clauses in DML commands.

3. Formulate the SQL required to select the total number of employees from the `employee` table with a last name, `last_name`, that starts with *H*.

4. What is the general syntax for the `INSERT` statement?

5. What is the general syntax for the `UPDATE` statement?

6. What are the four standard types of table rights you can grant to or revoke from a user?

7. How do you paint a SQL statement that returns all the employees from the `employee` table and their related department name, even if the employee is not in a department?

8. What is an execution plan, and how do you use it?

Putting PowerBuilder into Action

1. Open the DBA Painter.

2. Build a `SELECT` statement that selects all of the employee information in the employee table for employees whose department name is "Marketing." In case the department ID of the marketing department changes, you should use the name for your `WHERE` clause and not the department ID number.

3. Build an `INSERT` statement that will insert a new row into the department table. The row has a department id number of 600, and its name is `MIS`.

4. Build an `UPDATE` statement that will update the name of the MIS department to `Technology`. Don't go by the name; use the department ID of 600 as the key.

5. Build a `DELETE` statement that will delete the Technology department from the department table because everyone in that department seems to get laid off anyway.

6. Review the statements that you have created to ensure that you understand the SQL syntax that was generated.

7. Explain the SQL to see how the DBMS will execute it.

8. Execute the SQL statements in the DBA Painter.

Chapter

21

DataWindow
Definitions
(Objects)

In this lesson, you will learn about DataWindow Definitions. You will learn:

☐ How to create a new DataWindow Definition

☐ About the different parts of a DataWindow Definition

☐ How to preview your DataWindow Definition to see what it will look like

☐ How to set up your DataWindow Painter environment to meet your needs

☐ Several ways to control how the data in your DataWindow Definition will be represented

☐ Several ways to let the user modify the selection criteria of a DataWindow Definition

Showing Data in your Applications— DataWindows

If you remember when we talked about the Data Manipulation Painter, I mentioned that one of the most exciting features of PowerBuilder is the fact that you can take the very user friendly, intuitive functionality of the Data Manipulation Painter and easily incorporate it into your own applications. You can do this by using two PowerBuilder constructs called the *DataWindow Definition*, and the *DataWindow Control*. You use the PowerBuilder DataWindow Definition to define the structure and layout of the data that will be displayed. Later, in Chapters 23 and 24, you will learn about the PowerBuilder DataWindow Control, which you use to control the behavior of data in your DataWindow Definition. First, though, let's talk about how to define a DataWindow Definition.

Note: There is quite a bit of confusion among PowerBuilder developers about the use of the term *DataWindow*. This is because in PowerBuilder, there are three entities that contain the term *DataWindow* in their name. First is the *DataWindow Control*, which is the visual control that is placed on your window to allow the user to interact with data. As I've already mentioned, we'll talk about that in Chapters 23 and 24.

The second DataWindow is the *DataWindow Definition*, which you build in the DataWindow Painter and is referred to in the PowerBuilder documentation as a *DataWindow Object*. However, I have a problem with using the term *DataWindow Object* to define this PowerBuilder construct. Inside the DataWindow Definition are other entities that are referred to as the *DataWindow Objects*—the objects that are inside of a DataWindow Definition. When speaking to others about DataWindow Objects, the term *object* can be very ambiguous and confusing.

For this reason, throughout this book, we will refer to the DataWindow that you build in the Database Painter as a *DataWindow Definition*, and reserve the term

DataWindow Object for the objects that live inside of a DataWindow Definition. Although I can't guarantee that you won't continue to be confused when you read other PowerBuilder related documents, at least you will have half a chance because this lesson lacks that particular ambiguity.

To define a DataWindow Definition, you specify two things. First, you specify where the data that will be contained within the DataWindow Definition will come from, and then you specify how that data will be represented on the user's screen once it is inside. PowerBuilder offers three basic sources of data for the DataWindow. The first, and probably most obvious, is the result set of a SQL SELECT statement. PowerBuilder allows you to use a simple SELECT statement as the data source for your DataWindow Definition. Since Stored Procedures also can return result sets, PowerBuilder also provides a method for you to use the results of a Stored Procedure as your data source. Finally, you can specify that you want to fill your DataWindow Definition with data manually by using commands inside of your PowerBuilder scripts. There are a few variations on these three basic themes that we will talk about briefly in just a moment; but for now, these are the three places from which your DataWindow Definitions can obtain data.

In addition to specifying the data source of your DataWindow Definition, you need to specify the way the data will look, or the layout of the data on-screen. The layout is also made up of several components. First, you must specify the presentation style of the DataWindow Definition. Then, you must specify the position of each column in the window. Finally, you must specify the attributes of the specific columns inside the DataWindow Definition.

The DataWindow Presentation Styles

PowerBuilder offers a fair selection of DataWindow Definition *presentation styles*. The three most frequently used styles are the *Grid* layout, which looks and works much like a spreadsheet; the *FreeForm* layout, which looks and works like an on-line form with titles and fields laid out in vertical columns down a page; and the *Tabular* layout, which is identical to the FreeForm layout, except that it is laid out in horizontal columns across a page instead of vertically. Actually, the difference between a FreeForm DataWindow Definition and a Tabular DataWindow Definition has only to do with how it is initially built. After building a new FreeForm or Tabular DataWindow Definition, you can move your fields wherever you want on the page, and the "mode" of the DataWindow is the same for both. Besides these common presentation styles, there are also several other very important styles that may not appear in every application but can be very helpful anyway.

Included in this list of presentation styles is the *Group* style, which allows you to group your data based on the values in a particular column. For example, you may want to see the salaries of your employees grouped by state or by department. You can do this by using a Group style

DataWindow Definition. Incidentally, it should be pointed out that the Group style is identical to the Tabular and FreeForm style, except that it starts off with a grouping based on the column you specify and sets up some summary fields for you. You can, however, remove the grouping, and you will be looking at a FreeForm DataWindow Definition. In addition, you can take a FreeForm DataWindow Definition and create groups for it, and you'll learn just how to do that later this lesson.

The next style of interest is the *Crosstab* style, which allows you to see a cross-tabulated summary of your data in a grid format. Essentially, a crosstab report is like a two-dimensional group report. It allows you to use values in your table as the values of the X and Y axis, as well as the value of the resulting cell. For example, you may want to see the salaries of your employees not just by state, but by department and state. The X axis would be state, and the Y axis would be department. The resultant crosstab report might look like the one in Figure 21.1.

Figure 21.1.
The Employee Crosstab Report.

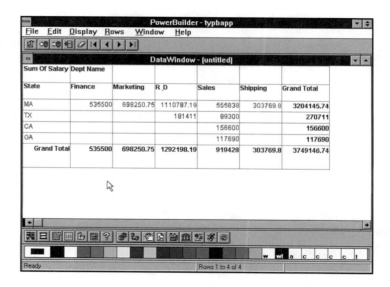

Another exciting style that you can use is a *Label* style. This style is meant specifically to support the printing out of mailing labels. In addition, PowerBuilder comes stocked with information on setting up labels of other types, including disk labels, file folder labels, and even business cards. Of course, there is enough flexibility in the system to let you design just about any label that you can dream up.

Another variation of the Tabular style is the *N-Up* style of DataWindows. This style is used to build a columnar DataWindow. The *N* in *N-Up* represents any number of columns. With the exception of the Crosstab DataWindow, all other DataWindow Definition styles that we have talked about so far only permit displaying one record's worth of information on a line or page.

However, using the N-Up style, you can split your row into multiple columns and display information from multiple rows on a single line or page.

One of the most exciting styles of the PowerBuilder DataWindow Definition is the *Graph* style. Just like it sounds, the Graph DataWindow Style allows you to use your data as the source for a graph on-screen. You can display Bar Graphs, Column Graphs, Pie Graphs, Line Graphs, Area Graphs, and Scatter Graphs in two or three dimensions. The data that is used to create the graph will be the data that is inside your DataWindow.

A very exciting feature of PowerBuilder is the capability to take DataWindow Definitions and store them inside other DataWindow Definitions. This is called *nesting*. For example, you can take one DataWindow Definition, which is a graph of your employee salary history, and place it inside a master employee DataWindow Definition. Then, each row in the master employee DataWindow Definition will display a salary histogram next to it. You can even place a vacation schedule or any other report on each row, and it will appear. In addition, you can create a DataWindow Definition using the *Composite Report* style, which does not have a base DataWindow but is just a collection of reports attached together.

Note: The different DataWindows inside a Composite Report don't actually have to be related to each other in any way; they can just be different collections of data stored in one DataWindow Definition. However, they usually are related to each other in some way, and in the next lesson we'll learn how to relate nested DataWindow Definitions.

21

The DataWindow Painter

You create your DataWindow Definitions in the *DataWindow Painter*. To open the DataWindow Painter, you can either press **Shift-F4** or click on the DataWindow button on the PowerBar. When you do this, you will be prompted to select a DataWindow Definition to open. To create a new DataWindow Definition, click on the **New** button. You will be presented with the New DataWindow dialog box, where you can select the Data Source and Presentation Style of the DataWindow Definition that you want to create (see Fig. 21.2). The bottom half of the screen lists the Presentation Styles and allows you to select the one that you want to use for your DataWindow Definition. The top half of the dialog box lists the available data sources for a DataWindow Definition. Earlier, we talked about three data sources for a DataWindow Definition. Here, though, there are five choices. This is because PowerBuilder gives you three different ways of loading a SQL Statement as the data source of your DataWindow Definition.

Note: Remember, you create DataWindow Definitions in the DataWindow Painter to define the layout and source of your data. You start off by specifying a presentation style and data source. In other PowerBuilder documentation, the DataWindow Definition may be referred to as a DataWindow Object. However, this can be confusing because there are some other things in PowerBuilder that are also referred to as DataWindow Objects. So instead, use the term *DataWindow Definition* to prevent confusion.

Figure 21.2.
The New DataWindow dialog box.

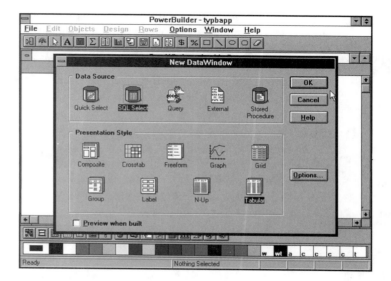

Warning: Before you go any further, be sure that the check box labeled Preview When Built is **unchecked**. If this check box is checked, you immediately will be thrown into DataWindow Definition Preview mode. We won't learn about Preview mode until after we have talked a bit about the DataWindow Definition itself, a little bit later. In the future, if you prefer to see what your DataWindow Definition will look like immediately after you define it, you can leave this check box checked. PowerBuilder will "remember" the way you last set it and leave it that way the next time you create a new DataWindow Definition.

The SQL Select Data Source

One method of building a SQL SELECT as the data source of your DataWindow Definition is with the **SQL Select** button. Let's start by taking a look at how it works. Click on the **SQL Select** button, then click on the Tabular Presentation Style, and then click the **OK** button. This will open the SQL SELECT Painter that we discussed in detail in the last lesson. Here, you can create a SELECT statement that will be used as your DataWindow Definition's data source using the same techniques that we discussed in the last section. Since we have already spent a significant amount of time learning about the SQL SELECT Painter, there's no reason to talk about it here again. Instead, let's go ahead and build a SQL SELECT Statement.

From the table list, select (you guessed it) the Employee and Department tables, and then click on the **Open** button. Now, let's select the dept_name column from the Department table, and the emp_fname, emp_lname, state, and salary columns from the Employee table. For now, let's leave out any WHERE clause or other special clauses. Instead, signal to PowerBuilder that you are done building your SQL Statement by selecting Design from the File menu, or by clicking on the Design button on the DataWindow PainterBar. When you do this, PowerBuilder will build a Tabular DataWindow Definition using this SQL statement as its data source, and it will be displayed inside the DataWindow Painter on your screen (see Fig. 21.3).

Figure 21.3.
A tabular DataWindow definition.

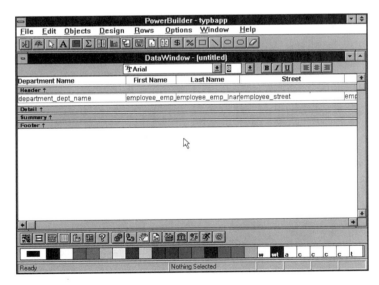

The Bands of a DataWindow

The DataWindow Painter is split into vertical sections, called *Bands*. Each band can contain different information and serves a different purpose. For example, the top band is called the *Header Band*. This band contains header information that will appear at the top of each page

of data in the DataWindow. You might place a report title and column headings in the Header Band. Beneath that, there is a *Detail Band*, which contains the information that will appear for each row of data in the DataWindow. In general, the Detail Band contains the data that was retrieved from the database. For example, you might want to display the employee name, department, and address information that we selected in our data source inside the detail band so that for each row of data that was retrieved, this information would be displayed. Underneath the Detail Band is the *Summary Band*, which contains the information that will be displayed after all of the data is displayed. This is a very good place to put computations like totals and averages when displaying mathematical data. Finally, the *Footer Band* contains the footer information that will be displayed at the bottom of each page, like the page number, date, and time. Although the preceding examples should help you understand how a DataWindow Definition allows you to create pretty, formatted reports, I should point out that these are just examples. In reality, there are a number of things that you can place inside of a band of a DataWindow Definition to display to your user.

The DataWindow Objects

The items that you can place inside of a DataWindow Definition are referred to as *DataWindow Objects*. Like the controls that go inside of a window, the DataWindow Objects are the visual components that are placed inside DataWindow Definitions to display information on the screen. These DataWindow Objects include your selected columns, as well as text objects, pictures, rectangles, and even other DataWindow Definitions. Each DataWindow Object has specific properties associated with it that you can set to meet your needs. You place these objects inside your DataWindow Definition by putting your cursor into control creation mode and creating them on your screen, much in the same way that you did when you placed controls on your window. In addition, most of the DataWindow Object attributes can be manipulated by double-clicking or right-clicking on the control that you want to edit, just like you did in the Window Painter. We'll talk more in detail about the DataWindow Objects as well as the different bands of the DataWindow in just a bit. But first, let's talk about what you see on your screen now.

> **Note:** DataWindow Objects are the objects (or controls) that you can place inside a DataWindow Definition. Don't confuse the term DataWindow *Object* with DataWindow *Definition*. Sometimes PowerBuilder documentation refers to the DataWindow Definition itself as a DataWindow Object, and that is why everyone is so confused.

When you build a tabular DataWindow Definition, PowerBuilder lines the selected columns up horizontally in the detail band, and places titles for those columns in the header band. In addition, you can place other DataWindow Objects inside your DataWindow Definition, even in other bands. Let's give our DataWindow Definition a footer that shows the date and the page number. In order to do this, we must first make room in the footer band for our new field. So, move your mouse over the gray band labeled Footer until the cursor looks like Figure 21.4. Then, click and drag the footer band down a bit, enough so there is room to fit one of the columns from above inside, about one and a half times the height of the band itself. Now, put your cursor into creation mode by selecting Today( ) - Computed Field from the **O**bjects menu, or by clicking on the **Today's Date** button on the DataWindow PainterBar. Then, click in an area inside the footer band of the DataWindow Definition, that is, above the footer band border. A small box with the word Today( ) should appear where you clicked.

Figure 21.4.

The mouse cursor to move the Footer band.

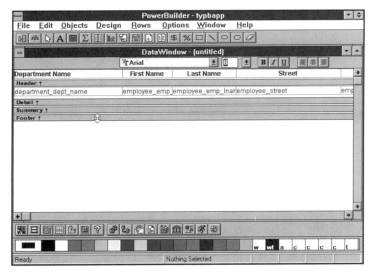

In order to help us know what we are looking at, let's create a summary of our data that tells us how many rows were retrieved. Open up the summary band in the same way you did with the footer band. Bring your mouse cursor over the band until it changes shape, and then click and drag the summary band about one and a half times its height down the page. In order to place a count object inside of your DataWindow Definition, you need to indicate what it is that you want to count. Since we want to count everything, we may as well just select any column in the DataWindow detail band. So, click on the box in the detail band that reads department_dept_name. Now, from the **O**bjects menu, select Count - Computed Field. Your mouse cursor now goes into count object creation mode. Click inside the summary band to place your count there. A field should appear inside the summary band that reads Count(department_dept_name for all). At this point, your window should look something like that which appears in Figure 21.5.

Figure 21.5.
Your DataWindow should look like this.

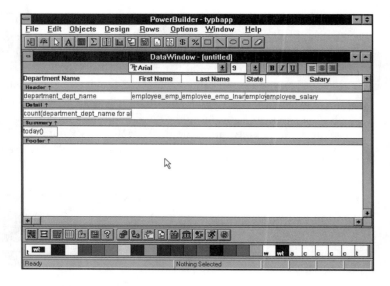

 Warning: You may not be able to see the entire contents of the count field on-screen—the field may be too small. That's okay, because we'll talk about how you can see what's inside this object in the next lesson.

Once you have placed a DataWindow Object onto your DataWindow Definition, your cursor returns to selection mode, and the item that you just placed in will be selected, indicated by small squares in the corners. In selection mode, you may move the items on the screen around, as well as edit their attributes. Before we begin talking about the attributes of our DataWindow Objects, though, let's take a look and see what we've got so far.

Previewing Your DataWindow

 Although I've described the different parts of a DataWindow Definition, like bands and columns, it is probably difficult to visualize how this all works itself into a pretty report. So, rather than continue discussing the details of manipulating the objects inside of your DataWindow Definition, I'd like to show you first the "meaning behind the madness." This way, you can understand how the different pieces of the DataWindow Definition come together to make really nice reports. Let's preview our DataWindow Definition by selecting Preview from the **D**esign menu, or by clicking on the Preview button on the DataWindow PainterBar. I bet you can guess where this will take you—to the Data Manipulation Painter. However, this time, instead of using the PowerBuilder data repository to figure out how to display your data, it uses your DataWindow Definition.

What you should see on the screen now is a report that displays a list of five department names along with the name and address information of the department heads of those departments (see Fig. 21.6). At the top line, in boldface, are the titles of each of the columns to make it easier to see what we are looking at. This line is represented in the DataWindow Definition as the Header Band, and reappears on top of each page of data in the Data Manipulation Painter. We'll demonstrate this in just a moment.

Figure 21.6.

Previewing the DataWindow Definition.

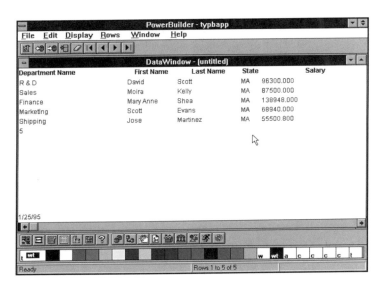

Beneath the header line are the five rows of data. Each column that we selected in our select statement is displayed underneath its heading from the header band. The reason for this is because of the column placeholders that appear in our detail band of the DataWindow Definition. Behind the scenes of the DataWindow Control, (the name I'll temporarily use to refer to the DataWindow that appears in the Data Manipulation Painter), there is a table buffer that holds the raw data from the result set of your SQL statement. In the foreground, the DataWindow Definition is used to format the data so that it appears nicely on the screen (inside the DataWindow Control). PowerBuilder loops through each row in the result set. As it hits a new row, it first places a new detail band inside of the DataWindow Control, copying all of the objects from the detail band, including columns placeholders, text items, rectangles and all. Then, it looks at the objects inside the DataWindow Definition. It finds all of the column placeholders in the DataWindow Definition, and replaces them in the current band of the DataWindow Control with the actual values stored in the current row of the result set. It then continues its other processing, like calculating computed expressions and formatting the data in the columns, until it is finished cleaning up this band-row of the DataWindow Control. Then, it can continue to the next row of data in the result set, and repeat the process. In reality, the process is slightly more complex, and is optimized so that it actually happens pretty quickly.

But for now, this overview will suffice. It is important that you understand conceptually what goes on when you display data in a DataWindow Control, even if it is implemented slightly differently.

After all of the rows of data are displayed, the information in the summary band is displayed. In this case, we placed a special type of column, called a *computed field*, inside of our DataWindow Definition to display a count of the number of detail rows that appear in our DataWindow Control in the summary band. After the last line of data in the DataWindow Control, you should see a small number 5 appear. The data in the summary band will appear only once per report, immediately after the last row of data in the detail band.

At the bottom of the page, you should see today's date (which will probably be different than the date that you see on the bottom line of the report in the figure). This is the date that you asked to have displayed in the footer of the DataWindow Definition. The footer will appear at the bottom of every page of data. The footer will move with the DataWindow Control, and automatically find the end of a page, and put itself there. To see what I mean, drag the corner of the current Data Manipulation Painter window, and make the window small enough so that there is a scrollbar with two (or more) pages of data inside of it. When you do this, the summary will disappear off to the next page, since the summary data appears only once, at the end of the entire set of data. However, today's date will still appear at the bottom of the page. In addition, if you scroll down to the next page with your vertical scrollbar, you will see that today's date appears at the bottom of this page, too. In fact, if you were to print the data out to your printer, and there were more than one printed page of data, the footer would automatically attach itself once to the bottom of each printed page. The difference between a summary line and footer line is often misunderstood, but that difference should be clear to you now.

Warning: The footer automatically attaches itself to the end of the page, whether it is a page on the screen or a page on the printer. It is important to recognize this because it means that what you see on your screen may look slightly different than what you get from your printer—the number of rows that will fit on a 640×480 screen (and still be readable) is smaller than the number of rows that will fit on an 8.5×11-inch piece of paper. You should take a look at your data in Print Preview mode, which you learned about in Chapter 20, to see on-screen exactly what your data will look like on paper.

Note: Again, the beauty of encapsulated, generic objects shows itself right inside the PowerBuilder environment. Rather than creating a separate PowerBuilder Data Browser to view data from the database, the PowerBuilder Data Manipulation

Painter is essentially nothing more than a DataWindow browser. When you attempt to view data using the Database Painter that we learned about in Chapter 16, or the DBA Painter that we learned about in Chapter 20, all that PowerBuilder does is dynamically create a DataWindow Definition based on the query that you built, using the extended attributes that you saved in the repository. Then it can simply open the Data Manipulation Painter with the DataWindow Definition that it created in the same way it might preview any other DataWindow Definition. The Data Manipulation Painter is really nothing more than a DataWindow previewer. That's why, if you recall, in the Database Painter you can view the contents of your table in Grid, FreeForm, or Tabular layouts—three of the standard DataWindow Presentation Styles.

How do I know this? Well, because the programmers of PowerBuilder at Powersoft were generous enough to give us the ability to do exactly the same thing. We'll learn a little bit about how to dynamically create DataWindow Definitions in our own applications in Chapter 24.

Now that we understand what we are trying to do, let's return to the DataWindow Painter and discuss in detail the means that we have to do it. Close the Data Manipulation Painter, and return to the DataWindow Painter, either by selecting **D**esign from the **D**isplay menu, or by clicking on the Design Button on the Data Manipulation PainterBar. You will then be returned to the DataWindow Painter, with your DataWindow Definition that you began painting earlier on your screen.

Controlling the DataWindow Painter Environment

Once back in the DataWindow Painter, there are a number of settings that you can control to make your environment meet your needs. Surrounding the edges of each of the DataWindow Objects is a gray border that is meant to make it easier to see the size and position of each of your items, especially since they can have transparent background colors. These edge markings will not be visible at runtime, but are there only to help you see what you are doing during development time. However, if you find these markings annoying, you can turn them off by unchecking the Sho**w** Edges menu item from the **D**esign menu. In addition, you can set the tab order for columns in the DataWindow Definition in much the same way that you set the tab order for controls in your window by selecting Tab **O**rder from the **D**esign menu. You can also set the Grid in the same way that you did in the window painter by selecting **G**rid/Ruler from the **D**esign menu. When you select this menu item, you will be presented with the Alignment Grid and ruler dialog box, which looks a lot like the Grid dialog that you saw in the Window

Painter, except that it includes an additional check box, labeled Show Ruler, at the bottom (see Fig. 21.7). If you check this box, the ruler will appear on your DataWindow Painter to help you align your objects on the screen (see Fig. 21.8).

Figure 21.7.
The Alignment Grid dialog box.

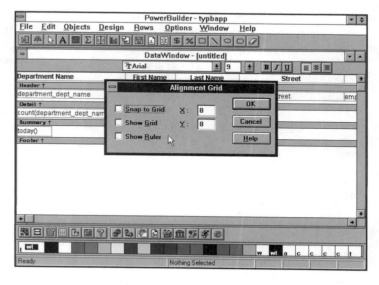

Figure 21.8.
The DataWindow Painter with the ruler.

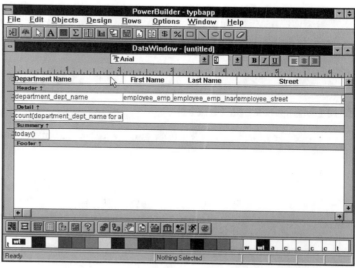

Finally, you can zoom your DataWindow Painter in our out by selecting **Z**oom... from the **D**esign menu. When you do this, you will be presented with the Zoom dialog box, which you also saw back in Chapter 20, when we discussed the Data Manipulation Painter (see Fig. 21.9).

If you change the zoom ratio, the dialog box will explain that Magnification is for view only. When you return to the DataWindow Painter with a new zoom ratio, the magnification will take effect, but all of the other menu items on the menu will be disabled until you reset the zoom ratio to 100%. Of course, to do this, you re-open the Zoom dialog box by again selecting **Z**oom... from the **D**esign menu.

Figure 21.9.
The Zoom dialog box.

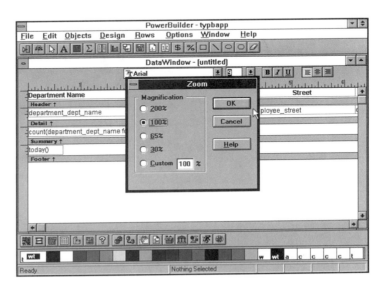

The Attributes of a DataWindow

In addition, you can manage some of the attributes of the DataWindow Definition itself that will be stored with the DataWindow Definition and used to display the data inside of it at runtime. You can set the background color, the pointer, and the units of measure by right clicking with your mouse in an empty area of the DataWindow. In addition, if you double click in the same empty area of the DataWindow, or if you select **D**ataWindow Style from the **D**esign menu, you will be presented with the DataWindow Style dialog box, from which you can set these attributes along with the Timer Interval of the DataWindow (see Fig. 21.10). As with windows, DataWindows also have timers associated with them, and by setting the timer interval, you can cause the timer event of your DataWindow Control to be triggered at regular intervals.

In addition to setting the style of the DataWindow Definition, you can also set its Print Specifications by selecting **P**rint Specifications... from the **D**esign menu (see Fig. 21.11). From the Print Specifications dialog box, you can specify the name that will be displayed in the print queue when data is printed from this DataWindow Definition. You can also specify the margin, in whichever units that you specified in the DataWindow Style. In addition, you can force data that is printed from this DataWindow Definition to use a specific orientation, paper size, or paper source. You can have the system automatically prompt the user with the standard Print dialog box (see Fig. 21.12) before printing the data. Finally, you can set the data to print out in newspaper column style, by specifying the number of columns that you want, as well as the width of each column.

Figure 21.10.
The DataWindow Style dialog box.

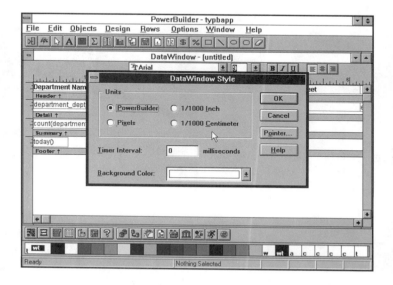

Figure 21.11.
The DataWindow Print Specifications dialog box.

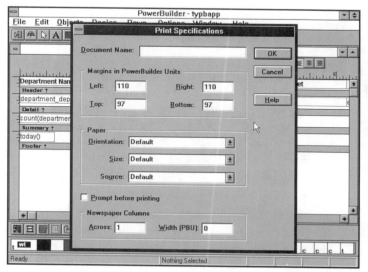

Figure 21.12.
The DataWindow Print dialog box.

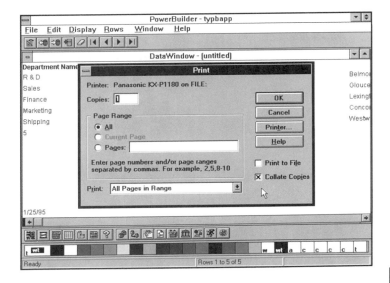

You can save a set of data to be stored right inside the DataWindow Definition by selecting **D**ata... from the **R**ows menu. When you do this, you will be presented with the Data Retained On Save dialog, which contains a spreadsheet-like data entry screen, listing the name of each of your columns in the title (see Fig. 21.13). From this dialog box, you can add, insert, and delete rows of data that will be stored in the DataWindow Definition by clicking on the appropriate button. In addition, by clicking on the **Retrieve** button, you can actually retrieve the result set of this DataWindow Definition into this dialog, and save it in the DataWindow Definition, and even manipulate it first if you want. This is an effective technique for storing static data in your application so that the user does not have to access the database to get it.

If you remember, back when you used the Data Manipulation Painter, you learned that you can sort and filter your data. Well, you can also have your data in your DataWindow sorted and filtered, and you can save a sort order and a filter criteria right inside your DataWindow Definition to do this. You define sort and filter criteria for your DataWindow Definition in the exact same manner that you used to define them in the Data Manipulation Painter. Select **F**ilter... from the **R**ows dialog box to open the Specify Filter criteria dialog box (see Fig. 21.14), where you can define your filter criteria using DataWindow expressions based on the DataWindow Objects that are displayed in the current DataWindow Definition. Select **S**ort... from the **R**ows dialog box to open the Specify Sort Columns dialog box (see Fig. 21.15), where you can define the sort order that will be used to display your data in this DataWindow.

Figure 21.13.
The Data Retained On Save dialog box.

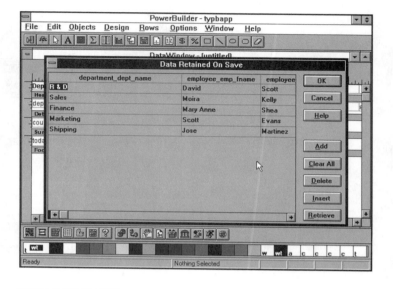

Figure 21.14.
The Specify Filter dialog box.

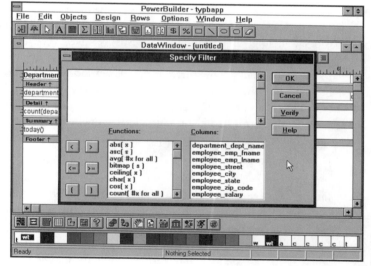

Figure 21.15.
The Specify Sort Columns dialog box.

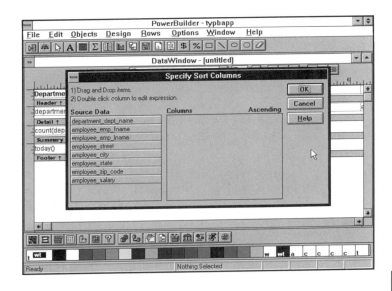

In addition to sorting your data, you may want to make the data in the DataWindow Control look even nicer by *Suppressing Repeating Values*. Suppose, for example, you have 75 employees in five different departments. If you sort on department, and suppress repeating department values, you will see department values displayed only when there is a new department value and on the first row of each page. To turn on suppression of repeated values, select Suppress Repeating **V**alues... from the **R**ows menu, and you will be presented with the Specify Repeating Value Suppression List dialog box (see Fig. 21.16). This dialog box works similarly to the Sort dialog box you just saw. You drag the column whose values you want to suppress from the left side, labeled Source Data, to the right side, labeled Suppression List.

Figure 21.16.
The Specify Repeating Value Suppression List dialog box.

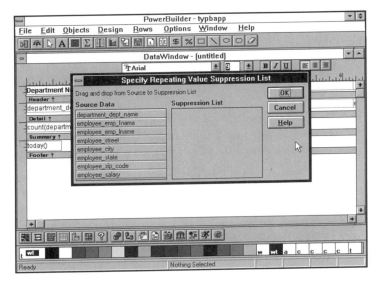

Normally, when you retrieve data into a DataWindow Control, the entire set of data is retrieved from the database and inserted into your DataWindow Control before anything else happens. However, when you have extremely large sets of data, you may want to provide the user with the ability to retrieve it a page at a time instead of all at once, so that the user doesn't have to wait for the entire set of data to come in before he or she can see it. Then, as the user requests to see a new page of data, more is retrieved if it is available. This feature is referred to as *Retrieve As Needed.* You can set your DataWindow Definition to retrieve data only as needed by checking the **R**etrieve Only As Needed menu item from the **R**ows menu.

Warning: There are a couple of rules to be aware of when using Retrieve As Needed. First, you should know that Retrieve As Needed is only useful if there is more than one page of data to be seen; otherwise, all of the data that is needed will be retrieved with the first page, and it won't matter anyway. Also if there is any sort criteria, or front end group definition (which we'll talk about a bit later), the DataWindow Control needs to retrieve all of the data in order to be able to perform the request, and so it will ignore a request to retrieve only as needed. Finally, when a user attempts to close a DataWindow Control that has results pending, you will need to tell the server that you are not interested in the rest of the results by using the DBCancel() function in your script to close the cursor to the database. You can also produce the same effect by turning off retrieve as needed and letting the rest of the data come in.

Additional Criteria Specification

In the real world, applications are generally built not just to display the same data to everyone, but to display specific data based on a user request. For example, all users may not want to see all employees, instead they may just want to see employees from a specific department. Essentially, the user wants to change the WHERE clause slightly so that he will see just the data that he is interested in. The PowerBuilder DataWindow Definition allows you to support this type of query from a user in three ways.

The first manner in which you can support this query is by dynamically changing the SQL statement inside your DataWindow Definition at runtime so that it meets the user's needs. This is a more advanced technique that we will learn about soon enough, in Chapter 24.

Two simpler techniques can be used to perform this operation, then. The first is to build *Retrieval Arguments* into your DataWindow Definition. Retrieval arguments are kind of like variables whose values are passed to the DataWindow Control when it is about to be *Retrieved*, for example, when the DataWindow Control is about to execute its SQL Statement and load up its result set. You can place these retrieval arguments inside of the WHERE clause of your

DataWindow Definition's data source, and when the values are passed in at runtime, they will replace the retrieval arguments in the WHERE clause. For example, we could have the following SQL Statement as our data source for this window.

```
SELECT department.dept_name, employee.emp_fname, employee.emp_lname
    FROM department, employee
    WHERE employee.emp_id = department.dept_head_id
    AND   department.dept_name = :ps_dept
```

Here we are using the exact same SQL Statement that we built early on, but instead have added a single condition to our where clause, where the department name is equal to something called :ps_dept. This thing, ps_dept, is in fact our retrieval argument, and is identified as such by the colon (:) in front of it. When the application runs, it will need to pass the value to use instead of this retrieval argument into the DataWindow (we'll learn how to do this tomorrow). So, if it passes the value R & D into the DataWindow, then the SQL Statement that will retrieve will be

```
SELECT department.dept_name, employee.emp_fname, employee.emp_lname
    FROM department, employee
    WHERE employee.emp_id = department.dept_head_id
    AND   department.dept_name = 'R & D'
```

In order to declare a retrieval argument, we have to go back into our DataWindow Source. To do this, select Edit Data Source... from the Design menu. When you do this, you will be returned to the SQL Builder with the SQL for this DataWindow Definition displayed. From there, you may select Retrieval Arguments... from the Objects menu. You will be presented with the Specify Retrieval Arguments dialog box, where you can specify your retrieval arguments (you can have as many as you want), along with their datatypes (see Fig. 21.17). For our purposes, enter in ps_dept, and specify that it is of type String. Now you can use your retrieval argument in any of your clauses inside the SQL Toolbox. Mostly, though, you will place your retrieval argument inside your where clause. So, to do this, click on the Where tab in the SQL Toolbox, and you will again be presented with the Where page. In the Column column, select "department"."dept_name". Then, in the Values column, you can either type in :ps_dept, or select it from a list of arguments which you can see by right clicking on the column and selecting Arguments.... This option was not available before because we never had any Retrieval Arguments. But now, since we do, it is a valid selection that will bring up a list of valid arguments that you can paste into your Values column. That's really all there is to it.

Now, if you select Design from the File menu, you will be returned to your DataWindow Definition, and it will contain your updated SQL Statement. If you preview your DataWindow now, you will need to specify the value that you want to use for your retrieval argument. Select Preview from the Design menu, or click on the Preview button on the DataWindow PainterBar. Before your DataWindow is populated, the Specify Retrieval Arguments dialog box will appear, and you will need to specify the value you want to use for your ps_dept argument (see Fig. 21.18). If you enter

R & D

then the single row that contains the department head for the R&D department should appear in the resulting DataWindow Control. Each time you re-retrieve your DataWindow, it will again ask for a new retrieval argument. Later, when we talk about using DataWindow Definitions in your applications, you will learn how to specify a retrieval argument in such a way that the user never gets prompted.

Figure 21.17.
The Specify Retrieval Arguments dialog box.

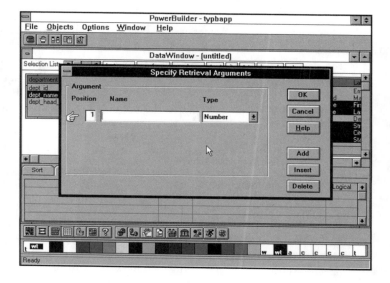

Figure 21.18.
Specifying a value in the Specify Retrieval Arguments dialog box.

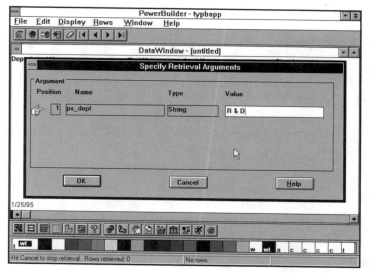

In addition to using retrieval arguments, PowerBuilder offers a feature referred to as *Query By Example* to allow users to specify dynamic query criteria. Query by example works in a similar manner to retrieval arguments, except that you don't specify anything in your WHERE clause. Instead, PowerBuilder prompts you for the criteria that you want to specify using the columns that are selected in the SELECT statement. It then uses your responses to determine how to update your WHERE clause all by itself. Since it knows which values you placed in which DataWindow columns, and how those DataWindow columns correspond to the columns in the database, it can build the WHERE clause based on the criteria you enter. To set up Query By Example, you specify which columns to include in the prompt for query criteria. Select **P**rompt For Criteria... from the **R**ows menu, and you will be prompted with the Prompt For Criteria dialog, where you simply highlight the columns that you want the system to prompt you for (see Fig. 21.19). Then, when you actually go to retrieve this DataWindow, you will be prompted to input the criteria that you want. Any criteria that you input will be appended to the WHERE clause of the query.

Figure 21.19.
The Prompt For Criteria dialog box.

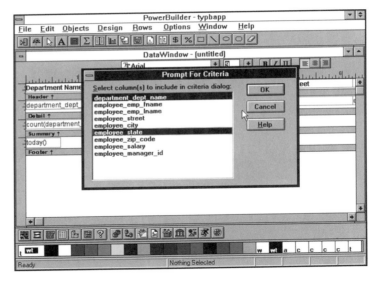

Let's try it. First, let's turn off the retrieval arguments that we set up in the last section. Even though it is legal to have both retrieval arguments and query by example, for this example, the retrieval argument will limit us to one row. So there won't be much to see unless we turn off the retrieval argument. Turn off the retrieval argument by selecting **E**dit Data Source from the **D**esign menu. Then, choose r**e**trieval arguments... from the **O**bjects menu, and delete the retrieval argument by clicking on the **Delete** button. Clear the retrieval argument from the WHERE clause by right clicking on the row in the Where tab of the SQL Toolbox and selecting Clear from the menu. Finally, to demonstrate our point even more, let's change the SQL Statement slightly.

Delete the current Join between the Employee and Department tables by clicking on the join box, and then clicking the **Delete** button from the Join dialog box. Now, create a new join by selecting Joins from the **O**bjects menu, or clicking on the Join button on the SQL PainterBar. Click with your join cursor first on the `dept_id` column of the Department table, and then on the `dept_id` column of the Employee table. This join will show all employees with their department name, instead of all departments with their department head employee information. Now, return to the DataWindow Painter by selecting **D**esign from the **F**ile menu, or clicking on the Design button on the SQL PainterBar.

Once back in the DataWindow Painter, select **P**rompt For Criteria... from the **R**ows menu, and highlight all of the columns listed there and click **OK**. Then, go back into Preview mode to see how it works, select **P**review from the **D**esign menu, or click on the Preview button on the DataWindow PainterBar. You will be presented with the Specify Retrieval Criteria dialog, where you can enter in the criteria you are interested in seeing (see Fig. 21.20). From this dialog box, you specify your criteria by entering values into cells under each column that you want to filter on. For example, if you just want to see people in the R&D department, enter

R & D

into the first cell in the `department_dept_name` column. Then, when you press **OK**, only those rows in the R&D department will be displayed (you should see 22 rows). However, if you wanted to filter only those rows in the R&D department that were in Texas, you could re-retrieve and specify this additional criteria. Select **R**etrieve from the **R**ows menu, or clicking on the Retrieve button on the Data Manipulation PainterBar to re-retrieve. The Specify Retrieval Criteria dialog box will again appear, and will still contain your old criteria in the `department_dept_name` column. Now, tab over to the `employee_state` column, and enter

TX

into the first cell in this column. When you click **OK**, only three rows will be retrieved, because only three employees in the R&D department live in Texas. Now, let's again retrieve the data, but this time, enter

Sales

in the second cell in the `department_dept_name` column. Now, when you press **OK**, you will see 22 rows appear. The rows that came up included employees from the R&D department in Texas, as well as **all** employees in the Sales department. This should indicate to you that each line in the criteria box is essentially an independent line, separated from the previous line by an OR clause, while each column on the line is separated by an AND clause. Therefore, the Texas state criteria that we entered is only used for the same line on which it was placed, ANDed together with the R&D department criteria, while the Sales department is completely separate. In other words, the criteria that was created in SQL would look something like this.

```
AND ( department.dept_name = 'R & D' AND employee.state = 'TX' )
OR  ( department.dept_name = 'Sales' )
```

Figure 21.20.
The Specify Retrieval Criteria dialog box.

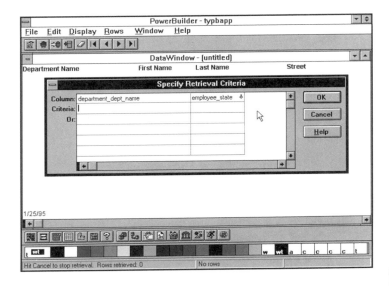

However, perhaps we wanted to see employees from Texas that are in either the R&D or Sales department. Then the criteria would have to be entered slightly differently. One possible way of specifying this query is to add the Texas criteria to the second line of the `employee_state` column in the criteria dialog. While this is legal, and will work, there are several more efficient ways of specifying this criteria all on a single line. Inside this criteria box, entering a value is equivalent to specifying equality. However, you can use relational operators other than equal in your criteria box. Simply specify the operator before the value. For our example above, then, you can remove the word `Sales` from the second line, and instead place the operator >= in front of the term `R & D` on the first line. So, the first line should read,

```
>= R & D
```

Now, when you press **OK**, you will only see five employees who all live in Texas, and work in either the R&D or Sales departments. However, the reason this worked was because we were lucky. There happens to be another department that is greater than or equal to 'R&D' called 'Shipping'. However, there are no employees in that department from Texas, and so we see what we wanted to see, even though it is not what we asked for. Had we wanted to see employees in Massachusetts, though, we would not have been so lucky. Once again, retrieve the data, but this time change the `employee_state` criteria from TX to MA. Now, you will get 39 rows, including nine from the Shipping department. But we don't want to see Shipping! So let's get rid of them by using the proper SQL Statement.

Retrieve your data one last time. This time, we are going to specify exactly what we want. If we were using standard SQL, we would probably say something like this.

```
WHERE department.name IN ( 'R & D', 'Sales') AND employee.state = 'MA'
```

In our prompt for criteria, we can even use an IN clause ourselves. Replace the >= R & D in the department_name column with the following:

```
IN ( 'R & D', 'Sales' )
```

Warning: Be aware, when using your IN clause in the prompt for criteria dialog, if the value that you are specifying is not a numeric value, you will have to place it in quotes, even though you didn't have to when you only entered a single value. This is because the comma (,) is used to separate the values, but is also legal inside of a character-based value, so if you did not enclose your values in quotes, there would be no way to determine whether a comma was part of a value or a separator character.

Now, when you click **OK**, you will see the 30 rows you want, containing only those employees who live in Massachusetts and work in either the R&D or Sales departments.

In addition to using IN clauses in your criteria box, you can also use a LIKE clause. For example, if you wanted to include employees in the states of California and Georgia in the preceding query, you could change the state criteria to read,

```
LIKE _A
```

This would include all states that ended in the letter A in your query. When you executed this query, your result would contain 36 rows. Finally, as we said before, values on the same row but in different columns are by default separated by AND clauses. However, you can override this by placing the word OR in front of your criteria, instead of placing it on a second line. The ability to let the user specify his own criteria in this manner can often be very exciting. In fact, PowerBuilder even gives you, the programmer, the ability to use this method to build your DataWindow sources, using the Quick Select data source that we briefly talked about earlier in this lesson.

Before we move on to the next topic, let's turn off prompting for criteria. Select **D**esign from the **F**ile menu or click on the Design button on the SQL PainterBar to return to the DataWindow Painter. Now, select **P**rompt For Criteria... from the **R**ows menu, and turn off prompting for each of the selected columns by clicking on them and unselecting them. Then, press the **OK** button to accept your changes. Now, let's continue.

Grouping Data

In the last section, we updated our SQL Statement so that we could see all employees with their departments. Then, we talked about ways to filter our data so that we see only one or two departments worth of employees. Now, let's make a report using this data that let's us see all of our employees, but splits them into groups that are of interest to us.

When we talked about the SQL Language a couple of lessons back (in Chapter 19), we mentioned that you can group your data using a special clause, called a GROUP BY clause. However, when you do this using SQL, you only see the summary information for each group and need to build a second SQL Statement to see the details of each row that make up each group. An alternative method of doing this would be to select your entire set of data into the front end (for example, the DataWindow), and build your summary information from the data after it is retrieved. PowerBuilder allows you to do this easily using DataWindow Groups.

To build a group, you select the Create **G**roup... menu item from the **R**ows menu. You will then be prompted with the Specify Group Columns dialog, where you can specify the columns that will make up the group that you want (see Fig. 21.21). For our purposes, let's group our data based on department. Drag the department_dept_name column from the list box labeled Source Data to the list box labeled Columns. At the bottom, you can specify that you want to have a new page between each new group value (for example, department), and/or to have each new group reset the page number to 1. For now, leave these options unchecked, and just hit the **OK** button. When you return to the DataWindow Painter, you will see two new bands appear (see Fig. 21.22). The first one, directly beneath the header band, is labeled

```
1: Header Group department_dept_name
```

The other one, beneath the Detail band, is labeled

```
1: Trailer Group department_dept_name
```

These new bands are there as headers and summaries for the group, and will appear at the beginning and end of each *group break* in the data. A group break occurs when the value for the column in the group criteria changes. So, for example, in our case, when the department name changes, a group break will occur. The previous group's trailer will be displayed, and then the next group's header will be displayed. Let's put some useful data, then, in the header and trailer for our department name group.

Make some room for a group header by dragging the group 1 header band down like you did with the summary and footer band before. Then, move the department_dept_name column from the detail band into the Group 1 Header band by clicking on it and dragging it up into the space that you just created. In addition, let's get some interesting summary information for the group. Select the employee_salary column in the detail band by clicking on it, and then select Sum - Computed Field from the **O**bjects menu, or click on the Sum button on the DataWindow PainterBar. PowerBuilder will place a new field in the Group 1 Trailer band that will show the sum of the salaries in the group. Now, let's also see the number of employees in each group. Select the employee_emp_fname column by clicking on it and select Count - Computed Field from the **O**bjects menu. PowerBuilder will place another field in the group trailer for us that will display the count of the employee first names (which will equate to the count of employees) for the group. The result should look something like the picture in Figure 21.23. In addition to creating the group, we also have to sort our values based on the group columns so that the group breaks occur only once per group. Select **S**ort from the **R**ows menu, and drag the department_dept_name

Σ

column into the Columns list on the left. Now, let's see what it looks like; preview the DataWindow by clicking the Preview button or selecting **P**review from the **D**esign menu. You should see a nice report that shows a list of all of the employees, grouped by department, and a summary line at the bottom of each group that shows the number of employees in that group, and the total salary for those employees.

Figure 21.21.
The Specify Group Columns dialog box.

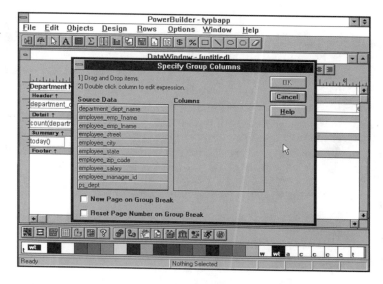

Figure 21.22.
The DataWindow with Group Bands.

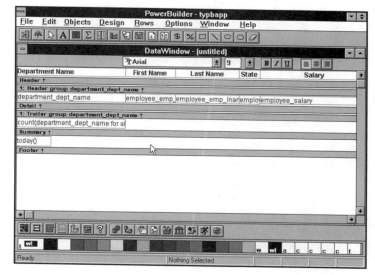

Figure 21.23.

The Department Name as a Group.

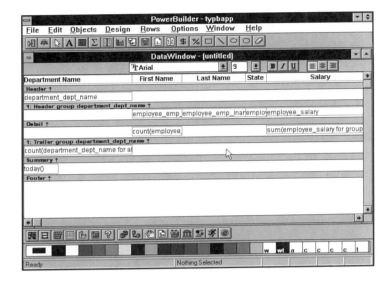

Using Your DataWindow Definition to Update the Database

So far, we have spent quite a bit of time discussing how the DataWindow can be used as a tool for displaying data. But the DataWindow is a data entry tool as well. To use the DataWindow as a data entry tool, you need to tell the DataWindow Definition how to build the proper statements necessary to update your tables. To specify this information, select **U**pdate from the **R**ows menu. You will be presented with the Specify Update Characteristics dialog box (see Fig. 21.24). Here, you can establish whether the DataWindow Definition supports updates or not by checking the Allow Updates check box. Then, you can specify which table will be used to update the database in the Table To Update drop-down list box. At the bottom of the dialog box, you can specify the columns that can be updated by highlighting them in the Updateable Columns list box. You also specify the columns whose values will be used to ensure that the right row is updated by highlighting them in the Unique Key Column(s) list box. You can quickly select the primary key of the update table as the DataWindow key if you click on the **Primary Key** button.

Note: You don't actually have to use the Primary Key of the table being updated as the key of your DataWindow Definition. Whatever columns you select as the key of the DataWindow Definition will be used to determine unique values in the table, even if the table doesn't enforce unique values for these columns.

Figure 21.24.
The Specify Update Characteristics dialog box.

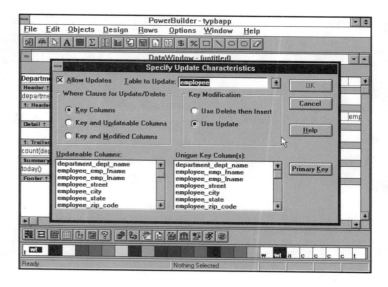

In the middle of the dialog box, you can specify how PowerBuilder will actually perform the update. On the right side, you can choose whether PowerBuilder will use a single UPDATE SQL statement to perform the update, or if it will DELETE the row that is going to be updated, and then immediately INSERT a new row with the new values. At the left side, you can specify whether the WHERE clause of the UPDATE or DELETE statement will use only the key values as the criteria, or if it will include other columns in the criteria, such as any columns whose values were modified or all of the updateable columns in the DataWindow Definition. By customizing your DataWindow Update criteria, you can specify how UPDATE (or DELETE/INSERT) statements will be generated by the DataWindow Control to update changes to the database when the user requests that his changes be saved.

Note: Although the difference between using UPDATE or DELETE/INSERT may seem insignificant, there are some important considerations. UPDATE is generally faster than DELETE/INSERT. In addition, when you use UPDATE, you don't need to include all of the columns in the table in your DataWindow Definition, since UPDATEs to a row can occur regardless of the value of other non-key columns in that row. However, when using DELETE/INSERT, you must include all non-nullable values in the DataWindow Definition in order for the INSERT to work. In addition, if you don't want to lose any values in the update, you will need to include **all** columns from the table. Realize that this holds true if you want INSERTs to work at all.

On the other hand, there is some merit to using DELETE/INSERT, too. When using an UPDATE statement, there is an error that can occur that will not occur when using DELETE/INSERTs. Let's say you attempt to swap the key values of two rows. When the DataWindow attempts to update the first row, it sends a statement to change the key value of the first row to the key value of the second. However, because it hasn't yet updated the key value of the second row, you will get an error that this key already exists. This condition can occur even if you were changing the key value of the second row to something other than the key value of the first. When doing a DELETE/INSERT, however, the DataWindow will first delete both rows, and then insert the rows with the new values, and everything will work fine. Of course, when only one row can be updated by the user at a time before the update is sent to the database, or if the user does not have access to change the key values, then this is not an issue, and you should use UPDATE.

In order for the user to be able to change the values in his DataWindow, you will have to set the tab order of the columns that he can edit to something greater than 0. Oh, and by the way, if you only select columns from one table in your DataWindow Source and also include the primary key of that table, PowerBuilder can figure out which tables and columns to use for updating, and will take care of all of that for you. It will even set your tab order for you. However, if you select more than one table in your data source, PowerBuilder has no way of knowing which table you want to use for updating, or even if you want to have any updates with this DataWindow at all, and so it leaves that up to you.

Morning Summary

You use the PowerBuilder DataWindow Definition to define the structure and layout of the data that will be displayed. PowerBuilder offers three basic sources of data for the DataWindow, from a SQL SELECT statement, from a Stored Procedure, or externally using commands in your scripts. In addition to specifying the data source, you also must specify the presentation style of the DataWindow Definition.

The DataWindow Painter is split into vertical sections, called *Bands*, that each contain different information and serve a different purpose. Inside of these bands you place *DataWindow Objects*. Like the controls that go inside of a window, the DataWindow Objects are the visual components that are placed inside DataWindow Definitions to display information on the screen.

You can preview your DataWindow Definition to see how it will look to the user. When you do this, you will be taken to the Data Manipulation Painter. However, instead of using the PowerBuilder data repository to figure out how to display your data, it uses your DataWindow Definition.

In the DataWindow Painter, there are a number of settings that you can control to make your environment meet your needs. You can show edge markings around your DataWindow Objects to help see where they are on the screen; set the Tab Order of your DataWindow Objects; turn on a grid and a ruler; zoom the magnification of your DataWindow Definition in or out. You can also edit the DataWindow Style and the Print Specifications; save data in your DataWindow Definition with the layout; filter and sort the data in your DataWindow Definition; suppress repeating values. You can also set the DataWindow Definition so that it will only retrieve data from the database as it is requested by the user.

You can also use Retrieval Arguments and Query By Example to dynamically control the data that will be retrieved by the DataWindow Definition. Using Retrieval Arguments, you can let the user supply a value or set of values that will be used in the WHERE clause of the SQL SELECT statement. Using Query By Example, you can prompt the user and let him enter in criteria for selected columns. Finally, you can split your data into groups based on the value of certain columns.

Finally, you can set up your DataWindow Definition so that it can update data that is entered into back to your database. You do this by specifying information about the table to update, the type of update statement to build, the columns that can be updated, and the key to use for the update statement. Since PowerBuilder knows the database names of your columns, it can use this information to build an update statement that will be accepted by the database.

22

Customizing Your Data Windows

In this lesson, you will learn more about how to customize your DataWindow Definitions. This includes:

- ☐ What the different DataWindow Objects are
- ☐ What the different attributes of these DataWindow Objects are and how to change them
- ☐ What computed columns are and how to create them
- ☐ How to specify default values and validation rules for your DataWindow columns

The Attributes of a DataWindow Column

When we first set up the DataWindow Definition, we selected the columns that would be selected from the database and displayed in our DataWindow. In the last lesson, we saw how the placeholders in our DataWindow Definition represented the data as it would appear in our DataWindow Control. Now let's talk about how we can manipulate these DataWindow column placeholders to make the data appear and react in the manner in which we desire.

You've already seen that you can select and move your columns around to different locations within the DataWindow Definition. In addition, there are many other attributes of your DataWindow columns that you can also control. Like window controls, DataWindow Controls have attributes that you set in order to control their appearance. Many of the ways in which you do this are similar or identical to the way that you control the objects in your windows.

Let's start, then, by talking about the mechanics of adjusting your controls. In addition to moving your controls, you can size them by dragging an edge or a corner of your control to the new desired position. When you last previewed your DataWindow Definition, you may have noticed that the Salary sum column wasn't big enough to fit the total salary of one of the departments (see Fig. 22.1). To make enough room, drag the left edge of the Salary sum (labeled Sum(employee in the trailer band of the Salary column) a bit further to the left so that the number will completely fit.

As with the controls on a window, the controls on your DataWindow Definition all have names that are used in your script to identify them. These names appear inside the columns so that they are easily identifiable on the screen. PowerBuilder assigns a default name when you create your DataWindow Definition. If you have selected only one table in your data source, then the default name of the column in the DataWindow will be the name of the column in the database. However, if you have selected multiple tables in your data source, then the default name will be the table name, followed by an underscore (_), followed by the database column name. This ensures unique default column names. However, you can change your column names, just as you can change the names of the controls in your window.

Figure 22.1.
The Total Salary by Department field doesn't always fit.

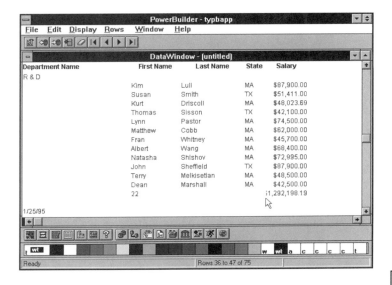

To change the name of a DataWindow Object, you can double-click on the object. For example, double-click on the column in the group 1 header currently called `department_dept_name`. You will be presented with the Column Name dialog box, which currently shows the current name of the column you selected (see Fig. 22.2). Change the name of the object by typing the name in the edit box, and clicking **OK**. Names of columns must be unique, so if you try to enter the name of a column that already exists in the DataWindow Definition, you will receive an error message indicating that the name is invalid or in use (see Fig. 22.3). Instead, let's change the name of the department name column to read `dept_name`.

Figure 22.2.
The Column Name dialog box.

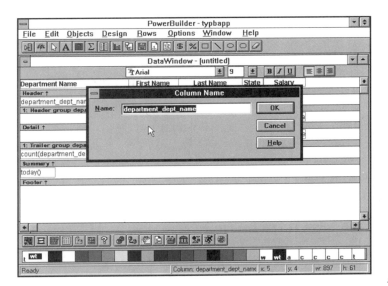

Figure 22.3.
*Column Name is
Invalid or In Use Error.*

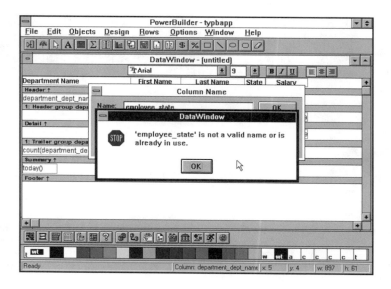

You should notice that the Column Name dialog box that you see in the DataWindow Painter is slightly different than the Control Name dialog boxes that you saw in the Window Painter. Here, there are no other attributes that you can edit from the dialog box as you could in the Window Painter. However, that doesn't mean that there are no other column attributes that you can edit. You can right-click on the column to see a menu of column attributes that you can modify, just as you did in the Window Painter (see Fig. 22.4). In addition, you can select **O**bject Style... from the **D**esign menu, and the right mouse menu will appear next to the currently selected control.

Figure 22.4.
*The Column right
mouse menu.*

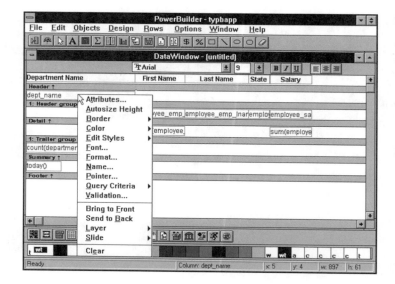

Many of the attributes that you can modify here are similar or even identical to the ones you worked with in the Window Painter. To see this, right-click on the dept_name column that we were working with earlier. For the moment, let's just look at the attributes that you are already familiar with. Skip down to the third attribute, Border. Here, there is a submenu from which you can select the border style of the column. This works in exactly the same manner as the border of controls in the Window Painter. Next is the Color menu item. This menu item also works in the same way as its counterpart in the Window Painter. You can select a color from this menu for the background or foreground of the control. In addition, I should point out that you can also continue to use the ColorBar that appears at the bottom of your screen, as you did in the Window Painter. In the same manner, you can change the font of the text that will appear inside of this control just as you did in the Window Painter, either by choosing **F**ont from the right mouse menu, or by using the StyleBar at the top of the DataWindow Painter. The **N**ame..., **P**ointer..., Bring To **F**ront, and Send To **B**ack menu items also work exactly like their Window Painter counterparts.

The Edit Styles of a DataWindow Column

Now, let's talk about some menu items that may look new to you, but whose functionality you saw when working with the Database Painter. The last time you saw the first six menu items of the **E**dit Styles menu, they appeared as buttons on the Edit Styles Maintenance dialog box. However, when you select any of these menu items, you will see that the dialog box you get is the exact same dialog box that you saw when you were maintaining your edit styles. This time, though, instead of creating new edit styles that will be saved in the repository, you can either assign an edit style to the current column by name (by selecting that edit style's name in the Name drop-down list box), or you can even create your own edit style from scratch. Instead of being saved in the PowerBuilder Repository, the edit style here is saved right in the DataWindow Definition, and will be used to control how your column will be displayed and edited when this DataWindow Definition is displayed in a DataWindow Control.

Note: You can also load a saved edit style from the repository, and then customize it for the column you are working on.

When we talked about maintaining your edit styles, we glossed over one of the edit styles that you can use called the *Drop-Down DataWindow*. Back then, we said that since you didn't know what a DataWindow is, there was no way that we could explain how to use it. Now that you at least have an idea of what a DataWindow is, we can talk a bit about the drop-down DataWindow edit style.

The Drop-Down DataWindow

The drop-down DataWindow is, in many respects, like a drop-down list box. When you build a column with the drop-down list box edit style, you store the list of values that will appear in the list box right in the DataWindow Definition. This is often referred to as *hardcoding* your data values. In practice it is often considered dangerous to hardcode any data-related information into your applications. Imagine if you hardcoded a value of A for Active status, and I for Inactive status in your application. Now, someone decides to change the status code to T for Terminated, and adds L for On Leave of Absence. In order to support this change, you would need to find every place in the code where a status code of I was found, recode it, and then recompile and redistribute your application. This would include any code tables that you may have created for your DataWindow Columns.

Instead of hardcoding your code tables into your applications, you could build your code tables in the database. Then, you could read in the code and decode values from the table, and use them in your application. Then, if someone decided to change the I to a T and an L, all they would have to do is update the code table. Since your application was reading decode information from the code table in the database, it would pick up the change automatically, and be able to deal with the new statuses. In PowerBuilder, there are ways to change the list of values in a hardcoded code table. However, when reading code/decode values from the database, it is much easier to use the drop-down DataWindow.

To create a drop-down DataWindow, you first have to create a DataWindow Definition that will represent the code table and will drop-down like a list box in the main DataWindow. Let's say that we are going to use the department table as a code table. The department ID is the code value, and the department name is the decode or description of the code that the user will understand. Let's create a DataWindow Definition that selects this information from the database. First, save the current DataWindow by selecting **S**ave from the **F**ile menu. You will be prompted with the Save DataWindow dialog box, where you can enter in the name and comments for your DataWindow Definition (see Fig. 22.5). Enter the name

`d_ch22-1`

and the comment

`The Employee/Department Join DataWindow from Chapter 22`

Now, let's build our new department DataWindow. Select **N**ew... from the **F**ile menu, and you will again be prompted with the New DataWindow dialog box. The SQL Select data source and Tabular style should still be selected, so you can just hit **OK**. This time, select only the department table. When the table comes up, select the `dept_id` and `dept_name` columns. Choose **D**esign from the **F**ile menu, or click on the Design button on the SQL PainterBar to create the DataWindow in DataWindow Painter. If you would like, you can preview your DataWindow. Now, save the DataWindow Definition with the name, `d_depts`, and comment, `The Department Drop-Down DataWindow`.

Figure 22.5.
The Save DataWindow dialog box.

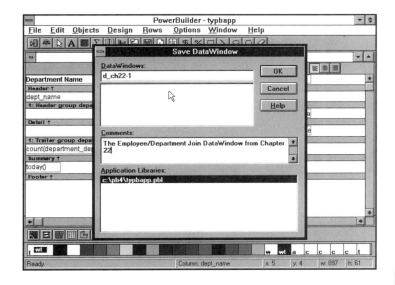

Now, let's create one more DataWindow Definition. This DataWindow Definition will be the main DataWindow that contains the drop-down DataWindow. Select **N**ew... from the **F**ile menu again. Click **OK** again to create a Tabular, DataWindow Definition from a SQL Select. This time, select the employee table. Select the `emp_id` and `dept_id` columns from the employee table, along with the columns from the employee table that you selected last time (`emp_fname`, `emp_lname`, `state`, and `salary`), and then open the DataWindow Definition. Preview your employee DataWindow Definition. Select Preview from the **D**esign menu, or click on the Preview button on the DataWindow PainterBar. As you may have expected, the `dept_id` column contains arbitrary code numbers that correspond to code values in the department table (see Fig. 22.6). Return to the DataWindow Painter by selecting **D**esign from the **F**ile menu.

To make things a little more visually appealing, size the `dept_id` column in the detail band so that its right edge meets the next column in your DataWindow, probably the `state` column. Now, right-click on the `dept_id` column, and select **D**rop-Down DataWindow from the **E**dit Styles menu. You will be presented with the Drop-Down DataWindow Edit Style dialog box that you saw back in Chapter 16 (see Fig. 22.7). In the drop-down list box labeled DataWindow: you can select the DataWindow that will be used as the code table for this column, which in this case is the department DataWindow that we created a moment ago, `d_depts`. Now in the drop-down list box labeled Display Column:, select the column from the drop-down DataWindow that will be used as the decode value. In this case, that will be the `dept_name` column. Finally, in the drop-down list box labeled Data Column:, select the code column, in this case `dept_id`. The other attributes that you can set in this dialog box are common to other edit styles, so we won't focus on them. Instead, click **OK** and let's see how it looks.

Figure 22.6.
The Department ID is really a number.

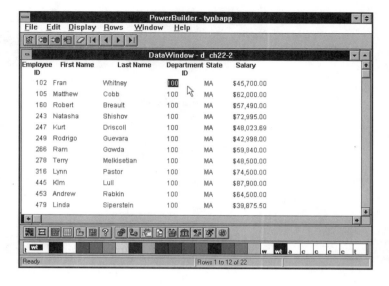

Figure 22.7.
The Drop-Down DataWindow Edit Style dialog box.

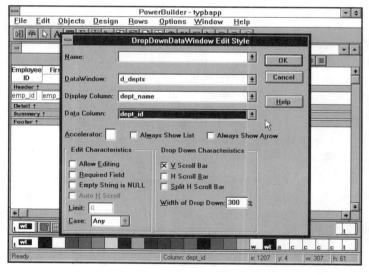

Preview your new employee DataWindow Definition. Select Preview from the Design menu, or click on the Preview button on the DataWindow PainterBar. You will probably need to re-retrieve the data for the changes to take effect, since PowerBuilder caches your last set of previewed DataWindow Painter results in the Data Manipulation Painter. Select Retrieve from the Rows menu, or click on the Retrieve button on the Data Manipulation Painter Bar. This

time, the `dept_id` column contains the names of the departments instead of the department ID numbers. In fact, if you click on the Department ID Column, you can see the drop-down DataWindow itself, with the department information inside of it (see Fig. 22.8). That's all there is to it!

Figure 22.8.

The Department Name as a Drop-Down DataWindow.

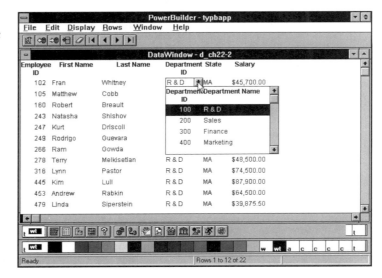

Other Column Attributes

Let's return to our discussion of column attributes. Return to the DataWindow Painter again, selecting **D**esign from the **F**ile menu. Right-click again on any of the columns in the detail band. If you select **F**ormat..., you will be presented with a dialog box that looks a lot like the dialog box you saw when you were maintaining your display formats from the Database Painter back in Chapter 16. The only difference is that the datatype is set to the datatype of the column, and of course you cannot change it. Also, instead of saving your format to the data repository, this format will be used to control how this column is displayed, and nothing else. The **V**alidation... menu item brings up a dialog box that you should also recognize from back in the Database Painter, that lets you build validation rules for the selected column. However, this time, instead of using the `@col` keyword to represent the column value that is typed in, you can use the `GetText()` function, which will return a string containing the data that the user typed. In addition, you can specify column names or numbers to represent other columns in the DataWindow. So, for example, the following would be a legal validation rule for the `salary` column:

```
Real( GetText() ) > 0
```

491

> **Warning:** The GetText() function will return a string value even if the datatype of the column is not a string type. For example, if the column is of type Real, and the user types in a value into this column, the GetText() function returns that value as a string, and you will need to convert it to a Real if you want to use it for anything. (That is why the validation above calls the Real() function.)
>
> At first glance, this may seem like a bug or an annoyance. It is not. The user can type anything into the DataWindow Column, even if it does not match the datatype of the column. A string is the only datatype that will hold all of the possible values that the user can type into a column. By returning the entry as a string, you can check it even if it does not match the datatype of the column.
>
> For example, you may have a Date field on your DataWindow Definition. In order to allow the user to quickly enter in today's date, you might want to allow the user to type **Today**. However, if GetText() returned a Date field, it could not return the value Today. Therefore, you would not be able to validate it and accept it as a legal value, which you would later convert to a legitimate date to prevent any real errors.

There are also a number of new items in the right mouse menu that you have never seen before. The first menu item in the right mouse menu is the Attributes... menu item. When you click on this menu item, you will be presented with the Attributes Conditional Expressions dialog box, which lists all of the column attributes that can be set based on a conditional expression (see Fig. 22.9). This includes things like the color, font, size, and position information. Normally, when you set an attribute of a column, the attribute is set to a specific value. For example, if you set the color of a column to Red, PowerBuilder internally assigns a specific number to that column's color attribute. The number is the RGB value for the color red, which is 255. However, certain attributes can contain expressions as values. For example, instead of setting the color attribute to Red, you can set the color value to be different based on the value of the column. You could set the color value of the salary column to be Red (255) if the salary value were less than 25,000, and Black (0) otherwise. To do this, you right-click on the salary column and select Attributes.... Then, you would search down the list for the Color attribute in the column labeled Attribute. If you double-click on that row, you will be presented with the Modify Expression dialog box (see Fig. 22.10). Here, you can build or enter in your conditional expression, in the same way that you have done in the past. In fact, if you prefer, you can type your expression right into the Attributes Conditional Expression dialog box. The expression that you would use to conditionally change the color of the salary column would look something like this:

```
if( salary < 25000, 255, 0 )
```

Figure 22.9.
The Attributes Conditional Expressions dialog box.

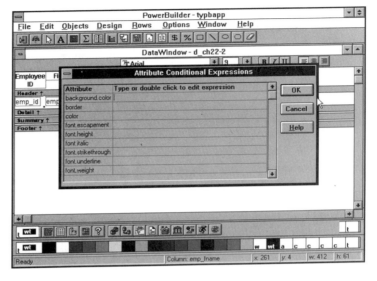

22

Figure 22.10.
The Modify Expression dialog box.

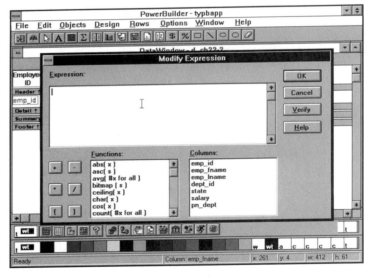

DO	**DON'T**

DO Use conditional expressions for your column attributes when you would like to have a column appear differently on different rows. You can even have one column's data be the value of the attribute of another column.

DON'T Confuse conditional expressions that control attribute values with expressions that make up column values or validation rules. Although they both are expressions that return a single value, the value is used for different things in each of the cases.

Beneath the Attributes... menu item is the **A**utosize Height menu item. If you have a column with the Auto VScroll attribute set, it will automatically word wrap data in that column to the next line. However, if the column is only one line high, then anything that is scrolled down to the next line will be cut off. But you can make the column automatically size its height so that any additional vertical lines of text inside will fit by checking the **A**utosize Height menu item. When you use the Autosize Height feature, the size of the autosized object will never shrink to a height that is less than the height specified in the DataWindow Painter. In other words, let's say you set the height of a column to fit two lines of text, and turn on autosize height. Even if there is only one line of text worth of data in the column, the height will *not* shrink to fit only one line. However, if there are three lines of text, the height will grow to fit all three. You can also autosize the detail band's height so that the detail band will grow to fit long text.

The next new menu item, **Q**uery Criteria, has two submenu items that control how this column will react to Query by Example (for example, when using the Prompt For Criteria dialog box that we talked about in the last lesson). If you check Equality Required, the user will only be permitted to enter in criteria using an equal sign. The user will not be permitted to use any of the other relational operators (<, >, and so on), nor will the user be permitted to use IN or LIKE clauses. If you check the **O**verride Edit menu item, the edit style for this column will not be used for entry, and the user will be able to type things that would be illegal if following the rules of the edit style.

The next new menu item is labeled **L**ayer, and also contains a submenu of different things. The first three items in the submenu are mutually exclusive. They control the layer of the DataWindow on which this object "lives." By default, a DataWindow Object lives in its band— the header, detail, footer, or any other band. However, you can also place objects in the foreground or background. If an object is in the foreground or background, it does not move relative to the page with the rest of the band information, but rather remains stationary in its position relative to the top right of the page. You can use this technique to place "watermark" bitmaps in the background, for example.

Beneath these three menu items are three other menu items. The first, Moveable, allows you to set the DataWindow object so that it can be dragged around inside the DataWindow Control at runtime in almost the same way that you can move your DataWindow Objects now. The second, **R**esizable, allows you to set the DataWindow Object so that its corners and edges can be dragged at runtime to change the size of the object, in the same way that you can size your objects now. The last menu item, **S**uppress After First, prevents the object from appearing in more than one column on a newspaper-column style page.

The last new menu item is the **S**lide menu item. You can set your DataWindow Objects to slide to the next closest object to close any gaps that may exist in a report. For example, let's say that you are making address labels. In your database, you have two street address fields, since some addresses may span two lines. However, most people have only one line for their street address. Normally, when you displayed a record that contained only one address line, you would have a big ugly empty space right between the first address line and the City line. Using the slide feature, though, you can get rid of that empty space by making the fields under it slide up to cover that space. There are actually two steps to setting a slide. First, you can set the slide mode of the columns that you want to slide. Your columns can slide upward or to the left. If they slide up, they can either slide up to cover space left empty from objects directly above them, or you can set it to slide up only if all objects above them have "disappeared." The second step is making sure that objects above (or to the left of) the slide columns actually disappear when they are empty. For standard columns, this involves simply checking the **A**utosize Height attribute. If there is no data in the column, the column will be autosized to disappear only if this attribute is set, and a column beneath it is sliding. However, there are some other objects that you can place in a DataWindow Definition that do not offer the capability to Autosize their height, and so we have to find other ways to make them appear and disappear.

Note: The difference between sliding directly above and sliding all above is subtle, so I wanted to spend a moment to discuss it in more detail. In either case, fields that slide above will slide upward on the page to fill in empty space. If a field is set to slide directly above, the field essentially looks straight up. If it sees room to move up, it moves up as far as it can go until it hits something. If the field is set to slide all above, it still looks up. If it sees room to move up, it moves up. However, it will be stopped by *any* field that is above it, even if that field is not directly in its path. Fields that are to the right and the left block the sliding field from moving upward, too.

22

Note: Although we won't spend much time discussing it, you can also right-click on some other areas of the DataWindow Definition to set attributes. If you right-click on any uncovered portion of the DataWindow Definition itself, you will be able to set the attributes of the DataWindow Definition. In addition, you can set the attributes of the different bands by right-clicking on the bands. All of these attributes that you can set are attributes that you are already familiar with because they are identical to attributes that you have seen for columns. So we won't spend any more time explaining them. You are invited to play with them at your leisure.

Creating Computed Fields

Let's say we want to create a text object (in other words, a label) that disappears if its corresponding data column contains no data. Earlier we talked about using expressions to set conditional attributes. We used conditional expressions to return a single value for specific attribute. One attribute, however, that we did not mention there that can be set is the actual value of the data inside the column. Using a special type of field, called a *computed field*, we can in fact set the data value of the column based on an expression, too.

To create a label that will disappear with its data column, you need to create a computed field whose value is null if its data column's value is null, and contains the text of the label otherwise. The formula to do this for the street column might look something like this.

```
if( IsNull( street), '', 'Street')
```

Which says if the value of the street column is null, then the value of this column is an empty string. Otherwise, the column contains the word Street.

There are many reasons that you might want to create a computed field. If you remember, in the last lesson, we created a few computed fields even though we didn't really know what we were doing. Do you remember? We created objects to figure out the Sum of our salaries, the number of our employees, the number of our departments, and even today's date. All of these are computed fields. Many of the most frequently used computed fields are listed as objects that you can create from the Objects menu. However, you can create just about any computed field that you can dream up by putting your cursor into Create Computed Field mode, and clicking on the DataWindow screen. To put your cursor into Create Computed Field mode, you can either select Computed Field from the Objects menu, or click on the Computed Field button on the DataWindow PainterBar. Then, when you place your computed field, you will be presented with the Computed Field Definition dialog box, which looks quite a bit like the Expression dialog box, except that you can also give your field an optional name at the top of the dialog box if you want to reference it in other places (see Fig. 22.11). Here, you can enter in your expression, and the value it returns will be displayed in your computed field.

Figure 22.11.
The Computed Field Definition dialog box.

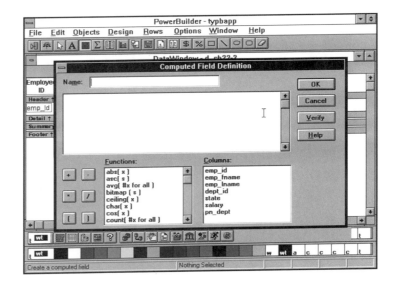

Nested Reports

In addition to data columns and computed fields, you can also place static text objects, pictures, rectangles, lines, ovals, round rectangles, which are rectangles with rounded corners (safe for the kids, you know), graphs, OLE objects, and *nested reports*. With the exception of the latter, all of these objects are simple and straightforward, and do not merit any further discussion. However, we should spend a moment to discuss nested reports, since they are a very useful feature of PowerBuilder, and you may find yourself using them quite frequently.

Nested reports are basically DataWindows inside DataWindows. Earlier we placed data from one DataWindow inside of another by using a drop-down DataWindow. Nested reports, however, allow you to take this a step further. Instead of having just a single display value from your other DataWindow, you can actually have the entire set of data in this other DataWindow be displayed. This is especially useful for master/detail situations where there is a one-to-many relationship between two sets of data.

To create a nested report, you can either select Report from the Objects menu, or click on the Nested Report button on the DataWindow PainterBar. When you do this, you put your cursor into Nested Report Creation mode. If you click on an empty space in the DataWindow Definition, you will be prompted to select the DataWindow Definition that you would like to use as your nested report (see Fig. 22.12). Then your report will appear where you had clicked your mouse, labeled with its report name.

Figure 22.12.
*The Select Report
dialog box.*

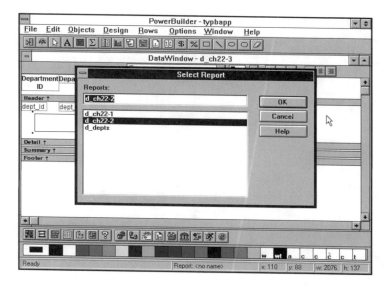

Let's go ahead and create a nested report. Edit the data source of the current DataWindow, and add a retrieval argument called `dept_id` of type number by selecting Retrieval Arguments from the Objects menu, and entering in the appropriate information. Then, add a line to the WHERE clause that has the column `dept_id` equal to the `:dept_id` retrieval argument that you just created. Now, return to the DataWindow Painter. Save the DataWindow Definition as `d_ch22-2`, with a comment of

```
The employee information DataWindow Definition
```

Now, let's go back and open the departments DataWindow Definition, `d_depts`. From the File menu, select Open, and then select `d_depts` from the list. When the DataWindow Definition comes up, drag the detail band down about twice its height. Then, select Report from the Objects menu, or click on the Nested Report button on the DataWindow PainterBar. Now, click in the empty space that you just made in your detail band. When prompted, select the `d_ch22-2` DataWindow Definition that you just created. When you're finished, your screen should look something like the picture in Figure 22.13. To prevent any "accidents," save this DataWindow Definition with a new name, `d_ch22-3` will do, by selecting Save As from the File menu.

This nested report works like a regular column in many respects. For example, if you right-click on the report, you will see that it has a number of attributes, most of which are identical to attributes that you saw for columns in your DataWindow Definition. However, there are two new attributes that you will not have seen before. The first one is the Criteria attribute. When you select this attribute, you are presented with the Specify Retrieval Criteria dialog box that you saw before when we talked about Prompting for criteria. The criteria that you can specify is for the nested report, not for the base DataWindow Definition.

Figure 22.13.

*The Department Master
with Employee Detail
Nested report.*

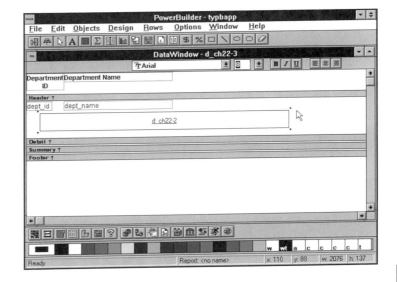

Additionally, there are two new menu items, **C**hange Report and **M**odify Report. The former allows you to change the report that will display inside your nested report DataWindow Object by prompting you again with the Select Report dialog box. The latter will allow you to actually edit the DataWindow Definition that makes up the nested report by opening the DataWindow Painter with that DataWindow inside. Finally, the last menu item is the Retrieval Ar**g**uments menu item. Using this menu item, you can set the value that will be used as the retrieval argument(s) for your nested report. When you click on this menu item, you will be presented with the Retrieval Arguments dialog box (see Fig. 22.14). However, this time, instead of typing in a value as the value of the retrieval argument, you can use any DataWindow expression, including the name of a column, in your base DataWindow. In other words, you can make the nested report relate directly to the data in the base report. For example, in our case, we want the nested employee report to list employees for a particular department. The employee DataWindow takes a single argument, pn_dept. In order for this DataWindow to work as a master-detail report, we must make the employee DataWindow retrieve all employees with a department ID that matches the department ID of the current row. So, as the value that will be used for the pn_dept argument, we must select the dept_id column from the list. This means that if the current row's department ID is 100, then the DataWindow will retrieve all employees whose department ID is 100 after this row. In order to really understand how this works, preview the results of this DataWindow Definition by selecting Pre**v**iew from the **D**esign menu, or clicking on the Preview button on the DataWindow PainterBar. You should be presented with a screen that looks a lot like that in Figure 22.15.

22

Figure 22.14.
The nested report Retrieval Arguments dialog box.

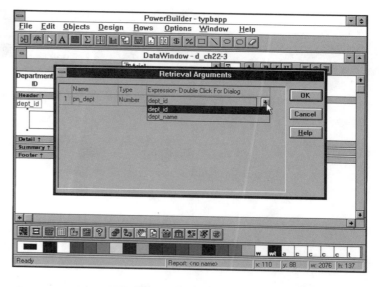

Figure 22.15.
The Department/Employee nested report.

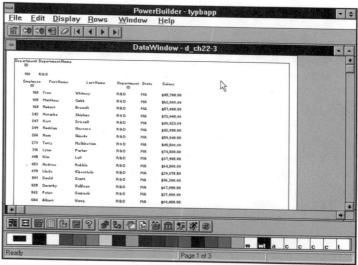

When you preview your nested report, pay attention to the status bar. If you pay attention, you'll notice that it actually retrieves the 5 department rows, and then it separately retrieves the data for the nested report (75 more rows). Now see what we've come up with. Each section contains a department number and name. Beneath that, tabbed over a bit, is a list of all of the employees

in that department. After the list of employees is the next department, followed by its employees, and so on. The list of departments is the master report, followed by the details of each department in the employee report. Although in this particular case there are other (and probably better) ways of listing this data, in the case of a real master-detail report you will find this feature most useful. After you are finished perusing the nested report, go ahead and return to the DataWindow Design by selecting **D**esign from the **F**ile menu.

> **Warning:** Notice, by the way, that when you opened the Data Manipulation Painter to preview your DataWindow Definition, it automatically came up in Print Preview mode. In fact, if you open the **F**ile menu, you will see that you cannot turn Print Preview mode off. Nested reports in PowerBuilder can only be viewed in Print Preview mode. Also, you should know that you can actually nest your nested reports more than one level. In other words, you could take the nested report that you just made, and use that as a nested report in another DataWindow. Then, you could take that nested report, and use it as a nested report in yet another DataWindow, etc.

22

Column Specifications

Well, after you have spent all this time working with your DataWindow Definition, perhaps you have deleted some columns, created some additional DataWindow objects, and given new names to your DataWindow columns. Maybe with all of this confusion, you have forgotten which DataWindow columns point to which database columns! Or maybe you just want to see a concise listing of the columns in your DataWindow with some important information about them. Well, you can see the specifications for each of the columns in your DataWindow by selecting **C**olumn Specifications... from the **R**ows menu. You will then be presented with the Column Specifications dialog box, which contains a list of the columns that are contained in this DataWindow Definition (see Fig. 22.16). In addition, for each column, it displays the column number, datatype, initial value, validation rule and error message, and database column name. The initial value and validation information that appear will be based on the initial value and validation settings in the database. However, you can change them here simply by typing values into the appropriate columns.

Figure 22.16.

The Column Specifications dialog box.

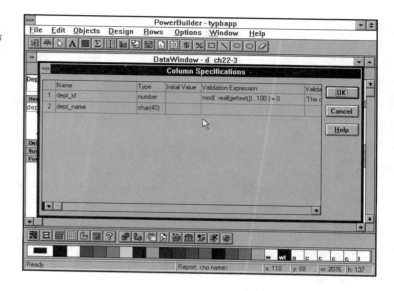

Afternoon Summary

Like window controls, DataWindow controls have attributes that you set in order to control their appearance. Moving and sizing your DataWindow Objects works the same way as it does in the Window Painter. You can change the name of the DataWindow Object by double-clicking on it. You can use the right mouse menu to edit other attributes of the DataWindow Object. Many of the attributes of the DataWindow Object are identical to attributes that you have seen in other places, like Name, Border, Color, and Font. You can also set the edit style, display format, and validation rule of your DataWindow columns from the right mouse menu.

In addition, you can set some attributes of a DataWindow Object based on a conditional expression, so that the attribute value is calculated dynamically at runtime. You can override how a column will react in a Prompt For Criteria dialog box. You can move a column to the background or foreground of the DataWindow Definition. You can make the column moveable or resizeable. You can force it to appear only once per row in a DataWindow Definition that has newspaper-style columns. You can also have your column slide up or left to fill in any gaps that may have been left by empty columns above or to the left of it. Using a *computed field* you can set the data value of the column based on an expression. You can create a nested report which is essentially a DataWindow contained in a DataWindow. Then, you can tie the criteria of the nested report to its parent DataWindow so that there is a relationship between the data in the two DataWindows. You can see a summary of the columns in your DataWindow Definition that includes information about which database columns each of your columns maps to, as well as default and validation information.

Q&A

Q I understand that extended column attributes are stored in the PowerBuilder repository on the database, but when I use them in a DataWindow are they applied at the database level?

A No, they are local to the DataWindow, a part of DataWindow intelligence. When you create your DataWindow Definition, extended column attributes are copied from the table column attributes and can be overridden in the DataWindow Painter. A good example of this occurs with validation rules, when a user enters a numeric field on a DataWindow that has a validation rule `Real(GetText()) > 0`, then the value entered must be a number, greater than zero. If the user tries to modify the field with an invalid number, a validation error message appears without any database access. The validation rule and message are both part of the DataWindow.

Q Is there any way to make computed fields reference other computed fields in the DataWindow Painter?

A Yes, PowerBuilder allows DataWindow expressions to reference other computed fields by name. When you create a computed field in the DataWindow Painter design screen, give it a name so that computer fields, sort expressions, group expressions and other DataWindow expressions can reference its value.

Q Within DataWindows, does the tab order just navigate the user between the fields?

A Yes and no. While tab order will navigate the user between fields in a fixed sequence, setting the tab order of a field to zero will prevent the user from modifying it. So not only will the field not be part of a tab sequence, but the field can never be modified directly by the user. They can, however, still be modified by the application in code. Master DataWindows in master, detail arrangements, and reports generally have the tab order on all the columns set to zero.

Q I created sort and filter criteria for a DataWindow then previewed it and modified some rows. Because I modified column values that I was using in the sort and filter criteria, I was surprised that the rows did not become sorted or filtered. Why did this happen?

A In the DataWindow Painter, both sort and filter criteria are only applied when data is retrieved from the database, or when new criteria is defined and applied automatically. Row insertions, modifications to columns and DataWindow updates will not cause the sort or filter criteria to be applied.

Q I created a DataWindow with some columns in the result set that I don't want users to see. Is there a way to hide these columns?

A Just delete them, press the **Delete** key when the column is selected in design mode or right-click on the column and select Clear. Deleting the column from layout of the

DataWindow Definition will not eliminate it from the result set. It will still have information stored in the DataWindow buffers like any visible column. If you want to place the column back on the DataWindow, then select Column from the Objects menu and click on the DataWindow where you want to place the column. The Select Column dialog box displays and allows you to select the column to place.

Q Can I modify and update a Composite report?

A Reports are generally not updateable. You will get the message "DataWindow does not have UPDATE capability" when you attempt a DataWindow update. Print preview mode, which is the only mode that can be used to display Composite and Nested reports, also does not allow the user to select and modify row information.

Q Is there another way, other than setting the tab order to zero, to prevent a user from modifying a column?

A Yes. The Protect attribute enables you to control user access to a field without modifying the tab order. This attribute can be set at the item level. In the DataWindow Painter, right mouse click on the column you want to modify the Protect attribute for and select Attributes... from the popup menu. When the Attribute Conditional Expressions dialog box opens, scroll down to the protect attribute and enter a value or expression. A value of 1 causes the item to be protected, and a value of 0 turns the attribute off.

Workshop

Quiz

1. Where will the items in the summary and footer bands of a DataWindow Definition appear when viewed?

2. What happens when a DataWindow Definition that expects arguments is retrieved without specifying values for these arguments? If there are a different number of arguments supplied than expected? If the argument datatypes don't match?

3. In addition to creating the groups themselves, what else must you do to properly present DataWindow information in a group format?

4. What mode are Composite and Nested reports viewed in?

5. Do you have to select a name from the Name drop-down list box when you are modifying a column's edit style in the DataWindow Painter?

6. What is a good reason to use a drop-down DataWindow instead of a drop-down list box in your DataWindows?

Putting PowerBuilder into Action

1. Go back and open the d_ch22-1 DataWindow Definition into the DataWindow Painter.
2. Create a new group. The new group will contain the employee_state column.
3. Add the employee_state column to the end of the sort specification.
4. Move the employee_state column DataWindow Object into the new group header band.
5. Change the background color of the DataWindow Definition to gray. Then, select all of the columns in the DataWindow, and change their border to 3D Lowered.
6. Change the employee_state column so that it does not use the edit style of the column when querying for criteria.
7. Turn Prompt For Criteria on. Select the Department name and State columns.
8. Preview your new DataWindow. Enter in different criteria values. It should now have your employees, grouped by state within department.
9. Turn off Prompt For Criteria before you save the DataWindow Definition because we won't want it on for the next lesson.

22

Chapter

23

DataWindow
Controls

In this lesson, you will learn how to take the DataWindow definition that we spent so much time learning about in the last lesson and use it in your application to display and edit data. You will learn:

- [ ] What the different DataWindow Control Attributes are
- [ ] What transaction objects are and how to use them
- [ ] The commands that you use to load and save your data
- [ ] The important events that occur in a DataWindow Control
- [ ] Some important DataWindow functions

Putting Your DataWindow into Your Window

After you have defined the layout of your DataWindow in your DataWindow Definition, you will want to display data using this layout in a window. You place a *DataWindow Control* in your window that will display the data using your DataWindow Definition. Then, you code the behavior of your DataWindow Definition in the DataWindow Control.

Open up the Window Painter by pressing **Shift-F2** or by clicking on the Window Painter on the PowerBar. Select the sheet that we created earlier, w_sheet_01, from the window. Now, you can place a DataWindow Control on your sheet by selecting **D**ataWindow from the **C**ontrols menu, or by clicking on the DataWindow Control button on the Window PainterBar. When you do this, your cursor goes into DataWindow Control Creation mode. Click in an empty space on the window, and an empty box will appear. This is the DataWindow Control, a shell that will hold a DataWindow Definition. If you double-click on this shell, you will be prompted to select the DataWindow Definition that will be contained within this shell with the Select DataWindow dialog box (see Fig. 23.1). Select the DataWindow that we created way back in Chapter 21, d_ch22-3. If you remember, this DataWindow contained a list of employees grouped and totaled by their department. This DataWindow Definition will be the *dataobject* attribute of the DataWindow Control.

DataWindow Control Attributes

After you click the **OK** button, you will be prompted with the DataWindow attributes dialog box, where you can modify the attributes of the DataWindow Control (see Fig. 23.2). Here, you can specify the name that will be used in your script to reference this DataWindow Control by typing it in the edit box labeled Name:. You can also specify the title of the DataWindow Control by entering it into the edit box labeled Title:. In addition, there are check boxes that you'll see beneath these two edit boxes that you are probably already familiar with. By changing the state of these check boxes, you can set whether your DataWindow Control is Visible, Enabled, or

Resizable. You can specify if it has a Title Bar, Control Menu, Maximize Box and Minimize Box, Horizontal Scroll Bar, and Vertical Scroll Bar. You can specify the type of Border it will have. Finally, there are two new attributes that you have never seen before that you can check here: Live Scrolling and Horizontal Split Scrolling.

Figure 23.1.

The Select DataWindow dialog box.

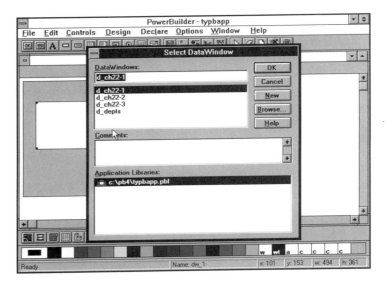

Scrolling, as you probably already know, is the process of paging through your data with the scrollbars. One manner in which you can page through your data is by dragging the *thumb*, the little square that shows your current scroll position, to a new position inside the scrollbar. If Live Scrolling is unchecked, then nothing will happen between the time you pick up the thumb and start moving it until the time that you drop the thumb on its new position, at which point the screen will "jump" to the new scroll position. If, however, Live Scrolling is checked, then the screen will scroll with the thumb. As you drag the thumb up, the screen will scroll up; and as you drag the thumb down, the screen will scroll down. Split scrolling allows you to split the scrollbar into two panes, each of which can be scrolled independently to display a different set of data from the page (see Fig. 23.3). This is very useful for large (wide) reports, that contain key information in the leftmost columns, and additional information along the row. You can split your DataWindow horizontally, leave the key information displayed in the left pane, and scroll through the data in the right pane, without having to worry about getting "lost."

In addition to these attributes, and the "usual" buttons that you see on a window control attribute dialog box, there is one additional button labeled **Change...** that when clicked, displays the Select DataWindow dialog box that you saw before. This allows you to change the data source and layout of this DataWindow Control by selecting a different DataWindow Definition to point to. Remember, the DataWindow Control is just a shell that is used as an interface between the Window and the source and layout of your data that you defined in the

DataWindow Painter. Although user interface behavior will be encoded into the DataWindow Control, the data source, structure, presentation, and layout are stored in the Data-Window Definition. And so, the DataWindow Definition is simply an attribute of the DataWindow Control.

Figure 23.2.

The DataWindow Control Attributes dialog box.

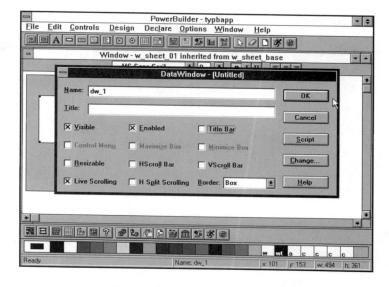

Figure 23.3.

A DataWindow using Split Scrolling.

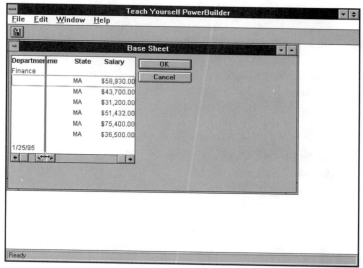

Note: I keep repeating this because you *must* understand the difference between a DataWindow Control and a DataWindow Definition if you want to take full advantage of this most powerful PowerBuilder feature.

While we're here, go ahead and change the name of this DataWindow to `dw_detail`. Give the DataWindow Control Horizontal and Vertical scrollbars. Make sure it is visible, and will scroll live.

Note: Like other window controls, you can also use the right mouse button to modify the attributes of the DataWindow Control if you prefer.

Transaction Objects to Talk to the Database

Once you have placed the DataWindow Control in your window and set up its attributes, you'll want to use the DataWindow Control to load, edit, and save data. There are several ways that you can get data into a DataWindow, but the most common method is to have it load data from the database based on the SQL Select of its dataobject. If you remember, when we talked about the Database Painter, we said that before you can work with your database, you need to connect to it. The Database Painter needs to know the "name and telephone number" of the database that you are working with so that it can make the proper "telephone call" to the DBMS.

In the same manner, in your application (for example, at runtime) you will need to connect the DataWindow Control to the database so that it knows the "name and telephone number" of the database that it is talking to. At runtime, there is no more Database Painter, however, and so the way in which you connect your DataWindow Control to a database is by using something called a *Transaction Object*. A transaction object is a PowerBuilder object that holds information about the connection to the database. Among other things, it contains attributes to hold the same things that you set up in your database profile. This includes the name of the DBMS, the name of the database (for example, the data source), the user ID and Password, and the Database Parameter string that contains the ConnectString that we discussed when we talked about connecting to the database. There are also several other attributes that you can set to control your database connection that we'll talk about in just a minute. You set these attributes just like any other object in code, by using dot notation to represent the object and attribute name, followed by an equal sign (=) and the value that will be assigned to that attribute.

23

SQLCA—The Default Global Transaction Object

If you recall, way back in the beginning of the book, we talked about the Default Global Variables that you can set in your Application Object, and you saw something called *SQLCA* that was defined as a transaction object. Well, that transaction object is the same transaction object that we are talking about here. SQLCA is a global instance of that transaction object that PowerBuilder sets up for you in all of your applications. You can also declare your own instances of your transaction object and instantiate them using the CREATE and DESTROY statements that you learned about when we talked about user objects. You can even extend the transaction object definition by defining a transaction object User Object, as we discussed in Chapter 14. But for the purpose of this lesson, let's stick to the use of SQLCA as the transaction object to prevent any confusion.

The Attributes of a Transaction Object

Table 23.1 lists the names and descriptions of each of the attributes that you can set for a transaction object. Some of these attributes are DBMS specific, meaning that the values they can accept are based on the DBMS you are using. We'll concentrate on the settings that you use for the ODBC driver to Watcom SQL because this is the package that comes with PowerBuilder. However, you can look in the PowerBuilder documentation to see what other settings are available for your DBMS.

Table 23.1. The Attributes of a Transaction Object.

Attribute Name	Description
Sent By User	
DBMS	The DBMS name (ODBC, ORACLE, Sybase, and so on).
Database	The name of the database to which you are connecting. (Not used in ODBC.)
ServerName [†]	The name of the server on which the database resides. (If you are using Watcom on a local machine, you can leave this blank.)
UserId	The User ID that will be used to logon to the database.
DBPass	The password that will be used to logon to the database.
DBParm [†]	Additional parameters that are passed to the database. For example, you can pass the ODBC ConnectString here to tell the ODBC driver which data source to use.
LogId [†]	The name or ID of the user who will log on to the server. (Not used for ODBC/Watcom.)

Table 23.1. continued

Attribute Name	Description
LogPass [†]	The password used to log on to the server. (Not used for ODBC/Watcom.)
Lock [†]	The lock isolation level. This has to do with how the DBMS will handle multiple users trying to access the same data at the same time.
AutoCommit	Whether PowerBuilder commits Database commands to the database automatically. If this value is FALSE (the default), PowerBuilder does not commit your database statements for you, and you must COMMIT or ROLLBACK your database statements yourself. If this value is TRUE, all database statements in your application will automatically be committed to the database immediately after they are executed, and you cannot ROLLBACK multiple statements, unless you perform your own transaction control with the database manually.
	Returned By DBMS
SQLCode	The result of the last Database command. A value of 0 means the Database command succeeded. A value of -1 means there was an error (you can then use the SQLDBCode and SQLErrText attributes to get the error code and error message). A value of 100 means the DBMS did not return any results.
SQLNRows [†]	The number of rows reported by the DBMS to have been affected by the Database command.
SQLDBCode [†]	The error code reported by the DBMS.
SQLErrText [†]	The text of the error message reported by the DBMS.
SQLReturnData [†]	Stores other information returned from the DBMS.

[†] May be different for other DBMSs

The table lists two types of transaction object attributes: *Sent By User* and *Returned By DBMS*. The former transaction object attributes are set by the developer in order to control how the database connection works. They control things like the login information, the name of the database, and the AutoCommit setting, which determines how PowerBuilder manages transactions. In your code, you will set these attributes before connecting to the DBMS to arrange for your "telephone line" to the database. Some of these settings (like AutoCommit) are used by PowerBuilder to control how each Database command is executed, and their value can be changed after you connect.

The DBMS sets the *Returned By DBMS* transaction object attributes in response to database commands that you execute in your application code. They return information like execution results, number of rows affected, and error information. In your code, you will read the values of these attributes to get information back from the database after executing a Database command. For example, the PowerBuilder database command that is used to connect to the database is coded as follows:

```
CONNECT USING SQLCA;
```

Note: Because SQLCA is the default global transaction object, PowerBuilder will use it even if you don't specify it by name, as in the following line of code:

```
CONNECT;
```

However, it is always preferable to prevent confusion by naming SQLCA explicitly, especially if you use multiple transaction objects in your application.

After you execute this command in your script, you will need to find out if it actually works. PowerBuilder interprets this command as a database command, reads the information that you set in the transaction object SQLCA, and performs whatever actions necessary to attempt to connect to the DBMS according to the information stored in SQLCA. Then, it fills the SQLCode attribute of SQLCA with a return code. If the connection succeeds, PowerBuilder sets the SQLCode to 0; otherwise, it sets SQLCode to -1, stores the error code that is returned by the DBMS in the SQLDBCode attribute, and stores the error message that is returned by the DBMS in the SQLErrText attribute. Now you can read the values out of these attributes to determine if your connection attempt was successful; and if it wasn't, you can find out what caused the failure.

As was briefly mentioned before, you can communicate with your transaction object using dot notation. You can set and read the values in this manner. The following code demonstrates how you might prepare a transaction object to connect to the PowerBuilder Demo Database that comes with PowerBuilder in the code of your application. This code also demonstrates the actual connection statement, as well as code to evaluate and respond to a connection error.

```
// Set up the SQLCA Parameters
SQLCA.DBMS="ODBC"
SQLCA.UserID="dba"
SQLCA.DBPass="sql"
SQLCA.DBParm="ConnectString='PowerBuilder Demo DB'"

// Attempt To Connect
CONNECT USING SQLCA;

// Check the Connection Return Code
IF SQLCA.SQLCode < 0 THEN
   MessageBox( "Database Error #" + String( SQLCA.SQLDBCode), SQLCA.SQLErrText)
END IF
```

This code sets the DBMS, Database, UserID, and DBPass attributes of SQLCA, and then attempts to connect. If the SQLCode returned is less than 0 (in other words, -1), then it displays a Message Box that shows the database error number and the database error message (see Fig. 23.4).

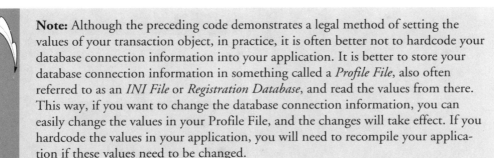

Note: Although the preceding code demonstrates a legal method of setting the values of your transaction object, in practice, it is often better not to hardcode your database connection information into your application. It is better to store your database connection information in something called a *Profile File*, also often referred to as an *INI File* or *Registration Database*, and read the values from there. This way, if you want to change the database connection information, you can easily change the values in your Profile File, and the changes will take effect. If you hardcode the values in your application, you will need to recompile your application if these values need to be changed.

PowerBuilder supplies a script that you can quickly paste into your application that will use the ProfileString function to read in SQLCA values from the PowerBuilder-supplied *PB.INI* file. This script is called *SQLCA.SCR* and can be pasted into your script by selecting **I**mport from the **F**ile menu of the Script Painter. This script reads as follows, but you can change it to meet your needs (for example, to read from a file other than PB.INI):

```
// This script will read all the database values from PB.INI
//   and store them in SQLCA.
SQLCA.DBMS       =ProfileString("PB.INI","Database","DBMS",              " ")
SQLCA.Database   =ProfileString("PB.INI","Database","DataBase",          " ")
SQLCA.LogID      =ProfileString("PB.INI","Database","LogID",             " ")
SQLCA.LogPass    =ProfileString("PB.INI","Database","LogPassword",       " ")
SQLCA.ServerName =ProfileString("PB.INI","Database","ServerName",        " ")
SQLCA.UserID     =ProfileString("PB.INI","Database","UserID",            " ")
SQLCA.DBPass     =ProfileString("PB.INI","Database","DatabasePassword",  " ")
SQLCA.Lock       =ProfileString("PB.INI","Database","Lock",              " ")
SQLCA.DbParm     =ProfileString("PB.INI","Database","DbParm",            " ")
```

23

In general, you will need to determine the best place to connect to your database. You can set up the SQLCA transaction object once in the Open event of your Application Object and even connect there. Or, if you prefer, you can place your CONNECT statement in front of each database command and then disconnect from the database immediately after you execute your database command using the DISCONNECT command. For now, though, let's just connect once when the application starts and disconnect when the application exits.

Open the Application Painter by pressing **Shift-F1** or by clicking on the Application button on the PowerBar. Then, edit the application script by selecting **S**cript from the **E**dit menu or by clicking on the Script button on the Application PainterBar. Right now, there should be only one line of code in this script that reads

```
Open( w_mdi_frame)
```

Figure 23.4.
The Database Error
Message Box.

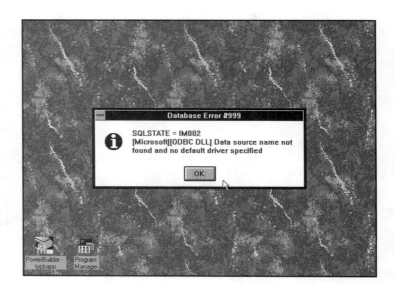

Replace that code with the following:

```
// Set up the SQLCA Parameters
SQLCA.DBMS="ODBC"
SQLCA.UserID="dba"
SQLCA.DBPass="sql"
SQLCA.DBParm="ConnectString='PowerBuilder Demo DB'"

// Attempt To Connect
CONNECT USING SQLCA;

// Check the Connection Return Code
IF SQLCA.SQLCode < 0 THEN
   // Error - Display Error Information
   MessageBox( "Database Error #" + String( SQLCA.SQLDBCode), SQLCA.SQLErrText)
ELSE
   // No Error - Open the MDI Frame.
   Open( w_mdi_frame)
END IF
```

This code will attempt to connect to the database. If it succeeds, it will open the MDI Frame as normal; otherwise, it will display the database error message in a Message Box and then exit. Now, have the database disconnect from the database when the application closes by changing to the Close script (from the Select Event drop-down list box) and by entering the following line of code:

```
DISCONNECT USING SQLCA;
```

Warning: The code that you placed in the Open Script of the Application functionally will work and is logically laid out. However, when you implement this code, the user will be waiting at an empty screen while the system attempts to connect to the database. If the connection is successful and the database is already started, this may not be all that bad because the user will not have to wait long at all. However, if there is a problem, either with the settings or the database itself, and the connection is not available, the system may take as long as a minute or even longer before it "gives up." If this happens, the user will basically be staring at the blank screen of a locked up machine for a full minute and will probably think that there was some problem starting the application itself and will reboot.

Alternatively, you can open the MDI Frame first, before you attempt the connection. Then, you could perform the connection after the MDI Frame is opened and close the MDI Frame if the connection fails. You could even post some message to the user indicating that you are attempting to connect. In doing so, the user knows what is going on and isn't afraid that the system is locked up. Furthermore, the user can better understand what is causing the problem if there is no connection because it will be clear that the problem is during connection time, and not part of the application startup itself.

Close the script painter by selecting **R**eturn from the **F**ile menu or by clicking on the Return to Application Painter button on the Script PainterBar. Then, save your changes to the application object by choosing **U**pdate from the **F**ile menu or by clicking on the Return button on the Application PainterBar. Now, your application is database active, and you can use the SQLCA transaction object to talk to the PowerBuilder Demo Database.

Note: Instead of using the global SQLCA transaction object, you may want to use your own transaction object for a variety of reasons. For example, you may have more than one database or server that you want to connect to, and so you create a transaction object in the manner described in Chapter 14. First, declare a variable of type transaction (or of the type of transaction user object that you may create in the User Object painter). Then, create it using the CREATE statement. Finally, when performing your embedded SQL Statements, including CONNECT, COMMIT, and ROLLBACK, refer to your transaction object in the command instead of the default SQLCA transaction object. The following example demonstrates the process:

```
Transaction ltrx_pb_db
ltrx_pb_db = CREATE transaction
// Set up the transaction settings, and then connect
CONNECT USING ltrx_pb_db;
```

Setting the Transaction Object of a DataWindow Control

After your transaction object is connected to the database, you can use that transaction object as a telephone line for your DataWindow Control to talk to the database. To do this, you assign the transaction object to the DataWindow Control. There are two PowerBuilder functions that you can use to do this: the SetTrans() and SetTransObject() functions. The difference between the two is small, but not insignificant. Both are used to assign a transaction object to a DataWindow Control, and accept as a parameter a reference to a transaction object. When you use the SetTransObject() function, your transaction object is used directly by the DataWindow to communicate with the database. However, when using the SetTrans() function, a *separate* copy of your transaction object is automatically created and used by the DataWindow Control. The new transaction object automatically connects to the database before each database command, and then disconnects from the database after the command is completed. While the SetTrans() method is slightly easier on the programmer, it also is slower and provides less control and so should be used sparingly. Use the SetTransObject() function if at all possible.

The format for both functions is as follows:

```
<DataWindow Control name>.SetTrans[Object]( <Transaction Object Name>)
```

Place the following code in the Open event of your w_sheet_01 window to assign the SQLCA transaction to the DataWindow that you placed in the window:

```
dw_detail.SetTransObject( SQLCA)
```

This will assign the SQLCA transaction object to the dw_detail DataWindow Control. Now your DataWindow Control can talk to the PowerBuilder Demo Database on the SQLCA phone line.

Loading Data into Your DataWindow

Once your DataWindow Control has a transaction object, you will want to load the data from the database into the DataWindow Control. You can do this by using the Retrieve() function. The format for the Retrieve() function is as follows:

```
<DataWindow Name>.Retrieve( [<argument1>, <argument2>, .. <argumentn>])
```

We'll talk more about the retrieval arguments in a moment. The Retrieve() function returns a 1 if it succeeds and a -1 if it fails. We'll talk about how to find out why it may fail a bit later. But for now, code the following line of code after your SetTransObject line, which will load the data from the database into the DataWindow, ignoring the result of the retrieve call:

```
dw_detail.Retrieve()
```

That's all there is to it! Now, you should be able to see your department data appear right inside your window. Return to the window painter by selecting **R**eturn from the **F**ile menu or by clicking on the Return to Window Painter button on the Script PainterBar. Then, you can run the application by selecting **R**un from the **F**ile menu or by clicking on the Run button on either the PowerBar or the Window PainterBar. You will be prompted to save the changes that you have made to this window—press **Yes** to save your changes. You'll notice that it takes a bit longer for the application to start up this time. This is because it is loading and connecting to the database before it opens the MDI Frame.

DO	DON'T

DON'T Connect to the database during the Open event of the application when building applications that will be used by other users. It makes you application "feel" like it is slow to the user because the user just sees a blank screen until the MDI Screen comes up. It's okay for your own use or for our example, but don't do it when creating distributable applications.

DO Use the PostEvent() function to post a user event from inside the Open event of the MDI Frame that will do your database connect after the MDI Frame has already appeared on-screen. This way, the MDI Frame will visually appear on-screen right away, and then the posted user event will take over and connect to the database. At this point, the screen already shows the user that the application has started. Managing user perception of time is half the battle in making an application whose performance is acceptable. You can use this technique for retrieving DataWindow Controls in a window Open event, too.

23

When the MDI Frame finally comes up, you can open your new Sheet by selecting **O**pen from the **F**ile menu. Again, it may take a little longer for the window to appear while the data is retrieved into the DataWindow Control from the database. Once it does come up, though, you should see all of your department data on-screen. It's just that simple! Go ahead and exit your application by selecting **C**lose from the System Menu, and you will be returned to the PowerBuilder Window Painter where you left off. (Again, it may take an extra few moments to get back while the application disconnects from the database and closes the Watcom Database Engine.)

Retrieval Arguments

If you remember, you also created a few DataWindow Definitions that had Retrieval Arguments in it that were used to specify the selection criteria of the DataWindow. When you have a DataWindow Definition that contains retrieval arguments, and you use the Retrieve()

function to retrieve your data, the same Retrieval Arguments dialog box that you saw in the Data Manipulation Painter will appear, allowing the user to enter in values for these retrieval arguments. However, you may not want to prompt the user with this dialog box, either because it just doesn't look all that nice, or because the user has already specified the value for the retrieval argument somewhere else or in some other manner (for example, by selecting a row in another DataWindow).

In order to do this, you can simply pass the retrieval arguments to the DataWindow as parameters to the Retrieve function, in the same order as they are defined in the DataWindow. Normally, you do this by passing variables that contain the value of the retrieval argument. However, you can also use literal values as your retrieval arguments. Let's try it.

Change the DataWindow Definition that is used as the dataobject of the dw_detail DataWindow. To do this, double-click on the DataWindow Control and click on the **Change...** button, or right-click on the DataWindow and select **C**hange DataWindow... from the menu. You will again be prompted with the Select DataWindow dialog box. This time, select the d_ch22-2 DataWindow Definition as the dataobject. If you remember, this DataWindow Definition contained employee data and accepted a retrieval argument for the department ID of the employees that will be retrieved. Now, without changing anything else, you can run the application again (save the changes like you did last time) and open the sheet again to see what happens. This time, as you open the sheet, you will be prompted to enter the department number with the Specify Retrieval Arguments dialog box that you saw yesterday. If you enter in the number 100, you will see the employees in the R&D Department (see Fig. 23.5).

Figure 23.5.

The Employees in the R&D Department.

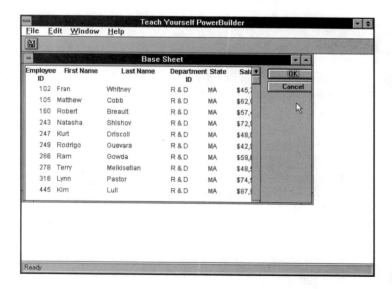

Exit the application, and let's fix it so that you are not prompted for the argument. Go ahead and edit the Open event script of the window. Now, change the line that reads

```
dw_detail.Retrieve()
```

to read

```
dw_detail.Retrieve( 100)
```

Close the script painter and run the application again. This time, the list of employees in the dw_detail DataWindow will come right up with the list of employees in the R&D Department.

We talked about using data from one DataWindow as the value of the retrieval argument of another. Of course, you already learned one method that you can use to do this, by using a nested report. But you may also want to set up an environment where the user can select a row in one DataWindow Control and use a value from that DataWindow as the retrieval argument value of a second DataWindow Control. In order to do this, however, you need to be able to figure out a few things about the first DataWindow, including the row that the user selected as well as the value contained in the foreign key column of that row.

Selecting and Scrolling DataWindow Rows

Let's start by talking about the rows of a DataWindow Control. In a DataWindow Control, only one row of data can be *active* at a time. Although it is possible that *no* row is active, you can never have *more* than one row active at a time. That doesn't mean that you cannot make a user interface where more than one row is *selected*, or highlighted. There is no limit to the number of rows that can be selected. However, the user can only click on or move to one row at a time, and this row becomes the currently focused, or active, row.

You can find out which row is the active row by using the GetRow() function. The GetRow() function returns the currently active row of the DataWindow Control. It's important to realize that the currently active row may not be the first row on-screen. In fact, it may not even be visible in the DataWindow Control. The user can click on a row in the DataWindow Control and then move it off the page by scrolling the DataWindow. Additionally, you can set the current row in code by using the SetRow() function. When you set the row, it will not automatically appear on-screen, either. If you want to set the row and have it appear on the page in code, use the ScrollToRow() function, which will set the active row and scroll it into the viewport of the DataWindow Control. The latter two functions take a row number as their parameter. In addition, you can scroll the DataWindow Control viewport in code without using the row number by using the ScrollNextRow(), ScrollNextPage(), ScrollPriorRow(), and ScrollPriorPage() functions, which scroll the DataWindow Control viewport forward or backward one row or page. These functions do not take any parameters, but do change the active

23

row by first figuring out which row is active, and then scrolling to the new row based on its own calculations. You can find out just how many rows there are in your DataWindow Control by using the RowCount() function, which takes no parameters.

The active row is not automatically highlighted, and by default, the user really has no way of knowing which row is currently active. However, there are two functions that you can use to indicate the current row to the user. The first is the SetRowFocusIndicator() function. This function allows you to specify the method to use to show the user the active row. It takes three parameters, although the last two are optional. The first parameter is the indicator that you want to use. You can specify the name of a bitmap, or you can specify one of two enumerated types: Hand! or FocusRect!. If you specify Hand!, PowerBuilder will display a picture of a hand next to the currently selected row in your DataWindow Control (see Fig. 23.6). If you specify FocusRect!, PowerBuilder will display a dotted rectangle (often referred to as a *caret*) around the active row (see Fig. 23.7). In addition, as was mentioned before, you can specify two other parameters. These two parameters allow you to specify the X and Y coordinates of the focus indicator relative to the top-left corner of the row. In other words, you can specify any bitmap as the row focus indicator and then specify how far from the edge of the row it will be placed. By default, the focus indicator is left justified and top justified with the detail band of the row. You can also turn off the focus rectangle by specifying the Off! enumerated value as the first parameter.

Figure 23.6.
The Hand Focus indicator.

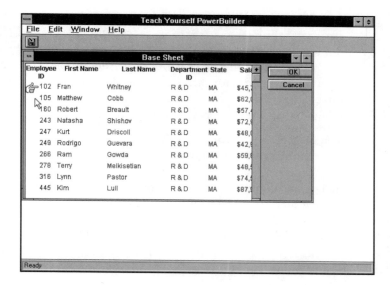

Figure 23.7.

The Focus Rectangle indicator.

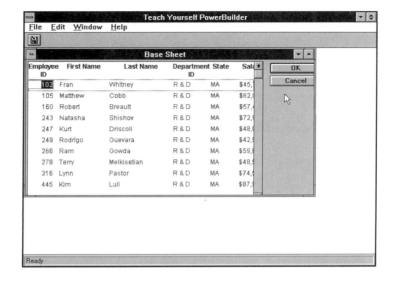

The second method of displaying which row is selected is by highlighting it. You can highlight a row by using the SelectRow() function. This function takes two parameters: the row number to select and the select state of the row. The row can either be selected or deselected. To select a row, specify a boolean value of TRUE as the second parameter, and to deselect it specify a boolean value of FALSE. If you specify a row number of 0, PowerBuilder will perform the specified selection action on all of the rows in the DataWindow Control. So, to quickly deselect all rows in the DataWindow, use

```
dw_detail.SelectRow( 0, FALSE)
```

You can use the result of the GetRow() function to highlight the active row, as in the following example:

```
dw_detail.SelectRow( GetRow(), TRUE)
```

Highlighting one row does not deselect any other rows in the DataWindow Control; you must code that logic in yourself. This allows you to let your user select multiple rows because you can leave more than one row selected. Then, you can determine the select state of a specific row by using the IsSelected() function. This function accepts a single parameter: the row number that you want to test. If the row is selected, it returns TRUE; otherwise, it returns FALSE. Also, you can quickly find the next selected row in a DataWindow Control by using the GetSelectedRow() function. This function will search the DataWindow Control to find a selected row. It accepts one parameter: the number of the row where you want to start the search. It returns the number of the first selected row it finds (after the row number you passed it). You can use these techniques to allow the user to turn on and off rows in DataWindows, and then process each selected row one at a time.

The *Clicked* Event

The user of your application will probably select rows by clicking on them. When the user clicks on a DataWindow Control with the mouse, it triggers a `Clicked` event. Then, any code that is contained inside of your `Clicked` event script will be executed. In general, then, the code to select your rows will be in the `Clicked` event. In addition, there is also a `DoubleClicked` event that you can script if you want to perform actions based on a double-click in your DataWindow Control. The `Clicked` and `DoubleClicked` events get fired between the time that the user clicks and the active row changes. In other words, if the active row of the DataWindow Control is the first row, and the user clicks on the second row, the active row of the DataWindow Control will not change to the second row until immediately *after* the script for the `Clicked` event is executed. This may sound silly, but it is completely intentional. You see, this allows you to see which row the user came from (using the `GetRow()` function). PowerBuilder supplies a special function called `GetClickedRow()` that returns the row that the user clicked on—the row that is about to become the active row. And so, during the `Clicked` event, you can figure out which row the user is coming from and which row the user is going to by using these two functions. This is critical in many cases to making a friendly user interface.

For example, you may want to ignore a click if it is on the current row. If you are doing a master-detail report where clicking on a row in one DataWindow Control retrieves data in another DataWindow Control, there is no point in re-retrieving data for the same row. So, you could test to see if the `GetRow()` and `GetClickedRow()` returned the same row number and only re-retrieved the new value if they were different. The most important thing to remember, though, is that when you use the `Clicked` and `DoubleClicked` events of a DataWindow, the row you will most likely be working with is the row number returned by `GetClickedRow()` function and not the `GetRow()` function.

Manipulating the Data in a DataWindow

After you know which row you want to process (either because it is the active row, clicked row, or selected row), you will then need to get the data out of it. Most likely, you will store this data into a variable. You use the `GetItemString()`, `GetItemNumber()`, `GetItemDecimal()`, `GetItemDate()`, `GetItemTime()`, and `GetItemDateTime()` functions to do this. The function that you use depends on the datatype of the value that you are getting. So, to retrieve a value that is stored in a string column, you use the `GetItemString()` function.

Note: These functions all work exactly the same and accept the same parameters. The only difference is that they return their values with a different datatype. And so, when referring to them as a group, I will use the notation. `GetItemXXX()`.

The format for the functions is as follows:

```
<DataWindowName>.GetItemXXX( <row>, <column> [, <buffer>, <original value>])
```

You must specify the row number and column of the cell from which you want to get the data. You can specify the column as a number or as a string by using its DataWindow Definition column name. In addition, you can specify from which buffer you want to get the value. The buffer is specified as an enumerated data type. The valid values are Primary!, which is the main buffer that is displayed in the DataWindow Control, Delete!, the deleted buffer that contains rows that have been deleted from the DataWindow Control, and Filter!, the buffer that contains rows that have been filtered out of the primary buffer. By default, of course, the Primary buffer is used. In addition, you can specify a boolean value to determine whether you will be given the original value or the current value of the cell. If you specify TRUE, the value returned will be the original value that was stored in this DataWindow Control, even if that is not what appears on-screen. If you specify FALSE or do not specify this parameter at all, the current value for this cell in the DataWindow Control will be returned. Although most of the time you will simply specify the first two parameters, row and column, the capability to get other information from your DataWindow Control by using this function can come in very handy at times.

Note: The term "original value" may be a slight misnomer here. In actuality, the value may not be the original value that was retrieved from the database. Instead, a value may have been retrieved from the database, modified, and then saved back to the database. If the value was saved back to the database, the DataWindow will treat it like it was the "original value" for the column, even though it wasn't. Perhaps a better term for this, then, would be the "persistent" value. No matter, as long as you understand the difference.

23

You can also change the value of your data by using a similar function: the SetItem() function. Unlike the GetItemXXX() functions, there is only one version of this function. It takes the following format:

```
<DataWindow Name>.SetItem( <row>, <column>, <value>)
```

Also, you can only set the value of the Primary buffer by using this function. You cannot set the value for any of the other buffers. The row and column specification works exactly like it did in the GetItemXXX() functions. The value that you specify is the value that will be placed inside the cell specified by the row and column of the function call. The datatype of the value that you attempt to place inside a column must be the same as the datatype of the column itself. For example, you cannot place a string value inside a column that is a number. In addition, although it wasn't mentioned before, the datatype of the cell from which you GetItemXXX() must match the datatype of the GetItemXXX() function that you use. For example, you cannot use the

GetItemString() function to get data from a cell that contains numeric data (stored as a number). Violating either of these restrictions will cause a SystemError to occur at runtime.

Putting It Together

Now that you know how to find out when a user clicks on a row in a DataWindow Control, what row the user has clicked on, and how to get the data out of that row, you can make your master-detail report. Make some room in the w_sheet_01 window by dragging the corner down and to the right. Move the buttons over to the right edge again so they are not in the way. Move the detail DataWindow Control down and out of the way toward the bottom of the screen. Create a new DataWindow Control in the window by selecting **D**ataWindow from the **C**ontrols menu or by clicking on the DataWindow Control button on the Window PainterBar and by clicking inside the top area of the window. Double-click on the new DataWindow Control. Select the d_depts DataWindow Definition as the dataobject for this new DataWindow and click **OK**. Then, turn on the vertical scrollbar and name this DataWindow Control dw_master. Now, open the script painter for the dw_master DataWindow Control. Select the dw_master DataWindow Control by clicking on it, and then open the script painter by selecting **S**cript from the **E**dit menu or by clicking on the Script button on the Window PainterBar. Then, select the Clicked event from the Select Event drop-down list box. Enter the following code into the script of the Clicked event of the DataWindow Control:

```
Long ll_row
Int li_dept
// Get the row the user clicked on.
ll_row = GetClickedRow()
// If it is a valid row, and is not the current row
IF ll_row > 0 AND ll_row <> GetRow() THEN
    // Deselect other rows, and Select the clicked row
    SelectRow( 0, FALSE)
    SelectRow( ll_row, TRUE)
    // Get the department id
    li_dept = GetItemNumber( ll_row, "dept_id")
    // and use it as the retrieval argument for the other DataWindow.
    dw_detail.Retrieve( li_dept)
END IF
```

This code will find the clicked row, select it, get the value of its department ID, and use that value as the retrieval argument for the detail DataWindow Control. Now, in order for this to work, you'll also have to give the new master DataWindow Control a transaction object. Since it is connecting to the same database with the same settings, you can simply assign it SQLCA like you did the detail DataWindow Control.

Return to the Window Painter from the script painter by selecting **R**eturn from the **F**ile menu or by clicking on the Return to Window Painter button on the Script PainterBar. Now, select the window by clicking on any empty area of the window (any area not covered by other controls). Now, open the script painter for the Window again by selecting **S**cript from the **E**dit

menu or by clicking on the Script button on the Window PainterBar. The Open event should appear with the code that you have set up inside. Place the following two lines of code in front of the line of code that is in there already:

```
dw_master.SetRowFocusIndicator( FocusRect!)
dw_master.SetTransObject( SQLCA)
```

Also, change the line that reads

```
dw_detail.Retrieve( 100)
```

to read,

```
dw_master.Retrieve()
```

so that the master DataWindow is retrieved when you open the Sheet. Now, return to the window painter and run the window. Save the changes when prompted. Open your Sheet again, and you will see a list of the departments in the master DataWindow. If you click on a department in the list, the employees in that list will be listed in the detail window. It should look something like Figure 23.8. Congratulations! You've achieved a very big step in building PowerBuilder applications!

Figure 23.8.
The Master/Detail window.

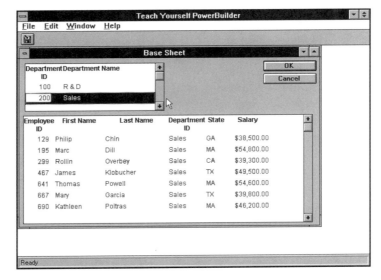

Morning Summary

In order to view your DataWindow Definition layout in a window, you place a DataWindow Control in your window and assign as its dataobject a DataWindow Definition. Then, you code the behavior of your DataWindow Definition in the DataWindow Control. The DataWindow Control has attributes of its own that specify things like its name, dataobject, and position. Most of these attributes are the same as attributes that are used in other window controls.

In order to use a DataWindow Control to talk to the database, you must set up a transaction object. PowerBuilder supplies you with a default transaction object, called SQLCA, that you can use, or you can create your own. The transaction object has several attributes that you can read and write that help you talk to the database. You use the User Controlled transaction object attributes to set up the database connection and to control how PowerBuilder will talk to the database. The DBMS communicates back to you by returning information in the DBMS Controlled attributes of the transaction object. Once you have set the transaction object attributes, you can then connect to the database by using the CONNECT keyword. Then, you can assign your transaction object to a DataWindow by using the SetTransObject() function.

After you have told your DataWindow how to talk to the database, you can ask it to load in its result set from the database by using the Retrieve() function. If you pass retrieval arguments to the Retrieve() function, the DataWindow Control will use those retrieval arguments instead of prompting the user. Once there is data inside your DataWindow Control, there are functions that you can use to get and set the active row, as well as to scroll through the data inside. You can also highlight the active row automatically by using the SetRowFocusIndicator() function or by manually using the SelectRow() function. If you do it manually, you will probably place some code in the Clicked event of the DataWindow that will get the clicked row and then select it.

In addition to cosmetic functions, there are also functions that you can use to get and set the actual data values inside the DataWindow Control. The GetItemXXX() functions are used to get a value from a cell in a DataWindow. The version of the function that you use depends on the datatype of the column whose data you are looking at. The SetItem() function is used to set data in the DataWindow.

Chapter

24

Working with DataWindows

In this lesson, you will learn:

- ☐ About the different DataWindow Events that get triggered in a DataWindow Control
- ☐ How to use these events to perform validation, trap errors, and control the behavior of your DataWindow Control
- ☐ How to insert and delete rows from your DataWindow Control
- ☐ How to update any edits back to the database
- ☐ How to dynamically modify the attributes of the DataWindow Definition that is used as the dataobject of the DataWindow Control

Editing Data in Your DataWindow Control

In the last lesson, we left you playing with your new master/detail DataWindows. You may have noticed that you can edit the data in these DataWindow Controls in almost the same way that you can edit the data in the Data Manipulation Painter. You can tab backward and forward through the columns and rows. Your edit styles, formats, and validation rules take effect in the same manner as they did in the Data Manipulation Painter. You can probably start to see how powerful DataWindows can be and how easy they are to set up.

Important DataWindow Events

What you may not realize, however, is that as you tab around and edit your data, you are actually triggering other important events in the DataWindow Control. There are several important events that we should talk about here that you may use to help your user to interact with data. Let's step through what happens as you work with the data in your DataWindow Control. Start by clicking on the first column of the top row in the Master DataWindow Control. Now, let's continue from there.

Change the department ID of the R&D department from 100 to 600. Then, press the **Tab** key. What you see is that the focus moves from the first cell in the DataWindow Control to the second one. Press the **Tab** key again, and the focus will move to the department ID cell of the next row. Behind the scenes, however, a couple of events have taken place; we'll ignore some of the less significant ones. First, as you type each number into the department ID cell, an event called EditChanged occurs. The EditChanged event occurs whenever the user edits data in a cell by typing. Then, as you press the **Tab** key, several events are actually triggered. First, the ItemChanged event occurs. This event occurs whenever a user changes the value of a column and then *accepts* the change by exiting out of the field (either with the mouse or the **Tab** key) or by pressing **Enter**, among other things. We'll talk a bit more about this event in a moment. After this, an event called ItemFocusChanged occurs. This event occurs as the current item in focus

moves from the department ID column to the department name column. When you press the **Tab** key again, the `ItemFocusChanged` event gets triggered again. This time, however, because you have not actually changed anything, the `ItemChanged` event never gets triggered. However, because tabbing causes the focus to move to a new row, the `RowFocusChanged` event is triggered, as the new row becomes active. In addition, there are several other important events that can occur in your DataWindow Control if everything does not go quite as smoothly as described here.

Validation Errors in the DataWindow Control

Change the department ID value of the second row to the number 20 and then press the **Tab** key, or click on another field. An error message should appear telling you that the department ID must be divisible by 100. The validation rule that you set up comes into action. As you attempted to tab out of the department ID column, before the `ItemChanged` event was triggered, some validation occurred, as well. First, the DataWindow Control attempted to validate the datatype of the data you entered. Because you entered in a numeric value, that validation succeeded. Next, it attempted to validate the data based on your validation rules. This validation failed. When this validation failed, a special event called `ItemError` occurred. By default, the `ItemError` event simply displays the error in a message box and then stops focus from moving to the next column. The `ItemChanged` event does not occur until *after* the validation rule test has passed. The order of these events may be important to you when you start to build real-world applications.

What's the point of all of these events? Well, the point is that you should be able to control the behavior of your DataWindow Control with respect to user input. And although validation rules, edit styles, and format masks allow you to easily control quite a bit of your user's editing environment, there are still limitations with using these alone. For example, you may find the need to validate data in a DataWindow based on the value of some other data. Perhaps the other data is from another row or even from another DataWindow Control. It would be difficult, if not impossible, to code such a thing into a validation rule.

Instead, PowerBuilder enables you to control things like validation using these events. Most specifically, the `ItemChanged` event is a very good place to put in any custom validations that you may not be able to fit into a validation rule in the DataWindow Definition, but would still like to have occur inside of your DataWindow Control after the user changes a value of a column (and changes focus to another column to accept the text). Remember, the `ItemChanged` event will be triggered after data in *any* column is changed. So, the first step in writing a validation rule in the `ItemChanged` event is to figure out which column the user has changed. To do this, you can use either the `GetColumn()` or `GetColumnName()` function. The `GetColumn()` function returns the current column number in the DataWindow Control, while the `GetColumnName()` function returns a string containing the name of the current column—that is, the column that the user

24

has just edited and is about to leave. Incidentally, as you may have guessed, you can set the current column in a DataWindow Control by using the SetColumn() function, which will accept either the column number or a string containing the column name as its parameter.

The Edit Buffer

After you have determined which column the user has just edited, you will want to find out what value the user has entered. If the GetItemXXX() function that we talked about in the last lesson immediately jumps into your mind, then you have a good head on your shoulders and should be very proud of yourself. If it didn't, that's okay because it's not the function that we want to use here anyway. In fact, we are going to use a new function called GetText() to find out what the user typed in. Here's why.

If you remember, we have talked about the different buffers of a DataWindow Control: the Primary, Delete, and Filter buffers. In addition to those buffers, there is one special buffer, the Edit buffer, that does not contain rows of data inside of it but instead contains only a single value. The value that the Edit buffer contains is the value of the cell that is currently being edited on-screen—that is, the cell that is currently active, or in focus. You see, visually the PowerBuilder DataWindow Control is nothing more than a dialog box that contains a picture of the latest data values on-screen. Behind the scenes (in memory) are all of these buffers full of data that are used to determine what data appears inside this dialog box. Hovering in front of this screen is a single edit control that moves around the dialog box based on the current row and column in focus. When you change the active cell, this little DataWindow edit control simply attempts to save its data back to the DataWindow Control. This is the point at which all of the validation occurs, along with the ItemChanged event. Then, if the validation succeeds, the DataWindow can accept this value from the edit buffer, update the buffer to hold the new value, and update the dialog box to display it. Then, the edit control will move itself to hover over the DataWindow Object that is next in the tab order of the DataWindow Definition. Although there is a little more to it because of things like edit styles and display formats, this is the general gist of it.

The GetItemXXX() functions allow you to inspect the value of the cell that is stored in the Primary buffer (along with the other buffers, as well). However, when the ItemChanged event gets fired, the value that is in the Primary buffer is still the value that was there before the user started typing in any changes. The value that the user typed in is still sitting inside the DataWindow edit control. The GetText() function will retrieve this value from the edit control as a string (even if the datatype is something else) so that you can inspect what the user has typed and validate it. The reason that this is always returned as a string is to allow you to inspect what the user typed, even if it does not conform with the datatype of the control. For example, if the user tried to type in the letter a into a column that was numeric, you might still want to read in that value. If the GetText() function returned data in the datatype of a column like the GetItemXXX() functions do, you would not be able to use that function to get the a that the user typed into that numeric column. This is because it is not a valid number and would not fit into a numeric variable. Using string variables allows you to retrieve just about any value, regardless of the real datatype of that

value. Of course, to do your validation, then, you will probably want to convert it to the proper datatype, if necessary. Incidentally, like the other DataWindow functions, there is a counterpart to the `GetText()` function that will change the text that appears in the DataWindow edit control. I bet you could have guessed that it is called `SetText()` and that it accepts a single string parameter containing the value that should be placed in the edit control. If you didn't guess that, then you can go sit in the corner with the folks who thought the `GetItemXXX()` function would be used to retrieve the data for validation!

Controlling Event Behavior

Once you have validated your data in the `ItemChanged` event, you will need some way to indicate to the DataWindow whether that validation has succeeded or failed. If the DataWindow validation has succeeded, you can let the default behavior of the `ItemChanged` event continue. By default, nothing happens in the `ItemChanged` event. When the code inside of it is finished executing, the process continues. So really, we only need to talk about a manner in which you can tell the DataWindow Control that the validation in the `ItemChanged` event has failed. The way in which you do this is by using a function called `SetActionCode()`. The DataWindow Control uses action codes to determine the action it will take after processing a specific event. While not all DataWindow events support action codes, each event that uses them has its own meaning for the different action code settings. The default action code setting is generally 0 and indicates to the DataWindow Control to continue processing normally. The action code is evaluated after the event script completes, so only the last action code setting in a script will have any effect.

24

Note: In PowerBuilder, no other control supports the use of action codes; they are specific to DataWindow Controls.

The `ItemChanged` event supports three action codes. The first of these, 0, is the default setting, as was mentioned earlier. When the action code of the `ItemChanged` event is 0, nothing extraordinary happens. The script for the `ItemChanged` event completes, and the DataWindow Control continues processing, assuming there is no problem. If you code your `ItemChanged` event and find a validation error, however, you can set the action code to 2 by using the following statement:

```
[<DataWindow Name>.]SetActionCode( 2)
```

Setting the action code to 2 in the `ItemChanged` event will cause the value to be rejected and changed back to the original value that is contained in the primary buffer of the DataWindow. The focus of the column will still change to the newly selected column if the user was trying to move to another column. However, the user-entered value will be rejected and ignored.

Alternatively, you can indicate failure more seriously by using an action code of 1. If you set the action code of an `ItemChanged` event to 1, it will prevent the focus from changing to the new column and will also trigger the `ItemError` event that was discussed earlier. Then, you can do your error processing in your `ItemError` event.

Like the `ItemChanged` event, the `ItemError` event also supports action codes. By default, this action code is 0, which in the case of the `ItemError` event will reject the value and cause the internal DataWindow Error message box to be displayed. The `ItemError` event also supports three other action code values. An action code of 1 will reject the value, prevent the focus from changing to the new column, but *not* show a message box. You can use this action code if you want to show your own message box instead of the system-defined one. In addition, you can use an action code of 2 to allow the value to be accepted (ignore the error) and an action code of 3 to reject and ignore the value but allow the focus to change, just like an action code of 2 in the `ItemChanged` event works.

Note: There are quite a number of events that support action codes so that you can totally customize the behavior of your DataWindow Control. Although we won't discuss them all here, be sure to check out the PowerBuilder documentation on DataWindow events if you need to figure out how to control the behavior of a DataWindow event by using an action code.

Inserting and Deleting Entire Rows

Besides allowing your user to edit data that already exists in the DataWindow Control, you may also want to allow the user to insert new empty rows into the DataWindow Control to enter data from scratch. You can insert a new empty row into a DataWindow Control by using the `InsertRow()` function. This function takes a single parameter: the row before which you want to insert. If you want the row to be inserted after all of the rows in the DataWindow Control, simply use 0 as your parameter value. The `InsertRow()` function returns the row number of the newly inserted row. If you specify a row number other than 0 in your function call, the number returned will be the same as the number you specified. If you specify a 0 as the row to insert, the row number returned will be the highest row number in the DataWindow. When you insert a new row into the DataWindow Control by using the `InsertRow()` function, any default values set as the Initial Values for a column will be present in the new row.

Warning: You again must recognize the fact that if you are inserting new rows and you have not selected all of the columns in your DataWindow Definition, you may have a problem later. This problem occurs when the DataWindow Control attempts to save the data back to the database if there are columns that are required by the database (that do not permit nulls) missing from the DataWindow Definition.

In addition to inserting new rows, you may want to delete a row from the database. You can do this using the DeleteRow() function. The DeleteRow() function also takes one parameter: the row number of the row that you want to delete. In addition, if you specify the row number as 0, it will delete the currently active row in the DataWindow Control.

Saving the User's Changes

All of these changes that you can make to your DataWindow Control are wonderful and exciting. The capability to insert and delete rows, to edit your data, and to exercise tight control over the data that the user enters into the DataWindow Control are wonderful features. These features make the DataWindow Definition/DataWindow Control combination a very programmer-friendly, easy, yet powerful method of controlling user interaction with a database. However, like the Data Manipulation Painter, the changes that are made are not stored back to the database until you specifically ask the DataWindow Control to save them for you. You do this by using the Update() function. The Update() function, like its Retrieve() counterpart, also returns a 1 if it succeeds and a -1 if it fails. In addition, however, it accepts two optional parameters, both of type boolean.

24

The first parameter to the Update() function specifies whether any pending edits in the DataWindow Control should be accepted. Remember when we talked about the ItemChanged event and the DataWindow edit control? We said that until the user actually accepts the changes, either by clicking on a different field, or by pressing the **Tab** or **Enter** key, the ItemChanged event does not get triggered, and the Primary DataWindow buffer does not get updated. Well, imagine if the user edited data in a DataWindow Control and attempted somehow to update the DataWindow without accepting the changes. This means that the last edit is essentially ignored because it has not been saved to the primary buffer. This, of course, would be very confusing to the user and would leave room for all kinds of problems. And so, when you Update your DataWindow Control, PowerBuilder by default causes the text in the edit control to be accepted, even if the user does not tab away. You can override this feature if for some reason you don't want this to happen by passing the first argument to the Update() function as FALSE. The default, of course, is TRUE.

The second parameter to the Update() function allows you to determine if the status flags will be reset after the update is completed. If you remember back when we talked about the DataWindow buffers in Chapter 18, we also talked about the status flags that are used to determine if a row has been modified and, therefore, if it needs to be updated into the database. Well, by default, after an Update() command succeeds, that DataWindow's status flags are reset so that the DataWindow recognizes that there are no more rows waiting to be updated to the database. When you change the value in a cell, the flag will once again be set to recognize that the front end is out of synch with the database, and the process will continue working. However, in some cases, it is useful to be able to prevent the Update flags from being reset automatically on Update(). For example, if you want to use a single DataWindow Control to update two tables, you will still need to know which cells need to be updated for the update of the second table. And so you will set this value to FALSE to prevent the flags from being reset on the first update. This way, you can change the table that will be updated by the DataWindow Control and execute a second Update() statement, and the DataWindow will still be able to find which values were changed to create its UPDATE SQL Statements. If you had left the second parameter its default value of TRUE, then the DataWindow Control would reset all cells so that they indicated that they were in synch with the database. The second Update() call would not execute any actual updates to the database because the DataWindow Control would think that it was already synchronized with the database, and no fields needed to be updated.

If you are updating a table and have the AutoCommit flag in your transaction object set to FALSE, you will need to make permanent any database updates that you make by committing them. And of course, if you find an error during the update process, you can instead roll them back. To commit an update, simply enter the following line of code:

```
COMMIT USING SQLCA;
```

To roll back any changes, you can code the following line:

```
ROLLBACK USING SQLCA;
```

Accepting the Last Edit before Updating

We spent a few moments discussing the importance of accepting the last change made by a user before an update is issued. We talked about how the Update() function may force this last change to be accepted automatically. But what if you want to do some validation before an update but outside of the scope of an ItemChanged event? For example, what if before the user attempts to update a DataWindow Control, you want to validate that the user has entered in values for each of the fields that are required? This cannot be checked in an ItemChanged event, but instead must be checked immediately before an Update() function call. Now, suppose that the user began entering data into the last required field when the Update button was pressed. However, the text of the entry has not yet been accepted. And so, the required field test will fail because the system doesn't recognize the input. How can you force the text to be accepted without calling the Update() function?

The answer is that you can use the AcceptText() function. The AcceptText() function forces the last change to be accepted, which may in turn force an ItemChanged or ItemError event to be triggered. In addition, if there is an error, the AcceptText() call will return a -1 so you can stop processing. If it succeeds, it returns a 1. You should always use the AcceptText() function if you plan on validating data in your DataWindow before updating. And even if you don't plan on validating, it probably wouldn't hurt to do an AcceptText() call immediately before an Update() call just to prevent bad habits.

DO	DON'T

DO Use AcceptText() to accept the last change in a DataWindow before validating the data if you are validating data outside of the DataWindow Control.

DON'T Ever call the AcceptText() function from the ItemChanged event. Because the AcceptText() function can trigger the ItemChanged event, this may cause a never-ending loop as the AcceptText() call causes the ItemChanged event to be triggered, which causes the AcceptText() function to be called, which causes the ItemChanged event to be fired, and so on.

Determining If Anything Has Been Changed

24

If you attempt to update a DataWindow Control that has not been modified, nothing bad will happen. PowerBuilder will determine that no data has been changed and will simply decide not to create any database update commands to change any data. However, if your application does other processing besides calling the Update() function when the user asks you to update changes (for example, validations), it is often useful to be able to determine if there have actually been any changes made to the DataWindow before spending valuable processing time trying to prepare for an update. If you recall, in the Data Manipulation Painter you were able to see a description of the rows in your DataWindow Control. It included the total number of rows displayed, the total number of rows modified, the total number of rows deleted, and the total number of rows filtered out. As you may have expected, PowerBuilder gives you functions that you can use to determine exactly that information in your code so that you can figure out, among other things, if any data has been changed. The functions that do this are, respectively, RowCount(), which we already briefly mentioned in the last lesson, ModifiedCount(), DeletedCount(), and FilteredCount(). Each of these functions takes no parameters and returns the total number of rows specified for the function. For example, the ModifiedCount() function returns the number of rows that have been modified. If you want to see, therefore, if any changes have occurred in a DataWindow Control, you can simply check if there are any rows that have been Modified or Deleted. If not, then there has not been any data change made to this DataWindow Control.

Note: The `ModifiedCount()` function returns the number of rows that have been modified in both the Primary and Filter buffers because they will all be updated when you execute the `Update()` statement.

After you know how many rows have been modified, you might actually want to search through and do something to the modified rows. Rather than search through *every* row in the DataWindow Control, you can quickly search through just the modified rows by using the `GetNextModified()` function. The `GetNextModified()` function takes two parameters: the first parameter is the row after which to start the search for the next modified row, and the second parameter is the buffer in which you want to search. If you specify a search row of `0`, the search will start from the first row of the DataWindow.

As you look at the modified rows, you will probably want more specific information about the type of modification that has been made. In other words, you will want to find out about the status of the update flags of the row that has been modified. To do this, you can use the `GetItemStatus()` function. The `GetItemStatus()` function accepts three parameters: the row, the column, and the buffer of the cell to get the status of. If you specify a column number of `0`, it will tell you the status of the entire row. There are four statuses that can be returned: `New!`, meaning that the row is completely new, that it has been inserted into the DataWindow with the `InsertRow()` function, and that it has not been changed; `NewModified!`, meaning that the row is new but has also been edited; `NotModified!`, meaning that the row or cell is not new, that it already exists in the database; and `DataModified!`, meaning that the row or cell is not new but that it has been edited and no longer matches its database counterpart.

Warning: The `New!` and `NewModified!` statuses apply only to rows and not to individual cells.

You can also change the item status of a row or cell by using the `SetItemStatus()` function. This function accepts four parameters: the row, column, and buffer of the cell whose status you want to change, and the new status that you want to give this cell. Like the `GetItemStatus()` function, if you specify a column number of `0`, the entire row will be changed to the new status. For example, the following line of code will change a row that is `DataModified!` to `NotModified!` so that it will not be updated to the database. (The row doesn't have to be `DataModified!`, but I will use this example to illustrate a point in a moment.)

```
dw_master.SetItemStatus( ll_row, 0, NotModified!)
```

While changes between `DataModified!` and `NotModified!` work as you may expect, there are some peculiarities when working with `New!` and `NewModified!` statuses. To change a `New!` row to `NewModified!`, you may not set its status to `NewModified!` directly. Instead, you change its

status to DataModified!. The first time you set a New! row to DataModified!, it will become NewModified!. If you really want it to be DataModified!, you need to set it again to DataModified!. In addition, to change a NewModified! row to New!, you may not set its status to New! directly. You must set the status of the NewModified! row to NotModified! instead. This will set the status back to New!. Then, if you really want it to be NotModified!, you must set the status of the now New! row to NotModified! again, at which point it will change to NotModified!.

In addition to changing the status of a single row or cell, you can also quickly reset the status of the entire DataWindow Control by using the ResetUpdate() function. This function takes no parameters. It resets the DataWindow Control as if it were updated to the database. That is, it resets all rows in the Primary! and Filter! buffers to NotModified! and then discards the rows in the Delete! buffer.

By using these techniques, you might create a script to validate and update your DataWindow Control that looks something like this:

```
// Accept any pending changes
IF dw_master.AcceptText() > 0 THEN
    // See if there are any changes
    IF dw_master.ModifiedCount() + dw_master.DeletedCount() > 0 THEN
        // Validate the changes to the DataWindow
        IF f_validate()  > 0 THEN
            // Update the changes
            IF dw_master.Update() > 0 THEN
                // Update succeeded. Commit the changes
                COMMIT;
            ELSE
                // Update Failed
                ROLLBACK;
            END IF
        END IF
    END IF
END IF
```

You might need to insert an artificial key into the key column of new rows, so your f_validate() function might look something like this:

```
Long ll_row
Int  li_max_dept
// Get the next department id (uses a different user function)
li_max_dept = f_get_max_dept()
// Get the first modified row.
ll_row = dw_master.GetNextModified( ll_row)
DO WHILE ll_row > 0
    IF GetItemStatus( ll_row, 0, Primary!) = NewModified! THEN
        // This row needs a key before it is inserted
        SetItem( ll_row, "dept_id", li_max_dept)
        li_max_dept ++
    END IF
LOOP
```

It's not the prettiest looking code in the world, but it does the job; and it does it properly, efficiently, and well.

Database Errors in a DataWindow Control

In the last section, we saw how to write a script that would (eventually) update a DataWindow Control. And in that script, besides rolling back, we essentially ignored any error that occurred from the `Update()` function. In fact, we didn't even test the `Retrieve()` function to see if it succeeded, although we probably should have. Even so, what happens if there is an error when updating the database? How will the user know about it?

Well, as you might have guessed, there is also a DataWindow event that will be triggered if there is a database error during the retrieval or update of a DataWindow Control. This event is called `DBError`. By default, when the `DBError` event is triggered, a message box appears displaying the error message that comes from the database. However, you can override this default behavior by changing the action code of this event to 1 with the `SetActionCode()` function. Then, you can use the `DBErrorCode()` function to find out the error code that was returned by the DBMS, and the `DBErrorMessage()` function to find out the database error message. These functions take no parameters. You can use the `GetUpdateStatus()` function to determine which row actually caused the error. This function takes two parameters. The first parameter is a variable of type `Long` and will hold the row number of the row that caused the error. The second parameter is of the enumerated type `dwBuffer!` and holds the name of the buffer (`Primary!`, `Filter!`, or `Delete!`) in which the row that caused the error lives.

You can use this information to react to database errors in your own way. For example, most DBMSs generate an error message if a row changes between retrieval and update. You can trap this error message and instead of just reporting an error, you can find out which row has changed and then reselect its data from the database by using the `ReselectRow()` function. This function takes a single parameter: the row to reselect. Or, you can just scroll to and highlight the row that caused the error, and make the user's life a little easier. But that's the beauty of PowerBuilder. It's easy to use the default functionality, and it's almost as easy to customize it to meet your needs.

Dynamically Modifying DataWindow Attributes

In PowerBuilder, all the objects that you build are stored using a special PowerBuilder language that the PowerBuilder compiler can interpret into specific attributes, behaviors, and instructions. The DataWindow Definition is not much different in that it also is made up of a language, called a *DataWindow Syntax*, that is used to store its definition. As you've already learned, PowerBuilder DataWindow Definitions store information in their syntax about the layout and data source of data in the database that can be used in DataWindow Controls inside your windows. At runtime, you can modify the attributes of a DataWindow Control like you might any other window control, simply by assigning a new value to that attribute in a script. And it also makes sense to assume that a developer might want to control the layout of the data displayed in the DataWindow Control, as well. In other words, the developer may want to control the attributes of the DataWindow Definition that is the dataobject of a DataWindow Control. Unfortunately, though, you cannot simply assign values to the attributes of a dataobject to modify them because there is no way in your script to refer directly to the attributes of a dataobject. Instead, then, you have to use special functions to control the attributes of the objects inside your DataWindow Definitions.

Setting Filters and Sort Keys on the Fly

The simplest attributes that you might want to change in a DataWindow Control at runtime are the Filter and Sort specifications of the DataWindow Definition that is its dataobject. You can use the SetFilter() function to specify a new DataWindow expression to be used as the filter criteria of this DataWindow Definition. The function takes a single parameter: a string containing the new filter expression. If the string is completely empty (""), then the filter will be turned off. If the filter string is NULL, the user will be presented with the Specify Filter dialog box that you also saw in Chapter 21 (see Fig. 24.1). Setting the filter expression does not actually perform the filtering of the rows, it only modifies the expression that will be used to evaluate whether a row will be displayed in the DataWindow. In order to actually perform the filtering, you must use the Filter() function. The Filter() function takes no parameters and filters out the rows that do not match the criteria of the filter expression, set either in the DataWindow Definition or in the last SetFilter() function call. In order to change the filter of a DataWindow Definition, then, you must call *both* functions, as in the following code:

```
dw_detail.SetFilter( "dept_id > 200")
dw_detail.Filter()
```

Figure 24.1.
The Specify Filter dialog box.

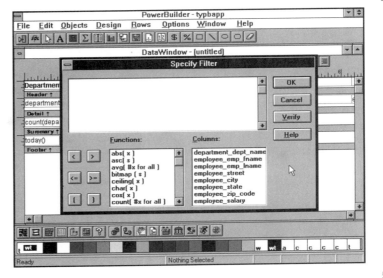

In addition to changing the filter criteria of your DataWindow Definition, you can also change the sort criteria of your DataWindow Definition by using pretty much the same technique. The SetSort() function allows you to specify the new sort criteria. The Sort() function actually performs the sorting. You specify the new sort criteria as a string containing the sort key column or expression, followed by a space, and the sort order, either an A for ascending order or a D for descending order. In addition, the SetSort() function accepts an empty string to clear the sort specification and a NULL string to prompt the user with the Specify Sort Columns dialog box that you also saw in Chapter 21 (see Fig. 24.2). And again, both functions must be called in order for a new sort key to take effect, as in the following example:

```
dw_detail.SetSort( "dept_name A" )
dw_detail.Sort()
```

Note: You can specify multiple sort keys simply by separating each sort clause with a comma, as in the following example:

```
dwDetail.SetSort( "dept_name A, state D)
```

Figure 24.2.
The Specify Sort Columns dialog box.

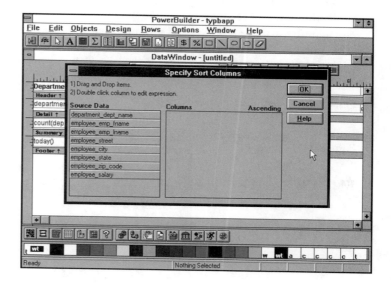

Other Attributes That You Can Set

In addition to the `SetFilter()` and `SetSort()` functions, there are functions that you can use to get and set tab order, validation rules, Border style, and code table values. You can use the `SetTabOrder()` function to change the tab order of a column in a DataWindow at runtime. The `SetTabOrder()` function accepts two parameters: the column name or number to change, and the new tab order value for that column. The function returns the old tab order of the column so that you can reset it later.

You can use the `GetValidate()` function to get the current validation rule of a column. Then, you can set that validation rule using the `SetValidate()` function. You can use the `GetBorderStyle()` function to find out the current border style of a particular column, and then set the border style by using the `SetBorderStyle()` function. You can get the code and decode values for a column with a code table by using the `GetValue()` function, which returns the code value followed by a tab character, followed by the decode value for the specified code table element of the specified column. You can set the value of a particular element of a column's code table by using the `SetValue()` function, which accepts the code and decode values also separated by a tab character.

Describing and Modifying Other Attributes

In addition to the "easy way" of modifying DataWindow attributes dynamically by using specific functions that modify or describe a specific attribute of a DataWindow Definition, there are also two functions that you can use to get almost complete control over your DataWindow Definition at runtime. These functions are the `Describe()` and `Modify()` functions. As you may have guessed, the `Describe()` function allows you to describe information about the DataWindow Definition, and the `Modify()` function allows you to change it. Both of these functions take a single string parameter containing code-like instructions on what to describe or modify, returning a different string containing the result of the instruction.

The instruction that you pass to the `Describe()` and `Modify()` functions is in a specific format. You specify the specific attribute of the DataWindow Object that you are interested in by using dot notation. The format of this attribute specification is

```
<DataWindow Object Name>.<Attribute Name>
```

If you are using the `Describe()` function, that's all you need—the attribute that you want to get a description of. If you are using the `Modify()` function, you must also specify the value that you want to assign to the specified attribute, in the following format:

```
<DataWindow Object Name>.<Attribute Name> = '<value>[~t<expression>]'
```

24

where `<value>` is any literal value, and `<expression>` is any legal DataWindow expression that returns a single value of the same datatype as the attribute. Incidentally, if you are assigning the attribute a numeric value, the quotes are optional. The DataWindow Definition will understand what you are saying whether you include them or not. However, the quotes are *required* for string values and for values with expressions, regardless of the datatype. If you are using an expression, even if the value is numeric, you *must* use the quotes. When specifying an expression, the value specified will be used as the default value of the attribute, but the expression will be used to dynamically determine the value of the attribute at runtime. This is the same attribute expression that you can also set in the DataWindow Painter when you select the Attributes... menu item from the Right Mouse Menu of an object.

The DataWindow Object Name can either be the DataWindow definition itself, referenced with the word `DataWindow`, or the name of any control in the DataWindow Definition, including columns, computed fields, text fields, bitmaps, rectangles, ovals, and all of the other objects that you can place in a DataWindow Definition, referenced by their DataWindow Name.

Note: In addition, when referencing columns, you can use the column number if you precede it with a number sign (#).

For example, to find out about the position of a DataWindow Object inside the DataWindow Definition, you might ask to describe that object's X and Y coordinates, as well as its Height and Width. You can describe the type of an object by using the `Type` attribute. The following example illustrates how you might read and write the width of a column:

```
ls_type  = dw_detail.Describe( "dept_id.Type")
ls_data  = dw_detail.Describe( "DataWindow.Data")
ls_width = dw_detail.Describe( "dept_id.Width")
ls_error = dw_master.Modify( "dept_id.Width = " + ls_width )
```

This code first stores the type of the department ID column of the detail DataWindow into a string variable called `ls_type`. Then, it retrieves all of the data from the DataWindow into a different string variable called `ls_data`. Then, it reads the width of the department ID column into a variable called `ls_width` and uses the value returned to set the width of the department ID column in the master DataWindow. Notice in the case of the width description that the value returned by `Describe` is always a string, even if the value being described is numeric. You can convert this value to its proper datatype in your code if you need to use it for calculations. If an error occurs, for example if you specify an invalid object or attribute, the value returned will be an exclamation point (!). And if the attribute that you are describing contains no value, then the `Describe()` function will return a question mark (?). The value returned by the `Modify()` function is also a string, which is empty if the modification succeeded, or contains an error message if there was a problem.

There is a wide range of attributes that you can describe and modify that are listed in Appendix A of the PowerBuilder Function Reference. You should learn about these different attributes. By using them, you can really make robust, user-friendly applications with exciting features like ad-hoc reports.

> **Note:** Incidentally, when using `Describe()` and `Modify()`, you can pass more than one instruction to the function at a time. To do this, you simply separate the list of instructions with a space. PowerBuilder will return errors in the usual way if there are any, and in the case of `Describe()` it will return any description back delimited with newline characters (~n). Chaining multiple commands inside a string in this manner and passing the string to the `Describe()` or `Modify()` function once is more efficient than looping and calling these functions multiple times. This is because there is an overhead involved in calling the function as well as redrawing the DataWindow Objects affected.

Creating and Destroying DataWindow Objects

In addition to modifying attributes by using the `Modify()` function, you can also create and destroy objects inside your DataWindow Definition at runtime. The syntax to destroy an object is relatively straightforward. You simply state

```
Modify( "DESTROY <object name>")
```

In general, this function call will destroy the specified object from the DataWindow Definition, removing it from the screen, and invalidating any references to it in the DataWindow Definition. However, if the object that you are destroying is a column, the data for that column will still exist in the DataWindow buffers, and references to that column will still be understood, but the visible component of the column will disappear from the DataWindow Definition. To completely eliminate the column, including both its visual and data components, you must specify to destroy the column itself, as follows:

```
Modify( "DESTROY COLUMN <column name>")
```

Creating objects in a DataWindow requires use of the CREATE keyword in the `Modify()` function. However, besides specifying the name of the object you are creating, you also must specify values for the attributes of the object that will be created. Some object attributes can be skipped in the CREATE statement if they can be given default values by the DataWindow Definition. The format for the CREATE statement is as follows:

```
Modify( "CREATE <object type> ( <attribute 1>=<value 1>,.. <attribute n>=<value
➥n>")
```

The details of dynamically creating DataWindow Objects involves discussing this DataWindow Syntax in quite a bit of detail. I won't bore you with a list of syntax rules, however. Instead, I will leave the details of the syntax itself up to you. You can read the PowerBuilder documentation for the details of the syntax of a DataWindow Definition. Or, you can export your DataWindow Definition object from the Library Painter and view its syntax in a text editor. Either way, the `Describe()` and `Modify()` functions give you a direct access route to the attributes contained inside a DataWindow Definition, and that is a power that is worth having. However, because this is an advanced topic, I will leave it up to you to pursue on your own.

In addition to creating columns and other objects, you can create entire DataWindow Definitions at runtime. To do this, you pass the syntax of the DataWindow Definition that you want to create to the `Create()` function. In addition, you can pass a string that will be used to return any error message when the `Create()` function executes. The `Create()` function must be run against a DataWindow Control on a window, which after successful execution will contain the DataWindow Definition specified in the first parameter to the function.

There are a few ways that you can get this syntax for your DataWindow Definition. You can read it from a file exported in the Library Painter, you can build it right inside your code by hand, or you can read out the DataWindow syntax of a different DataWindow Control by describing its `DataWindow.Syntax` attribute. And lastly, you can let PowerBuilder generate it for you from an SQL `SELECT` statement using the `SyntaxFromSQL()` function. The format for the `SyntaxFromSQL()` function is as follows:

```
<transaction object>.SyntaxFromSQL( <Select Statement>, <presentation string>
➥[, <Error Buffer>])
```

The presentation string that you pass is a string containing information about the initial presentation settings of the DataWindow that will be created. For example, you can specify the presentation style of the DataWindow, along with default values for certain attributes of the DataWindow Definition syntax that will be created. Again, I will defer details of this string to Appendix A of the PowerBuilder Function Reference. However, you should be aware that you can use this function to build DataWindow Definitions on the fly.

Afternoon Summary

As you tab around and edit your data in a DataWindow Control, you are actually triggering events inside of it that you can use to perform certain functions. For example, when you type values into a cell, the `EditChanged` event gets triggered. When you tab to another cell, the `ItemChanged` event gets triggered, and then so does an `ItemFocusChanged`. You can use these events to do things like validation and data manipulation in your code.

In order to perform validation, you will need to use the `GetText()` function to read in the value from the edit buffer because it has not yet been accepted into the Primary buffer of the DataWindow Control. Then, you can perform your validation and react to the user's changes.

By using the SetActionCode() function, you can tell the DataWindow Control what to do after it finishes executing your code. The SetActionCode() function causes different reactions in different events. For example, you can use it in the ItemChanged event to reject a value you determine to be invalid.

In addition to letting the user edit data, you can also allow the user to insert and delete rows by using the InsertRow() and DeleteRow() functions. Then, you can let your user save the changes back to the database by using the Update() function. When you do the update, by default, any pending changes in the edit buffer will be accepted to the Primary buffer. You can also force this to happen in your code by using the AcceptText() function, in case, for example, you want to do some validation first. You can also find out if any rows have been modified, deleted, or filtered out by using the ModifiedCount(), DeletedCount(), and FilteredCount() functions, respectively. You can quickly find modified rows using the GetNextModified() function. Then you can find out about the type of modification by using the status flags and the GetItemStatus() function, which returns the status of a cell or row. The status can either be New!, NewModified!, NotModified!, or DataModified!. You can change the status of a cell or row by using the SetItemStatus() function, and you can quickly reset the status of the entire DataWindow Control by using the ResetUpdate() function. In addition, successful execution of an Update() function call will reset the status flags.

During an update (or retrieve, for that matter), a database error can occur. If that happens, the DBError event will be triggered in the DataWindow. Inside that event, you can use the DBErrorCode() and DBErrorMessage() functions to get the error code and error message of the error that has occurred, and use the GetUpdateStatus() function to determine which row actually has caused the error.

In addition to modifying the data in the DataWindow, you may also want to modify the attributes of the DataWindow Definition at runtime. However, because the DataWindow Control doesn't give you direct access to the DataWindow Definition's attributes, you must use special functions to do this. You can change the filter specification of the DataWindow Definition by using the SetFilter() function. Then, you can perform the filtering out of the rows by using the Filter() function. In the same manner, you can set the sort criteria of the DataWindow Definition by using the SetSort() function, and then sort the rows by using the Sort() function. You can set the validation rule and message for a column by using the SetValidate() function, and read it by using the GetValidate() function. You can also get and set border styles and code table values by using similar functions.

In addition, you can use the Describe() and Modify() functions to describe or modify nearly any attribute contained within the syntax of the DataWindow Definition. These functions accept a single string parameter that specifies an instruction of what to describe or what to modify. You specify the name of the object and the name of its attribute, and in the case of the Modify() function, the value to assign to it. The Describe() function will return the information you ask for, and the Modify() function will assign the values you specify. You can also use the Modify() function to create and destroy DataWindow Objects, including columns. Finally, you can use

24

the Create() function to create a DataWindow Definition from scratch inside a DataWindow Control if you know the syntax of that DataWindow Definition. If you don't know it, you can let PowerBuilder build it for you from a SELECT statement by using the SyntaxFromSQL() function.

Q&A

Q I went into the Window Painter and clicked on the DataWindow icon on the PowerBar, and the DataWindow Painter came up! How do I place a DataWindow Control on my window?

A The DataWindow Control icon in the Window Painter looks *exactly* like the DataWindow Painter icon on the PowerBar, except that it is on the Window PainterBar with all of the other window control buttons, not on the PowerBar with all of the other Painter buttons. If you accidentally opened the DataWindow Painter when you meant to place a DataWindow Control on your window, it is because you clicked on the wrong one.

Q I am reading the script that you made in the Clicked event of the DataWindow Control to select the row that the user clicked on, but I am having some trouble understanding why you can't just select the row that the user clicked on. What's all that stuff in the beginning that you do?

A In a DataWindow Control, the Clicked event is triggered whenever the user clicks anywhere inside the DataWindow Control. However, the user does not always have to click on a row. The user may in fact click inside the DataWindow Control but not inside a particular row, such as in the header or footer band. If the user does this, the GetClickedRow() function will return a 0. Then, when the user attempts to highlight the clicked row, it will pass a 0 to the SelectRow() function. When the first argument to the SelectRow() function is a 0, it performs the selection (or deselection) on *all* of the rows in the DataWindow. So, when the user clicks on the header band, this will cause all rows in the DataWindow to be selected. In addition, if you perform any GetItemXXX() function calls with a row number of 0, you will generate a PowerBuilder Runtime Error because 0 is not a valid row in any DataWindow.

Q How can I get more information about what the user clicked on in the Clicked event? What if I want to react to a user clicking in the Header Band?

A You can find out which column the user clicked on with the GetClickedColumn() function (which returns only the column number, not its name). You can use the GetObjectAtPointer() and GetBandAtPointer() functions to find out which DataWindow Object and/or band the user clicked on, as well. These functions also return the row number of the object that was clicked if it is available.

Q Some of the DataWindow functions, like the `GetItemXXX()` and `SetItem()` functions, permit me to use either the column number or column name for their function calls. How do I know when I should use the name or number?

A Internally, there is no real difference between using the column name or column number in these functions. However, it is recommended that you *always* use the column name if you can because it is less dependent on the structure of the DataWindow Definition inside, and also because it is easier to read. Imagine if you coded a complex function that used only the column numbers. Now, six months later, you have to make a small change to the SELECT statement that is contained inside that DataWindow Control's DataWindow Definition—you have to insert a new column in the result set. Now, all of the column numbers in your script are invalid, and your code will stop working. However, if you used the names of the columns, you wouldn't have to change anything to keep your code working because the column names will be the same, even if their positions have changed.

Q There are all of these functions that have strings as arguments representing the names of DataWindow Objects and their attributes. Are these strings case sensitive?

A Yes and no. When referencing the name of a DataWindow Object, the string is in fact case sensitive, and you should always use lowercase letters. However, the attribute names are not case sensitive, and so lowercase `width` will refer to the same attribute as uppercase `WIDTH`.

Q I want to use the `Describe()` and `Modify()` functions to find out about a column whose name I don't know at development time. I do know the number of the column, though. How can I find out the column name in my code?

A You can refer to a column in the `Describe()` and `Modify()` functions by using its column number if you precede it with a number sign (#). Then, you can describe that column's `name` attribute, and it will return to you the name of the column, as in the following example:

```
ls_name = dw_detail.Describe( "#1.Name")
```

Workshop

Quiz

1. What is wrong with the following code segment? (Hint: It is not a syntactical or logic problem.)

```
dw_detail.SetTransObject( SQLCA)
dw_detail.Retrieve()
```

```
IF SQLCA.SQLCode < 0 THEN
   MessageBox( "Database Error #"  + String( SQLCA.SQLDBCode),
SQLCA.SQLErrText)
END IF
```

2. What other functions or statements must you execute before you attempt to `Retrieve()` data into a DataWindow Control?

3. If `AutoCommit` is set to `TRUE`, how many statements will be executed before a `COMMIT` is automatically sent to the database?

4. What is wrong with the following line of code, which attempts to set the value of the department name column in the `dw_detail` DataWindow Control to `"Marketing"`?

   ```
   dw_detail.dept_name.text = "Marketing"
   ```

5. What's the difference between the `SetFilter()` and the `Filter()` functions?

Putting PowerBuilder into Action

1. Let's make our `w_sheet_01` fully functional. Open up the `w_sheet_01` window in the Window Painter.

2. Edit the script of the `clicked` event of the `dw_master` DataWindow. Instead of just retrieving a row when the user clicks on it, you should first update any pending changes in the `dw_detail` DataWindow. Start by accepting any pending text edits. Then, if the `AcceptText()` succeeds, check to see if any data has been modified or deleted. If it has, update the changes in `dw_detail`. Only retrieve `dw_detail` if the update succeeds.

3. Edit the script for the OK button so that it updates both the DataWindows. Start by accepting the text of the two DataWindows. Then, if any data has been modified for `dw_detail`, update it without resetting the status flags. If the update of `dw_detail` succeeds, check to see if any data has been modified for `dw_master`. If there has, update `dw_master` (you can let the flags reset because they will only reset if the update succeeds anyway). If the update succeeds, reset the update flags. If everything succeeds, it closes the window.

4. Create a new button labeled `Insert` that will insert a new row into the `dw_detail` DataWindow at the end of the list.

5. Create a new button labeled `Delete`, that will delete the current row in the `dw_detail` DataWindow.

6. Make the Cancel button check if the any data has been modified in either of the two DataWindow Controls. If it has, prompt the user with a message box saying that there are changes pending and they will be lost. Then, close the window.

7. Run the application, open the `w_sheet_01` sheet, and try it out!

Using Structured Query Language (SQL) in Your Scripts

This chapter covers embedded SQL (Structured Query Language). For a discussion of SQL, see Chapter 19. In PowerBuilder, you can access your database using DataWindows, or you can code embedded SQL statements into your PowerScripts. Neither method is inherently better, but DataWindow support is one of the strongest features of PowerBuilder and, in general, should be considered the primary method for data manipulation. However, some types of database interaction such as data definition cannot be accomplished using DataWindows, and some types of data manipulation lend themselves to or require embedded SQL.

Before you can access the database, you must first have a valid connection. This connection is provided via transaction objects.

This morning, you will learn:

- ☐ Standard embedded SQL
- ☐ Error checking with embedded SQL
- ☐ Embedded Cursors
- ☐ Embedded Procedures
- ☐ Dynamic embedded SQL

PowerBuilder supports all of the features of this industry-standard language; however, some features depend on the specific DBMS that you are connected to. As a general rule, PowerBuilder supports all DBMS specific features, as long as they occur within a supported SQL statement for example, PowerBuilder supports DBMS specific functions within a SELECT clause). Any SQL that can be embedded in the PowerScript, including stored procedures and cursors, can either be written directly or "painted" by using an SQL Painter.

Standard Embedded SQL

PowerBuilder allows a subset of SQL to be coded directly in scripts. This is known as *standard embedded SQL*. For a complete list of standard embedded SQL statements and syntax, check the PowerBuilder Language reference manual. Coding standard embedded SQL is simple and straightforward. The following are simple examples of standard embedded SQL:

```
DELETE FROM phone_list WHERE customer.id = 1;

INSERT INTO phone_list (id,last_name,first_name,phone)
       VALUES (1,"Smith","Joe","7145551212");

UPDATE phone_list
       SET first_name = "Joseph"
       WHERE id = 1;

COMMIT USING SQLCA;
```

Note: In general, you should always perform error checking. For more information on handling errors, see the section "Error Checking with Embedded SQL," later in this chapter.

The preceding examples, except the COMMIT statement, aren't very practical. Hard coding information in your embedded SQL isn't something that will occur very often. However, they serve to illustrate a few key points. Foremost is that embedded SQL is terminated by a semicolon (;). Secondly, multi-line statements are simply continued and don't require the continuation character (&). Lastly, notice the USING clause on the COMMIT statement. Any valid transaction object can be specified; SQLCA is the default.

Tip: Embedded SQL is terminated with a semicolon (;). Do not use a continuation character (&) for multi-line SQL statements.

Instead of having to hard code information, PowerScipt variables can be substituted wherever constants are used in an SQL statement. The PowerScript variables must be preceded by a colon (:). Any valid PowerScript variable can be used. Let's take a look at some examples.

```
int li_cust_id = 1
DELETE FROM phone_list WHERE customer.id = :li_cust_id;

int li_cust_id
string ls_lname, ls_fname
_cust_id = 1
ls_lname = "Smith"
ls_fname = "Joseph"
INSERT INTO phone_list (id,last_name,first_name,phone)
     VALUES (:li_cust_id,:ls_lname,:ls_fname,"N/A");

int li_cust_id
string ls_lname, ls_fname, ls_phone
li_cust_id = 1
SELECT pl.last_name, pl.first_name, pl.phone
     INTO :ls_last_name, :ls_fname, :ls_phone
     FROM phone_list pl
     WHERE pl.id = :li_cust_id
     USING mytran;
```

The previous examples show the use of PowerScript variables. Variables can be used to provide as well as accept information in SQL. The SELECT...INTO statement is one of the most common standard embedded SQL statements. Variables *cannot* be used in place of SQL reserved words (for example, INSERT) or for SQL object names (for example, phone_list). They can only be used to supply values. Notice also that in the second example, constants and variables are used in the

same SQL statement. In the last example, the USING clause specifies a transaction object other than SQLCA. This transaction object must have been defined, populated, and used in a previously successful CONNECT statement before it can be referenced.

Note: A SELECT...INTO statement can only return one row; otherwise, an error will occur. If you need to return more than one row and you are not using a DataWindow, then use a "fetch loop" with a cursor or a stored procedure. Cursors and stored procedures are discussed later in this chapter.

Error Checking with Embedded SQL

When you use embedded SQL, you should follow it with SQL error handling. Transaction objects have attributes that allow you to check the results of the last SQL statement. SQLCode should be checked after every SQL statement: a value of 0 indicates a successful completion, 100 indicates that no result set was returned, and -1 indicates an error.

SQLCODE	Meaning
0	Successful completion
100	Successful completion, no result set returned
-1	Error; the statement failed

If SQLCode indicates an error (-1), you can use the DBMS specific SQLDBCode and SQLErrText to get more information about the error. Most times, SQLErrText is used in a message. SQLDBCode can be included in the message or used to control program flow.

If SQLCode contains a 100, no result set is returned. You must determine, based on the function being performed, if that is an error or not. SQLCA also contains SQLNRows, which indicates the number of rows affected and can be used to check the results of an operation. SQLReturnData may also help determine the status of your operation.

Warning: SQLDBCode, SQLErrText, SQLNRows, and SQLReturnData are DBMS specific.

Error checking requirements are application/function specific. However, most embedded SQL should be followed by error checking. The following are some examples of error checking.

```
SELECT pl.last_name, pl.first_name, pl.phone
    INTO :ls_last_name, :ls_fname, :ls_phone
    FROM phone_list pl
    WHERE pl.id = :li_cust_id;
```

```
if SQLCA.SQLCode = -1 then
      MessageBox("SQL Error", "Error retrieving information. Error: "
➡ +SQLCA.SQLErrText)
elseif SQLCA.SQLCode = 100 then
      MessageBox("Phone List", "Customer - " +string(li_cust_id) +" not found.")
end if

INSERT INTO phone_list (id,last_name,first_name,phone)
      VALUES (:li_cust_id,:ls_lname,:ls_fname,"N/A");

if SQLCA.SQLCode = -1 then
      MessageBox("SQL Error","Err #:"+string(SQLCA.SQLDBCode)+"-"
➡ +SQLCA.SQLErrText)
end if

CONNECT using mytrans;
if mytrans.SQLCode = -1 then
   MessageBox("DB connect error" String(mytrans.SQLDBCode) +"-"
➡ + mytrans.SQLErrText)
end if
```

For the SELECT, the SQLCODE of 100 is an error, but after the INSERT, we don't check for the 100 because we don't expect a result set. The last example shows error checking using a different transaction object. For advanced error checking, use SQLDBCode to perform more error specific processing; however, because these codes are DBMS specific, this would require the application to be table driven or DBMS specific.

Warning: Do not use this type of error checking after a retrieval or update of a DataWindow. Use the return code from the RETRIEVE or UPDATE function.

Embedded Cursors

SQL doesn't support multi-row SELECT operations. Instead, it is necessary to use something called a *cursor*. A cursor has an associated SELECT statement and after it is opened, it acts as a kind of pointer allowing you to access a row at a time from the result set.

A cursor must be declared before it can be opened. Once opened, you can access the rows one at a time by using the FETCH command. Special forms of the UPDATE and DELETE commands are also provided for affecting the current row. When you are finished using the cursor, you must close it.

Declaring a cursor is a non-executable command and is analogous to declaring a variable. Like a variable, the scope of a declared cursor is either global, shared, instance, or local, depending on where it is declared. The general form of a cursor declaration is as follows:

```
DECLARE cursor_name CURSOR FOR your select statement
```

The following are examples of cursor declarations:

```
DECLARE pl_active CURSOR FOR SELECT pl.last_name, pl.first_name, pl.phone
     FROM phone_list pl
     WHERE pl.status <> "DELETED";

DECLARE pl_all CURSOR FOR SELECT pl.last_name, pl.first_name, pl.phone
     FROM phone_list pl
     USING mytrans;

DECLARE pl_area CURSOR FOR SELECT pl.last_name, pl.first_name, pl.phone,
pl_last_act
     FROM phone_list pl
     WHERE pl.area_code = :ls_area_code;
```

The previous examples show different characteristics of the DECLARE cursor statement. The second example uses a user-defined transaction object, while the others use the default (SQLCA). The USING clause is only valid on the declaration; it is not valid with any of the other associated statements. The third example references a user-defined variable. As long as the cursor declaration is at the same or lower scope as the variable declaration, then this is not a problem. (You can't reference a local variable in a global cursor.)

An OPEN statement can be issued for any cursor that is within the same or higher scope. (You can't open a cursor in a global function that was declared at the local level.) The OPEN causes the SELECT statement specified in the declaration to be executed.

```
OPEN pl_active;

OPEN pl_all;
```

 Warning: Only one cursor per transaction object can be opened at a time.

Once a cursor is open, you can begin to process the result set. Opening a cursor does not return a row. You must use a FETCH statement to access each successive row. A FETCH returns a row of data into the specified variables. Fetching is similar to using a SELECT...INTO except that the column specification is defined in the declaration, so all you need to specify is the "into" variables. The variables must be specified in the same order as they are defined in the cursor declaration.

```
FETCH pl_all INTO :ls_lname,:ls_fname,:ls_phone;
```

 Note: Some DBMSs support formats of the FETCH other than the standard and default FETCH NEXT. Other formats include FETCH PRIOR, FETCH FIRST, and FETCH LAST. Each format will access the specified row.

Fetching is typically performed in a loop. The following is an example of a fetch loop that is governed by SQLCODE:

```
FETCH pl_all INTO :ls_lname,:ls_fname,:ls_phone;
do while mytrans.SQLCode = 0
        ... process the variables
        FETCH pl_all INTO :ls_lname,:ls_fname,:ls_phone;
loop
```

After processing the rows, or whenever you are finished with it, the cursor must be closed. CLOSE ends the processing of the cursor.

CLOSE pl_active;

CLOSE pl_all;

Besides the FETCH command, there are other commands associated with cursors. They are variations of the DELETE and UPDATE commands, "DELETE Where Current of Cursor" and "UPDATE Where Current of Cursor." They both act on the row where the cursor is currently positioned.

```
DELETE FROM phone_list WHERE CURRENT OF pl_all;
```

```
UPDATE phone_list SET status = "DELETED" WHERE CURRENT OF pl_all;
```

Note: Not all DBMSs support "DELETE Where Current of Cursor."

You have now seen all the commands associated with cursors. In order to use a cursor, it must be declared. You open it, fetch the rows, and finally close it. Let's take a look at a complete example of a locally declared cursor.

```
DECLARE pl_area CURSOR FOR SELECT pl.last_name, pl.first_name, pl.phone,
➡ pl_last_act
        FROM phone_list pl
        WHERE pl.area_code = :ls_area_code;

OPEN pl_area;
if SQLCA.SQLCODE = -1 then
        MessageBox("Database Error","Error starting update - "  +SQLCA.SQLErrText)
        RETURN
end if

FETCH pl_area INTO :ls_lname,:ls_fname,:ls_phone,:ldt_last_act;
do while SQLCA.SQLCode = 0
        ... process the row ...
        FETCH pl_area INTO :ls_lname,:ls_fname,:ls_phone,:ldt_last_act;
loop

CLOSE pl_area;
if SQLCA.SQLCODE = -1 then
        MessageBox("Database Error","Error finishing update - " +SQLCA.SQLErrText)
        RETURN
end if
```

25

Embedded Procedures

Stored procedures are pieces of code written in SQL (with extensions) and stored in the database. Stored procedures can return result sets. However, many stored procedures do not return result sets. To utilize a stored procedure in *embedded* SQL, you must declare it, execute it, and then fetch any results. In that respect, stored procedures are similar to cursors. There are many differences between stored procedures and cursors, but that is beyond the scope of this chapter.

 Note: Not all DBMSs support stored procedures.

Declaring a procedure is a non-executable command and is analogous to declaring a variable. Like a variable, the scope of a procedure is either global, shared, instance, or local, depending on where it is declared. The following are examples of procedure declarations. In order to declare a procedure, there must be a stored procedure in the database. This stored procedure is then associated with a procedure name in the DECLARE statement. The general form of a procedure declaration is as follows:

```
DECLARE procedure_name PROCEDURE FOR database stored procedure name.
```

The following are examples of procedure declarations:

```
DECLARE get_active_list PROCEDURE FOR sp_get_active_list;

DECLARE check_id PROCEDURE FOR sp_check_userid USING mytrans;

DECLARE get_list PROCEDURE FOR sp_get_list @status = :ls_status;

DECLARE get_order_num PROCEDURE FOR sp_get_next_number
        @num_type ="O";
```

 Note: Watcom 4.0 does not support the use of "@" symbols.

If you use SQL Server, output parameters can be indicated with the optional keyword "OUT" (for example, @ret_num=0 OUT)

The previous examples show different characteristics of the DECLARE procedure statement. The second example uses a user-defined transaction object, while the others use the default (SQLCA). The USING clause is only valid on the declaration; it is not valid with any of the other associated statements. The third example references a user-defined variable. As long as the procedure declaration is at the same or lower scope as the variable declaration, then this is not a problem (for example, you can't reference a local variable in a global procedure).

You can EXECUTE any procedure that is defined within the same or higher scope. (You can't execute a procedure in a global function that was declared at the local level.) An EXECUTE statement causes the stored procedure to be executed in the database.

```
EXECUTE check_id;

EXECUTE get_list;

EXECUTE get_order_num;
```

Now that the stored procedure is executed, you can process any results. Stored procedures don't have to return a result set. A stored procedure could return information via the return code (SQLDBCode). If a result set is returned, you must use a FETCH statement to access each successive result row. Fetching is similar to a SELECT...INTO except that the column specification is defined in the declaration, so all you need to specify is the "into" variables. The variables must be specified in the same order as defined in the stored procedure.

```
FETCH get_order_num INTO :ls_order_num;
```

If there are multiple rows, the fetching is typically performed in a loop. The following is an example of a fetch loop that is governed by SQLCODE:

```
FETCH get_list INTO :ls_lname,:ls_fname,:ls_phone;
do while mytrans.SQLCode = 0
        ... process the variables
   FETCH get_list INTO :ls_lname,:ls_fname,:ls_phone;
loop
```

If the procedure returns a result set, it must be closed after processing. CLOSE ends the processing of the procedure. You only need to close a procedure that returns result sets because PowerBuilder automatically closes procedures that don't. If no result set is returned and the procedure executed correctly, PowerBuilder sets SQLCODE to 100.

```
CLOSE get_order_num;
```

Now that you have seen all the commands associated with stored procedures, you know that in order to use a procedure, it must be declared and executed. If results are returned, you must fetch the rows and close the procedure. Let's take a look at a complete example of a locally declared procedure. This example returns a single row and therefore doesn't require a fetch loop. However, one row should always be returned; therefore, an SQLCode of 100 is considered an error.

```
DECLARE get_order_num PROCEDURE FOR sp_get_next_number
        @num_type ="O";
EXECUTE get_order_num;
FETCH get_order_num INTO :ls_order_num;
if SQLCA.SQLCODE = -1 or SQLCA.SQLCODE = 100 then
        MessageBox("Database Error","Error accessing order numbers - "
   ➥ +SQLCA.SQLErrText)
end if
CLOSE get_order_num;
```

25

Dynamic Embedded SQL

When PowerBuilder does not support a statement in standard embedded SQL, such as a Data Definition Language (DDL) statement, or when the input parameters or the format of the SQL is only known at run time, the application must specify the SQL dynamically. This is known as *Dynamic SQL*, and the parameters and statements can change each time the program is run.

This section covers the four dynamic SQL formats:

Format	Usage
Format 1	No result set; no input parameters.
Format 2	No result set, with input parameters.
Format 3	Result set format and input parameters are known at compile time.
Format 4	Result set format and/or input parameters are unknown at compile time.

Format 1 Dynamic SQL

Format 1 is the simplest form of dynamic SQL. Use this format to execute SQL statements that don't have any input parameters and don't produce result sets. Format 1 consists of the EXECUTE IMMEDIATE command that takes a string variable as its parameter. That string is then executed.

```
string ls_create
ls_create = "CREATE TABLE phone_list " &
+"(id integer not null,"&
+"(last_name char(30) not null,"&
+"first_name char(30) not null,"&
+"phone char(10) not null,"&
+"fax char(10) not null,"&
+"status char (10) not null",&
+"last_act date not null)"
EXECUTE IMMEDIATE :ls_create;
```

This example shows Format 1 being used for a Data Definition Language (DDL) statement. Almost any SQL statement can be built and executed this way.

Format 2 Dynamic SQL

This format is used to execute SQL statements that do not produce a result set but do require input parameters. Format 2 requires the use of a construct called the *Dynamic Staging Area*. The Dynamic Staging Area is a work area used by PowerBuilder for handling dynamic SQL. Format 2 consists of two parts : the PREPARE and the EXECUTE statement. The PREPARE statement takes a string of SQL as input. "?" can be substituted for cønstants in the SQL statement. The "?" acts as placeholder and will be replaced with the parameters that are part of the EXECUTE statement.

```
string ls_sql, ls_lname, ls_fname
ls_sql = "INSERT INTO phone_list (last_name, first_name) VALUES (?,?)"
PREPARE SQLSA FROM :ls_sql;
ls_lname = "QUINN"
ls_fname = "ROBERT"
EXECUTE SQLSA USING :ls_lname,:ls_fname;
```

Format 3 Dynamic SQL

This format is used to execute cursors or procedures that produce a result set, and the result set columns and number of input parameters are known when you are writing the script. Format 3 requires the use of the Dynamic Staging Area. Let's look at an example of a dynamic procedure.

```
string ls_num_type = "O"
int li_ret_num
DECLARE get_num DYNAMIC PROCEDURE FOR SQLSA;
PREPARE SQLSA FROM sp_get_next_number @num_type =?;
EXECUTE DYNAMIC get_num USING :ls_num_type;
FETCH get_num INTO :li_ret_num;
CLOSE get_num;
```

This next example illustrates a dynamic cursor.

```
DECLARE pl_area DYNAMIC CURSOR FOR SQLSA;
string ls_NY_area, ls_DC_area
ls_NY_area = "SELECT pl.last_name, pl.first_name, pl.phone, pl_last_act " &
      + "FROM phone_list pl" &
      + "WHERE pl.area_code = '212'"
ls_DC_area = "SELECT pl.last_name, pl.first_name, pl.phone, pl_last_act " &
      + "FROM phone_list pl" &
      + "WHERE pl.area_code = '202'"
if sle_state.text = "NY" then
      PREPARE SQLSA FROM :ls_NY_area USING mytrans;
else
      PREPARE SQLSA FROM :ls_DC_area USING mytrans;
else if
OPEN DYNAMIC pl_area;
FETCH pl_area INTO :ls_lname,:ls_fname,:ls_phone,:ldt_last_act;
do while SQLCA.SQLCode = 0
      ... process the row ...
      FETCH pl_area INTO :ls_lname,:ls_fname,:ls_phone,:ldt_last_act;
loop
CLOSE pl_area;
```

Similar to standard SQL, the DECLARE...DYNAMIC statement is non-executable and is analogous to declaring a variable. Like a variable, the scope is either global, shared, instance, or local, depending on where it is declared.

The FETCH and CLOSE statements are unchanged for standard embedded SQL. Dynamic cursors also support the other FETCH formats (for example, FETCH PRIOR, FETCH FIRST, or FETCH LAST) as well as the "Where Current of Cursor" variations of the DELETE and UPDATE commands.

25

> **Note:** Not all DBMSs support the extended FETCH formats or "DELETE Where Current of Cursor."

Format 4 Dynamic SQL

This format is used to execute a cursor or stored procedure that produces a result set, and the result set columns and/or number of input parameters are only known at run time. Format 4 requires the use of the Dynamic Staging Area and a construct called the *Dynamic Description Area*. The Dynamic Description Area contains attributes that describe the result set and input parameters. These are listed here:

Attribute	Description
NumInputs	Number of input parameters
InParmType	Array of input parameter types
NumOutputs	Number of output parameters
OutParmType	Array of output parameter types

The Dynamic Description Area also contains the actual values of the parameters. PowerBuilder provides functions for setting and accessing these parameters. These are listed here:

```
SetDynamicParm
GetDynamicDate
GetDynamicDateTime
GetDynamicNumber
GetDynamicString
```

These functions, along with the description arrays, allow you to analyze the input and output requirements of the dynamic SQL. The parameter types are enumerated data types. See the PowerBuilder Language reference for more information. Let's look at an example.

```
string ls_sql, ls_lname, ls_fname
int li_id, li_outputs, li_output

ls_sql = "SELECT id, last_name, first_name FROM phone_list WHERE status = ?"

PREPARE SQLSA FROM :ls_sql;
DESCRIBE SQLSA INTO SQLDA;

DECLARE pl_status DYNAMIC CURSOR FOR SQLSA;

SetDynamicParm(SQLDA, 1, upper(trim(sle_status.text)))

OPEN DYNAMIC pl_status USING DESCRIPTOR SQLDA;

FETCH pl_status INTO :li_id, :ls_lname,:ls_fname;
```

```
        li_outputs = SQLDA.NumOutputs
        for li_output = 1 to li_outputs
              *** allocate an array specific to the output types ***
        next
do while SQLCA.SQLCode = 0
        *** process the row using the array ***
        FETCH pl_status INTO :li_id, :ls_lname,:ls_fname;
loop

CLOSE pl_status;
```

PowerBuilder populates SQLDA.NumInputs when the DESCRIBE is executed. Utilizing that and SQLDA.InParmType, you can prompt the user for the required parameters if you can prompt using the column names. You can then set the input parameters by using the SetDynamicParm function.

PowerBuilder populates SQLDA.NumOutputs after the DESCRIBE command if the database supports output parameter description; otherwise, it populates it after the first FETCH. In a manner similar to input parameter processing, you can use SQLDA.OutParmType to call the appropriate function after the FETCH in order to retrieve the results.

Morning Summary

PowerBuilder contains extensive support for embedded SQL. Standard embedded SQL provides enough functionality to handle 95 percent of the requirements for typical SQL processing. Standard embedded SQL provides support for Data Manipulation Language (DML), including cursors and stored procedures. Standard SQL is coded right in the PowerScript and is terminated by a semicolon (;). Multi-line SQL does not require the continuation character (&).

Standard embedded SQL supports variable substitution, making the retrieval and updating of data flexible and powerful. PowerScript variables are preceded by a colon (:) and can be used in place of constants.

Transaction objects define a link between PowerScripts and the Database. Error handling is provided at two levels: generically using SQLCode and at the DBMS specific level using SQLDBCode. Other attributes of the transaction object can also provide information about errors. Through the use of transaction objects, PowerBuilder provides multiple connections concurrently.

If further SQL capabilities are required, PowerBuilder supports four different formats of Dynamic SQL. These formats range from the simplest (such as EXECUTE IMMEDIATE "your SQL") to functionality that allows almost completely Dynamic SQL including the number and types of input and output fields. PowerBuilder provides both the functions and the constructs to support this very dynamic functionality.

PowerBuilder provides this level of support of SQL on top of the easy-to-use functionality of their DataWindow objects.

25

Chapter

26

Using the
Debugger

In this chapter, you will learn:

☐ What the Debugger is and why you need it

☐ How to set up the Debugger

☐ How to use the Debugger

What Is a Debugger, and Why Do I Need It?

Even the most seasoned programmer finds bugs in his/her application, so you shouldn't be surprised to find a few in your PowerBuilder application. Luckily, PowerBuilder comes with a very powerful tool that can help you find and kill these bugs: the *Debugger*. The PowerBuilder Debugger allows you to view and manipulate variables and step through your scripts as your application executes. To use the Debugger, you simply select a break point or stopping point in your application scripts and run the application. When your application reaches a break point, the Debugger window will reappear. At this point, you may view and edit all variables and attributes, continue to step through the application one line at a time, or continue executing until the next break point is found. If you have never used a Debugger before, you will soon find it to be a very useful tool. If you have used a Debugger before, you will find that PowerBuilder's ranks among the best.

In this chapter, you will learn how to use the Debugger by placing stops in your scripts and viewing and manipulating variables. First, you will learn how to select scripts and place break points in them or edit any existing break points. After placing and editing a few break points, you will learn how to find, view, and edit variables and attributes. Finally, you will learn a few tips and techniques to further refine your ability to use the Debugger.

Setting up the Debugger

Using the Debugger is very easy. First, you have to start up the Debugger. To do this, click on the Debugger button on the PowerBar. Depending on whether or not break points have previously been set within the application, one of two things will happen: Debugger's Select Script window will open (see Fig. 26.1), or the Edit Stops window will open.

If break points have not previously been set within the current application, the Select Script window will appear after clicking on the Debugger button. (Note that if you are following along in PowerBuilder and the Edit Stops window appears, you can follow this portion of the tutorial by clicking on the **Clear All** button then the **Add** button to bring up the Select Script window.

Figure 26.1.
The Select Script Debugger window.

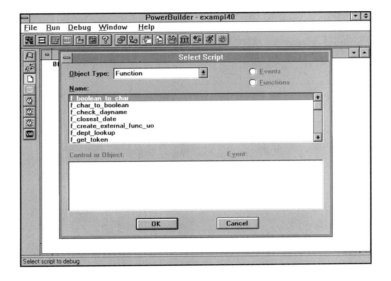

The Select Script window allows you to select a script in which you want to suspend execution in any of the current application's objects. This is done by selecting the type of object the script is in, defining whether the script is an event or a function, and selecting the script itself. The Select Script window contains the following controls:

- [ ] A drop-down list box entitled Object Type
- [ ] Two radio buttons entitled Events and Functions
- [ ] Two list boxes, one that is entitled Name and the other (below Name box) that changes titles depending on selections made in the window
- [ ] Two buttons: OK and Cancel

The Select Script window is a response window (application module) and there is no associated menu for it.

The Object Type drop-down list box contains a list of all of the PowerBuilder object types. The following selections are available: Application, Window, Menu, User Object, and Function. This drop-down list box is used to select the type of object containing the script in which you choose to suspend execution. For example, if you want to suspend execution in the open event of one of your application's window objects, select Window from the drop-down list box. If you want to suspend execution in a function in one of your user objects, select User Object. When a selection is made, the Name list box is repopulated to show the names of all of the objects of the selected type that are contained in one of the pbl files defined for the application.

26

The two radio buttons are used to define the type of script in which you want to suspend execution. If the script is any event—standard or user defined—then select the radio button marked Events. If the script is a function, then select the button marked Functions. When a selection is made, the bottom list box changes headings. Figure 26.2 shows what the headings look like when the Events radio button is selected. Figure 26.3 shows what the headings on the bottom list box look like when the Functions radio button is selected.

Figure 26.2.
The Select Script window when the Events button is selected.

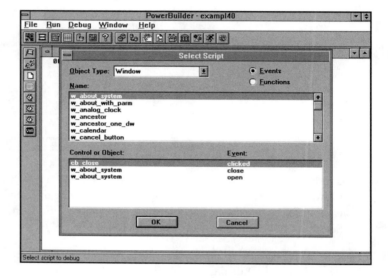

Figure 26.3.
The Select Script window when the Functions button is selected.

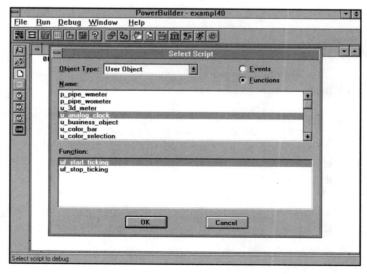

After selecting the script type, the bottom list box is repopulated. It shows the names of scripts of the selected type that are contained in the object highlighted in the Name list box. For example, if you want to suspend execution in the open event of one of your application's window objects, select the radio button marked Events. If you want to suspend execution in a function in one of your user objects, select the radio button marked Functions.

The Name list box contains the names of all of the objects in your application that are the type selected in the Object Type drop-down list box. Use this list to select the name of the object that contains the script in which you want to suspend execution. To do this, click on the name of the object. If the object name does not appear in this list, make sure you have selected the correct type of object in the Object Type drop-down list box. If the object name still fails to appear, leave the Debugger and make sure the pbl file that contains the object is defined for the current application. After finding and selecting the name of the object, the bottom list box is repopulated to show the names of all of the scripts of the selected script type that the object contains. For example, if you want to suspend execution in the open event of one of your application's window objects, make sure Window is selected from the Object Type drop-down list box and the Events radio button is checked. Then locate the name of the window object in the Names list box and click on it.

The bottom list box contains the names of the scripts in the selected object. If the script type you have selected is an event, you will have two columns in the list box (refer to Fig 26.2). The first column, entitled Control or Object, contains the names of all the controls on the selected object and the object name itself as it appears in the Names list box. The object name and name of each control will appear once in this list for each of its events that contain scripts. The event containing the script is displayed in the column to the right entitled Event. To select a script in a control, for example, the Clicked event for a button, find the name of the control containing the event. Then find the name of the event containing the script and click on that row in the list (refer to Fig. 26.2). To select an event on the object, for example, the Open for a window, find the object's name on the left side of the list. Then find the event on the right and click on that row.

If, on the other hand, the script type you have selected is Function, you will have only one column in the bottom list box titled Function (refer to Fig. 26.3). This column contains the names of all of the functions in the selected object. To select a function, find its name in the list and click on it.

Using the Debugger

You are now ready to enter the Debugger's main window (see Fig. 26.4). Select the point within the selected script in which you want to suspend execution. To accept the selected script and enter the Debugger's main window, click the **OK** button. To lose your changes and close the Debugger, click the **Cancel** button.

Figure 26.4.

The Debugger's main window.

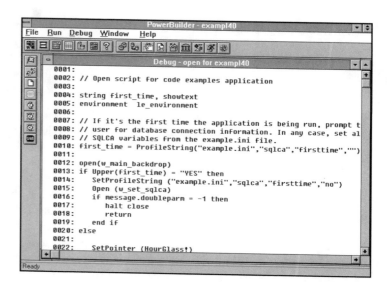

When the Debugger's main window opens, it will display the script you selected in the Select Script window (refer to Fig. 26.1). The Debugger also has a PainterBar associated with it that will be explored later in the chapter (see Fig. 26.5).

Figure 26.5.

The Debugger's PainterBar.

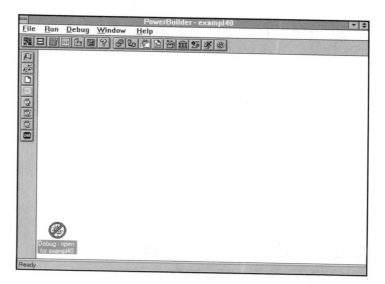

The first thing you need to know is how to place a break point in the script you have selected.

The term *break point* simply means the point in the application where you want to suspend execution. To set a break point in the script you have selected, simply double-click on the line in the script where you want execution to be suspended. You'll notice after clicking on a line that a small stop sign will appear to the left of the line. (see Fig. 26.6).

Figure 26.6.
Stop sign on the Debugger's main window.

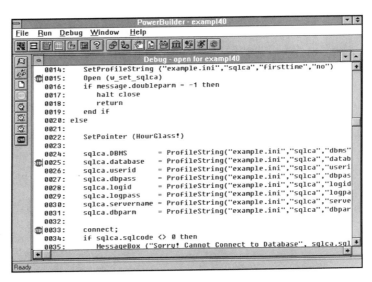

The stop sign denotes the location of break points in your script. You may place a break point on any line in any script, with the exception of commented lines. If you try to place a break point on a line that is commented out, PowerBuilder will beep at you, and the stop sign will not appear. One other exception I should note here is that if you have a command line that spans multiple edit lines (you have used the "&" character for easy reading), you must select the last edit line in the command.

You may select as many break points as you wish in a script, and you may select multiple scripts in which to place break points. If you want to select multiple scripts for placement of break points, select Se**l**ect Script... from the **D**ebug menu. This will reopen the Select Script window, allowing you to select another script. Don't worry about losing previously set break points; any break points you have set prior to doing this will be saved.

Now that you have learned how to select scripts and place break points, you need to learn how to edit the break points. To edit break points, simply pull down the **D**ebug menu and select Edit S**t**ops.... This will open the Edit Stops window (see Fig. 26.7). (Note: If you entered the Debugger with previously set break points for the current application, the Edit Stops window opened rather than the Select Scripts window.)

26

Figure 26.7.

The Edit Stops window.

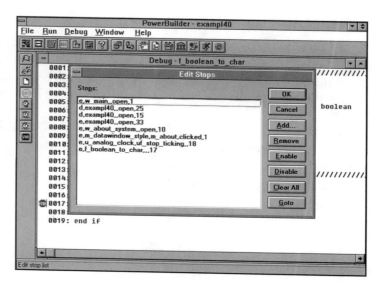

Within the Edit Stops window, all of the break points you have set appear in the list on the left side of the window. Each entry in the list is formatted in the following manner:

☐ The first letter is either *e* or *d*, denoting whether this stop is enabled or disabled, respectively.

☐ A comma followed by the object name the script is in.

☐ Another comma and the control name the script is in.

☐ Another comma followed by the line number on which the break point was placed.

The Edit Stops window has eight buttons. We will review the functionality of each.

The top button is the **OK** button. Like most **OK** buttons, selecting this button accepts your changes and closes the window.

The **Cancel** button also works like most cancel buttons; it loses your changes and closes the window.

The **Add...** button allows you to add another break point. Clicking this button closes the Edit Stops window and opens the Select Script window, allowing you to select a script to which a stop may be added.

The **Remove** button allows you to remove a stop you have placed earlier. To remove a break point, click on it (highlighting it). Then click the **Remove** button.

You may at some point want to disable a break point rather than remove it, allowing you to easily replace the break point if you should need it again in the future. The **Enable** and **Disable** buttons give you this capability. The **Enable** button enables a break point that was previously disabled.

To enable a break point, click on it (highlighting it), and then click the **Enable** button. The **Disable** button disables a break point. To disable a break point, click on it (highlighting it), and then click the **Disable** button.

The **Clear All** button removes all of the break points in the list.

The **Goto** button allows you to move between scripts that have break points assigned to them. To use this feature, select the break point you want to move to from the list and click the **Goto** button. The Edit Stops window will close, and the main Debugger window will display the script containing the selected break point.

Now that you have learned how to place and edit break points in your application, it is time to learn to use the Debugger to help you resolve bugs in your application. To do this, you must learn how to use the Debugger's many features. Most of the features for the Debugger are accessible through the PainterBar (refer to Fig. 26.5). The PainterBar will, therefore, be our starting point.

The first button on the painter bar is the Start button. Use this button to start your application running in Debug mode. In order for your break points to be recognized, you must run the application from this button or its associated menu item. (If you run the application by using the Run button on the PowerBar, your break points will not be recognized, and the application will run normally without debugging.) When the Start button is pressed, your application will open and run normally until it reaches the first break point. Once the first break point has been reached, execution will be suspended, and the Debugger window will display. You will notice that the PainterBar has changed (see Fig. 26.8).

Figure 26.8.
The Debugger's PainterBar during application suspension.

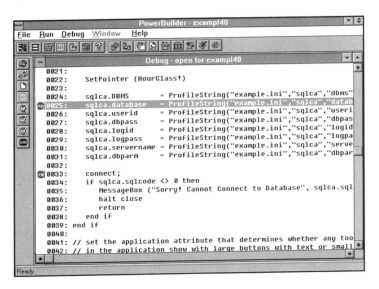

On the Debugger's PainterBar, the Start button has been replaced with the Continue button. The Continue button will hide the Debugger window and continue the execution of the application until either the next break point is found or the application is terminated. (Note that if you are following along in PowerBuilder, don't press the Continue button at this point; explanation of the use of the Debugger during suspension of the application follows.) Now that the application is suspended, you may add new break points or edit existing ones if you want to use the features described later to begin debugging your application.

The next button on the Debugger's PainterBar is the Step button. This button is used to step through the lines in your scripts one at a time. Each time you click this button, PowerBuilder will execute the line of script currently highlighted. If that line of script triggers an event or calls a function, that event or function's script will be loaded into the Debugger, and you will see it on the Debugger's main window. If you continue to step through this script until it terminates, you will be returned to the script that has your break point in it. In this way, the Debugger allows you to follow through the events in your application without having to put break points in each one. For example, if you were to put a break point on or stepped to a line in a script that opened a window, the next time you pressed the Step button, the open event for that window would be displayed. If you were to continue stepping through to the end of the open event (and any events or functions called by the open event), you would return to the calling script unless, of course, the window you were opening was a response window. In that case, you would not be returned to the Debugger until the response window was closed. If all this sounds confusing, don't be discouraged. It's really not difficult, and you'll get the hang of it once you experiment with this a few times.

The next two buttons on the PainterBar are the Select Script button and the Edit Stop button. These buttons correspond to the Select Script... and the Edit Stops... menu items we used earlier in this chapter. There is no difference between using these buttons and selecting the corresponding menu items.

The next three buttons on the list are the Watch buttons. I will put off discussion of these buttons until we have discussed the last button on the PainterBar, the Show Variables button. Clicking the Show Variables button causes the Debugger's main window to split vertically. The top half of the screen still shows the current script, but the bottom half now shows a hierarchical list of application variables by scope (see Fig. 26.9).

This hierarchical list works much like the Library Painter or File Manager. The icon for each row in the list tells you whether or not double-clicking on it will cause an action to occur or will expand the list further. (For example, in File Manager, double-clicking on a row that has a file folder expands the list to show the files for that subdirectory, but double-clicking on a row that shows the File icon launches the application associated with the file.) The yellow box to the left of each row on the Variables list tells you whether or not double-clicking that row will expand the list further or allow you to edit the variables or attributes on that row. If there is a plus sign

in the square, then double-clicking that row will expand the list to the next level. The plus sign will then change to a minus sign to indicate that the level is fully extended. If the square has nothing inside it, then double-clicking on that row will bring up an edit box allowing you to edit the value of the variables on that row. This is one of the best features of the Debugger. You can manipulate dynamically the values of your variables as you move through the application. This allows you to test different scenarios for your scripts.

Figure 26.9.
The Debugger's main window with Variables list.

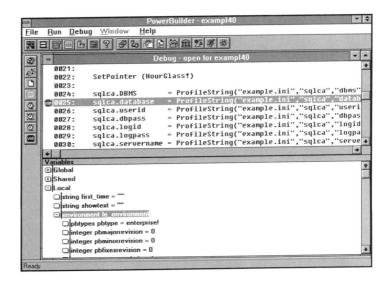

In order to be proficient in using the Variables list, you need to know how to find the variables you are looking for. When the Variables list is first displayed, you will see three groupings of variables (refer to Fig. 26.9): Local, Shared, and Global. Under the Local grouping will be the local variables for whatever script is currently displayed in the upper portion of the screen. The Shared grouping contains the shared variables for the object the script in the upper portion of the window sits on. For example, if the script were a window open event, the Shared grouping list would contain all of the shared variables declared for that window. The Global grouping contains not only the global variables you have declared for the application, but also the attributes of each instance of an object currently open in the application. What is noteworthy here is that an object's instance variables are treated as attributes of each instance. So if you are looking for an instance variable, you will find it in the Global grouping under the name of the instance of the object. For example, if the script were a window OPEN event, the instance variables for the window would be found in the Global listing under the name of the window (see Fig. 26.10).

Figure 26.10.
*Finding an instance
variable.*

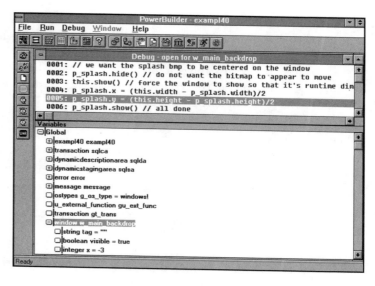

As you can see, finding and keeping track of variables and attributes can be a tricky thing; and the larger your applications get, the more difficult this becomes. Thankfully, the Debugger comes with a feature that helps find and track variables and attributes. This is where those PainterBar buttons we skipped earlier come into use. The Show Watch button causes the Debugger's main window to split verticaly yet again (see Fig. 26.11).

Figure 26.11.
*The Debugger's main
window with Variables and
Watch lists.*

The Watch list allows you to single out variables and attributes that are important and place them on the list for tracking. This way, you don't have to scroll through the Variables list while you are debugging. To add a variable or attribute to the Watch list, find and select it (by clicking once on it) in the Variables list, then click on the Add Watch button. The variable or attribute you select will now also appear in the Watch list. To remove a variable or attribute from the Watch list, select it from the list and click the Remove Watch button.

Both the Show Variables button and the Show Watch button work like toggle switches. So if you want to close one of the lists, just click on the button for that list again, and the list will disappear. Many people put all of their important variables in the Watch list and close the Variables list to give them more room on the screen to see the script. Others never use the Watch list and keep it closed all the time; and some (like myself) use both, closing and opening the lists as needed. It's really a matter of personal preference.

Helpful Hints for Using the Debugger

To be successful in using the Debugger, it is important that you know where to place the break points. If you place a break point too soon, you may wind up spending a long time stepping through your code before you get to the actual bug. On the other hand, if you place a break point after a bug occurs, you may miss seeing the bug occur. There is no one great method for figuring this out; but in general, it is helpful to have some idea as to which script is causing the problem. However, this is not always possible. When you are uncertain as to which script is causing the problem, it is best to start with the script of the last event the user initiated prior to the bug's occurrence. Following is a real-life example to illustrate this point.

You are asked to maintain an application you didn't write. One of the windows has a bug that occurs right after the user clicks a certain button. The Clicked event for that button triggers other events or calls other functions. Since you didn't write this code, you're not sure which function or event contains the bug. In this case, you should place a break point in the first line of the Clicked event for the button. This way, you can step through the code until you find the bug. Once you have found the bug, it's a good idea to place a break point just before it and remove the first one. Doing this will allow you to get right back to the bug without having to step a line at a time the next time through. After all, you don't always fix them the first time!

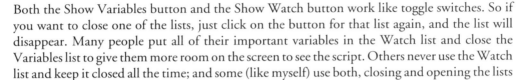

There are some things that you should avoid doing in the Debugger. Never place a break point in the Lose Focus or Other event for a window because the Debugger itself seems to trigger these events. What happens is that you end up in an endless feedback loop that eventually causes PowerBuilder to become unstable. Never step through the Close event for a response window. This will cause PowerBuilder to become unstable. Before Version 4.0 came out, I had a lot more things for you to avoid, but they all seem to be fixed in the new version!

Afternoon Summary

You will often find bugs in your PowerBuilder applications (especially when you first start developing in PowerBuilder!), and the Debugger is designed to help you find and kill them. To use the Debugger, you simply select a break point in your application scripts and run the application. The term "break point" is a point in the application where you want to suspend execution. To set a break point, simply double-click on the line in the script where you want execution to be suspended. The PowerBuilder Debugger allows you to place as many break points in your application as you like. When running your application from the Debugger, execution will be suspened as soon as the first break point is encountered. At this point, you may step through your application one line at a time using the Debugger's Step feature. During the suspension of the application, you may delete or add stop points as you please.

The Variables list section of the Debugger displays three groupings of variables: Global, Shared, and Local. You use this list to view and edit the values of your application's variables during execution time. Double-clicking on a variable will bring up an edit box allowing you to edit the value of a variable on that row. This allows you to manipulate dynamically the values of your variables as you move through the application.

Because the Variables list can get very large, the Debugger comes with a facility to allow you to track them. The Watch list allows you to single out variables and attributes that are important by placing them on it for tracking. This way, you don't have to scroll through the Variables list while you are debugging.

Q&A

Q Why would I want to use embedded SQL over DataWindows?

A Although DataWindows should be considered the primary method of data manipulation, some types of updates don't require the overhead of DataWindows and would be more efficient with embedded SQL. Accessing only a small amount of data (one or two columns or one row) can be much more efficient if using an embedded SELECT...INTO.

Q Can I create a table on the fly in PowerBuilder?

A By utilizing Format 1 of dynamic SQL, a table definition can be built and submitted to the database. Other database objects can also be dynamically created.

Q What type of embedded SQL is used to control a database transaction?

A PowerScripts supports both the COMMIT and the ROLLBACK statements as standard embedded SQL. (AUTOCOMMIT must be set to False.)

Q Why do I need the Debugger; isn't it obvious where the bugs are located?

A On smaller applications for which you have written the code, you may be better off not using the Debugger. The Debugger is most useful on larger applications where the bug may be imbedded deeply in the code. The Debugger is also great for finding problems in applications you are not familiar with.

Q Why don't I see my posted events execute?

A The Debugger will not display the scripts for events that have been posted unless you have placed a stop in that script. However, if a stop is encountered in a posted event, be careful not to step through the end of the script as this will cause the Debugger to become unstable.

Q Can I use the Debugger on an executable version of my application?

A No, you may only use the Debugger on the interpreted version of your application. If you need to debug an application currently in production, you must go back to the application's source libraries and run it in interpreted mode.

Workshop

Quiz

1. What are the two most important fields in a transaction object for error handling?
2. What are the valid values for SQLCode?
3. What character is used to terminate SQL statements, and how do you continue multi-line SQL statements?
4. Where can I use a PowerScript variable in SQL, and how do I indicate that it is a variable?
5. Can transaction objects other the SQLCA be used with embedded SQL?
6. Can a SELECT...INTO return more than one row?

26

Putting PowerBuilder into Action

1. Start the Debugger from the PowerBar.
2. Select the Window object w_sheet_01 to place a break point in.
3. Select the Clicked event for the DataWindow control dw_master.
4. Place a break point on the fourth line in the script. The line should read
   `ll_row = getclickedrow().`

5. Run the application from the Debugger.

6. Find the place in the application that will cause the break point to be recognized and cause the event. (Tip: Remember that it's in a Clicked event for a DataWindow.)

7. Step one line down the script.

8. Observe the value of ll_row and change it to a new value.

9. Continue execution of the application and observe the results of your editing.

27

Creating an Executable

In this chapter, you will learn:

- [ ] What an executable version is and why you need it
- [ ] File type definition and uses
- [ ] How to create an executable using the Project Painter
- [ ] How to creating an executable using the Application Painter

What Is an Executable Version, and Why Do I Need It?

Now that you have learned to build an application in PowerBuilder, you need to know how to distribute it to your users. To do this, you need to create an *executable version* of your application—a version that can be run on its own, outside of the PowerBuilder development environment. This is really just a matter of packaging appropriately the various pieces your application needs. In order to get the most efficient executable, you need to know how to pick the correct pieces and use the right model for packaging them together. In this chapter, you will acquire this knowledge and use the packaging tools that PowerBuilder provides to create an executable version of your application.

A PowerBuilder executable application can contain one or more of the following files:

- [ ] One executable file
- [ ] Any number of PowerBuilder dynamic library files
- [ ] Other resource files

In order for you to decide which of these files is needed for your application, you need to know what they are. The following section will explain each of these file types in detail.

File Type Definition and Uses

You will always create exactly one executable (.EXE) file for each application you want to distribute to your users. A PowerBuilder executable contains the PowerBuilder bootstrap routine, which enables your application to run as a native application on its target platform. This allows Windows users to start your application by double-clicking on the executable file's icon in Program Manager; Macintosh users can double-click the icon on the desktop.

Depending on the way the application has been built, the executable file will also contain one or more of the following:

- [ ] Compiled versions of objects contained in the application's libraries. The executable file may contain all of the PowerBuilder objects needed for the application. This is usually done so that you need to distribute only one file. For larger applications, you

may want to divide your application into one executable file and one or more PowerBuilder dynamic libraries. You will learn more about these libraries later in this chapter.

☐ An execution library list that is used by the PowerBuilder execution system to find objects and resources in the PowerBuilder dynamic libraries packaged with the application.

☐ Resource files used by your application, such as bitmaps (.BMP), icons (.ICO), and cursor (.CUR) files.

It is a good idea to keep your executable files smaller than 1.2MB. If you have a large application, you may decrease the size of your executable file by distributing some (or all) of its objects in one or more PowerBuilder dynamic library (.PBD) file. PowerBuilder dynamic libraries (DLLs) are like executable files in that they contain compiled versions of the application's objects. PBD files are a subset of a PowerBuilder library (.PBL) file. The PBD file contains only the compiled form of each object in the PBL file. PBD files work much like Windows dynamic link libraries in that they are linked to the application during execution. However, PBD files are not interchangeable with DLLs as they have a completely different internal structure.

Unlike executable files, PBD files do not contain the PowerBuilder bootstrap routine. As a result, they cannot be executed independently. Instead, PBD files are used by the application to provide objects and resources (such as icons) that are not contained in the executable file. There are a number of other reasons besides reducing the executable file size that you may choose to use PBD files. They are as follows:

☐ **Efficient Memory Usage.** Because PowerBuilder loads only the object needed rather than the entire PBD file into memory, it uses far less memory. Also using PBD files will make your executable size smaller in memory, making it faster to load and less obtrusive to the operating system.

☐ **Maintainability.** By allowing you to distribute the components of your application separately, maintenance of your application is simplified. If you need to distribute an upgrade or a bug fix, you don't need to redistribute the entire application. Instead, you can just distribute the PBD files that have been modified.

☐ **Greater Flexibility.** PBD files allow you to provide objects that are only referenced dynamically at runtime; for example, a user object whose name is contained only in a string variable. Objects like these, with the exception of DataWindows, cannot be put in an executable file.

☐ **Reusability.** You may share PBD files among any number of applications and concurrent users. This allows you to create common object libraries to be used by many (or all) of your applications.

Your PowerBuilder application may use external resource files such as icon (.ICO) or bitmap (.BMP) files. Following is a list of all the resource file types that may be referenced by a PowerBuilder application:

27

- [ ] Icons: ICO files
- [ ] Pictures: BMP, RLE, and WMF files
- [ ] Pointers: CUR files

These resource files must be distributed with your application. There are three different ways you may choose to distribute them:

1. Include your resource in the application's executable file.
2. Include your resources in the application's PBD files.
3. Distribute your resource files separately.

Each of these methods is discussed here:

1. **Include your resource in the application's executable file.** When an executable file is built, PowerBuilder automatically includes all of the resource files it finds referenced in all of its compiled objects. However, just like dynamically referenced objects, dynamically assigned resources are not included. In order to include these resources, you must create a PowerBuilder resource (.PBR) file.

   A *PBR file* is a text file containing a list of resource file names and dynamically referenced DataWindow objects. Use a text editor (like Windows notepad) to create your PBR files. List the resource file names that you want to include in the EXE file. To list a resource file in your PBR file, enter the name of each file on a separate line. The file name in the PBR file must exactly match the way the resource is referenced in your application's scripts. If the reference in the script contains the DOS path of the resource file, it must contain the DOS path in the PBR file. If the reference in the script does not contain the DOS path, it must not be in the PBR file, and the resource file must be in the directory that will be current when the executable is built. In order to include a dynamically reference DataWindow in the PBR file, you must enter the name of the PBL that contains it, followed by its object name enclosed in parentheses. The following is an example of a PowerBuilder Resource File:

```
check.bmp
clear1.bmp
clear2.bmp
copy1.bmp
copy2.bmp
cut1.bmp
cut2.bmp
paste1.bmp
paste2.bmp
delete.bmp
tree.ico
house.ico
```

```
swap.ico
watch.cur
reports.pbl(d_expenses)
reports.pbl(d_sales_summary)
common.pbl(d_exception)
```

Including resource files in your executable is the fastest approach because it requires the least amount of searching at execution time. Keep in mind, however, that you want to keep your executable size fairly small (under 1.2MB). Therefore, this may not always be the best place for them.

2. **Include your resources in the application's PBD files.** There are advantages to including resources in your PBD files. For example, if you have a common object PBL file that is shared among multiple applications, you may want to package any resources that are referenced by the objects in the PBL. This will allow you to distribute the PBD file knowing that everything it needs is contained within it. Unfortunately, unlike creating an executable, PowerBuilder does not automatically copy resources into the PBD when it creates it. So you need to build a PBR file that tells PowerBuilder what resources to include in the PBD file.

3. **Distribute your resource files separately.** Just include all of your resources in either the same directory as your application or in any directory listed in your DOS path. Although this method of distributing resources will allow you to easily revise and redistribute them in the future, it is the slowest at execution time.

Creating an Executable Using the Project Painter

Now that you have learned what an executable version of your application is and why you need to create one, you are ready to learn how to build one. There are two different ways to create an executable:

1. **Use the Project Painter.** The Project Painter should be used if you are creating a large application or one that uses PBD files.

2. **Use the Application Painter.** The Application Painter can be used to create smaller applications that do not use PBD files.

The Project Painter allows you to generate executable and PBD files. The information used for building these files is contained in PowerBuilder Project objects. The Project Painter is used to create and maintain these objects. Project objects contain the following information:

☐ The executable's file name.

☐ The PBD files used for the executable version of your application.

☐ The executable file's PBR file name.

☐ Each of the PBD files' PBR file names.

Creating an executable version of your application using the Project Painter is fairly straightforward. To create a new Project object, follow these steps:

1. Start the Project Painter by clicking on the Project button on the PowerBar. The Select Project response window appears (see Fig. 27.1).

Figure 27.1.
The Select Project window.

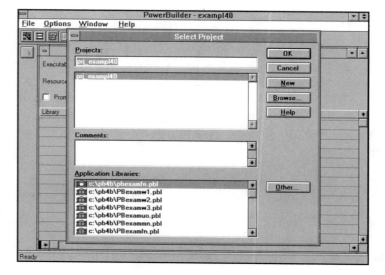

2. Click the **New** button to Create a new project object. The Select Executable File window appears (see Fig. 27.2).

3. Select the drive and directory in which you want to build the executable version of the application.

4. Enter the file name for the executable file to be built and click **OK**. The Project Painter Workspace window appears (see Fig. 27.3). The executable file name you just entered will appear in the Executable File Name entry box.

5. If you have created a PBR file for your executable, you may either enter the PBR file name in the Resource File Name entry box, or select Paste Executable's Resource from the **O**ptions menu to browse your drives and directories for the name.

6. If you want PowerBuilder to warn you prior to overwriting any existing PBD or EXE files, select the Prompt For Overwrite check box.

Figure 27.2.
The Select Executable File window.

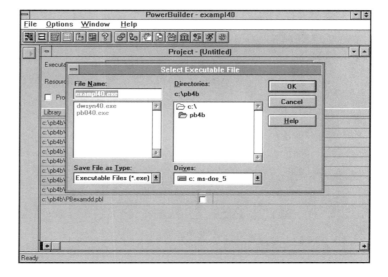

Figure 27.3.
The Project Painter Workspace window.

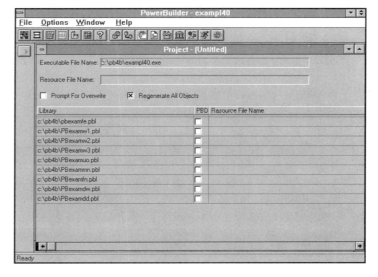

7. If you want PowerBuilder to regenerate all of the objects in the application's libraries, select the Regenerate All Objects check box. This is usually a good idea because it ensures that you have a clean copy of each object prior to creating the executable version for your users.

8. In the Library column, PowerBuilder lists the current application's libraries. To build a library into a PBD file rather than include its objects into the EXE file, select its corresponding PBD check box.

9. If you have selected a library to be built as a PBD and have a created a PBR file for it, you may either enter the PBR file name in the corresponding Resource File Name Column, or select Paste **D**ynamic Library's Resource from the **O**ptions menu to browse your drives and directories for the name.

10. After defining the Project object, and prior to building the executable version of your application, save your work. To save the Project object you have created, select Save **A**s from the **F**ile menu.

11. To finally build the executable version of your application, click the Build icon on the Project Painters Toolbar. PowerBuilder will then create the executable version of the application.

Creating an Executable Using the Application Painter

If you are creating only a small executable (with no PBD files) that you will probably not re-create, you may want to create it in the Application Painter. Prior to Version 4.0, this was the only way to create an executable. Frankly, I believe it is still included solely for compatibility reasons. The Project Painter is a far easier and more powerful way to build an executable version of your application. However, I will briefly cover the use of the Application Painter in this section.

To create an executable version of your application from the Application Painter, follow the these steps:

1. Start the Application Painter by clicking on the Application Painter icon on the PowerBar. The Application Painter window will appear (see Fig. 27.4).

Figure 27.4.
*The Application Painter
Workspace window.*

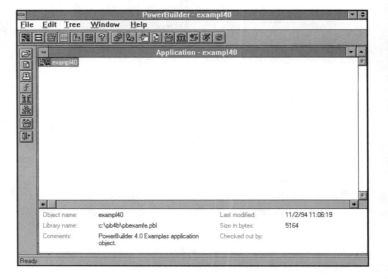

2. Click on the Create Executable icon on the Application Painter's toolbar. The Select Executable File window will appear (see Fig. 27.5).

Figure 27.5.
The Select Executable File window.

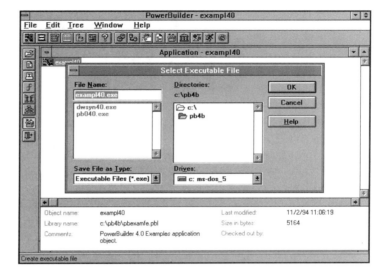

3. The current application's name with an .EXE extension will appear as the default executable name. You may overwrite this name with any valid file name you want. Windows users must be sure the file name ends with the .EXE extension. Click **OK** to accept the executable file name, and the Create Executable window will appear (see Fig. 27.6).

4. If you want to change the executable file name, either overwrite it in the Executable File Name entry box or press the **Change** button to bring back the Select Executable File window (refer to Fig. 27.5).

5. From the Directories listing, select the drive and directory in which you want the executable to be created.

6. If you plan on creating PBD files for this executable, select them from the Select Dynamic Libraries box. Objects from any library that you do not select from this box will be compiled into the executable file.

7. If you have created a resource file for this executable, enter its file name in the Resource File Name Entry box or click the **Files** button to bring up the Select Resource File window (see Fig. 27.7). This Window allows you to browse through your drives and directories to select a PBR file for your executable file.

8. Click the **OK** button on the Create Executable window to create the executable file and store it in the selected directory (refer to Fig. 27.6).

27

Figure 27.6.
The Create Executable window.

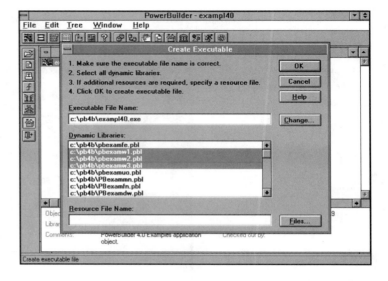

Figure 27.7.
The Select Resource File window.

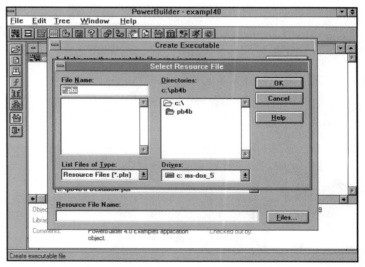

Morning Summary

After you have built an application in the PowerBuilder development environment, you will want to distribute it to your users. An executable version of your application is a version that can be run on its own. An executable version of your application can contain an executable file as well as any number of PowerBuilder dynamic library files and resource files.

The executable file contains the PowerBuilder bootstrap routine, which enables your application to run as a native application on its target platform. It also contains compiled versions of objects contained in the application's libraries, an execution library list, and resource files.

PowerBuilder dynamic libraries files do not contain the PowerBuilder bootstrap routine but are similar to executable files in all other ways. PBD files are used to provide more efficient memory usage, better maintainability, greater flexibility, and reusability for the executable version of your application.

A PowerBuilder resource file (PBR file) is a text file containing a list of resource file names and dynamically referenced DataWindow objects. This list is used at compile time to include external resources in your executable version. An example of some external resource files are ICO files for icons, BMP files for pictures, and CUR files for cursors.

The Project Painter allows you to generate executable and PBD files. The information used for building these files is contained in Project objects. Project objects contain the executable's file name, the executable's PBR file name, the PBD file names, and their corresponding PBR file names. After you have defined these items, you may save the Project object and create the executable version of your application.

If you are building a small application, you may alternatively choose to create an executable version of it in the Application Painter. To create an executable version of your application from the Application Painter, click on the Create Executable icon on the Application Painter's toolbar. Select an executable file name and directory, select the PBD files for the application, and select the PBR file for the executable file.

27

Chapter

28

Advanced Topics

In this chapter, you will learn about:

☐ The project life cycle

☐ Reusable common objects

☐ Performance and tuning

☐ The Windows API

☐ Caching data to eliminate joins in database queries

The Project Life Cycle

A software engineering project progresses through various stages. These stages include requirement analysis, design and development, and testing and user acceptance. The rapid emergence of Object Technology has modified the project life cycle to a certain degree.

Object-oriented design provides a model to support analysis and design. It is an iterative process: The design has to be revisited a number of times as new classes and methods are identified and new relationships are identified between different classes.

Requirement Phase

The first stage of the project is the requirements analysis phase. In this stage, it is determined what the system is required to do and what solutions it is required to provide. The functional requirements of the system and the scope of the domain of the application are identified at this stage.

Analysis Phase

The next stage of a project is the analysis stage. At this stage, the problem domain is analyzed, and the key objects that will be required to provide the desired functionality are identified. The logical design of the project is accomplished at this stage, and object reusability needs to be kept in mind. Objects designed in this application may be reused in other applications that provide similar functionality. Key classes and their definitions and operations are identified, and the relationships between different classes to provide the key system functionality is illustrated.

Design and Development Phase

The project progresses to the design and development stage after the analysis stage is completed. At this stage, the physical data objects are identified from the business objects formulated in the analysis stage. The architecture for the system is proposed, and the different classes and objects to provide the desired functionality are implemented. These objects can be broadly divided into visual or interface objects, and data management or business rules objects. A prototype is used

to familiarize the user community with the look and feel of the system, to consolidate the design of the interface classes, and to review the functional requirements of the system. The feedback from the actual users facilitates the improvement of the look and feel and points out any shortcomings in the requirements of the system.

> **Note:** The design stage is fairly iterative. As this stage progresses, new classes are identified and at the same time, certain classes are abandoned. Relationships between classes are modified and new ones established. Identifying classes and their behavior fairly accurately is critical in designing a scaleable and resilient system.

Testing Phase

The system is released to the users and enters the testing stage. A systematic and methodical approach is to implement a testing plan for the system. Each class or component of the system should be tested thoroughly to ensure that it exhibits the desired behavior and at the same time integrates with other components and modules in the system. If the system is designed using a distributed object architecture, then integration testing assumes critical importance.

It is recommended to perform regression testing as functional enhancements are made and undesirable behavior amended in different components. Using an automated testing tool to implement the testing plan facilitates the testing process.

Reusable Common Objects

With the advent of object technology, many applications are constructed using *object libraries*. Object libraries consist of reusable objects. The concept of object libraries is enhanced to design an application framework that provides the foundation to start building new applications. From this, it is evident that system architects and designers should design and build all classes and components with a high reuse factor.

Object libraries, besides providing ready-made components, also provide access to debugged and reliable code. An application framework, on the other hand, as mentioned earlier, provides the foundation to build a new system. Object libraries coupled with an application framework provide the ideal combination to minimize the time required to deliver reliable applications that address new business problems.

Let's briefly discuss two new terms that have been introduced. *Object libraries* can be described as a collection of well encapsulated objects, each describing a well-defined behavior. These objects may be designed to address certain functional requirements or may be very specific and provide business related functionality.

An Application framework provides components to rapidly build a reliable application, which provides a specific functionality.

Components in any application should be constructed as user objects if there is any indication that the set of behaviors they exhibit will be required in another module or even another application. For example, if one of the requirements in your system is to visually display the hierarchical relationship between the data elements, then the object built to satisfy this requirement should be constructed as a generic user object. This is because this is a common relationship between data elements, and there is an even chance that this requirement will surface in another module or application. This is a single reusable object that we have developed. It is database independent and can be used in any database application that needs to visually display the hierarchical relationship between data elements.

Similarly, in your application development effort you identify a number of objects that can be reused: a set of DataWindows that exhibit a master detail relationship encapsulated in a custom user object; a transaction manager derived from the PowerBuilder transaction object with added functionality for a specific DBMS; a non-visual user object container having a number of utility functions commonly referenced; a tab folder object that gives the tab folder look and feel; and so on. These objects can then be packaged in a library and used by different development teams to expedite their development efforts.

In the development of a system, you may identify a strategy to expedite developing a system that provides a certain functionality. For example, if there is a requirement for many reporting systems, you can architect an ad hoc reporting engine and a query by example engine configurable from a repository database. These reporting engines can be bundled with a transaction manager and an exception manager to create an application framework. Building a new reporting application will then involve configuring the repository database. The system will also provide flexibility to add new reports by inserting their definitions in the repository database.

Object technology is very powerful. New applications can be assembled from reusable objects as opposed to constructing afresh. The application development time is vastly reduced, the look and feel is uniform as the same objects are utilized by different applications, the applications are more reliable because object libraries provide access to debugged and functional objects, and well encapsulated objects ensure that the application is resilient to change.

Warning: Here is a word of caution for your endeavors to build reusable objects: Remember the theory of conservation of complexity. The complexity of a system is constant. It shifts from one part of the system to another. The trick is to evenly distribute it throughout your system. Try to refrain from building overly complex objects.

Performance and Tuning

The success of an application, among other factors, depends on its response time. Your PowerBuilder application, being a client/server application, can have its performance affected by many factors: performance of the DBMS; configuration of the client machine; network traffic; design and code quality of the PowerBuilder application; number of concurrent users; and so on. Of all the factors mentioned, you as a developer are responsible for the design and programming techniques used in constructing the PowerBuilder application, and it's your responsibility to ensure that the PowerBuilder application performs optimally.

Performance aspects of a PowerBuilder application can be broadly lumped into two categories: *database access* and *code execution*. The response time of a database access depends upon a number of factors: the mode of database access, the performance of the network, and the tuning of the query/database. The performance of the PowerScript code depends on the "quality" of the code, the design of the application, and the client machine configuration.

In this section, I will present some handy "power programming" tips and advice that will help you optimize the performance of your PowerBuilder application.

Let's initially discuss techniques that will hasten the opening or "painting" of windows in your application because the delayed opening of a screen can even disgruntle the user of an ergonomic and "snazzy" application. A common error made by novice PowerBuilder developers is to perform a lot of processing in the open event of a window. This tends to delay the painting of the window; you should try to minimize the processing in the open event of a window. If your window does require extensive processing when it opens, then create a custom user event and judiciously distribute the code between the open event and this custom user event. Post this custom user event so that it gets called after the window has opened. Some windows in your application may be required to display many data elements when they open up. Try to access the database once to get the required data. If this single query delays the opening of the screen, give the user the perception of speed by initiating the database access in the posted event and by displaying the data after the window has opened.

> **Tip:** The open event of a window should have minimal code. A custom user event posted from the open event should be used to do any extensive processing. This does not slow down the painting of the window and gives the user the perception of speed.

28

Controls on windows are another factor influencing the performance of the application. They should be designed for optimal performance and should give the application a uniform look and

feel. The time it takes for a window to open increases as the number of controls placed on it increases because PowerBuilder has to create each control at runtime and process events for them. Each control has a handle that is stored in the 64K Windows User Heap, thus utilizing Windows resources. Limiting the number of controls not only increases performance but also makes the screen ergonomic and intuitive, rather than overwhelming the user with a wealth of data.

Tip: Reducing the number of controls on a window speeds up the painting of the window.

DataWindows, apart from being a mechanism for data access and manipulation, let you display columns of data in the form of drop-down list boxes, check boxes, radio buttons, and edit controls. No matter how many columns are displayed, the DataWindow is still one control. If there is no database access and a window can either use a standard control or a DataWindow to satisfy the functional requirements, then you should use a DataWindow, reducing the number of controls on the window and the Windows resources used. The number of user objects created dynamically should also be reduced.

Tip: The number of dynamically created objects should be reduced. DataWindows should be used, wherever possible, to replace controls like check boxes, radio buttons, and so on.

PowerBuilder allows you to declare global functions. These functions are stored in PBL files and accessed like other objects. In the runtime environment, any call made to these functions in your application requires the application to search for it in the .EXE and the .PBDs affecting the performance. It is recommended that you declare object level functions if the functionality is local to an object, or encapsulate global functions in a nonvisual user object instantiated globally. This way, functions loaded in memory are referenced enhancing performance.

Tip: Limit the use of global functions—object level functions should be used.

Now, let's go over some PowerScript coding techniques. PowerBuilder has an extensive application programming interface (API) that provides over 400 functions. It is useful to get acquainted with it as soon as possible so that you don't end up writing functions in PowerScript that provide the same functionality as standard PowerBuilder functions.

> **Tip:** Use standard PowerBuilder functions wherever possible instead of creating functions that perform similar tasks using PowerScript.

It is bad practice to call the a function repeatedly that returns the same value. Assign the value to a variable and use the variable for any processing. This is illustrated in the following example:

```
//do not call a function repeatedly
for li_loopCounter = 1 to dw_1.rowCount()
    ....

    ....
next

//assign the value to a variable
li_numRows = dw_1.rowCount()
for li_loopCounter = 1 to li_numRows
    ....

    ....
next
```

> **Tip:** Do not call a function repeatedly in a loop.

Here is a handy tip for initializing dynamic arrays. When a dynamic array grows, Windows must allocate a new memory block large enough for the existing array and the new elements. When you initialize a dynamic array in a loop, you can improve performance by allocating the memory once if you fill the dynamic array backwards. It is recommended to pass arrays by reference to functions because if the array is large and passed by value, then double the memory is used as a copy of the array is passed. An example of initializing elements of a dynamic array is shown here.

```
//initialize the 50 elements
for li_loopCounter = li_numArrayElements to 1 step -1
    arrayElement[li_loopCounter] = .....
next
```

You should try to avoid the getItemString and setItem functions for manipulating large chunks of data cell by cell in DataWindows. Try to use the dwDescribe and dwModify functions. If there is no recourse but to use the getItemString or the setItem function, then turn the DataWindows redrawing off before the processing and force a redraw after it is over. This will significantly improve performance. Unnecessary retrieval of data should be avoided; you should use the dwShare or the importString function to share data between DataWindows.

28

Tip: Addressing data elements individually in DataWindows should be avoided—use the dwShare or importString functions.

Optimizing database access will significantly improve the performance of your application. You should only permit database access through DataWindows, and their datasource should be stored procedures if your DBMS supports them. Stored procedures provide access to compiled and optimized database code. Performance can be optimized by restricting the volume of data returned from the database server and by reducing the number of requests sent to the database server. Large volumes of data returned by the server not only increase network traffic but also use up client memory. Try to limit the number of rows returned, and don't retrieve columns that are not required.

It is not good practice to use the setTrans function to set the transaction object of a DataWindow. This is because the DataWindow issues a connect request to the dataserver before the retrieval and a disconnect after the retrieval; connect and disconnect are expensive operations for both the client and server.

Tip: Use the setTransObject function instead of the setTrans function to assign the dataobject of a DataWindow.

An important consideration in designing multi-user database applications is to have small logical units of database work. You should issue a commit immediately after an insert or update statement to release locks on the database tables, if you have set the database connection parameter autoCommit to False.

Tip: You should Commit or Rollback a transaction immediately if you have set the autoCommit parameter of the database connection as False.

Performance diminishes rapidly as the number of joins increases in a query. You can eliminate joins made to "thin and short" reference tables by caching the reference tables in DataWindows when your application starts up. You can then use these DataWindows as drop-down DataWindows in columns where the decode of the code value is to be displayed.

An application may not perform at the desired performance level if the executable is not built correctly. You can build the executable of your application with all the objects in one executable file (EXE file) or distribute the objects between an executable file and one or more dynamic

libraries (PBD files). As a rule of thumb, do not let the EXE file be larger than 1.2MB. You should consider breaking up the application into PBD files. Using dynamic libraries has other advantages. You can share components between applications by sharing dynamic libraries, and you can incorporate changes in the application by upgrading the appropriate dynamic library instead of replacing the entire EXE file.

At execution, PowerBuilder first searches for a referenced object in the EXE file and then searches the dynamic libraries in the order they are specified in the library list. It then loads the desired object into memory. It is recommended to build frequently referenced objects into the EXE or place them in a dynamic library that is at the beginning of the library list.

Tip: You should distribute objects in your application between an executable file and one or more dynamic libraries.

Dynamic libraries and EXE files do not include bitmaps, icons, cursors, and DataWindows that are referenced dynamically in scripts. You can use PowerBuilder Resource (PBR files) files to include these resources in dynamic libraries or EXE files. PowerBuilder searches for resources on the Windows search path if they are not built into the EXE or a dynamic library. The resource cannot be used in the application if the search path does not include the directory where it is located.

The Windows API

The *Application Programming Interface (API)* of Microsoft Windows provides developers of Windows applications access to functions, messages, files, datatypes, and data structures. This API is accessible from PowerBuilder. You have to declare the functions called from any of the several libraries in the API as external functions. The *Windows API*, which can be sub-divided into three modules or libraries, augments the extensive PowerBuilder API.

One of the libraries is the *User Application Programming Interface*. Functions in this group enable developers of Windows applications to create windows and to provide information about and modify their state and attributes. It also has functions that create menus and provide access to their attributes. This module has the message data structure and functions that process messages. The message data structure provides information about the state and events within an application. The events include standard input and timer events, events that require specialized processing and response, and requests for information from an application. The functions in this group include caret functions that mark a location in a windows client area for input; cursor functions that manipulate the cursor; dialog box procedures that create dialog boxes to prompt the user for additional information about command selections; hook functions that enable an application to gain access to the message stream; message functions that enable applications to get, process, and dispatch messages; painting functions that provide painting and miscellaneous graphics operations; property functions that enable manipulation of the property list, which is a storage area that contains handles for data that the application needs to associate with a window; scroll functions that provide functionality to scroll windows and controls and set scroll attributes; window creation functions that create, destroy, modify, and obtain information about windows.

The second module of Windows API, the *Graphics Device Interface (GDI)*, includes device independent graphic functions. It includes functionality to create line, text, and bitmap output on a variety of printers and displays of varying resolution and plotter devices.

Functions in this group include device context functions that provide functionality to manipulate links between a Windows application and the following: a device driver and an output device; color functions; color palette functions; drawing attribute functions that set the attribute of line, brush, text, or bitmap output; mapping functions that map the output in logical space to the display; coordinate functions that convert client coordinates to screen coordinates or vice versa; line output functions that create different types of line output; ellipse and polygon functions that are used for drawing and charting applications; and metafile functions (*metafiles* are a set of device independent GDI commands that create desired text or images).

The third module of the Windows API is the *system* or the *kernel interface*. This module contains functions that do the following: allocate and manage memory; manage tasks; load program resources; translate strings; alter the Windows initialization file; carry out communications; create and manipulate files; do resource and atom management; and sound functions.

The Windows API uses the Pascal calling convention: parameters are pushed onto the stack from the left to the right in the order in which they appear in the function call.

Let's go over an example of making a Windows API call. You can call the Windows function GetFreeSpace() from your PowerBuilder application if you want to determine the amount of available memory. This function is stored in the standard Windows DLL, Kernel.Exe. You will first have to declare it as an external function, as shown next, either globally or locally in the object where it will be called from.

```
FUNCTION long GetFreeSpace() Library "KERNEL.EXE"
```

Caching Data to Eliminate Joins in Database Queries

In the section on performance and tuning, I mentioned a technique to eliminate joins to speed up queries. Let's examine it in detail. Performance of database queries decreases as the number of joins in them increases. Joins to "short and narrow" reference tables can be eliminated if you cache them in your application at startup. You can open a window invisibly that retrieves or

caches reference tables in a DataWindow. If your database stores reference data in multiple tables, you should retrieve them into one DataWindow. This DataWindow should have three columns: `reference_type`, `code`, and `decode`. Let's name this window `w_cache` and the DataWindow `dw_cache`. This window should have a function to provide access to the cached reference data. The parameter to the function should be reference datatype. This function should filter the DataWindow for that particular reference type, and return the reference data in a tab-delimited format. A function that provides this functionality is shown here:

```
/*********************************************************
* f_get_reference_data
* Parms:     pi_referenceType int by value
* Returns:   string
* Descr:     This function returns the specified reference
            data
*********************************************************/

string ls_Data

//Filter the DataWindow for the specified reference data
dw_cache.setFilter&
    ("reference_type=" + String(pi_referenceType))
dw_cache.Filter()
//get the data into a tab separated string format
ls_Data = dw_cache.dwDescribe("DataWindow.Data")
//reset the filter on the DataWindow
dw_cache.setFilter("")
dw_cache.Filter()
//return the data string
return ls_Data
```

Let's suppose that you are retrieving a particular employee record. You will have to join with three tables to display the name of the department, name of the division, and the designation of the employee. This join with three tables will slow the query significantly. Here is a way to eliminate the three table join.

Construct a DataWindow that retrieves all the fields from the employee table without joining to the three reference tables. In this DataWindow, specify the style of the `department_id`, `division_id`, and `designation_id` columns as `dropDownDataWindow`. Set the `dropDownDataWindow` to be the same DataWindow that caches the data in the invisible window. Set the display column as `decode` and the code column as `code`. Now programmatically insert a blank row in each of these `dropDownDataWindows` to suppress them from retrieving data. Now after retrieving the employee DataWindow, call the function `f_get_reference_data` in `w_cache` for each of the three reference types to get the reference data. Populate each of the three `dropDownDataWindows` by using the `importString` function. Let's assume that the `reference_code` for department reference data is 1, for division reference data is 2, and for designation cache data is 3. The following code will give you an idea about performing joins in memory, whose functionality is given here:

28

```
/*********************************************************
* f_retrieve_emp_data
* Parms:    None
```

```
* Returns:   None
* Descr:     This function retrieves the employee data
             returns and does the three table join in memory
**********************************************************/

int li_deptCacheID = 1, li_divCacheID = 2
int li_designtnCacheID = 3
DataWindowChild ldwc_dept, ldwc_division, ldwc_designation
string ls_deptCol = "dept_id", ls_divCol = "div_id"
string ls_desigCol = "desig_id"

//Get  the handles of the dropDownDatawindows
dwGetChild(ls_deptCol, ldwc_dept)
dwGetChild(ls_divCol, ldwc_division)
dwGetChild(ls_desigCol, ldwc_designation)

//insert a blank row in each of them to prevent retrieval
ldwc_dept.insertRow(0)
ldwc_division.insertRow(0)
ldwc_designation.insertRow(0)

//set flicker off
dw_employee.setRedraw(False)

//retrieve the employee DataWindow
dw_employee.retrieve()

//set the cached data in the drop down DataWindows
ldwc_dept.importString(&
    w_cache.f_get_reference_data(li_deptCacheID))
ldwc_division.importString(&
    w_cache.f_get_reference_data(li_divCacheID))
ldwc_designation.importString(&
    w_cache.f_get_reference_data(li_designtnCacheID))

//force a redraw
dw_employee.setRedraw(True)
```

You should now see the name of the department, name of the division, and the designation of the employee appear instead of the IDs. This is significantly faster than performing the three table database joins in the query and, moreover, the reference data is available in memory.

Afternoon Summary

In this chapter, we have covered certain topics that should help you design an effective PowerBuilder application. A PowerBuilder application development project goes through various stages in its life cycle. The initial stage of the project, requirements analysis, determines what functionality is desired from the application. The logical design of the system is done in the next phase, the domain analysis phase. The classes identified during the domain analysis are implemented in the design phase. A working prototype should be built in this phase to validate the design and architecture and to get constructive feedback from users. The final phase is the integration and testing phase, where the different components in the system are tested and

integrated to provide the desired functionality. Design of a system using the Object Oriented Paradigm is an iterative process. Classes and their relationships are revisited at every stage of the development process.

It is critical to design and build well-encapsulated and reusable objects. This gives other application development efforts access to well-designed and well-tested objects. The reusable objects can be packaged in a library, or they can be loosely assembled to provide a template for rapidly developing an application in what is called an application framework.

The performance of a PowerBuilder application depends not only on the efficacy of the design but also on the coding techniques adopted in the application. Unnecessary database access should be eliminated, and database queries from the PowerBuilder application should be optimal and tuned. Reference tables should be cached to eliminate unnecessary joins in database queries.

The performance of a PowerBuilder application also depends on the executable created for the application. The executable can be a single EXE file or a EXE file along with one or more PBD files. As a rule of thumb, the EXE should not exceed 1.5MB. Commonly referenced objects should be placed in the EXE file or in the PBD file that is at top of the library list.

PowerBuilder has an extensive API; this is extended by the Windows API.

Q&A

Q Why do I need to create an executable version of my application?

A If your application has users other than yourself, you will want them to be able to run it without the PowerBuilder development environment.

Q Can I use the Debugger while running the executable version of my application?

A No, you can only use the Debugger while in the PowerBuilder development environment.

Q Do I need anything besides an executable file to run a PowerBuilder executable?

A Yes, if your users do not have the PowerBuilder development environment, you must distribute the PowerBuilder runtime libraries as well. There are some licensing issues here. Call Powersoft for more information.

Q If I reference external functions from dynamic link libraries (DLL files), can I include them in either the executable file or PBD files?

A No, PowerBuilder does not support the functionality. If you reference external DLL files, you must distribute them with your application.

Q I want to check if there is another instance of the application running in the open event of the application. There is no PowerBuilder function I can use to accomplish this. Do I have to write a C DLL?

28

A You can call C functions in the standard Windows libraries by declaring them as external functions. To check if there is another instance of the application running, use the function `GetModuleUsage` in the library `Kernel.exe`

Q **I have to keep on revisiting the base classes and modify their behavior while developing the PowerBuilder application. Is there a flaw in the basic design of my classes?**

A PowerBuilder provides an object-oriented development environment. Object-oriented design is an iterative process; new classes are added, and existing classes and their relationships with other classes are modified.

Q **I have a couple of functions that are used by many windows in the application. Does declaring them as global functions affect performance?**

A Yes, it does affect performance. The executable has to search the EXE file and PBD files if any. Instead, you can declare them as functions in the base window class of your application, or you can declare these functions in a non-visual user object and instantiate it globally. This way, all functions accessed are in memory.

Q **I have to locate a particular employee in a DataWindow based on the `employee_id`. The DataWindow has 500 records, looping through the entire result set slows the application. Is there a faster method to locate the record?**

A It is advisable to be familiar with the PowerBuilder API and use the appropriate functions. Instead of looping through the entire result set, you can use the `dwFind` function.

Workshop

Quiz

1. I want to share data between two DataWindows, but when I filter one, the other gets automatically filtered. How can you share data between two DataWindows without this limitation?

2. How do you retrieve a large result set into a DataWindow and give the user a perception of speed?

3. How do you speed up scrolling of DataWindows with bitmaps?

4. How do you speed up setting the values in a large number of cells in a DataWindow using the `setItem` function?

Putting PowerBuilder into Action

1. Start the Project Painter from the PowerBar.
2. Rename the executable file from the default typbapp.exe to firstexe.exe.
3. Select a new drive and directory in which to build the executable.
4. Make sure PowerBuilder warns you before overwriting any existing files.
5. Make sure all objects in the application are regenerated prior to creating the executable version.
6. Create a PBD file from the typbapp.pbl file.
7. Create the executable version and run it from the Windows Program Manager.

28

Appendix

Answers to Quiz
Questions

Answers to Quiz Questions

Day 1 Answers

1. So you've bought PowerBuilder, and you have this pretty, purple package in front of you. What do you have to do to be able to start?

   The first thing that you must do is install PowerBuilder on your computer. Installing PowerBuilder copies the proper files to the appropriate places on your hard drive. You must run the setup program from the first disk to install PowerBuilder. The setup program will install PowerBuilder onto your computer, copying the proper files to the right places on your hard drive. To run setup, select the Run menu item from the File menu and enter `a:\setup` in the entry box.

2. What kind of different buttons can you put on your toolbar?

   There are two different types of buttons that you can place on your toolbar. First, you can place standard buttons that map directly to items that appear on your menu, and perform internal PowerBuilder functions when they are clicked, for example opening the Application Painter or printing the current screen. Additionally, you can place custom buttons on your screen that will run external functions that are not part of the PowerBuilder environment. For example, you can create a button that runs Solitaire or Write, or that runs a report or query. There are two types of standard buttons: those that are accessible from anywhere within PowerBuilder that can appear on the PowerBar, like the button to open the Application Painter, and those that perform functions that are only available at specific times, like when the Application Painter is open, that go on the PainterBars.

3. How do you move the toolbar?

   You can move the toolbar in two ways. You can pick up the toolbar with your mouse pointer and drag it to its desired position on the screen. Click with your mouse button inside the edges of the toolbar, but without clicking on any of the buttons on the toolbar. This will "grab" it with your mouse. Don't let go of the mouse button, but drag the toolbar around the screen. If you prefer, you can also move the toolbar by right clicking with your mouse button on the toolbar. This will display the toolbar's right mouse menu, where you can specify its desired position. Finally, you can select Toolbars... from the File Menu, which brings up a window where you can specify the desired position of the toolbar.

4. How do you select menu items?

   The most direct way to select a menu item is to click on it with your mouse. When you click on a main menu, it will bring up the submenu for that item. Then, you can click on the menu item that you are interested in. Additionally, you can select menu items by pressing the **Alt** key to bring your focus to the menu bar and pressing the accelerator letter of the menu items that you are interested in. You can take this shortcut even further by pressing the **Alt** key at the same time as the accelerator letter of the main menu, for example **Alt-F** to open the File menu. Finally, if the menu item of interest has a key combination listed next to it, pressing that key combination will cause that menu item's function to be performed.

Day 2 Answers

1. What's the first step in creating a PowerBuilder program?

   The first thing that you must do once you have installed PowerBuilder is create an Application object.

2. What are the different attributes of the application object?

   The Application Object contains the following attributes that you can access directly from the Application Painter:

   ☐ The Icon
   ☐ The Default Global Variables
   ☐ The Default Fonts
   ☐ The Library List

   In addition, there are other attributes of an application that we cannot access directly from the painter, but that we can access with code. However, we have not learned about those yet.

3. What do you use to interface with your user?

   You interface with your user with Windows and Window Controls, like buttons, list boxes, text boxes, and so on.

4. What are the different methods that you can use to change the style of your windows.

   You can change the style of your window by double-clicking on it. Double-clicking on the window will bring up a dialog box that allows you to edit your window's style. Also, you can edit certain attributes of your window from the menus that appear in the Window Painter. Finally, you can right-click on the window to see a menu of items that you can manipulate that way.

Day 3 Answers

1. Name two ways that you can edit the attributes of a control.

   Actually, there are five ways that you can edit your control's attributes, but if you got any two, give yourself credit. You can edit the attributes of a control either by double-clicking on the control, or by right-clicking on it. Additionally, you can edit certain attributes with the StyleBar and ColorBar. Finally, you can also edit some attributes like position and height and width from the menus in the Window Painter.

2. Which control would you use to allow the user to enter in a number?

   You could use a SingleLineEdit control, an EditMask control, or a MultiLineEdit control, all of which allow the user to enter data by typing it in.

3. Which event will get triggered when your user actually enters a number into the control?

The `modified` event will be triggered when the user modifies the data in one of the above three named controls. However, you should be aware that this event does not get triggered until the user either hits the **Enter** key or changes the focus of the control.

4. Which control would you use to allow your user to close your window?

This is a trick question. You probably said, "A CommandButton." And if you did, you are not wrong at all. In general, most windows either have an **OK** and **Cancel** button, or a **Save** and **Close** button, all of which, except **Save**, cause the window to close. However, you don't really *need* a button to allow your user to close the window, he can close it simply by double clicking the control menu, or choosing `Close` from the control menu. However, offering the user a more friendly way to close his window, via a button, is a good practice. (Later, you'll also learn how to make a `Close` menu item of your own.)

5. In which event would you place the code to perform the closing of the window?

If you used a command button, you would place the code to close the window in the `clicked` event of the command button. If you noticed that there is a `close` event in the window itself, that's good. But that event doesn't cause the closing of the window. Instead, it is the event that gets run by the window as it is about to close, after the command button told it to.

6. When the user clicks on that button, and closes the window, what other events do you think will be triggered?

Well, I've already told you that the `close` event of the window will get triggered automatically. But before that happens, the `closequery` event of the window will get triggered. The `closequery` event of the window allows you to execute code before the close and even potentially cancel the close. This is where you might put a message asking the user to save his changes before closing.

Day 4 Answers

1. Throughout this book, object and variable attributes are set and accessed using the dot notation. What is the general syntax of this notation?

`Object_name.attribute` or `variable.attribute`.

2. Why are naming conventions so important?

They allow greater maintainability, readability, and understandability.

3. Name two ways arguments can be passed to a function.

By value or by reference.

4. What's the difference between a shortcut key and an accelerator for a menu item?

A shortcut key will activate the menu item when the user presses the indicated shortcut key(s). An accelerator must be accessed first by selecting the menu then by entering the menu item underlined letter, the accelerator.

5. How do you associate a menu to a window?

    Within the Window Painter, double click on the window to enter the `Window Style` dialog screen. Check the Menu check box and select a menu from the drop down list box.

Day 5 Answers

1. How do I delete a library?

    You can delete library files by using the Library Painter or the Windows File Manager. Consider creating a backup of library files you plan on deleting just in case you need to get them back later. Always use extreme care when deleting library files.

2. How do you create an MDI sheet? What is the Window Type of an MDI sheet?

    First, you must create a window. Since there is no window type of MDI sheet, you can save your window as any of the other window types. Then, to open the window as an MDI sheet, you must use the special `OpenSheet()` function, telling it the name of the window, and the MDI frame in which you want to open it.

3. Which common sheet arrangement types *cannot* be used as the initial arrangement sheet type of an MDI sheet?

    You cannot open an MDI sheet in `Tile!` or `TileHorizontal!` mode.

Day 6 Answers

1. What is the general syntax for calling ancestor scripts and functions?

    `CALL ancestor_object::event`

    `CALL ancestor_object'control::event` (control event)

    `ancestor_object::function()`

2. List three frequently used script pronouns other than `Super`.

    `This`, `Parent`, and `ParentWindow` (used in menu script).

3. Name the four variable scopes.

    Local, instance, global, and shared.

4. Give the three access levels you can declare for variables and functions.

    Public, Private, and Protected.

5. List the different types of User Objects.

    Class: Custom, Standard, (C++)

    Visual: Custom, External, Standard, VBX

Answers to Quiz Questions

Day 7 Answers

1. How do you declare access rights for variables?

   You can declare access rights as Public, Private, or Protected. The rights can be assigned one line at a time or to multiple lines of variables.

   ```
   //One line variable declaration
   protected long il_row
   //Multiple line variable declaration
   private:
   long il_row
   string is_text
   ```

2. How do Public, Private, or Protected access rights limit a variable's use?

   Public rights mean the variable can be accessed from any script in the application if the object the variable is contained within is available. Private access is only from the object in which the variable exists, inherited descendants cannot access the variable. Protected access is from the object in which the variable exists plus descendant objects.

3. What is the main reason to create a Standard Visual User Object?

   To extend the object's functionality and use it as a class for further object inheritance or object reuse.

4. How do you use a Class User Object in script?

   You must first define a variable of its type, then instantiate it with the CREATE statement. When finished with The User Object, destroy it to free resources.

   ```
   //user object of type transaction, named u_trans_pubs
   //declare class user object
   u_trans_pubs ltrx_pubs
   //instanciate, or create a copy of user object
   ltrx_pubs = Create u_trans_pubs
   //use transaction ltrx_pubs within your script then destroy it
   Destroy ltrx_pubs
   ```

5. List some benefits of encapsulation.

   Encapsulation protects an object's attributes and scripts from other User Objects. Maintenance of encapsulated objects is simpler because the code is in one place. Other objects that send messages to encapsulated objects will not require code changes if changes to the object are internal.

6. What is the syntax for using TriggerEvent() on an object's Clicked event and a declared user event, ue_custom_event?

   Standard events are recognized as enumerated data types while declared events must be entered as strings.

   ```
   //script for user object uo_1, from another window control
   uo_1.TriggerEvent(Clicked!)
   uo_1.TriggerEvent("ue_custom_event")
   ```

The compiler checks only that a valid enumerated data type or any string value is used.

Day 8 Answers

1. What is a primary key and why is it used?

    A primary key uniquely identifies each row of data in a table and enforces data integrity and row uniqueness.

2. What is a foreign key and why is it used?

    A foreign key associates one or more columns of a table to a unique constraint on another table, usually a primary key. It is used to ensure referential integrity between the two tables, and also relates the table information together.

3. What is table normalization?

    Normalization is the process of analyzing and reducing data base redundancy while still maintaining correct business rules. It helps maintain referential integrity.

4. What is the main purpose of table indexes?

    Speed selection of data.

5. What are views?

    A view is like a virtual table: it has no data of its own, only the definition exits. It provides data security because most users can not update it. A view provides an easy method for users to view data in different ways.

6. What is the display format definition for a date with style Jan/11/94?

    `mmm/dd/yy`

Day 9 Answers

1. What are three referential integrity rules that can be associated with a foreign key?

    `RESTRICT`, `CASCADE`, and `SET NULL` dependent deletes.

2. List some extended attributes of table columns stored in the PowerBuilder repository.

    Display format, edit style, validation rule, header, label, comment, initial value, width, height, and justification.

3. Besides viewing, modifying, inserting, and deleting table data, what is another use for the Data Manipulation Painter?

    The Data Manipulation Painter lets you view extended column attributes set for the table and see how they would behave in a DataWindow.

4. From the Data Manipulation Painter, how do you save table data to a text file or a file of another format?

With the rows you want to save displayed in the Data Manipulation Painter, select Save **A**s... from the **F**ile menu. A dialog box opens that allows you to select a format and enter a name for the file.

5. How do you bring text files into the Data Manipulation Painter and update the information to the database?

Select the table in the Database Painter that you want to update. Enter the Data Manipulation Painter and select **I**mport from the **R**ows menu, and then select the text file to import. If the file imports successfully, you will see the rows of data and can then update the rows to the database by selecting **S**ave Changes to Database from the **F**ile menu.

6. What rows go into the Filtered buffer when a filter is created and applied?

Rows that do *not* meet the filter criteria are placed in the Filtered buffer. If the filter is `emp_id > 200`, rows with `emp_id <= 200` are put in the filtered buffer. The remaining rows, with `emp_id > 200`, show in the Primary buffer, available for you to view.

Day 10 Answers

1. What are four main commands in Data Manipulation Language (DML) used to access the database?

`SELECT`, `INSERT`, `UPDATE`, and `DELETE`.

2. List the three main components or clauses in DML commands.

`SELECT`, `FROM`, and `WHERE`. In addition, there are `GROUP BY`, `HAVING`, `ORDER BY`, and other clauses that are used less frequently.

3. Formulate the SQL required to select the total number of employees from the `employee` table with a `last_name` that starts with *H*.

```
SELECT count(*)
FROM employees
WHERE last_name LIKE 'H%';
```

4. What is the general syntax for the `INSERT` statement?

```
INSERT INTO <table>
{<column list>}
VALUES(<value list>)
```

5. What is the general syntax for the `UPDATE` statement?

```
UPDATE <table>
SET <column 1> = <value 1>,
<column 2> = <value 2>,
   ...
<column n> = <value n>
WHERE <criteria>
```

6. What are the four standard types of table rights you can grant to or revoke from a user?

   SELECT, INSERT, DELETE, and UPDATE.

7. How do you paint a SQL statement that returns all the employees from the `employee` table and their related department name, even if the employee is not in a department?

   After placing a join between `employee.dept_id` and `employee.dept_id` in the Database Administration Painter SQL Painter, create an outer join on the employee table by selecting the join box option = `department.dept_id = employee.dept_id` and `rows from employee that have no department`.

8. What is an execution plan, and how do you use it?

   An execution plan is a plan of how the database will execute a SQL statement. In the Database Administrator, write or paste the SQL you want to examine. From the **O**bjects menu, select Explai**n** SQL to generate the execution plan.

Day 11 Answers

1. Where will the items in the summary and footer bands of a DataWindow Definition appear when viewed?

   The summary appears at the end of the entire set of data, while the footer appears at the bottom of each page.

2. What happens when a DataWindow Definition that expects arguments is retrieved without specifying values for these arguments? If there are a different number of arguments supplied than expected? If the argument datatypes don't match?

   An error will occur if you attempt enter arguments of the wrong type, or you enter an incorrect number of arguments. If no arguments are entered and some are expected, the Specify Retrieval Arguments dialog box will display for the user to enter the argument values.

3. In addition to creating the groups themselves, what else must you do to properly present DataWindow information in a group format?

   You must also sort the values based on the group columns to ensure all the rows within a group appear together, not scattered in many groups throughout the report.

4. What mode are Composite and Nested reports viewed in?

   Both Composite and Nested report formats display in print preview mode.

5. Do you have to select a name from the Name drop-down list box when you are modifying and column's edit style in the DataWindow Painter?

   No, you can just enter the edit style's attributes without selecting a predefined edit style.

6. What is a good reason to use a drop-down DataWindow instead of a drop-down list box in your DataWindows?

Changes in the data values can be implemented at the database level much easier with a drop-down DataWindow because data is retrieved directly from the database. Changes to data values for a drop-down list box may require a repository update of the list box attributes and modifications to all DataWindows that use it.

Day 12 Answers

1. What is wrong with the following code segment? (Hint: It is not a syntactical or logic problem.)

```
dw_detail.SetTransObject( SQLCA)
dw_detail.Retrieve()
IF SQLCA.SQLCode < 0 THEN
    MessageBox( "Database Error #"  + String( SQLCA.SQLDBCode),
SQLCA.SQLErrText)
END IF
```

You should not use the transaction object to return values for handling of database errors in a DataWindow. Instead, you should use the DataWindow Control's DBError event and use the DBErrorCode(), DBErrorMessage(), and GetUpdateStatus() functions to retrieve the error information in that event. The Retreive() and Update() functions will return a -1 if there was an error so that you can stop executing other code if you have to, and the DBError event will handle the error itself for you.

2. What other functions or statements must you execute before you attempt to Retrieve() data into a DataWindow Control?

At a minimum, you must initialize a transaction object and connect to the database with it. Then you must assign that transaction object to the DataWindow Control by using the SetTransObject() function.

3. If AutoCommit is set to TRUE, how many statements will be executed before a COMMIT is automatically sent to the database?

None! (Surprise!) The way PowerBuilder implements AutoCommit is that it never starts a transaction in the first place. This way, there is no need for a COMMIT statement to be sent because every command is automatically and immediately executed by the DBMS. The effect, however, is as if there was a COMMIT statement after each and every database command that was executed. (So if you said 1, give yourself at least half credit.)

4. What is wrong with the following line of code, which attempts to set the value of the department name column in the dw_detail DataWindow Control to "Marketing"?

```
dw_detail.dept_name.text = "Marketing"
```

You cannot use this notation for referencing columns in a DataWindow. You must use the `SetItem()` function to set a column value in a DataWindow Control. There are two reasons for this. First of all, if PowerBuilder were to offer this kind of notation, they would also need to provide you with some way to specify the row number of the value that you are changing because it is not included in that notation. They could probably come up with some notation that you could use, but there would still be a problem. The DataWindow Definition is not physically "attached" to the DataWindow Control. The name of the dataobject is one of the attributes of the DataWindow Control, but that can be changed at runtime. In fact, you don't even have to assign your DataWindow Control a dataobject at runtime. Because of this, there is no way for the PowerBuilder compiler to recognize the DataWindow Objects like column names as keywords. This is why you pass this information as strings by using functions like `GetItemXXX()`, `SetItem()`, `Modify()`, and `Describe()`.

5. What's the difference between the `SetFilter()` and the `Filter()` functions?

    The `SetFilter()` function sets the filter criteria of the DataWindow but does not actually perform the filtering of the data. It is the `Filter()` function that performs the filtering of the data.

Day 13 Answers

1. What are the two most important fields in a transaction object for doing error handling?

    `SQLCode, SQLErrText`

2. What are the valid values for SQLCode?

    `0` indicates a successful completion, `-1` indicates an error, and `100` indicates success with no result sets.

3. What character is used to terminate SQL statements, and how do you continue multi-line SQL statements?

    The semicolon is the SQL termination character, and multi-line SQL statements are simply continued—no continuation character is required.

4. Where can I use a PowerScript variable in SQL, and how do I indicate that it is a variable?

    Variables can be used to replace constants in SQL statements. Variables cannot be used for reserved words or object identifiers. Variables are prefixed with a colon (:).

5. Can transaction objects other the SQLCA be used with embedded SQL?

    Yes.

6. Can a `SELECT...INTO` return more than one row?

    No. If a multi-row result is required, use a DataWindow or a "fetch loop."

Answers to Quiz Questions

Day 14 Answers

1. I want to share data between two DataWindows, but when I filter one, the other gets automatically filtered. How can you share data between two DataWindows without this limitation?

   Do not retrieve the DataWindow; you already have the data in a DataWindow in your application. You can export the data from that DataWindow into a tab delimited string by using the `dwDescribe("DataWindow.data")`, and then importing it in the DataWindow by passing this string to the `importString` function.

2. How do you retrieve a large result set into a DataWindow and give the user a perception of speed?

   Set the DataWindows `retrieve as needed` attribute on.

3. How do you speed up scrolling of DataWindows with bitmaps?

   Instead of using bitmaps, use characters from the Windows special character set.

4. How do you speed up setting the values in a large number of cells in a DataWindow using the `setItem` function?

   The `setItem` function call forces the DataWindow to redraw, affecting performance. You set the DataWindows redrawing off by calling the `setRedraw` function and passing it the parameter `FALSE`. Set the values using the `setItem` function. Force the DataWindow to redraw, again calling the `setRedraw` function and passing it the parameter `TRUE`, after the processing is over.

620

Index

& and menus

Column Values command

ODBC

Remove Watch button

text

SAMS
Learning
Center

SAMS
PUBLISHING

windows

Add to Your Sams Library Today with the Best Books for Programming, Operating Systems, and New Technologies

The easiest way to order is to pick up the phone and call

1-800-428-5331

between 9:00 a.m. and 5:00 p.m. EST.

For faster service, please have your credit card available.

ISBN	Quantity	Description of Item	Unit Cost	Total Cost
0-672-30695-6		Developing PowerBuilder 4 Applications, 3 Edition (Book/Disk)	$45.00	
0-672-30564-X		PowerBuilder 4 Developer's Guide (Book/CD) (Available in March 1995)	$49.99	
0-672-30520-8		Your Internet Consultant: The FAQs of Online Life	$25.00	
0-672-30617-4		World Wide Web Unleashed	$35.00	
0-672-30612-3		The Magic of Computer Graphics	$45.00	
0-672-30413-9		Multimedia Madness, Deluxe Edition! (Book/Disk/CD-ROMs)	$55.00	
0-672-30638-7		Super CD-ROM Madness (Book/CD-ROMs)	$39.99	
0-672-30590-9		The Magic of Interactive Entertainment, 2nd Edition (Book/CD-ROMs)	$44.95	
		Shipping and Handling: See information below.		
		TOTAL		

❏ 3 ½" Disk

❏ 5 ¼" Disk

Shipping and Handling: $4.00 for the first book and $1.75 for each additional book. Floppy disk: add $1.75 for shipping and handling. If you need to have it NOW, we can ship the product to you in 24 hours for an additional charge of approximately $18.00, and you will receive your item overnight or in two days. Overseas shipping and handling adds $2.00 per book and $8.00 for up to three disks. Prices subject to change. Call for availability and pricing information on latest editions.

201 W. 103rd Street, Indianapolis, Indiana 46290

1-800-428-5331 — Orders   1-800-835-3202 — FAX   1-800-858-7674 — Customer Service

Book ISBN 0-672-30676-X

PLUG YOURSELF INTO...

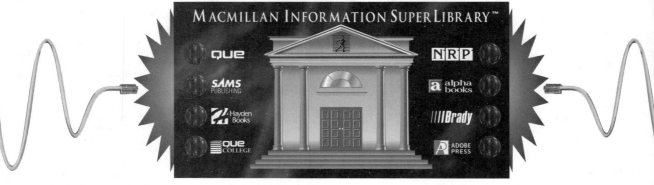

THE MACMILLAN INFORMATION SUPERLIBRARY™

Free information and vast computer resources from the world's leading computer book publisher—online!

FIND THE BOOKS THAT ARE RIGHT FOR YOU!

A complete online catalog, plus sample chapters and tables of contents give you an in-depth look at *all* of our books, including hard-to-find titles. It's the best way to find the books you need!

- **STAY INFORMED** with the latest computer industry news through our online newsletter, press releases, and customized Information SuperLibrary Reports.

- **GET FAST ANSWERS** to your questions about MCP books and software.

- **VISIT** our online bookstore for the latest information and editions!

- **COMMUNICATE** with our expert authors through e-mail and conferences.

- **DOWNLOAD SOFTWARE** from the immense MCP library:
    - Source code and files from MCP books
    - The best shareware, freeware, and demos

- **DISCOVER HOT SPOTS** on other parts of the Internet.

- **WIN BOOKS** in ongoing contests and giveaways!

TO PLUG INTO MCP: ➔

WORLD WIDE WEB: http://www.mcp.com

GOPHER: gopher.mcp.com
FTP: ftp.mcp.com